OPHELIA FIELD was educated at Christ Church, Oxford and the London School of Economics. Ophelia is the author of *The Favourite: Sarah, Duchess of Marlborough*, and has written for the *TLS*, *Literary Review* and *Sunday Telegraph*, among others. When not writing, she has directed programmes at a number of refugee and human rights organisations, including Human Rights Watch and the writers' association, PEN.

www.opheliafield.com

From the reviews of *The Kit-Cat Club*:

'[Field] has a native gift for historical retrieval so that we see the past in close-up, as it were, as well as in wide view' *The Times*

'It is a testament to Field's skill that the members of the Club come to life in such vivid and dynamic ways. There is a great deal of panache and pungency alongside the unfussy explication of the finer points of Georgian political intrigue' *Scotland on Sunday*

'A fascinating and elegant book . . . giving a full and brilliant picture of one of the most interesting periods in English history' *Scotsman*

'Magnificent . . . After reading this stimulating book, it is shocking to realise that the Kit-Cat Club has had to wait so long for its influence to be recognised. Field offers rich compensation, in a book that is both instructive and engrossingly readable' *Guardian (Book of the Week)*

'Highly intelligent . . . Field argues persuasively that the club transformed both politics and English cultural identity' *Observer*

'A hugely enjoyable study of male friendship' *Independent on Sunday*

'Field's clear and scholarly account of both the politics and the personalities shows how one man's idea that began in a pie shop became "the cultural institution, literary clique and political think-tank" that helped shape a nation' *Independent*

'This enterprising club required an enterprising commentator, and in Ophelia Field it has found one' *Irish Times*

'This is a wonderful book, which puts most popular history to shame by its intelligence, clarity and powerful story-telling . . . a brilliant portrait of England at the beginning of the modern age' *Mail on Sunday*

'What particularly distinguishes this book is the humane perspective in which the writer places her protagonists . . . As an essay in group biography her book presents an authoritative portrait of a genuinely revolutionary era' *Sunday Telegraph*

'Elegantly written and deeply researched . . . A fitting memorial to a remarkable body of men who contributed so much to British politics and culture' *Sunday Times*

'No record of what was said at the Kit-Cat Club meetings survives. The author turns this to her advantage, allowing the book to meander eruditely, rather like an 18th-century conversation' *Economist*

'What a wonderful subject Ophelia Field has found, and how adroitly she has handled it' *Spectator*

'This tale of the bawdy and bustling world of literary gossip and infighting, *Tatler*, politics, booze and Fleet Street in the 1690s is a must-read' *City A.M.*

'Vivid and massively detailed' *Time Out*

'[A] bold and hugely entertaining book' *Standpoint*

'The sort of brainy, literate history that most publishers have forsworn. It reminds you of an England where values were not determined by retailers . . . The *Kit-Cat Club* is a wonderful subject for a book and Field has handled it beautifully' *New Statesman*

By the same author

The Favourite: Sarah, Duchess of Marlborough

OPHELIA FIELD

The Kit-Cat Club

HARPER PERENNIAL
London, New York, Toronto, Sydney and New Delhi

Harper Perennial
An imprint of HarperCollins*Publishers*
77–85 Fulham Palace Road
Hammersmith
London W6 8JB

www.harperperennial.co.uk
Visit our authors' blog at www.fifthestate.co.uk

This Harper Perennial edition published 2009
1

First published in Great Britain by Harper*Press* in 2008

A catalogue record for this book is available from the British Library

ISBN-13 978-0-00-717893-3

Typeset by Palimpsest Book Production, Ltd, Grangemouth, Stirlingshire

Printed and bound in Great Britain by Clays Ltd, St Ives plc

FSC
Mixed Sources
Product group from well-managed
forests and other controlled sources
www.fsc.org Cert no. SW-COC-1806
© 1996 Forest Stewardship Council

FSC is a non-profit international organisation established to promote the responsible management of the world's forests. Products carrying the FSC label are independently certified to assure consumers that they come from forests that are managed to meet the social, economic and ecological needs of present and future generations.

Find out more about HarperCollins and the environment at
www.harpercollins.co.uk/green

To Paul, and the other members of the
Second Hungarian Literary Society

All the good talk over the pies and wine, Congreve's wit, Wharton's fascinating impudence, and Addison's quiet humour, is lost forever without record. The Kit-Cat had no Boswell.

G. M. TREVELYAN, *The Times*, 10 March 1945

Persons in great Station have seldom their true Characters drawn till several Years after their Deaths. Their personal Friendships and Enmities must cease, and the Parties they were engaged in be at an end . . . [I]f an English Man considers the great Ferment into which our Political World is thrown at present, and how intensively it is heated in all its parts, he cannot suppose that it will cool again in less than three hundred Years.

JOSEPH ADDISON, *The Spectator*, no. 101, 25 June 1711

Remember that a free State is only a more numerous and more powerful Club . . .

SIR WILLIAM JONES, *The Principles of Government, in a Dialogue between a Scholar and a Peasant*, 1783

CONTENTS

A detailed chronology and other additional material may be found at www.opheliafield.com

LIST OF ILLUSTRATIONS

Integrated images

First Plate Section

Jacob Tonson by Sir Godfrey Kneller (1717) © National Portrait Gallery, London.

Charles Sackville, 6th Earl of Dorset, by Sir Godfrey Kneller (*c.* 1700–6) © Private Collection.

George Stepney by Sir Godfrey Kneller (1705) © National Portrait Gallery, London.

Charles Montagu, 1st Earl of Halifax, by Sir Godfrey Kneller (*c.* 1703–10) © National Portrait Gallery, London.

Matthew Prior by Sir Godfrey Kneller (1705) © by permission of the Master and Fellows of Trinity College Cambridge.

Sir John Vanbrugh by Sir Godfrey Kneller (c.1704–10) © National Portrait Gallery, London.

Detail from 'The Distrest Poet' by William Hogarth (1736) © Birmingham Museums and Art Gallery.

William Congreve by Sir Godfrey Kneller (1709) © National Portrait Gallery, London.

William Congreve by Richard van Bleek (1715) © Photograph courtesy of Paul Laes, part of the collection of the museum M-Leuven, Belgium.

'Pope's Introduction to Dryden at Will's Coffee House' by Eyre Crowe (1860–1910) © Photograph courtesy of Sotheby's Picture Library.

'The Duke of Kingston introducing his Daughter, Lady Mary Montagu, as Toast to the Members of the Kit-Cat Club' by William Frederick Yeames (1884) © Christie's Images Ltd, 1996.

Henrietta Godolphin, 2nd Duchess of Marlborough, by Sir Godfey Kneller (1705) © Photograph by R. G. Silverwood, reproduced by kind permission of His Grace the Duke of Marlborough, Blenheim Palace Image Library.

Lady Mary Wortley Montagu, attributed to Jonathan Richardson (*c.* 1725) © Private Collection / The Bridgeman Art Library.

'View of the Queen's Theatre from the Rotunda, Stowe House, Bucks, with Lord Cobham and Charles Bridgeman' by Jacques Rigaud (1681–1754) © Private Collection / Photo © Christie's Images / The Bridgeman Art Library.
Castle Howard © The Castle Howard Collection.

Lady Steele (née Mary Scurlock) by Sir Godfrey Kneller © National Portrait Gallery, London.
Sir Richard Steele by an unknown artist (probably Christian Richter) (*c.* 1720) © National Portrait Gallery, London.

The Spectator, as printed on 7 June 1711 © 2000 RU Special Collections and Archives / Courtesy of Montclair University.
Illustration from front cover of 1759 *Tatler* featuring Isaac Bickerstaff on his chair © Courtesy of the Department of Special Collections, Spencer Research Library, University of Kansas.

Henry Fiennes-Clinton, 7th Earl of Lincoln, and Thomas Pelham-Holles, Earl of Clare and Duke of Newcastle, attributed to Sir Godfrey Kneller (*c.* 1721) © National Portrait Gallery, London.

While every effort has been made to trace the owners of copyright material reproduced herein, the publishers would like to apologise for any omissions and would be pleased to incorporate missing acknowledgements in any future editions.

PREFACE

The Kit-Cat Club existed at a pivotal point in British history, and its members participated prominently in the cultural, constitutional and social revolutions of their times. The Kit-Cat Club's story can therefore be read as a study of how the political stability Britain experienced after 1720 was constructed and defended from the 1690s onwards. For over twenty years – from the aftermath of the Glorious Revolution in 1688, through two long and expensive wars against Catholic France, into the reign of George I after 1714 – nearly all roads in British politics and culture led through the Kit-Cat Club, or took their direction in opposition to it.

That is the most objective explanation of why I wanted to write the first full biography of the Kit-Cat Club, but there were other reasons. This is, above all, a book about friendship. Having previously written on a female friendship in the early eighteenth century – the relationship between Queen Anne and her favourite, Sarah Churchill – I wanted to examine the more reticent but equally powerful male friendships of the same period. I was also interested in universal questions of how much we should be in business for ourselves, or how far we should be prepared to broker favours for friends, and nothing could better dramatize these dilemmas than the Kit-Cats' relationships with one another.

Of the fifty-odd Kit-Cat members, I have concentrated on a dozen, and within that dozen, on a literary quintet who are relatively well known today: Joseph Addison, William Congreve, Richard Steele,

John Vanbrugh and the publisher Jacob Tonson. This is therefore also a book about being a writer. Those who look back to some hypothetical golden age, before commercialism corrupted the arts, will be consoled by how similar the anxieties of the Kit-Cat authors were to those of many authors today. The Kit-Cat Club existed at the threshold between aristocratic and professional writing, and so developed a form of collective patronage for literary production that was suited to both. I was first drawn to the Kit-Cat authors by the fact that theirs were hardworking writing lives, supplemented by day-jobs and by a sense of wider public duty. I was curious to examine creative lives unprejudiced by the later Romantic cult of the artist, which still has us largely in its thrall.

Richard Steele once called for readers of his paper, *The Spectator*, to send in descriptions of their working lives, to 'give a lively Image of the Chain and mutual Dependence of Human Society'. This book traces the chain of dependency that connected the Club's writers and patrons; at times, researching it felt like drawing one of those diagrams in magazines showing how everyone successful in British culture is privately linked to everyone else. As an exposé of such connections, this is also a book about class in Britain. As an immigrant to Britain myself, I share the Kit-Cats' interest in the nature of 'Englishness', particularly the origins of the London elite that defines itself by education and cultural appreciation, while my own lack of strong national identity means that those who hold strong communitarian values, whether in relation to a club or a country, always intrigue me.

To write a book about the Kit-Cat Club is to describe a fabulous conversation extending over two decades, not one word of which is reliably recorded. Many of Jacob Tonson's papers were pulped by the 1940s. Addison asked that most of his personal letters be destroyed, and his correspondence with Steele seems to have suffered this fate. Robert Walpole destroyed many of his personal papers and ordered the confiscation and destruction of many left by other Kit-Cat politicians. William Pulteney destroyed papers that might have shed light on the Club's final days. There is, moreover, no surviving rule or minute book for the Kit-Cat Club. Not one regular diarist has emerged from among its members. The Club's authors seldom wrote autobiographically, and when they did, they rarely described interior worlds or private feelings. In this sense, however, a group biography is an apt form for a book about the Kit-Cats: they believed creative forces came from the 'commerce' or 'intercourse' between men's minds, as opposed to later beliefs in subconscious, individual sources of creativity. They believed that their Club was more, in other words, than the sum of its parts.

Viewing each life through the lens of the Kit-Cat Club is necessarily selective, as every man had many personal and professional relationships, and intellectual influences, unconnected with the Club. While I have occasionally mentioned the most important non-members so as not to skew the historical record, it has been impossible to give every non-Kit-Cat patron, relation, colleague and friend his or her full biographical due. I hope the champions of these figures will forgive me.

Note on Dates, Money, Spelling and Punctuation

Before the English calendar changed in 1752, New Year's Day was 25 March. To avoid confusion for modern readers, all dates in this book, unless indicated, take 1 January as the beginning of the new year, such that a date which would have been '5 February 1699', for example, is given here as '5 February 1700'. In addition, the 'Old Style' (Julian) calendar was ten or eleven days behind the 'New Style' (Gregorian) calendar used on the Continent. Unless otherwise stated, all dates are Old Style.

I have often followed an original value in pounds, shillings and pence (or guineas) with an approximation of its relative purchasing power today, though such calculations are notoriously problematic.

I have followed modern usage with respect to spelling and punctuation, but – to keep a dash of original flavour – not always with respect to capitalization. Abbreviated words have been expanded in all instances except titles of printed works, or where poetic metre demands.

I have also, for the sake of efficiency, used a number of modern words that did not exist in the late seventeenth or early eighteenth century, such as 'journalist', 'scientist' or 'publisher' (Addison was the first to use the word 'editor' in its modern sense in 1712).

Acknowledgements

In a book containing so much about patronage, I must start by thanking my own patrons for their generosity, in particular Flora Fraser and the judges of the inaugural Elizabeth Longford Award, as well as Mr Douglas Blythe, and the Society of Authors. My warmest thanks also go to my agent Lizzy Kremer and to my editor Arabella Pike, as well as Gail Lynch, Alice Massey, Annabel Wright, Katharine Reeve and Carol Anderson.

In a book about friendship, I also wish to thank my own friends who have helped with my research in innumerable ways: Tim Richardson for guidance on eighteenth-century gardens and countless other tips; Rodolph de Salis for finding some obscure answers; Sara Payne for revealing local landmarks; Sir Kit Booth for advice on Dr Garth; David Dudding for the reference to the Yale Kit-Cat; Peter Tregear for advice on opera; Peter Parker for advice on Isherwood's Kit-Cat; Frances Wilson, Tom Dyckhoff, Jane Ridley, Juliet Carey, Norma Clarke, Caroline Maclean, Kirsty Crawford and others for their advice and encouragement; Nadette, Marie and Michael for accommodating me in Dublin; Audrey and Austin Burton of Green Hammerton for their hospitality in Yorkshire; Giles Macdonogh for advice on the history of drink; Ed Kemp for advice on Congreve; and my mother, Michele Field, for her constant supply of clippings and references. In addition, I thank: the staff of the British Library, particularly Dr Frances Harris, and the staffs of the Beinecke Library at Yale University, the Gilbert Collection in Dublin, the Guildhall Library in the City of London, the Westminster Archives, the New York Public Library and Columbia University Library; Corin Fawcett and Sarah Colborne at the University of Nottingham Department of Manuscripts and Special Collections; Amanda Bevin and others at the National Archives, Kew; Mrs Cottrell-Dormer and Sheridan Strong at Rousham House; Rhys Griffith at the Herefordshire County Archives; Eddie Smith at Westminster School; David Onnekink at the University of Utrecht; Roy Wolper at the *Scriblerian* journal; Aileen Douglas at Trinity College Dublin, as well as Maire Kennedy, Charles Benson, Gerry Lyne and Dennis

McCarthy in Dublin; Kate Harris at Longleat; Dr Chris Ridgeway at Castle Howard; Tim Rowse at Harvard University; Ray Barker at Beningbrough Hall, North Yorkshire; Mr and Mrs Stuart Shepherd of Northampton; Paul Cox, Francesca Odell, Robin Francis and their colleagues at the Heinz Archive, National Portrait Gallery, London; Shane Burris at Pennsylvania State University's Palermo Library; Shona Robertson at the National Theatre Archives, London; Lesley Whitelaw at Middle Temple Library, London; Philip Carter and Matthew Kilburn at the Oxford Dictionary of National Biography; Margaret Ryan and Elaine Alahendra at the Foreign and Commonwealth Office archives; Hayley Whiting at the Bank of England archives; Jonathan Smith and William St Clair at Trinity College, Cambridge; Laura Edmundson in the British Pictures department at Sotheby's; Peter Milburn and Huw Colwyn Foulkes at the Harper's Trust, Bedford, as well as Tom Brown and Patricia Debens; Richard Knight at the Archives Centre, Holborn Library; Alice Sherwood and the other members of London's current Kit-Cat Club; Malcolm Taylor at the English Folk Dance and Song Society; Catherine Hall at the Theatre Museum, London; Carol Siegel at the Bough House Museum; Brian Perry at the Beaverbrook Art Gallery, New Brunswick; Kim Kitson and Andrew King at Claremont Landscape Gardens; Caroline Dalton; Victoria Glendinning; Brian Masters; Cedric Reverand; James Winn; Eveline Cruikshanks; David McKitterick; James Sambrook; Katherine Bucknell; and Dr Christine Ferdinand.

Above all, I wish to thank those friends and experts who generously gave their time to provide comments and corrections to the text, especially Paul Laikin, Martha Redding and Stuart Handley. Responsibility for what Richard Steele called 'squint-eyed Error' in this book, however, is entirely my own.

PROLOGUE
DRYDEN'S FUNERAL, MAY 1700

> Thy Wars brought nothing about;
> Thy Lovers were all untrue.
> 'Tis well an Old Age is out,
> And time to begin a New.
>
> JOHN DRYDEN, *Secular Masque* (1700)

ON A WARM London afternoon, 13 May 1700, a crowd of mourners assembled beneath the turret and weathercock of the Royal College of Physicians, then a handsome brick building on the west side of Warwick Lane, near Newgate Prison. They were attending the funeral of former Poet Laureate, John Dryden. Among the writers, actors, musicians, patrons, politicians and publishers gathering to pay tribute to the man generally acknowledged as the greatest writer and critic of his generation were over a dozen members of a controversial dining society known as the Kit-Cat Club.

One of Dryden's patrons, Kit-Cat member Charles Sackville, 6th Earl of Dorset, had earlier arranged for Dryden's embalmed body to be exhumed from the local churchyard of St Anne's in Soho, so that it could be reburied, with due pomp and ceremony, in Westminster

Abbey. The Kit-Cat Club financed this second funeral at the suggestion of Dr Samuel Garth, another of the Club's members, who was both Dryden's personal physician and one of his literary disciples. Any of the aristocratic Kit-Cats with good credit could have single-handedly paid the funeral's bill, totalling only £45. 17*s*. (or around £5,500 today), but by transforming the occasion into a communal gesture the Club was demonstrating its generosity and good literary taste to Londoners. Though both Whigs and Tories attended the funeral, no public occasion could take place in the 1700s without one of these two political parties attempting to dominate it, and in this case the Tories resentfully acknowledged that the Kit-Cats were posthumously appropriating Dryden to their distinctively Whig narrative of English literature.

At four o'clock, Dr Garth and the other Fellows descended from the oak-panelled Censors' room on the Royal College's first floor to host a drinks reception, with music and 'funeral baked meats',[1] for the assembled mourners. Garth, who wore a distinctive red cloak, delivered a Latin oration that offended several attendees for being addressed to the 'great god Apollo'.[2] Such an unchristian oration cleverly avoided the issue that the man whom the Kit-Cats were about to bury in an Anglican abbey had died a Catholic. One of Garth's literary enemies claimed the physician delivered the oration standing on a rotten beer barrel that collapsed halfway through. This slapstick moment was probably a fabrication, however, since another anti-Kit-Cat observer, who said Garth 'threw away some words and a great deal of false Latin', fails to mention it.[3]

At five o'clock, the coffin – containing the body wrapped in a flannel shift, tied at the feet like a fishtail and packed in bundles of rosemary – was loaded into a horse-drawn hearse adorned with black feathers. Eight musicians in mourning scarves led the procession playing crape-covered oboes and trumpets. At the head of the cortège walked the College beadles, carrying staves. There were three other funeral coaches, one carrying Dryden's widow and son. Over fifty private coaches followed behind.

Departing the Royal College's forecourt, they processed down Warwick Lane and Ludgate Hill, passing the Fleet, a former tributary of the Thames that had dried into a fetid ditch. The carriages following the hearse became entangled with several 'moveable Bawdy-houses' (prostitutes in hackney coaches) as they passed Chancery Lane,[4] the passengers bracing themselves as horses reared and carriages lurched against one another on the cobbles. The jam then cleared as they slowly proceeded west along the Strand, where gaps between the buildings offered glimpses of the equally traffic-clogged Thames below. At the hour Dryden's cortège passed, the Thames would have been at low tide, revealing the large mud-brown beach onto which shoeless children and scrap collectors were able to wander unimpeded, no embankments yet having been built. The procession finally turned down Whitehall, past the higgledy-piggledy buildings of Old Westminster Palace, towards the Abbey. In the surrounding streets, crowds gathered to watch the strange spectacle of England's nobility, dressed in unseasonably heavy wool mourning suits, paying their humble respects to a near-bankrupt author.

What really bothered several contemporary observers about this Whig-dominated event was the promiscuous mingling of England's social classes. As government ministers, dukes, earls and knights abandoned their carriages and liveried footmen in the Abbey's yard, they found themselves literally on an equal footing with tradesmen, actresses and lowly born 'Playhouse Sparks'. Tom Browne, a satirist, mocked the impropriety of the motley congregation as 'A Crowd so nauseous, so profusely lewd, / With all the Vices of the Times endued . . .'[5]

The procession was led through the Abbey by a figure whose runtish stature was undisguised by his high-crowned periwig and high-heeled shoes. This was Charles Montagu, King William III's former First Lord of the Treasury and another key Kit-Cat member. Tom Browne considered Montagu the epitome of what was loathsome about the new, affluent class of Whig politicians: 'grown sleek and fat', proud, corrupt and pretentious, flattering himself as the 'Chief of Wits'.[6] That Browne was able to publish such insults with impunity indicated, however, the reality of Montagu's situation in May 1700: he had fallen far enough from the King's favour that he would be openly attacked in the next parliamentary session.

Montagu's Kit-Cat colleagues, who knew his virtues of generosity, loyalty and intelligence, probably granted him pride of place in the procession to demonstrate their support for him during this difficult time.

Hobbling behind Montagu, leading a 'Troop of Stationers', came Dryden's half-crippled publisher and the Kit-Cat Club's founding father, Jacob Tonson. Tonson was grieving for the loss of his most lucrative and prestigious author, whose poem *Absalom and Achitophel* had launched Tonson's publishing career two decades earlier. Dryden had recognized Tonson as a cut above the Grub Street printers who seemed to 'live by selling *titles*, not books',[7] telling Tonson: 'I find all of your trade are Sharpers & you not more than others; therefore I have not wholly left you,' and signing a letter 'not your Enemy & maybe your friend, John Dryden'.[8] The longevity of the two men's collaboration, on numerous publications and as co-editors on a series of best-selling poetic *Miscellanies*, suggested an intellectual empathy greater than they had ever openly acknowledged to one another.

Next came Dryden's fellow authors, not yet recognized as a professional category and considered by many onlookers as even lower than the tradesmen: 'such as under Mercury are born, / As Poets, Fiddlers, Cut-purses and Whores'.[9] Pre-eminent among these was Kit-Cat playwright and poet, William Congreve. Congreve was an insouciant, cynical young Irishman, armoured by quiet confidence in his own talent. He had known Dryden since at least 1692, by which date Congreve had assisted the older poet with various Latin and Greek translations. Dryden quickly felt that in Congreve he had found a worthy literary heir, and, in begging Congreve to be 'kind to my Remains',[10] Dryden had effectively designated the young man his literary executor.

After Congreve, Dr Garth was considered next in line to inherit Dryden's poetic mantle, having published *The Dispensary* the previous year: a much-applauded mock-epic poem about Garth's battle to persuade the Royal College to dispense free medicine to paupers. Congreve and Garth had been among Dryden's circle at Will's Coffee House, the social centre of London's literati before the Kit-Cat Club.

The death of Dryden, 'To whom the tribe of circling Wits, / As to an oracle submits',[11] was a blow from which Will's Coffee House's 'Witty Club' would never recover, clearing the way for the rise of the Kit-Cat Club.

Rather than Dryden's favourites, Congreve or Garth, however, another Kit-Cat author, John Vanbrugh – 36 years old and with four plays under his belt – had been the one to offer practical assistance when Dryden lay dying. Vanbrugh organized a benefit performance, knowing Dryden would otherwise have little to leave his wife and children. Dryden's last dramatic work, his *Secular Masque* (1700), took new beginnings as its theme and was intended to be performed at the Theatre Royal, Drury Lane, on 25 March 1700: that is, on New Year's Day according to the Old English calendar – the first day of the new century. The production was not ready for this historic opening night, however, and the masque was probably not performed until after Dryden's death, when the third-night profits, which traditionally went to a play's author, would have been donated directly to Dryden's widow.

A number of other Kit-Cat members – including Members of Parliament, army officers and diplomats – accompanied Dorset, Montagu, Tonson, Garth, Vanbrugh and Congreve as they paced through the dimly lit Abbey to the solemn knelling of bells. When the mourners were all assembled under the Abbey's vast transept, a prebend began to read the service, and the choir sang an epicedium.

Several Tory eyewitnesses started the story, later repeated by Dr Johnson, that the funeral descended from a Christian solemnity into a kind of raucous party,[12] the playwright George Farquhar concluding with a sigh: 'And so much for Mr Dryden; whose burial was the same as his life: variety and not of a piece – the quality and mob, farce and heroics, the sublime and ridicule mixed in a piece – great Cleopatra in a hackney coach.'[13] Whether touching or absurd, sublime or ridiculous, Dryden's funeral served several purposes for the Kit-Cat Club: it raised the Club's profile with the man in the street; it claimed a Whig share in Dryden's reputation; and it expressed gratitude to a man who had mentored many of those present. The event further demonstrated that the Club was not cowed by the religious censors who had recently attacked the morality of Dryden's plays in the same breath as Congreve's and Vanbrugh's.

One of the mourners, frail old Samuel Pepys, would surely have thought back to another Westminster Abbey funeral he had attended in the company of the 27-year-old Dryden in 1658: that of Oliver Cromwell. Since then, England had seen a royal restoration and a revolution, but the turmoil and bloodshed of the Civil War still felt like recent history. Families and communities torn apart by the previous century's conflicts were still healing these divisions. With the new century only a couple of months old by the terms of their calendar, a sense of excitement hung in the air that spring, but the nation still lacked confidence, and feared the possibility of slipping back into barbarity.

Dryden's death proved a turning point for the Kit-Cat Club, after which it self-consciously set about trying to direct the course of English civilization in the new century, particularly the course of the two arts most beloved of Dryden: literature and music. None of Dryden's admirers, or 'Apollo's sons',[14] not even Congreve, felt up to carrying this torch alone, but together – through subscriptions and collaborations – the Kit-Cats assumed what they considered their patriotic duty: to guide and nurture native talent. No grouping before or since has worked towards such an ambitious vision of national reform, encompassing every high art form and seeking to dominate every aspect of Britain's social and intellectual life.

By compensating for the especially sizeable gaps in royal patronage of English poetry, theatre and music, the Club would contribute to a shift in authority from the Court to private citizens. More than their monarchs, they would fulfil the country's need for new role models, in fashions, manners and morals. This helped turn the Court into 'the highly symbolic, sober, secluded, and slightly strange institution it has since become',[15] while at the same time laying the foundations for the exponential growth of cultural consumption that would occur in the later eighteenth century. The Kit-Cat founders were born into an age of plague, fire and civil strife; the younger members would live to see the self-consciously 'civilized' age of Samuel Johnson, Joshua Reynolds and Robert Adam.

Similarly, when the Kit-Cat founders were born, most Britons would have said their monarch ruled them, but by the time the youngest members died, the majority would have said they were governed by an elected House of Commons. The Club was to be both a cause and a symptom of this shift in the political culture, from individual to collective accountability, and its leading members would also be closely involved in turning Britain from a 'ramshackle federal state'[16] to something significantly closer to a modern 'nation state'. The political stability of Britain after 1720 owed much to a sense of common purpose and values among those who wielded power, and the Kit-Cat Club was the prime example of a political grouping formed and sustained around shared ideological and cultural values, 'Alike in Morals, and alike in Mind',[17] rather than around bonds of kinship. Its members would pursue an ultra-Whig political agenda for over twenty years, such that an opponent could plausibly describe the Kit-Cat in 1704 as a 'Club that gave Direction to the State',[18] and such that its final generation of members, most notably Robert Walpole, came to dominate the first half-century of Georgian politics.

The Enlightenment philosopher John Locke wrote in 1690 that, alongside Divine Law and Civil Law, the third type of law was 'the law of opinion . . . praise or blame, which, by secret and tacit consent, establishes itself in the several societies, tribes and clubs of men in the world'.[19] The Kit-Cat Club continued this seventeenth-century tradition of 'clubs of men' carving out negative freedoms from the state, not least of which was the right to hold meetings and discuss their opinions freely. Kit-Cat members would help shape the nation's taste, character and international image in the coming decades, planting a particular idea of 'Englishness' in the popular imagination and contributing to the building of a more prosperous, polite and self-confident society.

On this evening in 1700, however, the Kit-Cats were first and foremost a remarkable group of friends, several of whom had known each other since childhood. Self-identification by their Kit-Cat name, and demonstrations of unity such as the funding of this ceremony, were now public vows confirming the men's personal and professional commitment to each other – nuptials of Whig fraternity. Dryden's death, several years after the Kit-Cat Club's foundation, marked the Club's coming of age.

I
SELF-MADE MEN

You will make Jacob's ladder raise you to immortality.

WILLIAM WYCHERLEY, addressing a poet soon to be published by Jacob Tonson[1]

ON ANY DAY but the Sabbath in 1690s London, ships from around the world disgorged Chinese tea, Indian sugar cane, Japanese porcelain, South American medicines and Persian silk at the eastern docks. Many of these cargoes were then carried by barge and cart to the Royal Exchange, 'a kind of Emporium for the whole Earth', built a couple of decades earlier between Cornhill and Threadneedle Street.[2] Entering the Exchange from the south, the visitor faced an elegant chessboard courtyard surrounded by two-storeyed arcades, containing over two hundred stalls, with the Mediterranean merchants to the right and American plantation traders to the left. At 'high exchange' (that is, in the early morning) the courtyard thronged with brokers, salesmen and 'stock-jobbers' trading in both tangible products and grand ideas. Upstairs, young girls sold ribbons and other 'toys' for ladies' dresses, while downstairs old beggar women sold the morning shoppers warm bags of walnuts, their shells littering the floor. Beadles patrolled, on the look out for trouble from the 'mumpers' (beggars) or the crowds of haggling Armenian, Jewish and Dutch merchants. For those unthreatened by London's role as a leading global centre of trade and commerce, in these years before there was a British Empire, the Exchange was a place to throw oneself into the urban melting pot.

Around 500,000 people lived in London at the end of the seventeenth century, out of five to six million in England as a whole. The city's population was densely packed into a small area of low buildings with only a few high steeples rising clear of the rooftops. One particularly large windmill sat on the south bank of the river close to the site of today's London Eye. Brick buildings were replacing wood after the Great Fire, and the West End was just beginning to emerge from open countryside. The Thames' northern bank was the southern perimeter of the city proper, with the old borough of Southwark south of the river, filled with prisons, shipyards, seedy inns and brothels, stinking tanneries and breweries. The other perimeters of London were the several royal palaces of St James's to the west, Old Street and Holborn to the north, King's (later Soho) Square to the northwest, and Whitechapel to the east. It was a time of thriving property developers: 'New squares and new streets [are] rising up every day to such a prodigy of buildings that nothing in the world does, or ever did, equal it,' Daniel Defoe declared.[3]

The Glorious Revolution of 1688 – the armed invasion that deposed the Catholic James II and installed a Protestant Dutchman, William of Orange, and his wife (James's daughter), Mary, on the English throne – had had social repercussions as profound as its constitutional consequences. Ordinary people began to re-examine and loosen the bonds that had tied them to their homes and class. For thousands of ambitious younger sons and rural labourers in search of trades or professions, this meant migrating to London, where everything seemed up for grabs – and within reach. Records for 1690 show three-quarters of London apprentices were born outside the city. London was also simmering with energy thanks to an influx of skilled Huguenot refugees and Dutch immigrants, as well as soldiers and sailors on their way to or from William's current war against France, the War of the League of Augsburg, then being fought in Flanders and Ireland. Army and navy commissions were briskly traded, allowing many men to pull themselves up by their bootstraps. Financing the war, meanwhile, required landowners elected to Parliament to start coming into the capital every winter (rather than merely every few years, as during previous reigns) to vote through the army supplies. These landowners were building townhouses and inventing new urban pastimes to amuse themselves through the long, cold parliamentary season.

William's government, as an institution, was itself a social parvenu, and the image of William as a foreign occupier, rather than rightful king, still flashed dangerously in the corner of the English people's collective vision. What mattered was that educated Englishmen should not question the legitimacy of the new regime, nor view the post-Revolutionary constitutional balance, with its greater emphasis on the House of Commons, as too nouveau or alien. Everything had to be overhauled, and new authorities made palatable. Adherents of the Whig party, on the whole more ideologically comfortable than the Tories with the Revolution and the post-Revolutionary social mobility, put their shoulders to this wheel.

Two such self-made Whigs were John Somers, one of the King's leading ministers, and Jacob Tonson, London's most prestigious publisher. Both were flourishing and fattening into comfortable middle age in the 1690s. Their characters were perfectly suited to the times – ambitious and ingenious, yet fundamentally pragmatic – and each was willing to play his part in the national effort of self-reinvention.

Tonson had grown up in central London. A 5-year-old in 1660, the year of Charles II's Restoration, Tonson's father was a barber-surgeon, a freeman of the City of London and a constable of High Holborn, while his mother's family were booksellers with successful shops at the gates of Gray's Inn. At 15, Jacob was apprenticed to the stationer Thomas Basset, where he laboured for the next eight years, elbow-deep in printer's ink and bookbinding resin from morning to night. Tonson read the books in Basset's shop voraciously, acquiring a love of literature, a dose of Latin and a practical understanding of the book trade. The world of books absorbed and comforted Tonson because he was lame in one leg and less physically able than other young men his age.

That his nickname 'left-legged Jacob'[4] signified more than mere clumsiness is confirmed by a physician's reference to Tonson's conscience being 'more paralytic and lost to all Sense of Feeling than his Legs'.[5] Tonson was also teased throughout his life for his ginger hair and wide, freckled face 'With Frowsy Pores that taint the ambient Air'.[6]

After completing his apprenticeship, Tonson immediately established his own firm, with premises at the Judge's Head in Chancery Lane. Kit-Cat authors later feared sending their manuscripts to this chaotic office in case they were lost amid all the 'lumber'.[7] Tonson was determined from an early age to buy rights to the work of major authors, living and dead, and so establish his reputation as a professional – some say the first professional – English publisher.

Tonson was the first to commission critical editions of Milton's poetry, notably *Paradise Lost*, and to make substantial profit from a literary backlist. He also had a nose for new talent. Alexander Pope later wrote of 'genial Jacob' bringing forth poems and plays from 'the Chaos dark and deep, / Where nameless *somethings* in their causes sleep'.[8] This idea of a publisher bringing forth creativity – rather than being merely a mechanical maker of books – was unprecedented. That the same publisher should be trusted to make critical amendments to manuscripts was even more unheard of. While Victorian antiquarians would snobbishly try to portray Tonson as merely a grubbing tradesman, there is clear evidence he was a man of great intellect and wit: Tonson later boasted, for example, that in the 1680s he had written various commendatory verses for new editions and passed these off as the work of his star authors, John Dryden and Edmund Waller. (This is also evidence, of course, that the publisher was not above corrupting the corpus of his authors' works in order to boost sales.)

Being published by Tonson was soon seen as an author's shortcut to the richest, most powerful readers, thanks to the publisher's gift for networking. Tonson aspired to be considered a gentleman, on a level with his clients and authors, and so would have felt insulted when called the 'chief merchant to the muses'[9] or a great 'wit-jobber' (that is to say, no better than a City 'stock-jobber').[10] He wished to set himself apart from other publishers and booksellers who were increasingly sullied by association with the hack writers of 'any mean production' in Grub Street.[11]

Though one contemporary bitingly remarked that Tonson 'looked but like a bookseller seated among lords, yet, *vice versa*, he behaved himself like a lord when he came among booksellers',[12] Tonson, in fact, succeeded in his social climbing: his correspondence shows that his authors accorded him the same terms of politeness that they employed to address their aristocratic patrons.[13] He was treated as their friend, not their servant. There is some disagreement as to how Tonson won this respect – one fairly impartial contemporary called Tonson a man who would 'Flatter no Body',[14] while another described him as shamelessly obsequious whenever there was a profit to be gained.[15] Certainly, from early in his career, Tonson made extravagant but well-calculated gestures of hospitality to both social inferiors and superiors. A bill survives for a 1689 dinner at a French-run 'ordinary' (a restaurant, usually run by Huguenot refugees) at which Tonson helped pay for a 'great table' of food, along with 20 gallons of claret, 6 of 'Canary', 4 of white wine, unspecified quantities of 'Rhenish' and champagne, 42 bottles of ale, musicians, servants, a constant fire, candles, pipes and tobacco, as well as a hired coach to pick up and deposit the guests – which, when added to compensation for 'glasses broke', came to £31. 8*s*. 6*d*. (around £4,000 today).[16]

John Somers was one of those invited to Tonson's parties before the Revolution[17] – one of the 'gentlemen of genius and quality' Dryden complimented Tonson on cultivating so assiduously.[18] Born in 1651 to the son of a Worcestershire attorney, Somers had quickly established a reputation as a brilliant legal mind while studying at Middle Temple – an Inn of Court that the sons of professionals 'ambitious of rule and government'[19] were attending in increasing numbers. Somers' father had stood on the Parliamentary side during the Civil War, and, in the same spirit, Somers fell into the Whig party's political camp. The Whigs opposed James II's moves towards Catholic emancipation during the 1680s, and so, in June 1688, Somers acted as counsel for seven bishops who signed a petition against James's order for a pro-Catholic Declaration to be read from pulpits. Somers distrusted this Declaration because it was brought in by royal prerogative rather than parliamentary statute, and because of his deeply ingrained prejudice that the Catholic Church – with its centralization to Rome and absolutist principles – was intrinsically 'unenlightened'. The invitation to William of Orange to invade was carried from a set of Protestant English nobles on the very day that the seven bishops' acquittal was celebrated in the streets by ordinary Londoners.

Following the Revolution, Somers' Whig credentials and intellectual reputation ensured his rapid promotion in government. He chaired the committee that drafted the Bill of Rights, the cornerstone of the new constitutional monarchy, and guided William towards accepting its limitations on royal prerogatives. Somers helped mount a retroactive public relations campaign, portraying the change of monarch as the triumph of 'Reason' – a simple expression of John Locke's 'contract theory', whereby unworthy rulers deserved to be deposed. In reward, Somers was appointed Solicitor General and then, in 1692, Attorney General, the latter a profitable office with extensive scope for patronage. Less than a year later, Somers was made Lord Keeper of the Great Seal, in charge of the Court of Chancery, and Speaker in the House of Lords, though he himself did not yet have a peerage. By 1695, Somers was one of four men who formed the 'Junto' of leading Whigs – the Cabinet within the Cabinet when in the King's favour, and when out of it, a kind of unofficial opposition or 'shadow' Cabinet. The Junto's power came from its ability to form block votes in the Commons and to raise from the City of London the extra funds necessary to supply William's costly war.[20] Somers was a particularly talented fundraiser, having no prejudice against the City's 'money men'. He was appointed one of the Lord Justices or regents entrusted with the administration of the kingdom whenever the King was on the Continent running the war.

At home, Somers was an incurable bibliophile. His library in Powys House, the impressive brick residence the King had granted him in Lincoln's Inn, was dominated by the legal texts in which the Tonson family firm specialized. Like Tonson, Somers' claim to gentility depended on his display of learning, and this library was the most tangible proof of that education. Tonson was careful not to lose touch with his increasingly powerful friend. He kept Somers' shelves well stocked and met him regularly to 'unbend' over an after-work drink in a tavern near Temple Bar, where the commerce of the City intersected with the politics and law of Westminster.

Tonson also flattered Somers' learning by offering the statesman opportunities for dispensing patronage to various authors in Tonson's publishing fold. Being unmarried and without significant extended family to support, Somers was free to put his patronage to such use. His beneficiaries included Dryden, though Somers allegedly authored an anonymous poem critical of Dryden's Catholicism and regretting, 'The knot of friendship is but loosely tied / Twixt those that heavenly concerns divide.'[21] Dryden in turn introduced younger authors to Tonson and hence to Somers' purse. Two such authors who arrived in London during these exciting post-Revolutionary years would quickly become the leading playwrights of their generation: William Congreve and John Vanbrugh.

Congreve had been 4 years old when his father, an English army officer, was posted to Ireland in 1674. A perk for those, like Congreve's father, in nominal service to the Lord Lieutenant of Ireland was free education for their sons at the best Irish grammar school, Kilkenny. Some sixty pupils were enrolled at the school in the early 1680s and Jonathan Swift was enrolled two years behind Congreve. Congreve went on to Trinity College Dublin at age 16 in 1686, with Swift following a few years later; these two talented young men lived together in the small community of students for several years without leaving any surviving trace of a particular attachment to one another.

Beyond Trinity's Elizabethan red brick walls, Dublin remained something of a frontier town, a place of opportunity for entrepreneurs and rough justice for criminals, including pirates, smugglers, deserters and horse-thieves; a place where disgraced Englishmen bought cheap land and acquired new identities. The Glorious Revolution was neither quick nor bloodless in Ireland. Instead, it haemorrhaged into the War of the Two Kings (between William III and James II, or 'Liam' and 'Seamus'), with violence that pushed out large numbers of Anglo-Irish refugees. When Trinity College closed in 1689 because of the upheavals, Swift fled to England, where he found his first job as secretary to a retired diplomat. That spring, as the deposed King James tried to retake Ireland with the aid of French troops, 19-year-old Congreve likewise fled to England where his family had well-off relatives happy to put them up. Congreve lodged first with his grandfather in Staffordshire, where, recuperating from an illness, he picked up a pen and began to compose his first play.

Two years later, Congreve arrived in London, a fresh-faced 21-year-old looking for an edgier and more fashionable existence than that on offer in Staffordshire. He was admitted to study law at Middle Temple in March 1691, but was described by a friend as having 'a wit of too fine a turn to be long pleased with that crabbed, unpalatable study'.[22] Middle Temple was not overly concerned if he neglected his legal studies to pursue a 'coffee house education' instead, since for many so-called 'amateur' students the Inns of Court were merely gentlemen's finishing schools, providing congenial central London lodgings.[23] Congreve himself described the education of Middle Temple as being more social than professional – 'Inns o' Court breeding', he said, was mainly about learning to snub one's country relations when they came to town.[24]

Congreve's wit quickly made him many friends among his fellow students – several of whom would end up as his fellow Kit-Cats in the years ahead. He went drinking with them in the self-consciously literary taverns and coffee houses of Covent Garden, northwest of the Temple. In that neighbourhood, according to one Kit-Cat poet, lawyers traded their robes for the lace coats of dandies, country girls lost their noses to syphilis, 'Poets canvass the Affairs of State', and all classes 'blend and jostle into Harmony'.[25]

In the centre of Covent Garden was Will's Coffee House, where Dryden held court among literati of all political shades. Congreve was probably introduced to this circle by one of the other ageing Restoration dramatists of London: Thomas Southerne or William Wycherley, whom Congreve knew through some cousins. Dryden's court at Will's was imperious: those allowed to take a pinch from his snuffbox comprised his inner circle, while his special chair had a prescribed place by the fire in winter and on the balcony in summer, which he called 'his winter and his summer seat'.[26] Yet, at the same time, Dryden carried himself with a charming humility that impressed Congreve deeply: Dryden was, Congreve remembered, 'of all the Men that ever I knew, one of the most Modest'.[27] The next generation of writers would say much the same of Congreve.

Dryden soon declared 'entire affection' for Congreve: 'So much the sweetness of your manners move / We cannot envy you, because we love,' he wrote.[28] Congreve, in return, said he was 'as intimately acquainted with Mr Dryden as the great Disproportion in our Years could allow', concluding quite simply that he 'loved' the old man.[29] Congreve showed his Staffordshire manuscript to Dryden, who declared he had never seen 'such a first play in his life', but added that 'it would be a pity to have it miscarry for want of a little assistance'. What the comedy, entitled *The Old Batchelor*, needed, Dryden declared, was only 'the fashionable cut of the town'.[30] Though ostensibly a plot of romantic intrigues, the real seduction of the play lies in the enviably quick wit exchanged between its male characters – it is a love letter to the urbane world Congreve must have imagined in his teens and in which he was now becoming accepted. Taking Dryden's suggestions on board, Congreve spent summer 1692 in Derbyshire reworking the text. By Michaelmas, thanks to Dryden's endorsements, Congreve was directing rehearsals of *The Old Batchelor* at the Theatre Royal on Drury Lane.

It was likely during these rehearsals that Congreve fell in love with the woman who would become his muse throughout the next decade: the actress Anne Bracegirdle, or 'Bracey'. Since adolescence, Bracey had acted under the tutelage of Mr and Mrs Betterton, two experienced members of the United Company, the theatre company based at the Theatre Royal. A brunette with dark sparkling eyes, a blushing complexion and a miraculously perfect set of even white teeth, it was said of Bracey that 'few Spectators that were not past it could behold her without Desire'.[31] Congreve met her when she was 'blooming to her Maturity'[32] and already a star.

It was more respectable to claim infatuation with Bracey than with most actresses, since she was reputed to be as chaste as the virgins she played. She lived with her mother in rented lodgings on Howard Street, where Congreve paid drawing-room visits. If their

Northamptonshire family was related to the Staffordshire Bracegirdles, they may even have been distantly related to Congreve. But away from the decorum of Howard Street, backstage at the theatre, Congreve pursued Bracey with fervour, writing her a love poem that lamented her chastity:

> Would I were free from this Restraint,
> Or else had hopes to win her;
> Would she could make of me a Saint,
> Or I of her a Sinner.[33]

The Old Batchelor opened in March 1693 to a 'Torrent of Applause' that would have fulfilled any young writer's most immodest fantasies.[34] The debut was such a success that 'many persons of Quality cannot have a Seat, all the places having been bespoken many days since'.[35] Jacob Tonson needed no further persuasion to become Congreve's publisher. Tonson printed, then quickly reprinted, the text of *The Old Batchelor*; he would thereafter hold exclusive rights to all Congreve's plays.

Around Michaelmas 1693, Tonson moved from above his shop in Chancery Lane to a house at the south side of Fleet Street, near the gate of Inner Temple. Soon after, according to poll tax records, Congreve moved out of Crane Court and became Tonson's lodger at this Fleet Street house. The two men, publisher and author, lived together, along with their several domestic servants, for seven years, until 1700. A later imaginary dialogue, written by a mutual friend of theirs, has Tonson exclaiming to Congreve that during these Fleet Street days, 'While I partook your wine, your wit and mirth, / I was the happiest creature on God's earth!'[36]

As Congreve's *Old Batchelor* had its debut on the London stage, 29-year-old John Vanbrugh arrived in the city, in circumstances unlike those of most other ambitious young newcomers. His boat had come from France, where since 1688 Vanbrugh had spent the best part of his twenties, detained without trial and on charges that had been forgotten almost as soon as the key turned in his cell door. The French had arrested Vanbrugh because they had miscalculated the status of his family, believing he would make a valuable bargaining chip to trade for a high-profile French prisoner. Though Vanbrugh's mother did have various noble relations, his late father had been a merchant in Chester, trading in property, lead, grain and Caribbean sugar, and his grandfather was a penniless Flemish refugee. When Vanbrugh's father died soon after the Revolution, Vanbrugh had inherited only a small sum and the burden of responsibility for his numerous siblings.

Some of Vanbrugh's captivity was spent in the Bastille, where his health suffered. Now, in 1693, having been traded for an insignificant Frenchman thanks to his mother's tireless lobbying, he returned to England a free man and, to use his own phrase, as 'sound as a roach'.[37] Imprisonment was a formative experience for Vanbrugh: it gave him a real appreciation of what arbitrary government could mean, and a violent aversion to boredom. He was determined not to waste another minute of his life.

After his return from France, Vanbrugh stayed in London for only a year before leaving 'that uneasy theatre of noise'[38] to join a marine regiment. Purchasing an officer's commission both advanced his social position and promised a secure income. In wartime, however, it was also an act of patriotism: Captain Vanbrugh saw action at a disastrous naval battle and was lucky not to be recaptured by the French. He borrowed some money from a fellow army officer, which he repaid when back in London by writing a play for the Theatre Royal, where his creditor was a patentee. *The Relapse* opened there in November 1696 and proved an overnight sensation, reviving the sinking fortunes of the United Company and more than repaying Vanbrugh's debt. Its success inevitably introduced Vanbrugh to Tonson and the coveted cultural patrons – like Somers – for whom Tonson acted as gatekeeper and broker. Congreve and Vanbrugh therefore started climbing 'Jacob's ladder' to fame and fortune as undeclared rivals, with only three years between their brilliant entrances into the London theatre world and Jacob Tonson's circle of highbrow friends. Soon, however, Tonson would find a solution to make the way less steep for them both: he and his patrons would found the Kit-Cat Club – an institution which would support the two authors throughout the rest of their lives.

II
FRIENDSHIPS FORMED

> [W]e very often contract such Friendships at School as are of Service to us all the following Part of our Lives.
>
> *The Spectator* no. 313, 28 February 1712[1]

THE SENSE OF unbounded possibility felt by many individual Englishmen in the 1690s owed much to what one historian has dubbed the 'educational revolution' of the earlier seventeenth century.[2] A surprisingly high proportion of England's sons (though none of its daughters) attended grammar schools, dissenting academies or the liberally endowed foundation or charity schools, so that teaching was no longer the preserve of the clergy and private tutors in noble households. For the generations of boys who enjoyed this expansion in primary and higher education, there were lifelong side effects: the formation of friendships that felt as important to them as family bonds, and a lasting enthusiasm for all-male camaraderie that would express itself subsequently in all-male clubbing.

Westminster School, refounded by Elizabeth I, was a private London school that was now expanding its intake and supplying a new breed of gentleman to government offices and the professions.

Jacob Tonson once explained that whereas Eton was 'very much filled by the Sons of Quality & who are not to be much pressed to study', Westminster produced 'manly Orators, & the very air of London brings on the Improvement of Youth for any business of the world . . .'[3] There, in around 1680–2, a gang of three schoolboys, known among themselves as 'Matt' (Matthew Prior), 'Chamont' (Charles Montagu) and 'Cat' (George Stepney), formed a bond of friendship that would not weaken for a full two decades, until the day when one of them dramatically betrayed another.

The three boys slept in a dilapidated former granary next to Westminster Abbey, where, in fireless rooms reeking of damp wool socks and cheap candles, they spent their evenings translating and memorizing passages from classical authors, preparing to be tested at six the next morning. Amid mild malnutrition, older boys could receive extra food from the table of the headmaster, Dr Busby, if they composed particularly well-turned Latin epigrams. The template was set: food in exchange for wit. 'Chamont' shared the scraps of meat his epigrams won with his two younger friends, and with his earnest little brother 'Jemmy', also at the school.

Enduring the hardships of Westminster's regime not only formed firm bonds of male friendship but also made the three boys mistake themselves for social equals, despite widely varying family backgrounds. Matt Prior had by far the humblest origins and was only at the school thanks to a fairytale stroke of good luck. One day in the 1680s, he had been working at the Rhenish Wine House, a fashionable Whitehall tavern owned by his vintner uncle, when the ageing Restoration rake, Charles Sackville, 6th Earl of Dorset, came in with some friends and noticed that Matt was working behind the bar with a copy of Horace in his hand. To test whether the boy understood what he read, the noblemen asked him to translate one of Horace's odes into English, and they were impressed when he quickly returned with a translation in metric verse. No matter how many times they repeated the test, Matt delivered. Dorset learned that Matt's joiner father had sent him to Westminster School some years earlier, where he had been taught Latin, but then, when his father died, his uncle had withdrawn him 'in the middle of the third form' to work at the

Rhenish.[4] Dorset remedied this situation by asking the Dean of Westminster to readmit Matt to the school at the Earl's personal expense, thereby becoming Prior's first patron.

At the other extreme, Charles Montagu was the grandson of the 1st Earl of Manchester, whose London residence, Manchester House, stood imposingly across from the Rhenish Wine House. Despite his venerable family name, however, Montagu was a younger son of a younger son and knew his future would depend largely upon his own efforts. George Stepney (nicknamed 'Cat' because he always seemed to land on his feet) similarly had no expectation of a significant inheritance, while being acutely aware of his own intelligence. Stepney's father, though briefly a Groom of Charles II's Privy Chamber, had essentially been a grocer and died in debt. His widowed mother survived by renting out properties in Scotland Yard. Stepney's rank therefore fitted roughly equidistant between Prior's near-total obscurity and the ancient lineage of the Montagus.[5]

Montagu, Prior and Stepney resolved to stay together at university. As Westminster's top scholar, Stepney could afford to turn down a place at Christ Church, Oxford, to join Montagu at Trinity College, Cambridge, to which Montagu had been elected some years earlier. In 1683, Prior joined them in Cambridge, attending St John's, where he was able to gain a scholarship and so save Lord Dorset considerable expense. Matt's background would have been less unusual at Cambridge than at Westminster since the majority of Cambridge students were non-gentry by this date. Prior had several advantages over most of his ambitious fellow students: Dorset's vested interest in his future, a naturally magnetic wit, and epicene good looks, with bright blue eyes under a mop of dark hair.

While he was at Cambridge, Prior maintained his connection with Dorset, sending an epistolary poem comparing the poor mutton at St John's with the 'kindest entertainment' he had enjoyed at his patron's table.[6] Then, in February 1685, Montagu, Prior and Stepney decided to build on Lord Dorset's interest in Prior and bring themselves collectively to the Earl's notice. It was a good moment to apply to Dorset as he had recently inherited his family seat at Knole in Kent, and expected further enrichment through his second marriage to a 17-year-old heiress. Prior, Stepney and Montagu therefore each wrote Dorset a poem on the death of Charles II, criticizing the accession of his crypto-Catholic brother James. These poetic offerings led Dorset to invite Prior's two chums to London to receive the benefit of some high society introductions. Montagu accepted Dorset's invitation, but Stepney believed he could not afford to enter London society without an income. Montagu therefore used his family contacts to help Stepney find a diplomatic posting in Hamburg, to which he travelled directly from Cambridge. The pretence of the boys' social equality was already beginning to wear thin.

In 1687, Montagu and Prior sat over a bottle in the Middle Temple rooms of Montagu's brother Jemmy and composed a parody of a recent Dryden poem about the Catholic and Anglican churches. They correctly guessed that the Whiggish Lord Dorset would be pleased by such a parody, which they entitled *The Hind and the Panther Transvers'd To the Story of The Country-Mouse and the City-Mouse*. Dorset circulated the poem widely among his political allies who opposed James II's religious policies during the tense year preceding the Revolution. Prior later claimed he did nothing more than take dictation from Montagu when they collaborated on the *Mouse* poem, but it is hard to know whether this was just Prior's way of flattering his friend after the latter became a rich and powerful man. If true, it would be less unjust that Dorset's recompense for the poem was to promote Montagu but not the more needy Prior, prompting the wry observation that 'one Mouse ran away with all the Bacon, whilst the other got Nothing but the empty Cupboard'.[7] When William arrived in England the following year, the Dutchman already knew of the poem; Dorset introduced the impish 27-year-old Montagu as its author, 'Mouse Montagu', and the soon-to-be-crowned King gave 'the Mouse' £500 'to make a man of him'.[8]

From this point on, Montagu determined to follow Dorset's example and be more statesman than struggling poet.[9] Montagu left a frank explanation of this choice, in which he is likeably without illusions:

I less affect to fiddle than to dance.
Business and Poetry do ill agree,
As the World says, and that's enough for me;
For some may laugh and swagger if they please,
But we must all conform that Love our Ease.[10]

Montagu also made an advantageous match in 1688 to a rich sexagenarian widow whose first marriage (six years before Montagu's birth) had been to his relation, the 3rd Earl of Manchester. When Prior heard the news, he composed a poem about how 'Chamont' would be elevated above his reach by the marriage, comparing the wedding to an apotheosis: 'Pleased that the Friend was in the God improved.'[11] Montagu, however, sent his old school friends assurances that the married state would not lessen his desire for 'a constant friendship and correspondence' with them.[12]

In reward for having escorted James II's younger daughter, Princess Anne, in her midnight escape to join the rebel forces in 1688, Dorset was appointed King William's Lord Chamberlain, the Court's chief functionary. Montagu, Prior and Stepney became popularly known as 'Lord Dorset's Boys', though Stepney at first received favours and 'protection' from Dorset only indirectly, and may not have met the Earl in person until a visit home from the German states in 1693. Prior remembered 'Sneaking . . . among the Crew' of 'Crowding Folks with strange ill Faces' who came to beg favours from Dorset after his appointment.[13]

While Prior was 'sneaking', Montagu's career advanced at speed, thanks to brilliant performances in the Commons. By 1692, Montagu was a Privy Counsellor, alongside Somers and Dorset, a Lord of the Treasury, and the youngest addition to the Whig Junto. Montagu won the King's particular favour by loyally supporting the army supply Bills and promoting a Treasury plan to raise a million-pound loan for the government – a loan identified by the nineteenth-century historian Macaulay as the 'origin' of England's national debt, and still admired by recent historians, such as D. W. Jones, for its ingenuity.[14] Montagu thereafter became a dispenser of patronage in his own right – someone to whom Prior addressed epistolary poems, seeking patronage, much as Montagu had addressed Dorset only a few years earlier.

Montagu was also responsible for shepherding through Parliament the Act founding the Bank of England in 1694, in return for which he would gain the post of Chancellor of the Exchequer. Montagu personally pledged £2,000 (equivalent to some £235,000 today) to the Bank's first subscription, and was joined by many friends. Tonson, probably at the encouragement of Somers, subscribed £500. The new institution was closely tied to the interests of the Whig party, and to financing the Anglo-Dutch alliance. The Tories were less invested (literally and metaphorically) in finance capital. They felt increasingly insecure in the midst of this 1690s financial revolution, and Montagu was an easy figurehead for them to attack. His Tory enemies said Montagu was 'a party-coloured, shallow, maggot-headed statesman'[15] who caressed those who approached him with projects until he had all the details then mysteriously cooled towards them before stealing their ideas. Montagu thought of it merely as keeping an open door to proposals that might benefit the new nation.

While Montagu helped Stepney advance his diplomatic career, Dorset found a diplomatic posting for Prior in The Hague, the Anglo-Dutch allies' headquarters. Stepney often broke his journeys from Berlin back to England with a visit to Prior in The Hague, where the two would sit before 'a good turf fire',[16] roasting chestnuts, getting drunk and offloading their professional and private problems. Prior's lover at the time, a cook-maid nicknamed 'Flanders Jane' whom Prior declared he loved 'above Interest or lust',[17] would have refilled their glasses on these occasions. Stepney was meanwhile sowing his wild oats across central Europe during the early 1690s, writing frankly to a lady in Dresden who had romantic designs on him: '[T]o make love perfectly, methinks Body is as necessary an Ingredient as Brandy is in Punch. Your Wit and Friendship are very good sugar and nutmeg, but there must go something more to make the Dose complete.'[18]

At their sessions before the turf fire, Prior and Stepney also discussed the financial strain of living like gentleman-diplomats when they were entirely dependent upon the Treasury to reimburse their expenses. Both were aware that their humble births mattered more in Europe than at Westminster or Cambridge. Prior referred to himself as 'Albion's meanest son',[19] while Stepney was hurt when someone told the Elector of Saxony he was not of noble birth, which prevented the Elector from inviting him to dine for a month. In answer, Montagu and Dorset had Stepney made a Gentleman of King William's Privy Chamber, and Montagu arranged an advance on Stepney's salary, for which Stepney thanked Montagu warmly, calling him his 'good Angel at the Brink of the Pool'.[20] On another occasion, Stepney told his mother he had declined a £1,000 personal loan from Montagu for reasons that show the men remained, in the early 1690s, more old school friends than patron and client: '[I]t is the last use any man should make of his friend, & which I should be sorry to be reduced to,' Stepney declared.[21] Prior had less scruple about begging for cash from his old friend: 'If you can get me any ready money, it would be more charity than to give alms to the poorest dog that ever gave you a petition; if not, patience is a virtue, and a scrap or two of Horace must be my consolation.'[22]

Like Somers, Montagu believed in the Ciceronian ideal that literary endeavour was an essential qualification for being a great statesman, and if one was not writing oneself, then playing patron to poets was the next best thing. Montagu and Dorset therefore ensured that Tonson published the witty, self-mocking verses that both Prior and Stepney continued to write in between the 'prose affairs' of international diplomacy.[23] Pursuing identical courses, and consulting one another on their poems in manuscript, they would not have guessed that Stepney would be remembered as one of England's first modern diplomats, while Prior would be remembered primarily as a poet.

Montagu, Prior and Stepney all wrote elegies on the occasion of Queen Mary's death in December 1694, to demonstrate their loyalty to the widowed King. The Tories had always felt more at ease with Mary, as a Stuart daughter, than with her husband's largely parliamentary claim to the throne, and Mary's death now meant William had to renew his bid for popular support. William's childlessness also placed increased importance on Mary's sister Anne, now William's heir apparent, and on Anne's choice of friends. From The Hague, Prior observed the political upheavals consequent upon Mary's death in a letter to Montagu:

> These matters will be decided before the King's coming over, so we must have a vigilant eye. I call it 'we', for you, Sir, have always regarded my interest as if it were your own; and when I consider that you have taken your poor neighbour and made a friend of him, and solicited for that friend as if he had been your brother, I doubt not but you will have the reward you deserve (though a good while hence) in the Court of Heaven; and I the credentials I do not deserve to some Court or Republic a little nearer.[24]

Another writer to produce an elegy on Mary's death, published by Tonson, was a young Fellow of Magdalen College, Oxford, named Joseph Addison. Addison was, like Prior and Stepney, a product of the late seventeenth century's widening access to education. He had attended Charterhouse, a charitable school and hospital then located near to today's Barbican Centre that was considered one of the best grammar schools in England. It took in forty nominated scholars for free, alongside sixty fee-paying non-boarders or 'town boys'.[25] Like Westminster, Charterhouse ran a long, spartan day from six in the morning to six in the evening in summer, with an hour's later start in winter, and taught the classics (mainly Cicero and Horace) with a heavier dose of stick than carrot.

Entering as a scholarship boy in 1686, the 14-year-old Addison formed a close friendship with another scholar the same age, who would become his lifelong companion and collaborator. This boy, Richard (or 'Dick') Steele, had already been at the school for two years when Addison arrived.

Steele's father, an Anglo-Irish gentleman from Dublin, died in his early childhood, a fact Steele believed left him calamitously hyper-sensitive forever after. Steele dramatized the event in a later essay:

> I remember I went into the Room where his Body lay, and my Mother sat weeping alone by it. I had my Battledore [a toy] in my Hand, and fell a-beating the Coffin, and calling Papa; for I know not how I had some slight Idea that he was locked up there. My mother catched me in her Arms, and transported beyond all Patience of the silent Grief she was before in, she almost smothered me in her Embrace, and told

> me in a Flood of Tears, Papa could not hear me and would play with me no more, for they were going to put him under Ground, when he could never come to us again.[26]

Steele's mother – whom he remembered as 'a very beautiful Woman, of a Noble Spirit'[27] – sent him away from Ireland, to live with his wealthier, childless aunt and uncle in England, and it was they who entered him at Charterhouse in 1684. His mother died that same year, orphaning him fully.

Steele's uncle was private secretary to the 1st Duke of Ormonde, the same Lord Lieutenant of Ireland served by Congreve's father, and it was Ormonde who, as a governor of Charterhouse, arranged for Steele's admittance. One letter from the schoolboy Steele to his patroness-aunt survives. It includes a formal apology for not writing more often, mixed with a pained awareness of his dependency, expressed with less than complete humility: 'Madam, should I express my gratitude for every benefit I receive at Your Ladyship's and my good Uncle, I should never sit down to meat but I must write a letter when I rise from table.'[28] Steele addressed successive patrons with similarly mixed feelings throughout his life.

Their intellects, and the loss of their mothers when they were 12, were what Addison and Steele had in common; the rest was all contrast. Steele was short and square-bodied, with a 'dusky' complexion that, combined with his fading Irish accent, would have been interpreted by contemporaries as indicating lowly birth;[29] Addison was tall for his age, with pale blue eyes and the pallor of a bookworm. Soon the advantage of Steele's previous years at the school was erased as he came to idolize his new friend.

Addison invited Steele home for the holidays. Addison's father was Dean of Lichfield, having settled there after an exotic life as chaplain to the British garrisons at Dunkirk and Tangier. Addison had immense respect for his father, who imbued him with a profound belief in self-control. In 1686, the Dean was raising four children alone – three boys and a girl, of whom Joseph was the oldest. Steele admired how the Dean taught his sons to vie for his favour and called it 'an unspeakable Pleasure to visit or sit at a Meal in that Family'.[30] Steele was warmly welcomed into the Lichfield deanery that school holiday, and recalled how Addison's father 'loved me like one of them'.[31]

Addison only stayed at Charterhouse for a year before being elected to his father's former Oxford college, Queen's, at the age of 15. This confirmed Steele's belief in Addison's superiority; Steele remained ever after several steps behind his friend academically. Steele entered Christ Church, Oxford, in December 1689, by which time Addison had been elected to one of the 'demyships' (scholarships offering free lodging) at Magdalen College. Christ Church, to which Steele was sent thanks to his uncle's connections, did not suit him well. It had stood on the losing side of the previous year's Revolutionary politics (in contrast to Magdalen, which had resisted James II's demands) and contained more nobly born students than the rest of Oxford's colleges. When Steele went up, his aunt gave him a pair of gloves and a sword to help him fit in.

After a year, Steele asked his uncle to pull strings with the Dean of Christ Church to get him a scholarship, reporting that though he had gained his tutor's respect, 'these places are not given by merit but are secured by friends'.[32] When his uncle's efforts failed to produce the scholarship, Steele moved to Merton College to accept one there instead. Steele left Merton in May 1692 and enlisted in the army as a 'wretched common Trooper',[33] since he lacked the funds to buy an officer's commission. Years later, Steele recalled Oxford students who window-shopped, played billiards and bowls, and who were 'seized all over with a general Inability, Indolence and Weariness, and a certain Impatience of the Place they are in'.[34] Steele sounds as though he was well acquainted with these 'loungers', but he probably left university voluntarily, out of patriotic duty, rather than because he was expelled, as Jonathan Swift later hinted. Steele would have watched the fireworks in Oxford celebrating the Treaty of Limerick after William's victory in Ireland, and the troops returning from the Irish wars. Though Steele missed his chance to participate in this Protestant victory in his homeland, he could still serve the Protestant cause on the Continent. Since the regiment he joined belonged to his uncle's patron's son, enlisting may also have been a direct order from his uncle that Steele could not refuse.

Addison did not feel a similar pull towards the adventure of war. He remained to wander the water walks and gardens of Magdalen, translating and composing Latin poetry to the acclaim of his fellow academics. These pastimes between teaching duties sound more plausible from what we know of Addison than his later confessional lines referring to his 'heedless steps' upon 'the slippery paths of youth'.[35] One thing Addison never let himself be was heedless, and his decision not to enlist was decidedly careful of his own person.

When Addison sent a poem flattering Dryden's talent to the poet in London, Dryden and Tonson included it in the *Miscellany Poems* they co-edited in 1693.[36] Addison's 1694 poem, 'An Account of the Greatest English Poets', then summarized the history of English poetry, culminating – implausibly to modern judgement – with Charles Montagu at its pinnacle. Addison immediately found a flattered benefactor in the 33-year-old Chancellor of the Exchequer. Steele later recalled that Congreve was the instrument of Addison's 'becoming acquainted with' Montagu.[37] How Congreve and Addison first met, however, is uncertain. Most likely it was through Dryden and/or Tonson, following Addison's inclusion in the *Miscellany*, or perhaps Tonson invited Addison home to the Fleet Street house the publisher then shared with Congreve. Either way, there was soon mutual respect between Addison and Congreve, whose respective specializations in Latin and Greek literature spared them direct rivalry.

By 1695, Addison was studying to take orders, though he increasingly wished neither to follow his father into the Church nor to remain a university tutor. Addison therefore sought to add a further patron to his portfolio and did so in the traditional way: by poetic tribute. His verse 'On His Majesty, Presented to the Lord Keeper [Somers]' was a bold move on the young academic's part, since he had never met Somers, and had no family connection to justify the presentation. Somers must not have minded, since he let Tonson and Congreve bring the poem's author to meet him. Until now, Addison had been not so much a Whig as Whig-leaning, but these two poems, courting Montagu and Somers, marked his first clear declaration of political allegiance.

Addison's friend Steele had more enthusiasm but less opportunity to serve William's government. Steele too wrote an elegy for Queen Mary: 'The Procession: A Poem on Her Majesties Funeral, By a Gentleman of the Army'. Steele's, however, was not printed by Tonson, but by a lesser firm, probably at Steele's own expense. If Addison and Steele corresponded during these years while following such starkly divergent paths, the letters are lost. Addison seems not to have shared any of his impressive new literary contacts with his former school friend.

Steele had by this time seen active military service in Flanders during 1692–4, for a salary of about 4 shillings (now around £20) a day. Steele had thereby 'wiped off the Rust of Education',[38] and depended, as a soldier puts it in one of Congreve's plays, 'upon the outside of his head [rather] than the lining'.[39] Nonetheless, in the army as in international diplomacy, promotion could be secured by demonstrating literary wit in flattery. As a result of dedicating his elegy on Queen Mary to Baron Cutts, a war hero turned governor of the Isle of Wight, Steele was permitted to switch to the Coldstream Guards, a more elite regiment that provided security at the royal palaces. Steele was made a captain, and, though Cutts was the Guards' nominal commander, much of the actual commanding was left to Steele, especially in early 1697 when he served as Cutts' private secretary. The prospect of a peace to end the War of the League of Augsburg spelled an end, however, to further army promotion for Steele.

Dick Steele would soon prove himself, like Tonson and Prior, an extremely enterprising man, in tune with this enterprising period of British history. This was the legacy of each of these three men's childhood struggles, in contrast to the more complacent confidence of Congreve and Addison – both of whom, despite the forced migrations of the Congreve family and the early death of Addison's mother, came from relatively stable and financially secure homes. Belonging to a club (or a political party) would always be a more primal need for Prior and Steele, both parentless, than for Congreve or Addison. Kindred spirits become far more important than kin if you have fewer kin to begin with.

III
THE SCENT OF THE PIE-OVEN

Who knows but by the dint of Kit-Cat's Pies,
You may, e'er long, to Gods and Monarchs Rise.

NED WARD, *The Secret History of Clubs* (1709)

A CONTEMPORARY ACCOUNT by a writer named Ned Ward states that the Kit-Cat Club originally convened at the Cat and Fiddle, a London tavern owned by one Mr Christopher (or 'Kit') Cat (or 'Catling'[1]), a pastry cook from Norfolk, whose supposed portrait shows a gnarly man with a white knotted handkerchief on his head. The Cat and Fiddle was on Gray's Inn Lane, a street then noted for its fresh air blowing down from open fields to the north of the city.[2] As a 'kit' was slang for a small fiddle, the Cat and Fiddle's signboard, jutting into the lane with its painted emblem of a fiddle-playing puss, may have been a punning reference to the tavern's proprietor.[3]

Ned Ward's account describes the meeting of this 'greasy' pie-maker, Mr Cat, and the 'amphibious' publisher-cum-bookseller, Tonson, when they were neighbours in Gray's Inn. Ward envisaged Tonson, his aspiring writers and wealthy patrons gathered sweatily together within the scent of Mr Cat's pie-oven to eat a 'collation of oven trumpery' – mutton pies, cheese-cakes, golden custards, puff-pastry apple tarts, rose-water codling tarts, and other ornate dishes requiring engineering in dough. As they became drunk, the guests composed doggerel in praise of Mr Cat's pastry creations. The 'voracious mouth' of the flaming oven swallowed what they bothered to write down on paper, suggesting it was as near to hand as a spittoon or wastepaper basket.[4]

The Kit-Cat Club thus began as an eccentric publishing rights deal, cooked up by Tonson,[5] and has also been called 'the first expense-account publisher's dinner on record'.[6] The publisher 'very cunningly' resolved to feed a gang of 'poetical young sprigs' – including his Fleet Street housemate Congreve – on a regular basis, with Cat's baked goods, provided the poets 'would do him the honour to let him have the refusal of all their juvenile productions'.[7] Beyond first options on the works of new authors, Tonson wished to forge professional loyalties in the heat of Cat's pie-oven, with an eye to longer-term profits.[8] Ever since Tonson's earliest ventures, he had been securing authors' loyalties through gifts of food and wine – sending exotic melons to Dryden when first wooing the dramatist into his publishing fold, for example – and hiding commercial motives under a veneer of pseudo-baronial hospitality. As early as the 1680s, Tonson had organized what he called 'Clubbing with Ovid'[9] – that is, assembling networks of translators to produce collaborative publications. Now he was simply clubbing men in the same way as he had previously anthologized their writings.

The exact date at which the semi-professional friendships between Tonson, his patron-readers (such as Somers, Montagu and Dorset) and his young authors (such as Congreve, Vanbrugh, Prior and Stepney) turned into 'The Kit-Cat Club' is unknown, but it was certainly during the final years of the seventeenth century. Thanks to his family's bookshops in the Gray's Inn neighbourhood, Tonson would have frequented the Cat and Fiddle long after moving his own premises from the area. Whereas Tonson's biographers tend to credit him with the foundational love of pies,[10] Somers' biographers claim it was the Lord Keeper who discovered Cat's bakery and took his drinking companion Tonson there one day to taste them.[11]

Although there had been clubs in England before, the Kit-Cat Club would be the first to have such wide-ranging interests and influence, combining cultural, political and professional purposes. Previously, trade and craft guilds, political cliques and literary coteries had kept to their own relatively distinct spheres – so, for example, Will's Coffee House had been the venue one evening for Dryden's 'Witty Club' and for the politicians' 'Grave Club' another.[12]

The Kit-Cat Club would draw many of its literary members from the Witty Club, but whereas the Witty Club members were both Whigs and Tories, being a Whig was to be as essential a qualification as wit when it came to joining the Kit-Cat. The republican and Whig clubs of the Civil War and Restoration periods had been notorious as hotbeds of subversion, insurrection and treachery. King William, who relied on the Whigs but 'believed the Whigs . . . did not love monarchy', remained suspicious of any club that might engender new republican conspiracies.[13] The Kit-Cat Club, through its emphasis on literature and other highbrow culture, would strive to shake off these inherited associations, and make clubbing into a respectable pastime for a post-Revolutionary Whig gentleman. In doing so, it would provide the template for the literary and cultural clubs that proliferated later in the eighteenth century, of which Dr Johnson's is the most famous.

Though the origins of the Club's name were disputed even within the members' lifetimes,[14] the majority of primary sources support Ward's assertion that it came from Mr Cat's mutton pies, known as 'Kit Cats',[15] on which the Club originally dined.[16] The contemporary poet Sir Richard Blackmore writes, for example:

> Indulgent BOCAJ did his Muses treat,
> Their Drink was gen'rous Wine and Kit-Cat Pies their Meat,
> Here he assembled his Poetic Tribe,
> Past Labours to Reward, and New Ones to Prescribe.[17]

A half-pun on the Club's name may also explain why it was adopted. A 1711 letter allegedly written by Mr Cat is signed with the variant spelling 'Ch Chatt'.[18] The slang 'chit-chat' for small-talk was commonly used, and practising the art of conversation was a central preoccupation of the Kit-Cat Club, so this name may have been thought amusingly apt. In addition, the name contained a classical allusion pleasing to the founders' Whiggish tastes: in ancient Rome, cats symbolized liberty since no animal less likes to be caged, and the goddess of Liberty was often represented with a cat at her feet. Though Tories and Whigs competed to claim many of the same patriotic principles, liberty was one rhetorical term used far more frequently by the Whigs.

The heat of the scene before the pie-oven, as evoked by Ned Ward, was similarly symbolic. Warmth was considered a Whig characteristic, as shown by the anecdote in which the Kit-Cats asked Mr Cat to bake some pies with the poetry of the comic dramatist Thomas D'Urfey used as baking paper, to test that poet's Whig principles and fitness for membership. The story goes that the members complained when the pies were not baked through, to which Mr Cat replied that D'Urfey's writings were so cold they were cooling the dough. They were not, in other words, sufficiently Whig.

Pies were certainly baked on discarded bits of writing in that paper-frugal century. Dryden described worthless pieces of poetry as 'Martyrs of Pies'[19] and Addison later mused with false modesty that his journalism would 'make a good Foundation for a Mutton-pie, as I have more than once experienced'.[20] The nice image of Mr Cat's customers picking the last of the 'kissing crust' (the old name for the soft under-crust of a pie) off a piece of blank verse, the ink transferring from browned paper to golden pastry, was not fanciful but real.

As pies and puddings were considered the best of English cookery, the Club's favourite dish would have signified the founders' self-consciously English, as opposed to French, tastes. The pies were also regarded as humble fare symbolizing the condescension (in its archaic, entirely positive sense) of aristocrats conversing with struggling, lowly born authors. This was made clear by one playwright's hope that his play, even if lacking in delicacy, might nonetheless suit the taste of great men just as 'A Kit-Cat is a Supper for a Lord'.[21]

The Kit-Cat authors were never literally starving for a meal, but they were certainly hungry for recognition and fame. Patrons such as Dorset, Somers and Montagu were therefore essential guests at Mr Cat's table. Throughout the Kit-Cat Club's several incarnations, from its 1690s' foundation to its demise some two decades later, patronage was to remain the single most important constant in the Club's story – the mechanism that made it tick.

Whereas writing for money was condemned by Renaissance critical theory as limiting an author's imaginative freedom, patronage allowed its recipients to profit without feeling sullied by the pecuniary motives of Grub Street hacks (one of whom, in their eyes, was Ned Ward). The Kit-Cat Club provided, in other words, the same 'cover' as verse letters – mimicking an earlier, courtly way of doing things. Verse letters in the 1690s pretended to have a readership of one, the aristocratic addressee, while actually having print runs of hundreds. The Club's authors pretended to be a carousing circle of amateurs with private incomes, when really they were piecing together their livings out of day-jobs, book sales and audience figures.

They hoped to be permitted exceptions to the rules of class, familiarity being among the most valuable gifts that a noble patron could bestow. For a writer to be admitted into a nobleman's 'conversation' implied a rise in status with tangible benefits in terms of one's creditors. It was not simply a flattering attention from a social superior; it was an asset that could be spent afterwards as though it were hard cash.

The tantalizing promise of patronage was meant to guarantee a certain level of conversational virtuosity at the Kit-Cat Club, in contrast to the conversation at the Witty Club, where Dryden's approbation was the only reward on offer. Though Will's Coffee House was supposed to be an 'Exchange for Wit', the fact that there was more profit in publishing a good line than throwing it away on one's friends caused the 'Wit-Merchants' to meet there, it was said, 'without bringing the Commodity with them, which they leave at home in the Warehouses'.[22] A character in one of Congreve's plays similarly refers to wit as an alternative currency, in which writers are naturally richer than their patrons: 'None but dull rogues *think*; witty men, like rich fellows, are always ready for all expenses; while your blockheads, like poor needy scoundrels, are forced to examine their stock and forecast the charges of the day.'[23]

A later satirical play about the Kit-Cat Club referred to certain members 'who only listen in it'[24] – these were the aristocratic patrons who came in the spirit of an audience, ready to exchange one currency for another. It was a fair exchange, in so far as a poet might determine a patron's reputation among contemporary readers (and voters) and in the eyes of posterity. Tonson shrewdly realized that busy, wealthy and powerful men would gladly pay for the glamour of association with popular writers such as Vanbrugh and Congreve, or at least would prefer to play patrons than become targets of their satire. As Ned Ward put it, some Whig grandees joined 'in hopes to be accounted wits, and others to avoid the very opposite imputation'.[25]

The Kit-Cat authors, in their poetry and classical translations, self-interestedly perpetuated the idea that a well-rounded nobleman must be a generous patron. They constantly reminded their superiors that there was a parallel value system, independent of inheritance, in which the nobly born were expected to compete, if not with their own literary talent then at least as discerning patrons. The Kit-Cat Club's broad membership implied a hierarchy based on values other than birth and wealth: 'Though not of Title, Men of Sense and Wit.'[26]

Prior and Stepney, for example, showed an imaginative sensitivity throughout their writings and classical translations to the theme of 'meanly born' men who led virtuous lives, or proved themselves great senators, lawyers or soldiers. In his translation of *Juvenal's Eighth Satire*, Stepney contrasted the great achievements of lowborn Cicero, or Tully 'the native mushroom', to highborn Rubellius whose useless life was no better than that of 'a living statue'.[27] It was an old Christian idea, given a fresh political edge: the natural corollary, or ultimate logic, of the Whig theory of kingship, that each man had to earn his own honour in this world.

Lord Dorset was flattered as 'bountiful Maecenas', especially after his appointment as the King's Lord Chamberlain. This was a reference to the Roman patron whose circle had included Virgil and Horace, and who was therefore the prime classical model for Kit-Cat patronage. Dorset had been a patron to Tonson's authors, including Dryden, since before the Revolution, and when Tonson published Congreve's second play, *Love for Love* (1695), it was with a dedication to Dorset attached – a transparent bid by Congreve to become another of the Earl's favoured 'Boys'. The publisher tended to broker the patronage of Somers when one of his prose authors needed subsidy, but that of Dorset when it was an aspiring poet or playwright.

The contemporary writer John Macky emphasized Dorset's role as one of the Kit-Cat Club's 'first founders',[28] alongside Tonson and Somers, and if this was indeed the case, then Dorset's motives were largely nostalgic and escapist. By the mid-1690s, Dorset was in his late fifties and his second marriage was souring because of quarrels over his wife's estate. He was therefore spending more time in town, pretending to a bachelor's lifestyle. At Charles II's Restoration Court, Dorset had enjoyed a dissipated youth, one of the 'Merry Gang' of poets and rakes alongside the infamous Earl of Rochester. Dorset had fought in street brawls and duels, been Nell Gwynn's lover and survived nearly fifteen years of nocturnal, riotous, self-destructive living. He had escaped frequent brushes with the law, including charges of murder and of gross indecency after a drunken appearance stark naked on a tavern balcony. Now in the 1690s, having a mid-life crisis, Dorset wanted to recapture the carefree spirit of his youth, or at least help the next generation of poets enjoy a similar camaraderie.

For Montagu, as for Prior and Stepney, nostalgia for the collegiality of Westminster and Cambridge was a significant motive in their clubbing. These men treasured memories of sharing the life of the mind, before the realities of the world had separated them. To their eighteenth-century minds, family was directly associated with nature, in contrast to friendship, which they associated with the power of reason to make discerning, civilized choices. Montagu, at least, sought a place where his intellectually noble friendships with Prior and Stepney might be preserved, despite all that had changed in their relative circumstances since Cambridge. He also sought to extend his reputation as a patron by supporting other authors beyond his childhood friends. *The Old Batchelor*, for example, had won Congreve

Montagu's patronage and friendship – something that may have aroused some jealousy from Prior and Stepney, since Prior once complimented Stepney's poetry by comparing it favourably to Congreve's weaker efforts.[29]

For the Whig government ministers, furthermore, solidifying friendships through new clubs and associations was part of a wider civic duty to resolidify the nation. Civil turmoil had meant not knowing who your friends were from one day to the next; post-Revolutionary peace and prosperity now required rebuilding trust between like-minded men. When Dorset or Montagu was flattered as a modern Maecenas, it was not simply because they were each generous literary patrons, but because their aims resembled those of the Roman governor who, via his literary circle, had tried to reconcile a fractured society and forge ideals of 'Roman-ness' in the decades following a civil war.

Over the years, many observers would complain that the Kit-Cat Club monopolized literary patronage. One imagined Tonson boasting:

> I am the Touchstone of all Modern Wit,
> Without my Stamp in vain your Poets write.
> Those only purchase ever-living Fame,
> That in my *Miscellany* plant their Name.[30]

Another saw the Club's monopoly of literary fame as a corruption of literary justice: 'But Mastiff Poets oft are doomed to Starve, / Whilst Lapdog Wits are hugged, who less deserve.'[31] Cognoscenti have been envied in every age, but the Kit-Cat Club's networking was more acutely resented because it was unapologetically partisan. The Whigs recognized, years before the Tories, the benefits of creating a 'sympathetic climate of opinion' through art, and set about establishing a patronage network to incubate this 'climate'.[32] Dr Johnson called Dorset and Montagu 'universal' and 'general' patrons, meaning they rewarded writers of either party, but the majority of their largesse was dispensed within their own political fold.[33] They did not regard the exclusion of Tory writers from the Kit-Cat Club as a corruption of the arts by politics, since they shared a belief in '*amicitia*' – a community in which political fellowship flowed naturally from virtuous characters thinking and acting in perfect accord. The Tories of the 1690s may have shared the same classical reference points, but their power base, centred on country squires and clergy, was – for the time being at least – intrinsically less 'clubbable' than that of the more metropolitan Whigs.

Another motive of the Kit-Cat patrons, to which Blackmore alluded in his verse account of the Club's foundation, was that 'warlike William' had no interest in English literature, so that authors 'met with small Respect' at Court and felt they must seek their rewards elsewhere. It had been, in fact, a deliberate policy on William's part to present himself as a warrior-king, too busy saving the Protestant world to bother with flattering poetic dedications. William avoided literary patronage partly in order to imply he had no need of propagandists – as a providential leader who needed no help but God's – and partly because he had little love for a language that was not his own. Hampton Court's competition with Versailles motivated royal patronage of the visual arts and architecture, but no similar royal bounty flowed towards English authors to match Louis XIV's patronage of writers such as Racine and De La Fontaine. Though the relative beneficence of previous English Courts to poets may have been exaggerated, the rising numbers of men attempting to pursue writing careers without private incomes under William III made it appear as if royal reward for wit was in short supply. This was the gap the Kit-Cats felt it their patriotic duty to fill.[34]

The Kit-Cats' sense of patriotic duty was linked to their sense of historical continuity with previous literary clubs during what they regarded as England's last golden age: the reign of Elizabeth I. They had in mind the legendary 'merry meetings' of Shakespeare, Beaumont, Fletcher, Ben Jonson and others at the Mermaid tavern, or the 'Apollo' wits Jonson gathered around himself at the Devil tavern in Temple Bar. This latter club fascinated Richard Steele (he described taking a party up to the Devil in 1709 and finding 'the rules of Ben's Club' were still to be seen 'in gold letters over the chimney'[35]), and Tonson once received an unsolicited poem that flattered the Kit-Cat Club by comparison to Ben Jonson's club at the Devil.

The dating of the Kit-Cat Club's foundation to the second half of the 1690s would place it in the context of a significant relaxation in attitudes to the public exchange of opinion. Sixteen ninety-five saw the second lapse of England's Licensing Act, after which there was a huge surge in the number of books, papers and pamphlets flying off London's presses – especially pamphlets which debated public affairs or satirized public figures.

Authors and printers could still be prosecuted under blasphemy, obscenity and sedition laws, particularly if they expressed Jacobite views (that is, supportive of James II's restoration), but there was now a feeling that just about anyone and anything could get published. It was no coincidence that the Kit-Cat's members chose Tonson as their chairman and secretary, emphasizing this link between their Club and the power of England's comparatively unfettered printing presses.

By the 1710s, there would be some 21,000 books published in Britain – far more than in any other European country – and, by approximately the same date, clubbing would be seen as a quintessentially English activity, John Macky observing: '[A]lmost every parish hath its separate Club, where the Citizens, after the Fatigue of the Day is over in their Shops, and on the Exchange, unbend their Thoughts before they go to bed.'[36] Freedom of commerce, association and expression went hand in hand.

The Kit-Cat Club, like many of the clubs that would follow it, had an ambivalent relationship to the birth of the new style of financial capitalism around it. On the one hand, the Club was a way to preserve the ancient loyalties and hereditary customs that its members feared the new modes of commerce might extinguish. London's worlds of politics, publishing and commerce were ruthless and unregulated, making people seek refuge in the gentler ideal of 'clubbability'. At the same time, as Whigs who generally appreciated and exploited the benefits of credit-based commerce and urban life, its members recognized that they needed to invest in social capital as much as financial capital, and the Club was formed to assist with such investment. This meant acquiring a reputation for learning and taste, and securing well-connected friends with inside information about both stocks and politics.

This was a period of great social anxiety, as boundaries between classes became increasingly blurred and the concept of gentility increasingly uncertain. In the seventeenth century, a 'gentleman' had been a man entitled to bear arms and with no need to work for a living, but by the 1690s gentility was becoming a more fluid matter of education, manners and taste. Outward indicators of a genteel education, such as the great private libraries of Somers and Montagu, could be imitated by anyone with money, as when a character in one of Vanbrugh's plays mocked the way gilt-covered books were valued as interior décor by the nouveau riche. Another Vanbrugh character was a 'fake' peer who purchased his peerage from the Crown for £10,000. To be a Kit-Cat, in this context, was to wear a badge of cultural honour that could not be faked or debased by imitation. For the first time, membership of a particular club became a recognized social credential.

It would be unfair, however, to describe the Kit-Cat Club as concerned only with preserving the reactionary cultural credit of the aristocracy in the face of entrepreneurial capitalism and social mobility. As would become clear in the following decade, the Club promoted a very particular, patriotic agenda, slicing through every art form, to raise the nation as a whole up to their cultural level, and for that they had to look outwards, far beyond their own charmed circle. Tonson's presses, pouring forth their texts for the literate public, were the first evidence of this engagement with the wider world.

It was not self-interest, self-improvement or civic duty that made these men leave their homes and go out to a tavern on a cold wet night, however, but rather a longing for relaxation, amusement and the sympathy of friends. The tasty wine and pies of Mr Cat and the enticingly warm wit of Congreve or Prior, were as crucial to the successful foundation of the Kit-Cat Club as any social or economic cost-benefit analysis at the back of its founders' minds.

IV
THE TOAST OF THE TOWN: A KIT-CAT MEETING, 1697

We taught them how to toast, and rhyme, and bite,
To sleep away the day, and drink away the night.

WILLIAM SHIPPEN, *Faction Display'd* (1704)

IN THE FADING light of a Thursday afternoon during the winter of 1697–8, the Kit-Cat members made their way – by foot, coroneted coach, carriage and swaying sedan chair – towards the Cat and Fiddle tavern in Gray's Inn, to attend a Club meeting that would end with an unusual visitor.

Tonson would have arrived early to ready the room. As a later Kit-Cat advised: 'Upon all Meetings at Taverns, 'tis necessary some one of the Company should take it upon him to get all Things in such Order . . . such as hastening the Fire, getting a sufficient number of Candles, [and] tasting the Wine with a judicious Smack.'[1]

When the other members arrived, each bowed to the gathered company before being relieved of his outer jacket or cloak, hat, gloves, cane or sword by a waiting servant. Disrobing elegantly was an art, and Congreve mocked country bumpkins who went too far and pulled off their boots on such occasions.

It has been suggested that the Club's seating arrangements mimicked an Oxbridge college dining hall, with a 'high table' for the grandest nobles and lower tables at right angles for everyone else, but it is more likely that such a sharp distinction between aristocrats and wits was deliberately avoided, to the mutual flattery of both. The Club's presidential pride of place, a wooden 'elbow chair' (armchair) at one end of the table, was occupied not by the Club's highest ranking peer, but by Tonson, while Matt Prior mentions that it was unnecessary to sit in one's seat for the duration of a Kit-Cat meal.

The diners first washed their hands in a basin, then the highest ranking member said grace. In 1697, this was the Duke of Somerset, Charles Seymour, the second highest ranking peer in the kingdom. He was a vastly wealthy and notoriously proud man, who spoke with an affected lisp and had once disowned his daughter when he awoke from a nap and caught her seated in his presence. Only 35 in 1697, however, such caricaturish excesses lay ahead of him. Somerset was at this time renovating his stately home of Petworth in Sussex, where he and his wife had spent the preceding summer, and he was the Chancellor of Cambridge University, responsible for re-establishing that university's press. Tonson's firm was collaborating with it to produce a series of Cambridge classics: a canon-forming list first shaped by Dryden and, after Dryden's death, by the Kit-Cats. Somerset may also have been personally responsible for Montagu receiving the title of High Steward of Cambridge University earlier in the year.

By now the Club had expanded beyond the first huddle of friends before Mr Cat's pie-oven, though it is uncertain whether it had already reached its later cap of thirty-nine members. Certainly a number of other dukes and earls had been admitted, and after Somerset finished the grace, these nobles were first to offer their plates to the carving man. They also initiated all calls for wine throughout the meal. The Kit-Cats' belief that it was vulgar to over-emphasize such distinctions of rank, however, would have blunted many rules of 1690s etiquette, good English breeding showing itself 'most where to an ordinary Eye it appears the least'.[2] The very English prejudice by which the confidence to flout class divides is considered the sign of real class was just emerging.

Some class divisions were beyond flouting, however: a number of waiters – footmen brought by the guests mixed with 'drawers' from the tavern below – would have stood discreetly against the walls for long hours. These silent observers took their opinions of the Kit-Cat Club to their graves, but one such 'Spectator of Gentlemen at Dinner for many Years' complained how masters expected their servants to be sober and chaste when the masters themselves – with the advantages of education and property – could not exercise the same self-control.[3]

The waiters would have laid out the first course, including 'pottages' (stewy soups) and large joints of meat, before the Club members arrived. Dorset, in line with his other Restoration tastes, loved lavish banquets where diners 'devour Fowl, Fish and Flesh; swallow Oil and Vinegar, Wines and Spices; throw down Salads of twenty different Herbs, Sauces of a hundred Ingredients, Confections and Fruits of numberless Sweets and Flavours'.[4] By mid-winter, however, the contributions of game and fresh produce, brought to town at the end of the summer from the landed members' estates, would have been running out. If there were a separate dessert course, it would likely have involved fruit and nuts in preserving syrups, or a spiced rice pudding called a 'whitepot'.

The vogue for decorative dishes in symmetrical or pyramidical shapes did not start until the latter part of the eighteenth century, so the Kit-Cat pies, with their decorative pastry, would have been the likely centrepieces. The menu almost certainly included native oysters, available then like sturgeon and lobster in cheap plenitude from the Thames. Fish, such as anchovy, was also used to make salty relishes to accompany meat, and passed around, like salt, on the tip of one's knife. Cutlery was just becoming commonplace, but using fingers and fingerbowls remained perfectly acceptable.

Eating the main meal of the day with friends in the mid-afternoon was an increasingly fashionable pastime, but also a civilizing duty. Only beasts, Epicurus taught them, dined alone. Congreve reflected that he disliked 'seeing things that force me to entertain low thoughts of my Nature. I don't know how it is with others, but I confess freely to you, I could never look long upon a Monkey without very

Mortifying Reflections, though I never heard anything to the Contrary, why that Creature is not Originally of a Distinct Species.'[5] Kit-Cat dinners demonstrated, among other more overt purposes, the members' distance from the apes – or, more to the point, from the London 'mob' outdoors. Public dining also, implicitly, demonstrated men's distance from women. Being a lady in this period required rejection of physical appetites, for food as for sex. It was no more polite for a woman to say she was hungry, or let men see her eating in public, than to mention if she was sweaty or lustful. The fact that the Kit-Cat was a dining club should therefore be seen as the corollary of its exclusively masculine nature; the first in a long line of clubs where men went to escape their uneducated wives and what they regarded as the intellectual wasteland of the domestic dinner table.

The men seated around the tavern table in 1697 brought a variety of experiences, worries and needs to the Club. Montagu, now 36, had been appointed First Lord of the Treasury in May, following the removal of the Tory-leaning Sidney Godolphin (known to his contemporaries and throughout this book as Lord Godolphin). Montagu had received this post only after managing, by the skin of his teeth, to save the country from financial mismanagement. In 1695, he and Somers had hatched a plan for a national recoinage, intended to deal with the problem of clipped coins. The policy was a disaster, however, forcing the new-minted Bank of England to renege on contracts such that army paymasters could not obtain supplies. With troops and sailors on starvation rations and the verge of mass desertion, the Dutch had had to bail out the English for several months. Luckily, a parallel economic crisis broke in France, leading both sides to look with sudden favour upon peace talks. Montagu extended £5 million of debt for just long enough to conclude such talks at William's palace of Ryswick, near The Hague, where Prior acted as his eyes and ears, checking the draft treaty's translations and sending copies back to Montagu, alongside cases of duty-free wine. The Treaty of Ryswick was concluded in September 1697. Among its terms was the return of North America to its state of pre-war division between France and England.

The conclusion to the War of the League of Augsburg, however, left Montagu in an even more difficult economic position than before:

peace did not immediately reduce the national debt, while making it harder to justify the taxation of landowners needed to service that debt. Physically and mentally exhausted, Montagu would therefore have come to the Kit-Cat that winter from his townhouse on Jermyn Street not only hoping to consolidate his political support but also to find solace in his old hobby of poetry and in his childhood friends.

This winter was the first time the Earl of Dorset and his three 'Boys' had been reunited in London for several years. Dorset, still at the Kit-Cat Club's 'suckling centre',[6] had been sanguine when the King paid him off handsomely to resign as Lord Chamberlain in April, so that the place could be given to a Dutch royal favourite. Dorset was relieved, in fact, to relinquish a post that required him, against his nature (and ironically in light of his past indiscretions), to play state censor of the theatres. The resignation, however, left Dorset with fewer occasions to see his Privy Council friends and greater interest, like Somerset, in attending the Kit-Cat Club to hear Court and Commons gossip. By 1697, several of Dorset's other old friends from his days of youthful debauchery were also members. Most notable among these was John Vaughan, 3rd Earl of Carbery, described by Pepys as 'one of the lewdest fellows of the age'[7] and particularly notorious for having sold his Welsh servants into slavery in Jamaica.

Dorset's original 'Boy', Matt Prior, was now one of the most dominant, entertaining personalities at the table, said to leave 'no elbow room for others'.[8] He was in London only briefly, having returned from the Peace Congress at Ryswick and expecting to be sent next to a position in Ireland he had pulled several strings to obtain. He had pleaded with Montagu for a post lucrative enough that he could 'come home again to dedicate the rest of his life *amicitiae aeternae*, and to the commands of my Master'.[9] Clearly, Montagu's rapid rise had altered their relationship: they were no longer pretended equals, but master and servant. In January 1698, however, Prior went not to Dublin but to the English embassy in Paris. By the time he departed for France, he would be suffering from weak lungs, which smoke-filled nights at the Kit-Cat had aggravated.

Stepney was also enjoying a brief sojourn in London, having returned in September after a series of postings in Hesse-Cassel, the

Palatinate and Trier. By this time, Stepney was considered an expert on tumultuous central European affairs. He was, therefore, an important international informant to the Whig Junto, though his London bosses thought he cared too much about his own popularity in foreign Courts, to the possible detriment of England's interests. At the beginning of the year, travelling back and forth across central Europe between Anthonie Heinsius, Grand Pensionary of Holland, and the various German rulers ('Electors') within William's alliance, Stepney had told Montagu he could not take much more of 'this vagabond life which is full of care and I fear will end in nothing but debts'.[10] Such complaints, combined with the end of the war, provided an excuse to bring Stepney home and remind him of his native loyalties. There were few better places to do this than at the Kit-Cat Club.

Prior and Stepney had profited from Montagu's rise to power. Montagu ensured Stepney was admitted to the Commission for Trade and Plantations (or 'Board of Trade'), which Somers had helped establish the previous year, and of which Montagu was an *ex officio* member. The Commission later became the administrative foundation of Britain's colonial empire. Stepney received his place in June 1697, with a £1,000 salary, and attended his first meeting after returning to London that September. It happened to be a historic meeting: the first time that independent statistics were presented to a government body with the intention of guiding economic policy along scientific lines.

Montagu also admitted Prior and Stepney as Fellows of the Royal Society, of which he was President. The Society had started as a private members' club, dedicated to furthering scientific knowledge, in a London tavern in 1660. After 1677, however, the Society had published no reports for nearly forty years, even though 1687–97 was a decade of high-voltage scientific and mathematical creativity following the publication of Newton's *Principia*. Though the Kit-Cat Club existed on the verge of the first mechanical-industrial age, none of its members were what we would consider scientists. Dorset and Somers were also Royal Society Fellows, but such Kit-Cats were so honoured because they had influence at Court, not because they were engaged in the work of empirical or experimental discovery.

Since 1695, Somers had been among the seven regents administering England during the King's absences, and his loyalty was rewarded in December 1697 when he finally accepted a barony, alongside valuable estates in Surrey to finance the expense of this peerage. Somers was by then Lord Chancellor, overseeing the appointment of all judges and Justices of the Peace. He had spent the summer in retirement at Clapham and Tunbridge, in poor health, but by the winter he was back at Powys House, in daily contact with Montagu and the two other Junto lords. The Kit-Cat Club was one of the key venues where three of the four Junto lords conferred outside Whitehall. Its congenial, alcohol-mellowed atmosphere no doubt minimized the risk of division while they argued policy and political strategy.

The third Junto Kit-Cat, attending this dinner besides Montagu and Somers, was Baron Wharton. A 49-year-old, large-souled man with a pock-scarred, open face that his contemporaries felt better suited to a tavern keeper than a baron, 'Tom' Wharton had composed a marching tune called 'Lillibullero' that became the popular anthem of the Glorious Revolution. Afterwards, it had been he who proposed that William and Mary should reign jointly, and, for the better part of the decade, Wharton was Somers' and Montagu's closest political ally and the Whig party's unofficial manager. Wharton and Montagu defined the Junto's tactics by leveraging their way into power through the collective strength of their followers in the Commons. Now, in 1697, Wharton remained a man to be reckoned with, thanks to extensive electoral influence derived from his estates and income (some £13,000 per annum, equivalent to around £1.2 million today).

His influence also derived from his leadership of the Dissenters' wing of the Whig party. Raised a Calvinist in the era of Charles II's anti-Dissenter Test Acts, young Wharton had been barred from attending Oxbridge, and educated at home by tutors and among the Huguenots in France. Throughout his career, promoting toleration of Dissent was his personal crusade, even as he embraced the apparent hypocrisy of 'conforming' to the Church of England in order to hold public office himself. Sitting at this Kit-Cat dinner, however, Wharton was not feeling at the top of his game; he had not won a place in the King's recently reshuffled ministry. Wharton was Comptroller of William's Household and was given various appointments in April – Lord Lieutenant of Oxfordshire, Chief Justice of Eyre, and Warden of the royal forests south of the Trent – but these were far from the real power he coveted. Compared to his younger Junto colleague Montagu, Wharton felt underappreciated.

To be a Kit-Cat now required more, in terms of political allegiance, than being a Whig: it required allegiance to the Junto (although the fourth Junto member, Lord Orford, was never a Kit-Cat). Accordingly, the six or so young MPs who belonged to the Club during these early years were each aligned to a Kit-Cat patron.[11] At this dinner, they would have tried to impress their patrons when the Club's conversation turned to politics and discussion of the war's end. Despite public celebrations around a temporary triumphal arch constructed in St James's Square, and celebratory poems on the new peace, insiders like Montagu and Somers understood that the peace of Ryswick was merely a breathing space in which to rearm. Louis XIV had recognized William III as lawful King of England, and promised not to aid any further Jacobite invasions like the attempt he had funded in 1692, but too much remained at stake for the peace to be more than an uneasy truce.

The Treaty of Ryswick left unresolved the fundamental question of who would succeed the last of the Spanish Habsburgs, Carlos II, and so control the balance of power in Europe. William therefore wished to maintain a 'standing army' of over 24,000 men, but needed Parliament's consent. The Junto members supported this policy, and were therefore considered leaders of the 'Court Whigs', while a number of other 'Country Whig' MPs formed an opposition coalition with the Tories. The Country Whigs opposed the standing army, believing that the King might abuse it and turn it into a tool of domestic tyranny, while the Tory landowners opposed the tax burden of paying for it. The young MP Robert Harley headed this anti-Junto coalition, and exchanged fierce words with Montagu over the issue in the Commons that winter. Montagu argued 'that the Nation was still unsettled, and not quite delivered from the Fear of King James; that the Adherents to that abdicated Prince were as bold and numerous as ever; and he himself [James II] still protected by the French King, who, having as yet dismissed none of his Troops, was still as formidable as before'.[12]

Harley and his followers, who met at the Grecian tavern on the Strand, organized propaganda, calling for the army to be reduced to its 1680 levels. In response, Somers authored an anonymous pamphlet, in the form of a letter to the King, defending the royal policy. In it he argued that, in the end, 'we must trust England to a House of Commons, that is to itself'.[13] It was a debate about the balance between national security and civil liberties. The Kit-Cat Club was a place for Somers to run this pamphlet's arguments past his friends, and to encourage others to pick up a pen in service of Court policy. Prior supported Montagu and Somers with *A New Answer to An Argument against a Standing Army* (1697) – a poem that asked:

> Would they discreetly break that Sword,
> By which their Freedom was restored,
> And put their Trust in Louis' Word?

It concluded that those opposing a standing army in the name of limiting William's powers would ironically find themselves responsible for the return of the more absolutist Stuarts. Organizing production of such propaganda was one of the Kit-Cat Club's earliest collective political activities.

The standing army debate was the first face-off between Harley and the Junto – a foretaste of the rivalry that would flare over a decade later and almost destroy the Junto Whigs and the Kit-Cat Club. In 1697, Harley had triumphed: a Commons resolution was passed that a Disbanding Bill should be introduced. This crisis, and analysis of the Junto's tactics in the press and in the Commons, would therefore have carried the Kit-Cats' conversation through several courses.

The literary conversation of the Club that winter is equally easy to deduce. Around half of the members had just subscribed to Dryden's new translation of the *Works of Virgil*, which Tonson had published with an introduction by Addison. Dryden said the book was only for the 'most Judicious' audience. Though the 500 subscribers were both Whig and Tory, and Dryden, with his Jacobite sympathies, gave the work several Tory dedications, the publication still had a distinctly Whiggish colouring; the author was grimly amused, for example, to find Tonson had made an illustration of the hero Aeneas bear a marked resemblance to King William.

Subscription editions were a bargain way for the nobility to patronize writers: a hybrid solution at a time before the general public was literate and prosperous enough to act as the greatest patron of them all. By advertising their names as subscribers in the publications, aristocrats shifted from commissioning books towards being their celebrity promoters. This was Tonson's answer to issuing more specialist or scholarly works with high unit costs. In the case of Dryden's *Virgil*, besides the deluxe editions sent to the subscribers, Tonson also published a cheap edition, for the general public to buy from his shop. Dryden and Tonson's collaborations before the Kit-Cat's foundation had helped popularize classical translation in England, and Dryden and Congreve's translation of Juvenal and Persius in 1693 ushered in the notion of the translated author, as Dryden put it, 'speak[ing] that kind of English, which he would have spoken had he lived in England, and Written to this Age'.[14] Such accessible publications, with their attractive illustrations and lack of scholarly paraphernalia, were part of the Kit-Cat's patriotic agenda to better educate their literate countrymen and did much to pave the way for the neoclassical populism of the later eighteenth century.

One Kit-Cat subscriber to *The Works of Virgil*, whom Dryden described as 'without flattery, the best Critic of our Nation',[15] was William Walsh. Walsh's reputation as a critic must have been based on his conversation at the Witty Club rather than his writing, since what little Walsh had published (through Tonson) was mostly amorous poetry and boasts of his exploits with women. Walsh was an object of ridicule for his excessive love of fine clothing and his wig containing over three pounds of powder that produced little puffs of cloud with every sharp movement of his head. In 1697, Walsh was in his mid-thirties and beginning to suspect his name would not become immortal. His estate, by this date, was reportedly 'reduced to about £300 a year, of which his mother has the greatest part'.[16] Though he had been seeking patronage from Somers since 1693, this winter marked a turning point, after which Somers' support was decisive in getting Walsh elected to a parliamentary seat for Worcestershire.

At Dryden's Witty Club, Walsh had drunk and quipped with Dr Samuel Garth, who was now also his fellow Kit-Cat. Garth attended that winter, eager to see Stepney and Prior after their long stints overseas. Garth had known 'Lord Dorset's Boys' at Cambridge and had written a poem praising Prior and Stepney as the best and brightest hopes of English literature. Like them, Garth had had to make his own way in the world after receiving a mere £10 legacy from his family. Now, at 37, he was a respected physician, but still writing poetry – largely revisions of his mock-epic *Dispensary*. He had subscribed five guineas (some £700 today) to Dryden's *Virgil*.

Though many Kit-Cat patrons dabbled in authorship, there was no real risk of confusing the bluebloods with the literary thoroughbreds at the Club's table. At this meeting of 1697, Congreve was the leading literary man. He was overseeing a new production at Inner Temple of his three-year-old hit, *Love for Love* (1694). This play, his third, was originally the debut production of a new theatre company that had splintered off from the United Company in 1695. The defection had been led by Bracey's mentors, the Bettertons, so she went with them, and her suitor Congreve devotedly followed, promising to write for the new company. More importantly, Congreve used his credit with Dorset to obtain an audience with the King for Bracey and the Bettertons, thereby gaining a royal charter for their new company. Congreve was offered shares in it by way of thanks.

Betterton's company set up in an old tennis court building at Lincoln's Inn Fields, and the King himself was in the audience on the opening night. Bracey played the complex lead role of Angelica in *Love for Love*, and also spoke the Epilogue, in which Congreve had her complain of men who 'wanting ready cash to pay for hearts, / They top their learning on us, and their parts.' There may have been self-mockery in this, given the lewd pun in 'parts' and the fact that Congreve certainly remained short of 'ready cash' at that date.

Montagu showed his approval of *Love for Love* by appointing Congreve in March 1695 to a commission for regulating and licensing hackney and stagecoaches, with a salary of £100 (around £10,000 today) plus a percentage fee for each licence issued. Congreve could lease out the actual work to a clerk at a much smaller salary, pocketing the difference. This commission was a clear example of the Kit-Cat Club's *modus operandi* for literary patronage, the patrons frequently dispensing public offices rather than cash from their own private pockets. (Such 'jobs for the boys' were, of course, of little use to the female authors whom Tonson published, the most notable of whom were Aphra Behn, Katherine Philips and Susanna Centlivre.)

In April 1697, Congreve was further made one of eleven managers of the Malt Lottery, a government scheme for raising duties on malt used for brewing and distilling. The following month, Montagu added yet another post for licensing hawkers and pedlars. All this added up to a secure but still modest income for the playwright. Congreve's work in progress that winter was a poem, 'The Birth of the Muse', which would be dedicated in gratitude to Montagu, 'by turns the Patron and the Friend', when Tonson printed it the following year.[17]

Congreve's involvement made Montagu into a 'great favourer' of Betterton's new theatre company, in preference to the United Company at Drury Lane.[18] Though the two companies' rivalry was never partisan, both being essentially Whig, the Kit-Cats clearly backed the new house at Lincoln's Inn. Montagu, who, like Tonson and Somers, had taken a sudden interest in Vanbrugh's career after the success of *The Relapse* the previous winter, saw Vanbrugh's second comedy, *The Provok'd Wife*, in manuscript and persuaded (perhaps paid) the playwright to adapt it to better suit Betterton's company. For Vanbrugh, this was a smart move, as he now had access to a more talented cast: *The Provok'd Wife*'s portrayal of marital misery was brilliantly brought to life by Mr Betterton, now in his sixties, and the ageing actress Mrs Barry. Bracey played Belinda.

In 1697, therefore, Congreve and Vanbrugh were showing their work on the same stage. They avoided direct competition thanks to the fact that Congreve produced a tragedy instead of a comedy for the same season as Vanbrugh's *Provok'd Wife*. Congreve's tragedy was *The Mourning Bride* and, as usual, the lead role was written for his beloved Bracey. Both Vanbrugh's comedy and Congreve's tragedy were hits, with the playhouse 'full to the last'.[19] When his plays gained universal applause, Vanbrugh, flamboyant and sociable, relished the attention. Congreve pushed himself forward in less obvious ways: when he put his name as author on a playbill in 1699, Dryden remarked that this was 'a new manner of proceeding, at least in England'.[20]

A contemporary critic said Vanbrugh's writing seemed 'no more than his common Conversation committed to Paper'.[21] This is tribute to the artfulness of 1690s conversation as much as to the seeming artlessness of Vanbrugh's writing, and if conversation was an art form, the Kit-Cat Club was its medium – the reality that Vanbrugh and Congreve refined and amplified. Indeed, their shared love of writing in naturalistic speech explains their general preference for comedy over tragedy, a genre in which more formal verse was expected. The playwrights' writing methods, however, were stark contrasts: while Vanbrugh rapidly churned out 'new' plays translated from classical or French sources, Congreve wrote and revised laboriously, relying on original if convoluted plots.

The surprising absence of reference to one another's work in their critical writings, and the fact that Congreve's library did not contain a single Vanbrugh play when it was sold after his death, suggest rivalry between the two men. On the other hand, there are generous compliments to Vanbrugh's 'sprightly' talent in two anthologies by Congreve's close friends,[22] and Congreve would have a middle-aged portrait of himself painted reading a Vanbrugh play.

Congreve explained to an old friend from Kilkenny School, Joe Keally: 'I need not be very much alone, but I choose it, rather than to conform myself to the manners of my Court or chocolate-house acquaintance.'[23] It was as if Congreve found adopting his public mask – his Kit-Cat persona as a 'man of wit' – almost an insult to his intelligence; as if he hated to feel like a trained monkey brought in for the amusement of his literary patrons. Congreve's plays contain characters that can be viewed as at least partial caricatures of the less intellectual Kit-Cat patrons: in *The Double Dealer*, for example, Congreve presents the peers of England as sexually and intellectually impotent. Their pretensions as wits and writers are the idle pastimes of trivial minds, and Lord Froth fancies himself a theatre critic who thinks he will look more knowledgeable if he does not laugh at a play's jokes. In *Love for Love*, Sir Sampson mocks the servant Jeremy for having ideas above his station, yet Jeremy is better educated than a 'gentleman' named Tattle, who thinks the head of the Nile is a Privy Counsellor. Such were the literary messages by which Kit-Cat authors began to detach class from birth, and pin it more squarely on a person's taste and education. It was not a new comedic device to show servants sharper than their masters, but this time it had a fresh and more pointed cynicism. At the Kit-Cat that evening in winter 1697, however, the dukes and earls seated around Congreve detected no disdain or boredom lurking beneath his indulgent smile and patient remarks: 'No one, after a joyful Evening, can reflect upon an Expression of Mr Congreve's that dwells upon him with pain,' Steele later recalled.[24]

The end of the meal would have been signalled by Tonson, as Secretary, or by Somerset, as highest in rank, throwing down his napkin and calling for a larger washbowl. Then, after the board was cleared of the final course, the servants brought 'every man his bottle and a clean glass',[25] and Tonson turned the diners' attentions to the only official order of business: the nomination of 'beauties', and the recitation of light verses in their honour. Tonson, as one of Prior's poems put it, 'bawls out to the Club for a toast'.[26]

As a drinking and dining society first and foremost – Addison called it a club 'founded upon Eating and Drinking'[27] – the Kit-Cat Club was contemporaneous with another known as 'The Knights of the Toast' or 'The Toasters'. These Toasters raised their glasses to nominated 'beauties' among the ladies of the town, without, it would seem, any ulterior political or cultural motive. They were just men who fancied themselves gallant connoisseurs of fine wine and women, as mocked by a 1698 ballad depicting them flirting outrageously during a church sermon. At least seven men were members of both clubs. Many Toasters never joined the Kit-Cat Club, however, disqualified from the latter by their Toryism.

Steele wrote the most famous description of how toasting a beauty worked:

> The Manner of her Inauguration is much like that of the Choice of a Doge in Venice; it is performed by Balloting; and when she is so chosen, she reigns indisputably for that ensuing Year; but must be elected anew to prolong her Empire a Moment beyond it. When she is regularly chosen, her Name is written with a Diamond on a Drinking glass. The Hieroglyphic of the Diamond is to show her that her Value is imaginary; and that of the Glass, to acquaint her that her Condition is frail, and depends on the Hand which holds her.[28]

A manuscript letter confirms that this passage describes not only the Toasters' but also the Kit-Cats' ritual and that a complimentary verse on each toasted beauty was engraved beside the name on each glass.[29] No glass complete with lady's name or verse appears to have survived the centuries. (The glasses today known as 'Kit-Cat' style are erroneously named and date from the later eighteenth century.) That the toasting was *in absentia* allowed toasts to be made by married men, to married women. A Tory authoress named Mary Astell sarcastically rebuked the Kit-Cats for how their toasting could bring respectable society ladies unwanted attention: 'When an Ill-bred Fellow endeavours to protect a Wife, or Daughter, or other virtuous Woman from your very Civil Addresses, your noble Courage never fails of being roused upon such great Provocations.'[30]

The only two essential qualifications to be a Kit-Cat toast were beauty and Whiggery. Many women were chosen as toasts purely as compliments to their fathers, uncles or husbands. Many were girls in their teens, toasted unashamedly by middle-aged men in a period when the legal minimum age for marrying or having sex with a girl was ten, and when a male reader could write a letter to a paper protesting that it was a gentleman's natural privilege to fornicate with 'little raw unthinking Girls'.[31]

Steele's statement that women should 'consider themselves, as they ought, no other than an additional Part of the Species . . . shining Ornaments to their Fathers, Husbands, Brothers or Children'[32] may be belittling, but an ornamental role was for many women an improvement upon living as victims of casual molestation or beating. The Kit-Cat members set themselves up as gallant models for reforming men like Vanbrugh's character Sir John Brute in *The Provok'd Wife*, who beats his wife simply because he has the right to do so. Their rituals were the beginnings of a more 'polite' and chivalric treatment of women that would become codified in the later eighteenth century. A few of their toasts contain salacious puns, but they are relatively lacking in libido compared to the verses of the earlier Restoration rakes. Dorset when young, for example, had asked: 'For what but Cunt, and Prick, does raise / Our thoughts to Songs, and Roundelays?'[33] Now the answer seemed to be that the one-upmanship of literary competition was as rousing as lust. A 1700 poem, *The Patentee*, contrasts the Kit-Cats 'swollen with wit' to the Knights of the Toast 'with lechery lean',[34] suggesting not only that the Toasters were less overweight, but also that they composed toasts to seduce women, while the Kit-Cats wrote more for the sake of impressing one another.

As a prologue to the nominations of toasted beauties for 1697, Congreve would have recited a standard 'Oath of the Toast':

> By Bacchus and by Venus Swear
> That you will only name the fair
> When chains you at the present wear
> And so let Wit with Wine go round
> And she you love prove kind and sound.[35]

No list of toasted beauties exists this early in the Kit-Cat Club's history, though it is likely that one of the five surviving verses dedicated to Lady Carlisle dates from this period. She was the wife of the 28-year-old Charles Howard, 3rd Earl of Carlisle, having married him when he was 19 and she just 13. Dr Garth sought the patronage of Carlisle when he composed and recited the following toast to Lady Carlisle:

Carlisle's a name can every Muse inspire,
To Carlisle fill the Glass and tune the Lyre.
With his loved Bays the God of day shall Crown,
Her Wit and Beauty equal to his own.

It is uncertain how boisterous Kit-Cat toasting became. If the texts of the Kit-Cat toasts are anything to go by, the atmosphere was ludic but not lewd. When Montagu once sent poetry to Stepney in Hamburg, however, he had added with a wink that 'There are some others which are fitter to create mirth over a glass of wine than to be put into writing.'[36] One example may be a poem that survives among the Kit-Cat manuscripts about a lady's use of a massive candle as a dildo. Such poetry, produced alongside the toasts but unfit to be published by Tonson's press, would have been another obvious reason for keeping women away from Kit-Cat meetings. This evening, however, an exception would be made.

Though there seems to have been a rule that members could not toast their own wives, one member decided that evening, 'on a whim', to make the unusual nomination of his own daughter. The member was a widower named Evelyn Pierrepont, 5th Earl of Kingston-upon-Hull. Kingston argued that his daughter, Mary Pierrepont, though not yet 8, was far prettier than any of the candidates on the list. No objection was made to Mary's age, but there was another rule that forbade members from electing a lady whom they had never seen. 'Then you shall see her,' declared the Earl, and 'in the gaiety of the moment' sent orders to a house in the village of Chelsea, where Mary was then lodging, to have the child finely dressed and brought to him at the tavern.[37]

By the time Mary reached Gray's Inn, the other toasts had been balloted and drunk. Entering the sybaritic atmosphere of that tavern room was, by her own account, an overwhelming experience for the sheltered girl: dozens of men around the table and spitting fire, all eyes fixed on her, greasy chins shining, like the silver and pewter, in the guttering candlelight, the stinking smoke from their long thin pipes mixed with the stew of their bodies and the whiff of the piss-pot in the corner. She must have first gone to curtsy to her handsome 30-year-old father, seeking his approbation for her outfit, which, in the style of the 1690s, was much like a grown woman's in miniature. Her heart beat nervously against her stays.

Years later, Lady Mary recalled she was received 'with acclamations' and 'her claim [as a toast] unanimously allowed'.[38] The members, raising their brimming glasses in her direction, then drank her health. Pride blushed over the little girl's face under the spotlight of the men's attentions and stayed with her for years afterwards as a vivid memory – a highlight, she said, of her life: 'Pleasure . . . was too poor a word to express [my] sensations. They amounted to ecstasy; never again . . . did [I] pass so happy a day.'[39] She is the only Kit-Cat toast to leave us a proud record, albeit verbal and repeated perhaps inaccurately by her granddaughter, of how it felt to be so honoured.

Lady Mary's name was then 'engraved in due form upon a drinking-glass'.[40] She certainly saw the glasses, since in one of her private letters as an adult she laughs about a chamber pot being engraved like a Kit-Cat glass. She was also, it seems, toasted by the Club as an adult, in 1712 and 1714, though no verses in her honour have survived.

The image of the 8-year-old 'kitten' being handed round by the Kit-Cats, including so many members of the King's Cabinet, is a striking embodiment of patriarchy. A woman's beauty equated to tangible value on the marriage market, and Mary Pierrepont would later confound her own beauty's 'value' in this sense by eloping with her preferred suitor, who could not pay her father's asking price. Under her married name of Lady Mary Wortley Montagu, her poetry, letters and conversation would then win her a reputation as the most brilliant female wit of her generation.

Lady Mary attributed her own wit partly to Congreve, who was to take as much interest in her mind as her beauty as she grew up, and whom she described as her wittiest friend. Though her father was, like most gentlemen of his generation, unconcerned with his daughter's education, Mary secretly educated herself to a high level starting the year after she visited the Club. Lady Mary is also remembered for bringing the concept of vaccination back to England from Turkey, introducing this practice into British society by convincing her aristocratic friends to try it. She thereby saved future generations from smallpox's life-threatening risk and the disfigurement she herself suffered in 1715, a year after she was last toasted as a beauty by the Kit-Cats.

Writing three years before this 1697 meeting took place, Mary Astell asked her fellow Englishwomen: 'How can you be content to be in the world like tulips in a garden, to make a fine show and be good for nothing?'[41] Astell believed the way forward was through female education and therefore tried to form an early female academy. It would not be until the succeeding generation, however, that women would see far greater, albeit short-lived, educational opportunities. By the mid-1760s, Elizabeth Montagu and her bluestocking friends would be able to sit and discuss books and politics with willing men, in imitation of the French salons; in 1697, such a mixed gathering was unthinkable.

We know the Club could carouse until the early morning hours. Dawn may even have been breaking by the time Kingston took his daughter home. Tonson would not have covered the enormous bill of every meeting now that the Club was so rich in noble patrons. Ned Ward said the Kit-Cat wits performed their verses and then the richer members 'would manifest by their Liberality, when the Reckoning came to be paid, the Satisfaction they had found in the witty Discourses of their wiser Brethren'.[42]

Stupefied with wine, the members said their loud farewells, leaving the exhausted servants of the Cat and Fiddle to deal with the feast's debris. Linkmen carrying lanterns were waiting outside to escort those who did not have carriages. From the overheated tavern, the Kit-Cats emerged into the damp, foggy night air in the labyrinthine alleys south of Gray's Inn. Wharton headed back to Gerrard Street, Somers to Powys House, Somerset to Northumberland House on the Strand, Carlisle to King's Square, Vanbrugh to his lodgings next to the Banqueting House in Whitehall, and Congreve and Tonson returned together to their shared house on Fleet Street. Unified by their Whig beliefs and an implied promise of mutual support, they had fortified themselves against the political risks that the final years of the 1690s would throw at them.

V
CULTURE WARS

There the dread phalanx of reformers come,
Sworn foes to wit, as Carthage was to Rome,
Their ears so sanctified, no scenes can please,
But heavy hymns or pensive homilies.

DR SAMUEL GARTH,
Prologue to *Squire Trelooby* (1704)[1]

THE KIT-CAT MEMBERS' relaxed attitudes to religion and morality were both ahead of their time, predicting later Georgian rationalism, and a remnant of the Restoration rakes' godless cynicism. As opinion-makers, the Kit-Cats tried to promote religious tolerance and moderation, in reaction to the 'enthusiasm' (fanaticism) they felt had inflamed the Civil War, the persecution they associated with Catholicism, and, as Voltaire noted when he saw the crowds in the Royal Exchange, because toleration was good for business. Although there was 'less Appearance of Religion in [England], than any other neighbouring State or Kingdom',[2] many of the 'middling sort' who were profiting most from the growth of trade and commerce in the 1690s were devout Protestant churchgoers who felt they were clinging to the remnants of Christian morality amid a 'debauched age'.[3]

The beginning of a correlation between one's faith and social position showed itself in the theatres where there was a mismatch between the censorious bourgeois audiences after 1688, on whom the permanently near-bankrupt theatres were dependent, and the authors who were still writing for a small, elite intelligentsia of morally and religiously liberal patrons. The Kit-Cats and their friends could support a playhouse for one night, but theatre managers needed the plays to be uncontroversial to draw regular crowds. All this came to a head in the Kit-Cats' battle with clergyman Jeremy Collier.

In April 1696, Collier, a middle-aged Cambridgeshire clergyman, attended the Tyburn execution of two men condemned for plotting to assassinate King William. Alongside his fellow 'non-jurors' (clergymen who had refused to swear allegiance to the new monarchy), Collier ascended the scaffold and, by laying on hands, offered the plotters absolution for their treachery. Since this was a serious crime under English law, Collier thereby condemned himself to living as an outlaw. Over the following months, he published, semi-anonymously and from hiding, views that challenged King William's 'false' authority and the Church of England's feeble acceptance of this authority. Collier portrayed post-Revolutionary England as in need of urgent salvation.

Many non-Jacobites agreed with Collier on the last point. The first Society for the Reformation of Manners was established in the Strand roughly contemporaneously with the Kit-Cat Club's foundation in Gray's Inn. This society vowed to spy out and report offenders against the laws on immoral behaviour, and monitor which Officers of the Peace were effective or negligent in enforcing these laws.

After Queen Mary's death in 1694 and the end of the War of the League of Augsburg in 1697, William needed a new way to legitimize his rule and was fearful of alienating or antagonizing the Society for the Reformation of Manners' army of grassroot Christian activists. He therefore deliberately set about becoming the leader (rather than target) of those seeking to reform the loose morals of the age. In December 1697, to offset the unwelcome news that peace with France would not bring a drop in taxes, he promised the Commons that he would commence a kind of *Kulturkampf* at home – a crusade against 'Prophaneness and Immorality'.[4] This encouraged certain zealous MPs to present an address to him in February 1698 concerning suppression of unchristian books and punishment of their authors, ultimately resulting in 'An Act for the more effectual suppressing of Atheism, Blasphemy and Prophaneness'.

The previous month, on a freezing day in January 1698, a fire destroyed most of Whitehall Palace. Certain Jacobite pamphleteers, including Collier, played upon people's Sodom-and-Gomorrah-ish superstition that God had frowned upon the Williamite Court. Some suggested William enjoyed sodomy with his male favourites. Vanbrugh faced a similar accusation of bisexuality in an anonymous poem alleging that the playwright did 'Active and Passive, in both Sexes Lust'.[5] Vanbrugh was specifically accused of sodomy with Peregrine Bertie, with whom he lodged in Whitehall, and therefore blamed for the fire that destroyed the Palace.[6] While a manuscript of 1694 confirms Bertie and Vanbrugh were intimate friends, nothing more is known of their relationship.[7]

Vanbrugh's sexuality was attacked because his satirical plays had made plenty of enemies in church pulpits. When *The Relapse* (1696) was first performed, with its comparison of church congregations to social clubs and its depiction of a careerist chaplain, Vanbrugh was saved from the Bishop of Gloucester's wrath only by his friends' 'agility'.[8] In the Preface to the first printed edition of *The Relapse*, Vanbrugh answered his attackers:

> As for the Saints (your thorough-paced ones I mean, with screwed Faces and wry Mouths) I despair of them, for they are Friends to nobody. They love nothing, but their Altars and Themselves. They have too much Zeal to have any Charity; they make Debauches in Piety, as Sinners do in Wine, and are quarrelsome in their Religion as other People are in their Drink: so I hope nobody will mind what they say.[9]

Vanbrugh's scepticism about the moral conversion of the husband in *The Relapse* implied allegorical scepticism about the country's moral reformation, but it was a scepticism he could not afford to voice more openly.

Immediately after the Whitehall Palace fire, capitalizing on London's *fin de siècle* mood, Collier published *A Short View of the Immorality and Prophaness of the English Stage* (1698). This book censured immorality and profanity in recent plays by the so-called 'Orange Comedians',[10] foremost among whom were Congreve and Vanbrugh. It did so in a style of close textual analysis that would be highly influential on future critics, both Christian and secular. It opened with the premise that 'The business of Plays is to recommend Virtue and discountenance Vice', and ended with a section complaining that sinful characters were escaping dramatic justice. *A Short View* was rancorous, pugnacious and literal-minded, but also intelligent and biting. It was an instant bestseller.

As an outsider, ostracized by Williamite society, Collier did not hesitate to attack the biggest literary names of the day, including Dryden, Congreve and Vanbrugh, whom he called 'snakes and vipers'. Though Collier said he wanted only to reform the theatres, his *Short View* fanned the flames of a popular movement driven by an abolitionist impulse. It was not the first shot fired in the culture wars, but it was the loudest, and the one aimed most directly at the Kit-Cat Club's authors. The Club's own name was not yet, in 1698, well known enough for its members to be attacked as a collective entity, but the battle against Collierite attitudes was one of the struggles that helped bond the Club's friendships in these early years.

Collier attacked the representation of women in the plays of Vanbrugh and Congreve as bold, libidinous and knowing creatures. He blamed the playwrights for allowing women to act these roles on stage, 'to make Monsters of them, and throw them out of their kind'.[11] As early as 1693, when Congreve's *Double Dealer* was first performed, ladies were so outraged by the realism of his female characterization that, in ironic defence of their modesty, they shouted out protests during the performance and hurled things at the stage. Congreve responded that the ladies in his audiences could no more expect to be flattered by a satire than 'to be tickled by a surgeon when he's letting 'em blood'.[12]

Collier particularly criticized the Orange Comedians' disparaging view of marriage. In one sense, the Orange Comedians' attitude was simply an old joke inherited from Restoration drama, but they treated it with greater seriousness, bringing out the true dramatic tension of claustrophobic, bitter marriages. As one critic has observed, if today we are living through the death throes of the nuclear family, the Kit-Cat authors were living through its birth pangs,[13] and Vanbrugh and Congreve explored their fears of this new social unit in their work while assiduously avoiding such commitment in their own private lives. In Congreve's *Old Batchelor*, Bellmour summed up the author's own attitude to the married state:

> Bellmour: Could'st thou be content to marry Araminta?
> Vainlove: Could you be content to go to heaven?
> Bellmour: Hum, not immediately, in my conscience, not heartily.

Vanbrugh's *Provok'd Wife* leaves its marital problems unresolved at the end of the play – a radical ending for a comedy but also a bitter truth in an age when divorce was a great rarity. Whether or not he was bisexual, Vanbrugh was certainly a confirmed bachelor in the 1690s, morbidly mocking his Kit-Cat friends whenever one of them became engaged. He gossiped to a fellow Kit-Cat, for example, that another Club member, Anthony Henley, was tying himself to 'a mettled jade'[14] – this was, in fact, Mary Bertie, a cousin of Vanbrugh's friend Peregrine. Mary's chief attraction for Henley was probably her fortune of some £30,000 (well over £3.6 million today, and more than enough to cover Henley's debts of £10,000). Surrounded by mercenary matches, Vanbrugh's cynicism was understandable.

The Junto members conducted their love lives not unlike the libertine characters in a Restoration or Orange comedy, and Collier's criticism of the theatre was fired by rumours about the conduct of playwrights' patrons. Wharton was described as 'something of a libertine', and an anonymous satire referred to his whoring.[15] He kept a mistress for many years during his first marriage, then in 1692, at

44, he married 22-year-old Lucy Loftus, who became a Kit-Cat toast in 1698 and was referred to as 'the witty, fair one'.[16] Though Wharton seems to have been unfaithful to his young wife, Lucy was rumoured to be just as 'abandoned' as her husband.[17]

Montagu, similarly, never treated his marriage to the dowager Lady Manchester as any impediment to his long-standing affair with a Kit-Cat toast named Mrs Catherine Barton, the niece of Sir Isaac Newton. The Duchess of Marlborough laughed at Montagu's playing the ladies' man, with 'a great knack at making pretty ballads', though he was so short and 'hideously ugly'.[18] A Tory satire accused Montagu of lining his pockets with public funds that he 'whored away or pissed against the walls'.[19] That this accusation may not have been simple libel is suggested by a Whig friend's joking remark that, when Prior and Stepney left London in 1698, Prior for Paris and Stepney for Saxony, their departures caused the business of a certain London brothel to nosedive.

Collier attacked the Kit-Cats not just for being sexual liberals but also for their godlessness. Beyond their anti-clerical one-liners, the plays of Vanbrugh and Congreve contain a fundamentally secular and cynical worldview that challenged Collier's religious faith to its core. Congreve's *Way of the World* has a character swear an oath on Tonson's *Miscellany* rather than on the Bible. While his plays epitomized the grace and elegance of the coming eighteenth century, Congreve's philosophy, at its darkest, was closer to twentieth century nihilism. He believed social conventions and good humour kept a thin lid on dark passions and the 'power of baseness'.[20] Vanbrugh's view of life, meanwhile, was more martial and combative – a constant struggle in which God's mercy and justice played little part: 'Fortune, thou art a bitch by Gad!' exclaims Young Fashion in *The Relapse*.[21]

There was virtually no avowed atheism (any more than avowed republicanism) among Whigs, yet this was the obvious accusation for Tory satirists to hurl. These satires claimed the Kit-Cat Club fomented 'free-thinking': one written in the voice of a Kit-Cat founder, for example, recalled that ''Twas there we first instructed all our youth, / To talk profane and laugh at sacred truth.'[22] Another later proposed that the 'great discoveries' of atheism 'be adapted to the capacities of the Kit-Cat . . . who might then be able to read lectures on them to their several toasts'.[23] Individual Kit-Cat patrons notorious for irreligion included: Wharton (who never repaired the damage done to his image by a notorious incident in 1682 when he and some friends allegedly urinated and defecated on the altar and pulpit of a Gloucestershire church); Somers, who, though a member of his local vestry, was branded a deist (that is, one sceptical about revealed religion though not the original existence of God); and Dr Garth, whose choice of profession derived from, or reinforced, his innately sceptical outlook. One Tory satire imagines Garth speaking to a dying clergyman: '"Why, Sir, have you the vanity to think that religion ever did our cause any service?! . . . I'll tell the Kit-Cat Club of you, and it shall be known to every man at C[our]t that you die like a pedant."'[24]

In May 1698, inspired by Collier's attack and the King's call for moral reform, the Middlesex Justices of the Peace prosecuted Congreve for having written, five years earlier, *The Double Dealer*. Tonson and the printer Briscoe were prosecuted for publishing the play. Nobody was imprisoned or fined, but Congreve was forced to revise the play to prevent further prosecution. These revisions involved the character of the chaplain, Mr Saygrace, and deletion of allegedly profane and indecent language.

Congreve, embittered by this interference in matters literary, published *Amendments of Mr Collier's False and Imperfect Citations* (1698) in reply to *A Short View*. His main line of argument was that his words should not be judged out of context: the same justification often used against censors today and an early instance of a writer complaining against deconstruction of his text. Congreve added wit by emphasizing that smut was in the eye of the beholder: '[T]he greater part of those examples which he [Collier] produced are only demonstrations of his own impurity; they only savour of his utterance and were sweet enough till tainted by his breath.'[25] The charge of prurience was fair – Collier did seem to take great pleasure in spying out immorality – but Congreve's defence was weakened by the need he felt to claim some alternative reforming purpose for his satire.

Vanbrugh was thicker-skinned than Congreve ('Fortunately, I am not one of those who drop their spirits at every Rebuff – If I had been, I had been underground long ago'[26]) but his own response to Collier, *A Short Vindication of 'The Relapse' and 'The Provok'd Wife'* (1698), got off on an equally wrong foot by accepting Collier's premise that the purpose of theatre was to 'recommend Virtue and discountenance Vice'.[27] King William had expressed approval of *A Short View* to demonstrate his sympathy with the moral crusaders, even permitting its Jacobite author impunity to come out of hiding. Knowing the King was content to see the theatres gagged, playing to the vocal Christian reformers, must have forced Vanbrugh to pull his punches and choose his words carefully.

Whereas Congreve pretended Collier's insults were too exaggerated to be wounding ('He would have poisoned me, but he overdosed it, and the Excess of his Malice has been my Security'[28]), Vanbrugh admitted *A Short View*'s undeniable popularity now made it, as another Kit-Cat admitted, a 'thing no farther to be laughed at'.[29]

More self-confident defence came from a non-Kit-Cat writer also targeted by Collier, the neoclassical critic John Dennis. A friend of Congreve's since 1691, Dennis suffered from an absurd prickliness of temper, a quality that probably disqualified him from Kit-Cat membership, if he sought it. Dennis' response to Collier's *Short View* rightly linked the 'high flying'[30] Jacobite author with those censors at the opposite end of the religious and political spectrum: the Puritans.[31] Dennis defended the stage without denying its appeal to 'passions' above reason, and did not bother to claim that drama need serve a reforming purpose. One enemy asserted Dennis 'sat at the head of a Club' to 'impeach' Collier,[32] which suggests that the Kit-Cats deferred to an ad hoc grouping of anti-Collierites to handle the matter. In his *Defence of the Short View* (1699), Collier stated he would only continue the debate with writers like Congreve and Vanbrugh, not with small fry like Dennis.

By 1699, there were nine Societies for the Reformation of Manners working across London, and by 1701 there would be almost twenty. Moral reformers in the Commons and Lords continued to introduce legislation that intruded into the private sphere, with the King's approval. Somers and his Kit-Cat colleagues in the Lords were among those to vote down a 1699 Bill to make adultery a misdemeanour punishable under the common law, for example. Somers had personal reasons for doing so: from as early as 1694, he had been the lover of his Herefordshire 'housekeeper', Mrs Elizabeth Fanshawe Blount, whose husband was in prison. One Tory satire accused Somers of having had Mr Blount arrested in order to bed the wife, whereas Somers' friends portrayed him as having rescued her from a negligent, shiftless husband.[33]

In February 1699, William proclaimed that actors must avoid using profane and indecent language – disregarding the role of his own Cabinet ministers, Somers and Montagu, in encouraging and financing the writing of the allegedly profane and indecent plays in the first place. When Congreve's *Double Dealer* was revived in March 1699, it was in the expurgated version.

The Kit-Cat Club survived Collier's attacks on its members because it did not attempt to defend the imaginations of Vanbrugh and Congreve as they really deserved to be defended. Instead, the Kit-Cat critics emphasized the points on which they agreed with Collier: that wit without decency is not true wit; that smut should not be used to compensate for a deficit of 'sprightly Dialogue',[34] and that mobbish audiences needed elevation and education, for the whole nation's sake. While the Kit-Cat patrons supported the Club's authors in defiance of the censors, the more ambitious Whig politicians also recognized that they needed to work on their public image, and that a new, more 'improving' literature was required to win the moral highground back from the Tories. Congreve and Vanbrugh were not, however, willing to produce it.

It would be the stars of the following generation of Kit-Cat authors – Addison and Steele, not yet members in 1698 – who succeeded in bridging the gap between the Club's libertine, Restoration founders, led by Dorset, and Collier's puritanical strictures. Steele, who was at heart a faithful Christian, later admitted to having privately admired much that Collier preached, 'as far as I durst, for fear of witty Men, upon whom he had been too severe'.[35]

In 1698, at the height of the culture wars, Steele was known as

'Captain Steele' – one of the many demobilized officers whose uniforms reddened the theatre audiences after the peace of Ryswick. Steele was then living either with his aunt and uncle at their Bond Street house, or at the Whitehall home of his boss, Lord Cutts. Steele said Cutts treated him like a son and provided him with 'an introduction into the world', so it may have been through this military patron that Steele first entered Dryden's outer orbit at Will's Coffee House. There was already, of course, the connection established with this circle through Addison, though Addison lived in Oxford until 1699.

Steele seems to have charmed Congreve, in particular, with whom he passed 'many Happy Hours'.[36] This was quite an honour, since Congreve confided to Joe Keally that he was 'not apt to care for many acquaintance, and never intend to make many friendships'.[37] Steele, for his part, said that he felt the 'greatest Affection and Veneration' for Congreve, admiring, in particular, Congreve's poem 'Doris'.[38] No evidence survives to tell us whether Steele felt a similarly warm regard for Vanbrugh in the late 1690s; as a soldier-turned-playwright, Vanbrugh was the obvious role model for Steele at this juncture.

Steele also appears to have befriended Congreve's housemate, Tonson, by 1698. That year, Tonson moved his firm's offices from Chancery Lane to his family's old premises in Gray's Inn, where they would remain until 1710. A satirical advertisement appeared cruelly referring to Tonson's 'Sign of the two left Legs, near Gray's Inn Back-Gate'.[39] Steele was often to be found at this shop during 1698. There he could sit for hours and read for free, with a glass of wine by his side, as bookshops then were more like paying libraries where, for a small subscription, one could read the most recent publications on the premises, leaving a bookmark in a volume if not finished at a single sitting.

An additional attraction at Tonson's shop was the publisher's 18-year-old niece Elizabeth, an assistant in the business. In 1699 or 1700, she gave birth to an illegitimate daughter by Steele, christened Elizabeth and given the surname of 'Ousley', after Dorothea Ousley, a nurse who raised illegitimate infants and orphans in the neighbourhood. How Tonson felt about Steele, an insolvent Irishman, ex-soldier and aspiring playwright, having impregnated his unmarried niece is not recorded, nor is there evidence that Steele's guardian aunt and uncle ever found out about the baby.

Steele felt that an illegitimate child was deeply shameful, not an everyday occurrence. He must have known how Addison disapproved of the 'Vermin' who carelessly produced bastards and whose punishment should be, Addison joked, transportation to a colony in need of population.[40] The person to whom Steele therefore turned during the crisis was not Addison, nor any of his witty male friends, but Mrs Mary Delariviere Manley, an unconventionally worldly woman who had been a confidante to Charles II's mistress, the Duchess of Cleveland, and who had lived with several men in London, starting with John Tilly, a lawyer and warden of Fleet Prison. Steele met Mrs Manley through Tilly, who in the mid-1690s had joined Steele and another old university friend as gullible investors in some alchemical research.

Manley claimed Steele dealt with two unwanted pregnancies in the late 1690s – one baby died, the other was presumably Elizabeth Ousley. It is unclear whether Elizabeth Tonson was the mother in both instances. Mrs Manley explained that she had stood as guarantor for Steele when he needed credit with a midwife, though whether for an abortion or a birth is unclear. Steele never paid the midwife's bill, so she threatened to sue and make the matter public. A note in Steele's hand confirms this story, referring to blackmail by a Mrs Phip[p]s in Watling Street, near St Paul's, 'at the sign of the Coffin and Cradle', through her 'threatening to expose the occasion of the debt. It is £22. – £5 of it is paid'.[41]

Steele's refusal to return the favour and lend Mrs Manley some 'trifling sum' ended their friendship some years later.[42] She complained of his ingratitude, to which Steele responded that he only refused because he did not have the ready cash to lend. He still had, he insisted, 'the greatest Sense imaginable of the Kind Notice you gave me when I was going on to my Ruin'.[43]

This guilty sense of his own 'ruin' was the source of Steele's sympathy for Collier's coinciding jeremiads about national ruin, though Steele was too much of a Whig to think the Williamite world any more sinful than its Restoration predecessor. Steele's comment about Collier having been 'too severe' on witty men was similarly born of his growing friendship with Collier's targets, Congreve and Vanbrugh. Steele recognized that Tory efforts to caricature the Whigs and their wits as unfaithful individuals, both sexually and politically, ignored a certain code of honour upheld by these men, who proved, in fact, as emotionally loyal to their mistresses as they were to their 'Revolution Principles'.[44] Their fidelity to one another as friends, through the Kit-Cat Club, was also an important way in which they sought to counter these Tory accusations and attest their virtue.

During the first five years of the new century, the Collierites and their allies did not slacken in their efforts to force moral reform on the theatres and society as a whole – over thirty pamphlets on the controversy would be published by the end of 1700 alone, including *A Second Defence of the Short View* by Collier himself. This pushed the Kit-Cat Club to display its defiance of these repressive religious forces more overtly, as on 9 January 1700, when the Club went to the theatre 'in a body', to see a performance designed as a rebuff to denunciations of the Whig theatres. The day before, Matt Prior, in London, wrote to Abraham ('Beau') Stanyan, one of Congreve's friends from Middle Temple student days and now a fellow Kit-Cat, serving as a diplomat in Paris: 'Tomorrow night, Betterton acts Falstaff, and to encourage that poor house the Kit Katters have taken one side-box and the Knights of the Toast have taken the other.'[45]

The two clubs were, it seems, putting on a show of friendly rivalry for a common cause. The 'poor house' was Betterton's theatre in Lincoln's Inn Fields, under the patronage of Montagu and the rest of the Kit-Cat Club. Betterton's low rumbling voice and round belly made him perfect for the part of Shakespeare's Falstaff. Prior, meanwhile, had penned 'a Prologue for Sir John [Falstaff] in favour of eating and drinking',[46] which teased the Knights of the Toast for living on 'meagre Soup and sour Champagne' instead of good English fare like Falstaff. It also teased Jacob Tonson as looking like 'old plump Jack [Falstaff] in Miniature'.[47]

It is significant that the Kit-Cats so honoured Falstaff, a character moderating tragedy with comic excess and abundance, resilient in his frivolity, regenerative in his adaptability, and a patriotic nobleman who fondly mentors young Hal, the future King of England. Falstaff could be viewed as a hero of English paternalism and materialism, while his love of food and drink was a straightforward connection to Kit-Cat dining. As *A Kit Cat C—b Describ'd* (1705) put it: 'None but Sir John Falstaff's of the Party: Fat, Corpulent Lords, Knights and Squires, were to be Admitted into [the Kit-Cat] Society by the Laws of its First Institution.'[48] Falstaff's capacious love of life was contrasted to images of rectitude, chastity and neo-Puritanism in the performance. The Club, which counted 'keeping up good Humour and Mirth' as an objective equal to 'the Improvement of Learning',[49] was making the case for a new style of Whiggism – with hedonistic appetites, yet with heart, honour and national pride.

The plan for the 9 January theatre outing was for the Kit-Cats to dine at Dorset's townhouse then proceed to Lincoln's Inn. Prior had had difficulty breathing a few days earlier, so he went to the dinner intending only to 'sit down to table when the dessert comes, eat nothing but roasted apples, and drink sack and water'.[50] The others would have honoured the Falstaffian spirit of the evening with a hearty meal. Their drunken posse, when it turned up at the theatre, must have looked the epitome of privileged debauchery to the servants sent ahead to save their seats. A satirist described Montagu in the theatre 'sitting on the Kit-Cat side, and Jacob T[onson] standing Door-Keeper for him'.[51] The Toasters, on the other side, were led by the Earl of Carbery, acting as 'general of the enemy's forces', despite also being a member of the Kit-Cat Club by this date.[52]

Congreve described the theatre as an open arena full of 'washy rogues' to whose semi-illiterate judgement he reluctantly submitted his 'repartee and raillery'.[53] Elsewhere, he despised the 'swarm of Scribblers' and City men who arrived before three o'clock to make sure they had enough elbow room, and who ate plum cake while watching the play.[54] If the people in the pit did not approve of the performance they blew on little toy whistles called 'cat-calls'.

The constant, defensive reference to the verdict of the pit by Congreve, Vanbrugh and other Kit-Cats hints at major tension between these writers and their audiences, and reflects their anxiety about the coarsening of the culture. The Kit-Cat Club emerged while popular culture was perceived as expanding at an unprecedented rate, and highbrow authors sought to cling to the opinions of the tasteful, educated few. The Kit-Cat critics were unified, for example, in their distaste for the popular entr'acte entertainments (rope dancers, singers, trained animals, tumblers and acrobats) added to even the most serious plays. They also distrusted mechanical innovations in scenery and special effects that appealed to the pit. Prior's Prologue for Falstaff, in this case, urged the audience to 'save the sinking stage' by preferring English comedy to the 'Apes' of French farce.[55]

Watching this performance, which probably consisted of extracts featuring Falstaff rather than an entire history play, the Kit-Cats would have been as much part of the show as the actors: Dorset boasting his ribbon of the Garter; Garth in his distinctive red cloak; Walsh with his heavily powdered wig. The key difference between theatres in this period and those in the Restoration was a larger forestage, so most of the action took place in the middle of the audience. Theatres remained well lit throughout the performances, and after 1690 there was some reintroduction of seating on the stage itself, further blurring the demarcation between the play's intrigues and those in the audience.

The plan to assist Betterton's theatre succeeded beyond expectations. Nearly three weeks later, a Londoner wrote: 'The Wits of all qualities have lately entertained themselves with a revived humour of Sir John Falstaff . . . which has drawn all the town more than any new play that has been produced of late.'[56]

The Kit-Cat Club continued its outings to the theatre over the next few years. In 1700, one satire referred to the Dorset Garden Theatre on the Thames at Whitefriars, 'Where Kit-Cats sat, and Toasters would be seen.'[57] They could attend either the opening night and support the theatre and its company, or the third night to support the playwright. Such excursions were an ideal way for the Club to publicize itself and its patronage, showing London society it was no gang of political conspirators skulking down a back alley like the regicide, republican clubs of the seventeenth century, and that the Kit-Cat's members refused to be cowed by the Collierites' moral condemnation of their dramatic poetry.

Congreve's new comedy of manners, *The Way of the World*, began rehearsals at Lincoln's Inn soon after the Falstaff performance closed. Again, the hopes and incomes of Betterton's company were pinned on the new play, with Vanbrugh remarking that 'if Congreve's Play don't help 'em, they are undone'.[58] The play, however, though costing its author some 'care and pains' to write,[59] was a risky work which Congreve said he doubted London's degenerate audience would appreciate, rather than one designed for popularity. Betterton's actors no doubt felt some ambivalence about the work – so brilliant, yet so difficult – as they rehearsed it. Congreve knew that parts of the play were provocative: two fingers stuck up to those who wanted less cynicism and more moral certainties on the English stage. The Prologue, for example, to be spoken by Betterton and concerning the author's intentions to entertain rather than reform, addressed itself sarcastically to any Collierites in the audience:

> Satire, he [Congreve] thinks, you ought not to expect;
> For so reformed a town who dares correct?
> To please, this time, has been his sole pretence,
> He'll not instruct, lest it should give offence.

The Way of the World, like Congreve's earlier plays, reflected the author's view of the urbane society in which he moved: the primacy of male friendships, bonded as much by clubbing and card-playing as business contracts and kinship. Congreve complicates theatrical stereotypes by making the play's hero, Mirabell, one of these suave and socially adept young London gentlemen – qualities traditionally belonging to morally suspect stage villains. Mirabell's final proof of integrity in the play, furthermore, is his kindness to Mrs Fainall, his former mistress. Even today, the question of one's moral duties to one's ex-lovers would be subtle territory for a play; in 1700, facing an audience of Collierites, it was an astonishing question to pose.

Congreve laughs at the affectations of Mirabell's friends, in the characters of Witwoud and Petulant, yet at the same time invokes sympathy for the social insecurities that require such pretences, as when Witwoud laughs at Petulant's attempts to feign popularity by saying he will dress up in costume and 'call for himself, wait for himself, nay and what's more, not finding himself [at home], sometimes leave a letter for himself'.[60] The mutual exposure of faults and fears is simultaneously cruel and affectionate, as male friendships so often are. The author showcases the men's conversation, and hence his own, while implying that they are balancing on their tightropes of wit above great social uncertainty.

When the play moves on to women, courtship and marriage, it mixes traditional complaints against the marriage yoke with a more honest account of which partner really lost their rights through marriage in the 1700s. In the famous 'proviso scene' where Millamant and Mirabell lay out their conditions of engagement, Millamant tries to preserve her rights, while her lover, Mirabell, tries to encroach upon them. The scene has often been complimented for showing equality between the sexes, yet it is a deceptive sort of equality: the couple are well matched in their knowledge of literature and parity of wit, but for Millamant her wit and coquetry are her only means of exercising some small power. She asks for a less conventional marriage because she fears to 'dwindle into a wife'.[61]

Congreve was troubled by the discordance between patriarchal laws and the reality of several strong women he knew and admired. In 1695, he wrote, 'We may call them the weaker Sex, but I think the true Reason is because our Follies are Stronger and our Faults the more prevailing.'[62] In *The Way of the World*, Congreve emphasizes that women are often less delusional in love than men, and in Millamant – a part written with Bracey specifically in mind – he celebrates the attractions of an intelligent, spirited woman. Mirabell's speech explaining why he loves Millamant is the writing of an author who loved, at this point, without illusions: 'I like her with all her faults, like her for her faults. Her follies are so natural, or so artful, that they become her; and those affectations, which in another woman would be odious, serve but to make her more agreeable.'[63]

As late as September 1698, nearly six years since their first meeting,

Congreve was still being teased that he 'need not covet to go to Heaven at all, but to stay and Ogle his dear Bracilla, with sneaking looks under his Hat, in the little side Box'.[64] Tom Browne commented sceptically on Bracey's famed chastity, noting that Congreve 'dines with her almost every day, yet She's a Maid; he rides out with her, and visits her in Public and Private, yet She's a Maid; if I had not a particular respect for her, I should go so near to say he lies with her, yet She's a Maid'.[65] Several later satires suggested Congreve and Bracey secretly married, though this is improbable since, when Bracey died in 1748, her will described her as a 'spinster'.[66]

The Way of the World went over the heads of its first audience in March 1700, as its author had expected, one observer saying it was 'hissed by Barbarous Fools in the Acting; and an impertinent Trifle was brought on after it, which was acted with vast Applause'.[67] Dryden was too ill to attend its opening night, but there is something poignant about the fact that Congreve's masterpiece, so far ahead of its time and predictive of so much later eighteenth-century literature, was one of the last works Dryden read before he died. He recognized its genius, and told Congreve not to mind its disappointing reception by everyone but, as Steele put it, 'the Few refined'.[68]

The Way of the World was to be Congreve's last play; he retired from dramatic writing at 30. This was not a fit of pique because his masterpiece failed to gain universal acclaim, as is sometimes said. Rather, he felt he had reached the height of his powers and had nothing further to prove to an audience becoming increasingly censorious, bourgeois and unimaginative.

Just as the play's early closure was a blow for Betterton's struggling company, so too Congreve's retirement from playwriting in 1700 must have been a blow for his publisher, Tonson, so close upon the death of Dryden. Dryden's name had been a critical seal of approval on any book that bore it in the preface or dedication. The editions of *Miscellany Poems* Dryden had edited for Tonson since 1684, for example, had become the most prestigious anthology of England, such that Tonson continued to produce the series long after Dryden's death. As one poem in the third *Miscellany* put it, Dryden's opinion was like a monarch's face stamped on a coin, giving value in an otherwise uncertain age.

A Satyr against Wit (1699), by Richard Blackmore, reversed this metaphor to mock the authors mentored by Dryden and the patrons assembled by Tonson. Describing the writings of those Montagu patronized as being like clipped or devalued coin, a sideswipe at Montagu's failed recoinage scheme of 1696, Blackmore suggested that Congreve and Vanbrugh would be left with little reputation were their work cleansed of its impurities. Blackmore further proposed Somers, Dorset and Montagu should underwrite a 'bank of wit' to reform the currency of English poetry, meaning that they should give their support to worthier poets, like him.[69] Garth, Steele and Walsh contributed, on behalf of Dryden and his Witty Club, to a collected volume of verses as a counter-attack to Blackmore,[70] and this literary skirmish on the eve of Dryden's death did much to consolidate the Kit-Cat Club's sense that it must ensure Dryden's critical standards for English literature were not forgotten. In June 1700, a young man wrote to Garth on behalf of a group of unknown poets who had compiled a collection of elegies for Dryden, asking forlornly, 'who shall make us known, and stamp Esteem, / On what we write...?' He begged for the book to be commended by Dr Garth, even though the young man and his friends had no 'swelling Kit-cat' patron on their title page.[71]

After Dryden's death, Tonson used the Kit-Cat Club's collective opinion as a replacement for Dryden's critical taste when evaluating works submitted for publication or when compiling the *Miscellanies*, letters of acceptance from Tonson to various writers often referring to work having passed the test of the 'best judges'.[72] One Tonson biographer has even conjectured that the anonymous poems in the later *Miscellanies* 'as a whole represent the literary activities of the Kit-Cat Club'.[73]

Critical taste was understood to require cultivation, so that a true critic was made, not born. The paradox that this was believed by some of the highest born men in England was awkwardly explained by another shared belief: that a gentleman who had no need to work or seek a patron should, thanks to such independence, be the most impartial critic and arbiter of taste. Fresh works were therefore submitted to the Kit-Cat Club's 'peer review' not merely to seek patronage but also because of a residual respect for aristocratic opinion, according to classical theory. In an age that believed 'Fame consists in the Opinion of wise and good Men',[74] the Kit-Cat Club sought to be the makers of fame. As its own fame grew, the Club became a whetstone for sharpening its members' critical faculties, and a practical help to Tonson's publishing firm in the absence of paid editorial staff.

Dryden's Witty Club had been attacked for being self-serving, self-important and malicious. The Kit-Cat Club now became the new target for such envy and resentment, as it sat and decided what writing should go to Tonson's presses and what into the tavern fireplace. Ned Ward was among those who questioned the Whig lords' right to sit as the self-styled custodians of English literature and who complained that the Kit-Cats, unlike Dryden, now made the critical process too Whiggishly ideological: '[T]hey began to set themselves up for Apollo's court of judicature, where every author's performance, from the stage poet to the garret-drudge, was to be read, tried, applauded, or condemned, according to the new system of Revolutionary Principles.'[75]

Soon the Kit-Cats were to give the same ideological treatment to other art forms, including architecture.

During the summer of 1699, while Somers and Montagu were visiting Somerset and others at their country seats, and several fellow Kit-Cats were touring France, Vanbrugh – who had seen enough of France during his long captivity there – toured the great houses of northern England. He travelled by high-speed 'calash' (a light two-wheeled carriage with a removable hood) and stayed with at least two Kit-Cat friends: William Cavendish at Chatsworth for four or five days, then, in July, with his distant kinsman, Carlisle. Carlisle's membership of the Kit-Cat Club rested on his proven influence in the 1695 Cumberland election, and on the fact that, though Carlisle's Howard ancestors were prominent Catholics, his grandfather and father had been Whigs and his own Whiggery was fervent. Carlisle's love of books would also have recommended him to Tonson and the Kit-Cat collectors; he catalogued his family's libraries and added to them constantly. In the summer of 1697, Carlisle had stayed with the Somersets at Petworth and admired it with an envious eye, developing his own ambitions to become an architectural patron – ambitions that would be spectacularly realized in his later building of Castle Howard.

By 1699, Carlisle had been appointed a Gentleman of the Bedchamber – a Court place to add to his other honours: Governor of the town and castle of Carlisle, Lord Lieutenant of Cumberland and Westmorland, and Vice Admiral of the seacoasts for those two counties. Thinking his future income secure, and eager to lend additional status to his title, which dated back only as far as his grandfather, Carlisle decided to build the Howard family a new seat, on a scale that would allow him to entertain royalty.

Carlisle had already invited the architect William Talman to develop plans for a house at Henderskelfe, northeast of York. Talman, who designed much of Chatsworth, was Carlisle's first choice because he was the King's favoured architect, and the project could demonstrate shared tastes with William III in one of the few artistic spheres where the King took interest. By July 1699, however, when Carlisle invited Vanbrugh to the same site, it appears Talman had been dropped. Whether Talman's designs simply disappointed Carlisle, or whether Kit-Cat favouritism displaced a more qualified man, is hard to know. Talman, at any rate, thought he had been unfairly dismissed and threatened to sue.

The ebullient Vanbrugh, who seemed to have no fear of failure despite his near-total lack of architectural experience, described his earliest designs for what would become 'Castle Howard' to one of the Kit-Cat patrons as being for 'a plain low building like an orange house'.[76] This does indeed describe Vanbrugh's earliest, amazingly plain sketches. Such consultations with Whig patricians were probably the source of the legend that Vanbrugh designed Castle Howard on a napkin or scrap of paper during a Kit-Cat Club dinner. It is true that Vanbrugh designed the house by committee – a way for Carlisle to enjoy the prestige of undertaking such a project long before there was a finished product to show off – but there is no specific Kit-Cat dinner that can be credited with the house's conception. As Vanbrugh wrote, 'There has been a great many Critics consulted upon it since, and no objection being made on't, the Stone is raising and the Foundations will be laid in the Spring [of 1700].'[77] This prediction was, as Vanbrugh's predictions of time and cost almost always were, unrealistic. The foundations were not laid until the spring of 1701. First the villagers and small farmers of Henderskelfe had to be evicted and the property enclosed. (A contemporary said Carlisle was zealously concerned for those on his lands, but this was more a concern for their obedience at the polls than their rights.) During the two years between the first designs and the first work on site, the Kit-Cats were consulted and various elaborations added.

King William also reviewed the plans in June 1700. As with a poem dedicated to a monarch or noble patron, so architecture was not only an expression of status and power but also a bid to obtain them. To build on such a scale, albeit in the Continental baroque style, was seen as a patriotic act that ought to bring cultural prestige to the nation and royal favour to the owner. The English baroque expressed the 'communal will' of the Kit-Cat Club in architectural form, taking 'its emotion from the sense of grandeur and confidence enjoyed by the old Whigs of the 1688 revolution'.[78] Carlisle was 30 when he commissioned Castle Howard, five years younger than Vanbrugh. So, although of the 'old Whig' generation, Carlisle acted in the ambition of youth. He was the first and most important of six Kit-Cat architectural patrons who would help make Vanbrugh into one of Britain's greatest architects.

For all his social climbing, Vanbrugh knew how to pull someone else up the ladder behind him. He introduced the experienced builder and designer Nicholas Hawksmoor to Carlisle, and got him a salary almost twice what the average craftsman was paid. Vanbrugh was not paid at all; his rewards consisted of jobs and sinecures. Not only did this shift the expenditure from Carlisle's pocket to the Crown, but it also permitted discretion within the Club: the tactful illusion that members were not divided into employers and employees.

Vanbrugh used the time between first design and commencement of building, while living on half-pay from the Second Marine Regiment, to gain some little experience by building himself a house in London. In July 1700, soon after he reviewed the plans for Castle Howard, the King granted Vanbrugh permission for what would be the first of a series of private houses on the burnt-out ruins of Whitehall Palace. Private property was replacing royal property in much the same way that privatized aristocratic patronage was replacing royal patronage.

Vanbrugh's townhouse was built quickly during 1701. When complete, it served as a life-sized demonstration model and advertisement for his skills. Jonathan Swift (by this time a clergyman and published author, ambiguously seeking Court Whig favour in London while writing anonymous lampoons against the same Whigs) described it as 'resembling a Goose Pie' and sneered at Vanbrugh turning to architecture 'without Thought or Lecture'. He suggested Vanbrugh had been inspired by watching children build houses of cards and mud. Swift also emphasized, enviously, that the architect of the 'Goose Pie' house had enjoyed a meteoric professional and social ascent, thanks solely to whom he knew in London high society: 'No wonder, since wise Authors know, / That Best Foundations must be Low.'[79]

At least Vanbrugh was finding that his architectural designs, no matter how lusty, were not, like his plays, subject to accusations of blasphemy and immorality. Neither Vanbrugh nor Congreve stopped writing as abruptly as sometimes portrayed, but both lost interest in dramatic writing at the height of their literary careers thanks in part to unrelenting pressure from the Collierite censors. When Betterton's company revived Congreve's 1695 hit *Love for Love* in Easter 1701, a legal action was brought against the players for 'licentiousness',[80] despite the fact that the production had been staged for a Christian charity (for 'the Redemption of the English now in Slavery . . . in Barbary'[81]). Similarly, when Vanbrugh's *Provok'd Wife* was revived, both the author and the players (including Bracey) were charged with using indecent expressions and sentenced to fines of £5 (almost £700 today) each.[82] The old fear of the semi-illiterate audience acting as judge and jury was becoming a sinister reality.

As Vanbrugh shifted his energies to architecture, Congreve likewise turned after 1700 to art forms less scrutinized in terms of morality: music and lyric poetry.[83] Both men's diverted careers, however, continued to be bound closely to the political fates of their patrons in the Kit-Cat Club; in the political situation of 1700, those fates seemed extremely uncertain.

VI
THE EUROPEANS

I hate the idea of causes, and if I had to choose between betraying my country and betraying my friend, I hope I should have the guts to betray my country.

E. M. FORSTER, *Two Cheers for Democracy* (1951)

THE KIT-CATS CONSIDERED themselves not only urbane but also cosmopolitan sophisticates, looking beyond England's shores culturally and politically, and defining themselves in comparison to other nationalities. Theirs was an outward-facing club, trying to build an outward-facing nation, and trying to stereotype their Tory rivals as old-fashioned, parochial isolationists (despite, paradoxically, the Jacobites' supranational loyalties to the Pope in Rome and the exiled Stuart Court in France). Being ruled by a Dutchman underscored the extent to which England's domestic politics were enmeshed with the struggles between the major Continental powers: France on the one hand and the Habsburg realms on the other. When this clash of empires was temporarily paused after the 1697 peace, several Kit-Cats seized the opportunity to expand their education of European languages and politics through travel. Others – Lord Dorset's Boys

– continued working on the Continent as a new breed of professional diplomat. For one of them, parliamentary debates about England's international relations would dramatically reveal his betrayal of his fellow Kit-Cats.

The culture wars raging in England at the turn of the century formed the backdrop to more straightforward political confrontations between parties. Spring 1698, for example, saw the Kit-Cats and other Court (Junto) Whigs preparing for a general election at a time when England's Protestants were feeling reprieved from the potential dangers of a Jacobite assassination plot against the King (the so-called Fenwick Affair of 1696) or the spectre of a French invasion (no longer an immediate risk during the peace). The Junto Whigs' power and influence disintegrated alongside this lessening level of public alarm, and the Tories' ambitions rose in inverse proportion. The Junto Whigs therefore knew they had an electoral fight on their hands, despite the fact that they now had the King's backing, William having been deeply angered by the 1697 opposition call for a Disbanding Bill. The Kit-Cat politicians took concerted actions across a number of marginal constituencies. Somers, for example, gifted legal title in Reigate burgages (freehold properties) to his friends, including Congreve, Tonson and several other Kit-Cats, so that they became propertied voters, able to win that seat to his interest. Despite such dubious tactics, however, the Junto lost control of the Commons in July to Harley's alliance of Country Whigs and Tories.

Montagu kept his seat representing the borough of Westminster only after an expensive campaign. On the same night as his embarrassingly narrow victory was announced, so too was the death of his elderly wife, Lady Manchester. This meant the loss of an annual £1,500 (today £142,000) jointure, which automatically transferred to Montagu's stepson. This stepson was another Kit-Cat, also named Charles Montagu, who was exactly the same age as his stepfather, cousin and namesake. He had inherited the title of 4th Earl (later 1st Duke) of Manchester, and is hereafter referred to as 'Manchester' to avoid confusion.[1]

The King was losing patience with Montagu's inability to muster parliamentary support to defend the Court and defeat the Disbanding Bill. Before the election, Montagu had succeeded in raising revenue for the King and army by navigating through the Commons a £2 million flotation of a New East India Company. The Old East India Company, the only major London corporation run by Tories, was forced to invest in the New, which became a rich source of employment and dividends for Montagu's Kit-Cat friends. After the Whig election defeat, however, the Old East India Company took advantage of the King's impatience with Montagu and petitioned for a renewed right to trade. At the same time, a passionately argued pamphlet in favour of disbanding the army, *A Short History of Standing Armies*, seemed to win the press war over that issue in favour of Harley's opposition. Prior reported from Paris that the Jacobite Court-in-exile at Louis' chateau of St Germain-en-Laye was rejoicing at the prospect of the English army dismantling itself, and in January 1699, the Disbanding Bill passed, despite all Montagu's blocking efforts. To the King's outrage, England's army was required to reduce itself to 7,000 'native born' men. Everything achieved by the Whigs in the first half of the 1690s seemed to be unravelling.

During the long 1698–9 parliamentary session, therefore, the Kit-Cat Club was an important forum for holding together the Junto Whig faction while it was under strain, and for monitoring the precarious international situation through its younger members' Continental travels and diplomatic postings. In this context, Montagu encouraged Addison, still a cloistered tutor at Magdalen College, not to enter the Church but instead seek a political or diplomatic career. '[H]is Arguments were founded upon the general [de]pravity and the Corruption of Men of Business [i.e. government], who wanted liberal Education,' recalled Steele. '[M]y Lord ended with a Compliment that, however he might be represented as no Friend to the Church, he never would do it any other Injury than keeping Mr Addison out of it.'[2]

Addison at this time was struggling to reconcile his own worldly ambitions with his father's lessons in Christian humility. He wrote a draft sermon, published many years later as an essay on 'The Folly of Seeking Fame', asking whether God's purpose in giving us the 'passion' of ambition was to drive forward our 'sedentary' souls, and whether ambition is less sinful when it is commensurate with ability: 'How few are there who are furnished with Abilities sufficient . . . to distinguish themselves from the rest of Mankind?'[3] Ambition for fame, he wrote, is the same instinct that makes us vulnerable to criticism, and the pleasure of fame is inevitably 'precarious' because it rests on the fickle and fallible opinion of mortals, rather than God's judgement.

Addison seems to have reconciled his ambition with his conscience by his twenty-seventh birthday, which coincided with the 1699 May Day celebrations at Magdalen. The following morning, Addison caught a coach to London, quitting forever the university where he had lived and worked for over a decade. Through Montagu, Addison received a £200 (over £20,000 today) government stipend to travel and study French. Somers partnered Montagu in supporting Addison's European education, as a letter of thanks from Addison to Somers confirms: 'I have now for some time lived on the Effect of your Lordship's patronage . . . The only Return I can make your L[or]d[shi]p will be to apply myself Entirely to my Business and to take such a care of my Conversation that your favours may not seem misplaced.'[4]

Addison's trip started, in August 1699, on a literal wrong foot, with a fall into the sea as he disembarked at Calais, a succession of 'dismal Adventures' ('lame post-horses by Day and hard Beds at night') and misunderstandings because of his feeble French. 'I have encountered as many misfortunes as a Knight-Errant,' Addison laughed in his first letter back to Congreve, adding that he liked French statues and paintings only because 'they don't speak French'.[5] Without the language, Addison was left to enjoy the sights of *grand siècle* Paris, with Louis XIV's magnificent, strictly regulated rebuilding projects making it appear unlike any city that had previously existed. The city's ramparts had only recently been dismantled to allow the building of the new boulevards, including the Grand Cours along the line of today's Champs Elysées, and the Place Vendôme was just about to be inaugurated.

Yet Paris, in contrast to London, did not feel like a city in its prime. The city's famous street life was increasingly policed out of sight, even in the Marais, and the social hierarchy had ossified around a limited number of titled families. The capital was also suffering from the absence of the Court, which had moved to the Palace of Versailles. Yet the Louvre and other royal buildings still stood, hollowly hogging land throughout the city's centre – a fact seen by another Protestant English visitor as symbolic of Louis' despotic disregard for his own people: 'Here the palaces and convents have eat[en] up the People's dwellings and crowded them excessively together.'[6]

Addison soon sought familiarity and conversation among the expats at Paris' English embassy, which then had no fixed address but moved to each ambassador's private residence. At this date, Montagu's stepson Manchester had just been appointed ambassador, inheriting Prior as his secretary. The 'docile'[7] Beau Stanyan, who had already served as Manchester's secretary at the English embassy in Venice, arrived in Paris in June 1699 to replace Prior, but Prior remained for a period of handover. All three Kit-Cats – the ambassador and his two secretaries – were therefore working together at the Paris embassy when Addison arrived. Vanbrugh jokingly congratulated Manchester on fulfilling his ambition to host every English gentleman coming to France, but Addison would have been a particularly honoured guest as he carried introductions from Somers and the ambassador's stepfather, Montagu. Addison became good friends during this time with both Manchester and his wife. Lady Manchester was a beauty, reportedly toasted 'with an Exemplary Constancy' at the Kit-Cat Club by the Earl of Carbery.[8] When Addison himself eventually joined the Kit-Cat, he would patriotically toast Lady Manchester's natural complexion in contrast to French 'haughty Dames that Spread / O'er their pale cheeks an Artful red'.[9]

Prior likewise remarked on the overpainted Parisian women, with the result, he told Montagu, that French men 'make love to each other to a degree that is incredible, for you can pick your boy at the Tuileries or at the play'.[10] Prior seems to have preferred heterosexual flirtations with English ladies in Paris – a business as separate from his relationship with his live-in lover Jane, he told her, as love poetry is from prose:

What I speak, my fair Chloe, and what I write, shows
The diff'rence there is betwixt nature and art.
I court others in verse; but I love thee in prose:
And they have my whimsies, but thou hast my heart.[11]

When a newspaper in London falsely reported that Prior was engaged to a certain Lady Falkland, Prior joked to Montagu that such a courtship was impracticable:

> She is an old Troy that will not be taken in ten years, and though fifty strong fellows should get in to her by stratagem, they might even march out again at a large breach without being able to set her on fire; but one single sentinel as I am with a thin carcass and weak lungs might lie before her walls till I eat horse-hides and shoe-leather, unless you kindly sent me some refreshments from the Treasury.[12]

Prior thus used gossip about his own love life as an excuse to beg cash, and to all such requests Montagu remained a responsive friend: 'Of all my correspondents,' Prior told him, 'you are certainly the best, for you never write to me, yet *do* always what I beg of you. I am extremely obliged to you for the two last hundred pounds.'[13]

On another occasion, not long before Addison's arrival, Prior begged Montagu: 'For God's sake, will you think of a little money for me, for I have fluttered away the Devil and all in this monkey country, where the air is infected with vanity, and extravagance is as epidemical as the itch in Scotland.'[14]

Montagu never reproached Prior for these 'dunning' letters, though he once defined 'men of honour' as being those who asked no favours of their friends: 'Free is their service, and unbought their love.'[15] Prior required some finesse to keep the two relationships, of patronage and friendship, in balance; he signed off one letter: '*Adieu*, Master; Nobody respects the Chancellor of the Exchequer more, or loves dear Mr Montagu better, than his old friend and obliged humble servant, Matt.'[16] Inversely, as Dorset moved into retirement, his relationship with Prior became more that of a friend than patron: 'I could almost wish you out of all public affairs,' Dorset told Prior, 'that I might enjoy your good company oftener and share with you in that ease and lazy quiet which I propose to myself in this latter part of my life.'[17]

Steele once declared that a gentleman should travel 'to get clear of national Prejudices, of which every Country has its share',[18] yet Addison's time among the Kit-Cats in Paris only reinforced his prejudices. This experience underpinned Addison's lifelong patriotism and dedication to resisting the French model of unmediated and unlimited power, vested in a single monarch: 'As a British Freeholder, I should not scruple taking [the] place of a French Marquis; and when I see one of my Countrymen amusing himself in his little Cabbage-Garden, I naturally look upon him as a greater Person than the Owner of the richest Vineyard in Champagne.'[19]

Addison adopted Prior's opinions on nearly everything they encountered in France, and most of those opinions were extremely critical. Prior complained to Montagu about the hypocritical pretence of cordial diplomatic relations with France during this lull before war was sure to resume: 'We took our leave yesterday of this Court, from whom we had a great many compliments and a damned dinner . . . they are very obliging to us one day and the same to King James the next.'[20]

Elsewhere he observed frankly: 'These people are all the same: civil in appearance and hating us to hell at the bottom of their heart.'[21] Prior described Louis XIV as living 'like an Eastern monarch, making waterworks and planting melons' while his nation starved.[22] He showed the elderly French king as a grotesque, vainly picking at his few remaining teeth, and described the exiled James II as 'lean, worn and rivelled'[23] – telling the English ministers, in other words, exactly what they wanted to hear: that their enemies were literally toothless and impotent. Addison, though wondering at the luxury of the French palaces, similarly criticized the disparity between rich and poor, and the displacement of whole villages at Louis' orders, just 'for the bettering of a View'.[24]

Addison's only concession to the French was that they had the advantage over the English in good humour. In rural France, he wrote, 'Everyone sings, laughs and starves.'[25] The French were also much more at ease in their conversation, especially compared to Addison, whose natural reticence in groups was accentuated by his poor French. Later, in his essays, Addison would try to convert his own self-conscious personality into the general image of English national character, in contrast to the French: 'Modesty is our distinguishing Character, as Vivacity is theirs.'[26]

Addison was caught in the middle of a certain tension between Prior and Manchester during Prior's final months in Paris. Prior described how even the servants there, including his girlfriend Jane, considered Manchester's manners too crude for a diplomat – blowing his nose into his napkin, spitting in the middle of the room, or laughing too loudly. A rude letter from Manchester, complaining how Prior wasted money and left his post with tasks half-done, suggests the dislike was mutual. Though Prior had proved himself useful at Ryswick, Lord Manchester's diplomatic record in Venice had been less impressive – he was assessed as being 'of greater application than capacity' and 'of good address but no elocution'.[27] Manchester's noble birth, however, protected him from explicit criticism, while Prior grew resentful at how little remuneration or simple thanks he received after compensating for the failings of his nobly born superior. When Prior returned to London, he travelled the last leg of the journey from The Hague in the company of both King William himself and the Tory Earl of Jersey, who had been Prior's boss at the Paris embassy before Manchester and was now allied to William's rising Dutch favourite, Arnold van Keppel. Prior not only caught a chill while crossing the Channel but also sensed which way England's political wind was blowing: away from the Junto Whigs. From this point onwards, Jersey, though in opposition to Prior's Kit-Cat friends, superseded Montagu and Dorset as Prior's leading patron.

Addison lodged at the Paris embassy until October 1699, then retreated to study French at a remote abbey at Blois, in the Loire, for a year. Stanyan kept Addison supplied from Paris with updates on international developments, though it is likely neither man was informed of the most important but top secret development – the signing by France and England, in October 1699, of a 'Partition Treaty' to peaceably divide the Spanish Empire, including the

Americas, after Carlos II's death. Earlier in the summer, Somers had used his power as Lord Chancellor to permit the King to negotiate such a treaty without informing Parliament. It was not illegal for Somers to do this, but it would create severe problems for Somers when the Treaty, and its successor, the second Partition Treaty signed in March 1700, were later discovered by Parliament.

Addison was in Blois when he belatedly heard news that, thanks to sustained pressure from Harley's opposition, his patron Montagu had resigned from the Treasury and hence as the King's chief minister. Montagu's resignation and move to a less powerful but more lucrative post (as Auditor of the Receipts of the Exchequer) was a blow to his friends and followers. It confirmed Prior in his decision to shift patrons, discarding the bonds of friendship formed by school, university and, latterly, by the Kit-Cat Club.

Prior said that after Montagu's resignation he expected Somers, the only Kit-Cat and Junto member remaining in the King's inner circle, to be next 'fallen upon' by the Tories, 'though God knows what crime he is guilty of, but that of being a very great man and a wise and upright judge'.[28] Prior was prescient: when a Commons vote against Somers' probity was very narrowly defeated in April 1700, the King was reluctantly forced to dismiss Somers. Montagu's outrage at this decision showed his deep personal loyalty to Somers, yet neither he nor other politico Kit-Cats resigned *en bloc* to protest their friend's martyrdom. It would hardly help Somers if all his political allies fell on their swords and thereby left the King wholly in other hands: 'You may easily think Lord Somers cannot but have a great many friends, but they may show their friendship and yet continue their duty to the King,' Manchester advised Prior.[29] The Club instead showed its solidarity with both Montagu and Somers in more subtle ways – its members' show of public unity at the Falstaff theatre outing and at Dryden's funeral had this as specific political motive, alongside defiance of Jeremy Collier.

All three Lord Dorset's Boys were reunited in London at the time Somers was forced to surrender the Great Seal. Stepney was working on the Commission of Trade and Plantations, where in June 1700 he formed a sub-commission to negotiate the boundaries of Hudson's

Bay in Canada with the French. Soon after, Prior, who had given little outward sign of his shift towards Jersey's patronage, was appointed to the same Commission of Trade, replacing the retiring Commissioner (and famous Enlightenment philosopher) John Locke. With Montagu a member of the same Commission, this was possibly the only time the three old friends worked side by side.

With his Commission income, Prior bought a large townhouse on Duke Street, overlooking the promenades and dairy fields of St James's Park, and he entertained there in a manner consistently beyond his means. He invited Dorset, Montagu and Stepney to dinners there of 'Bacon-Ham and Mutton-shin'.[30] Such hospitality disguised Prior's deepening involvement with the Tories, and allowed him to gather information from his old Whig friends to pass on to the rival party.

That same summer of 1700, Montagu flexed the strained muscles of his remaining influence to procure another sinecure for Congreve: the post of Customer of the Poole Port – a post Congreve held for just over two years. Congreve's portfolio of sinecures, totalling just under £200 a year, now gave him some degree of financial security. He (and his beloved dog 'Sappho') moved out of Tonson's house, but he continued to live as a rent-paying lodger, this time with a married couple named the Porters who lived on Arundel Street. Mrs Frances Porter was Bracey's sister.

Congreve's move from Fleet Street did not signify any falling out with his publisher, as shown by the fact that the playwright accompanied Tonson to Europe in the summer of 1700. Congreve let his friends know of their safe arrival in Calais, after which he travelled to Het Loo (William's palace and hunting lodge in Guelderland), then Rotterdam. Congreve would have been quizzed by the Dutch courtiers about the latest news from England, which was causing disquiet among Europe's Protestants. Princess Anne's only son and heir, the 11-year-old Duke of Gloucester, had just died unexpectedly in July. This threw the English Crown's Protestant succession back into doubt, making the Whigs fear that the post-Revolutionary regime, under which, for all their present problems, they had generally thrived, could yet be reversed. In August, the Junto lords stayed together at a country house near Hampton Court, and they there decided that Stepney should take advantage of his good standing with Sophia, Electress Dowager of the German state of Hanover and the Protestant granddaughter of England's James I, to ask informally whether she and her heirs would accept the English succession. This letter, in Stepney's own humble name, was sent from London in late August or early September 1700.[31]

October 1700 saw another pivotal royal death: that of Carlos II of Spain. Carlos, it emerged, had bequeathed his Spanish Habsburg Empire, including its lucrative Spanish American trade, to Louis XIV's grandson, Philippe Duc d'Anjou, rather than to the Austrian Habsburgs. When Louis XIV decided to defend his grandson's inheritance, thereby disregarding the two Partition Treaties signed with England, the stage was set for a new European war. The English and Dutch saw that a merger of the French and Spanish empires would upset the balance of world power. The Junto Whigs in particular, being most closely allied with the Dutch and Dissenting interests, advocated mounting a new defensive war against Louis XIV. As the Tory Charles Davenant put it, the mood of the Junto Whigs in 1700 was all '"To your tents, O Israel!"'[32]

Tipped that war would soon break out, Congreve and Addison accelerated their European travels. Addison gave up improving his French, 'which has been a Rock in my way harder to get over than the Alps,'[33] and sailed for Italy. He travelled with a former Oxford pupil, named George Dashwood, son of the Lord Mayor of London and '*un bon gros et gras bourgeois*',[34] as well as Edward Wortley, a nephew of Montagu's, and former Middle Temple chum of Congreve's and Stanyan's. By chaperoning these two young men through Italy, Addison was paid enough to cover his own expenses. In Rome, Addison watched Pope Clement XI officiate for two hours at St Peter's, and purchased twenty volumes of European manuscripts for Somers.

Congreve was back in London by December 1700, at which time he gave an Irish friend advance notice of Montagu's elevation to the House of Lords as 'Baron Halifax'. The patent for Montagu's title, drawn up by Prior, referred to Montagu having provided the 'sinews of war' by establishing the Bank of England and generally restructuring

English commerce in the 1690s, which was no more than the truth.[35] The peerage, however, was less royal thanks for services rendered than acknowledgement of Montagu's growing impotence in the Commons since the last election.

It was said Lord Halifax (as Montagu shall henceforth be called) 'brought up a familiar style' to the House of Lords, which made the tone of debates there far more informal.[36] While the Kit-Cats admired this style, just as they admired Wharton's rumbustious colloquialisms whenever he spoke in the upper house, a Tory critic snobbishly described it as 'Billingsgate rhetoric', unfit for a peer.[37] Such remarks point to the close relationship between the conversational style of the Kit-Cat Club, which increasingly behaved like a mock-parliament in its meetings,[38] and the tone of actual parliamentary debate – one elite talking-shop echoing another.

Dickens famously remarked that the House of Commons was 'the best club in London'.[39] With its nepotism, cronyism and oligarchic management, government at the beginning of the eighteenth century was indeed a giant club – MPs were not called 'members' for nothing, and those who held government places, voting with the Court in the Commons, were sometimes known as 'the Club Men'.[40] Kit-Cat spirit translated to wider Whig party loyalty, which magnified itself into national patriotism, and collective identities forged in a tavern's backroom evolved into national identities. Such collective identity was formed most deeply during periods of political adversity, as during the winter of 1700–1.

The King was back to relying, against his own inclinations, on Tories like Laurence Hyde, Earl of Rochester, and the Treasury management of Lord Godolphin. This necessity was confirmed by another Tory-dominated Parliament returned after the election in January 1701.

The Kit-Cat Club's lifespan was characterized by unusually frequent and highly contested elections, averaging one every second year. Individual Junto members' electoral influence, through direct patronage, but also through circular letters and regional party whips, was therefore key to the Club's wider influence. In particular, England saw a notable rise in 'carpet-bagging' and boroughs 'succumb[ing] to affluent, absentee candidates in preference to indigenous minor gentry or merchants'.[41] The Kit-Cat Club contributed to this, in so far as it established bonds between the nobility and London gentlemen who were not their kinsmen, which were then imported into Parliament.[42] Not all MPs who were handed seats without contest failed to serve their constituents honourably, but nor was such an MP likely to challenge his patron's instructions. Lady Mary Wortley Montagu, despite her personal fondness for the Club, remarked that its members were 'dupes to their leaders'.[43]

As in 1698, the Kit-Cats had tried to influence voters in 1701 in ways considered unconstitutional by many at the time: letters from Lord Carlisle to rally support for Whig candidates around the country, for example, led to a Commons vote against peers meddling in elections beyond the counties where they owned property. Halifax and Wharton so aggressively used their interests in Wiltshire to secure election of New East India Company supporters that the Tories afterwards sent the unlucky Whig election agents to the Tower.

After the 1701 election defeat of the Junto Whigs, Robert Harley's supporters nominated him for the Commons' Speakership. It is telling that the Junto did not organize its resistance to this move via the Kit-Cat Club but rather via another Whig club that ran in parallel – the Whig Rose Club, which met at the Rose tavern in Covent Garden. The Rose Club was a far less exclusive and yet more narrowly focused society than the Kit-Cat, founded at around the same time and used by Halifax and Wharton as a place to whip underling Whig MPs into line. Over seventy-five such MPs met at the Rose to coordinate their opposition to Harley's appointment as Speaker, but were defeated at the vote in February 1701.

The following month, the Commons passed the Act of Settlement, ensuring the English Crown would pass to the House of Hanover (Electress Sophia, followed by her son George) should both William and Princess Anne die childless. The ministry, including Lord Godolphin and Robert Harley, supported this crucial constitutional measure, and the Act was voted through 'without any dispute',[44] since no MP of either party could openly oppose the Protestant succession and hope to retain a career in Williamite government. Behind the scenes, however, certain Tories tried to obstruct the clauses intended to consolidate the Whig model of limited parliamentary monarchy, such as limits on any future monarch's power to dictate foreign affairs. The Junto argued to retain such limitations and so believed themselves the true defenders of English liberties (even against William, if need be). The Act also sounded the death knell for the old Stuart idea of the monarch as God's Anointed, ruling by Divine Right. The succession was explicitly being determined, after all, by an Act of Parliament, not by God. After 1701, allegiance to the Hanoverian succession became an inviolable tenet of the Kit-Cat Club, as for most Whigs – a tenet the Kit-Cats would need to defend with all their energy in future. The Act of Settlement had secured the succession on paper, but it was a long way from being secure in practice.

The inseparability of the Kit-Cat Club's cultural and political pursuits is well demonstrated by the relationship between the parliamentary debate over 'election' of England's royal heir and the debate then raging between subjective (Lockean) and objective (classical) theories of criticism. Congreve dramatized the subjectivists' viewpoint in March 1701, just as the Act of Settlement was being passed, in a new musical masque entitled *The Judgment of Paris*. Congreve turned this piece – about goddesses competing in a kind of beauty pageant – into an actual competition for English composers, with the *London Gazette* advertising for new songs, the best of which, as voted by the audience, would win £200 (over £26,000 today). Tonson administered the competition. As with the Falstaff performance and Dryden's funeral, the event was a way for the Club to reassert itself culturally during a time of political difficulty, while making a case among intellectuals for a particularly Whiggish theory of critical judgement. They wished to show that, whether choosing one's leaders or one's entertainment, the same enlightened exercise of reason and good taste was required.

Only four musicians entered the competition because it was unfairly believed that the event, like a parliamentary election, would be fixed. A good audience, however, attended to hear the four alternative performances at the Dorset Garden Theatre, which had been lined with tin to improve its acoustics, and prettily decorated with extra candles. 'The boxes and the pit were all thrown into one; so that all sat in common,' wrote Congreve, 'and the whole was crammed with beauties and beaux, not one scrub being admitted.'[45] Free hot chocolate and cool drinks, including 'ratafia' (liqueur flavoured with almond or fruit kernels) and white wine, were served between the pit and the stage. Bracey, or 'Our friend Venus' as Congreve fondly called her, 'performed to a miracle'. She and the other actresses playing the goddesses judged by Paris were at one point in the masque ordered to disrobe and partially did so, making it an extremely erotic performance for its day.

The Kit-Cat patrons dominated the all-Whig subscription supporting this production and competition, with Halifax being its prime sponsor, and Somerset lobbying for his favourite contestant to win. Ironically, as in the last two parliamentary elections, it was not the Kit-Cat candidates who triumphed, however, but another young man, John Weldon, who later became the King's organist.

There was soon little time for such cultural contests, as another parliamentary crisis erupted around the 'discovery' of the two secret Partition Treaties. Harley, who only wanted an excuse to further decapitate the Junto Whigs, promptly led his coalition of Tories and radical Country Whigs (who feared William's secret diplomacy as a return to the autocratic ways of Charles II) to attack the Treaties' makers. Declaring passionately that Somers had to be punished or 'our posterity will curse us',[46] Harley tried to persuade his fellow MPs to impeach Somers.

On 14 April 1701, Somers delivered a half-hour speech in his own defence to the Commons, 'with great plainness and presence of mind', explaining he had only been following the King's orders.[47] He then withdrew before the House voted on his case.

Prior was one of the MPs sitting in the Commons that evening. He had obtained his East Grinstead seat three months earlier through the influence of his childhood patron, Dorset. Though he had written to Dorset in 1698 complimenting William's wisdom in concluding the first Partition Treaty (in which Prior himself had had a significant hand), Prior now took the extraordinary step of voting with

Harley and the Tories in favour of impeaching Somers for 'a high Crime and Misdemeanour' in the Lords. If the Kit-Cats had not suspected the shift in Prior's loyalties before, it was now made dramatically evident. As Prior voted, he must have avoided the eye of fellow Kit-Cat William Walsh, acting as teller. Though there was often the odd deviancy on a division list, such outright defection away from a political party and its patrons was observed with shock. Prior further voted with the majority, 198 to 188, to bring impeachment charges against two other Junto lords: Orford and – incredibly, in light of their long friendship – Halifax.[48]

Afterwards, the Kit-Cats unanimously denounced Prior as an ungrateful Judas, concerned only with keeping his place. One remarked that Dorset had not raised Prior from tavern-sweeping obscurity for disloyalty such as this. Halifax's brother Jemmy, now the eminent jurist Sir James Montagu, struggled as only a lawyer could to excuse their old school friend, explaining that Prior must have felt voting otherwise would have turned the guilt for the two Treaties upon the King himself. The Kit-Cat Club was unconvinced, and though Prior was not expelled from the Club straight away, he was unwelcome at its meetings from this date onwards.

A little lament, written by Prior in 1701, may suggest he regretted the price paid for his political choices that year:

> Reading ends in Melancholy;
> Wine breeds Vices and Diseases;
> Wealth is but Care, and Love but Folly;
> Only Friendship truly pleases.
> My Wealth, my Books, my Flask, my Molly,
> Farewell all, if FRIENDSHIP Ceases![49]

At the same time, another Prior verse conveys his overriding pragmatism, which had led him to act as he did:

> For conscience, like a fiery horse,
> Will stumble, if you check his course;
> But ride him with an easy rein,

And rub him down with worldly gain,
He'll carry you through thick and thin,
Safe, although dirty, to your inn.[50]

Stepney, the third Lord Dorset's Boy, could not easily forgive Prior's betrayal. That summer, he told Halifax that the second 'mouse' had been 'nibbling towards drawing me into a correspondence with him, but I waived it in as cold a manner as I could'.[51] What Halifax's own feelings were when he learned that his friend of almost twenty years was among those who voted for his impeachment can only be guessed.

Somers and Halifax coordinated a press campaign against the impeachment charges, using the Kit-Cat Club to liaise with Whig writers in their defence. A Tory complained that those who were 'solicitous for the nation' were being libelled as Papists, Jacobites and French spies, as 'given out in a certain printed ballad, said to be written by a certain club of great men, which was then held not far from the King's Head tavern in Holborn [on Chancery Lane, hence plausibly the Kit-Cat Club at Gray's Inn] . . . The mob took the hint . . . and gave it out for gospel in an instant.'[52]

Jonathan Swift, who had watched with envy as Congreve received favours from the Kit-Cat patrons, contributed an anonymous pamphlet in defence of the impeached lords. Somers and Halifax sought the acquaintance of the pamphlet's author via its printer, and were, boasted Swift, 'very liberal in promising me the greatest preferments I could hope for, if ever it came in their power'. Swift claimed he 'grew domestic' with Halifax during 1701, and was 'as often with Lord Somers as the formality of his nature (the only unconversable fault he has) made it agreeable to me'.[53] Nonetheless, Swift was not invited to join the Kit-Cat Club.

Congreve turned his legally trained eye to the various charges against Somers and concluded, in June 1701, that the impeachment would never go through, 'for there is neither matter nor proof'.[54] After a tussle between the lower and upper houses, his fellow peers acquitted Somers and dismissed the other charges against Halifax and Orford. This was a crucial political moment, at which a Whig-dominated Lords overrode a Tory-dominated Commons, allowing the Tories to thereafter cast the Whig Junto as an anti-democratic force, for all their talk of English liberties. It was a crisis that polarized the parties and set the terms for heated Whig/Tory debates throughout the decade to follow. As one Tory muttered, these impeachment proceedings had launched 'a feud that I fear will not die'.[55]

VII
THE WHIGS GO TO WAR

[T]o say 'these are my friends' implies 'those are not'.

C. S. LEWIS, *The Four Loves* (1960)

SOMERS AND HALIFAX had to advise the King 'behind the curtain', as the contemporary phrase went, after their narrow escape from impeachment. In the summer of 1701, they also encouraged less prominent Kit-Cat friends who sat on Grand Juries throughout the country to petition the King and so make it appear as though the nation was crying out to resume war with France, and for another general election that might return a more Whiggish House of Commons. The Kit-Cat patrons simultaneously commissioned pro-war propaganda, such as Stepney's *Essay upon the Present Interest of England* (1701), arguing that Louis' record of breaking international treaties made another war a necessary evil.

William needed no persuading. He had every intention of taking the country back to war, and had sent John Churchill, then the Earl of Marlborough, to The Hague as a plenipotentiary, to negotiate a new 'Grand Alliance' between the Austrian Habsburgs, the United Provinces and England. This confirmed the political rehabilitation of Marlborough, previously out of favour with the King, and the start of a vital alignment between the international objectives of Marlborough and those of the Kit-Cat Club. Stepney, who had finally been appointed Envoy to the Imperial Court in March, did what he could from Vienna to assist Marlborough with the negotiations.

The second Treaty of Grand Alliance was signed in August 1701. Soon after, when James II died in exile, Louis XIV took the decisive step of recognizing the deposed king's son, James Edward Stuart (known to the Whigs who alleged he was illegitimate as 'The Pretender' and then later as 'The Old Pretender'), as James III of England and James VIII of Scotland. France and Spain also imposed an embargo on English goods. These actions persuaded many previously reluctant Tories to support the coming war and resupply the army they had so recently pressed to disband. Even so, the Tories believed England's only hope of victory was at sea, since the French army comprised between a quarter and half a million men and was considered invulnerable on land, especially if allied with the Spanish forces. The King, who favoured fighting on his home turf in Flanders, therefore dissolved Parliament as a prelude to a new election, just ten months after the last, in the hope that more Whigs, who would back his war strategy, might be returned. At the election, the Kit-Cat lords once again emptied their purses and pulled strings on behalf of their candidates, Wharton influencing the return of some twenty-five MPs to the Commons. A Tory poem accused the Kit-Cat Club of disseminating libellous election propaganda via street hawkers who were hired by 'Trusty Secretary Jacob'[1] and licensed by Congreve's Office.

The composition of the Commons after this election was more evenly balanced between the parties, and certainly more in favour of war. A series of promotions followed for the Whigs, especially the Kit-Cats. Though Marlborough, now Commander-in-Chief of the Armed Forces, was willing to work with the Junto for the sake of the forthcoming war effort, his closest ally, Lord Godolphin, had resigned as First Lord of the Treasury before the elections, stating he refused to serve the Junto's will in place of the King's. The Kit-Cat Carlisle was given this top Treasury post in December, and

Manchester was appointed Secretary of State for the Southern Department (whose responsibilities included France, southern Europe, the plantations and American colonies, Ireland, and a share of domestic policy, including law and order). Addison wrote to Lord Manchester from Italy with congratulations and offering his services.

It was too soon after the impeachment crisis for Halifax or Somers to be officially rehabilitated. Somers remained without official appointment, dividing his time between his townhouse in Leicester Square and his country retreat of Brookmans Manor, in Bell Bar, Hertfordshire. Halifax meanwhile remained Auditor of the Receipt, continuing to grant profitable administrative places to impecunious writers. One of these was a Kit-Cat named Arthur Maynwaring, who would become the Club's leading propagandist in the decade ahead. He had been a friend of Congreve's since Middle Temple days, at which time Maynwaring was just sloughing off his early Jacobite sympathies and converting – with all the fervency of a born-again believer – to post-Revolutionary Whiggism. He had been among Dryden's literary disciples at Will's Coffee House, then another of Lord Dorset's protégés, and now in 1701 he was passed along from Dorset to the care of Halifax's patronage, thereby gaining a place as a Commissioner in the Customs House.

Addison remained another of Halifax's charges. He was travelling north from Florence to Geneva at the end of 1701, just as Halifax and Somers were beginning to regain their influence, and as he crossed the Alps, 'shivering among the Eternal snows', Addison claimed he distracted himself from his vertigo by composing, upon horseback, a verse 'Letter from Italy to Lord Halifax'.[2]

Richard Steele, meanwhile, spent the summer of 1701 lodging in Wandsworth with a woman who tutored girls – an experience that may well have shaped his later views in favour of promoting female literacy. Steele was working hard on his first play, *The Funeral*, while spending his leisure time with Congreve, who was passing the summer just across the river in Chelsea. Tonson had already published Steele's first work, a didactic moral tract entitled *The Christian Hero*, suggesting that no overly hard feelings remained over the seduction of Tonson's niece. Given the impeachment proceedings that were commencing at the time, Steele had dedicated the tract not to any Junto lord, but to his army boss Lord Cutts. The primary aim of *The Christian Hero* was to make its author some quick cash, and indeed the book proved a bestseller in those Collierite times, running to twenty editions. Steele's literary friends, however, teased him as a hypocrite given his recent sexual indiscretions, including a dalliance with a woman called 'Black Moll' and a duel fought in Hyde Park against another Irish army officer, most likely over a woman. The wits 'measured the least levity in his words and actions, with the character of a Christian Hero'.[3] Whether due to these friends' teasing or the reflective exercise of writing the book, Steele does appear to have reformed his sex life after 1701. His spending habits were less easily cured, however. In a letter to an army friend at this date, he confided that 'nothing can really make my heart ache but a dun'.[4]

Steele wrote *The Funeral*, like *The Christian Hero*, with an eye to commercial success, aiming to please censorious theatre audiences, but also to 'to enliven his character' in the eyes of his literary friends,[5] since, as he put it, 'Nothing can make the Town so fond of a Man as a successful Play.'[6] For good measure, the play's anti-French jokes capitalized on the town's rising mood of bellicose Protestant patriotism. Even in December 1701, however, when the play opened and went to the printers, Steele remained politically cautious: he dedicated it to the wife of William's Dutch favourite, Keppel, rather than to an Englishman of a particular party or faction. *The Funeral* was, as hoped, an instant hit, performed more than 170 times over the next five years. Steele's reputation as a popular (if not erudite) writer was made, as was his career in the rearming army: as reward for his literary success, he was given a commission as Captain in the new 34th Regiment of Foot.

Two days before Steele received his commission, on 8 March 1702, King William died following a fall from his horse, and his sister-in-law Anne assumed the throne. Intelligent and diligent, Anne could also be stubborn and oversensitive. Innately Tory, she believed it her royal duty to stand above party and resented any attempt by political factions to force her decisions, begging Lord Godolphin, whom she appointed as Lord Treasurer, to help her keep out 'of the power of the Merciless men of both parties'.[7] Anne was, furthermore, devoutly religious, personally repelled by what she regarded as the gross immorality and open impiety of the Junto lords. The Tories played upon Anne's High Church prudishness, increasing their efforts to expose the Kit-Cat politicians' private sleaze, not only to shock Anne and the Collierites, but also to challenge the Whigs' claim to be 'dispassionate' men.

Anne held a grudge against Halifax, Wharton and Somers for their role in supporting her expulsion from William and Mary's Court back in the early 1690s. Several Kit-Cats complained in the House of Lords upon the publication of a history by one Dr Drake, who implied that the Junto had treated Anne disrespectfully and done everything it could to prevent her succession. Another Tory, Charles Davenant, wrote a pamphlet in which a Whig character confesses that preventing Anne's succession 'was the Discourse of all our Clubs'.[8]

The Junto Whigs' rising hopes and ambitions therefore collapsed upon Anne's accession. Somers, who even in his unemployment had maintained an advisory relationship with William, was now *persona non grata* at Anne's Court, not even permitted to continue as a magistrate in his native Worcestershire. Halifax and Wharton were immediately dismissed from the Privy Council. The man replacing Wharton as Comptroller of the Royal Household, the Tory Sir Edward Seymour, declared in the Commons what a pleasure it was 'to have a Queen that was entirely English'.[9] Jack Smith, the leading Kit-Cat in the lower house, replied indignantly that 'none but one whose heart was truly French would make a reflection on his late Majesty'.[10] Defence of King William's memory quickly became the new litmus test of Whig allegiance.

Vanbrugh foresaw the sudden demotion of his patron Carlisle, who handed the Treasury back to Godolphin after less than three months in the job. Vanbrugh therefore bought a new army commission to keep himself afloat were Castle Howard's construction put on hold. Carlisle had also organized for Vanbrugh to be appointed Comptroller of the Board of Works – a part-time job, paid accordingly, but with several houses attached, which Vanbrugh could rent out for profit. In this way, a state income relieved the Earl of the personal expense of paying Vanbrugh's salary as an architect. The appointment came through in May 1702, with Vanbrugh supplanting William Talman for a second time. In fact, the Earl continued to build Castle Howard with additional vigour after his dismissal, as if not to lose face. By the end of 1702, there was a roof on the east wing and work starting on the central block.

Manchester also lost his job as Secretary of State for the South following Anne's accession. Lingering in Geneva, Addison had hoped that, through the influence of Manchester or Halifax, he might be appointed as English representative to the army camp of Prince Eugene of Savoy, the Imperial Commander and Marlborough's most useful ally in the impending war. However, with news of William's death and of the demotion of so many Kit-Cat patrons, Addison's hopes were dashed.

The Kit-Cat Club would function as a centre of opposition to Anne's first, Tory-dominated administration. Anne's ministerial favourites – Godolphin, Marlborough, and later Harley – tried, futilely, to claim they stood aloof from party like the monarch herself, but, like Anne, all three leaned instinctively towards the Tories. Anne chose to retain just two non-Harleyite Whigs in her first ministry, one of whom was the Duke of Somerset – his reward for having stood by Anne and the Marlboroughs during their 1690s quarrels with William and Mary. Somerset, in turn, was able to retain and even promote his personal Kit-Cat clients. Most significantly, Harry Boyle, a cousin of Somerset's, remained Chancellor of the Exchequer. A fictionalized record of a Kit-Cat meeting in the weeks before King William's death had depicted the Club, like a mock-parliament, passing a motion that 'Harry Boyle's head of hair be demolished and afterwards burned by the hand of the Common hangman'. Apparently, Boyle's wig had turned rancid with the pomatum (gum or grease) used to thicken it, and was offending their noses. Now that the political ground had shifted, leaving so few Kit-Cats in government, Boyle became a much more important figure, worthy of respect.

The Whigs feared Anne might desert the Grand Alliance and shy away from war with France, perhaps even making a deal with her exiled half-brother, The Pretender, to undo the Act of Settlement. These fears were unfounded. Marlborough and Godolphin shared the Whigs' conviction about the need to contain French imperialism, and when, in February 1702, Louis' troops seized Dutch fortresses in the Spanish Netherlands, Anne reassured Europe she would not break the Alliance. On 4 May 1702, England formally declared war on France.

As the War of Spanish Succession began, Steele, who had spent the spring travelling through Essex and Norfolk hiring his company of soldiers with money borrowed from friends, found his whole regiment quartered at the dilapidated Landguard Fort in Harwich. It was a bleak, windy spot where Steele's men fell sick from chills, a place far removed from Steele's recent success in the London theatres and with little opportunity for either heroism or promotion. Steele at least had time to write. Local tradition has it he wrote his second play, *The Lying Lover*, on his off-duty evenings at the Queen's Arms in Harwich.

Addison meanwhile continued his European travels within Allied territory during the first campaign of the war. He visited Stepney's embassy in Vienna in the summer of 1702, then Hamburg that winter, complaining of being unable to see the German landscape because everything was so covered in snow that the dirty linen on inn beds was the only thing not white. As Addison was travelling on a tight budget, it was all the more welcome when Stepney opened doors for him with letters of introduction to the Electoral Courts of Dresden and Hanover, and by obtaining dinner and opera invitations from the Prince of Liechtenstein and the nobility in Hamburg. Addison likely sent Stepney an early draft of his Italian travel journal, later to be dedicated to Somers, which Addison said was passed around so many friends in manuscript that it 'made a greater voyage than that which it describes'.[11] More than any of his literary tourism in Italy, these months among the northern European Courts, under Stepney's tutelage, would prove useful to Addison in future.

Somers told Halifax he now saw their role as fighting at home the war that Marlborough was to fight on the Continent. By this he meant that it was their responsibility to run the Whig publicity machine in support of Britannia's crusade in Europe – selling a woolly conflation of liberty and national destiny not dissimilar to American patriotism in later centuries. Somers edited and Tonson published *Several Orations of Demosthenes . . . (English'd from the Greek by several Hands)* (1702), for example, which included speeches calling the Athenians to war. Four of seven contributors to this book were Kit-Cats.[12]

When it came to whipping up Whig Protestant patriotism, the Kit-Cats were hindered by the profiles of the monarchs fate handed to England: first William, a Calvinist Dutchman, then Anne, an unattractive Tory woman, and finally the prospect of a Lutheran German from Hanover. Marlborough was therefore quickly chosen to become 'the hero of the Whigs, though he was never a Whig hero'.[13] This was made possible largely thanks to Marlborough's wife Sarah, who was a vehement Whig and spent much of the following decade pressing her husband to side with, or at least work with, the Whig leadership. Like Sarah, the Kit-Cat Club was eager to absorb the Allied Commander into its party, and from 1702 onwards recruited a series of Marlborough relations and supporters as the next best thing to the man himself, who protected his political independence. A Tory satire, written after Marlborough received his dukedom, described a typical Kit-Cat member as being a 'humble servant' of Marlborough 'from the Teeth outwards', but 'the Duke will not be led by the Nose by him, which very much alters his [the Kit-Cat's] inward Respect' for the Duke.[14]

The clearest example of this forcible assimilation of the Marlborough 'brand' is the admission of Francis, Viscount Rialton and future 2nd Earl of Godolphin, who was both son and heir of the Lord Treasurer Sidney Godolphin and husband of Marlborough's eldest daughter Henrietta. In a Kit-Cat toast to Henrietta, she is complimented in terms clearly referencing her father: 'Her conquering race with Various fate surprise / Who 'Scape their Arms are Captive to their Eyes.'

Marlborough's other daughters were also repeatedly nominated as Kit-Cat toasts after 1702. Similarly, the Kit-Cat Club membership of Edmund Dunch can be explained by his marriage in spring 1702 to Elizabeth Godfrey, daughter of Marlborough's sister Arabella. Two other Kit-Cats later married a daughter and a granddaughter of the Marlboroughs. Dr Garth's importance within the Club rose significantly after he became Marlborough's personal physician, and after Garth helped Marlborough's younger brother avoid murder charges, earning Marlborough's lasting gratitude.

Another Kit-Cat member who was admitted thanks to his links to Marlborough was Charles, Lord Mohun. By 1702, Mohun had stood trial for murder no less than three times, escaping conviction in at least one case thanks to the value of his vote in the Lords, which he gave to King William in exchange for clemency. Following his return from a trip to Hanover to meet with Electress Sophia, Mohun was teased for putting on 'a Politician's Face' for the Whigs.[15] Kit-Cat membership sometime between the autumn of 1701 and May 1702 therefore fitted neatly with Mohun's resolution to rectify his 'slips of youth' and become a political player.[16] It would also have fitted, cynically, with his need for more friends in the Lords in order to win a complicated inheritance dispute that began in 1701. At his first attendance at the Kit-Cat Club, Mohun 'broke down the gilded emblem on the top of his chair', giving Tonson the opportunity to allude slyly to Mohun's wayward past by complaining that 'a man who would do that would cut a man's throat'.[17]

A number of military men were also admitted to the Kit-Cat after 1702, all of whom, almost inevitably given the limited size of the army's officer class, had links with Marlborough.[18] Most important of these was James, 1st Earl of Stanhope, eldest son of the respected diplomat Alexander Stanhope. By May 1698, when James Stanhope served briefly alongside Prior at the Paris embassy, a friend told Alexander that his son was the 'greatest hope in England, and I believe no man of his age hath by his own personal merit made himself so many friends and rendered himself so universally acceptable'.[19]

King William had at first been charmed by Stanhope's precocity and outspokenness, but cooled towards him when the young man wrote in favour of disbanding the army after Ryswick and argued with one of the King's Dutch friends. This anti-Court positioning alone excluded Stanhope from the Kit-Cat Club when it was first formed in the late 1690s. Stanhope also lost royal favour at the outbreak of the culture wars in 1698 because of his overt anti-clericalism. When Anne came to the throne, however, Stanhope was one of those lucky enough to survive the Whig purge thanks to Somerset's protection. Somerset supported Stanhope in gaining a parliamentary seat for Cockermouth in Cumberland, and probably a simultaneous seat at the Kit-Cat Club, in summer 1702. Stanhope's erudition, particularly as a translator of Greek, and his exquisite family seat of Chevening in Kent, qualified him for the Club from a cultural standpoint, one contemporary calling him 'the best scholar perhaps of any gentleman of his time'.[20]

At the outbreak of the War of Spanish Succession, Stanhope had been posted to the Iberian Peninsula, but, after commendation for his part in storming Vigo Bay in October 1702 – England's first significant victory – he had been transferred in 1703 to serve directly under Marlborough in Flanders. Stanhope developed a good working partnership with Marlborough, who recognized that Stanhope possessed a mixture of soldierliness, diplomatic charm and intellect not unlike his own.

Another of the Kit-Cat Club's new military members after 1702 was James, future 3rd Earl of Berkeley, a naval officer admitted on the same day as Mohun. Richard Boyle, 2nd Viscount Shannon, also joined the Club soon after leading the grenadiers who stormed the fortifications at Vigo with Stanhope in October 1702.[21] Two soldier brothers, John and James Dormer, may also have entered the Club, simultaneously or in succession, soon after the war began. A 'Mr Dormer' is recorded as dining at Wharton's house on Dover Street, alongside four other Kit-Cat members, on 5 December 1702, and again with three Kit-Cats on 27 December.[22]

The only military Kit-Cat whose membership certainly predated 1702 was Colonel John Tidcomb, a Restoration Court pal of Dorset's who had led deserting troops towards William's invasion force in 1688 and was now enjoying the Club in his retirement. Tidcomb and Dorset provided the prototypes for the admission of Kit-Cat soldiers who possessed enough cultural refinement that their conversation did not, as Addison put it, 'smell of gunpowder'.[23]

Thanks to the additional military members who joined during 1702 and 1703, the Kit-Cat Club needed to move to a more spacious venue: likely the Fountain tavern on the Strand. Whig conspirators had clubbed in this tavern before the Revolution and this subversive history now held added appeal for the Kit-Cats as they entered an indefinite phase of political opposition to another Tory-leaning Stuart monarch. Some sources state that Mr Cat sold the Cat and Fiddle to buy the Fountain with a loan from Tonson, just as Cat moved his home and shop from Gray's Inn down to Shire Lane, a street that ran through the middle of where the Royal Courts of Justice stand today.

In addition, for summer gatherings, the Kit-Cat Club planned to erect some sort of clubhouse, referred to as a 'convenient reception', in the fresher air of Hampstead. The village of Hampstead was then visited mainly for its proximity to the Bellsise (today Belsize) Gardens – pleasure gardens like those in Kilburn, Vauxhall and St Pancras where Londoners could enjoy music, dancing, gambling and sex amid the shrubbery. The original proposal for the Hampstead venue in May 1702 was signed by fourteen members of the Club who each promised to contribute ten guineas (each guinea was worth 20–30 shillings or £130 to £200 today), with Wharton listed as 'Controller of the Society'.[24] The building was to be finished by the spring of 1703, but it may be that it was never begun. Though a 1708 poem does refer to the Kit-Cats dining on Hampstead's 'airy Head' in the summertime,[25] no clubhouse has ever been identified there, and there is an oral tradition that they met in the gardens of the Upper Flask tavern, known for its 'races, raffles and private marriages', rather than in any purpose-built venue.[26]

When in power, the Kit-Cats always imagined themselves in terms of heroic, patriot governors, modelled on classical Roman senators – men whose friendship formed the pillars of civilization – but when out of power, Renaissance and humanist models came to the fore, and they imagined themselves a private circle in retreat from a repressive state. During these first years of Anne's reign, when all the Kit-Cats but Somerset had been unceremoniously ejected from the Queen's Cabinet, but when the country was embarking on a war most intensely desired and bankrolled by their party, the Kit-Cats were ambivalent about which image to cultivate: the Fountain politicians or the Flask revellers.

VIII
KIT-CAT CONNOISSEURS

If eating or drinking be natural, herding is so too.

3RD EARL OF SHAFTESBURY, *Characteristicks of Men, Manners, Opinions, Times* (1711)[1]

IN EARLY 1703, Tonson acquired another summer home for the nomadic Kit-Cats. He leased a country house at Barn Elms, about seven miles west of London on the south side of the Thames, just west of Putney. The surrounding area was a picnic resort for Londoners, mentioned by Pepys as a place for strolls among the majestic elms and by Congreve as one of dubious morals. It was best reached by barge from Whitehall, rather than by the road (the original King's Road) that ran through the open country of 'five fields' and was notoriously plagued by highwaymen.

Elizabeth I had once stayed at Barn Elms' manor house. Tonson's property was a much more modest residence to the north of the manor, possibly its dairy. Taking the lease was nonetheless an expression of Tonson's social aspirations. The westerly migration from the stink of London into fresher air represented both his own and the Club's rising status since the 1690s. The proliferating villas of

Twickenham and Clapham would soon become a clichéd image of new money's encroachment, as Whig 'Cits' (City citizens) imitated the rural idyll of the landed gentry but within commuting distance of the town. Like them, Tonson wanted to live within easy reach of London, but this Barn Elms property was unusual in being a status symbol not only for a private individual but also for a collective group.

Tonson may have been allowed to use the unspent Kit-Cat subscription monies, collected to build a Hampstead venue, to renovate the Barn Elms house instead. He hired Vanbrugh to fit up the house's interior. Like Vanbrugh's 'Goose Pie' house in Whitehall, Tonson's small property was good practice for the self-taught architect before working at Castle Howard, though in the latter case Vanbrugh would largely leave Hawksmoor to design the interior. Both houses, small and large, reflected their owners' desires to be judged more on how they spent their money than on how much money they had – in Tonson's case because he had more than was considered decent for an untitled merchant, and in Carlisle's case because he had less than his title suggested. As with membership of the Kit-Cat Club, the fad for architecture and interior design, and thereby the demonstration of one's taste, was a way to set oneself apart from an ever-increasing number of prosperous but perhaps less educated neighbours. A diverse range of luxury furnishings available at this date – thanks to the East India Company's imports of cotton, chintz and porcelain, for example – made it as easy for Tonson as for Carlisle to participate. As Defoe wrote when he saw a tradesman's house filled with velvet hangings, embroidered chairs and damask curtains, it was now common for such a man to own 'Furniture equal to what, formerly, sufficed the greatest of our Nobility'.[2]

The first time Tonson took Vanbrugh down to Barnes to survey the property, the men shared a simple supper in the kitchen, which Vanbrugh would remember fondly some twenty years later as 'the best meal I ever ate'.[3] Tonson thus became Vanbrugh's second architectural patron, after Carlisle. By this date Tonson and Vanbrugh were also close personal friends. Tonson allocated a bedroom for

Vanbrugh's permanent private use at Barn Elms, and a poem by a mutual friend contained a fictionalized dialogue in which the character of Tonson says of Vanbrugh: '. . . so much I dote on him, that I / If I were sure to go to Heaven, would die'.[4]

Tonson convened the Club in London in March 1703, telling the members it would be the last meeting for some time, as he would be travelling to Holland on book business. Stepney, who was in Vienna cajoling Emperor Leopold into devoting greater military resources to the Grand Alliance, sent his 'hearty affections to the Kit-Cat; I often wish it were my fortune to make one with you at 3 in the morning'.[5] This March 1703 meeting seems to have been a particularly late and lively one. A dangerously indecent poem by an unidentified Kit-Cat was recited, mocking Queen Anne for her phantom pregnancies. In the poem, Anne knights her doctor with her bare, gouty leg, in a fit of pleasure when he declares her pregnant. It is a nasty piece, reflecting the Junto Whigs' disgruntlement, out of office thanks to what they considered a woman's ignorant and irrational prejudices.

The Kit-Cats' published propaganda was more restrained. Tonson's press, for example, published *The Golden Age Restor'd* (1703), which was a sarcastic call to arms, suggesting the Jacobites should oust the few remaining Whigs at Court as the prelude to a Franco-Jacobite invasion.[6] Written by William Walsh, the poem was printed anonymously and its authorship mistakenly attributed to Arthur Maynwaring, who almost lost his commission at the Customs House as a result. Yet Maynwaring did not break ranks and betray the poem's true author. The Kit-Cats stood collectively behind the publication's anonymity, just as the Tories concealed the author of their reply, *The Golden Age Revers'd* (1703), which reviled the Kit-Cat Club as a gang of hubristic conspirators.[7]

Tonson departed for Holland soon after the March meeting. Now 47 and balding ('spacious brow[ed]', as one poet delicately put it[8]), he travelled this time with the youngest Kit-Cat: the indolent 19-year-old Charles Fitzroy, 2nd Duke of Grafton (grandson of Charles II and his mistress Barbara Villiers), who had joined the Club upon reaching his maturity. Vanbrugh thought Tonson would find it amusing to hear that the Tories suspected the bookseller of travelling as a Junto messenger destined for Hanover, and that his subscription list to a new edition of *Ceasar's Commentaries* was rumoured to be a sinister list of rebels plotting to overthrow Queen Anne. While Tonson's subscription lists were not without political subtext, there was no such undercover mission. It was simply a trip to acquire new texts, typeface and paper from the Continent.

Tonson left his nephew, Jacob Tonson Junior (brother to Elizabeth and uncle to Steele's illegitimate child; referred to hereafter as 'Jacob Junior' to avoid confusion) in charge of the publishing firm. This partnership would continue after Tonson's return, and from this date forward it is often unclear which of the two Tonsons was responsible for particular publications or business decisions. Despite the trust placed in Jacob Junior, however, there is evidence that he did not feel unalloyed affection for his domineering uncle.

Vanbrugh, trusted as closely as Tonson's nephew, was left in charge of the renovation work at Barn Elms. He travelled there to inspect the site amid unseasonably heavy rains in June 1703, and reported to Tonson that the carpenters had been neglecting the job for the past fortnight: '[E]very room is chips – up to your chin!' The neighbours had also failed to steal the peas and beans from Tonson's kitchen garden, so that they hung rotting on the vine. Vanbrugh assured Tonson, with a gentle jibe at Tonson's aspirations for the modest property, that the house would soon be ready 'for the reception of a king'.[9]

Other Kit-Cat Club members took an active interest in the Barn Elms works, supporting the theory that it was intended to become a Club venue. Congreve told Tonson in Amsterdam: 'I believe Barn Elms wants you and I long to see it but don't care to satisfy my curiosity before you come.'[10] Vanbrugh wrote, meanwhile, that 'the Kit-Cat wants you much more than you ever can do them . . . Those who remain in town are in great desire of waiting on you at Barn-Elms.'[11]

This last statement emphasizes how central Tonson remained as Club secretary and chairman, even now that the Club's membership had expanded to include more than a dozen peers of the realm. A month later, Vanbrugh complained again: 'The Kit-Cat . . . will never meet without you, so you can see here's a general stagnation for want of you.'[12] The Duke of Somerset sent the same message, though in a more imperious tone: 'Our Club is dissolved, till you revive it again; which we are impatient of.'[13] Congreve, Vanbrugh and Halifax drank a toast to Tonson's quick return one day that summer at Hampton Court, 'as we were sopping our Arses in the Fountain, for you must know we have got some warm weather at last'.[14]

Yet Tonson's position remained, at the same time, precarious. Though still the Club's convener and nominal host, he seems to have also been the butt of the Club's raillery during repeated rifts between the publisher and his Kit-Cat authors. A satirical advertisement was printed in January 1704, ostensibly composed by Tonson to deny that he was 'infamously expelled a certain Society called the K-t C-t Club' as a result of his 'ill-timed freedom with some of the Principal Members at the Reading of a Late Satire upon his Parts and Person' and also to deny he was 'since Clapped up in a Madhouse'. To the contrary, the advertisement explained, Tonson had withdrawn himself voluntarily 'in scorn of being their Jest any longer' and 'walks the public Streets without a Keeper'.[15] The notice has the tone of an inside joke, meriting speculation about the incident behind it. What was the 'Late Satire'? Was it *Faction Display'd* (1704), William Shippen's poem which incorporated three lines mocking Tonson's freckles and lameness? And what was Tonson's 'ill-timed freedom'? Could it be, as the phrase suggests, that the tradesman had finally taken a liberty too far?

Another poem, *The Kit-Cats*, written sometime before June 1704, seems to refer to the same rift. Structured around an allegory in which the Club's literary members rebel against Tonson's authority ('They cry he Sep'rate Interest Carries on, / Pretends their Profit, but designs his own'), the poem is the literary bruise remaining after a fight which history has forgotten.[16] Again, two sources dating to 1705 refer to Tonson being so severely teased by the Club's members that he talked of leaving them: a poem referred to Tonson being 'Sullen through his late ill-Usage' at the Club,[17] while a play called *The Quacks* showed 'Stationer Freckle' feeling aggrieved when his authors teased him in their verses. A private letter from Halifax to another Kit-Cat confirms Tonson bore the brunt of the Club's raillery, and was growing sick of it: 'Our friend Jacob seems to have abdeclared [i.e. abdicated] his government of the Chit-Kat . . . [T]hey had teased him so unmercifully of late that I fancy he intends to leave them.'[18] Another, later poem described Tonson as having 'more Humours than a dancing Bear' but ultimately being persuaded to reconcile with his Kit-Cat authors.[19]

As Vanbrugh helped Tonson realize his social aspirations at Barn Elms, so he continued to help Carlisle confirm his family's status – as well as Carlisle's personal educational and cultural status – at Castle Howard. With time on his hands since the Queen had relieved him of his Treasury office, Carlisle was able to personally oversee the construction site there. That summer of 1703, some 200 men were working on the Yorkshire house and gardens. When work had hardly begun, Carlisle took a party of friends, including Kit-Cats Kingston, Grafton, Wharton and William Cavendish, for an impromptu site inspection, demonstrating that the project was, from the start, distinctly Whiggish.

Carlisle's aesthetic, like Vanbrugh's, seems to have gained definition through exchanges at the Kit-Cat Club. Though the Kit-Cats published no manifesto, we can retrospectively discern an unwritten manifesto directing all their cultural projects, whether literary or architectural. This manifesto involved competing with French culture but not, as might be expected, rejecting it wholesale. The Kit-Cats drew from French comedies, architecture and gardening manuals, just as they imported other Continental models from Venice or Vienna, but they aimed to modify all these European imports and so establish a more 'modern' and distinctively English brand of neoclassicism. Vanbrugh tried to temper the baroque style, associated as it was with Europe's absolute monarchies, with historical English elements – for example, long Jacobean galleries – and with numerous visual allusions to the Roman republic that the Whigs considered the classical parallel to their constitutional monarchy.

The question of why the Kit-Cat Club felt such an urgent need to define England's national style is a complex one. There was a sense that pre-Revolutionary elites had been lapdogs to the French, a sense that the large number of immigrants in London and at Court during William's reign had further diluted English identity, a sense that European baroque architecture had left England lagging behind, and a wish, in light of England's rising commercial power, to hold their heads high and build properties exuding new-found national self-confidence. There was no English school of architecture to constrain Vanbrugh, and he was lucky that his Kit-Cat commissioners gave him great imaginative freedom during a time of stylistic transition. The Kit-Cat Club directed him only by endorsing his search for a new, distinctively English style. Perhaps his own sense of coming from a family of recent migrants sharpened his personal passion for this quest.

One of the most radical, innovative aspects of Castle Howard was its location – that someone should build such a palatial home on a windswept hillside in Yorkshire. Carlisle saw himself as extending the reach of civilization by importing Continental styles he had seen on his travels into the depths of the English countryside, for his neighbours' edification. The project brought direct economic benefits to the local craftsmen it employed, and the emulation of such great Whig houses by more minor nobility and gentry – such as the building of Beningborough by John Bourchier in Yorkshire in 1716 – was to have trickle-down economic benefits.

Castle Howard was also a Whiggish project in the sense that its contents boasted of English trade and manufacture. Its interior was started after 1706, though interior designs had been a part of the house's overall plan from the beginning, with Vanbrugh commissioning Hawksmoor to design the 'Eating Room' interior, for example. This was a new way of working, reflecting the fact that a private citizen's private rooms could now make public statements, as only royal palaces' interiors had previously done. Carlisle engaged several London merchants to do the upholstering and make the furniture for his rooms, and collected delftware and other exotic decorative items from the London importers. The house's bedchambers were hung with oriental silk damasks, its dressing rooms with India wallpapers, and the Earl's Grand Cabinet with angora mohair imported by the Turkey Company. The whole house, in other words, became a receptacle for the luxuries of British trade, but with its owner constantly aiming to emphasize that he was a collector and connoisseur, not just a greedy shopper.

The magnificent building, as it rose, provoked the ire of some smaller Yorkshire landowners, resentful of raised wartime taxation and of peers like Carlisle who were aligned to the City of London's interests. Had they known the extent to which Carlisle's income had dwindled, and how watchful he had to be of expenditure on building a house financed largely through credit and card winnings, they might have felt less aggrieved.

Carlisle had the power to bestow heraldic rewards through the College of Arms, and therefore was able to pay Vanbrugh for building Castle Howard by making him a 'Carlisle Herald' in June 1703, an appointment from which Vanbrugh was then promoted to the lucrative place of 'Clarenceux King of Arms'. This required only that Vanbrugh occasionally appear at the College of Arms in ornate costume. A contemporary's reaction to news of the appointment was pragmatic: 'Now Van can build houses.'[20] Suspicions that Carlisle and Vanbrugh were treating the heralds' internal hierarchy with cynical disrespect, however, were confirmed when Vanbrugh later referred to this appointment as 'a Place I got in jest'.[21] To Tonson in Amsterdam, Vanbrugh confided that several Kit-Cats had ridiculed his heraldic investiture with their own drunken ceremony. Carlisle's brother-in-law, neighbour and fellow Kit-Cat, Algernon Capel, 2nd Earl of Essex, had done the honours, said Vanbrugh, 'with a whole Bowl of wine about my ears instead of half a Spoonful'.[22]

In Amsterdam, Tonson was missing Vanbrugh's company, being stuck instead with that of Addison, recently returned to Holland after his tour of the German Courts. Since Addison would never support himself outside academia solely on the proceeds of Latin translations, Tonson tried to think of a day-job for his author. Reviewing his portfolio of Kit-Cat patrons, Tonson knew that only Somerset was flourishing politically under Anne's Tory-led ministry, and so enquired whether Addison might become an escort and tutor for Somerset's son. When Somerset replied positively, offering a salary of 100 guineas (some £14,000 today), Addison wrote back: 'As for the Recompense that is proposed to me, I must take the Liberty to assure your Grace that I should not see my account in it but in the hopes that I have to recommend myself to your Grace's favour and approbation.'[23]

Somerset took offence at this hint that he would owe Addison future patronage and that the salary was ungenerous; he withdrew the offer. Addison, never one to offend the rich and powerful intentionally, hurriedly apologized, but it was too late. Tonson, having stuck his neck out for Addison in seeking the favour from Somerset, was unimpressed by how it had been handled. While he appreciated Addison's intellect, Tonson never warmed to Addison as to Congreve and Vanbrugh, and incidents like this help explain why.[24]

Addison was tiring of expat society in Holland, focused as it was on purely material, mercantile and military concerns. He complained of being forced to become conversant with the market price for nutmeg and pepper because, 'since the coming in of the East India fleet, our conversation here runs altogether on Spice'.[25] By September 1703, he was back in London after five years of travel. Tonson probably returned on the same ship, bringing a supply of Dutch type that was to improve the appearance of English printed books dramatically, as well as various purchases on behalf of his favourite Kit-Cats: a copy of Palladio's architectural plans for Vanbrugh, ivory mathematical instruments for Halifax, and a set of new linen for Congreve.

Following Addison's return to London, he rented a garret on the street today known as the Haymarket (thanks to then being the location of one of London's largest stables and hay markets). It neighboured Dr Garth's handsome, fully staffed townhouse on the street's eastern side. Addison's despondency and anxiety about his career and income at this date were understandable. He had given up a safe path in the Church for the ambition of becoming a government servant and writer, but neither of his recent prose publications on Italian tourism or Roman medals was attracting much interest beyond his friends. Somers, Halifax and Manchester remained

Addison's nominal patrons, having invested in his European education, but there was no fresh idea of how to employ him since he had blown his chance with Somerset. Addison lived off his small inheritance, conscious of being the eldest yet least settled of his siblings, at 32 the walking embodiment of unfulfilled intellectual potential.

Lady Mary Wortley Montagu (who had high standards) declared Addison the best company in the world, and Steele, always Addison's biggest fan, asked Congreve to agree that an evening alone with Addison was like 'the Pleasure of conversing with an intimate Acquaintance of Terence and Catullus, who had all their Wit and Nature heightened with Humour, more exquisite and delightful than any other Man ever possessed'.[26] Yet Addison had a natural aversion to large gatherings, saying there was 'no such thing as real conversation between more than two persons'.[27] It was less a matter of principle than personality. He described himself, using a metaphor from Congreve's *Double Dealer*, as a man who could draw a bill for a thousand pounds but had not one guinea in his pocket, meaning that he could express himself with perfect fluency on paper but then grew tight-lipped and tongue-tied in public. He felt this was a disability partly because he shared the widespread belief that a writer would produce better work if part of a stimulating literary circle – that dinner parties and drinking friendships were essential ingredients in highbrow creativity, as for the Roman Augustans.[28] Addison saw the Kit-Cat Club as a place where writers' 'Conversation fed their mutual Flame'[29] and so, against the grain of his own personality, he forced himself to join the Club, to which so many of his friends and patrons had long belonged, in 1704.

Ironically, the practical result of Addison's reticence when at a Kit-Cat Club dinner was that he had to get quickly drunk to relax. Addison was especially fond of Canary wine and 'Barbadoes water' (an alcoholic cordial flavoured with citrus),[30] and Steele was almost certainly thinking of Addison when he described a friend whom you could seldom get into a tavern, but 'once he is arrived to his pint and begins to look about and like his company, you admire a thousand things in him which before lay buried'.[31]

The amount usually drunk at the Kit-Cat Club is disputed.

One contemporary said they 'refresh themselves with a glass of wine, but with great moderation'.[32] Individual members' household alcohol bills, however, suggest that they were often well soaked,[33] and a Tory poet described the Club as inspired by intoxication: 'Oft do they in high Flights and Raptures swell, / Drunk with the Waters of our Jacob's Well.'[34]

Vanbrugh's personal punch recipe also suggests that there were some lethally strong cocktails besides the wine on offer at the Club: 'water or small beer; mead, port – two glasses each; rum, saffron – a very little of each; nutmeg, poker [i.e. warmed by inserting a hot poker], orange or lemon peel in winter; balm etc in summer'.[35]

Addison's travel book on Italy had reviewed the wine in every place he visited, and this wine connoisseurship was something he shared with other Kit-Cat members. In 1704, when Congreve noted 'Good wine scarcer than ever',[36] Addison joined the Kit-Cat Club partly because it was one of the few places where one would have been served the finest, lighter French wines. Imports of French wine were heavily taxed during the war, and though the Kit-Cat lords and MPs supported this protectionism in Parliament, they privately made full use of the privilege allowed to the Privy Counsellors among them to import large quantities of duty-free wine. In 1706, Congreve complained London 'affords not one drop of wine out of a private house'.[37] His distinction between what they were drinking in public and private is telling.

Since the Methuen Treaty of 1703, Portuguese wine could be imported at a third less duty than French. Port was 'patriotic and Whig and woollen; claret was Francophile and Jacobite'.[38] Kit-Cat Anthony Henley quipped that the Tories were unpatriotic because 'they are for bringing in French claret and will not sup-Port'.[39] Among the Whigs, champagne and claret became truly guilty pleasures, and much black-market French wine was labelled as port to get it through customs. Between 1705 and 1714, Congreve was one of five Commissioners for licensing wine, which, combined with his job at the Customs House, placed him perfectly – alongside Maynwaring – to assist his patrons with defrauding the system.

In the early 1700s, when heavy drinking had not yet exploded into the epidemic depicted in Hogarth's 'Gin Lane' but rather remained the preserve of the upper classes (as in the phrase 'drunk as a lord'), alcoholism was not regarded as a serious issue. Even the Collierites and Societies for the Reformation of Manners never focused on temperance. However, Addison, self-critical of what he must have known was a personal weakness, lectured young men never to boast of drunkenness, since it distorts the intelligence and 'displays every little Spot of the Soul in its utmost Deformity'.[40] He published an essay advising his readers to drink as follows: 'the first Glass for myself, the second for my Friends, the third for good Humour and the fourth for mine Enemies'.[41] One reader, possibly a teasing friend, commented that 'there was certainly an Error in the Print, and that the Word *Glass* should be *Bottle*'.[42]

Addison was far more abstemious about food than alcohol, having too delicate a digestion for the richer dishes at the Kit-Cat feasts. The Kit-Cat Club remained a dining club, even as it assumed its range of other identities as cultural institution, literary clique and political think-tank. It was imitated as a dining and toasting club by the 'Beefsteak Club', another Whig club that started sometime before 1705.[43] But, though many Kit-Cats were dedicated food lovers, only one member's admission rested primarily on his reputation as a gourmand. Charles Dartiquenave (or 'Dartineuf'), known to his friends as 'Darty', was a member when Addison joined. Darty was rumoured to be a bastard son of Charles II, but in fact his father was a Huguenot refugee. Darty had written a volume of poems in Greek and Latin while a boy, and as an adult became known as a great punster. He was appointed an Agent of Taxes in 1706 and later Paymaster of the Royal Works, being described by one contemporary as 'the man that knows everything and that everybody knows'.[44] Anecdotes about Darty, however, focused on only one thing: his obsessive love of food.[45] Pope wrote an epigram: 'Each mortal has his pleasure: none deny / Scarsdale his bottle, Darty his Ham Pie.'[46] It is unsurprising that a man who became known as 'a most celebrated sensualist and glutton'[47] should have sought admission to a club founded upon pie-eating.

Addison's indifference to good food was shown by Edward Wortley

Montagu's explicit refusal to share lodgings with Addison unless he hired a better cook. In a famous essay on the 'Gluttony of a modern Meal', Addison imagined each rich dish on the table as a dish of gout, dropsy or fever. Addison said his prescriptive diet would be one dish per meal, with simple sauces – closer to our modern norm. He recommended that if one must eat a large dinner, one should balance it with some days of abstinence.

Addison's arrival coincided with the Kit-Cat Club's move after 1704 to Barn Elms, where there was fresher produce to enjoy besides the stodgy pies. Following a summer visit to the property, Vanbrugh told Tonson there were a 'hundred thousand apricocks [*sic*]' in the orchards, along with strawberries, redcurrants 'red as blood', gooseberries, peaches, pears, apples and plums sufficient 'to gripe the guts of a nation'.[48] Addison would later take great pride in his own kitchen garden, full of cabbages, 'coleworts' (half-grown cabbages) and herbs,[49] so he would have taken a keen interest in Tonson's kitchen garden and orchards at Barn Elms, but more as a gardener than gourmand.

A Swiss visitor in 1719 observed many people in England 'never eat any bread, and universally they eat very little: they nibble a few crumbs, while they chew the meat by whole mouthfuls'.[50] Meat was a status food and a taste for it (in pies or as roasts) was considered manly, but people also ate more fruit and vegetables than is sometimes supposed. The Kit-Cats would have disdained Italian cookery for its relative scarcity of meat, though Carlisle – with a taste for Continental imports in food as in architecture – once ordered, from an Italian warehouse on London's Suffolk Street, 'some choice figs', parmesan cheese and four or five pounds of 'French raisins'.[51] The Kit-Cat diet was, in other words, not as unvaried as one might think. Addison described a dinner conversation about gastronomic antipathies like eels and parsnips, which proceeded 'till we had worked up ourselves to such a Pitch of Complaisance that when the Dinner was to come in, we enquired the Name of every Dish and hoped it would be no Offence to any in Company'.[52]

The balancing of the Club's meat with more fruit and vegetables in the summer paralleled, symbolically, a balancing of the Club's masculinity with more 'polite', feminine tastes. After the Barn Elms renovations were completed, Vanbrugh, Carlisle and Garth hosted a 'Barns Expedition' by barge to show the house off to a party consisting of Marlborough's wife Sarah and other noble Whig ladies. And it was after the Club settled at Barn Elms (and the Fountain tavern) that the Kit-Cats added a larger dash of delicacy to their meetings with bespoke drinking glasses and decorative silverware.[53] Vanbrugh always referred to the Barn Elms house by the feminine pronoun and, in one letter to Tonson, personified it as Tonson's mistress. This was an allusion to a quip in Wycherley's play *The Country Wife*,[54] but also a way of countering accusations that an interest in interior design was in any way effeminate.

The metaphor of 'appetite' versus 'taste' was used in relation to all forms of connoisseurship, with the idea that 'consumption' should be refined and one's palate exercised: 'Conversation with Men of a Polite Genius is another Method for improving our Natural Taste,' Addison wrote.[55] At the dinner table, the expectation of conversational pleasures to be served by one's fellow diners was equal to the expectation of good food. Every dinner party in London was said to need at least one Kit-Cat guest, or 'Flat was the Wine and tasteless was the Cheer.'[56]

Addison had joined the Club, however, not for its wine or conversation, but to remedy his unemployment. Resisting lethargy, he helped select the poems for another edition of Tonson's *Miscellany*, but this took only a little of his time and attention. Nothing could have come as more of a relief, in these circumstances, than an unexpected visitor bearing good news in the late summer. Harry Boyle, the Chancellor of the Exchequer with the stinking wigs, personally climbed the three flights of stairs to Addison's garret to deliver an important message directly from Lord Treasurer Godolphin. Boyle was possibly selected, or volunteered, as messenger because he was a Kit-Cat and this was a Kit-Cat-inspired business.

Halifax had suggested to Godolphin that Addison be commissioned to write a poem for the government, in exchange for a post as Commissioner for Appeals and Regulating the Excise (a virtual sinecure, worth £200 a year or some £26,500 today). Godolphin himself was 'not a reading man',[57] but the three Kit-Cat Junto leaders had persuaded him that the war effort needed a patriotic poem to celebrate Marlborough's great victory against Louis XIV and the Bavarians in August 1704 at the battle of Blenheim.

The battle of Blenheim had saved Austria from French invasion, against all odds. Marlborough's troops had killed or captured three-fifths of the Franco-Bavarian enemy. It was a victory that seemed beyond providential, almost miraculous, and which suddenly propelled England into being a front-rank military power. Many date the decline of French hegemony from this defeat, together with that at Schellenberg six weeks earlier. Though several Kit-Cats had been close to Marlborough beforehand, Blenheim marked the point at which support for the war became synonymous with support for Marlborough. Though Marlborough's inclinations may have been Tory, and his stance ostensibly non-partisan in 1704, the Junto Whigs were the ones keenest to celebrate his crushing defeat of the French.

For Addison, patriotism was 'the most sublime and extensive of all social virtues'.[58] He shared the Kit-Cat belief that heroic verse befitted the heroic, post-Revolutionary times through which the Whigs felt they were living, or at least their faith that heroic verse might help create such a heroic age. Though his patrons were Whigs, Addison also shared with Godolphin and Marlborough a forlorn hope that Whig and Tory brands of patriotism might be harmonized, if only the words of his poem were chosen carefully enough. Valorization of Marlborough, whose deeds in Europe 'proudly shine in their own native light',[59] was the perfect theme for such an anthem of national unity.

Addison's ode to the victory of Blenheim, *The Campaign*, was circulated to the Kit-Cats in manuscript during the autumn of 1704, and published by Tonson in December. Steele wrote a poem of his own puffing *The Campaign* before its publication, suggesting the former schoolfellows were back in touch. Steele's theme is a self-deprecating comparison between his own 'slender stock of fame' and that of his friend.[60] Given that Steele had written a bestselling book and hit play by this date, while Addison had only studied and travelled, it is telling that Steele envied his friend as the more 'famous' of the two – the one whose poetry and intellect were admired by the critical elite. It was a symptom, too, of Steele's deeply ingrained assumption of inferiority to Addison.

In *The Campaign*, Addison apotheosized the newly created Duke of Marlborough as one who 'rides in the whirlwind, and directs the storm', an image cleverly reminding readers of the previous autumn's Great Storm and suggesting Marlborough could face down such heavenly portents. That single image was applauded for a century afterwards as an early instance of the Sublime in English poetry. A few contemporary Tory critics smelled something fraudulent in the poem, jeering at the effeminacy of a Kit-Cat patron who would 'much rather judge of Addison's Poetical History of the Battle of Blenheim than be in it, and is fitter to write the second part of *The Campaign* than to make One'.[61] But for the most part, and with the readers who mattered, including Marlborough himself, the poem was a critical success.

Godolphin rewarded Addison with the promised Excise post, while Halifax gave Addison another unpaid 'job' in the summer of 1704, asking him to supervise the tuition of the 7-year-old son of a lady whom Halifax was then courting: the Countess of Warwick, wealthy young widow of Mohun's rakish friend, the 6th Earl of Warwick. Addison was closer to the Countess' age than 43-year-old Halifax, however, and Addison's concern for her son's welfare appears to have had an aphrodisiac effect. By the end of 1705, after Addison received the secure salary of his Excise post, the diarist Thomas Hearne recorded 'for certain' that the Countess and Addison had married.[62] They had not, but it was true that they were at the start of a protracted courtship, as Addison struggled to climb several more rungs of the social ladder and become a fit husband for a countess and stepfather for an earl. That such a report was circulating so soon after an identical rumour in August 1704 about an engagement between the Countess and Halifax suggests there must have been some interesting exchanges between Kit-Cat patron and client during the intervening eighteen months.[63]

Daniel Defoe, at this time the 'infinitely obliged humble servant' of Robert Harley (who had freed him from Newgate Prison in 1703), was one contemporary who resented the unfair advantages and rewards of patronage he saw the Kit-Cat authors enjoying. Addison's high-profile poetic commission to write *The Campaign* was a prime example. Demurring from the general applause, Defoe accused Addison of being no better than a mercenary Grub Street hack, writing: 'Maecenas [Halifax] has his modest fancy strung, / And fixed his pension first, or he had never sung.'[64]

IX
BY SEVERAL HANDS

> Music hath Charms to soothe the savage Breast, to soften Rocks, or bend a knotted Oak.
>
> WILLIAM CONGREVE, *The Mourning Bride* (1697)

WHILE EMPLOYED ON the Barn Elms and Castle Howard works in the summer of 1703, Vanbrugh commenced a third venture drawing on both his theatrical and architectural talents: the building of a new London theatre on the site of the stables neighbouring Dr Garth's house and Addison's garret lodgings. The idea had been prompted by Betterton's theatre company's need for a more permanent home than the old Lincoln's Inn tennis courts, but also by the lack of any London stage spacious enough for the performance of operas.

Encouraging English music and opera was one of the Kit-Cat Club's clearest, but most consistently overlooked, goals. Posterity has agreed that England was, before Handel's arrival, in an age of (non-folk) musical dullness; the Kit-Cats felt it their civic duty to address this. More self-interestedly, they knew music was the art form that the weak-sighted Queen most enjoyed, and they understood from the Hanoverian heirs, who regularly enjoyed operas in Herrenhausen and Venice, that the present dearth of good music in London would be a matter of future royal displeasure.

In a period before being an opera or music aficionado was considered a requirement for a London gentleman, many Kit-Cats were both: Maynwaring was an accomplished singer and harpsichordist, and one of the first Englishmen to espouse Italian opera; Anthony Henley played several instruments well, composed songs for a play by fellow Kit-Cat Richard Norton, and was considered a leading music critic;[1] Manchester, Stanyan, Prior and Stepney saw numerous operas while travelling across Europe – indeed a poem of thanks to 'Co. Carlo di Mankester' shows Manchester played patron to the Venetian opera while serving as English ambassador there.[2] An anecdote about Prior at the Paris opera has him annoyed by a man next to him who unconsciously hummed and sang along. Prior started muttering insults about the singer on stage until his irritating neighbour overheard and argued in the star's defence. 'I know all that,' Prior replied, 'but he sings so loudly I couldn't hear you!'[3]

John Evelyn's diary records Italian opera in London as early as 1674, yet opera still seemed to most Englishmen in 1703 'not a plant of our native growth, nor what our plainer appetites are fond of, and is of so delicate a nature that without excessive charge it cannot live long among us'.[4] Dryden had attempted, but failed, to found an indigenous operatic tradition with his musical adaptation of *Paradise Lost* in the 1670s. Though the Kit-Cats preferred the 'plainness' of oratorio to the frippery of French or Italian productions, they sought to nurture a home-grown style of English opera. A publication compiled by Congreve's friend John Abell, *A Choice Collection of Italian Ayres* (1703), to be sung in the north of England and 'at both Theatres in London', therefore included a song entitled 'The Kit-Cat'. This approach to musical reformation paralleled the Kit-Cats' emergent approach to architecture: inspire English taste using imported baroque elements, in the hope that some distinctively Whiggish hybrid might take root.

The only English-born composers to have earned critical regard during the Kit-Cats' lifetimes were the Purcell brothers, Henry and Daniel. Henry Purcell set several Congreve poems to music before he died in 1695, and Vanbrugh's play *The Pilgrim* (1700) included music by Daniel. Among the Kit-Cats, Vanbrugh and Congreve were particular enthusiasts for the Club's musical mission. Congreve had fallen in love with Bracey partly thanks to her singing voice, and placed great importance upon the songs, set by John Eccles, in *Love for Love* and *The Way of the World*. By the 1700s, though still in his thirties, Congreve was suffering from cataracts and could only read or write with the help of a thick magnifying glass. His love of music, like Queen Anne's, therefore grew in proportion to his failing eyesight.

At first, the building of the new Haymarket theatre was solely Vanbrugh's initiative – undertaken not only for the public good but also as a property development project from which he personally hoped to profit by retaining and renting out the land and vaults under the theatre. Vanbrugh's design was approved in model form by the Kit-Cat patrons and was 'very different from any Other [Play]House in being'.[5] No original plan survives, and the theatre burnt down in 1789, but these differences probably related to its acoustics and a deeper stage to allow for elaborate scenery. For its operatic purpose, there was to be the innovation of an orchestra pit – previously musicians in English theatres played behind the scenes, on the stage, in a side-box, or perched above the proscenium arch. In addition, the dramatic action was to be removed from the middle of the audience and set back into a world of suspended disbelief. It was, in other words, the first theatre resembling the classic nineteenth-century design still familiar today.

By mid-June 1703, Vanbrugh was telling Tonson (in Holland): 'I finished my purchase for the Playhouse and all the tenants [of the stables] will be out by Midsummer Day [24 June]; so then I lay the cornerstone and, though the season be thus far advanced, have pretty good assurance I shall be ready for business at Christmas.'[6] This was an over-optimistic forecast. The theatre – which came to be called the Queen's Theatre – would take three times as long to build as Vanbrugh predicted.

Work had not yet begun on the theatre's construction by November 1703 when, following Tonson's return from Amsterdam, the Kit-Cat Club resumed its regular Thursday meetings. The Kit-Cats' anti-government mood came to a head on 4 November 1703, the eve of the anniversary of King William's landing at Torbay, which the Whigs celebrated as if it were a national holiday, in pointed preference to other official celebrations at Anne's Court. A London contemporary refers to the anniversary being celebrated with illuminations and bonfires 'in the chief streets all over town' and '[A]t the Kitcat 'twas very great. Lord Hartington [William Cavendish], Duke of Somerset etc were there. The glass sent down was to the immortal memory of King William. They had all new clothes etc.'[7] Aside from the usual four-line toasts to female beauties, Vanbrugh that evening presented his witty verses 'To A Lady More Cruel Than Fair', but most of the conversation probably focused on matters political, not literary.

The three Kit-Cat Junto lords would all have attended this Williamite anniversary, though Somers and Wharton had been critically ill earlier that year. Wharton, thinking he was dying, had called his servants and the Whig voters of Aylesbury to his bedside, shaken their hands, then 'recommended himself heartily to the Kit-Cat' before falling asleep and awaking 'out of danger' the following day.[8] The Tories also cursed Dr Garth for having cured Somers' possibly syphilitic symptoms. Halifax, much younger than his colleagues, was in sound health but still trying to recover from his political demise: the Lords had acquitted him of committing 'breach of trust' as Auditor in January 1703, but he remained barred from promotion in the Treasury due to Lord Godolphin's position there.[9]

Three weeks after this dinner, on the night of 26 November, London was hit by the full-scale hurricane that became known as the Great Storm of 1703. Congreve reported that he and his friends 'very narrowly escaped the hurricane on Friday night last'. All the trees in St James's Park were flattened, and the leads of church roofs 'rolled up as they were before they were laid on'.[10] The roofs were also stripped off the King's Bench Walk buildings of Inner Temple, ships and boats were destroyed at sea, and the roads of southern England were left impassable. The wind ripped through Congreve's bolted back door and blew his furniture and papers together into a giant heap.

The second evening of the storm coincided with a performance of *Macbeth* at Drury Lane, where the witches' scene needed no artificial sound effects. Jeremy Collier immediately published his interpretation of the storm's devastation as 'the Voice of an Angry Heaven' pronouncing on the London theatres, just as he had seized on the opportunity of the Whitehall fire five years earlier.[11] John Dennis dryly replied that, if such was God's purpose, the punishment was unfairly meted out to nations as far away as the Baltic States.

This post-Storm revival of the Collier controversy soon led Queen Anne to step into her late sister Mary's shoes as leader of England's moral reformation. A fast day was decreed for 19 January 1704 to repent national indecency, a royal decree being issued that 'no plays be acted contrary to religion and good manners, on pain of being silenced, and that no woman wear a vizard [mask] in either of the theatres'.[12] The play Steele had written in Harwich, *The Lying Lover*, was an experiment in whether comedy could be as 'moral' as Collier exhorted, and was performed under this decree's restrictions. No great applause resulted, however, and Steele passed the following year amassing debts and commuting between London and his languishing regiment at Landguard.

Evading the censors, and not awaiting Vanbrugh's theatre, the Kit-Cat Club also organized a series of ten musical recitals for an exclusive subscription audience, at the Drury Lane and Lincoln's Inn theatres, between November 1703 and March 1704.[13] This 'Subscription Music', modelled on the 1670s fad for music 'consorts' in private houses, developed a party political colouring: 'Music has learned the discords of the State, / And concerts jar with Whig and Tory hate.'[14] Somerset and other Whigs patriotically championed a singer named Katherine Tofts, rival to a Tory-sponsored French singer named Marguerite de l'Epine. Tofts, however, complained the Whig 'Lord Subscribers' forced her to sing 'Even songs that were not proper for her, which gave room to her Enemies to endeavour to lessen her Credit [reputation]'[15] – further evidence that the Kit-Cats were often amused by bawdy material at their private soirées. The way that the Kit-Cats moved musical performance in and out of private and public venues also indicates that this was a transitional period in the economics of cultural consumption. Subscription performances were a compromise between parties by private invitation and the more democratic approach of selling tickets to anyone who could pay. They reflected a Whig way of doing business: a semi-mercantile approach to aristocratic patronage of the arts.

On the last night of the Kit-Cat recital series, a three-act comedy 'by several hands' was performed 'as a compliment made to the people of quality at their subscription music'.[16] Congreve, Vanbrugh and William Walsh had, over the course of two mornings, collaborated to translate the Molière play *Monsieur de Pourceaugnac*, retitling it *Squire Trelooby*. Garth added a prologue. The final product, which appears never to have been published, though approximate versions survive, was staged at the old Lincoln's Inn Fields theatre. It is a rare example of an explicitly collaborative work by the Kit-Cat authors.

Vanbrugh was also turning the Haymarket theatre project into far more of a communal, Kit-Cat one. First, there was a plan to raise a subscription for the theatre's completion, collected and administered by Tonson's firm during the spring of 1704. Each subscriber paid 100 guineas (each guinea worth £130–£200 today) in four instalments, and was promised free lifetime admission to 'whatever Entertainments should be publicly performed'[17] and 'certain other privileges'.[18] Of twenty-nine subscribers, thirteen were Kit-Cats. The second indication of the Kit-Cat Club's cultural as well as financial investment in the theatre was an invitation for Congreve to become Vanbrugh's partner in managing it. Vanbrugh would have argued that joining the management was the only way to extract fair profit from their literary properties, given that playwrights then held no copyright and received no payments after the original production, and Vanbrugh would also have played on Congreve's long-standing loyalty to Bracey and Betterton's Company. Congreve, who had just failed to secure another hoped-for sinecure because of the decline in his patrons' influence under Queen Anne, agreed. Spring 1704 therefore found Congreve and Vanbrugh becoming close collaborators, both on the page and in business, for the first time since the Kit-Cat Club began. It was a professional rather than 'bosom' friendship, however, with Congreve complaining sadly at around this time: 'I know not how to have the few people that I love as near me as I want.'[19]

In April 1704, though construction was already well underway, the theatre's foundation stone was ceremonially laid by Somerset and/or by a Kit-Cat Club toast: Anne, Countess of Sunderland, Marlborough's favourite daughter who was married to a radical Whig politician named Charles Spencer, 3rd Earl of Sunderland. On one side of the stone was engraved 'Little Whigg' – the Countess' nickname, in honour of her political fidelity.[20] On the other side, in case there was any doubt about who was responsible for the theatre, they engraved simply 'Kitt-Catt'.[21]

Addison looked down on the new theatre's building site from his bird's-eye casements with ambivalent feelings, having once told Stanyan he 'would as soon be in a neighbouring wood as at the Opera'.[22] Many Englishmen at this date took a perverse pride in their reputation as Europe's most unaffected people, and Addison disdained operatic artifice in just this way. He considered opera a decadent art form because it appealed to the senses, not to reason, yet it failed to recall the existence of God, like a scenic view or birdsong.[23]

A Tory satirist saw in the new theatre's humble location, on top of a stinking stable, an allegory of the self-made Whigs' impertinent social ascent, and Harley's follower Defoe attacked the venture in similar terms: 'Apollo spoke the word / And straight arose a Playhouse from a turd.'[24] Dr Garth, however, took pride in the miraculous social transformation that the building rising beside his house represented:

> Your own magnificence you here survey,
> Majestic columns stand where dunghills lay,
> And cars triumphal rise from carts of hay.[25]

In one building's transformation, Garth implied, lay hope for transforming the whole English nation. The Kit-Cat Club was to be a vehicle of this transformation: raising taste from the lowest dross to loftier heights. The subscription to the Queen's Theatre was intended to be the artistic equivalent of the Royal Society's patronage of Greenwich Observatory in the 1670s – support for what was considered a weakness in the national culture: 'the cradle and forcing-ground for the Italian opera in England'.[26]

The Kit-Cats did not draw attention to the fact that they were compensating for Anne's lack of patronage, at least in comparison to Louis XIV's generous patronage of French opera; they instead sought her backing for their project. In November 1704, there was a preview performance for the Queen in Vanbrugh's 'almost finished'[27] theatre on the Haymarket – effectively an application for her to approve its licence. Received by the theatre's attendants liveried in scarlet in her honour, she was conducted into the main auditorium where the ceiling had been painted with 'Queen Anne's Patronage of the Arts', depicting Anne surrounded by the Muses, against a sky-blue, cosmic background. Chandeliers and flickering sconces lit the auditorium, reflecting in the plentiful gilt decorations on the baroque arch. Seating surrounded the orchestra pit, and eight large columns supported concentric circles of galleries. With seating for over 900, this was far larger than Mr Rich's theatres in Drury Lane or Dorset Gardens. Tonight they did not have to worry about filling it, playing for a royal audience of one.

The performance consisted of a music recital – a safe choice. The Collierites, however, were outraged at this royal visit to the Kit-Cat theatre, and even more outraged when, in December 1704, Anne issued a licence for the new theatre company, 'reposing especial trust and confidence in Our Trusty and Well-beloved' Vanbrugh and Congreve that they should reform 'the Abuses and Immorality of the Stage'.[28] These two playwrights, who had been in the frontline of godless dramatists attacked by Collier, were now – in the name of theatrical reformation – artistic directors of the Queen's Theatre. The licence was surprising, and scathingly satirized by those obsessed with England's moral decay. The Society for the Reformation of Manners published an open letter of protest to Archbishop Tenison, calling Congreve and Vanbrugh the worst offenders 'in equal Abhorrence to the Church and State'.[29] A mock-advertisement appeared for the 'New Hospital in the Hay-market for the Cure of Folly',[30] and the female Tory writer Mary Astell referred to the Kit-Cats as men 'who desire to be more taken notice of' by means of their subscriptions, criticizing the fact that they donated more to the new playhouse than to 'the building or repair of a Church'.[31] The replacement of church-going by cultural consumption worried people like Astell, and for good reason.

The precise political context for these attacks, and also for a Tory poem depicting the Club's leaders as republican-atheist conspirators,[32] was a religious debate then raging in Parliament. In mid-November 1704, High Church Tory MPs, the most vocal defenders of the Church of England's institutional privileges, introduced the Occasional Conformity Bill, aimed at eradicating the superficial observance of Anglicanism by which Protestant Dissenters, a crucial wing of the Whig party and a tight-knit community of rising economic power, could hold public office and enter Parliament. It was the third time the Tories had tried to introduce such a Bill, but this time they 'tacked' it onto another Bill for supplying the army, hoping such blackmail of the pro-war Whigs would force it through the Lords. This 'tacking' was defeated in the Commons, but Godolphin and Marlborough had to rely on the Junto Whigs, combined with Robert Harley's management of his supporters, to achieve this result. Once the anti-Dissenter Bill was 'untacked', the Junto was unable to prevent its passing through the Tory-dominated Commons in December 1704. The Kit-Cat played its part in organizing opposition to the Bill that winter, just as Oldmixon recorded that the High Church Tories were meeting at the Vine tavern on Long Acre to rally the Bill's supporters. Wharton, thanks to his upbringing as a Dissenter, spoke with particular passion against it in the Lords, while Stanhope returned from Portugal (after his regiment's capture and his own near-death from illness) in time to add his equally vehement voice. The Tory Bill failed to pass through the Lords, slain by Kit-Cat oratory and the Whigs' remaining majority in the upper house.

The Queen, High Church woman that she was, had supported the Occasional Conformity Bill at its first attempt in 1702, even though she was married to a Dissenter who himself practised occasional conformity, the Lutheran Prince George of Denmark. She had then refused to listen to the alarmism of the Whigs when it appeared for a second time (maintaining that she saw 'nothing like persecution in this Bill'), but this third divisive and reckless attempt of the 'tackers' proved as unpopular with the Queen as it did with the public, elated with national pride by Marlborough's brilliant victories.

Anne's licensing of the Queen's Theatre therefore indicated a softening in her feelings towards the Whigs, and hence the Kit-Cat Club's projects, at the end of 1704. She was disillusioned with the behaviour of certain Tory leaders, like Sir Edward Seymour and the Earl of Jersey, who were making life difficult for her commander, Marlborough. The Junto and their Kit-Cat clients therefore dared to feel some optimism as they met that winter and planned how to bargain their way back into power sharing.

Following Marlborough's hero's welcome to English shores in December 1704, Godolphin and the Queen discussed a fitting monument for the Blenheim victory that would also serve as a personal reward. It was decided that the Treasury should fund the building of a private house near Woodstock in Oxfordshire – the building that eventually became known as Blenheim Palace. Over Christmas, Marlborough approached Vanbrugh regarding its design. His choice of an architect who was a Kit-Cat was deliberate; as the Queen and the nation showed their gratitude to Marlborough, so, by choosing Vanbrugh, Marlborough signalled his gratitude to the Junto for having defeated the tackers and pushed the army supply Bill through Parliament. The beginnings of the house acknowledged the beginning of a new alliance between the Godolphin–Marlborough duumvirate and the Junto Whigs.

Like Addison's poem celebrating the battle of Blenheim, Vanbrugh's designs for Blenheim Palace depicted Marlborough and the War of Spanish Succession in epic mode, on a par with the men and deeds of classical antiquity. As with Castle Howard, this was ideological architecture in the sense that it was a palace for a private citizen, symbolizing a shift in authority from the Crown to the relatively self-made aristocracy. It was also a monument of new nationhood, reflecting the beginnings of Britons' grander ambitions, fanned by military victory and the Junto Whigs' Protestant patriotism, to lead Europe and acquire an empire.

Blenheim and the new Queen's Theatre on the Haymarket were products of Vanbrugh's theatrical ego and imagination, and both were criticized as metaphors for the hollow, selfish ambitions of the Junto Whigs, epitomes of style over content: 'For what could their vast columns, their gilded cornices, their immoderate high roofs avail, when scarce one word in them could be distinctly heard?'[33] In the case of the Haymarket theatre, this was a literal flaw in the acoustics, the 'vast triumphal piece of architecture' with its high-domed ceiling being excellent for the 'Swell of a Eunuch's holding Note'[34] but hopeless for hearing actors' speaking parts.

Oddly, in view of the theatre's original purpose and acoustics, Congreve and Vanbrugh could not settle on whether to open with a play or an opera. As late as February 1705, Congreve told a friend: 'I know not when the House will open, nor what we shall begin withal; but I believe no opera. There is nothing settled yet.'[35] A Dryden play was considered, to which Garth was asked to write a new prologue. The prologue Garth penned, however, contained a near blasphemous streak of anti-clerical wit, describing the modern theatre as a new temple that should replace the 'pious pageantry' of a corrupt Church of England.[36] When Vanbrugh and Congreve read this they must have known it would be a red rag to a bull, making a mockery of the Queen's proclaimed reformist purpose in licensing their theatre. They therefore switched back to the plan to open with an opera, with Congreve deciding to write an original libretto in English for an opera entitled *Semele*, to be set by the very English composer John Eccles.

The *Semele* libretto, written in spring 1705, is full of sexual desire. It was written at a time when Congreve was infatuated with a new lover – Henrietta, the wife of Congreve's fellow Kit-Cat, Francis Godolphin (Viscount Rialton), and the eldest child of the Duke of Marlborough. Henrietta, a wise old woman of 24, had been married to Francis for seven years, and Congreve had admired her for at least two. Congreve presented Henrietta with a poetic lament on the death of her little brother, the Marquess of Blandford, in 1703, and faced the angry disapproval of Henrietta's mother, the Duchess of Marlborough, after that date – the beginning of a disagreement concerning Henrietta's carelessness of her own reputation that slowly extinguished Henrietta's little remaining affection for her over-controlling mother. At one stage, the Duchess even sent her son-in-law Francis condolences on his wife's infidelity, promising she would never breathe a word to her friends of 'a proceeding that must appear so strange and monstrous'.[37]

Henrietta was made a Lady of the Bedchamber to the Queen and the toast of the Kit-Cat Club on several occasions. After Blenheim, Maynwaring used a Kit-Cat toast to flatter her father, for example:

> Godolphin's easy and unpractised air
> Gains without Art and Governs without Care
> Her conquering race with Various fate surprise
> Who 'Scape their Arms are Captive to their Eyes.[38]

But Henrietta also aspired to be thought a literary wit. Her mother observed that Henrietta was seduced by the flattery of literary dedications, giving '100 guineas to a very low poet that will tell her she is what she knows she is not'.[39] Though Henrietta never published anything, she possessed a share of her mother's frighteningly sharp intelligence and impatience with slow men – including her husband. Congreve therefore seduced Henrietta with his literary reputation, in spite of his lack of noble birth, his gout and semi-blindness that made him seem far older than his 35 years.

The memoirist Lord Chesterfield later described Henrietta's husband Francis as a man of little ambition, who went to the House of Lords only to sleep, whatever minor posts he acquired being thanks to his powerful father and father-in-law. Whether this was fair, it does seem Francis preferred a quiet life, and chose a complaisant attitude towards his wife's barely concealed affair. When Henrietta and Congreve consummated their romance is unknown, but it was soon referenced in several published satires. There must have been a little awkwardness when Congreve and Francis Godolphin met at the Kit-Cat Club, but in general Francis seems to have ignored his cornigerous condition. Attitudes to adultery were changing during this decade, allowing more room for negotiation. *The Athenian*

Mercury published letters from cuckolded readers declaring their forgiveness of wayward wives to be not weakness but a new form of male gallantry. The character Fainall in Congreve's *Way of the World* overlooks his wife's adultery because it gives him space to conduct his own. Though the historical record tells us nothing about Francis Godolphin having extramarital liaisons, they may merely have been lower profile than his wife's affair with Congreve.

Congreve remained a lodger with the Porters, while the Countess lived with her husband and young children at the Lord Treasurer's house at the corner of St James's Palace, yet Henrietta spent so many hours with Congreve and his friends that the Duchess of Marlborough would later adopt her granddaughter Harriet on grounds of Henrietta's neglect. Lady Mary Wortley Montagu confessed some jealousy when Henrietta began to monopolize her friend and mentor Congreve, and Bracey may also have felt displaced. The actress continued to work with Congreve at the Queen's Theatre, seeing him almost daily during the London seasons of 1704–6.

Congreve once explained that he was not a man to turn every feeling into a poem: 'I feel sensibly and silently for those whom I love.'[40] Nor do private love letters survive between the Countess and Congreve to further characterize their attraction to one another. It was, however, an affair that would last for the rest of Congreve's life, and would haunt Henrietta long after his death.

Unfortunately, for all the passion of Congreve's *Semele* libretto, Eccles' static score did nothing to stir the blood, and Congreve agreed the opera should not open the new theatre. Instead, after further delays and changes of plan, the Queen's Theatre opened, on 9 April 1705, with Jakob Greber's Italian pastoral opera, *The Loves of Ergasto*.

The Kit-Cat subscribers would have filled their private side-boxes for this opening night, though Congreve, Vanbrugh and Tonson had some trouble mustering their members, as many of the army officers were setting sail for the Continental battlefields,[41] while the peers and MPs were headed to their estates and constituencies. Various sources state that the Club met to dine at the Queen's Arms in Pall Mall, just around the corner from the Haymarket, before the performance. Most of the audience entered the gallery through a small door in Maiden Lane, on the west side of the theatre, but the Kit-Cats and other subscribers could enter through a 'patrons' entrance' to the north of the auditorium. The start of a performance was delayed for the Club's arrival.

Ergasto was a disaster. It was sung in Italian, by singers procured by Lord Manchester in Venice, but one audience member remarked that these singers were 'the worst that e're came from thence'.[42] Some felt the managers had lost their nerve in starting with an Italian opera instead of 'a good new *English* opera'.[43] Tonson published a version of the libretto ready for its first night, like a programme, in which the Italian was innovatively translated into English on the opposing pages. A Tory satirist, parodying this bilingual libretto, reprinted the opera's prologue with a prose paraphrase on the reverse that gave the prologue a Collierite gloss. Its author mocked the Kit-Cat writer-managers for hubristically fancying themselves 'Creators, Givers of Being and God Almighties'.[44] Similarly, Charles Leslie's Tory *Rehearsal* included several swipes against the Queen's Theatre: 'The Kit-Cat Club is now grown Famous and Notorious all over the Kingdom. And they have built a Temple for their Dagon: the new Playhouse in the Hay-Market.'[45]

Like the Temple of Dagon, the god worshipped by the Philistines, failure soon literally brought down the Kit-Cat theatre's ceiling. Although the theatre had been built for a mass audience rather than for the elite few, Congreve perversely penned a scathing Epilogue to *Ergasto*, snobbishly attacking the audience for demanding vulgar novelties and promising (with dangerous disregard for the Queen's licence) future performances with more 'bold strokes' of satire and smut. The rest of the season contained few novelties and no bold strokes. Apart from a couple of new plays by a Mrs Pix, probably performed thanks to Congreve's influence since he often promoted female authors, the rest of the performances were revivals.[46] Located some way west of the traditional theatre district and a dangerously long distance to expect ladies and gentlemen in silk shoes to walk comfortably for an evening's entertainment, the Queen's Theatre audience numbers quickly dropped off. The half-empty seating had a depressive effect and the theatre ran into almost immediate financial trouble. Vanbrugh therefore agreed to make alterations to the auditorium, transforming the theatre back from an opera-house into a playhouse by lowering and flattening the roof. As a result, the beautiful ceiling depicting Anne and the Muses was destroyed. As the foundations of Blenheim started to rise, Vanbrugh's workmen hacked the Queen's image from the sky, and the Kit-Cat Club concluded, with regret, that the English were not yet ready for opera.

X
THE COMEBACK KITS

Did not I find you out the secret to become Famous by making you Praise one another against the Opinion of the whole Town!? And brought the Club to that Reputation that those who only listen in it are Wits everywhere else. Are not my Lord Clack and Colonel Silent reckoned Wits only for being of it?

'STATIONER FRECKLE' [Jacob Tonson] in *The Quacks, or, Love's the Physician* (1705) by Owen Sweeney[1]

SEVENTEEN HUNDRED AND FIVE WAS A turning point for the Kit-Cat Club, after which the mood and membership shifted to become far more political. *A Kit-Cat C—b Describ'd* (1705) emphasized that the Club was now much more than an innocent dining or drinking club, being 'not for diversion, but for business'.[2] Another Tory satire identified the shift in the Kit-Cat Club's priorities from arts to politics, saying that its members 'are fallen off the Design of their first Institution; and from turning Critics upon Wit, are fallen into Criticisms upon Policy; I might say AGENTS in it'.[3]

Tory satires correctly identified the fact that, following the defeat of the tackers in late 1704, the Club's political leaders were making their individual and collective comebacks. In 'A New Ballad Writ by Jacob Tonson and Sung at the Kit-Cat Club on the 8th of March, 1704' (that is, 1705 by our calendar),[4] King William's ghost triumphantly sings about the Duchess of Marlborough holding 'Nanny' (Anne) in her clutches, while the Whigs plot to regain power in the forthcoming May–June 1705 general election. The ballad is clearly a fiction, maliciously misattributed to Tonson's authorship, yet the specificity of the date – falling on a Thursday – suggests the Club really had met that evening to commemorate the third anniversary of King William's death. Negotiations were certainly underway regarding what concessions the Junto would leverage from the Marlborough–Godolphin ministry over the course of these months. During these negotiations, Lord Godolphin sometimes expressed surprise at the Junto's greater interest in promoting their friends than their family. On the occasion, for example, when Halifax had the choice of protecting Stepney from demotion or promoting one of his Montagu relatives, he opted to protect Stepney. Though Godolphin and Marlborough felt a deep mutual loyalty to one another, such giving of patronage to friends above kinsmen was not what Godolphin would have expected. The Kit-Cat Club was only a particularly large bump in the generally uneven, nepotistic playing field of eighteenth-century power, but it is important to appreciate that the Club's patrons believed themselves meritocrats in the sense of selecting their friends for employments, on the basis of those men's talents, ethics and personal merits, rather than favouring half-wit relations.

The Tackers Vindicated; or, an Answer to the Whigs New Black List (1705) was another Tory satire published in the run-up to the summer election, suggesting that the Kit-Cat membership list should be used by the Tories as a blacklist of enemies to Church and Queen. The Whigs too had their blacklists, and Matthew Prior's name had been on them since his treacherous Commons vote in 1701. Though Prior should in theory have flourished under Anne's first, Tory-dominated administration, the Marlboroughs mistakenly believed he had been responsible for writing anonymous satires against them, and so blocked his preferment at every turn. This misfortune had left Prior stuck in a no-man's-land between the Marlborough–Godolphin ministry and the Kit-Cat friends he had abandoned, writing in June 1703: 'I had mistaken the path of life proper for me; I was not born a Courtier, being in my temper too passionate and too open in my conversation.'[5]

It was probably after the distance between Anne's ministry and the Whigs narrowed in late 1704, and after old Lord Dorset, who retained a nostalgic affection for Prior, became so unwell that he could no longer attend Club meetings, that the Kit-Cats felt bold enough to formally expel Prior.[6] Another member, the theatre critic Richard Norton, was also banished from the Club in 1705, for having 'refused to Subscribe' (presumably to the Queen's Theatre), but more seriously for failing to 'Advance and Forward their Whiggish elections'.[7] Norton had effectively retired from public life by this date, and so was of little more use to the Club.

Prior's and Norton's emptied seats may have permitted space for Steele's admission to the Kit-Cat Club in the spring of 1705. That season, Steele's play *The Tender Husband* debuted at Drury Lane only a fortnight after the Queen's Theatre had opened. It was a play about the nature of Englishness, defined by wartime Francophobia. Steele's central characters, the Clerimonts, act with Continental affectation, and the husband lets himself fall prey to excessive Latin jealousies. Order is restored only when the Clerimonts learn to exercise moderation and toleration, traits presented as essentially English. It was a sell-out hit, though Steele made only £13. 5*s*. 8*d*. (less than £2,000 today) from its performance.

Steele said he received help with the script from Addison, who gave it 'many applauded strokes' and a prologue.[8] This is the first firm evidence of Addison and Steele collaborating on a literary work, and the first sign that, after some years, the men had renewed their childhood friendship. Steele addressed the printed dedication of the play to Addison in a way suggesting a desire to fix their friendship as something more 'inviolable' in future: 'My Purpose, in this Application, is only to show the Esteem I have for You, and that I look upon my Intimacy with You as one of the most valuable Enjoyments of my Life.'[9]

Steele's admission to the Club likely resulted from *The Tender*

Husband's success. Congreve and Vanbrugh badly needed to lure a popular playwright away from Drury Lane, while the Club's political patrons knew of Steele's reputation as a vehement Whig and hoped he would prove a useful party writer. Steele's nomination for membership of the Club was also helped by his improved financial prospects. In April 1705, Steele wrote from his lodgings (above an apothecary's shop near St James's) to his former army patron Lord Cutts, explaining that he was in financial trouble but expecting his problems to be solved by marriage to a Barbados heiress named Margaret Ford Stretch. Mrs Stretch's Barbados estate – including 700 acres of sugar plantation and over 200 slaves – was worth £850 (almost £120,000 today) in annual rents. Steele therefore borrowed £400 (over £56,000 today) from Addison, secured against his fiancée's fortune. One acquaintance commented that 'Captain Steele may make use of a widow's jointure to advance himself, but he's not a stake to be depended upon.'[10]

Steele was behaving not only like the fortune-hunting character Captain Clerimont in *The Tender Husband*, but like a sharp joke in Congreve's *Love for Love*, where Sir Sampson says he is tickled 'to see a young spendthrift forced to cling to an old woman for support, like ivy round a dead oak'.[11] Mrs Stretch's age and state of health when she married Steele in the spring of 1705 are unknown, but it seems Steele was less than surprised when she died that December. As she had no other surviving male relatives, Steele inherited her entire estate.

In many ways, the question is why Steele was not invited to join the Kit-Cat Club sooner, given his many friends and acquaintance among the members. Tonson (whom one source said had the sole prerogative to convene 'Chapters' of the Club to consider changes in membership, as if the Club were an order of knights[12]) knew Steele well, and Steele's family connection to the Duke of Ormonde linked him to several other Club members: Tidcomb, another of Ormonde's old clients; William Cavendish, the Duke of Devonshire's son and Ormonde's kinsman; and Vanbrugh, whose mother had been distantly related to Ormonde.

Steele further counted Maynwaring and Congreve as drinking

companions, and had known several other Kit-Cats since Will's Coffee House days. Garth, in particular, was loved by Steele as the embodiment of philanthropy and generosity: '[I]t is as common with Garth to supply Indigent Patients with Money for Food as to receive it from Wealthy ones for Physic,' Steele flattered,[13] adding that Garth was only ever present at Kit-Cat dinners with half a mind: '[O]ur Mirth is often insipid to You, while You sit absent to what passes amongst us, from your Care of such as languish in Sickness.'[14] Another anecdote, however, has Garth coming to the Club one afternoon, saying he had to leave early because he had patients to see, but then getting drunk and forgetting them. When Steele reminded him, the doctor pulled out his list and said: 'It's no great matter whether I see them tonight or not, for nine of them have such bad constitutions that all the physicians in the world can't save them; and the other six have such good constitutions that all the physicians in the world can't kill them.'[15] Steele also gave Garth the epithet of the 'Best Natured Man', adding, 'You are so universally known for this character that an epistle so directed would find its way to you without your name.'[16]

Steele paid equally fulsome compliments to Lord Somers, whom he said had ascended to the heights of power purely through 'a certain Dignity in Yourself, that (to say the least of it) has been always equal to those great Honours which have been conferred upon You'.[17] Steele emphasized not Somers' public achievements in this dedication but the charms of the private man known only to those who 'are admitted into your Conversation'.[18] This phrase beams with Steele's self-satisfaction at his own admission to Somers' inner circle, the Kit-Cat circle, by the time of writing.

Joining the Kit-Cat Club meant a great deal to Steele, not only in terms of social status and expectation of patronage, but also in terms of his sense of himself as a cultured, cosmopolitan gentleman. Steele once described himself as a 'Stranger upon Earth', a mere 'Looker-on' compared to Lord Halifax.[19] Though Steele never entirely lost that outsider's perspective, the promise of the Club was that it treated its members as equals in conversation – as men who each *belonged*. He contrasted its atmosphere and motives with those of Tory hospitality:

> A vainglorious [Tory] fox-hunter shall entertain half the county for the ostentation of his beef and beer, without the least affection for any of the crowd about him. He feeds them, because he thinks it a superiority over them that he does so, and they devour him, because they know he treats them out of insolence.[20]

Whig lords, Steele implied, lived in the same style but a different spirit. Fed on Kit-Cat pies and wine by his social superiors, Steele flattered himself he was being fed with 'affection'.

Steele's and Addison's admissions introduced a more guilty attitude towards the Club's nocturnal bacchanalia. Although Addison had left Magdalen recognizing there was life beyond the cloister, he remained a fundamentally pious man, with a more melancholic personality than friends like Congreve, Vanbrugh, Prior or Stepney. The need for faith, he wrote, 'must be very evident to those who consider how few are the present Enjoyments of the most happy Man'.[21] Addison knew that a virtue of the English character was to consider excessive religious feeling unfashionable, but he concluded that religious hypocrisy was less dangerous than 'open Impiety',[22] and thought that was exactly what the other Kit-Cats verged on. Tonson once remarked that Addison, 'ever thought him[self] a priest in his heart'.[23]

There is an anecdote about Addison and Steele unwisely inviting Benjamin Hoadly, the Latitudinarian Bishop of Bangor, to be an honorary guest at a Whig 'club meeting' to celebrate the November anniversary of King William's landing in England. Another Club member entered the tavern room on his knees and in that posture toasted William's immortal memory with a tankard of ale. Watching this slapstick, Steele leaned over to the Bishop and whispered: 'Do laugh. 'Tis humanity to laugh.' This touching story of Steele protecting his wit-challenged friend has a less edifying conclusion: Steele proceeded to get so drunk he had to be carried home and put to bed by his friends. The next morning, he sent an apology to Hoadly for his disgraceful behaviour.[24]

In his writing, Steele condemned excessive drinking because it stopped a man being 'master of himself' – a resonant phrase for

Steele, who craved independence from his superiors above all else.[25] Steele also observed that drink could start by making men into warmer friends, but ended by removing the capacity for empathy:

> You may indeed observe in People of Pleasure a certain Complacency and Absence of all Severity, which the Habit of a loose and unconcerned Life gives them; but tell the Man of Pleasure your secret Wants, Cares, or Sorrows, and you will find that he has given up the Delicacy of his Passions to the Craving of his Appetites.[26]

Steele regarded Dorset, in particular, as a man whose 'shining Qualities' made self-destructive living ('drinking till they cannot taste, smoking till they cannot see, and roaring till they cannot hear') misleadingly attractive.[27] He and Addison may have been as fond of drink as Dorset, Tidcomb or the other earlier Kit-Cats, but they were both men who regretted their drunkenness and apologized to bishops in the morning.

This attitude seems to have spread from the new admissions to the older members of the Club. Congreve, who when younger had only disapproved of drunkenness if you spat or 'bepiss[ed] yourself', advised a friend in 1706 that '[n]othing but an absolute and continued regularity' could counteract past years of excess.[28] He still loved his wine, and his 'usquebaugh' (an Irish whiskey), but he no longer treated heavy drinking as a macho competition or a requirement for poetic wit.

Soon after Congreve's appointment to the Commission for licensing wine, arranged by Halifax,[29] Congreve – whom a fellow Kit-Cat described as having 'no head for business'[30] – bought himself out of Betterton's company and so quit 'the affair of the Hay-market', saying he had 'got nothing by it' and leaving Vanbrugh to deal with the failing theatrical enterprise alone.[31] It could not have been worse timing. In June 1705, Vanbrugh received the warrant to build Blenheim Palace and had to devote most of his time to that property (which Congreve's lover Henrietta stood in line to inherit since Marlborough had no living sons). Congreve's resignation may also have been the cause of a rift between Congreve and Tonson, which we know about thanks to a poem written on the later occasion of their reconciliation.[32]

Steele was fortunately on hand to help Vanbrugh pick up the pieces at the Queen's Theatre. In Congreve's place, for example, Steele composed a prologue for *The Mistake*, a play hurriedly translated from French by Vanbrugh for performance in December 1705. Vanbrugh knew, however, that though Steele shared his own entrepreneurial and soldierly energy, Steele had a sorry record in business. Steele was not asked to replace Congreve as a company investor or manager.

June 1705 also saw the election go decisively in the Junto Whigs' favour, though they failed to gain an outright majority. The Queen's recent indulgence of the Whigs, combined with the public's disgust at the tackers' tactics, had hurt the Tory vote. One young Whig MP who had played a key role in defeating the tackers was Robert Walpole, later to become Britain's first Prime Minister. Descended from a long line of Norfolk gentry and married to the daughter of a prominent London merchant, Walpole typified his party's alliance between county and City. Walpole's first patron, the Earl of Orford (a title Walpole would one day acquire himself), likely introduced Walpole to the other Junto members, whom Walpole quickly charmed. A fellow MP described the young Walpole as having 'the most friendly nature I have known'[33] and another contemporary referred to him as 'always . . . laughing and talking'.[34]

Stanhope, on the instructions of Halifax, had invited Walpole to lead the Junto Whig MPs in October 1703, the Junto having realized that they needed a new manager in the lower house.[35] Walpole effectively accepted this responsibility, and also joined the Kit-Cat Club at around the same time as Addison. Unlike Addison, he loved nothing more than hosting lavish meals for his Club friends – Walpole's personal accounts from later years show he spent over £1,000 a year (or nearly £150,000 today) on food.[36] He used the position he received on the Admiralty Council, as thanks for his Commons campaign against the tackers, to smuggle wine from Holland on navy vessels, which the Kit-Cat Club must then have enjoyed, and, in expectation of this appointment, Walpole moved his wife to a grand townhouse on Dover Street where he held a housewarming feast and ball to which every Kit-Cat would have been invited. Walpole's giddy younger sister, Dolly, came to London for the ball where her flirtation with the 56-year-old, married Wharton led to a minor scandal.[37] Walpole's ostentatious hospitality was competitive – trying to outdo others in the aristocracy – but also his way of blocking out the nagging worry of debt during years when the tenant farmers on his lands were unable to pay their rents.

After Christmas 1704, the tacking debate gave rise to a grouping of MPs, led by Walpole and Stanhope, who were sometimes known as the 'Kitlings'.[38] The others in this grouping were Spencer Compton, Jack Smith (though much older than the others), William Pulteney, and Walpole's former schoolmate, Charles, 2nd Viscount Townshend. Townshend was the only non-Kit-Cat in the group, either by choice or because he lacked the necessary charms (his diction was described as 'inelegant . . . frequently ungrammatical, always vulgar; his cadences false, his voice unharmonious'[39]).

Most of the Kitlings' extended families – the Walpoles, Stanhopes and Comptons – were divided by party, showing that ideology was increasingly trumping kinship when it came to determining men's loyalties. Some were even leaving their estates to political friends rather than relations: when Stanhope's 'bosom friend', the Whig Earl of Huntingdon, died in February 1705, for example, he bequeathed Stanhope £400 per annum (over £56,000 today) to 'defend the liberty and laws of his country, and the rights of the people'.[40] In April 1705, Stanhope was promoted to Brigadier-General and in May returned to Spain to drive forward the Allied campaign to place the Austrian Archduke Charles on the Spanish throne.

Spencer Compton, in his early thirties like Stanhope and Walpole, may already have been a Kit-Cat for several years by the time Walpole joined the Club. Compton's sister was married to Lord Dorset, so he first became acquainted with Tonson and all three of Lord Dorset's Boys in the 1690s.[41] Compton was not the sharpest pin in the box, explaining why the Kit-Cats did not ask him to lead the Kitlings in the Commons, but his natural hauteur carried him far enough.

In the summer of 1705, Jack Smith was elected Speaker in the

Commons – clear confirmation that the election results had favoured the Whigs. Somers had written to Whig peers telling them to ensure their 'friends' were all present in the Commons to vote for Smith.[42] It was a close contest, Smith finally winning by forty-three votes, and the Kit-Cat Club met to toast the victory that same evening. Smith was perceived as a relatively moderate Whig, not one whom, as Godolphin put it, 'nothing would satisfy but wresting the administration out of the Queen's hands'.[43] After becoming Speaker, Smith was seen as the creature of the Marlborough–Godolphin duumvirate, but where the duumvirate differed from the Junto, he still voted with his Kit-Cat friends. One Tory satirist criticized Smith as 'a State hermaphrodite – an ambidexter. Jacob Tonson, with his two left legs, makes not such an awkward figure as he does.'[44]

The final member of Walpole's clique of Kitlings was Pulteney. At 21 in 1705, Pulteney returned from his Grand Tour, won a seat in the Commons, which he held until 1734, and also a seat in the Kit-Cat Club. As a boy, Pulteney had inherited an enormous fortune and gained a reputation as a talented classicist. Congreve, perhaps seeking a malleable patron, was said to have consulted Pulteney on a draft of *The Way of the World* while Pulteney was still in his teens.

Addison was another who flourished thanks to Kit-Cat patronage after the 1705 election. Rather than being rewarded like Congreve with a mere sinecure, Addison was given a government office of substance. In July 1705, he was appointed Under-Secretary to Sir Charles Hedges, Secretary of State for the South. Though Hedges was a Court Tory and not a Kit-Cat, Addison obtained this important position primarily through the influence of Somers and Halifax. An Under-Secretary was paid about £400 a year (over £56,000 today), but the job was also worth at least £550 (over £77,000 today) in commissions on fees charged. For this salary, Addison worked long hours in his Whitehall office, managing news and diplomatic business from all the relevant countries; his letters to friends after the summer of 1705 constantly apologize for his lack of time. Luckily, several Kit-Cat friends were among Addison's diplomatic correspondents. He briefed Stepney in Vienna on war news from Spain and Portugal, and on the rise of Walpole's Kitling clique. Stanyan, meanwhile, was appointed Envoy Extraordinary to the Cantons of Switzerland in May 1705, charged with increasing the Swiss contribution to the Grand Alliance.

In November 1705, the faltering Tories misstepped badly. The Tory Lord Haversham suggested England invite Electress Sophia of Hanover to reside in England, so ensuring a smooth succession. Anne took offence at this proposal, believing it implied she was about to die or go mad; it reminded her of her son's early death, which had left the country without a nearer heir to the throne. Wharton set up the Whig attack on Haversham's motion in a speech dripping with irony about the Tories' sudden concern for a Protestant succession. Somers came up with an alternative proposal, more to the Queen's liking, for a regency council to govern temporarily in the event of Anne's incapacity or death, until the Hanoverians arrived on English soil. Wharton promoted and Somers drew up this vital piece of constitutional legislation (the Regency Bill), which passed through Parliament in February 1706, ending the 'invitation crisis'.[45] Wharton wrote to the future George I, explaining the new arrangements.

In December 1705, the Tories took yet another self-defeating step when they claimed the Church of England was 'in danger' because of Junto influence on Godolphin's ministry.[46] The pious Queen again took personally the suggestion that her reign might be endangering the Established Church, and enjoyed watching the Junto gleefully argue down the motion. Halifax declared that the only time the Church was in danger was before 1688, when 'those Patriots that stood up in [the Church's] Defence and endeavoured to prevent the Evils which might ensue from a Popish successor, were discountenanced and punished'.[47] Somers summarized the Whig case by saying that the 'danger' was a bogey, recklessly raised by the Tories to destabilize the country in time of war. The Whigs easily won the vote, and profited enormously from the chance to present themselves as defenders of Church and Queen.

The parliamentary session of 1705–6 saw other significant common law and equity reforms, spearheaded by Somers. The Junto was back pulling the strings of power, which were knotted together at the Kit-Cat Club. Walpole's arrival brought a new energy to the

Whigs in the Commons, but also a more narrowly political focus to a Club that had previously been as much, if not more, about literary and musical patronage. The Kit-Cat now became a Whig party inner sanctum – the place for policy to be debated on a Thursday evening before Anne's Council met after dinner on a Sunday.

As if symbolically marking the Club's shift of emphasis and atmosphere, Lord Dorset, who had kept the Restoration's spirit so long alive in the Club, died on 29 January 1706. Dorset had been infirm for some time – in 1700, he was rumoured to have finished himself off with a case-knife and had to 'make his appearance in all the coffee houses to convince the world of the contrary'.[48] Dorset had participated in Anne's coronation but after 1702 played little role in public affairs. Before his death, he lived at the spa in Bath, growing fat and, according to Swift, dull-witted in his dotage. Congreve disagreed. Visiting Dorset while he was dying, Congreve reported: 'Faith, he slabbers more wit dying than other people do in their best health.'[49] In October 1704, Dorset had outraged his family by marrying his housekeeper, Anne Roche, who was automatically assumed to be a gold-digger. An anti-Whig satire included Dorset falling asleep at a Kit-Cat Club meeting and rousing himself only to raise a toast to Roche. Another acquaintance saw the marriage as proof Dorset, in his early sixties, had 'entirely lost his senses'[50] (men were traditionally believed to lose their reason at the age of 63, their 'great climacteric'). Dorset's family complained that Roche had 'held him in a Sort of Captivity down at Bath' until he married her and changed his will.[51] Prior, who understood about loving women who were not 'ladies', took a more sympathetic view,[52] and Addison later wrote essays about a superannuated Restoration rake who bore more than a passing resemblance to Dorset and who chose as his wife 'an obscure young Woman, who doth not indeed pretend to an ancient Family, but has certainly as many Forefathers as any Lady in the Land, if she could but reckon up their names'.[53]

News of Dorset's death reached London on 30 January 1706, the anniversary of Charles I's execution and therefore a day on which Tory preachers went into zealous overdrive denouncing the Whigs from their pulpits as closet republicans. When the Kit-Cat Club met the following night, and feasted heartily to compensate for the national fast the day before, they surely would have drunk to Dorset's memory. Richard Boyle, 2nd Viscount Shannon, who had become Dorset's son-in-law in June 1704 by marrying Dorset's illegitimate daughter Mary, was likely among the Kit-Cat toasters. With Stepney abroad and Prior expelled, Halifax was the only former Lord Dorset's Boy there to raise a glass to the Maecenas of the 1690s and founding father of the Kit-Cat Club. Halifax was appointed one of the guardians of Dorset's 18-year-old son Lionel, now the 7th Earl of Dorset (referred to hereafter as 'Lionel' to avoid confusion), and Lionel was soon admitted to the Club in honour of his father.

Halifax was to take Lionel on an important Kit-Cat journey to the northwest German state of Hanover later that spring. Together with Addison, the two men were in Amsterdam in May 1706, awaiting the arrival of the fourth Kit-Cat in their party: Vanbrugh. They passed the time by attending a synagogue service of the Portuguese Jewish community, to hear prayers for the success of the forthcoming campaign against France – a gesture to compliment a community helping bankroll the war that no Tory delegation would have made. Halifax also familiarized himself with the Dutch leaders and generals Marlborough was constantly placating to keep the Grand Alliance united.

Officially, their mission was to invest the 23-year-old Electoral Prince of Hanover (the future George II of England, grandson to the then heir to the throne, Sophia) with the Order of the Garter, and to deliver the Regency Act and deeds of English naturalization to the Electoral family. Unofficially, the delegation's goal was to strengthen relations between the Whigs and the Hanoverians. Experience under William had taught the Junto that the Germans would bring various favourites and advisers into English politics; its members wanted to know what lay in store. Queen Anne had ordered the mission to demonstrate her commitment to the Protestant succession and to heal any offence caused by her refusal, during Haversham's 'invitation crisis', to let the Electress move to England.

As the herald appointed to perform the investiture, Vanbrugh was the most essential member of the delegation, but he had delayed his departure by a month, as it was an extremely inconvenient time for him to leave England. Blenheim's walls were just rising, and the central block of Castle Howard was nearing completion. Between these two sites, and managing the struggling Queen's Theatre, Vanbrugh's hands were full, but he could not refuse the Queen's command. He arrived in Amsterdam in mid-May 1706, together with a more junior herald and a vast load of heraldic ceremonial gear.

Vanbrugh was sent to Hanover not only as a herald but also to represent the best of English talent and manners, as a playwright, architect and fluent French speaker. Similarly, though Addison was officially sent as Under-Secretary of State, he was selected because he had impressed various Hanoverian courtiers, including the philosopher Gottfried von Leibniz, during his stay there just a few years earlier. If Addison and Vanbrugh had not spent much time together before, they now had weeks on the road from Amsterdam.

The trip to Hanover appears to have been open to other Kit-Cats and their friends. Congreve told Joe Keally, for example: 'I was out of town when Lord Halifax undertook his expedition. If you had been here, and inclined to such a ramble, I should not have avoided it.'[54] The presence of young Lionel, however, is what most clearly identifies the trip as a Kit-Cat junket. This was part of the Kit-Cats' campaign to mentor and flatter Lionel, hoping he would shortly prove a generous patron of the arts like his father. Prior had been the first to commence this campaign, having written to Lionel when he was only a 10-year-old schoolboy. The Kit-Cats would be disappointed, however: Lionel did not share his father's ambition to distinguish himself through patronage of the arts. Or perhaps Lionel listened to Kitling Spencer Compton, who warned him that his father had left many debts, so his son would need to live more frugally.

When they arrived at the Hanoverian frontier, the delegation paused, fearing they might be received without due ceremony if the Electoral family were indeed displeased with Anne's recent actions. Halifax sent Addison ahead to test the mood, smooth things over, and ensure the Hanoverian Court could not feign surprise at the delegation's arrival. Addison was pleased to report that he found Hanover willing to welcome them 'in great pomp and state'.[55]

The delegation was greeted with a grand reception in a private house, and accorded the royal honours of trumpets and kettledrums. Addison, who described the Hanoverian Court as 'the most Agreeable place in the world',[56] was made particularly welcome by Leibniz, who called the English delegation '*une fort bonne compagnie*' and arranged for Addison to sit at Sophia's table.[57] Upon being introduced to Sophia, Halifax handed over Anne's letter and the Acts of Parliament with various assurances of personal and national friendship, before being honoured by a private conversation with her son the Elector ('in very ill French' on Halifax's part). Halifax described the future George I as 'more easy, and familiar than I expected . . . but I think Him very dry'.[58]

The following day the delegation requested an audience with Sophia's grandson, the Electoral Prince. It was a sensitive business, they discovered, as the Prince and his father were in the middle of a family quarrel, so the Elector was pettily insisting that the ceremony to invest his son with the Garter be less elaborate than his own earlier investiture. The Prince's investiture was therefore a relatively simple affair a few days later: Halifax tied the blue ribbon onto the Prince's leg, propped up on a stool, while Vanbrugh read out the required words. This was followed by an early afternoon dinner in Sophia's apartments and, in the evening, a ball. Two days later, there was a further ceremonial presentation, and the delegation attended a thanksgiving service for Marlborough's recent victory at the battle of Ramillies.

Nothing could have reflected so well upon the English visitors as this exhilarating news of Marlborough's latest victory arriving during their sojourn in Hanover. Halifax described being awakened to hear the news in a 'transport' of happiness.[59] The significance of the victory was that it allowed the Grand Alliance's focus to shift from Holland and the other United Provinces to the eastern fronts of the war, of more direct concern to the Hanoverians. Tories critical of England fighting such a heavy land war argued that the Whigs only financed these eastern campaigns after 1706 to serve Hanover's national interests, and so curry favour with the future royal family at the English taxpayers' expense.

Between the investiture ceremonies, the Kit-Cat tourists enjoyed the sights of Hanover, which was considered the most sophisticated of the German Courts, heavily influenced by Venetian culture. They likely viewed the frescoes in the Herrenhausen Gallery and the Italian old master paintings collected by the Electoral family. Vanbrugh would have been fascinated by the Elector's project to rebuild Herrenhausen and its gardens, and flattered by the high status that the Court favourites, Leibniz and Johann von Kielmansegg, accorded to architecture as an art form.

The Kit-Cats were invited to stay in Hanover a few days longer than planned to attend the wedding of the Elector's daughter to the Prince of Prussia. This show of favour was noted in England as a sure sign that the future monarch would favour the Junto Whigs. Their Tory opponents must have observed the whole thing, through Hanoverian spies and as relayed in the English press, with jealous despair. If a wavering Tory had not previously contemplated restoration of James II's son as his party's best hope after Anne's death, he may well have begun to do so now.

XI
UNEASY UNIONS: 1707

Blest Revolution, which creates
Divided Hearts, united States.

JONATHAN SWIFT,
Verses Said to be Written on the Union (1707)

THE 1706–7 NEGOTIATIONS for securing a union between England and Scotland – nations which, despite a union of Crowns in 1603, maintained remarkable political and religious independence – were led, on the English side, by members of the Kit-Cat Club, in particular Lord Somers. The Junto Whigs had seen themselves as nation-builders since the heady days of constitutional change following the Glorious Revolution, as every piece of heroic verse blowing their own Whig trumpets made clear. Now they were involved in founding not a metaphorical new 'Age' but a literal new 'Britain' – an achievement of statecraft that was, for once, every bit as momentous as they boasted.

Since 1688, the Scots and English had done little but antagonize one another – King William thoroughly alienated the Scottish political class for the sake of his Continental wars, and tensions arose between the two peoples as England became one of the wealthiest European nations and its northern neighbour one of the poorest. An unusual alliance of anti-Union opinion formed between English merchants and High Church Tories: the merchants feared losing trading privileges and monopolies, while the Tories opposed further negotiations with the Presbyterian Scottish Establishment.

William's dying wish, however, echoed in Anne's maiden speech in 1702, had been for legislative union to succeed dynastic union between England and Scotland. Godolphin, Marlborough and what might be called the Whig war party (the Junto, Kit-Cats and their other followers) had persuaded Anne that this was necessary in order to strengthen the British Isles against Louis XIV and prevent the Scottish Crown being grabbed by her half-brother, The Pretender. Scotland and Ireland were seen as England's half-open back doors, in need of bolting against Jacobites and Catholics. The war with France also required troops and funds from Scotland, and centralization of government through legislative union would allow these to be secured more reliably and efficiently. The Junto, however, waited until their post-1704 political comeback to really push the unionist agenda. They needed to ensure their domination of the negotiating Commission so that the deals done would go in their own party's favour. They were also alarmed into action by the Scots passing the Act of Security in August 1703, which insisted upon Scotland's right to select its own monarch, separate from England.

By 1706, alternating strategies of carrot and stick had brought the Scots to the negotiating table. On 10 April 1706, while the Westminster Parliament was prorogued, thirty-one Commissioners were named by the Court, of which nine were Kit-Cats and a larger number were friends or kinsmen of the Kit-Cats. Congreve remarked to a friend on the similarity between merger negotiations then underway between the Queen's Theatre and Drury Lane and those his patrons were conducting at the national level: 'Have heard there is to be a Union of the two [play]houses, as well as Kingdoms.'[1]

Six days later, on 16 April, the Commissioners held their first meeting in Addison's Whitehall offices, 'The Cockpit', with the English Commissioners in one room and the Scottish Commissioners in another. Halifax, though a Commissioner, had just departed for Hanover, where he could represent the Junto as being the key promoters of an Act guaranteeing the Hanoverians a further Crown.[2] Somers told Lord Marchmont, former Lord Chancellor of Scotland, of his conviction that union was needed to secure Protestant domination and thus the liberties of both peoples: '[I]f we do not now become better friends than ever, we shall soon be less so.'[3]

The negotiations proceeded through written papers passed between the two Cockpit rooms, rather than face-to-face debate. Cash and personal promises also passed between the two sets of men. The negotiations of 1706 have been described as 'not far removed from a conspiracy',[4] with certain Scottish peers and lairds seeking rewards of money, pensions and titles, while offering such bribes in turn for their followers' votes. However, it is too simplistic to attribute the successful negotiations solely to venality and corruption; the £20,000 (over £2.5 million today) secretly paid to various Scots was too small an amount to be decisive. Most of the payments were merely confirmation of alliances between the Junto and the so-called 'Squadrone' of Scottish Whig magnates. More significant were various Scots' hopes to have a stake in 'The Equivalent' – £398,000 (or nearly £52 million in today's money), which England would pay to Scotland upon union, as compensation to creditors of the former Scottish government.

In mid-August 1706, the Kit-Cat delegation to Hanover sailed home from The Hague with the East India Company's fleet, and Somers expressed his relief at having Halifax back to help handle the more delicate points of the negotiations. September saw the leader of the Scottish parliamentary opposition to union, the Duke of Hamilton, undercut his own side and so leave the way open for passing the articles of the Act of Union in the Scottish Parliament.

The Scottish people were less easily convinced. When the articles were made public, numerous addresses to the Queen begged for a new general election, and there were riots in Edinburgh, Glasgow and the southwest lowlands. On 3 September 1706, Addison told Stepney in The Hague (where, in reward for his long hard years of diplomacy in Vienna, Stepney was now Envoy Extraordinary and

Plenipotentiary to the States General of the United Provinces, effectively administering the captured Spanish Netherlands): 'The Union at present takes up all public discourse, and 'tis thought will certainly be concluded at last, notwithstanding the late popular commotions.'[5] Stepney was asked to investigate whether any European power was funding intrigues or riots to prevent the union, and reported back that he thought only the French would bother with this. To his overseas correspondents, Addison passed on the complacent reassurance of his Junto bosses that 'not only the Parliament, but throughout the kingdom, the majority is for the Union'.[6] In fact, a pro-union Scottish Whig historian only twenty years later admitted that 'not even one per cent' of his fellow Scots supported the Act while it was being negotiated.[7]

To obtain the Scottish clergy's support for the union, the Junto Whigs ensured that an Act guaranteeing the Presbyterian Establishment was appended to the Act of Union – a concession from the English that was decisively influenced by the 'Dissenters' Friend', Lord Wharton. Wharton's key role was recognized the following month when the Queen created him Viscount Winchendon and Earl of Wharton. One address thanked him for single-handedly preventing the European war from being played out on Scottish soil.[8]

In December 1706, Marlborough's son-in-law Sunderland was appointed Secretary of State for the South, with the support of Somers and Halifax, who also ensured Addison did not lose his place as Under-Secretary in the change. Sunderland's appointment was celebrated not so much for its own sake as for being an augur of future Junto promotions. What Addison and his patrons failed to appreciate, however, was the depth of Anne's resentment at being forced to appoint Sunderland, a radical Whig, against her personal wishes.

After Sunderland's appointment, the Junto's interest in pushing forward the union seemed to wane. Some have interpreted this as evidence that they were less interested in union per se than in the leverage the union negotiations gave them over Godolphin's ministry.[9] Junto policy, however, did not essentially change: they still pursued union, though nervous that Godolphin might try to use the distribution of seats in the unified Houses of Parliament to undercut the Whigs' voting block. The Scots were understandably confused about how closely the ministry and the Junto were really working together.[10]

Such internal divisions in England were the only hope of the few Scottish politicians who, reflecting the ordinary people's mood, continued to oppose union: 'The Scots that can't hinder the passing of the Articles retard it as much as they can in hopes perhaps that Our English Parliament may by any unseasonable Heats or Reflections give them a Handle to break the whole Project,' wrote Addison to an English diplomat in Hanover.[11] Such Scottish opponents resented that the Treaty was being foisted upon them, though the truth – as between friends where one is much wealthier or more powerful than another – was more complicated.

The union negotiations preoccupied the Junto so thoroughly during the spring of 1707 that the Kit-Cat Club's meetings were temporarily neglected. Addison explained to one petitioner that Halifax was 'so much taken up about the Scotch Union and other public Business that it has been difficult to find an Opportunity of speaking with him' on matters of private patronage.[12] Addison was kept busy implementing his patrons' policies: by the end of 1706, a number of Scottish 'Incendiaries' protesting against the union had been arrested on Addison's orders, and he said he believed 'the Union will quickly be finished on the Scotch side'.[13] This optimism was justified. The Scottish Parliament passed all the union articles by January 1707, thanks to a combination of persuasion, bribery (cash and peerages) and compromise. In Westminster, the Commons Committee of the Whole House then met under Kitling Spencer Compton's chairmanship and followed suit within six weeks, passing the Bill almost without debate. On hearing the news, Addison exhaled: 'God be thanked.'[14]

A few weeks later, in March 1707, Addison was feeling tense for another reason: he had written the libretto of an opera, *Rosamund*, about Henry II's lover Rosamund Clifford, and it was to have its opening night at the Drury Lane theatre. Addison had altered the ending of Rosamund's true story to a falsely happy one: the reunion of Henry II and his murderous wife Eleanor. This was intended to make the opera an allegory for the Treaty of Union, with Eleanor representing the Jacobites of Scotland coming to be tamed. The Kit-Cat Club's long-held agenda of reforming English culture – particularly literature and music – was now, in theory at least, for the benefit of an expanded club of all Britons.

Addison's opinions about opera had been refined by the Kit-Cat Club's influence. He was now convinced that a new style of opera was needed in the new Britain, stripped of Continental absurdities and reflecting what he saw as the English national character. His authorship of a 'native' opera on a very English historical theme and written in the English language was a direct response to the Kit-Cat Club's nationalistic agenda for the arts – an agenda shared, admittedly, by a handful of prominent non-Kit-Cat Whig critics, and by other authors who had tried to write 'dialogue-operas' for 'the Right Noble, Honourable and Ingenious Patrons of Poetry, Music, &c The Celebrated Society of the Kit-Cat Club'.[15] Steele reported that there were 'People of Quality' now funding operas by subscribing 'some thousands of Pounds', and, in response, 'our English poets have not been behindhand with our English Heroes in reducing the French Wit to as low a state as their Arms'.[16] No statement could better express the Kit-Cat Club's image of itself as conducting a cultural campaign to parallel Marlborough's military campaigns. It was a type of battle Addison was willing to fight at his patrons' command: hence *Rosamund*.

The opera's subject allowed Addison to flatter the all-powerful Marlboroughs, since Rosamund Clifford's legendary bower was located on the grounds of Woodstock Park in Oxfordshire, where Vanbrugh was building Blenheim. Ten days before leaving for Hanover, therefore, Addison presented a draft of the libretto to the Duchess of Marlborough – the Duke having returned to the Continental battlefields after a winter spent socializing, thanks to his Whig wife, with the likes of Halifax, Wharton, Garth and Maynwaring.[17]

On the trip to Hanover, Addison, Vanbrugh, Halifax and Lionel, all of whom shared a keen interest in opera, must have debated the art form's merits, problems and future in England. If Vanbrugh did not originally suggest to Addison *Rosamund*'s patriotic story before they went to Hanover together, he certainly seems to have influenced the opera's eventual staging: a picture of Blenheim Palace, as it would look when completed, was painted on the pasteboard stage-set. It would have been the first time the audience had seen Vanbrugh's vision for the house, and there was a nice circularity to the gesture, since stage-set design had so influenced Vanbrugh's approach to architectural and landscape design. The allegorical link between the historical past and the yet-to-be-built future, the new nation born in 1707, was reflected in Addison's lyrics which described contemporary greatness bursting forth from the ruins of former greatness: 'Behold the glorious pile ascending! / Columns swelling, arches bending.' Vanbrugh also had an ulterior, more provocative motive in suggesting this set that he probably did not disclose to Addison: by reminding the public of the historical significance of Woodstock's ruins, Vanbrugh hoped to stop the Duchess of Marlborough from demolishing them as he already knew she planned to do.

Rosamund's performance at Drury Lane, rather than the Queen's Theatre, has obscured its distinctly Kit-Cat roots, but the reason Addison took it to the rival company was simple: a deal had been struck at the start of the season whereby the Queen's would perform only plays, while Drury Lane (and Dorset Garden) would perform only operas. Congreve, hearing of this deal, thought the 'houses are misapplied' – meaning that the monopolies should have been granted in reverse, to suit their acoustics.[18]

Rosamund opened on 4 March 1707. The omens must have looked good to its author, as he stepped past the shoeshine boy and the barber who camped, to serve theatregoers, in the doorway of Drury Lane's neighbouring Rose tavern. By the time Addison came out of the theatre, however, he knew his carefully calculated effort to establish an English style of opera (and to compliment his boss Sunderland's famous in-laws, the Marlboroughs) had failed dismally. *Rosamund* ran for only three nights – just long enough for Addison to receive his takings.

Thomas Clayton's inharmonious score ('a confused Chaos of

Music'[19]) was largely to blame, though the music had been previewed to a select audience and passed the 'Opinion of the Best Judges', for which read Kit-Cats.[20] Yet Addison took *Rosamund*'s failure to heart: it was the first major failure of his creative life, and seems to have piqued into definite antipathy his ambivalence about traditional Italian opera. Addison was soon complaining in a prologue to a friend's play that Italian opera, which was doing well with London audiences only a few years later, left one 'from the full fatigue of thinking free'. He objected that 'Our homespun authors must forsake the field / And Shakespeare to the soft Scarlatti [Alessandro Scarlatti, opera composer] yield.'[21]

Two months later, bottles of French wine posing as port were undoubtedly uncorked when the Kit-Cat gathered to celebrate the Treaty of Union as it came into force on Thursday, 1 May 1707. It was a day of national celebration for the new 'United Kingdom', the bells of St Paul's ringing out over London. Although the union had been as much a policy of self-interest as 'affection', the Kit-Cats retrospectively celebrated it as a visionary act on their part, just as they had retrospectively recast the Revolution of 1688 as 'Glorious' and high-principled. The ambivalent English feelings about union in 1707 have been compared to ambivalence surrounding German reunification in 1989, with even less populist pride since no restoration of a previous national entity was involved.[22] The Scots were even more sceptical – the immediate impact on them was a range of new taxes, the longer-term benefits of sharing a slice of England's global trade and colonial profits being not yet obvious. There was pride, however, in achieving the merger of two independent sovereign nations without bloodshed. The Whig leadership rejoiced in the solid fiscal and military national unit they had managed to create in the midst of a pan-European war against a much larger and more centralized enemy. Stepney sent congratulations from The Hague to his Kit-Cat friends in London.

This May Day of the new Britain's birth was also Addison's thirty-fifth birthday. It was also the day Steele officially assumed a prestigious new job as editor of the government mouthpiece, *The Gazette*. Steele owed this new post at least in part to Addison, since it had been in the gift of Addison's boss Sunderland. At the same time as Steele was given the editorial responsibility, Tonson's firm received the printing rights – a lucrative contract.

Steele's Kit-Cat membership had paid its first dividends the previous summer, in August 1706, when, through Halifax's influence, Steele was appointed to be a Gentleman-Waiter to Anne's husband George – a fly-on-the-wall place useful to the Junto's efforts to read the Queen's moods on a daily basis. More importantly for Steele, it was worth £100 a year (nearly £14,000 today) tax free, which he sorely needed, as two creditors had brought legal actions against him that year. When his Barbados heiress wife had died in December 1706, the short-term result was to worsen Steele's problems, as his debts were called in before he had cash in hand.

The post of gazetteer was previously a sinecure worth only some £60 a year and *The Gazette* was just a sheet reporting basic international news. With Steele's appointment, editing *The Gazette* became a nearly full-time job, the salary raised to £300 (almost £42,000), and the paper included more editorial analysis. The paper's content came to Steele through the two Secretaries of State, and Steele worked in Sunderland's Cockpit office, under Addison's daily supervision. Addison and his counterpart in the Northern Office, Thomas Hopkins (later to become a Kit-Cat too), received news from commanders and envoys, which they passed to Steele, who digested it for publication three times a week. Though Steele claimed he tried to keep *The Gazette* 'very innocent and very insipid',[23] the conduct of the war was becoming an increasingly partisan issue, requiring Steele to sift 'bloody News from Flanders'[24] through a pro-Junto, pro-war filter.

Addison and Steele not only worked as colleagues in the same government department, but also shared Addison's St James's lodgings that summer of 1707. In later essays, each man described the pleasure of waking early in central London, to the first rumble of hackney coach wheels and the sing-song cries of street vendors selling powdered brick, 'small-coal' or milk carried warm from the dairies just beyond St James's.[25] There were also criers selling Steele's *Gazette*, but Addison wryly suggested they could afford to sell it a little less energetically: 'Our News should indeed be Published in a very quick time, because it is a Commodity that will not keep cold. It should not however be cried with the same Precipitation as *Fire*.'[26]

August found each man in the middle of a courtship: Addison was visiting the Countess of Warwick and her son at Holland House, while Steele was falling head over heels in love with 29-year-old Mary Scurlock, a Welsh woman who had inherited money from her late father and was now living alone with her mother on Swallow Street, just off Piccadilly. It has been suggested Steele met Mary at his first wife's funeral in December 1706, though Steele's first surviving letter of courtship dates from 9 August 1707.

Dressing to impress Mary on 15 August, Steele would have 'shifted himself' into one of his finer outfits. This included his neckcloth or 'band', worn starched like a cleric's at this date, a hat from his haberdasher John Sly, and a topcoat that might have cost as much as £80. Steele always spent lavishly on his appearance, even when, as in 1707, he was indebted to several friends. He said it was 'a comfort to [be] well dressed in agreeable company.'[27] Steele therefore never 'rode out' without a black, full-bottomed, high-crowned, dress periwig of the most expensive kind, which he hoped made his face appear less stubby.[28] Such a periwig, made of hair shaved and sold by the poor, had to be kept fresh with frequent perfuming. Addison referred to the 'Caul of a Wig, which is soiled with frequent Perspirations'[29] – especially, one imagines, when a squat, olive-skinned Irishman, with 'a shape like the picture of somebody over a farmer's chimney' and no private fortune, was presenting himself as a suitor.[30] On the way to Swallow Street, Steele likely stopped to be shaved at his barber, where he ran up annual bills as high as £50.

By contrast, Steele would have preferred if the object of his affections spent little on fashion and cosmetics, finding true beauty, he claimed, in the animation of a face and the embellishments of mind, manners and virtue. By Steele's account, Mary was naturally handsome, her inheritance being the only further adornment she needed. Despite her advanced age of 29, therefore, Steele was not Mary's only suitor that summer.

Flattering Mary's dislike of flattery, Steele wrote: 'I shall affect plainness and sincerity in my discourse to you, as much as other lovers do perplexity and rapture. Instead of saying I shall die for you, I profess I should be glad to lead my life with you.'[31]

Yet when Steele first called on Mary, and she was too busy to see him, he scribbled a fairly 'rapturous' love note while standing under the amused eyes of her servants in her hallway, saying he would return the following morning. The next day, he was admitted to sit with her, and the meeting must have gone well, as the following day Mary quickly wrote to her absent mother, asking permission to marry him. Mary argued the writer's intellect made up for his lack of estate and title, and said she intended not to have any 'public doings' but to marry privately, as was then common.[32]

Mary may not have told Steele her mind was so quickly made up, since she received numerous billets-doux from him throughout August 1707. In some cases, Steele wrote them in the office, while working on *The Gazette*, complaining his daydreams distracted him from his business. There is a sincerity to these little letters that suggests Steele was erotically and romantically excited at the prospect of this second marriage: 'The Day hangs heavily upon me and the whole business of it is an impertinent Guilty Dream in comparison [to] the happiness of a few moments of real Life at your House',[33] or, 'I Lay down last night with your Image in my thoughts and have awaked this morning in the same contemplation.'[34] Most tellingly, for an ambitious young writer and Kit-Cat: 'All books are blank paper, and my Friends intruders.'[35]

Mary's side of the correspondence is almost entirely lost, and at the start there may not have been much of it, with Steele making the running. He called upon Mary regularly, at a set hour. On 30 August, Steele explained: 'I am forced to write from a Coffee house where I am attending about business. There is a dirty Crowd of Busy faces all around me talking of politics and managing stocks, while all my Ambition, all my wealth is Love!'[36] The next afternoon, after church, was again spent hanging around the St James's Coffee House, where Steele laughed at how he was distracted by desire: 'A Gentleman asked Me this Morning what news from Lisbon, and I answered, *She's Exquisitely handsome*.'[37] If such flattery was even partly true, it

Jacob Tonson, publisher, bookseller, and founding father of the Club, shown holding Milton's *Paradise Lost*, which Tonson and other Kit-Cats helped place in the English literary canon.

Lord Dorset *(top left)*, another Club founder, and Kit-Cat portraits of the three men known, when young, as 'Lord Dorset's Boys': George Stepney *(top right)*, Charles Montagu *(bottom left)* and Matthew Prior.

Sir John Vanbrugh *(top left)* and William Congreve became celebrated playwrights, but started as 'distressed poets' in garrets *(top right)*, needing Kit-Cat patronage. Congreve looks radiant in his Kit-Cat portrait of 1709 *(bottom left)*, while a later portrait shows him reading a Vanbrugh play, surrounded by emblems of time, lost sight and aging *(bottom right)*.

Kit-Cat Toasts: Henrietta Godolphin *(left)*, Congreve's lover and wife of his fellow Club member, and Lady Mary Wortley Montagu *(below)*, before she was disfigured by smallpox, were among dozens of 'beauties' toasted by the all-male Club.

LEFT: The Kit-Cats were well-known figures to the Victorians, who re-imagined these two scenes: *(top)* Alexander Pope as a boy, brought into Dryden's 'Witty Club' at Will's Coffee House, meeting his early Kit-Cat patrons; and *(bottom)* Lady Mary Wortley Montagu, when seven, being introduced to the Kit-Cat wits.

Joseph Addison *(above)* and Richard Steele *(right)*, pioneers of modern journalism, were boyhood friends who joined the Club in 1704 and 1705, respectively. These Kit-Cat portraits reveal their contrasting, complementary characters.

Club Chaos and Order: The reality of Kit-Cat meetings lay between the comic disorder of Hogarth's famous 'Midnight Modern Conversation' *(above)* and the teetotalling politeness shown in the painting 'A Meeting of the Society for the Reformation of Manners' *(below)*. The Victorians mislabelled the latter as depicting the Kit-Cat Club.

'Those who could walk did, the others fell': Gentlemen leaving the drunken pleasures of a club meeting in the early morning hours. Though this painting is Dutch, clubs were perceived as a distinctively British enthusiasm in the early eighteenth century.

was a serious disability for the editor of *The Gazette*. '[A]ll that speak to me find me out, and I must lock myself up, or other People will do it for me.'[38]

On 3 September 1707, Steele laid out his financial situation in a letter to Mary's mother, stating he was comfortably off thanks to his first wife's legacy, with an annual income after deductions of £1,025 (over £133,000 today). More importantly, Steele said his 'Friends are in great power', meaning he and a future wife would have to keep up certain appearances 'that I may prosecute my Expectations in a busy Way while the Wind is for Me, with a Just consideration that, about a Court, it will not always blow one Way'.[39]

Steele seems to have persuaded Mary to marry him without awaiting her mother's approval, as the wedding is registered at the church of St Mary Somerset on Old Fish Street Hill, on 9 September 1707. The weekend before, Steele sat imagining, in a daydream full of erotic charge, how Mary's lips would move to shape the words of her wedding vows.

Steele's friends seem to have known nothing of the marriage at first. Even Vanbrugh, with whom Steele worked at the Queen's Theatre, wrote that same day to Lord Manchester without mentioning Steele's nuptials – a type of gossip Vanbrugh was normally quick to pass on. Because of this secrecy, Steele's wedding day did not go well. The new Mrs Steele insisted on returning to her mother's house that evening to maintain appearances, even though her sickly mother was still out of town and Steele had Addison's lodgings to himself that night. The frustrated groom exploded in anger, before returning alone to his rooms. Almost immediately afterwards, Steele sent a repentant letter, trying to erase the frightening impression his sudden 'ill-nature' must have made. A few stanzas of poetry in Mary's hand suggest she was filled with sudden doubts, now they were married, about the sincerity of her husband's previous abject declarations.

Mr and Mrs Steele had not yet started living together in early October 1707, as they awaited the return to London of Mary's mother, so that they could receive her formal blessing. Steele wrote to his mother-in-law, therefore, with heartfelt impatience for her swift recovery and return. In the meantime, he continued to lodge with

Addison, while Mary remained up the hill on Swallow Street. The situation wore on Steele's nerves, and he seems to have dealt with it by staying late at the office as often as possible. For weeks, Steele sent notes to Mary apologizing for being unable to join her for their main meal in the middle of the day, around 3 p.m., because of a heavy workload.[40] One night at 8 p.m., he wrote from the Fountain tavern, possibly from a Kit-Cat meeting: 'I beg of You not to be uneasy, for I have done a great deal of business today very Successfully, and wait an hour or two about my *Gazette*.'[41]

Steele's *Gazette* was reporting in October 1707 that the first Parliament of 'one united kingdom by the name of Great Britain',[42] including its 'new Brethren' from Scotland,[43] unanimously re-elected Kitling Jack Smith as its Speaker. By the end of the month, Steele had rented a house on Bury Street, around the corner from St James's Square, then a large open square empty of trees or fences. He planned to live there with his wife and mother-in-law, and promised Mary he would work with extra determination to ensure his new family was well provided for. Finally, in November, he moved his belongings out of Addison's lodgings and into Bury Street. Steele's mother-in-law had obviously returned and accepted her daughter's fait accompli.

According to family legend, a fourth person was brought into the Steele household soon after: his illegitimate daughter by Tonson's niece, now aged 9 or 10. It was said that Steele asked his new wife to accompany him on a visit he was making one afternoon without telling her where they were going, and drove her to a 'boarding-school in the environs of London'.[44] There he presented a young lady 'to whom Steele showed the greatest fondness, insomuch that his wife asked him if the child was his. On his acknowledging that she was: "Then," said the Lady, "I beg she may be mine too."'[45]

The girl's real mother, Elizabeth Tonson, after whom she was named, did not die until 1726. How Elizabeth felt about her daughter's adoption by Steele's new wife is not mentioned. There is a distinct lack of reference to Elizabeth in the Steeles' personal correspondence during the following years, leading some scholars to conclude that, if she was taken out of the boarding school or orphanage where she was reared, she was more likely taken to live with her mother's family, the Tonsons. Certainly Tonson and the girl's uncle, Jacob Junior, not Steele, arranged Elizabeth's marriage to a glove manufacturer from Herefordshire in 1720. Steele eventually left Elizabeth a legacy, however, so the oral tradition about Mary accepting the girl into her home is not wholly implausible.

During this honeymoon period, Mary must have been eager to please her new husband, and believed his reassurances about his bright career prospects as he set her up in such style amid the nobility of St James's. On 4 November 1707, a few days after moving into their barely furnished house and a week after the Kit-Cats 'distinguished themselves Extraordinarily' at a Club meeting to celebrate King William's birthday,[46] Mary celebrated her own birthday. Steele, though only 35, was suffering from gout but struggled downstairs on crutches to join her, together with a few close friends, in the parlour. There he sat, probably wearing the tasselled silk turban he often wore instead of his periwig when at home, watching his Welsh bride dance for him, swirling gaily around the room. Beneath the music, a few notes of discord – about money, sex and her family – must already have been sounding, but for now the birthday music drowned them out. The following day, King William's landing in 1688 was celebrated as usual with a Kit-Cat Club feast and by Whigs in taverns and pulpits across the country, all eager to see the current influence of the few Whigs favoured by Marlborough extend to the benefit – and profit – of an even wider circle.

XII
BESET

> For the man who keeps his eye on a true friend, keeps it, so to speak, on a model of himself.
>
> CICERO, *Laelius, de Amicitia*, 80

THE KIT-CATS' self-congratulation, following the Treaty of Union and the appointment to high office of their Whig ally Lord Sunderland, was short-lived. The unexpected loss of another much-loved founder member in the early autumn of 1707 was the first news suddenly to sober their collective mood.

At the beginning of 1707, George Stepney had travelled to Hesse-Cassel to negotiate a treaty on behalf of the Grand Alliance with Prince Charles of Hesse, an old diplomatic contact. The treaty sought to keep Hessian troops fighting against the French in Italy, despite lacking Allied funds to pay for them. It was a tricky negotiation, and Stepney failed to secure the terms his government wanted. During this time of strain, the Envoy's health deteriorated. Stepney had always thought of himself as having a solid constitution, but now, aged 44, he was diagnosed with an ulcer that may, in fact, have been cancer.

Stepney wrote to Lord Lexinton, Envoy Extraordinary to the Imperial Court in Vienna, hoping that he could retire soon: 'One successful Campaign more will, I believe, be attended by a happy, hon[ora]ble & lasting Peace – when I hope to set up my Rest upon some pleasing seat upon the Thames.'[1] This intention to serve until the end of the war was not fulfilled. Stepney collapsed and was forced to return to London at the end of August 1707. Thanks to Marlborough's personal intervention, a yacht was procured to sail the patient home as quickly as possible. In a letter of thanks, Stepney further asked Marlborough whether he would take Stepney's secretary under his 'Favour and Protection'.[2]

After returning to England, Stepney, who had never been able to buy property of his own, spent a fortnight at a friend's house on Paradise Row in Chelsea. The house was likely that of the elderly Kit-Cat Lord Carbery, with its gardens rolling down to the banks of the Thames. In some such tranquil setting, the 'pleasing seat' he had hoped for, Stepney died on 15 September 1707.

Addison was by Stepney's side at the end. The two men had corresponded frequently (and, rarely for Addison, as equals) during the ten months Stepney served as Envoy in The Hague. When Stepney received the appointment in September 1706, Addison had written with obvious personal warmth:

> I beg leave to congratulate you upon your removal to a province that requires all those great abilities for which you are so deservedly celebrated . . . I have often had an opportunity of mentioning my obligations to you, and the great respect I shall always have for so extraordinary a character.[3]

Stepney had taught Addison how to treat government service as a profession rather than a hobby, yet simultaneously to maintain a self-image as a man of letters. Much affected by his friend's sudden death, Addison therefore reported the news to Manchester: 'I need not tell you how much he is lamented by everybody.'[4]

Stepney's will asked for him to be buried in Westminster Abbey, this 'being the place of my Education', and for Halifax and Prior to be tasked with enumerating the achievements of his life and diplomatic career at the funeral, since Stepney knew they would do it 'with plainness and truth'. Halifax was left a golden drinking cup, and instructed to select from Stepney's private library 'a hundred Tomes, if there be any which may deserve to have place in his Library'. As for Prior, Stepney only provided that he should be forgiven fifty guineas of debt,[5] but behind this provision lay a larger message of forgiveness for the Lord Dorset's Boy who had betrayed his friends. Stepney's will also ordered his private letters be destroyed, which, on the whole, they were.

Stepney's Kit-Cat friends probably bore the expense of his Abbey funeral a week later, on the night of 22 September, much as they had borne that of Dryden. The pallbearers consisted of two dukes, two earls and two barons – a remarkable tribute to the son of a minor courtier, and further evidence of the Kit-Cat Club's power to level social classes. A Latin epitaph, transcribed by Tonson, was engraved on Stepney's tomb, listing Stepney's intimacy with 'men of the highest position' as an achievement in its own right.

Stepney was hardly cold in the ground when an unseemly scramble started among several Kit-Cats to obtain his post in The Hague and place on the Board of Trade. The candidates included Stanyan, Stanhope, Lord Berkeley and William Walsh. The most tactless application came from Prior, who wrote to Halifax about the post while their friend still lay mortally ill in Chelsea. Such behaviour could only be explained by Prior's now desperate financial situation. Prior apologized to Halifax for remaining the latter's debtor 'as to Pecuniary Matters', and protested that, though it was 'too late to recapitulate the differences that have happened between us, or to dispute the reasons', his 'respects to yourself and your family are inviolable'.[6] No reply from Halifax survives.

Superficially the Junto was, as Steele put it, back 'in great power' at this time, but underlying tensions were starting to fester between Club friends. The first tension was political. Wharton and Halifax were losing patience with the fact that their mounting influence had not yet returned them to high office. While staunchly supporting the war effort, they recognized the paradox that the worse the war went, the more dependent Godolphin's ministry became upon them. When it came to the crunch, the General and Treasurer were dependent upon Whig Junto votes in the Commons to pass Bills of army supply. When, for example, the loss of some British ships and the failure of Britain's Allies to fulfil their pledges of troops and supplies led the Tories to propose Britain transfer its forces from Flanders to Spain, where they could focus on protecting sea trade routes to Italy and the Levant, Marlborough and Godolphin had to look to Somers and the Whigs to block this unwelcome initiative. The debate, with Somers saving the day for the ministry, was a clear instance of how Tory attacks increased the Junto's power. In December 1707, a non-Junto Whig loyal to Godolphin told a friend: '[T]he Kit-Cat & Junto, have changed their principles so often upon the score of dominion that I doubt not your Lordship will see . . . how little a free nation ought to rely upon them.'[7]

Other Kit-Cats, however, disapproved of the Junto's tactic of capitalizing on this paradox – particularly several moderates (Somerset, Smith, Walpole, Compton and Harry Boyle) who started to identify themselves as the 'Treasurer's Whigs' because they were willing to form alliances with the Tories in support of Godolphin's ministry and the war, thereby loosening the Junto's parliamentary grip. Walpole, in particular, spoke out against Halifax's and Somers' attempts to pry the Queen's husband from the head of the Admiralty. This internal party division, between the Junto Whigs and Treasurer's Whigs, put a freeze on Kit-Cat meetings for much of the winter, Congreve remarking that he only saw Addison 'once by accident' in January 1708.[8]

The Whigs were united, however, against Robert Harley, who had been carrying on a backstairs intrigue throughout 1707 to convince Anne he could offer a coalition government independent of the Junto Whigs. In February 1708, Marlborough and Godolphin, spurred on by the Junto lords and Marlborough's wife Sarah, told Anne that either they or the intriguing Mr Harley, then Secretary of State for the North, would have to go. At first the Queen resisted, but Addison was soon telling Manchester 'a Secret here at present: that the Queen has just now demanded the seals of [Harley]'.[9] The audacity of having forced Anne to demand a resignation, against her will, made the development one to be relayed in an excited whisper across half a continent. Four days later, Harley resigned, and Wharton moved that Harley's personal secretary be tried as a Jacobite.

Tories and supporters of Harley resigned in solidarity, and were replaced by Whigs.[10] Though each of the promoted men was a Kit-Cat, they were all from among the Treasurer's Whigs, making this faction even more pivotal. Wharton complained that Jack Smith, whose opinion 'no man valued', was being consulted on appointees, rather than the 'whole body of the Whigs' – meaning Wharton and his friends.[11] The Junto, on the other hand, saw it would be wise to work alongside their fellow Kit-Cats who were now in the Cabinet. 'This Revolution,' Addison observed, 'has already had the good Effect to Unite all old friends that were falling off from one another.'[12]

Meanwhile a heated debate about the battle of Almanza, a disastrous defeat suffered by the Allies in Spain, was underway in the House of Lords. Appointed Envoy Extraordinary to the Spanish Court of Carlos III (formerly Archduke Charles of Austria) in 1706, Stanhope had directed the Spanish campaign in tandem with his Commander-in-Chief, Lord Peterborough, for the past year. When an offensive strategy, recommended solely by Stanhope, led to the defeat at Almanza in April 1707, Peterborough and the anti-war Tories held Stanhope personally responsible for the terrible loss of life and territory.

Kit-Cat Major-General Shrimpton was one of those humiliated at Almanza, and relatives of Kit-Cat members were among the thousands killed. It was a defeat as disastrous as Marlborough's victories in Germany had been miraculous, and Stanhope was forced to defend his actions in the Commons that winter. With Marlborough's and the Junto's help, however, Stanhope was cleared of all charges, and even promoted to assume Peterborough's command in the next Iberian campaign of spring 1708. Addison described the Almanza debate, coming before another general election, as one that 'fixed all men in their proper parties and thoroughly established the present [Whig-dependent] Ministry'.[13]

On the subject of the war, there was now little distinction between

Whig and Court propaganda. In spring 1708, the Kit-Cat authors seem to have collectively answered a call from their Junto patrons to turn their hands to pre-election campaign literature. Halifax and Somers commissioned Addison to produce a pamphlet, *The Present State of the War* (1708), arguing for continued engagement until the separation of France and Spain was guaranteed. In it, Addison acknowledged that the War of Spanish Succession was primarily about trade rather than religion, but labelled as unpatriotic anyone seeking peace under current conditions. A war that began with cross-party support was fast becoming a Whig enterprise, just as the ministry, which had begun as moderately Tory, would soon be propped up almost entirely by Junto-managed votes.

Tonson printed and widely distributed another anonymous pamphlet, *Advice to the Electors of Great Britain* (1708), which argued that, since certain Tories were suspected of plotting with France to restore The Pretender, all who cared about defending a Protestant Crown should vote Whig. A High Church Tory reported that the pamphlet was written by 'Lord S[ome]rs or some eminent member of the Kit-Cat' and 'for the style, the character and the lies there is in it, seems worthy of the mind of Jacob T[onso]n'.[14] It was, in fact, written primarily by Arthur Maynwaring.

Electoral propaganda in the event proved superfluous, as the Whigs received the pre-election gift of an unsuccessful invasion attempt by James II's son and his French allies. Addison and his boss Sunderland were among the first to receive reports of the invasion forces gathering at Dunkirk. Heavy mists in the North Sea provided cover for the enemy ships when they set sail on 6 March 1708. The French were testing whether the Scottish back door remained ajar; Addison characterized the invasion as 'the last Effort of the party that opposed the uniting of the two Nations'.[15] By this he meant the Jacobites, feared and vilified as the terrorist cells of their day.

Britain was put into a state of emergency. Addison, despite failing eyesight and temporary lameness, worked day and night to mobilize the nation's defences. Internal freedom of movement was suspended, with Englishmen requiring permits to travel north. When Sir George Byng prevented the French landing and captured one

Jacobite ship, Addison was the man at Westminster to receive this welcome report. By 23 March, the Jacobite Duke of Hamilton was in custody. A month later, some fifty Jacobite prisoners were sent to the Tower of London to stand trial.

The immediate effect of the abortive invasion was to strengthen the Whig hand. On 9 March, the Queen reshuffled her Cabinet, and there was talk that Wharton and Somers would soon finally receive high office. The second major effect was a swing in favour of the Whigs in May's election, where they won their first Commons majority of Anne's reign – a notable exception to consistent Tory election victories throughout the 1690s and 1700s.

Sunderland had recommended Addison as a parliamentary candidate for Lostwithiel, in Cornwall, a traditionally Tory seat that Addison won in May 1708 despite his total lack of personal connections there. Addison took his seat when the House reassembled in the autumn, alongside the Duke of Somerset's son – the young man he had unsuccessfully applied to tutor not so many years earlier. There was a fly in the ointment, however: the Tories claimed the Lostwithiel electoral rolls had been rigged – not difficult when the franchise only extended to some twenty-four men. As a result of these allegations, the result was 'set aside' in December 1708, and Wharton had to come to the rescue by handing Addison another pocket borough, that of Malmesbury. For several years, Addison served that constituency alongside Thomas Farrington, another possible Kit-Cat returned thanks to Wharton.

Wharton spent up to £80,000 (over £8.6 million today) on campaigns across the country in 1708, proving responsible for the return of over a dozen MPs. As his annual income was only £16,000, this expenditure was enough to bring bailiffs to the door of Wharton's Dover Street mansion. Abel Boyer eulogized Wharton as a man of unshakeable Whig convictions ('the most active, most strenuous, and most indefatigable Asserter of Liberty'[16]), and Steele remarked upon Wharton's fidelity to those he supported: '[H]e helped more of his Friends to places than any one of the Ministers themselves; his Lordship being the best Friend and the best Solicitor in the World when he was pleased to Honour a Man with his Protection.'[17]

Wharton had a way with the man in the street, described as demagogic or democratic depending on whether one was his enemy or ally. One anecdote recorded by Steele described Wharton during elections in the Buckinghamshire borough of Wycombe: two Tory candidates spied him going into the local shoemaker's shop and asking where Dick was, at which the woman in the shop said her husband was out but 'his Lordship need not fear him, she would keep him tight [to vote Whig]'. 'I know that,' Wharton said, 'but I want to see Dick and drink a Glass with him.' Wharton then asked the woman, 'How does all thy Children? Molly is a brave Girl I warrant by this time . . . Is not Jemmy breeched [in breeches] yet?' At which, Steele said, the two eavesdropping Tories jumped on their horses and fled the election, since any peer who knew the names and ages of a local shoemaker's children must be unbeatable. Steele, of course, brought Whig bias to this story, but it is telling that Wharton's common touch was highlighted with such pride.[18]

Vanbrugh and Congreve never stooped to pre-election pamphleteering or sought seats in Parliament, leaving such work to the newer Kit-Cat members, like Addison and Steele. Congreve remained consumed by his affair with Henrietta: 'If I have not ambition, I have other passions more easily gratified,' he confessed.[19] The management of the Queen's Theatre, meanwhile, was again consuming Vanbrugh. Its company had swapped monopolies with Drury Lane in December 1707 and was now producing only operas – an arrangement 'to the general liking of the whole Town'.[20] Vanbrugh, who had temporarily sold the theatre's management, now bought back his shares.

At first Vanbrugh counted on Kit-Cats and other wealthy Whigs to subscribe for the costs of bringing over Italian opera singers, but the Kit-Cats appear to have let him down. Vanbrugh was therefore forced to apply to the Queen for a subsidy. He hinted to Manchester (currently on his second stint as Envoy in Venice, with Stanyan as his secretary) that this royal grant was as good as promised, so if 'Nicolini' and 'Santini' would come to England, they could divide as much as £1,000 (over £116,000 today) between them. 'Nicolini' was a famous castrato, Nicolo Grimaldi, who later arrived in London and demanded crippling fees every season, which Vanbrugh failed to persuade the Queen to pay. Receipts from performances remained so low that Vanbrugh was forced to sink his own money into the theatre to keep it solvent, 'and this Distresses me to the last Degree'.[21]

Part of the problem was that Vanbrugh was competing against private musical performances at the houses of certain Kit-Cat lords, free from overheads. Addison referred, for example, to an opera 'played several times' at Halifax's house, its score sent from Venice by Lord Manchester.[22] The other problem, according to Vanbrugh, was that gallery audiences of the 'middling sort' were not buying tickets in sufficient numbers, even after he reduced ticket prices in February 1708. The Collierite campaigners were continuing to hurt the theatre's audience figures, and a manuscript account book from April 1708 shows Vanbrugh taking a loss of £1,146 (or some £133,000 today) on every performance. Before the season ended, in May 1708, he was forced to resell his shares in the theatre company,[23] thereafter collecting only rent on the building. 'I lost so Much Money by the Opera this Last Winter that I was glad to get quit of it,' Vanbrugh admitted. '[Y]et I don't doubt but Operas will Settle and thrive in London.'[24] He would never again entirely recover his financial stability.

The Kit-Cat Club had not ceased its patronage of the Queen's Theatre when that theatre had abandoned operas. A Kit-Cat document had been produced early in the previous year's season 'all in Lord Halifax's handwriting' for 'a subscription of four hundred guineas for the encouragement of good comedies'.[25] This seems to have evolved into a Club scheme, 'for Reviving Three Plays of the best Authors, with the full Strength of the Company; every Subscriber to have Three Tickets for the first Day of each Play, for his single Payment of Three Guineas'.[26]

These three plays – Shakespeare's *Julius Caesar*, Beaumont and Fletcher's *The King and No King*, and a composite play made of Dryden's *Marriage à la Mode* and *Maiden Queen* – were performed in January and February 1707, and proved highly popular with audiences. Garth and Steele did their bit by launching *The Muses Mercury*, an innovative monthly arts newspaper, reporting on theatre and opera, in January 1707. Its editorial assumption was that if there was a shortage of new writing in England, this was simply due to a scarcity of patronage, '[f]or we have no Reason to doubt but there are Geniuses now living'.[27] Once again the Kit-Cat manifesto about native art was at work: with the revival of the three comedies, the Club hoped to kick-start England's literary future by celebrating its past.

Bracey, now in her mid-thirties, performed as Portia in this 1707 production of *Julius Caesar*. Audiences that season, however, made plain their preference for a younger actress: a girl named Ann ('Nancy') Oldfield. Nancy had been Maynwaring's mistress for several years, and was living with him openly by 1707. One critic described her as acting 'very well in comedy but best of all, I suppose, in bed. She twines her body and leers with eyes most bewitchingly.'[28] Bracey, eclipsed by Nancy's sex appeal, decided to make it her last season. The Kit-Cats heard of Bracey's retirement and were about to raise a toast to her when Halifax proposed that they pledge something more substantial: a gift of 200 guineas. The others added to this until there were 800 guineas (some £156,000 today) on the table. It was a larger lump sum than the Kit-Cat Club had ever given to any of its male authors, Congreve included.

Just as Vanbrugh asked Manchester to import Italian opera singers in 1708, so Manchester brought over the Italian painter Pellegrini to work on Castle Howard's interior in August 1708. There is no clearer example of how the Kit-Cats applied the same principles of importing and adapting European talent across the different arts. Vanbrugh's search for an English architecture, mixing old castellar forms with neoclassical geometry, was most apparent at this time in the rebuilding of Manchester's country seat of Kimbolton Castle, near Cambridge. Vanbrugh told Manchester he planned to give the house 'Something of the Castle Air, though at the Same time to make it regular'.[29] Just as English opera was imagined as something that would take an emasculated Continental model and defeminize it, so Vanbrugh said he aimed to create a 'very Noble and masculine Show' at Kimbolton.[30]

Racing by calash between London, Kimbolton and Woodstock, Vanbrugh would nonetheless have made an effort to attend the Kit-Cat Club when Tonson reconvened it in the summer of 1708. The venue was probably Barn Elms, where it was 'a most miserable Year for fruit'.[31] In June 1708, a Tory observer relayed the following gossip to the Club's now avowed enemy, Robert Harley:

> The last Kit-Cat has afforded much diversion. Jacob Tonson, in his cups, sitting between Dormer and Walpole, told them he sat between the honestest man in the world and the greatest villain; and explained himself that by the honest man he meant Dormer, the other was a villain forsaking his patrons and benefactors the Junto, for which poor Jacob was severely bastinadoed.[32]

To be 'bastinadoed' means to be beaten with a stick on the soles of one's feet, and Tonson's verbal beating was because he had drawn unnecessary attention to the rift between the Junto Whigs and Treasurer's Whigs at a time when, after the election victory, the Club was trying to forgive and forget. Dormer had remained a loyal Junto follower, while Walpole was a Treasurer's Whig, challenging the party whip of Halifax, Somers and Wharton. In the reshuffle after Harley's fall, Walpole's appointment as Secretary-at-War was reward for what some (including Tonson) saw as his leadership of the 'traitors'. To outsiders, these divisions were overshadowed by Whig monopolization of every branch of government and culture.

Stepney's death was followed by two other unexpected Kit-Cat deaths in 1707–8 (of William Walsh and Major-General Shrimpton) leaving seats at the Kit-Cat table vacant. Thomas Hopkins was therefore elected into the Club sometime in early June 1708. One spy on the Club reported:

> Jacob, who always hated him [Hopkins], bantered him by telling him his election was a banter, for the company then there was but a committee and that all elections were to be in a full meeting. Upon this, the new elect made a speech and told them he hoped his election would be confirmed by the whole society, for which calling [in]to question the power of that company then present, he was turned out of doors.[33]

Tom Hopkins' qualifications for admission were numerous. He now worked as the other Under-Secretary to Sunderland alongside Addison at Whitehall, and together the two helped keep the peace between their Junto-aligned boss and the Godolphin–Marlborough duumvirate. Hopkins was a perfect, neutral candidate for the Kit-Cat after the recent rifts among its members. He also had literary credentials and valuable family links to City financiers.

In July 1708, Addison, who was then living at Sandy End, a hamlet between Chelsea and Fulham not far from Barn Elms, wrote to a friend enclosing 'a Ballad fresh from the Kit'.[34] This may have been 'Jack Frenchman's Defeat' by Congreve, or the 'Toast to Mademoiselle Oudenarde', both celebrating Marlborough's recent victory at the battle of Oudenarde on 11 July. The latter has been attributed to Maynwaring, but was more likely a joint composition, with different Kit-Cats tagging on verses to 'smoke' one another. Subtitled a 'Dialogue in verse between Tonson, [Tom] Hopkins, [Richard] Topham and Lord Halifax', this ballad is an important Kit-Cat artefact, identifying Richard Topham as a Club member – possibly another new member, besides Hopkins, admitted that summer to fill Shrimpton's, Stepney's and Walsh's spaces.[35] The ballad refers to the Kit-Cat as a club 'at Service so hard' for the Whig cause, but quickly descends into a bantering competition, in which the members rib each other for their literary ignorance, lowly births and need for alcohol to fuel wit.

Aside from the fictional 'Mademoiselle Oudenarde', at least fourteen real ladies were toasted at a meeting that summer, most with some Marlborough connection. Each was awarded a flattering title. Francis Godolphin's wife and Congreve's mistress, Henrietta, was hailed 'The Desirable', Henrietta's sister and Sunderland's wife Anne 'The Miracle', while the Duke of Richmond's daughter Lady Louisa Lenox was 'The Bloom'. Dunch's wife, Marlborough's niece, who had an infamous gambling habit, came off less well as 'The Careless'.[36] The list tells us more about the political constellations of 1708 than about which women the various members admired. The Duke of Grafton's pursuit of Mrs Knight, a woman worth £70,000 (over £7.5 million today), for example, was a business matter, not material for a toast. Similarly, Addison would not have wanted to put on record his ambitious interest in the Countess of Warwick. Some ingratiating letters sent by Addison in late May to her 11-year-old son survive: offering to hunt for birds'-nests or inviting the Earl to hear the morning birdsong in a neighbouring wood, mixing these suggestions with quotes from Virgil or Cicero. For all their kindness, there is something unattractive in Addison's courting the mother via the child.

One existing member would have attended these summer meetings in a new guise. Lord Hartington, a Kit-Cat since at least 1702, inherited the title of Duke of Devonshire following the August 1707 death of his father, one of the Glorious Revolution's 'immortal seven' who invited William to invade. The dying 1st Duke also left his balding, 34-year-old son the properties of Chatsworth and Devonshire House in Piccadilly. The 2nd Duke, whom the Queen continued to favour for his father's sake, now became her Lord Steward and was sworn into her Privy Council in September 1707. The young man's title was a significant new ornament for the Kit-Cat Club, as discussed in a gossipy letter from Vanbrugh to Manchester. While Devonshire's father had been a generous patron of the arts at Chatsworth, the son's contribution was as collector of medals, prints and an impressive library.

Steele would have attended the Kit-Cat meetings that summer, pursuing patronage from the Junto, particularly Halifax, before his Barbados inheritance came through. Years later, Steele listed as a fault: 'Neglect of Promises made on small and indifferent Occasions, such as Parties of Pleasure.'[37] Though Steele admitted being guilty of this vice, he was probably remembering occasions when great men had promised, in their cups, to do him favours that never materialized. By the summer of 1708, still waiting to rise above the post of gazetteer, conscious of promises to his wife and mother-in-law and of debts incurred for their sakes, Steele badly needed a helping hand from his fellow Kit-Cats. Later he would reflect on his lifelong cap-in-hand relationship with these patrons: 'There is indeed something so shameless in taking all Opportunities to speak of your own Affairs, that he who is guilty of it . . . fares like the Beggar who exposes his Sores, which instead of moving Compassion, makes the Man he begs of turn away from the Object.'[38]

Since at least February 1708, Steele had been forcing his wife Mary, whom he called by the pet name 'Prue' (referring to her prudent but also prudish character), to deal with his creditors.[39] The couple spent a great amount on keeping up appearances over the spring of 1708: Steele often wrote home asking his wife to drop by the office in the afternoon, warning her to be well dressed and charming when introduced to anyone who could help his career. Part of keeping up appearances that summer involved the Steeles buying a second home in the village of Hampton Wick, near Hampton Court and not far from Tonson at Barn Elms and Addison at Sandy End. Steele referred to it self-deprecatingly as 'The Hovel', in contrast to Halifax's neighbouring residence of Bushy House.[40] In September 1708, Steele stayed at Addison's house on more than one night and was taken to visit Addison's sister Dorothy. Yet Steele's borrowing from Addison before receiving his conjugal inheritance must have strained their friendship, both men having been raised on the Roman motto that self-sufficiency was a precondition for true friendship – a view Steele echoed when he famously declared that 'Equality is the life of Conversation'.[41]

Dr Johnson recounted how, when a friend embarrassed by a debt started to agree with everything Addison said, Addison snapped: 'Sir, either contradict me, or pay me my money.'[42] While this obsequious debtor was not necessarily Steele, it gives a sense of how such financial imbalance would have exacerbated the men's already lopsided friendship. Addison, whose father had taught him to regard the proper use of money as a matter of moral rectitude, once remarked, 'When I hear a Man complain of his being unfortunate in all his Undertakings, I shrewdly suspect him for a very weak Man in his Affairs.'[43] Steele, on the other hand, was allergic to being beholden to anyone, even his most admired friend, and said the ideal benefactor was a man who gave assistance 'with the mien of a receiver'.[44] One suspects that Addison, for all his vaunted modesty, was not quite as devoid of condescension as that.

Steele's wife, who wished her husband was more like Addison, her 'Favourite' among Steele's friends,[45] continued her barrage of complaints about their straitened circumstances. Finally, in August 1708, Steele said he would not have his business governed by his wife's orders, no matter how much he loved her, and returned her letter so that 'upon second thoughts, you may see the disrespectful manner in which you Treat Your Affectionate Faithful Husband'.[46] When £9,300 of the first Mrs Steele's money finally came through, Steele repaid almost all his debts, and hired a footman, but this reprieve from debt was brief. In October 1708, Steele refused to deliver a note from his wife to his mother-in-law because he suspected it contained complaints of his 'unkindness', which he denied: 'If you want for anything it is that you will not supply yourself with it, for I very regularly send you wherewithal.'[47]

October 1708 brought a fresh disappointment to the Steeles. Queen Anne's husband Prince George sickened with asthma and died, despite the best attentions of Dr Garth and the royal physicians. Steele therefore lost his Court place as a Gentleman Usher to the Prince. When the seriousness of the Prince's illness had first become apparent, Steele had pursued another £300-a-year place as Gentleman Usher of the Privy Chamber by drinking all night with the Kit-Cat patrons until he was hung over the next day. Steele described himself as 'busy about the main Chance',[48] but nothing seems to have come of his networking.

While Steele stood on duty guarding Prince George's corpse on 28 October 1708, a bailiff (or 'bum') was standing stolidly outside the Steeles' front door on Bury Street, sent to collect the rent. Prue, pregnant with their first baby, had to face this harassment alone. Steele shortly after brought her to stay in Kensington with a friend, while his creditors sued him. The following month Steele borrowed cash from a tradesman, 'for I find Friendship among the Lowest when disappointed by the Highest'.[49]

On balance, the Queen's bereavement ended up profiting the Kit-Cat Club, sapping her energy to resist the Junto's political pressure. She promoted their members, friends and relations in the months that followed. Somers became Lord President of the Privy Council and Wharton was appointed Lord Lieutenant of Ireland. Wharton picked Addison to go with him to Dublin as his right-hand man. Jonathan Swift, looking on, described it as a 'new world'.[50]

The Junto credited the Duchess of Marlborough with having helped convince her husband, and thereby Godolphin and the Queen, to make these Whig appointments, especially Somers', which

Vanbrugh had thought hopeless as recently as July 1708. As a result, another poem 'to the tune of a French ditty' was added to the Kit-Cat repertoire in November, in which Hopkins and Topham ('the Wits / Of Windsor Town') toasted Marlborough's wife adoringly.[51]

The Junto's rapid elevation to high office healed the remaining divisions within the Kit-Cat Club; all Whigs now effectively became Court Whigs, lessening the pivotal importance of moderates like Walpole and Smith. A dinner at Smith's house marked the reconciliation between the former Treasurer's faction and the Junto.

Only three of the seventeen Kit-Cat MPs who convened at the opening of the new Parliament in November 1708 received no income, military or civilian, from the government. The dramatic expansion in State bureaucracy begun under William was continuing, with an increasing number of revenue offices created to raise war funds – the bureaucracy would treble its 1689 size by 1720, meaning treble the patronage opportunities for those with power over appointments. Encouraged by spyhole authors like Ned Ward, whose books on clubs were bestsellers, London readers were becoming fascinated by the Kit-Cat Club's enormous power and influence – the eternal fascination of the velvet rope. 'The Bath, the Wells, and every Fair, each Chocolate, Gaming House and Tavern, resounds with your Noble Exploits,' one contemporary, addressing the Kit-Cats collectively, remarked.[52]

In this context, Sir Richard Blackmore finally revised and published his 1704 poem, *The Kit-Cats*.[53] Blackmore admired the Kit-Cat Club's 'native Fire', which might rekindle and enlighten English arts, but also felt disgust at the cliquishness of Tonson and his friends. The poem describes an assault on the 'Kit-Cat State' by the God of Dullness and his forces. Echoes of the recent Jacobite invasion were intentional. The God of Dullness calls the Kit-Cat Club an 'Upstart Sect' threatening his empire by efforts to 'with Arts the British Heads refine'. The Kit-Cats are ironically presented (in light of the real war being waged at the time) as squadrons fighting a mock-defence of Wit. In the penultimate stanza, Blackmore predicts a glorious future will be sabotaged not by the God of Dullness but by political factionalism within the Club. Blackmore foretells that nothing will corrupt them like success, and that the Club, 'Embroiled in Feuds and sour with Discontent', finally

> Shall into various Warring Parties split,
> Which brings the Downfall of Imperious Wit.
> This Doom attends the Upstart Kit-Cat State,
> This shall be Wit's, this shall be BOCAJ's Fate.

This was a prophecy that would one day apply to another more fatal schism than that of 1707–8.

As prizes rained on others and the Kit-Cats' fame reached new heights, Steele told Prue he was chasing 'that life we both pant after with so much earnestness'.[54] He hoped to step into Addison's vacated post as Under-Secretary of State in the Southern Department. '[T]here is a thing in Agitation that will make me happy at once,' Steele wrote confidentially to his wife two days after Addison switched to his new, Irish post. 'Your Rival [for Steele's company], A[ddiso]n, will be removed and if I can succeed Him in His Office It will answer all Purposes.'[55] Addison suggested Steele for the job, and Steele lobbied for it with every spare moment.

Steele was to be bitterly disappointed: a Scotsman named Robert Pringle received the post instead. This period left a sour taste in Steele's mouth years later when he regretted wasting his life in 'Fruitless attendance' upon powerful men. Steele claimed to have known dependants of such men who 'have been for twenty Years together within a Month of a good Employment, but never arrived at the Happiness of being possessed of anything'. If someone else obtains the employment a man is after, Steele wrote, it is often someone who never even solicited for it, since great men thereby seek to expand the circle of those indebted to them; and if a man 'grow out of Humour' upon such a discovery, everyone will think him unreasonable.[56] Steele knew the real reason Somers had not secured the post for him: 'I am reckoned in general an ill manager, and know also that it is made a bar against doing for Me.'[57]

Steele must have given way to envy, depression and bitterness that winter, as London suffered sub-zero temperatures and heavy snowfalls. Only Dr Garth was not, it seems, oppressed by the Great Frost. Whenever anyone complained of the cold, he was said to reply: 'Yes sir, 'fore Gad, very fine weather, sir, very wholesome weather, sir; kills trees, sir; very good for a man, sir.'[58] Amid the snowstorms, Steele continued to attend the Kit-Cat Club, helping Tonson make selections for the sixth *Miscellany* of contemporary poetry. Defrosting his ink stand, Steele penned a note to his seven-month pregnant wife that he was 'indispensably obliged' to dine with Tonson, where papers were to be read after dinner 'whereof, among others, I am to be a Judge'.[59] The young Alexander Pope's poetry was among the work selected for this *Miscellany*, not only on Steele's recommendation but also on that of Garth, Congreve and Addison. Walsh, Halifax and Tidcomb had previously encouraged Pope's writing, though Pope was excluded from Kit-Cat membership and barred from receiving a Court or government place by his Toryism and Catholicism. The Kit-Cats' recognition of Pope's genius, however, demonstrates that Whig critics were never entirely blinded by ideology.

On 26 March 1709, Mrs Steele gave birth to a daughter, christened Elizabeth like Steele's first, illegitimate daughter. While Steele was seeking a gift or loan to keep a roof over his family's head, half the Kit-Cats were personally guaranteeing the national debt. In April, the Bank of England agreed to advance the government large sums without interest in exchange for the exclusive right to issue notes ('Exchequer Bills'). The subscription was swiftly filled, mainly by Whigs eager to demonstrate loyalty to the new Kit-Cat governors. It was the second such subscription in three months; the first, in February 1709, doubled the Bank's capital, its Charter having been extended by Parliament despite strong Tory opposition. The February subscription list was filled within a few hours, with many would-be signatories turned away. Among the names on the list are several Kit-Cats peers: Somers is down for £3,000, Somerset for £5,000 and Halifax for £10,000. Not only the peerage got in on the Bank's profits, however; by 1710, Kit-Cat Anthony Henley, for example, had at least £4,000 invested under his own name and an equal amount invested as part of a group. These enormous sums were a measure of how fully such men endorsed continuing the war at this critical juncture, when there was growing pressure from the Tories and others to negotiate a peace.

Originally, back in the 1690s, the Bank of England and deficit-financing had been criticized based on the argument that, when the personal wealth of MPs, peers and Cabinet members was tied up in government stock, they would be less independent and less ready to hold the monarchy accountable. In 1709, with the Whig leaders visibly less enthused than most of the nation about a possible end to the war, many felt these suspicions justified. This impression was reinforced when the Old and New East India Companies merged in 1709 to form the United Company, the former Whig directors and investors of the New Company holding the controlling majority. Whether there was ever truth in the accusations that the Kit-Cat Club monopolized literary patronage and the arts, the Club's members and associates certainly had a credit monopoly firmly in place by 1709.

Steele's career disappointments had one positive result: they forced him to concentrate on writing. *The Tatler*'s first issue appeared on 12 April 1709, less than a week after Steele's daughter's christening, as spring weather belatedly warmed London's icy streets. Hoping that this new production would be a money-maker, Steele told Prue to 'depend upon it that I shall bring you home what will make things have a cheerful aspect'.[60]

The Tatler consisted of a single essay per issue, on a folio sheet printed on both sides, and folded to create four pages. The first four issues were distributed free, to hook the largest possible number of readers. Steele had gained the confidence to launch the paper through editing *The Gazette*, but *The Tatler* would give him a much freer outlet for the views he could not express in the government press. Its essays were narrated by the fictional Isaac Bickerstaff, and the paper's stated purpose was to reach the man in the street or London coffee house, but also to create a new readership that aspired to emulate Bickerstaff's urbane life, with his club of friends who met at the Trumpet tavern (a real tavern halfway down Shire Lane, where Mr Cat lived).

Steele asked Halifax's 'favour in promoting' *The Tatler*, by means of a subscription, but wittily did so as if he were just an agent for his fictional creation, Bickerstaff, who was 'naturally proud' and therefore would only accept cash in excess of the subscription price if Halifax would take 'so many more books' in exchange.[61] *The Tatler* fast became the most popular paper in Britain, forging a new kind of community through print.

Bickerstaff addressed himself to women too – the result of Steele having learned to write for the mixed audience of the theatres. What this meant, in practice, was keeping the writing conversational, relying on analogies or allegories to explain big ideas, and leavening political news or debate with entertaining social observations and fanciful stories. Like the modernized translations of the ancient classics by Dryden and Tonson decades earlier, the central purpose was to educate and edify the nation, but the pill was mixed with a good deal of jam. As women took the paper with their real bread and jam, it created new reading habits in the domestic realm, and ended the idea that devotional books were the only fit reading matter for the female sex. At this date, literacy figures were around 45 per cent for men and 25 per cent for women, but the vogue for *The Tatler* actively expanded those percentages and helped turn Britain into a country of readers. Steele wrote for the merchants on the Exchange, the Customs men on the docks, the law students lying on the grass outside Gray's Inn and the shoppers in the Exchange – the whole litany of humanity that made London feel like a heaving world city – but also for the rest of the country who received *The Tatler* by subscription in the tri-weekly post. Nationwide debate could now be conducted at unprecedented speed, compared to previous pamphlet debates.

The periodical tried to answer, for example, all those who were wearying of a long, expensive world war. Tenant farmers and the landless poor were suffering hardships thanks to the heavy rains and bad harvests that followed the Great Frost, and landowners were unable to collect rents to pay the wartime taxes. In August 1709, Marlborough won the battle of Malplaquet only after enormous loss of life and high casualties among his largely conscripted men. Nor was it the decisive victory for which everyone had hoped. After the blood spilled at Malplaquet, Anne began to lose her stomach for war and joined the popular majority in seeking a speedy end to Britain's involvement.

The Queen blamed the collapse of peace talks in The Hague in May 1709 on the Junto's excessive demands. Afterwards, the parties publicly argued over whether the war should continue. Patriotic aggression had overtaken the Whigs' genuinely defensive grounds for starting the war, as they now sought total Bourbon surrender, not just the maintenance of a balance of power. Satirists scorned the Kit-Cats for dealing in poetry during wartime and for fine dining during food shortages: Ned Ward called the Kit-Cats 'Luxurious Heroes of the Pen', and criticized even the physically disabled Tonson as a mock-hero who only dared 'to storm the crusty walls' of Mr Cat's pies when his compatriots were storming the French town of Tournai.[62] Mary Astell's sarcastic dedication 'To the most Illustrious Society of the Kit-Cats' in *Bart'lemy Fair: or, an Enquiry after Wit* (1709) was similarly scathing about the Club's self-congratulation while soldiers died every day in Flanders: 'You who are our Household Gods could not indeed be permitted to leave the Island and expose your precious Lives.' Astell wondered whether Marlborough could ever have brought home a victory if 'his Army were composed of such Men of Wit and did they allow themselves time to think'. She further commended the Kit-Cats, tongue in cheek, for having 'Fortitude to let the Cries and Tears of whole Troops of Orphans and Widows go unregarded, but who will suffer no part of Voluptuousness to pass by them, nor meanly curb any of their loosest Desires'.[63]

Steele's *Tatler* became a crucial mouthpiece for the Kit-Cats and other pro-Marlborough Whigs in answering such attacks, the paper's fifth issue, for example, containing a panegyric on Marlborough. What Steele did most brilliantly was to report the news in a seemingly impartial tone, while slipping in a good deal of Whig editorializing. He avoided the usual tone of the propagandist – superlative praise of one side, personal insults of the other, dogmatic-sounding assertions – instead giving Bickerstaff the voice of a charming, tolerant man of sense. In many ways, Steele wrote Bickerstaff to sound like Addison – the man Steele (and Steele's wife) essentially wished he could be.

Steele sowed the seeds of Whiggish attitudes in countless *Tatler* essays. One allegory about a scholar, a tradesman and a courtier who were cousins, for example, taught the interdependence of England's classes and professions – a central tenet of Whig political economy. Another essay lectured on how poor commoners should be appreciated for their 'Heroic Virtue' as much as the famous, powerful or rich – the same kind of socially levelling lesson taught by the translations of Stepney or Prior in the 1690s.[64] *The Tatler* successfully occupied the political centre ground with claims to neutrality and detestation of factionalism, but at the same time, everyone knew Steele and his friends were Whigs. The publication thus transformed Whiggism from a purely political ideology into a wider moral code, claiming a monopoly on common sense and good taste (a 'monopoly of our Sense', as Prior put it[65]). To spread urbane values was never politically neutral; the London boroughs remained more Whig than the rest of the country, so making provincial society more like London society was a way to make it more inclined to think, and vote, Whig. Steele thereby helped transform the Whig party's longer-term fortunes by making its policies seem the thinking-person's only reasonable choice, however hostile the current electoral climate. No Tory writer was ever as adept at such beguiling, almost subliminal, cultural propaganda.

In May 1709, six weeks after his daughter's birth and during *The Tatler*'s first month of publication, Steele was arrested for a debt of £120 (£11,500 today). To add insult to injury, debtors' prisons charged fees and rent. During his imprisonment, Steele tried to prevent Prue from panicking, telling her: 'There is no doubt but We shall be easy and happy in few days.'[66] It was a tradesman who bailed Steele out, while fellow Kit-Cat Spencer Compton, then a royal Paymaster, secretly advanced Steele his pension as Gentleman Usher to the late Prince George, enabling him once again, temporarily, to clear his debts. Addison's gesture of assistance was to write an anonymous contribution to *The Tatler*. It was to be the start of a journalistic collaboration between the two men that would extend beyond *The Tatler* and forever change the art of journalism.

By October 1709, Steele was again begging Halifax for cash because 'I am at this time in danger of being torn to pieces for £150.'[67] Cash and credit problems were ubiquitous at this period, even if someone lived frugally, which Steele did not. Members of the gentry often settled bills no more than once a year, and there was little distinction between business and household expenses or income, often obscuring a man's real financial situation. Steele later wrote, with some envy: 'Our Gentry are, generally speaking, in debt; and many Families have put it into a kind of Method of being so from Generation to Generation.'[68] Steele's own debts seem to have arisen from 'imprudence of generosity, or vanity of profusion'[69] – what he called 'Faults of a Person of Spirit'.[70]

Whatever his financial situation, Steele felt that drinking with Kit-Cat friends would improve his prospects. Prue was less convinced, scolding him when he regularly came home drunk to Bury Street. While Bickerstaff was a bachelor, having only the 'family' of a cat and dog awaiting him by the fire every evening, Steele was greeted by Prue's recriminations, and it seems he sometimes responded with violent outbursts. *The Tatler* exhorted men to reform their violent tempers, both in public life and at home; for Steele this was a mission of self-reform – an effort to live up to the models of Bickerstaff's good nature and Addison's self-control.

XIII
IRELAND: KIT-CAT COLONY

> [A]s I am an Englishman, I am very cautious to hate a Stranger, or despise a poor Palatine.
>
> ADDISON AND STEELE,
> *The Tatler* no. 111, 24 December 1709

After Wharton's appointment as Lord Lieutenant of Ireland in autumn 1708, his choice of Addison as Irish Secretary meant that the two highest executive posts in that kingdom were occupied by Kit-Cats. In addition, Tom Hopkins was Addison's primary correspondent in the Southern Department, which administered Irish affairs from Whitehall, and Harry Boyle was the Lord Treasurer of Ireland, also based in London. A Kit-Cat therefore held every senior post in Ireland's colonial administration in 1709, with the exception of the Club's close ally Lord Sunderland at the head of the Southern Department. The reason for the Club's monopoly on Irish government, like everything else at this date, related to the War of Spanish Succession: following their triumphant suppression of the Jacobites in Scotland, they were now focused on shutting another back door to The Pretender and French invasion. Ireland's coastal defences remained on alert in 1708–9, and the Protestant populace were 'almost frightened out of their wits'.[1] At the same time, since the Catholics were as much an internal as external threat in Ireland, the Kit-Cats' short rule would reveal the dark, repressive underside of the Whigs' aggressive Protestant patriotism – to be replicated throughout Britain's empire in the centuries to come.

Addison's career so far had been almost entirely guided by Kit-Cats – Halifax, Somers, Manchester and Wharton. Wharton was a very different character from the other three, and it has often been assumed Addison had trouble respecting his new boss for the same reasons Queen Anne found Wharton personally offensive: his blaspheming, gambling, wild living and brash manner. Macaulay contrasted Wharton's crude masculinity to the Irish Secretary's 'gentleness and delicacy'. They were, in a sense, personifications of the Kit-Cat Club's double nature – the crude mixed with the refined.

But Addison did respect Wharton, who, though no intellectual, 'had too much Penetration to be shuffled with', as well as a natural gift for politics.[2] When Addison and Steele later penned a dedication to Wharton, they carefully complimented him less on his vision than on his 'utmost Industry'.[3] Addison also perceived an element of self-parody in Wharton's swaggering and backslapping, as if he were playing up to his reputation, distracting opponents from his acuity. Addison was fastidious almost to the point of asexuality, yet his letters suggest he sometimes envied Wharton's gregarious, relaxed manner, which must have been popular with the Irish. Steele testified Wharton had, in return, 'a particular Esteem and Friendship for him [Addison] to his Death, consulting him on the most important Affairs'.[4]

Wharton was in his early sixties when he was posted to Ireland. His fair eyebrows were white underneath the fringe of his eternally youthful periwig and his waistline had expanded to the point of no return, but he was otherwise in good health. Wharton was appointed Lord Lieutenant partly because he had a vested interest in Irish prosperity; his family owned land in the Irish counties of Carlow and Westmeath. Through his second marriage to Lucy Loftus, a Kit-Cat toast of 1698, Wharton acquired a large estate in

Rathfarnham, southeast of Dublin, worth several thousand pounds in rents.

Wharton's departure for Ireland was delayed, officially by the illness of his wife, but unofficially to benefit his colleagues, who recognized Anne was sending him to Dublin partly to remove his influential voice from Westminster. By mid-April 1709, departure could be deferred no longer. Wharton and Addison sailed a week after Steele's *Tatler* launch. The crossing to Dublin took three days and involved risk of capture by French privateers who often forced ships to St Malo. When Wharton and Addison arrived on 21 April, Dubliners were glad not only for their governors' safety but also to receive news from England, since the last packet boat from Holyhead had been captured, and its mailbags thrown overboard.

As Wharton's yacht sailed up to Dublin's Wooden Bridge, escorted by convoys of small boats, greeting crowds waited on the Strand. Large numbers of the Irish nobility and gentry had turned out in their coaches to watch the governors' procession up troop-lined streets to Dublin Castle, the viceregal residence and English secretariat. Dublin was predominantly an army town, the military list far exceeding the civil, so the quayside would have been filled with bright uniforms, mixed with the distinctive dark dress of the town's Quakers and other Dissenters.

Ireland's Dissenters were an economically successful, fast-expanding minority. In Ulster, over half the population were Presbyterians and others who had fled from political persecution and economic hardship in Scotland. The Reverend Joseph Boyse was the chief Dissenter in Dublin at this date and would certainly have been out to welcome Wharton as 'the Dissenters' Friend'. Before leaving England, Wharton helped pass a Whig Bill to naturalize foreign Protestants living in England (thus creating many new citizens likely to vote Whig). This Bill was a litmus test of Whig loyalty; every Kit-Cat MP voted for it. The Irish Dissenters therefore celebrated Wharton's appointment as Lord Lieutenant, believing it would improve their rights. They saw Wharton as their co-religionist, even if he conformed in appearances to Anglicanism and was a religious sceptic in private.

While Irish Dissenters were mostly shopkeepers, tradesmen and merchants, the Established Church's members tended to come either from 'the quality' or the urban poor. A class conflict therefore underlay the confessional one. In Dublin, social ascents could be dramatic: Sir William Robinson, the city's Surveyor-General and Accountant-General in 1702, for example, started life as a scullery boy. Most of the Irish nobility, on the other hand, were, like their Scottish equivalents, living on incomes inadequate to match their pretensions, thanks to low Irish land rents. This made competition for sinecures, pensions and government posts especially fierce, and the Protestant Establishment deeply defensive of their privileges, especially the right to hold office.

It would therefore have been with some trepidation that William King, Archbishop of Dublin, welcomed Wharton. The Irish Establishment could not comprehend a man whose religious convictions were subservient to his political ideology. As Steele put it, Wharton 'often declared that he was a Friend to the Dissenters, not taking them in a Religious but a civil Capacity, because they were always Friends to the Constitution'.[5] Wharton's prominent role in ensuring the Scottish Presbyterians were tolerated within the 1707 Act of Union did not recommend him to the Anglo-Irish either; as Swift wrote: 'We make a mighty difference . . . between suffering thistles to grow among us, and wearing them for posies.'[6]

Swift, a prebend in the Irish Church at this date, reassured Archbishop King that Addison, '*le plus honnête homme du monde*',[7] was a much more God-fearing man than Wharton and could be trusted to defend the Irish Establishment. Swift described the new Secretary as 'a most excellent Person; and being my most intimate Friend, I shall use all my Credit to set him right in his Notions of Persons and Things'.[8] It was true that Addison and Swift were friends at this date: the previous summer in London, Swift had boasted that the 'triumvirate of Mr. Addison, Steele and me come together as seldom as the Sun, Moon and Earth' though 'I often see each of them, and each of them me and each other'.[9] But Swift was underestimating the strong Kit-Cat bond between Wharton and Addison.

When Swift openly criticized Wharton, he was baffled to find Addison becoming 'nine Times more secret to me'.[10]

The crowd on the Dublin quay would not have represented the country as a whole. Contemporaries estimated there were six Papists to every Protestant in Ireland, while modern historians estimate that between two-thirds and three-quarters of the country's population was Catholic – those then referred to by Irish Protestants as 'the Irish'.[11] Since William III's victory at the Boyne, and the Treaty of Limerick that followed it in October 1691, the Protestant minority had been in the ascendant. Swearing religious oaths, including one denying the Pope's authority, became a requirement for holding office, practising law, joining the army or standing for election, and Catholics were required to pay tithes to the Anglican Church. Catholicism was further restricted by persecution of its clergy. The Catholics' poverty arose not so much from these Penal Laws, however, as from the peasantry's exploitation by landlords of both denominations and due to a rapid population increase that inflated rents. Swift saw the English as pursuing a deliberate policy of restricting trade and keeping Ireland poor, but not too poor, so as to limit the number of popular Catholic uprisings.

The year 1709 was one of high food prices in Ireland. In March 1709, a proclamation banning food exports declared that 'the poorer sort of the Inhabitants of this Kingdom are in danger of perishing' thanks to a bad harvest and then to bulk-buying by merchants who, ignoring the famine, exported what corn, grain and meal there was 'to parts beyond the Seas'.[12] Dutch merchants had been attacked in Cork by hungry mobs, and along the Dublin quayside many curious spectators out to greet Wharton and Addison would have depended on the relief granted by their English governors in the form of the city's single workhouse and a small cash fund for widows.

The two Kit-Cats probably looked down from their carriage upon the mob with a large dose of English bigotry. Swift said he and his fellow Protestants thought the Catholic poor 'as inconsiderable as the Women and Children',[13] yet he knew his English friends did not think much more highly of the Protestant ruling class:

> As to Ireland, they know little more than they do of Mexico; further than that it is a Country subject to the King of England, full of Boggs, inhabited by wild Irish Papists; who are kept in Awe by mercenary Troops sent from thence: And their general Opinion is that it were better for England if this whole Island were sunk into the Sea.[14]

Addison would not necessarily have been disabused of such prejudices by his friendship with Steele, who once remarked the Irish were 'more harmless' but also 'more stupid' than other races.[15]

The Anglo-Irish nobility had been suffering an identity crisis since the 1690s. The greater sharing of sovereignty between the Crown and Parliament since England's constitutional changes of 1689 meant it was more awkward for Irishmen to argue that their loyalty was to the English (now British) Crown, not the Westminster Parliament. Addison observed that the Irish were always harking back to the ancient pacts between the English and Irish kings, hating to have it thought that 'they are a conquered and dependent kingdom'.[16]

But conquered and dependent was what they were. Lord Lieutenants like Wharton were answerable not to the Irish Parliament but to Westminster and the Queen, so there was less need for a Kit-Cat Club equivalent in Dublin to jerk the strings of electoral influence. Wharton could convene and prorogue the Irish Parliament, and though that institution could submit Bills to Westminster for approval, and could still obstruct the granting of war supplies, it had no control over amendments the Privy Council in London might then make.

England resisted full legislative union with Ireland, however, on economic grounds, preferring to protect its own markets. After the Treaty of Union with Scotland, the English treated Ireland as an even more subordinate colony, filling places in the Irish government with Englishmen – like Wharton and Addison – rather than with locally born Anglo-Irish. The only bright side of this colonialism was that repression of the Catholic population would likely have been even more ferocious if it had been left entirely in the Protestant electorate's hands. The view of themselves as external moderators between religious zealots allowed the Kit-Cats to reconcile their Whiggish principles about governmental accountability with their near total lack of such accountability to the Irish freeholders.

As the viceregal procession moved off from the waterside, gunfire saluted the new arrivals, followed by bell ringing and bonfires that continued through the night. A contemporary observed that to be Lord Lieutenant came nearer to kingship in 'train and state' than any comparable office in Europe.[17]

The city that the two men found in 1709 had a population of 60–75,000, but it had rapidly expanded from only 15,000 in 1660, and was crammed into a small geographical area. The town's boundaries were, by today's landmarks, St Stephen's Green to the south, College Park to the east and St Audeon's church to the west. Visible on one hill was the Royal Hospital at Kilmainham, completed the previous year, and another prominent landmark was the tower of the Tholsel (law courts), which afforded the best view over the city. Ormonde's Quay was a large open square with docks on the bank of the river, dominated by the Custom House. Walled embankments were being built along the river, but were not yet complete; improvements in the harbour were also underway, Dublin and Cork being the main ports for American trade. Around Temple Bar stood Dutch-style 'Billies': tall, thin, gabled, brick terraces built by Huguenot immigrants. Other than this, the city centre's basic layout in 1709, before it was expanded by Georgian squares, was remarkably similar to that of today.

The procession's final steps were along Castle Street, Cork Hill and Cole's Alley, which led up to the Castle's ornate armorial gate. The Castle's viceregal lodgings had a view out through this gate, while Addison resided on the side of Upper Castle Yard. Back in January 1709, Addison had sent his second cousin, a triple-chinned fellow named Eustace Budgell, ahead to Dublin 'to make my Lodgings Inhabitable'.[18]

Addison secured Budgell a place as a clerk under him, but tasked him first with ensuring there was a well-stocked wine cellar at Dublin Castle. In 1709, French wine was more easily available in Ireland than in England, and was often smuggled from Dublin to London as Portuguese or 'Irish wine'.[19] If Budgell did his job well, therefore, Wharton and Addison would have enjoyed their first night at Dublin Castle sampling their new cellar and toasting friends back in Westminster,[20] only to be awakened at dawn by the Castle's kettle-drummer, trumpeters and the racket of soldiers with their horses and dogs in the yard outside.

Thanks to his Kit-Cat contacts, Addison had plenty of Dublin acquaintances eager to introduce him to the town's treacherously complicated local politics. Congreve's friend Joe Keally, for example, was now living at his estate of Keally Mount in Kilkenny, sitting as MP for Doneraile and as Attorney General for the Palatinate of Tipperary. In May 1709, Congreve encouraged Keally to offer his services to Wharton. When Keally suggested that Congreve, who was a regular dinner companion of Wharton's in London, should do the same, Congreve demurred: 'The hint you give me is very kind, and need not seem unfeasible to any who does not know particular persons and circumstances as well as myself.'[21] Since Congreve wrote warmly in other private letters about Wharton's political skills and Addison's character, this is a somewhat cryptic answer. It may have been merely his polite way of saying that his life (and lover Henrietta) lay in London and that he preferred not to become a serious civil servant like Addison.

Wharton and Addison had had the whole winter to prepare for their rule of Ireland, and arrived with a clear plan, hammered out over Kit-Cat dinners in late 1708 and fine-tuned on the voyage over. Their priorities were simple: to secure Irish funds and soldiers for the war, and to ensure Ireland's Catholics and Tories provided no foothold for foreign Jacobites. When Wharton made his first speech to the Irish Lords at Chichester House on 5 May 1709, these were his simple messages. He asked them to vote for war supplies, reassured them the Irish troops on the Continent would soon be relieved, suggested they consider increased fortifications and construction of an armoury in Dublin, and called for new legislation to promote the Protestant interest and prevent 'the Growth of Popery'.[22] Notably absent was any mention of helping the Dissenters by repealing the Test Acts, an omission that instantly won grateful support from the Anglo-Irish MPs and Lords.

Addison, who probably helped word the speech, commended Wharton's wisdom in not raising the issue of Dissenters' emancipation immediately, so as to ensure that other measures – most importantly the war supply – would first be voted through. Allowing the Irish parliamentarians to come up with their own proposals for further excluding and controlling the Catholics was also clever. 'I question not but . . . he will be able to lead them into anything that will be for their real interest and advantage,' Addison assured Halifax in London.[23] Congreve, when sending news of the failing 1709 peace negotiations at The Hague, responded to praise of Wharton's political instincts and oratory: 'I am glad His Excellency pleases so well. Nobody knows better how to do it.'[24]

The following day, 6 May 1709 (on which, in London, Steele was released from debtors' prison), Wharton and Addison received the freedom of the City of Dublin. On the same day, a vote by the City of Dublin Corporation was the first spark in a Whig–Tory dispute that would escalate into a major political row a few years later. A senior alderman was passed over as Chief Magistrate in favour of a more junior Whig: a result orchestrated by, or designed to please, Wharton. Dublin's Tory leaders, who clubbed at the Swan tavern near Lucas' Coffee House, complained that this infringed the Corporation's charter. They swore to reverse the appointment if they ever regained power in Dublin Castle.

This matter showed that the Irish 'political nation' was becoming almost as polarized as England by the labels of Whig and Tory. The Irish Tories tended to have Old English, pre-1641 settler roots, whereas the local Whigs tended to descend from families settled after Cromwell. Unlike England, where a normally Tory Parliament was going through an exceptional period of Whiggism, the Irish Parliament remained evenly split between Whig and Tory MPs, united by membership of a single minority – the High Church Anglo-Irish squirearchy. A centre grouping usually voted with whichever party was sent over from London to govern. The handful of former Catholics in the Irish Parliament always voted with the Tories, however, and an association between Tories and Jacobites was inevitably imported from English political discourse. In 1708–9, therefore, the Whig hand was strengthened by rumours that The Pretender planned to invade again; even more than in England, the Irish ruling class feared the Jacobites because a Stuart restoration would reverse the current arrangement of land tenure in Ireland.

Addison, who made himself personally popular with men of both parties in Ireland, was returned to the Irish Parliament in May 1709 as Member for Cavan – a seat acquired by nomination rather than contest. There is an anecdote about Addison's first speech in either the British or Irish Commons, at which he was said to have stood up and stammered 'Mr Speaker, I conceive . . .' three times, before, conceiving nothing, sitting down again.[25] Addison wrote repeatedly in his later journalism about 'Oppressions of Modesty' creating an incapacity for public speaking, and how this could let down even the most intelligent and educated man, so there was probably some truth in the story.[26] Addison's praise for Wharton's effective delivery of speeches takes on added significance in this light: Addison must have felt a mixture of emotions about his more extrovert patron, 'envying his Impudence and despising his Understanding'.[27] Steele hit the nail on the head, perhaps, when he wrote an essay about men held back by 'their fear of failing at indifferent things' like public speaking, and attributed such fear to vanity, since it showed 'they would be too much pleased in performing it'.[28]

During this first session of the Irish Parliament, the Quakers addressed the Queen, via Wharton, expressing thanks for their freedom to worship, proclaiming their loyalty, and begging for mercy 'where we cannot actually Obey some Laws', meaning their refusal to pay tithes or swear sacramental oaths.[29] Various poetic dialogues about the Quakers not paying tithes were published in Dublin in 1709, prompted by Wharton's arrival. While Wharton knew the Irish Parliament would pass no overt proposal to free Dissenters from the Test Acts or give them greater freedom of education, he did what he could to alleviate the discrimination suffered by 'his people'. Wharton supported a subscription fund to assist Dissenters fighting 'unreasonable prosecutions', for example.[30]

In subsequent speeches to the Irish Parliament, Wharton hinted he would like to see the Test Acts repealed, but the Irish oligarchy ignored his hints. Wharton's underlying theme was always the need for the Protestants of Ireland to unite against the Catholic threat: 'It is not the Law now passed, nor any Law that the Wit of Man can frame, will Serve you against Popery, whilst you continue divided amongst yourselves.'[31] Unfortunately, the Church of Ireland knew that in a crisis the Presbyterians and Quakers would always back them against the Catholics, so there was little incentive to establish a friendlier accord with these economic rivals. In fact, granting equal rights to Protestant Dissenters was the one 'threat' that could unite Irish politicians of both parties, such that Englishmen often mistook Irish Whig MPs for Tories when they voted against toleration of other Protestant denominations.

When it came to repressing Ireland's Catholic masses, Lord Lieutenant and Parliament were on adjacent, if not identical, pages. Wharton's invitation to Parliament to come up with additional Penal Laws was hungrily accepted, with new Bills proposed before the month was out and passed by the end of August 1709. These were the laws Edmund Burke would later describe as the 'ferocious acts of Anne', which were 'as well fitted for the oppression, impoverishment, and degradation of a people, and the debasement in them of human nature itself, as ever proceeded from the perverted ingenuity of man'.[32] They completed the transfer of property from Catholics to Protestants; made the oath of abjuration (swearing Anne was rightful Queen and denying The Pretender's claims) a requirement for every Irishman over 16; offered rewards for reporting unregistered Catholic priests; and ensured children of declared converts received a Protestant education.

The size of the Irish Catholic population made strict enforcement of the Penal Laws impossible. The Catholic bishops had been banished since 1697, but many survived clandestinely. A 1709 letter from the Bishop of Elphin tells how he lived on the run, too poor to keep a horse or servant. As Catholic priests died, it was illegal to replace them, so that one Englishman wrote, '[I]t will appear plain enough that the Romish religion is on its last legs in Ireland.'[33] In January 1704, one Penal Law had required every Catholic priest to register with a local magistrate, stay at one address and provide securities against absconding or other suspect behaviour. For several years, the rural magistrates had left the parish clergy fairly well alone, with only one priest prosecuted at the Cork Assizes in April 1709. However, the new law offering increased rewards triggered a spasm of priest-hunting that summer after the Kit-Cats arrived, with several bishops captured and transported. A particularly zealous 'priest-catcher' named Oxenard received large rewards from Dublin Castle.

There were also increased rewards for 'discoverers' – Protestants who, having found a Catholic breaking the Penal Code by purchasing land or taking a long lease, filed a 'bill of discovery' and won entitlement to the property in question. This aspect of the Code divided families. Any Catholic who joined the Established Church could deprive his Catholic relations of all but a life interest in their property by 'discovering' them. After the 1704 extension of the Penal Laws, fewer than ten landowners 'conformed', whereas after 1709, some 500 did so, fearing they would be deprived of their estates. In June 1709, under Wharton's gaze, two prominent Catholic nobles renounced their Catholicism in St Andrew's Church, Dublin. Nonetheless, other members of the Catholic elite continued to own land, and though excluded from public office, had the right to vote. The majority of their compatriots continued to treat them with respect.

The inability to own land pushed many young Catholics into trade, which was still permitted, even if they could not join a guild. This was encouraged by a 1707 Penal Law ordering the transportation of 'such as pretend to be Irish gentlemen and will not betake themselves to any honest trade or livelihood, but wander about demanding victuals'.[34] During the spring 1709 debates, it was proposed that Catholics should be debarred from trade as well, but Addison recorded with some relief that this clause was 'after great debates entirely flung out'.[35]

It was also debated whether Catholics should be entirely deprived of the franchise. Addison's summary of this debate illustrates the complex dynamics of a country ruled by an insecure minority grappling with Lockean principles of government:

> It was urged . . . that it was unreasonable so great a body of people should be bound by laws which were not made by their representatives . . . that religion should have no part in the considerations but as it endangered the State, and that therefore all who could comply with the oath of abjuration should be qualified as voters.[36]

It remains unclear to what extent Wharton and Addison encouraged elaboration and enforcement of the Penal Laws, or whether their mediation softened the impact of a system amounting almost to apartheid. The Lord Lieutenant's power and patronage were so great that some influence can be presumed. Swift claimed Wharton would override the Irish Privy Council whenever he and Addison had not managed them into the desired position, saying simply, 'Come, my lords, I see how your opinions are, and therefore I will not take your votes.'[37]

Steele's biographical sketch complimented Wharton on his mercy and humanity in protecting the English Papists from being plundered and attacked after the Glorious Revolution, but the same piece also boasted Wharton did more to suppress the Irish Catholics in the first three months of his government than his Tory predecessors in the previous three years. As a result, 'the Native Irish, the ragged Teagues and beggarly Papists did not crowd after his Coach and howl him along the Streets as they have done some who preferred an Affection of Popularity to the Destruction of the Popish Interest'.[38] Swift, on the other hand, gossiped that Wharton liked to 'whore with a Papist'[39] – a detail which, if true, suggests his anti-Catholic prejudices were more pragmatic than visceral.

Wharton and Addison, viewing the situation in its European, wartime context, feared the Catholics above all for their treasonous French sympathies. Many Gaelic Irish were suspected of lending support to French pirates and privateers, and when Dr Lambert, Wharton's chaplain, sermonized against Catholic pilgrimages to holy wells, he did so believing they had a politically seditious purpose. Addison served on a number of committees involved in drafting Penal Laws while Parliament was adjourned during June and most of July 1709.

As Kit-Cats, Wharton and Addison felt patronage of the arts in Dublin – what they and later Whig historians saw as bringing civilization to the hinterlands – to be an important part of their colonial duties. Of course, this civilizing mission only concerned itself with Protestant Irish society, trusting in a trickle-down effect to civilize the 'superstitious' and 'barbarous' Catholics. They did not commence any private palatial building projects in Ireland (back in England, Vanbrugh was nearing completion of Castle Howard's exterior that summer of 1709), but one of Wharton's first decisions was to support an Irish parliamentary petition to the Queen for a £5,000 donation (almost £480,000 today) to found a library in Trinity College to promote 'good literature and sound Revolution Principles'.[40] This is the beautiful library that remains the pride of the College today. Addison became particular friends with one of the Fellows of Trinity, the great philosopher George Berkeley, who was just publishing his *Essay Towards a New Theory of Vision* (1709).

When it came to musical edification, the Kit-Cat governors imported people from London. Thomas Clayton, the composer of Addison's failed opera *Rosamund*, accompanied them to Dublin to direct 'Court diversions'. He presented a season of operas between April and September 1709, including *Arsinoe, Queen of Cyprus* and *Rosamund*. The Aldermen and other chief citizens of Dublin were invited with their wives to these operas at the Castle, where Lady Wharton presided – 'Never was there a Court at Dublin so accessible, never a Lord Lieutenant so easy to be approached . . . The Day was for Council, the Night for Balls, Gaming Tables and other Diversions.'[41] The balls were famously good, to the extent that Wharton's name was used in one poem as a verb – 'to Whartonize', meaning to party.[42]

Plays were performed at Dublin's Theatre Royal (known as the Queen's Theatre, like Vanbrugh's in the Haymarket, for the duration of Anne's reign). The repertoire was imported from London, albeit authored by many Anglo-Irish playwrights like Congreve and Wycherley, and Wharton invited a London comedian named Anthony Aston to Dublin to act in a comedy and musical.

There was no programme of patronage for Anglo-Irish writers

comparable to that of the Kit-Cat Club in London, however. For all his ballad and toast writing, Wharton had less interest in literature than Halifax or Somers. Wharton encouraged the reprinting of certain English political tracts in Dublin, but did not commission original works of propaganda.

Dublin was little different from numerous medium-sized English towns in mimicking, after an inevitable lag, the fashions and values of London. An increasing number of Irish nobles were purchasing townhouses in Dublin where they spent the winters; the coaching ring in Phoenix Park imitated that in Hyde Park; and foreign tutors were setting up shop to teach Anglo-Irish boys French for their Grand Tours. The city's councillors were increasingly concerned with Dublin's image, as shown by a complaint about butchers throwing animal hides into the streets, 'by which evil practices this city has suffered in its reputation and character abroad'.[43]

Traffic between Dublin and London was also increasing. With Irish private bills and court rulings open to appeal in Westminster, each Anglo-Irish family had to send at least one representative to London to manage its affairs. Meanwhile, many English Whigs took advantage of Wharton's rule to visit Dublin. Steele wrote that Wharton's Court 'was crowded with People of Quality who came from England on purpose to have the pleasure of his Conversation'.[44] Tonson promised to visit, but Congreve was soon observing that 'Mr Addison surely knows Mr Tonson too well to think he will come to Ireland for having said so, unless some considerable subscription may be set afoot to induce him.'[45]

Unlike York or Oxford, fashions, goods, news and even ideas could enter Dublin directly from Europe or the other English colonies, without having to transit London first. 'We hear by our East India ships lately arrived in Ireland that the Factory at Borneo has been ruined by the Natives, who it is said rose upon Our Countrymen and cut their throats,' Addison wrote.[46] Ships from Jamaica, which often docked first at Galway, if they made it past the French privateers, carried luxuries like sugar and indigo, while ships from Spain, which docked in Kinsale and Cork, brought wine, brandy, salt, oil and lemons. Six days after Wharton and Addison arrived, a ship from

Bilbao brought these foodstuffs, which were as quickly shipped up to Dublin as across to London. Added to plentiful supplies of Irish butter, cheese, beef and honey, all among Ireland's major exports to England in 1709, Dublin did not lag behind London in culinary terms. The dinners hosted at Dublin Castle by the Kit-Cat colonialists must have rivalled the feasts at Barn Elms or the Fountain, minus Mr Cat's pies.

Addison was responsible, in the summer of 1709, for pushing a less popular import upon the Irish. In July 1709, a proposal of the Privy Council of Ireland, of which Addison was a member, was sent to Anne suggesting a group of war refugees from the Palatinate (a territory on the Rhine, including the cities of Heidelberg and Mannheim) be resettled in Ireland. These Palatines were currently in Kent, where their presence was provoking protests from the locals who thought the refugees were taking their jobs and parish charity. Some 10,000 were encamped on Blackheath. Stepney had educated Addison on the persecution of the Protestants in places like the Palatinate, which Stepney witnessed at first hand during his diplomatic travels – the French army's complete destruction of Heidelberg in 1693, for example, was often held up as incontrovertible evidence of Louis XIV's savagery. Later Addison wrote against the use of torture as the 'Method of Reasoning which has been made use of with the poor Refugees'.[47] Wharton and Addison saw that resettling some Palatine refugees to Ireland would alleviate the tensions they were creating in England, while bringing in 'such a Colony of Protestants could not but add to the Security and Advantage of the English Interest' in Ireland.[48]

It was not so simple politically. Since the Palatines were not Anglicans, they would add to Ireland's much-resented Dissenting population. Thomas Lindsay, Bishop of Killacoe, called the refugees 'a parcel of beggars' that Ireland could ill afford.[49] Wharton lobbied to persuade the Irish MPs and clergy that the refugees should be admitted, and encouraged the reprinting in Dublin of English tracts describing the persecution of the Palatines. In the end, with the agreement of the Kit-Cat-dominated Board of Trade in London, over 800 Palatine families (some 2–3,000 individuals) were brought over from

England to settle in Limerick and Kerry. It is a tribute to the skill of Addison and Wharton that the Irish Commons declared they would 'cheerfully embrace' the resettled refugees ('Their Calamitous Circumstances justly remind us how lately we were turned Out of our Dwellings by Violence and Oppression and forced to seek shelter in England'), though the Irish MPs coolly asked for £5,000 (£480,000 today) a year from the Treasury in London as compensation.[50]

The refugees received discounted rents and financial support, but it was difficult finding work around Limerick and Kerry, so many drifted towards Dublin, where there was already a sizeable Huguenot refugee population, or back to England. Some refugees did settle in western Ireland – on the estate of Sir Thomas Southwell near Rathkeale, for example, where the remnants of that engineered Protestant community remain discernible in the area today.

In mid-July 1709, Wharton retired to the Lord Lieutenant's allocated country house, Chapelizod, with fifty armed guards, their tents pitched in the grounds. Addison and his staff of clerks followed. Chapelizod was known as 'The King's House' because William III had retired there after his victory at the Boyne. It lay to the left of the road out of Dublin that skirted the banks of the Liffey. The Temple family owned the land surrounding it, and famous Dutch gardens adjoined the house.

Before leaving town, Wharton sent a letter back to the Southern Office warning Sunderland that any attempt by the Privy Council to amend the Irish Money Bill (for taxes to supply the war) would offend those he was trying to win over to the Whig side in Dublin. Amendments were made, however, as the English and Scots tried to protect their wool and linen producers against the Irish. When the Bill returned thus amended to Dublin, it was an embarrassment to Wharton, who looked as if he lacked the London ministers' full support.

Steele said the Tories in London hoped to keep Wharton out of the way in Dublin for the winter session of 1709–10, as the political contest between the Junto and their Tory opponents was heating up. Wharton, however, cunningly sent Lady Wharton to the Queen to beg she might see her husband in London one last time before she gave birth that winter, so Wharton was allowed home.

After a fortnight's holiday in Ireland, touring the east coast and visiting the site of the battle of the Boyne, Addison also planned to head home to England – crossing paths with the Palatine refugees who were being shipped in the opposite direction. Before departing, however, he met briefly with Jonathan Swift.

The expectations that Halifax's and Somers' flattery of Swift had raised in 1701 had soured by the time Swift dedicated *A Tale of a Tub* (1704) to Somers. While at first glance this dedication bid for Somers' patronage, its wording had an undertone of facetious resentment, which Somers was too intelligent to miss. Congreve expressed a relatively cool opinion of his old schoolmate's bestseller, and it was Addison and Steele who had been invited into the Kit-Cat Club in 1704–5, not Swift. Swift later disparaged Halifax's literary discernment in the same breath as he expressed his disillusionment with Halifax's unfulfilled promises: 'His encouragements were only good words and dinners . . . I never heard him say one good thing, or seem to taste what was said by another.'[51] Swift's awkward combination of unctuousness, social insecurity, sarcastic pride and quirky genius did not, at any rate, suit Halifax's palate.

Swift unsuccessfully lobbied Godolphin, Halifax and Somers on behalf of the Irish clergy (regarding their taxes) for two years after 1707. Swift's letters to Halifax in 1709 are such an odd mixture of obsequiousness and veiled insult that it is easy to understand why this lobbying failed (in one, for example, Swift tells Halifax that His Lordship is 'universally admired by this tasteless People [the Irish]'[52]).

In 1709, Swift then switched his attention to the new Lord Lieutenant, Wharton, but was no more successful. At Swift's first attempt to seek a meeting, Wharton told him to return another day, and when he did so, Wharton received him 'dryly' and broke off the interview in a temper. Swift tried one last time, but when he was heard with no greater sympathy, he left Wharton's office bitterly offended, and humiliated by the failure he was forced to report to Archbishop King.

Swift acknowledged Wharton to be a man of political conviction ('in Point of Party…[Wharton] is one to be confided in'[53]) but considered his toleration of Protestant Dissent to be both religiously and constitutionally reckless. It was this attitude that ultimately precluded Swift from developing or maintaining solid friendships with the Kit-Cats, including Addison.

Wharton's first year of government in Ireland had avoided the contentious issue of Dissenters' rights almost entirely, yet Wharton and Addison also avoided granting the Irish Church any new benefits. 'During the greater part of [Wharton's] government, I lived in the country, saw the Lieutenant very seldom when I came to town, nor ever entered into the least degree of confidence with him,' Swift later wrote.[54] Indeed, Wharton's snubbing of Swift pushed the latter decisively in the direction of the Tories and made Wharton into Swift's personal *bête noire*. In December 1710, Swift would anonymously publish *A Short Character of His Excellency Thomas Earl of Wharton, Lord Lieutenant of Ireland*, vilifying Wharton,[55] and in the marginalia of a history book Swift jotted down his damning verdict beside Wharton's name: 'The most universal villain I ever knew.'[56]

Wharton – who was capable of having a man dismissed from his place one day, then the next, 'as if nothing at all had passed, lay[ing] his hands with much friendliness on your shoulders'[57] – hardly noticed the deep offence he had caused Swift by snubbing him. It is unknown whether, when Addison and Swift crossed paths in Dublin in the late summer of 1709, Addison recognized how a little seed of resentment had been planted in the soil of Irish religious politics that would soon grow to produce, from Swift's pen, the most toxic anti-Junto and anti-Kit-Cat propaganda. As Swift hitched a lift back to England on the Lord Lieutenant's yacht, there was already lying among his papers just such a piece of sulphurous invective against Wharton that would deeply wound its victim the following year.

XIV
THE MONOPOLY BROKEN: WHIG DOWNFALL

A Party Man indeed, and such most of Us are or must be, is an Animal that no Commentator upon Human Nature can sufficiently explain. He has not his Opinion . . . in his own keeping. *Quo ad hoc*, he is Mad.

MATTHEW PRIOR, *An Essay Upon Opinion*[1]

THE END OF the previous year, 1708, had seen the Junto Whigs at the zenith of their power and influence, dominating commerce, trade, government and culture. The attainment of this dominance, however, coincided with military setbacks for Marlborough and with growing public anger about the financial and human cost of the war. It was no longer possible to tell whether Kit-Cat interests were based on a principled vision of the national good, as they claimed, or whether they defined that public good only by what was good for themselves. Soon the argument between these two viewpoints would burst into the public realm through a ferocious 'paper war' between Whig and Tory propagandists.

A man widely seen as a living stereotype of Whig greed and self-interest, Sir Henry Furnese, joined the Kit-Cat Club in 1709. Furnese embodied all the social alliances, formed since the Glorious Revolution, which the Tories feared and hated: a Dissenter, a self-made merchant turned financier, married into old money and land, then raised to a baronetcy in 1707. Furnese did vast deals with Halifax's Treasury during the 1690s, and made private loans to Tonson in the early 1700s, around the same time that he became Marlborough's personal banker. In 1705 Godolphin's Treasury gave Furnese a six-month monopoly on remittances to the Low Countries, Germany and Portugal, on which he received substantial commissions. By the time he joined the Club, Furnese's combined holdings in the Bank of England and East India Company were over £16,000 (some £1.5 million today). The high interest rate on Furnese's loans meant the Tories and rival Whig investors characterized him as a wartime profiteer, though, without such loans, for which Furnese sometimes personally shouldered the risk, the Grand Alliance might have collapsed on several occasions.

Furnese's admission to a Club already containing some of the richest private citizens in Europe was offensive to those who opposed the war not only because of the resources the war consumed but also because it accelerated unwelcome social changes in England. Mary Astell sarcastically declared that the Kit-Cats 'cease not to endeavour, by the Assistance of your darling Luxury, that great Leveller and Transferrer of Property, to make the Tradesman equal to the Lord'.[2]

In November 1709, Furnese – whose 'correspondents' had extended further enormous loans to the English and Allied governments that spring – hosted a dinner for the Kit-Cats to celebrate his 'promotion' into the Club. Maynwaring told the Duchess of Marlborough that her husband had intimated he might attend Furnese's Kit-Cat feast, and that Furnese had promised, if the Duke did attend, to

> carry the Club into the City, and give such an entertainment as never was seen there . . . [I]f his Grace shall be at leisure to be there next

> Thursday, it will be an honour which every member will be proud of . . . and they will certainly testify their gratitude by some public act.[3]

Marlborough was successfully brought to Furnese's feast, a publicity coup of enormous significance for the Junto Whigs. Tory non-members gossiped that he was 'admitted extraordinary to the Kit-Cat Club, and Jacob Tonson ordered to dedicate *Caesar's Commentaries* to him and not to the Duke of Ormonde, as he has promised, and six of the members are to write the epistle [dedication] to him'.[4]

The first point of this gossip was false – Marlborough never joined the Kit-Cat Club, but the Whigs were happy to let the story circulate that he had. Twenty-four Kit-Cats subscribed to *Caesar's Commentaries* prior to its publication, demonstrating their support for its new dedicatee, Marlborough, at a time when he was under increasing pressure from the Tories, after the failed spring 1709 peace talks and the bloody battle of Malplaquet.[5]

On the Saturday morning following Furnese's feast, Maynwaring congratulated the Duchess of Marlborough 'upon the victory which your servant, Sir H. Furnese, obtained last Thursday in the Kit Cat Club'. Maynwaring said Wharton, who distrusted Marlborough as a Tory at heart, tried to obstruct the admission of the Duke's banker, while Lord Mohun, so loyal to Marlborough that he later offered to second the Duke in a duel, 'prepared to open the debate' in support of Furnese. In the end, 'the members were so visibly on the knight's side that there was not a word said against him, and he was peaceably introduced to a place which he had as much a mind to as all the world has to places of another kind'.[6]

A few days before Furnese's feast, Dr Henry Sacheverell, a High Church, High Tory firebrand, had preached a sermon in St Paul's Cathedral challenging the country's post-Revolutionary constitution. Sacheverell had been invited to do so by the Tory Lord Mayor, but the Mayor could not have guessed how inflammatory the sermon would be – threatening the current government of 'False Brethren' with 'the lake which burns with fire and brimstone'. In 1688, Tory defenders of the Church of England had ultimately set aside their religious doctrine of 'non-resistance' or 'passive obedience' to the supremacy of the Crown and helped oust James II; now Sacheverell condemned their pragmatism, implying the Revolution should be reversed.

It was Sacheverell's second anti-Whig sermon of the year. A war-weary populace, strained by inflation and food shortages, and resenting the refugees arriving in London when a quarter of their countrymen were receiving parish relief, were excited by Sacheverell's militancy. They bought copies of the printed sermon in their hundreds of thousands.

The Kit-Cats were alarmed by this charismatic preacher rallying the mobs for the Tory cause, and rose to the Tory Lord Mayor's bait. A letter from one Tory to another in December 1709 reported that a plan to impeach Sacheverell before Parliament had been 'some time since fully concluded upon at the Kit-Cat Club, where my Lord Marlborough, they say, was present, assented to it, and has actually enrolled himself a member of that detestable society'.[7] This suggests the impeachment may have been discussed at Furnese's feast. Another source says the decision to impeach Sacheverell was taken by the Junto at some 'consultation' where the Duchess of Marlborough was also present 'to fill out their tea and wash their cups'[8] – probably not, therefore, a Kit-Cat meeting but a mixed-sex gathering around the Duchess' tea-table.

Wherever the idea was first mooted, it was finally resolved upon at another unofficial ministerial confab in mid-December 1709, including many Kit-Cat politicians but also non-Kit-Cats like Godolphin, Sunderland and Orford.[9] One source has Wharton and Sunderland as the most fervent proponents of impeachment, overcoming Somers' cautious preference for a lower-profile approach, while another, contradictory source states that no man was 'so pressing' as Somers 'to have Dr Sacheverell tried; and one of his arguments . . . was that if they did not do it, the Queen would be preached out of the throne and the nation ruined'.[10] Whoever was responsible, the decision to impeach would prove a terrible miscalculation.

A junior Whig MP first formally raised the matter in the Commons on 13 December, and the Whig-dominated House swiftly agreed that Sacheverell should face trial. During the following two months, while the trial was being prepared, the Tories elevated Sacheverell to their mascot and martyr. When the trial finally commenced at the end of February 1710, the streets surrounding Westminster Hall were lined with excited crowds of anti-government, pro-Sacheverell demonstrators. Feelings were running as high as when the seven bishops were tried on the eve of the 1688 Revolution. Then, young John Somers had been a counsel for the defence, with the mood of the people behind him; now, as Lord President, he must have sensed he and his friends were working against the popular will.

There were twenty 'managers' on the prosecution side, of whom eighteen acted in the trial. Nine were lawyers and, of the remaining nine who were MPs, five were Kit-Cats – or, more precisely, 'Kitlings': Walpole, Stanhope, Compton, Harry Boyle and Jack Smith. On the first day, Halifax's brother, Attorney General Sir James Montagu, was one of the first speakers for the prosecution. On day two, Walpole and Stanhope spoke to great effect. Walpole's speech was peppered with jibes against the Tories that amused the audience. He was feeling confident from his recent promotion to Treasurer of the Navy. He focused on the contradictions of the Tory position: 'To recommend themselves to the Queen they condemn that Revolution without which She never had been Queen . . . [and] to manifest their Aversion and forever to blast all Hopes of the Pretender, they advance and maintain the Hereditary Right as the only true Right to the Crown.'[11]

Stanhope's speech, though the last of the day, was the most effective of all. Using few notes, he delivered a passionate attack on Sacheverell as a thinly disguised Jacobite intent on sedition. The Lieutenant-General turned Tory texts on their heads while playing upon the latitude allowed him, as a soldier, to speak heatedly:

> There is such an Affinity, my Lords, between this Sermon and the Doctrines which are preached and propagated by a certain Set of Men . . . They are the Pure and Undefiled Church of England! The only Men of Loyal and Steady Principles! They never took the Oaths to the Government; never bent their Knee to Baal! . . . We are all

Schismatics, that is, all the rest of England are Schismatics, Heretics and Rebels! . . . If they are in the right, my Lords, what are the consequences? . . . All the Blood of so many brave Men, who have died (as they thought) in the Service of their country, has been spilt in Defence of an Usurpation, and they were only so many Rebels and Traitors.

On the third day, Compton spoke, followed by Smith, Chancellor of the Exchequer, who delivered a clear extempore speech on Whig views about toleration of Protestant Dissent. The latter condemned Sacheverell on Christian grounds, for, 'instead of preaching peace and charity and other moral virtues', taking upon himself 'to raise jealousies, foment divisions and stir up sedition'.[12] Harry Boyle made the last speech of the day to a restless, exhausted audience.

That night, Tory mobs went on the rampage and central London saw more street violence than it had during even the peak of the Civil War. Armed rioters burnt down Dissenting chapels and meeting houses, and attacked the homes of Wharton and Furnese – from the mob's viewpoint, though Wharton had objected to Furnese joining the Kit-Cat, these men were birds of the same feather. Many Kit-Cats felt in personal danger as their most alarmist fears about Jacobite rebellion seemed suddenly to be realized.

The morning after the riots, the trial proceeded, in a state of muted shock, to hear Sacheverell's defence. Sir Simon Harcourt was widely agreed to be the most eloquent defence manager, but Sacheverell also presented his own case brilliantly. Using the dock as a pulpit, the Doctor spoke to the city and countryside beyond Westminster Hall, knowing his speech would be published and disseminated before the trial's verdict. On some points Sacheverell remained unrepentant, but on the charge of sedition he declared his innocence before God, 'the Searcher of Hearts', and, as many in the audience cried with pity for his martyrdom, he prayed with seeming magnanimity for his prosecutors to be delivered from sin and error.

Addison was one Kit-Cat unable to attend Sacheverell's trial, having gone to Malmesbury to campaign for that seat – if winning the votes of only thirteen gentlemen, most of whom were thoroughly under the thumb of his patron Wharton, can be described as campaigning.

Addison's interest in the trial was personal as well as political, since Sacheverell was a former roommate from Magdalen – yet another case of a man whose flamboyant self-confidence had attracted modest Mr Addison. It is unknown whether Addison was aware of Sacheverell's 'high-flying' views about the Church and Divine Right of Kings during those university years, but Sacheverell had preached against Dissenters as 'crafty, faithless and insidious persons' for almost a decade since.[13] Addison was therefore particularly grateful for news of the trial in letters sent by Steele, who attended the trial every day and met with Kit-Cat friends to debrief on the proceedings in the evenings. Steele developed a particular friendship with Stanhope during this episode.

On 9 March, the prosecution replied to Sacheverell's defence, and on 16 March the lords began considering their verdict. Among some thirty peers who spoke that day, Wharton was one of the boldest. He dared argue, before Anne, that 'if the Revolution were not lawful, many in that House and vast Numbers without were guilty of Blood, Murder, Rapine, and Injustice; and the Queen herself was no lawful Queen'.[14] Conscious that, though they might win the vote in the Lords, they had lost in the court of public opinion, Halifax and Somers said little and sat looking grim.

When the trial ended on 20 March, Sacheverell was found guilty by a margin of only seventeen lords' votes. He received a light sentence, escaping imprisonment, but was banned from the pulpit for three years, with copies of his sermons and speeches to be confiscated and destroyed. Though Carlisle had proposed this light sentence, in order to salvage some of the Queen's favour for his party, other Kit-Cats were outraged. Smith muttered that this was a 'ridiculous judgment' that would deter nobody from Jacobite sedition.[15] Most depressing for the Kit-Cat Club, the Duke of Somerset was among five lords absent from the critical vote. Somerset claimed ill health, but his absence was interpreted as confirming his decision to defect and join with Harley against the Junto. There had been rumours since September 1709 that the flame-haired Duchess of Somerset was becoming Anne's personal favourite, supplanting the Duchess of Marlborough, while Harley, with the Queen's tacit approval, was urging Somerset to abandon his old Whig friends and colleagues. After Somerset's no-show at the Sacheverell trial, he and Shrewsbury (back from Italy) became leaders of a splinter grouping of Whigs willing to work with Harley and the Tories to form a ministry dedicated to ending the war.

The rest of the Kit-Cat Club, led by Wharton and Somers, remained firmly behind Marlborough and the policy of pursuing the conflict until the French were thoroughly contained and Spanish trading rights firmly secured for England. Halifax came closest to being seduced by Harley's offers of cross-party cooperation, since he had long nursed resentment about receiving no high office (being considered a man of 'unreasonable vanity' and ambition by Marlborough and Godolphin, and coveting Godolphin's own Treasury job[16]). It was Wharton who gave Halifax some ideological backbone and persuaded him not to go the same way as Somerset.

An emergency meeting of the Kit-Cat Club, to discuss and condemn Somerset's 'elopement' with Harley,[17] was convened in April 1710. The 'good-natured'[18] but rarely sober Charles Lenox, 1st Duke of Richmond, was chosen to host it because of his high rank and birth (an illegitimate son of Charles II by Louise de Kérouaille), and because he had been a Kit-Cat for as long as Somerset, since the 1690s. Maynwaring said it was considered essential for 'a thing of that consequence to be done in a Full House' – using parliamentary jargon to describe the Club's proceedings.[19] Whether the lisping Somerset deigned to attend his own expulsion is unknown, but non-members, hearing about it on the political grapevine, reported the meeting's outcome, saying Somerset 'was expelled the Chit-cat by a vote brought in ready cut and dried by Ld Wharton: the crime objected, the words of the vote say, was for being suspected to have held conferences with Robin the Trickster [Robert Harley]'.[20] Addison, supporting Wharton, commented that Somerset seemed, by aligning with Harley, 'to have pulled down the pillars like Sampson to perish among those he destroyed'.[21]

Another place in the Club also became vacant because of the Earl of Essex's sudden death in January 1710. The members most likely to have filled these two vacancies were 25-year-old Richard Lumley, later

2nd Earl of Scarbrough, and 20-year-old John, 2nd Duke of Montagu. Scarbrough was the son of a loyal old Whig signatory to the invitation to William, yet said to be without 'the least pride of birth or rank'.[22] An MP for East Grinstead after 1709, Scarbrough inherited his peerage upon his elder brother's death in 1710, and established himself as 'one of the best speakers of his time' in the Lords.[23] The young Duke of Montagu, meanwhile, was Halifax's cousin – a boy of 9 at Boughton House when Congreve stayed there in 1699, working on *The Way of the World*. Montagu was eccentrically generous and soft-hearted, loved childish pranks, and held radical views about educating African slaves.[24] In 1709, he had inherited his dukedom and fortune, including Montagu House, in central London, and Boughton. Montagu was also Marlborough's son-in-law, married to Henrietta's younger sister, the hot-tempered Mary, so his admission was a further signal of the Club's definitive positioning as Marlborough's defenders.

While the Kit-Cat Club was busy restocking its members, and getting into tavern brawls with Tories over whether Sacheverell should be toasted or cursed,[25] Sacheverell was celebrating as if he had been acquitted rather than convicted. The Whigs saw, from reports of the crowds that greeted Sacheverell as he toured the country, that their party would lose the next election if the Queen called it anytime soon. The Tories, seeing the same thing, organized addresses to the Queen from every corner of England, begging her to do so.

In the spring of 1710, Addison returned with Wharton to Ireland for their second year as colonial governors. Addison had become a regular contributor to *The Tatler* – and hence Steele's secret collaborator behind the mask of Isaac Bickerstaff – over the preceding winter. Now *The Dublin Gazette*, 'at the request of several Persons of Quality' (namely Addison and Wharton), advertised that *The Tatler* would be reprinted locally three times a week, as in England, so long as the packet boats brought the originals over safely.[26]

As Wharton and Addison made the same ceremonial procession up to Dublin Castle in 1710, their mood was very different from that on the same occasion a year before. Their success in winning over the majority of the Irish Parliament during 1709 was now irrelevant. Their Dublin opponents were emboldened by reports that their governors' friends no longer had the Queen's backing and were likely to lose control of the English Commons at the next election. Members of the lower (predominantly High Church and High Tory) Irish clergy disseminated a message to local churches to pray for 'Thomas Wharton, being very sick and weak' – a genuine request from the wife of a sick Dublin butcher named Thomas Wharton, put to malicious use.[27] Reports of civil unrest in England, surrounding Sacheverell, probably also emboldened the Irish: the first signs of what would later become widespread agrarian unrest were seen in Connaught in 1710, when evicted tenants protested by 'cattle-houghing' (cutting the sinews or tendons in their landlords' cattle's legs).

The Irish Parliament convened in May 1710, Wharton promoting several local men tolerant of Dissenters, and granting a pardon to a Presbyterian preacher at Drogheda. Repealing the Test Acts was now even more of a non-starter than in 1709, and the Irish Commons, particularly its Tories, more assertively resisted approving the war supply. They argued that Irish taxes should be saved for Irish armaments and fortifications, or for suppressing domestic Catholic unrest, such as the 'riotous tumult' of 'about Ten Thousand Papists' that Wharton's soldiers quashed in County Meath in June.[28] Wharton's parliamentary skills were once again evident as he overcame these objections and got Marlborough's supplies voted through. Numerous other small political defeats in Ireland, however, reflected the Whigs' coming fall from power in London: the appointment of a Tory Provost at Trinity College Dublin; the vandalization by Tory students of a statue of William III; a delay in funds from London to demolish the Tories' favourite tavern in order to build a wider entrance to Dublin Castle.

Addison – preparing to lose his income as Secretary for Ireland after the next general election in England – purchased a lifelong sinecure as Keeper of Records of Bermingham Tower in Dublin Castle. This post had been worth only £10 per annum, but Addison had the salary raised to £400 (over £42,000 today), as a kind of pension. Addison once defined a corrupt man as one 'who upon any Pretence whatsoever receives more than what is the stated and unquestioned Fee of his Office',[29] and the evidence suggests that he lived up to this probity in all his offices,[30] while feeling no guilt about giving himself a post and then raising its salary.

A second, unexpected fortune came to Addison at about the same time. Addison had had his younger brother Gulston appointed President of the United East India Company's Council and Governor of Fort St George in Madras in December 1708. It was a job worth up to £20,000 a year (or over £2 million today). Now Addison received news that Gulston had died in suspicious circumstances at Fort St George, bequeathing Addison his United East India Company holdings.

Steele's finances were also improving, in keeping with his rising status within the Kit-Cat Club thanks to *The Tatler*'s unprecedented popularity. Steele was no longer simply Addison's sidekick, though Addison still complimented his friend on particular *Tatlers* in the tone of a teacher patting a pupil on the head. In January 1710, before the Sacheverell trial announced the reversal of their political fortunes, the Kit-Cat patrons saw to it that Steele received a Commission in the Stamp Office, worth £300 a year (some £32,000 today). Nearly forty Kit-Cats and Kit-Cat relations also recognized *The Tatler*'s achievement by subscribing to the publication of a first collected volume of its essays. Tonson collected the subscriptions at his new premises, marked by the sign of Shakespeare's Head, on the south side of the Strand, facing Catherine Street, which then cut across today's Aldwych.

In July 1710, Steele dedicated this collected *Tatler* volume not to any patron with deep pockets, but to his Kit-Cat colleague, Maynwaring, declaring nobody had a 'nobler Spirit for the Contempt of all Imposture'.[31] This dedication recognized that Maynwaring, keenly observant under deceptively heavy eyelids, and said to be 'the ruling man in all conversations',[32] had assumed the role of the Whigs' unofficial chief of propaganda since the 1708 election. The most political *Tatlers* that summer (nos. 187 and 193) were written by Maynwaring, or based on his hints. Maynwaring persuaded Steele that the time had passed for Isaac Bickerstaff's cosy, avuncular reports from his club – that a new political situation demanded less subtle rhetoric. *The Tatler* therefore started risking more essays that explicitly defended the current Whig ministry. Steele filled one issue that should have celebrated the Queen on her birthday, for example, with a celebration of her leading ministers instead. This 'Constellation' of talent, he wrote, reflected 'a lustre upon each other, but in a more particular manner on their Sovereign',[33] suggesting power and influence now shone in a radically reversed direction, from subject to monarch. This was the great Whig inversion of traditional political philosophy, to which Steele subscribed all the more enthusiastically after listening to the Sacheverell trial's contest of ideologies. It was the kind of journalism, subtly undermining the Queen's authority, which caused the Tory leader Henry St John to denounce 'all the Pains which have been taken to lessen her Character . . . by the Wits of the Kit-Cat'.[34]

Steele continued to struggle in his private life. A disgruntled letter in April 1710 told Prue, who seems to have passed the last month of another pregnancy at Addison's summer cottage at Sandy End, that she was neglecting the simple wifely duty of companionship: 'Rising a little in a morning and being disposed to cheerfulness . . . would not be amiss.'[35] Mrs Steele's moodiness is explained when we learn that, despite his sizeable Stamp Office income, Steele was once again confined to a 'sponging house', an institution for debtors kept by a bailiff or sheriff's officer, later that same month. Swift recorded that Steele was only 'a little while in prison',[36] but other published pamphlets suggest he was still required to sleep in the sponging house six months later. During the daytime, Steele worked to pay off his debts, writing little notes to Prue to send him clean laundry before various business meetings. Tradesmen friends, rather than Kit-Cat patrons, kept him in pocket money. 'Why should it be necessary that a Man should be rich to be generous?' Bickerstaff asked in *The Tatler*, which continued to appear despite its editor's incarceration.[37]

Steele would therefore have been in curfewed custody when his son Richard was born on 25 May 1710. Two Kit-Cats, Halifax and Hopkins, stood as godfathers at the boy's baptism at St James's Church, Piccadilly, in June. Steele must have been bitterly amused that he could summon such powerful and wealthy godparents, and receive the whole town's applause for *The Tatler*, yet could not find the relatively small sums needed to buy his own freedom.

That same spring, legislation colloquially known as the 1709 Copyright Act passed into law. It was the first statutory protection of literary property in England, and Tonson was a prime mover behind it. Tonson's motive in lobbying for the Act was not to secure better rights or incomes for authors like Steele, struggling to make ends meet, but to address the growth of piracy. Grub Street publishers like Edmund Curll printed pirated editions of plays or poems circulating in manuscript, without the author's permission, and though Tonson might ultimately profit from such piracy if the unauthorized edition prompted the author to print a 'correct' one afterwards, more often the author's text was gazumped at the last minute by some inferior imitator. Tonson therefore used his Kit-Cat contacts to lobby for the new law, and Addison established a committee to consider 'amendments made by the Lords in a Bill to encourage learning by vesting the property in printed books in their authors and publishers'.[38] Addison and Steele also raised public awareness by writing in *The Tatler* of professional authors' hardships, comparing themselves to merchants who come home after long voyages and find their countrymen can immediately plunder whatever they bring into port.

The Copyright Act passed through the Lords on the third attempt,[39] recognizing and protecting authors' rights for the first time in English history. The law had significant impact in other, unforeseen ways: it made authorship seem a more respectable profession and reduced authors' dependence on aristocratic patrons like those of the Kit-Cat Club. The Act also inadvertently increased the importance of the author as individual originator, rather than anonymous collaborator.[40] If Tonson, Addison and Steele could have looked into the future, they would have seen how copyright contributed to the decline of the Kit-Cat Club's idiosyncratic methods of literary subsidy.

In the short term, the new Act protected Tonson's rights to his unrivalled backlist of English classics, including Shakespeare's plays, though the penalties for piracy were not effectively applied until after Tonson's lifetime. It was no coincidence that the Act was introduced in the same year as Tonson published the first critical edition of Shakespeare, edited by the dramatist Nicholas Rowe – a volume reprinted frequently until Tonson's copyright ran out in 1731, and which was largely responsible for repopularizing Shakespeare in the eighteenth century. Tonson also promptly registered his ownership of all Congreve's dramatic works and brought them out in collected form, authorized and edited by the playwright himself. Both English literature's Renaissance and more recent past were being fixed as objects of veneration for a new generation of self-confident Britons.

The Copyright Act was one of the last pieces of legislation passed by the Whigs before the Tories made their push for power in the summer of 1710. '[I]n England, a man is less safe as to politics than he is in a bark upon the coast, in regard to the change of wind and the danger of shipwreck,'[41] wrote Prior, whose long-leaking ship was finally about to come into port.

In June 1710, Sunderland – the strident Whig whom Anne had appointed as Secretary of State against her own inclinations – was dismissed and replaced by a Tory. It was the first sure sign that the Whigs and Marlboroughs were about to fall. In August, Godolphin was dismissed as Lord Treasurer, and was replaced by Harley. Kit-Cat Jack Smith, Chancellor of the Exchequer, was a heartbroken witness to this unceremonious dismissal, resigning in protest. An anonymous Tory published some verses on Godolphin's fall:

> Behold the Man who bore the powerful Wand
> Ensign of Treasure and supreme Command
> Reduced by an offended Monarch's Wrath
> To bowl [i.e. booze] with Hopkins and be praised by Garth.[42]

Dr Garth published a broadside eulogy to Godolphin, regretting the 'star sinister' that threw the Treasurer from office.[43] Steele and Hopkins (dismissed as Under-Secretary of State for the South when Sunderland was dismissed as Secretary) went to pay their respects to the former Treasurer at Putney shortly afterwards. Though Marlborough remained in command of the army, the writing was on the wall for him too. Congreve was shocked: 'No man that I know (without exception of any) is able to make any conjecture of what is intended by the proceedings at Court.'[44]

On 19 September, a group of Kit-Cat ministers – Somers, Devonshire, Boyle – resigned in protest at the prospect of serving under Harley.

Two days later, Anne dissolved Parliament and called a general election, without consulting the Privy Council. Wharton and the last leading Whigs were removed on the 26th. Walpole was told he would be replaced as Secretary-at-War, but survived Tory corruption charges and became leader of the Whig opposition in the Commons. He began to host dinners for the deposed Whigs, supplementing those of the Kit-Cat Club, at his London home in winter and in Chelsea during the summer. With these ministerial changes, the Queen's wishes were signalled to every electoral patron across the country.

The calling of the 1710 election marked the outbreak of the 'paper war' between the Whigs and Tories. Before *The Tatler*, the only regular paper aside from the government *Gazette* had been Daniel Defoe's *Review*. By the end of 1711, some 200,000 copies of newspapers and periodicals were in circulation every week. Godolphin's government had 'ever despised the Press, and never could think a nation capable of being influenced' by its productions,[45] but the Kit-Cat Club patrons felt otherwise. Maynwaring took orders through the Kit-Cat Club to marshal the Whig writers, including Benjamin Hoadly. Harley, meanwhile, paid liberally for the production of numerous anti-Junto newspapers, satires and pamphlets.

One anonymous anti-Whig ballad was titled 'A Song at the Kit-Cat Club' and anticipated the *Beggar's Opera*'s analogy between petty and political crime:

> What signifies a Whore or two,
> To Bridewell sent and whipped,
> Whilst the great Rogues unpunished go
> And all the Kingdom's stripped?

Another anonymous ballad, likely commissioned by Harley, described the Kit-Cats as 'Hard-mouthed Sots' advancing 'their Canting State' by any Machiavellian means.[46] A third, authored anonymously by Swift, ridiculed the Junto's political impotence by analogy with the ageing Kit-Cats' collective sexual impotence. This was a poem claiming to have been found in the cabinet of one Mrs Anne Long, a former Kit-Cat toast, entitled 'An Essay to Restore the Kit-Cat

Members to their lost Abilities, for the sake of the LADIES who admire 'em':

> Are these Men for Their Business fit?
> Shall one of these Men think to come,
> With Claret reeking, reeling home,
> To do a longing Lady Right,
> That has expected him all Night?[47]

Such verses appealed beyond the educated elite, while Whig propaganda was usually limited to prose works addressed to local office-holders and landowners. Whig writers usually only penned *ad hominem* attacks on the Tory hacks in Grub Street, but Tory journalists attacked Whig leaders directly. Like government ministers who spoke with pride of ignoring public opinion, the Whig writers could not let go of Drydenesque snobbery about writing for the uneducated. Only Maynwaring was happy slinging mud to popular tunes, composing an updated 1710 sequel to his lively anti-Harley hit of 1708, 'A New Ballad: To The Tune of Fair Rosamund'.[48] Two country-dances, entitled 'The Kit Cat Club (1 and 2)' and first printed in the 1710 edition *Playford's Dancing Master* may also have been part of the Whig election campaign.

Harley hired literary henchmen (and women) able to match or better those of the Kit-Cat Club. Defoe, who had done the odd writing job for Kit-Cat patrons whenever he felt their commission was in keeping 'with my Reason, my Principle, my Inclination and the Duty every man owes to his country and his posterity',[49] now turned his *Review* into a mouthpiece of the Harleyite Whigs. Mrs Manley also wrote for Harley as a Tory and settled an old personal score by portraying Steele as 'Monsieur le Ingrate' in a bestselling satirical romance.[50]

Harley also recruited former Lord Dorset's Boy and Kit-Cat, Matthew Prior. In September 1710, between Godolphin's dismissal and the 1710 elections, Prior wrote in *The Examiner*, a new Tory journal he helped found, criticizing the Kit-Cats as monopolizers of literary fame. Prior referred to his own expulsion from the Club (which still rankled), and mocked Furnese's literary pretensions in gaining admission. Prior went on to ridicule Garth's eulogy to Godolphin. As recompense for *The Examiner*, Harley paid Prior enough to buy a modest house in Essex – a richer reward than any diplomatic posting or salary advance Prior had ever received from Dorset or Halifax.

Addison accepted Maynwaring's invitation to write for the Whig cause after his return from Ireland in August 1710. When Prior's *Examiner* piece appeared, Addison answered with a new paper called *The Whig Examiner*. Published weekly until early October 1710, Addison wrote three issues before the elections and two while they were in progress. Defending the Junto ministry, *The Whig Examiner* also defended Garth's poetry. On politics, it preached to the coverted, with elegantly expressed but rather stale arguments. As Swift remarked, the Whigs' problem was that they wrote propaganda '[n]ot with a View of convincing their Adversaries, but to raise the Spirits of their Friends'.[51] Addison's ethics were also a hindrance: '[I]t shows a good Mind to forbear answering Calumnies and Reproaches in the same Spirit of Bitterness with which they are offered,' he said.[52] Addison was, moreover, too willing to admit both parties exaggerated their cases: 'How many Persons of undoubted Probity and exemplary Virtue, on either side, are blackened and defamed?'[53]

Maynwaring closed the toothless *Whig Examiner* after its fifth issue, and tried replacing it with another paper called *The Medley*. Whether or not the Kit-Cat Club's dinners were used to plan press strategy, the paper war more closely united the Kit-Cats in friendship and partisan solidarity. Garth was asked to edit *The Medley*, but limited himself to becoming a contributor, alongside Addison, Steele, and Anthony Henley, who wrote pieces in the personae of tradesmen, peasants or servants.[54] *The Tatler* also continued to serve the Whig Junto's cause, making Harley's government determined to close it down, despite its popularity. On the eve of the election, the Tory *Moderator* reported, menacingly, the imminent death of Isaac Bickerstaff, which would be 'much lamented by the Gentlemen of the Kit-Kat-Club and all true Republican Spirits'.[55]

When the country went to the polls in October 1710, the Tories won by a landslide, gaining a majority of nearly 200 MPs, around fifty of whom openly expressed Jacobite sympathies. Since the Commons was the engine of Whig power, this meant total defeat for the party. Exactly two years earlier, Swift had called the Whig takeover a 'new world'; now he used the same phrase to describe another, in reverse.[56]

The Kit-Cat MPs fared better than other Whig candidates, since their Club patrons allocated some of the safest seats to them. Since early September, the Junto had been conferring about who to put forward as candidates where, and in the end only five Kit-Cat MPs were not returned.[57] The most surprising and significant unseating was that of Stanhope. He had returned to Spain by the time of the election, but none of the Kit-Cats worried much when a Tory brewer challenged him in his Westminster seat. Stanhope's status as a war hero made him seem a racing certainty against a lowly tradesman. Addison published an essay in which a Stanhope-like character declares, 'Let it not avail my competitor that he has been tapping his Liquors while I have been spilling my Blood . . . !'[58] But Tory satires published before the election undermined Stanhope's claim to heroic masculinity, accusing him of sodomy (an accusation made seven years' previously in another Tory satire, over which Stanhope ignored Stepney's advice to sue[59]). The satirists focused Londoners' anti-war feelings against the Commander, and the brewer won the seat by a landslide. Walpole urged Stanhope to return from Spain as soon as possible after the results came in: 'Dear Stanhope, God prosper you and pray make haste to us that you may see what you would not believe.'[60]

While Wharton lost many seats previously under his control, he at least managed to see Addison returned, uncontested, in Malmesbury. Swift nonetheless attributed the victory to Addison's personal qualities, remarking that if Addison 'had a mind to be chosen king, he would hardly be refused'.[61] Addison was, at this moment, in Swift's favour thanks to various flattering letters Addison had sent Swift in an effort to woo the satirist away from Harley's patronage. Three days after Addison's victory, he dined with Swift and Garth at the Devil tavern on Fleet Street, but it was clear that Harley was winning the contest for Swift's allegiance, flattering him with one-to-one meetings and sensitive information of the kind that the Junto had always refused him.

Harley never intended to lead a purely Tory administration. He had hoped for a more evenly split Parliament that would allow him to rule as an unfettered power broker, above a coalition of Tories and anti-war Whigs. He was therefore almost as alarmed as the Whigs by the Tory landslide, forcing him to serve a single party. At first, Harley and his closest colleague, Henry St John, tried to retain a few junior Kit-Cats in the administration, but one by one their loyalty to their Whig patrons made their positions untenable. Nor did Harley have any great wish to purge Congreve, who had always maintained personal friendships with Tories as well as Whigs, from his 'little Office' for licensing wines. When Halifax asked Harley to leave Congreve alone, Harley readily assented, quoting from the *Aeneid*: 'We Tyrians are not so devoid of sense / Nor so remote from Phoebus' influence'.[62]

Swift therefore had little grounds to boast, as he did, of having saved Congreve's job. Swift's lobbying for Congreve was not evidence of their friendship, in fact, so much as evidence of how much Swift enjoyed playing patron to a man he had envied since they were boys in Kilkenny. Swift's *Schadenfreude* seeps through his descriptions of how physically incapacitated Congreve had grown by the age of 40, describing him as gout-ridden and 'almost blind with cataracts'.[63] As Swift catalogues long hours spent at Congreve's lodgings during this period, one reads between the lines that the invalid host could not risk offending Swift by asking him to leave.[64]

The reluctance of Addison, who despite his own eye troubles remained far more robust and self-sufficient than Congreve, to accept Swift's help as an intermediary with Harley is clear from one of Swift's journal entries that October;

> I was this morning with Mr Lewis, the Under-Secretary to Lord Dartmouth, two hours, talking politics, and contriving to keep Steele in his office of Stamp-paper . . . in the evening, [I] went to sit with Mr Addison and offer the matter at distance to him, as the discreeter person, but found party had so possessed him that he talked as if he suspected me, and would not fall in with anything I said. So I stopped short in my overture and we parted very dryly; and I shall say nothing to Steele and let them do as they will.[65]

As Swift sought out Addison that autumn, both men appear to have been under similar instructions from their respective superiors to cultivate one another's company and report back any intelligence gained. Swift dined with Addison and Garth again on 27 October, and with Addison and Vanbrugh on 8 November, just six days after Swift's first anonymous attack on Marlborough appeared in *The Examiner*.

Swift complained the Kit-Cats were 'insufferably Peevish' after their loss of power.[66] He was as alienated by their reluctance to accept his help as he had been by the reluctance of Somers, Halifax and Wharton to grant him their patronage in earlier years. Addison's and Congreve's esteem for Swift has been consistently overestimated, most of the evidence of their 'friendship and dearness'[67] coming from Swift's diaries or from letters containing flattery clearly intended to prevent Swift from writing against them. In truth, the Kit-Cats were always wary of Swift, even when he seemed their ally, and Swift sensed this distrust. Swift always spoke of Addison and Steele as a pair, calling one ungrateful for favours done to the other, and his journal entries reek with envy of the two men's friendship. Now he found they liked him even less in the self-importance of his attentions from Harley. Tellingly, when Addison and Steele resisted Swift's offers to represent them, Swift described them as choosing instead to 'club' with one another.[68]

Despite resolving to wipe his hands of the Kit-Cats, Swift arranged two appointments for Steele to call on Harley in November 1710. Swift's assumption that Steele would plead to keep his position in the Stamp Office failed to take account of Steele's unbreakable Kit-Cat allegiances and genuine political convictions. Steele appears to have missed both appointments, in at least one case deliberately. Steele claimed he was actively choosing principles over profit: 'I rejoice that I had spirit to refuse what had been lately offered Me.'[69] This referred to a new carrot Harley's intermediaries had waved before his nose if he would break with the Junto: the job of managing the Drury Lane theatre.

Addison, as expected, lost his place as Irish Secretary when Wharton was replaced as Lord Lieutenant of Ireland by a Tory, just days after their return from Dublin.[70] Swift could not comprehend why Addison did not want to keep a post under a non-Whig ministry, 'which by a little compliance he might have done'.[71] Soon after,

Wharton was threatened with impeachment for having pardoned the Presbyterian preacher in Drogheda and for removing an Irish officer solely so he could resell the commission for profit. Addison corresponded with friends in Dublin about the injustice of the charges against his patron, saying he felt 'bound in Honour to do him what Right I can'.[72] The proceedings were eventually dropped.

Addison also corresponded about a private business scheme by which he hoped to cushion the loss of his Irish income. He seems to have tried out a sideline as a shoe importer to Ireland, probably intending to sell them to army regiments, but in September 1710, he received 'Ill news of my shoes being damaged' at sea,[73] and came to regard the venture as worthier of Steele than himself. Addison never risked anything similar again.

Swift dined with Addison and Steele yet again on 10 November 1710. They must have suspected that he was the anonymous author of the piece that had appeared in *The Examiner* the previous day: the beginning of a concerted press attack on Wharton. This attack was the start of Swift's revenge for all the snubs he had suffered while lobbying Wharton on behalf of the Irish Church. He wrote savagely of the Whigs in his journal: 'Rot 'em for ungrateful dogs; I will make them repent their usage.'[74] In December, Swift also published anonymously the piece of invective against Wharton he had had in hand on the yacht home from Dublin the previous summer. *A Short Character of His Excellency Thomas Earl of Wharton, Lord Lieutenant of Ireland* sold 2,000 copies in two days[75] and inflicted lasting damage on Wharton's reputation. It denounced him as 'a public robber, an adulterer, a defiler of altars'. Swift wrote that no Irishman 'now possesseth more than what the Governor's Lust and Avarice have overlooked; or what he was forced to neglect out of mere Weariness and Satiety of Oppression',[76] and indeed there is some contemporary evidence to support these charges that Wharton profited exorbitantly (a personal profit of at least £45,000, or around £4.8 million today) from his time as Irish Lord Lieutenant. Swift, behind the anonymous mask of *The Examiner*, wrote of 'the wonderful Delight of libelling Men in power, and hugging yourself in a Corner with mighty Satisfaction for what you have done'.[77] Smug with the power of his pen, Swift was possibly also the author of a verse satire in which the Kit-Cat members ask themselves with punning hindsight:

> Disgraced, Undone, and made the Nation's Sport,
> From Places turned, and banished from the Court,
> Why did we not (Fools as we were) foresee,
> Our *Swift* Destruction in a Monarchy?[78]

Wharton tried to appear unaffected by *A Short Character* and other journalistic attacks, telling the House of Lords that 'I matter 'em not', but he was shaken by the onslaught. Addison referred to *A Short Character* as 'a scurrilous little book',[79] and, perhaps suspecting the identity of its author, started steering clear of Swift: 'Mr Addison and I are different as black and white, and I believe our friendship will go off by this d[amn] business of party,' Swift told a friend. 'He cannot bear seeing me fall in so with this Ministry; but I love him still as much as ever, though we seldom meet.'[80]

During the 1710 election, the only Tory clubs were those organized by Tory MPs in certain counties.[81] Over the winter of 1710–11, however, a group of Tory backbenchers formed what became known as 'The October Club' (either in honour of the Tory election landslide that October or because the members drank 'October Ale'), dedicated to influencing the policy of Harley's government. It met at the Bell tavern in King Street, Westminster, and had nearly 150 members, whom Defoe denounced as 'oath-taking Jacobites, self-contradicting, moon-blind high-flyers [ultra-conservative Anglicans]'.[82] That a journalist in Harley's pay should take such a line indicates Harley was as troubled as the Kit-Cats by these extremist Tory backbenchers. The Octoberites were angry that Somerset or any Whig had been invited into the government; they called for the impeachment of all Whig leaders and merciless suppression of Dissenters.

Harley countered the October Club's political organization with the much more exclusive 'Saturday Club': dinners held at his home each Saturday, to which Harley invited Henry St John, Sir Simon Harcourt and two or three other close colleagues to discuss policy and strategy, just as the Whig Junto did on Thursdays at the Kit-Cat. Swift was immensely flattered to be invited too.

Steele, for all his talk of sacrificing income to principle, may have cut a deal with Harley in early 1711 by which he would be permitted to keep his Stamp Office job on the understanding that he closed *The Tatler*. The 'death' of Isaac Bickerstaff therefore came on 2 January 1711, when the last *Tatler* appeared. The writer John Gay, then a young man just arrived in London, reported on how even Tories mourned the loss of this witty and wise periodical.

In the last number, Steele revealed his authorship (which had been effectively known, at least in literary London, for some time) and hinted heavily at Addison's large number of contributions. Steele may not have had his friend's permission to drop such hints, as Addison remarked that he was 'surprised'[83] to be so unmasked and left for Bath the following morning, saying he needed to drink the waters for his eyesight. There was, Addison remarked, 'something very barbarous and inhuman in the ordinary Scribblers of London'[84] and he was reluctant to be known as one of them. Around the same date, Maynwaring was writing optimistically to the Duchess of Marlborough that 'it is possible to scribble these men [Harley's ministry] down'.[85] Such contrasting Kit-Cat remarks show the gap between Addison's view of journalism as literature and Maynwaring's view of it as propaganda.

In March 1711, probably thinking of Swift's attacks on Wharton, Addison lamented satire without signature as 'Arrows that fly in the dark', which inflict 'a secret Shame or Sorrow in the Mind of the suffering Person'.[86] Swift's role as the leading contributor to *The Examiner* was made public by a Whig pamphlet in May, forcing him temporarily to lay down his pen to avoid prosecution for libel.

Luckily for Swift, the Tories were clasping him firmly to their political bosom that spring, by establishing a club specifically intended, Swift said, 'as a rival to the Whig Kit-Kat Club'.[87] Henry St John and several Tory literati, such as Dr Arbuthnot (the Tories' caustic equivalent to Dr Garth), founded the 'Brothers Club',[88] and by June 1711 Swift had joined. Prior also became a member, grateful to have new comrades to replace those who disowned him in 1701.

The Brothers took in 'none but men of wit or men of interest; and if we go on as we begin, no other club in this town will be worth talking of,' Swift boasted. The Club took the Kit-Cat model of mixing literary men with politicians and patrons, who footed the bills for meals, though 'with none of the Extravagance of the Kit-Cat'.[89] It even met on Thursdays, at the same time as the Kit-Cat, sometimes at the Thatched-House tavern near St James's, but also – unlike the Kit-Cat – at members' homes, including Prior's on Duke Street. (There is an anecdote, with a nice touch of unintentional irony, about Prior trying to feed these Tory friends the kind of humble fare he ate in his Kit-Cat days, leading Swift to complain of indigestion: '[M]ade a debauch after nine at Prior's house, and have eaten cold pie, and I hate the thoughts of it, and I am full, and I don't like it.'[90])

St John was the Brothers' chief patron, as only the sons of Harley and Harcourt were admitted, not their ministerial fathers. Though Harley appears to have made financial contributions towards the Brothers, the Club soon turned into a base for St John's personal rivalry with Harley, and patronage through the Kit-Cat model of dispensing government offices was tricky for St John to organize alone.

After *The Tatler* closed, Steele shifted his political views to other publications. Realizing Steele would not be gagged by the threat of unemployment, Harley and the Brothers started to encourage Tory propaganda depicting Steele as a Grub Street hireling and republican menace – a smear campaign to be relentlessly pursued for several years. The charge of being a hack was unfair: Steele, more than most, believed that when he wrote for the Whigs he was 'writing for his country'. He was, literally and intellectually, deeply invested, and willing to pay the price of his beliefs.

XV
IN THEIR OWN IMAGE

> [W]ho is there so remarkable in any sort of Learning that would not be content to part with all his past Reputation to be able for the future to write like the *Spectator*?
>
> ARTHUR MAYNWARING in *The Medley*, 4 April 1712[1]

THE PUBLIC'S SORROW at *The Tatler*'s closure in January 1711 turned, on 1 March 1711, to excitement at a new dish, served fresh six mornings a week: Addison and Steele's *Spectator*. Like its predecessor, it sold for a penny, consisted of a single essay by a narrator ('Mr Spectator'), and often incorporated both real and fictional readers' letters. Steele was the paper's instigator, but Addison, with time on his hands since his dismissal, committed to writing an equal share of the daily essays. Soon, thanks to Steele's reverence for his friend, Addison dominated the paper's tone and editorial line.

The Spectator would have an immediate and lasting influence on British society, journalism and literature, creating a whole new style of conversational criticism and engagement with contemporary culture. Addison's 1954 biographer concluded that its influence in Britain 'might be found to exceed that of any other work except the Bible'.[2]

The Spectator's authorship was again anonymous, but the first issue acknowledged the biographical curiosity of readers, which the unmasking of Isaac Bickerstaff had recently intensified: 'I have observed,' wrote Addison, 'that a Reader seldom peruses a Book with Pleasure till he knows whether the Writer of it be a black or a fair Man, of a mild or a choleric Disposition, Married or a Bachelor.'[3] Most readers would have believed that Mr Spectator was Steele (not least because he gave the narrator his own short face and body) with occasional assistance from several others. Few beyond their closest friends knew the extent of Addison's contribution.

Thanks to their patrons' political demise, Addison and Steele were now more equal in their material circumstances than at any time since their schooldays. Each retained one English salary: Addison his Magdalen fellowship; Steele his Stamp Office pay. Knowing he could not push his luck too far with the latter, Steele agreed the new paper should take a politically moderate stance: Mr Spectator's manifesto was to 'observe an exact Neutrality between the Whigs and the Tories, unless I shall be forced to declare myself by the Hostilities of either side'.[4] The first part of this statement showed Addison's influence – having 'bridled' Steele's Whig zeal[5] – while the second part remained a coded warning that *The Spectator* would not be intimidated by Harley.

A dozen or so retailers collected the advertisements that financed the paper, including Steele's friend Charles Lillie, a perfumier and snuff-seller on the Strand. Addison wrote on *The Spectator*'s economic benefits, boasting it would 'consume a considerable quantity of our Paper Manufacture, employ our Artisans in printing, and find Business for great Numbers of Indigent Persons' (as its hawkers). Journalism was, in his eyes, a compassionate capitalist venture, 'providing Bread for a Multitude'.[6] By late 1712, it was providing a great deal of 'bread' for Tonson, whose firm printed it jointly with Sam Buckley. *The Spectator*'s profits amply repaid all Tonson's investment in the Kit-Cat Club.

The paper's earliest issues were written by the two friends working side by side. Addison would make rough notes through the day ('a whole Sheet full of Hints that would look like a Rhapsody of Nonsense to anybody but myself'[7]), then compose his essays orally, declaiming as he paced the room, while Steele, with healthier eyesight and residual deference, was tasked with 'throwing it upon Paper'.[8] At the end of the essay, they would look into their books, 'consider which of the Ancient Authors have touched upon the Subject', and insert a Latin or Greek motto at the start.[9] Addison then spent hours editing the piece, even interrupting a print run to correct his own prose. Steele, by contrast, wrote quickly, volubly and somewhat carelessly, relying on Addison for overall editorial cohesion.

As time wore on and *The Spectator*'s parameters became established, Addison and Steele worked much more independently. Addison wrote alone in his study, in an armchair with a lamp burning at his elbow, while Steele was one of those rare writers who liked to write in crowded public places, perhaps because such spots were less distracting than his household of unhappy wife, demanding mother-in-law, bawling infants and probing debt collectors. A bookseller in Lincoln's Inn Fields claimed Steele wrote his first 'rudimental Essays in Spectatorship', and sorted through readers' letters, at a table in his shop front,[10] and Steele worked so often at Tonson's shop on the Strand that he kept a personal stock of wine there. The difference in the two men's habits also reflected Addison's nervousness about his authorship being revealed, while Steele was happy to be celebrated, through knowing winks, as Mr Spectator. The fictional persona added gravitas to Steele's opinions and blended Addison's writing seamlessly with his own. Steele would readily have credited Addison's work if Addison had wished it, but it suited both that he did not.

Like *The Tatler*, *The Spectator* operated at the level of innuendo. It gently indoctrinated its readers not by demonizing Tories and Jacobites but by making them seem silly and unfashionable. Such prejudice-setting was lethally effective when it came to those readers in the 'middle condition' in London, the provinces and England's new colonies, who wanted to be told how to behave, what to read and what to think. These readers sought a moral education outside the Church, a critical education without pedantry and a social education without condescension. In providing all this, Addison and Steele transformed the journalistic profession into one as much about shaping taste and opinion as communicating facts.

The Spectator's second issue introduced the literary conceit of the 'Spectator Club',[11] which would be used sporadically thereafter. This imaginary dining club included representatives of many different professions and classes – as if the Club was the nation's body politic in miniature. The two most dominant characters were Sir Andrew Freeport, a Whig entrepreneur, in whom many saw Sir Henry Furnese ('He made his Fortunes himself; and says that England may be richer than other Kingdoms by as plain Methods as he himself is richer than other Men'[12]), and Sir Roger de Coverley, a Worcestershire landowner, Tory baronet and fox-hunter. Sir Roger was presented as harmless, eccentric and lovable, but also old-fashioned and dim-witted.

While Sir Andrew Freeport won Spectator Club arguments on issues like the nature of charity and prosperity, Sir Roger won the reader's affection, especially in his behaviour towards those below him. 'When he comes into a House,' Steele wrote of Sir Roger, 'he calls Servants by their Names and talks [to them] all the way upstairs to a Visit.'[13] Addison, who was the primary creator of Sir Roger, was playing on the old literary theme of the town's superiority to the country, while at the same time, in making Sir Roger so likeable, advocating reconciliation between the 'Landed' and 'Monied' interests. It was an approach much influenced by earlier Kit-Cat authors: Vanbrugh's *Relapse* (1696), for example, presented a Jacobite character, Young Fashion, as essentially sympathetic and redeemable, and that play's ending found redemption in the symbolic marriage of town and country.

The Tories believed the 'Monied Interest' had been perverting government since the 1690s, and *The Spectator* was launched during a particularly fierce Tory backlash against new money. The Tories passed the 1711 Landed Property Qualification Act, for example, to exclude all but landowners from becoming MPs, but this only resulted in men who had become rich through commerce buying country estates, making older families feel even more dispossessed and squeezed. Preaching the mutual interdependence of town and country in this context, while ostensibly neutral, was therefore a Whig project. It became a debate about which class was the truest repository of English virtues: the urban 'middling sort' or the nobility or peasantry. The Whiggish *Spectator* championed the 'middling sort', determined to spread the culture of the capital throughout the country.

C. S. Lewis wrote that fondness for *The Spectator*'s Sir Roger expressed the superiority that 'the victorious party so easily accords to the remnants of a vanishing order'.[14] If so, the Kit-Cats' superiority was either prophetic or nostalgic, since Sir Roger was conceived at a time when the Whig elite had every reason to doubt its political survival, and when Addison and Steele had to project a confidence in their own futures that they did not feel.

The subliminal message was that neither Sir Roger nor Sir Andrew was a party zealot, as demonstrated by their belonging to the same club. Given that Addison and Steele did not belong to such a non-partisan club, this might have laid them open to charges of hypocrisy, but by inviting Tory friends like young Alexander Pope to contribute to *The Spectator*, they used the publication to supplement the partisanship of their Kit-Cat careers (and, they hoped, declaw Pope as a potential enemy). By not making the Spectator Club a venue for cultural patronage, they sidestepped direct comparisons with the Kit-Cat.

Some readers, reasoning that Steele could not write so many essays single-handedly, believed the Spectator Club really existed, the members taking turns writing; or suspected the Spectator Club was an apolitical front for the paper's collective authorship by the Kit-Cats. The real relationship between the Kit-Cat Club and *The Spectator* was less direct but more profound.

Most superficially, the Kit-Cat Club was the two authors' primary source for the experience of what it was like to attend an all-male dining club, since neither were members of any other clubs prior to 1711. More interestingly, *The Spectator*'s much-admired prose style was a flower grown from the bed of Kit-Cat conversation. Virginia Woolf observed that all the great eighteenth-century writers seem to have learned to write by talking, and the Kit-Cat Club was one of the most demanding arenas in which Addison and Steele exercised their conversational skills. Steele felt writing second best to the simplicity and sincerity of unpremeditated speech, and directly equated a man's personal charm with his charm on the page: 'The good Writer makes his Reader better pleased with himself, and the agreeable Man makes his Friends enjoy themselves rather than him.'[15] Style in speech and prose was part of a single project of elegant self-depiction and self-projection.

Many *Spectator* essays move from a particular anecdote into a wider, generalized discussion – a classic format for clubbable conversation. The *Spectator* essays gain additional strength through their cross-referencing, such that they formed an ongoing conversation with regular readers from week to week, flattering them into feeling 'in the club' and encouraging them to participate by sending in their letters.

Other facets of *The Spectator*'s style also derived from earlier Kit-Cats' writings, such as Congreve's aphorisms, or Garth's combination of allegorical, mock-epic elements with a socially reforming message in *The Dispensary*. The trick of writing apparently non-political literature that contained strong Whig subtexts was learned from plays such as Vanbrugh's *The Relapse* (1696), in which a child's rebellion against an 'arbitrary' parent is an allegory of a nation's rebellion against its 'arbitrary' king.

As the periodical progressed, its authors made less use of the Spectator Club device, but the club theme never entirely disappeared, thanks to *The Spectator*'s obsession with classifying people. Addison's first *Spectator* essay on the subject of 'those little Nocturnal Assemblies, which are commonly known by the Name of *Clubs*' mentioned the Kit-Cat, but, like Ned Ward, mixed real with fictional clubs invented for satirical effect. There was the Club of Fat-Men where a man could not be a member if he could fit through the door, the Hum-Drum Club of men who smoked their pipes in silence, and the Club of Duellists (which 'did not continue long, most of the Members of it being put to the Sword or hanged'[16]). In another essay, Addison described the Everlasting Club, whose members sat in twenty-four-hour rotation so that there was always company to be found for a drink. It claimed to have started during the Civil War, treating 'all other Clubs with an Eye of Contempt, and talks even of the Kit-Cat and October [Clubs] as a Couple of Upstarts'.[17]

Whether the Kit-Cat Club met to toast *The Spectator* on the Thursday it was launched is not recorded, or whether it convened at all that difficult spring, while Harley's ministry was enjoying a peak in popularity. In March 1711, a French spy, the Marquis de Guisard, made an attempt on Harley's life that won the chief minister public sympathy and disproved Whig allegations that his ministry was in league with Louis XIV. While these allegations were indeed an exaggeration, it was true that Harley and St John intended to conclude a peace deal with France. This was a grave national danger in Mr Spectator's eyes, which he referred to by innuendo, cautioning his readers against importing indecent French habits such as male servants for ladies' dressing-rooms.

One of *The Spectator*'s first essays was an allegory of Public Credit, depicted as a beautiful but fragile virgin on a golden throne. The phantoms of Jacobitism and Republicanism rush in to frighten her, until she is calmed by a host of friendly spirits, including the Hanoverian heir, who replenish her bags of gold. Addison wrote this allegory in the context of mounting tension between the Whig City and Harley's Exchequer. The latter, according to Swift, needed to raise £5.6 million but 'the Whigs will not lend a groat, which is the only reason of the fall in stocks, for they are like Quakers and fanatics that will only deal among themselves'.[18] This tension culminated at the April 1711 elections of Bank of England and United East India Company directors, where Tory shareholders turned out in high numbers to try to dislodge the Whig management of each. Dr Sacheverell purchased the £500 of Bank stock necessary to participate, and was hissed by the Whig shareholders when he turned up to vote. The Kit-Cat Club's political members played their usual role in 'whipping up' Whig shareholders and succeeded in narrowly averting the Tory takeovers.[19]

In the Commons, the Whigs had no such majority to rally, and failed to prevent a parliamentary resolution, on 14 April, that bringing Palatine refugees into England was a 'scandalous

Misapplication of the Public Money, tending to the Increase and Oppression of the Poor of this Kingdom'.[20]

In *The Spectator*'s tenth issue, Addison estimated there were twenty readers for each of the 3,000 issues printed, suggesting that copies were circulated within households and coffee houses, and that public readings were spreading the paper's influence beyond a literate audience. In July 1711, Addison said his bookseller reported 'Demand for these Papers increases daily', and spoke of his 40–50,000 readers as a kind of composite patron.[21] Whether the figures were accurate, it is significant that Mr Spectator hears of having a mass readership 'with much Satisfaction', rather than aristocratic embarrassment at being applauded by the common mob.

Mr Spectator repeatedly declared he was taking knowledge from where it was 'bound up in Books'[22] to where it could 'dwell in Clubs and Assemblies, at Tea-Tables and Coffee-Houses'.[23] *The Spectator* was a product of the Kit-Cat Club for this reason if for no other: Addison and Steele had been taught to seek popularity, on condition of not appealing to the lowest common denominator, by the elder generation of Kit-Cat authors and literary patrons. This popularizing principle was the legacy of Dryden, Congreve, Stepney and Prior, who had written vernacular translations of classical authors (though Addison recommended another translator's Virgil as being 'finer' than Dryden's,[24] his 'tepid homage'[25] to Dryden becoming, over the years, a bone of contention between Addison and earlier Kit-Cats like Congreve and Tonson[26]). Now the commercial success of *The Spectator* vindicated the Kit-Cats' popularizing principle as no dramatic or poetic work had before. '[T]he general Reception I have found,' boasted Mr Spectator, 'convinces me that the World is not so corrupt as we are apt to imagine.'[27]

By the issues numbered in the 200s, it was clear from readers' letters that the paper was a place to issue national announcements and that Mr Spectator wielded enormous social influence, tangible and immediate, in readers' lives. When Steele published an essay against 'Fribblers' (irresolute men who court women they never ask to marry), for example, fathers across Britain began closing their doors on such gentlemen callers.[28] Contemporaries often noted the paper's far-reaching impact on the nation's manners, ordinary conversation and attitudes. Throughout the newly formed nation, anglicization, through *The Spectator*, meant 'Kitcatization'. There is also evidence of the influence of the paper on Englishmen far beyond Britain's shores, such as a letter from an English merchant living in Sumatra who said that, besides the Bible and John Locke's essays, *The Spectator* and *Tatler* were his 'constant Companions'.[29]

The diversity of *The Spectator*'s correspondents – gentlemen, businessmen, clergymen, actors, servants, ladies and schoolboys – was as striking as its readership figures. It was continuing *The Tatler*'s success in expanding the size of Britain's literate culture, including the number of women readers. Alongside the Kit-Cats who subscribed to the journal's collected edition published in 1712–13, there were many merchants and minor office-holders, but also some thirty-six women, including several of the 'middling sort'. In the fourth issue, Steele stated his intention to provide lessons for women readers on their duties and behaviour: 'I shall take it for the greatest Glory of my Work, if among reasonable Women this Paper may furnish *Tea-Table Talk*.'[30] Addison agreed, asserting that 'there are none to whom this Paper will be more useful than to the female World'. He bemoaned the trifling concerns of 'ordinary Women', such that 'the right adjusting of their Hair [is] the principal Employment of their Lives'.[31] The obvious paternalism of these remarks is somewhat mitigated by the fact that many of the 'women' they were advising on whom to marry and how to live were, in fact, girls of 13 or 15.[32]

As a publication considered decent for discussion in mixed-sex company and among every class of person, *The Spectator* was usurping the pulpit in defining Britain's moral order. Addison used his essays – particularly his Saturday essays – to sermonize in a spirit of rational piety. The Glorious Revolution had slackened the Episcopal Church's hold in England, if only because William was not raised an Anglican, and many Whigs – certainly most of the Kit-Cats – were instinctively anti-clerical. *The Spectator*'s popularity was partly explained by the British search for secular guidance on decency and manners, though the authors would have said they were prescribing Christian living and churchgoing, not offering an alternative.

Mr Spectator's sermonizing tone tapped into the national zeal for self-improvement fomented by the Collierites and other moral reformers over the past decade. The British were trying to settle their own values during Anne's reign – a campaign of self-mastery and self-civilization less than half a century before they set out to master and civilize the rest of the world. They believed themselves more enlightened than the generation that had fought the Civil War, yet with less refined and cohesive culture than many of their European neighbours. *The Spectator* therefore declared itself for the 'wearing out of Ignorance, Passion and Prejudice' among the English.[33]

Constructing an image of the 'national character' was the first order of business. When Addison remarked on how Frenchmen could converse with a warmth and intimacy that 'abundance of wine can scarce draw from an Englishman',[34] he was generalizing his own taciturnity and reserve into a national characteristic. In *Spectator* no. 135, Addison summarized the English language as befitting the English temperament in being 'modest, thoughtful and sincere'[35] – a description of his own better qualities, as man and author, rather than something that could be proved of his countrymen as a whole. By 1850, according to Paul Langford, there was near universal agreement on the key traits of the English character being energy, candour, decency, taciturnity, reserve and eccentricity.[36] Addison and Steele, who together could claim every quality on this contradictory list, deserve a large share of the credit for forming this consensus.

Marlborough's victories since 1702, and the expanding strength of British trade, were by now giving Britons a sense of themselves as a 'chosen people' in the same way that Americans would feel in later centuries. As royal bloodlines had been so easily thrown aside by the Revolution and the Act of Settlement, Whig patriotism stressed a providential view of the nation, bonded by Protestantism and political principles, rather than by blood. This they saw as a more 'modern' kind of nationhood. It was also the only patriotism they could logically assert between 1710–14, when their only powerful allies in London were the envoys of the Imperial and Dutch governments.

In *The Whig Examiner*'s last issue, Addison had told his readers: 'Passive Obedience and Non-Resistance are the Duties of Turks and Indians.' He contrasted these Tory and High Church tenets to the more critical, rationalist mindset of Englishmen. The Tories, Mr Spectator repeated in July 1711, were like 'wild Tartars'.[37] To be British, in other words, was to be Whig.

Paradoxically, the Whigs managed to incorporate a certain cosmopolitanism into their image of Britishness that the Tories – associated with the rural nobility and peasantry – seemed to reject. *The Spectator* is full of respectful references to Oriental and Islamic cultures, shown to be admirable and even superior to European cultures. Drawing on his father's books about North Africa and 'Muhammadanism', Addison remarked on his 'particular Pleasure' in finding analogies to Christian belief in different cultures and countries.[38] Similarly, Addison and Steele admired the commerce and internationalism of the Jews, as the invisible 'Pegs in the Building' of European civilization.[39]

People supporting both parties were invested in Britain's international trade, but the Whigs claimed the lead in championing a mercantile model of political economy. Mr Spectator showed his Whig worldview by arguing that a commercial nation could never have too many traders, drawing parallels between military and mercantile glory. He repeatedly exhorted younger sons of the nobility and gentry to make themselves useful by joining some market-oriented profession. Addison and Steele were breaking down the traditional assumption that a life of aristocratic leisure was the height of individual freedom. In refreshing contrast to the later nineteenth-century preoccupation with making the poor more productive and deserving, they focused on reforming the unproductive rich. It was a view drawn from their own experiences as authors who had always needed to earn an income, yet did not feel their consciences, intellects or art were prostituted by that fact.

Though *The Spectator* declared the education of women a priority, the paper was just as interested in reforming men. The new, urban British society needed a 'new man', if only as a way around the rising rivalry between old blood/land and new money.

The model of masculinity Addison and Steele presented was, again, one learned largely under the Kit-Cats' tutelage. They mocked excessive, Francophile refinement in men, just as Vanbrugh mocked Lord Foppington in *The Relapse* (1696), while stressing that a man was not effeminate if he avoided resorting to violence – the same message taught by the character of Sir Brute in Vanbrugh's *Provok'd Wife* (1697). If Addison's and Steele's many complimentary poems, dedications and letters to Dorset, Somers, Halifax, Manchester, Wharton and others are to be even half-believed, these Kit-Cat patrons were Mr Spectator's measure of civilized male behaviour. Even Manchester and Wharton, for all their unrefined habits and youthful duels, were admired as models of a new synthesis between Restoration Court manners and the country squire's 'old English Plainness and Sincerity'.[40]

In one of *The Spectator*'s many lessons on how an Englishman should comport himself, Addison advised that 'an unconstrained Carriage and a certain Openness of Behaviour are the height of Good Breeding . . . our Manners sit more loose upon us'.[41] It was the same philosophy by which Prior once flattered Dorset in referring to the relaxed 'freedom' of Dorset's dinners 'which made every one of his guests think himself at home'.[42] Today it remains a trait of the British upper class that less is considered more, and displaying wealth too ostentatiously is considered bad breeding. *The Spectator* adopted the Kit-Cat ethos of superficially underplaying distinctions of rank and advised pretentious provincial readers it was now *outré* to make too many formal bows to superiors, or to take the 'trouble' to serve one's dinner guests strictly according to their rank. 'There is infinitely more to do about Place and Precedency in a Meeting of Justices' Wives,' observed Addison, 'than in an Assembly of Duchesses.'[43]

C. S. Lewis wrote in 1945:

> I sometimes catch myself taking it for granted that the marks of good breeding were in all ages the same as they are today – that swagger was always vulgar, that a low voice, an unpretentious manner, a show (however superficial) of self-effacement, were always demanded . . . Even to this day, when we meet foreigners (only think of some *young*

> Frenchmen) who have not been subjected to Addisonian 'reform', we have to 'make allowances' for them.[44]

These remarks emphasize the momentousness of *The Spectator*'s reform of national manners, its reimagining of national character. Addison and Steele were not inventing these manners out of thin air, however, but teaching the nation to copy manners they themselves had been taught over the years by their Kit-Cat patrons.

The English 'have no adequate Idea of what is meant by "Gentlemanly, Gentleman-like, or much of a Gentleman"', Steele observed.[45] The authors saw it as less important to be a gentleman in the technical sense than to behave in a gentlemanly way, less important to be a lady than to be ladylike. Many letters to Mr Spectator were anxious about this state of affairs. They came from people fearful of being duped by fake charm, unable to distinguish the genuine article from its replica, or fearful of not passing the test themselves. Social mobility begat status anxiety. *The Spectator*'s readers started to bind up issues of the paper on single themes to form homemade sets for easy reference, making the publication physically resemble the Christian conduct books that preceded it.

The Spectator's didacticism flowed in only one direction: outwards from London, which contained around a tenth of Britain's seven million people by 1711. This direction was most obvious in the realm of fashion. One letter – likely concocted by Addison while out of town during the summer of 1711 – mocked the outmoded fashions in provincial society. Among many other lessons, Mr Spectator was teaching Britain what not to wear. Increasing fashion awareness in rural backwaters incidentally profited Whig cloth manufacturers and traders, like Furnese.

Congreve, writing from Tunbridge Wells, complained that society there was 'of that sort who at home converse only with their Relations; and consequently when they come abroad, have few Acquaintances, but such as they bring with them'.[46] In 1711, Mr Spectator visited Tunbridge Wells to make similar, superior observations (on the indecency of swinging women upside down during country dancing, for example), knowing his pronouncements when printed would directly alter public behaviour in Tunbridge and every town of its kind. Steele explained the philosophy of making urbanity synonymous with the best of British – an attitude he and the other Kit-Cat authors learned at Dryden's knee – when he allied himself to 'The Town' in preference to the City or Court: '[T]he word Town implies the best People in the whole, wherever they are pleased, or are disposed, or able to live. The Town is the upper part of the World, or rather the fashionable People . . . everyone would be in Town if they could.'[47]

Only a minority of Kit-Cats, like Tonson, were born into urbanity. Many, like Carlisle or Congreve, grew up in the sticks then migrated to London for their education, parliamentary seat or advancement. Their snobbery about the countryside was, therefore, largely self-fashioning. It represented the experiences of large numbers of less prominent migrants to urban jobs in service, business or trade, thanks to the seventeenth-century beginnings of the agricultural revolution that were already displacing people from the land. *The Spectator*'s role in educating socially ambitious newcomers on how to navigate London society and wear the mask of urbanity was important for thousands of these migrants.

The Spectator, however, also exported urban habits to those who stayed at home in the provinces. The Kit-Cat Club, filtered through the Spectator Club, was imitated in the most literal sense by the formation of local clubs and societies across the land, for example. *The Spectator* directly inspired the formation of the 'Edinburgh Easy Club' in 1712, where Scotsmen gathered to polish their conversation, and the 'Gentleman's Society' at Spalding, south Lincolnshire, which started meeting in a coffee house for literary conversation at around the same date. *The Spectator* also recommended Englishmen follow the French salon model by spending more time in women's company, since 'where that was wholly denied, the Women lost their Wit and the Men their good Manners'.[48] While the essayists constantly joked about women's senseless prattle and denigrated female friendships as less sturdy than male, there is a defensive ring to these jokes, as if they privately realized women were the more naturally adept gender when it came to personal communication and friendship. In this light, the Kit-Cat Club and its many imitators were like remedial classes where men could practise these arts removed from the pressure of female scrutiny – places for men who, as Steele put it, 'cannot talk without the help of a Glass at their Mouths, or convey their Meaning to each other without the Interposition of Clouds [pipe smoke]'.[49] These men were urged to smooth the rough edges off their manners and drop their tendency to pedantry by taking their wit into ladies' drawing rooms.

Mr Spectator wrote in the grammar of balance, always setting one element against its antithesis ('to appear free and open without Danger of Intrusion, and to be cautious without seeming reserved'[50]). This style of rhetoric suited a time when success depended upon steering a middle course between political extremes. Addison's famous 'middling' style was not only learned from the Romans but was a specific product of 1710–12's polarized political atmosphere. Much of this tone of moderation and reason in *The Spectator* derives from its sense of humour, seen as another vital ingredient of the new national character. As early as 1695, Congreve wrote: 'I look upon Humour to be almost of English Growth' because of the 'great Freedom, Privilege and Liberty which the Common People of England enjoy'.[51] This sense of humour was vital, Congreve argued, because the English were otherwise so depressive:

> Is there anywhere a People more unsteady, more apt to discontent, more saturnine, dark and melancholic than ourselves? Are we not of all People the most unfit to be alone, and most unsafe to be trusted with ourselves? Are there not more Self-murderers and melancholic Lunatics in England, heard of in one Year, than in the great part of Europe besides?[52]

Congreve argued – replying to Collier – that London needed its comic plays just to cheer itself up. With the same faith in literature to reshape national behaviour, Addison now used the ironic register of Mr Spectator to teach pragmatic humanism and stoicism to his readers (though Addison and Steele thought the philosophy of Stoicism inferior to Christianity). These qualities, far more than the melancholy Congreve described, remain the essence of how other nationalities still view Englishmen today: at best an understated courage, at worst an emotional autism.

Addison stated that *The Spectator*'s vast readership was 'more just than private Clubs or Assemblies in distinguishing between what is Wit and what is Ill-nature'.[53] Steele, who privately sympathized with Collier's critique of the London stage, similarly condemned the 'unhappy Affectation of being Wise rather than Honest, Witty [rather] than Good-natured'[54] among the London literati. This was where, he implied, the town's elite had something to learn from the country's moral majority. Addison and Steele thought the best recipe was a mixture of the old aristocratic code – taken from a manual like *The Gentleman's Recreation* (1710), which recommended every would-be gentleman to see the works of Congreve or Vanbrugh – and the more bourgeois, pious tone of a handbook like *A Help to National Reformation* (1700). Mr Spectator resembled, on the one hand, a spying informer working for the Society for the Reformation of Manners, and on the other, an expansively generous Sir John Falstaff, telling his readers to avoid giving of themselves only 'upon the Tilt' so that the recipient has to 'Taste of the Sediments' from the cask of one's soul.[55]

The Spectator's effort to make Whiggery synonymous with Englishness did not go unchallenged by the Tories, who could still count upon widespread anti-war, anti-Junto feeling at this date. The year after *The Spectator* started, Dr Arbuthnot published his pamphlets on *The History of John Bull* (1712). The first pamphlet was entitled *Law is a Bottomless Pit* and was an anti-Marlborough tract complaining about crippling wartime taxation. In it, the Scottish-born Arbuthnot portrayed the English Everyman, 'John Bull', as a small cloth merchant duped by his lawyers into pursuing a long and costly lawsuit. This was an allegory for the British public being duped by the Junto into pursuing a long and costly war for the Junto's personal profit.

Arbuthnot portrayed Bull as 'an honest, plain dealing fellow, choleric, bold and of a very unconstant temper'. The irony was that there had always been something of this character within the Junto and the Kit-Cats, in the uncouth habits of men like Wharton and

Manchester, or the dumb-but-honest characters of Shannon and Grafton, or the crude ballads of Maynwaring. Even Steele, the rear end of the pantomime horse that was ultra-polite 'Mr Spectator', was known to get drunk and disgrace himself at the Kit-Cat Club. They had a clear ideal of how a gentleman ought to behave, with moderation and wit, but it was not always how they did behave.

John Bull morphed, in the later eighteenth and nineteenth centuries, into the iconic image of the Whig nation, growing increasingly obese and obdurate. But, before the Tory-invented British bulldog became the dominant satirical image, the Kit-Cats tried to project a far more positive image of an enlightened, cultured and well-travelled Englishman. Their agenda for improvement of the arts had continued after the Whig fall in 1710, with Lord Manchester, for example, bringing George Frederick Handel, the *Kapellmeister* and star composer at the Hanoverian Court, to London.

Handel's first opera in England, *Rinaldo*, was performed at the Kit-Cat-built Queen's Theatre in February 1711. It proved such a phenomenal success that it offended the national pride of Addison and Steele, who feared the popularity of Handel's Italian operas would retard the development of indigenous English music, and steal audiences away from English drama. They tolerated imported Italian singers, but believed they should only sing compositions in English. Five days after *Rinaldo*'s premiere, *The Spectator* ran a letter from a tone-deaf Englishman, complaining there was nothing for him to enjoy at the opera since he spoke no Italian. Addison, still smarting from *Rosamund*'s failure in 1707, mocked the ludicrousness of audiences listening to operas in a language they did not understand. He predicted it would be a short-lived fad that would mislead later historians into imagining the average eighteenth-century Londoner understood Italian fluently. *The Spectator* also published scathing reviews of the crowd-pleasing special effects used during *Rinaldo*, including a flock of sparrows and finches released in the theatre that defecated on the audience's heads. In April 1711, Mr Spectator lectured that the Italian ingredient in English music was too overpowering a flavour: 'Let the Infusion be as strong as you please, but still let the Subject Matter of it be English.'[56] This position was derived from a wider aesthetic philosophy that music should be subordinated to words, as passions to reason.

The castrato Nicolini was therefore paid to sing an 'English Opera' (English words set to Italian music) called *Calypso and Telemachus* with a libretto by a protégé of Addison's. This production had no greater success than *Rosamund*, leading Mr Spectator to tell English musicians to forget opera and write church music instead. Steele meanwhile attempted to rival Handel's operas by producing a series of music and poetry recitals to showcase British talents like Thomas Clayton, alongside foreign musicians. The venue was a hired, crumbling hall in York Buildings, on Buckingham Street near Charing Cross, between the Strand and the river. The opening performance was on 24 May 1711. The day before, Harley was created Earl of Oxford and Mortimer (and shall henceforth be referred to as 'Lord Oxford' or 'Oxford'). Steele invited Oxford to the show in a spirit of party neutrality, hoping this would attract a larger audience. Despite *The Spectator*'s support, the event was not a success, ticket sales failing to fill the 200-seat hall for the rest of the series. Steele lost money, just as Vanbrugh had lost money pursuing the Kit-Cat's patriotic agenda at the Queen's Theatre a few years earlier.

Robert Walpole, with time on his hands while out of political office, also contributed to the Kit-Cats' cultural programme by organizing a burlesque show, mocking Italian opera, in the winter of 1711. In contrast to Steele's approach of inviting Tories to his audience, Walpole reportedly stood at the theatre entrance, checking no Tories were admitted who might try to wreck the show.

Addison and Steele used *The Spectator* as a vehicle for theatre criticism beyond denigration of Handel's operas. Soon they found that, though they could not direct the nation's musical tastes, they could exercise unprecedented power to make or break literary careers by reviewing, endorsing and advertising plays. When Addison's friend, a lean young poet named Ambrose Philips, produced a new English tragedy, *The Distressed Mother*, to which Steele wrote the Prologue and Addison's cousin Budgell, under Addison's supervision, wrote the Epilogue, *The Spectator* endorsed the play shamelessly. Both its authors invested in the production, and Maynwaring's mistress, Mrs

Oldfield, played the lead role. Tonson published the script shortly after the opening night, dedicated to the Duke of Montagu's wife Mary. A less biased critic said *The Spectator*'s glowing review won the play an undeservedly large audience, especially after the paper reviewed it a second time through the fiction of Sir Roger de Coverley going to see it.

Addison reviewed the theatre audience as much as the plays, reprimanding people who were noisy and immodest in imitation of what he called French audience manners, or who were too engrossed in themselves to appreciate the play. Addison rebuked fashionable young wits who exaggerated their indifference because they were 'supposed [to be] too well acquainted with what the Actor is going to say to be moved at it', regretting the popular preference for bawdy comedy over any 'inward Sentiment of Soul'.[57] At times, Mr Spectator sounded not unlike killjoy Collier, but laying the blame for the theatre's degeneracy more on hard-hearted audiences than the country's godless dramatists.

Mr Spectator's theatre reviews were an innovation – far more conversational and accessible than the scholarly forms of criticism shared among the elite before. Unfortunately Addison and Steele never retrospectively reviewed the restaged works of their fellow Kit-Cats, the Orange Comedians. Perhaps, given the extent to which they shared qualms about the cynicism and anti-clericalism of those plays, it was tactful not to do so. Whenever they referred to their friend Congreve, however, it was with the implication that everyone with sense knew he was a great writer. In one essay, Addison remarked that since Congreve and Vanbrugh had retired as dramatists, no one had equalled them.

Critical taste became, in a new and Whiggish way, an essential aspect of being an English gentleman. Mr Spectator in one essay observed that all a self-made man needed for social acceptance was at least two suits of new clothing a year and 'the Words "Delicacy", "Idiom", "fine Images", "Structure of Periods", "Genius", "Fire", and the rest, [which] made use of with a frugal and comely Gravity, will maintain the figure of immense Reading and depth of Criticism'.[58] Pleasantly surprised to find that there was a popular market for such literary criticism, Addison produced in May 1711 a further week-long essay series on comedy. He introduced the series with a statement that demonstrates how much *The Spectator* was about making learning accessible to a wider public:

> I shall endeavour to make what I say intelligible to ordinary Capacities; but if my Readers meet with any Paper that in some Parts of it may be a little out of their Reach, I would not have them discouraged, for they may assure themselves the next shall be much clearer.[59]

In one of these essays, Addison summarized John Locke on the difference between 'Wit' and 'Judgement' (as, respectively, the facility for rapidly combining ideas and discriminating between them), and added his own thought that wit must also 'Delight and Surprise'.[60] The series owed much to Congreve's *Letter Concerning Humour* (1695), with its criticism of those who used wit to stir up social discord and its belief that satire should be compassionately aimed only at faults we are able to change. Addison further declared his purpose was to 'banish' certain 'Gothic' tastes in wit and so reform 'Our general Taste in England'.[61]

Addison continued this English literature course – remarkable for appearing at a time when no such course was taught in any school or university – with essays on the virtues of the old English ballad form, like the ballad of 'Chevy Chase'.[62] To give such a 'low' form serious critical attention, comparing it to Virgil, was radical, and several parodies promptly appeared, scornful of *The Spectator* in the same way that some people today might scorn a doctoral thesis on rap lyrics. Once again, this populist strand must be credited to the Kit-Cat Club: Mr Spectator referred to the late Lord Dorset as having collected old English ballads, which he admired for their simplicity. 'I can affirm,' Addison added, 'the same of Mr Dryden, and know several of the most refined Writers of our present Age who are of the same Humour.'[63]

The Spectator's literary criticism returned in January 1712, with Addison publishing essays elucidating Milton's *Paradise Lost*: one every Saturday until 3 May. This epic poem had some success before

Tonson bought the rights to it, but did not sit on the pedestal in the English literary canon that it does today. Tonson devoted much energy to increasing public appreciation (and sales) of the poem at the start of his career, and by 1711 he was printing its ninth edition. Addison now promoted Milton as a specifically English genius and his epic as 'an Honour to the English Nation'.[64] It is debatable which of the two men, publisher or critic, did more for the dead poet's reputation, but together they may be credited with Milton's subsequent reputation.

As in his 1694 poem flattering Charles Montagu, Addison wrote in September 1711 on the subject of literary genius, distinguishing between 'Natural' and 'Learned' genius. The former category included Shakespeare. The second group – those whose writing is more like a well-tended garden than a wild landscape – included Milton and Sir Francis Bacon. Addison added a new emphasis on originality and individuality, which gestured towards the Romantic age to come, stating that 'very few Writers make an extraordinary Figure in the World who have not something in their Way of writing and expressing themselves that is peculiar to them and entirely their own'.[65] In another *Spectator*, Addison went further and suggested that poetic genius showed itself, rather like the best personal manners, in knowing when to break rules: 'Our inimitable Shakespeare is a Stumbling-block to the whole Tribe of . . . rigid Critics,' he declared.[66]

After Milton and Shakespeare, the English author most often named in the essays of Addison and Steele was Edmund Spenser. *The Faerie Queene* inspired the allegories in *The Spectator*, and Spenser's chivalric, Protestant imagery appealed to the Whigs during the decades of war against Catholic France. Sounding like Congreve when he argued that English comic dramas were a necessary antidote to national melancholia, Addison argued that Spenser's 'fairie way of writing' was needed to entertain the fancies of a nation generally disposed to gloom.[67] Though several Tory critics and poets also admired and imitated Spenser in the 1700s, it was the first generation of Kit-Cat members who initially rehabilitated Spenser's reputation, most notably Tonson and Somers with the republication of *The Faerie Queene* in 1692. Somers, when painted for his Kit-Cat portrait, chose to wear no badge or staff of office but held an octavo edition of Spenser's *Faerie Queene.*

To revive a golden age of English literature, the Kit-Cats sought to teach their countrymen to take pride in the Elizabethan authors above all others. British national identity during the following 200 years formed around the heritage of English literature to a remarkable extent, and *The Spectator* (educated by the Kit-Cat Club) was one of the first and most influential sources of this pride at a time when English was not yet considered a major European language.

As Mr Spectator held forth on tragedy, comedy, ballads, Milton, Spenser, the nature of literary genius and the pleasures of the imagination, the public thought Steele, not Addison, was writing these scholarly essays. The essays that were in fact composed by Steele increasingly relied on lengthy quotation of readers' letters, Steele supplying just an introductory line or two. The vitality and gaiety of his stories provided welcome relief from Addison's intellectual criticism, but – now that scholars have separated whose essays were whose – we can see that the efforts of the men's contributions were growing increasingly unequal. Perhaps Steele's assumption that his friend was the greater writer and thinker was so deeply ingrained that it did not even cross his mind to compete or keep up.

In 1712, having been friends for twenty-six years, they both turned 40 – an age at which, Addison noted, 'there is no dallying with Life'.[68] The strength of friendship between Addison and Steele at this time of intense creative collaboration is difficult to measure, largely because their private correspondence has not survived.[69] In print, we know Steele unequivocally called Addison 'the man I best loved'.[70] As if to compensate for the rather tight-lipped, strait-laced persona Addison sometimes projected, Steele testified in print to Addison's 'smiling Mirth', 'delicate Satire' and 'genteel Raillery' when he was 'free among Intimates'.[71] No matching declaration of love for Steele was ever penned by Addison, though he did compose the following lyrics for a hymn in 1712:

Thy Bounteous Hand with worldly bliss
Has made my cup run o'er,
And in a kind and faithful Friend
Has doubled all my store.[72]

For Addison, the more private the conversation the better, and most friendships, even in a club like the Kit-Cat, remained too politic – too driven by professional *quid pro quo* – to be trusted.[73] Addison quoted Cicero, Bacon and Ecclesiastes on the need to have 'a bosom Friend',[74] or 'one Counsellor of a Thousand', rather than friends who are each 'a Companion at the Table, and will not continue in the Day of thy Affliction'.[75] Steele was such a friend, though Steele's 'days of affliction' were so much more numerous than Addison's that their friendship had become something of a one-way street. And when Addison was ever in trouble, he turned not to Steele but to his former travelling companion, Edward Wortley Montagu.[76] Wortley Montagu, in return, confided in Addison that he was conducting an affair with Lord Kingston's daughter, Lady Mary. Mary's father opposed the match, forcing the couple to elope in 1712, and afterwards Addison owed some apology to his Kit-Cat colleague for having kept secret his bosom friend's plans.

Alexander Pope described how Addison sometimes teased Steele for holding him in such high regard, and when Steele described their collaborative working relationship, Steele's excitement at his own submissive position is palpable: 'I rejoiced in being excelled, and made those little talents, whatever they are which I have, give way and be subservient to the superior qualities of a friend whom I loved.'[77] As a further compliment to his friend, Steele described Addison's contribution to *The Tatler* as eclipsing his own: 'I fared like a distressed Prince who calls in a powerful neighbour to his aid. I was undone by my auxiliary; when I had once called him in, I could not subsist without dependence on him.'[78] There is an unintentional hint of resentment here – like the hint of resentment Steele barely concealed towards all his patrons and benefactors – and in the end Steele could not help remarking on his galvanizing role (living up to his own name) in persuading Addison to publish journalism and in getting the paper out six days a week. As Steele fairly put it, whatever he owed to Addison, the world owed Addison to Steele.

The Spectator's role in advocating national unity and moderation depended largely on Addison's personality. Though Addison had a strong sense of life's hardship, in *Spectator* no. 26 he admitted (as Mr Spectator) having no personal experience of true depression or melancholy. Therefore, when Addison admired the poise of the British constitution as though it were a gentleman's well-balanced character, he did so in a spirit of personal as well as patriotic vanity. Addison's greatest fault was pride: in *The Spectator* issue where Addison declares his ambition to bring philosophy out of 'Closets and Libraries', it is less often noted that the author describes himself in the preceding sentence as Socrates reincarnated.[79] One could say that the new national character Addison and the other Kit-Cats promoted also suffered from this fault – the fault that would lead Britain into the chauvinism and atrocities of empire.

When Dr Johnson reached middle age in the 1760s, he took Addison as his personal model – to the extent of finding his Steele in the young James Boswell. Boswell said he would prefer to imitate a composite of Addison's wisdom and Steele's gaiety – the composite character of Mr Spectator, in other words. It was a nice irony of *The Spectator*'s anonymous authorship that the public criticized Steele for not living up to all the paper's strictures – on frugal spending, for example – when so many of those strictures came from Addison's pen. Steele was expected, in other words, to embody the virtues of his more sensible, cautious friend. Yet Dr Johnson, for all his reverence of Addison's genius, concluded: 'Of this memorable friendship, the greater praise must be given to Steele. It is not hard to love those from whom nothing can be feared, and Addison never considered Steele as a rival.'[80]

What Addison most needed from Steele was Steele's inexhaustible optimism about their collaborative projects, and the permanent pose Steele struck as Addison's greatest fan – an ever-attentive listener. 'Good Breeding,' Steele wrote in October 1712, 'obliges a Man to maintain the Figure of the keenest Attention, the true Posture of which . . . I take to consist in leaning over a Table, with the Edge of it pressing hard upon your Stomach.'[81] In *The Christian Hero*, Steele had said conscience was the ballast 'in the Voyage of Life', as ambition was 'our Sail', and he quoted himself again on this in his forties.[82] He was still living at full tilt, like a boat with a sail puffed full of ambition, always in danger of collapse.

This difference in Addison's and Steele's characters is discernible even in the portraits of each man painted by Sir Godfrey Kneller: Steele seems to be leaning slightly forward, towards the viewer, while Addison leans slightly back. These paintings were part of Kneller's famous series depicting the Kit-Cat Club's members, painted at irregular intervals between roughly 1702 and 1721.[83] Steele's was painted in 1711, around the time he was launching *The Spectator*.

Steele sat for his Kit-Cat picture at the studio in Kneller's townhouse in Great Queen Street, near Lincoln's Inn Fields. Sunlight shone through a window to Steele's left, which overlooked Kneller's fine garden and that of his neighbour Dr Ratcliffe, whose servants sometimes crept through an adjoining gate to pick Kneller's flowers, much to the painter's annoyance. The house was quiet as Kneller worked – he had no children by his wife Susannah, though he kept an illegitimate daughter from an earlier lover at another address. As Kneller sketched out Steele's face, giving it what Steele later described as a 'resolute'[84] expression, the artist said he regretted that Annibale Carracci, the great sixteenth-century painter and draughtsman, was no longer alive to do it justice. This was Kneller teasing Steele's vanity with a hidden barb in the compliment, as Carracci was as famous for his cartoons of grotesques as for his serious portraits. Steele's account of the sitting, written many years later, suggests he was sharp enough to appreciate the ambiguity. The remark may, however, have led to a more serious conversation about what Kneller saw as a dearth of talented English portraitists at this date. Steele wrote an essay about painting ('a Poetry which would be understood with much less Capacity and less Expense of Time') being a neglected art in England – yet another art form to be added to the Kit-Cat Club's to-do list of national reform. The nineteenth-century critic William Hazlitt singled this out as the best critical piece in the whole *Spectator*.[85]

Today there are forty-three surviving Kneller Kit-Cat paintings showing forty-four portraits (one being a double), but there are also said to be four 'missing' portraits, which may or may not have existed, as well as a significant number of known members who were never painted for the series. Each picture in the Kit-Cat series measures thirty-six by twenty-eight inches. Like a close-up photograph, these portraits create a strikingly new sense of intimacy and informality. In contrast to Van Dyck portraits, for example, Kneller's Kit-Cats put themselves on the viewer's level, showing each man down to his waist and half turning towards the viewer. Seven of the portraits show the sitters wearing loose Indian shirts, and most of the other sitters are also informally dressed, with open collars, in relaxed poses. Lord Mohun, painted in 1707, is the essence of expensive informality in his blue velvet coat, gold brocade waistcoat and open shirt collar. He holds a snuffbox with an indistinguishable miniature in the open lid – the only woman to sneak into the Kit-Cat series. The majority of the Kit-Cats wear full-flowing wigs, but five sport turbans, making them more individualized to modern eyes. This naturalism, of course, involved theatrical artistry, rather like the banter in a Congreve play. Addison praised such informality in contrast to French portraiture, which he denounced as affected, with too much bright, fussy finery and 'a certain smirking Air'.[86]

Modern art critics have seen 'a certain smirking Air' on the faces of the Kit-Cats themselves – 'an image of the ruling oligarchy, cheerful and self-satisfied, with a little coarseness in the lips and insensitivity behind the eyes'.[87] They do seem a self-satisfied group, but this overlooks the fact that many of the paintings were completed at a time, between 1710 and 1714, when the Kit-Cats' political and personal fortunes were in ruins. Steele's portrait is a case in point. Here was a man who, in 1711, could hardly afford to replace the clothes on his back, borrowing money from Furnese, clinging on to his only regular income by his fingernails, and hounded by the Queen's chief minister and government-sponsored press for his political opinions. The pose of self-assurance was, in other words, even more artificial than the pose of informality.

The remarkable similarity of the portraits expressed the Kit-Cat Club's egalitarian spirit; the classical ideal of friendship among equals.

That some of England's highest ranking peers were presented in the same style as Mr Edmund Dunch or Mr Jacob Tonson, the old aristocracy beside a new meritocracy, was shocking to viewers at the time. The Kit-Cat Club as a society of equals had always been, of course, an 'idealization',[88] ignoring its members' widely varying circumstances, and the portraits are the most obvious sign of that idealization – equality being easier to achieve on canvas than in life.

Why Kneller ever started to paint such a large series is uncertain. One of the Club's members was said to have suggested giving Tonson 'some considerable token of our remembrance', and Tonson asked that this 'token' be their portraits.[89] Tradition has it that Somerset first presented his portrait to Tonson as a gift, then the others followed suit. In the absence of original bills or receipts, it is unclear whether the Club paid for the series by subscription or individually.[90] John Faber Junior, who made engravings of the paintings, confirmed they were donated to Tonson, and dedicated his book of engravings to Somerset as the first donor. The set, after 1704, was certainly hung, as each was completed, at Tonson's Barn Elms house:[91] a 1705 satire told readers that if they wanted to discover a certain Kit-Cat member's identity, they should ask Tonson to 'show you his Picture with the Rest that belong to the Club'.[92] Tonson's private collection was ahead of its time, prefiguring the later eighteenth-century craze for portraiture and home galleries.

We are lucky there is a Kit-Cat portrait of Congreve.[93] Not long before he sat for it in 1708, Congreve remarked that 'sitting for my picture is not a thing very agreeable to me'[94] – self-consciousness that explains why there are relatively few images of the famous writer. Congreve thought Kneller's image made him look 'too chuffy [chubby]', though elsewhere he admitted to having grown so fat he was 'puzzled to buckle my shoe'.[95] The Kit-Cats as a whole were large men – literally fat cats. Mohun was politely described as 'inclining to fat',[96] and most of the Kneller portraits show heavy jowls and double chins, with Charles, 4th Baron Cornwallis the most morbidly obese. When Steele asked Congreve's friend Joe Keally to send him a cheap tailored suit from Dublin, Steele instructed that it be 'every way too big for yourself', which, since Congreve teased Keally for being overweight, implies Steele was even larger.[97] In October 1709, Lady Mary Wortley Montagu laughed to describe a 200-yard running race down the Mall in St James's, featuring as contestants two of the fattest men in London, both Kit-Cats: Garth and Grafton. Grafton grew so fat and alcoholic as he aged that Lord Hervey would nickname him 'booby Grafton', whose body was 'as impotent now as his mind',[98] and Swift dismissed him as 'almost a slobberer'.[99] Similarly, when the Duchess of Marlborough witnessed her friend Dr Garth's spherical form trying to dance a minuet, she muttered: 'I can't help thinking that he may sometimes be in the wrong.'[100]

Congreve's Kit-Cat portrait does not show him as the gouty invalid he was by 1708: it makes him look sun-kissed and full of energy. It contrasts with one painted by Richard van Bleek in 1715, when Congreve was 45, which captures Congreve's more contemplative, reclusive side as he sits reading a Vanbrugh play, surrounded by poignant allusions to time, lost sight and ageing.

In Vanbrugh's Kit-Cat portrait, he holds a compass, the tool of his architectural draughtsmanship, and wears his badge as Clarenceux King of Arms, the heraldic appointment with which Carlisle paid him for Castle Howard.[101] There is no emblem of Vanbrugh's earlier, theatrical career.

In Tonson's portrait, painted late in the series, in 1717, the book he holds is not an emblem of friendship with one of his living authors, but a grateful acknowledgement of the work that first made him rich: *Paradise Lost*. Tonson's is one of the most pleasing portraits in the series. He sits alertly in the 'elbow chair' of the Kit-Cat Club, wearing a turban rather than hiding his jowls under a wig's thick side-curls.

Sir Godfrey Kneller, born Gottfried, son of Zacharias Kniller, the Surveyor of Lübeck, emigrated to England in 1674. After early successes painting the Duke of Monmouth and Charles II, Kneller became a favoured Court artist, a Knight of the Realm and Justice of the Peace. Kneller was never a Kit-Cat himself, however, as some have claimed.[102] The fact that a self-portrait by Kneller later hung in the same Barn Elms room as the Kit-Cats' has erroneously led to the painter's inclusion in the Club, while Kneller's paintings have confused the record of who was a member almost as much as they have clarified it. At most, Kneller was, like Marlborough, an honoured and exceptional guest.

Kneller once remarked that history painters 'do not begin to live themselves until they are dead', whereas 'I paint the living, and they make me live.'[103] Some have interpreted this as an admission of unabashed commercialism, for which Kneller was as much criticized as Tonson, but Kneller more likely meant that painting the famous assisted his own fame. The statement proved truer than he realized: Kneller's name has lived on in posterity largely because of whom he painted rather than how he painted, and the Kit-Cats were, until as late as the 1950s, some of his most famous subjects. There was a wonderful *quid pro quo* in the end: the Club was immortalized by Kneller, and Kneller was immortalized by the Club.

In so far as the Kit-Cat Club was about styling oneself by choice of friends, the pictures give the elusive art of friendship a monumental solidity. The fact that Tonson wanted to fill his house with portraits of his friends emphasizes how much the Club was about replacing social networks based on blood by those based on merit and mutual regard. Ironically, Kneller's style added a certain similarity to the men's physiognomies, as if they were all distant cousins. Perhaps it was merely the mimetic quality of friendship, which was then extended, through the paintings and publications like *The Spectator*, to a whole nation of Kit-Cat imitators.

There is, sadly, no painting of the Club as a group, gathered around a table in animated conversation or mingling in their clubroom, as in Reynolds' *Members of the Society of the Dilettanti*, Zoffany's *The Academicians of the Royal Society* or Hogarth's *Midnight Modern Conversation*. Thus there is no painting to help us understand who was closest to whom, who was central and who was peripheral. It is as if the Kit-Cats chose to preserve themselves as a series of individual essays instead of a group biography.

XVI
THE CRISIS

The KIT-CAT CLUB, generally mentioned as a set of Wits, were in reality the Patriots that saved Britain.

HORACE WALPOLE, son of Kit-Cat Robert Walpole[1]

By SUMMER 1711, the Kit-Cat Club had become an informal shadow Cabinet, orchestrating Junto strategy in opposition and maintaining Whig morale in the political wilderness. As at the beginning of Anne's reign, such periods of political adversity provided opportunity for gauging clients' loyalty to their patrons. It must have been a constant question for the Kit-Cat aristocrats whether the authors they supported sincerely liked them, or whether they were valued only for the favours they dispensed. Ned Ward, with no patron to liberate him from Grub Street, had accused the Kit-Cats of being a bunch of 'scabby friends' who lived by 'tickling each other with reciprocal flattery'.[2] To Ward's eye, the trumpeted 'new golden age' was a façade, hiding corruption. By protesting their friendship in private letters and public dedications, the Kit-Cats were fending off such cynical readings of their fellowship. Their self-image demanded they should believe themselves 'disinterested', their Club founded on mutual affection and Whig ideals rather than material deals between craven clients and narcissistic patrons.

Addison said he had suffered 'incredible losses' since losing his Irish post,[3] and pressed Steele to repay an overdue loan. Addison worried he might also lose his pension as Keeper of the Records in Dublin. He asked an Irish Tory friend to help him keep it, but also to downplay his financial desperation, since 'I know the most likely way to keep a place is to appear not to want it.'[4] Partly with an eye to retaining the Keepership, and partly out of genuine concern at the impact of rampant partisanship on British society, Addison instigated a series of *Spectator* essays seeking a truce with the Tories. He mourned the 'Malice of Parties . . . rend[ing] a Government into two distinct People and mak[ing] them greater Strangers and more averse to one another than if they were actually two different Nations'.[5] This, Addison argued, gave the advantage to Britain's foreign enemies and distorted relations between private individuals, to the extent that he feared to 'discover the Seeds of Civil War in these our Divisions'.[6] Soon after, in late July 1711, Addison and Steele dined with Swift for the first time in several months, to ask whether Swift would intercede to help Tonson's firm keep the printing licence for *The Gazette* and, presumably, help Addison retain his Irish Keepership. Swift described feeling 'as a twig' grabbed by the Whigs 'while they are drowning'.[7]

Addison then departed to spend the rest of the summer in Bath, leaving Steele in the emptied city to write August's *Spectators* single-handedly. 'Unbridled' by his friend's absence, Steele almost immediately abandoned the pretence of party neutrality. He used a report about the exciting news of Marlborough breaking through the French ('*Ne Plus Ultra*') lines as an excuse to attack Oxford's ministry, then suspected of cutting deals with France behind Marlborough's back. Several readers complained at this Whig tub-thumping, but Steele ignored them, penning a tribute to an idealized commander who was unmistakably Marlborough.[8]

'[N]ot a meeting of Friends, not a Visit, but like Jehu to Jezebel, *Who is on my side? Who? Who is for Peace? Who is for carrying on the War?*' wrote Daniel Defoe, his tone perfectly reflecting the high pitch of London politics in 1711 and the fact that war or peace was now the only question debated in the coffee houses and Commons.[9] Steele may have favoured at least one further military campaign, and believed that opening peace negotiations strengthened the resolve of the enemy, but he understood that the peace the Tories wanted would be hugely popular.

Prior, now 'a thin, hollow-looked man',[10] had been hired to open talks with the French, based on his personal acquaintance with the French minister, the Marquis de Torcy. Prior and a French cleric named Abbé Gaultier departed from London in July 1711, empowered to negotiate with Torcy at Fontainebleau. Neither Parliament nor British diplomats like Stanyan (still ambassador in Berlin, despite his friends' fall from power) were informed. When Prior returned to England from this first mission under a false name, a port official arrested him as a suspicious character. Thanks to this arrest and a leak from the Austrian Envoy, the negotiations became public knowledge by the end of August. Prior later recalled that Lionel, the young Lord Dorset, counselled him to 'save his bacon' by renouncing, even at this late stage, his work for the Tories.[11]

Prior hosted the continuing negotiations with French officials at his own house on Duke Street, St James's, most importantly on the night of 20 September 1711. A week later, Oxford and Henry St John signed the peace preliminaries, and Prior, now officially the Queen's ambassador and plenipotentiary (despite Anne noting his 'mean extraction'[12]), started commuting between London and Paris. St John instructed him in the following affectionate terms: 'For God's sake, Matt, hide the nakedness of thy country, and give the best turn thy fertile brain will furnish thee with to the blunders of thy countrymen, who are not much better politicians than the French are poets.'[13] Prior was obviously as loved and trusted by his Tory patrons as he had ever been by Dorset or Halifax.

Pro-Marlborough Whigs like those in the Kit-Cat Club regarded these open negotiations with impotent horror, as a betrayal of British interests and as leaving France's expansionist ambitions insufficiently checked. Steele called Oxford's government 'the French Administration' in sarcastic honour of its collaboration with the enemy.[14]

Prior and others in the Brothers Club encouraged Swift to produce a political tract that would discredit the war and demolish Marlborough's reputation, thereby preparing Parliament's conscience to accept both the peace terms and Marlborough's dismissal. This Swift did in spectacular fashion, producing *The Conduct of the Allies and of the Late Ministry* (1711). *The Conduct* sold thousands within days, and was reprinted six times. 'I lay it down for a Maxim,' Swift declared in its opening passage, 'that no reasonable Man whether Whig or Tory (since it is necessary to use those foolish Terms) can be of the Opinion for continuing the War upon the Foot it now is, unless he be a Gainer by it.'[15] The pamphlet's success in achieving its aims was an astonishing feat, given the extent of the Commander-General's popularity. Steele's *Englishman's Thanks to the Duke of Marlborough* (1711) was a weak riposte.

The Kit-Cats began to feel it was time to lay down their quills and take more direct action. Their sense of urgency was prompted not only by the peace negotiations but also by Queen Anne's declining health, with the fear that the French and Jacobites would seize upon her incapacity or death to venture another armed invasion. The Kit-Cats planned a pre-emptive show of strength: a procession through London, in which effigies of the Devil, Pope and Pretender were to be set alight. It was to take place on 17 November 1711, the anniversary of Elizabeth I's accession and a key date in the Protestant patriotic calendar. They laid out £1,000 'by contribution' to fund the demonstration,[16] and Steele and the Duke of Montagu were tipped to lead it. When the Kit-Cat Club dined the preceding Thursday, probably in a private 'Velvet room' at the Queen's Arms,[17] they discussed these plans, as well as other grants and subsidies to keep the wheels of their influence oiled while in opposition.

Though such 17 November processions were traditional – the 1st Earl of Shaftesbury's Whig club had financed those of 1679 and 1680, for example – Lord Oxford worried that 1711's would turn into an anti-government riot since it would coincide with Marlborough's return to London. At midnight on 16 November, therefore, the Queen's Footguards were sent to a house in Drury Lane to confiscate the Devil, Pope and Pretender effigies, Wharton later laughing that 'Their Disciples came by night and stole them away.'[18] The Whig journalist Abel Boyer claimed the banning of the procession, and the 'Trained Bands' of soldiers patrolling London for three days afterwards, were intended to inflame public paranoia about the Whigs as republican revolutionaries.[19]

Though Maynwaring did publish new lyrics to the 1688 anthem of 'Lillibullero', the Kit-Cats were not so naïve as to believe they could spark a full-scale revolution. They merely wanted to appeal to the disenfranchised, illiterate, yet influential London mob, much as Sacheverell had done, and hoped that Marlborough's personal magnetism, if he were to appear on the shoulders of such a procession, could rally such support.

An anonymous government author published a poem, *The Kit-Cat Clubs Lamentation for the loss of the Pope, the Devil and the Pretender, that were taken into custody on Saturday last by the Secretary of State. Written by Jacob Door-holder to that Society* (1711). The poem sneered at how the Club's leaders, once 'looked upon as Sages / Fit to be Canonised by future Ages', were now reduced to sedition and 'abortive insolence'. The poet accused them of Devil-worship and, bizarrely, of covert Jacobitism. Oxford also ordered a paper called *The Postboy* to insert a paragraph in its 22 November issue, explicitly accusing the Kit-Cat Club of

> a conspiracy to raise a mob, to confront the best of queens and Her ministry, pull down the houses of several honest and true worthy English gentlemen, having had money distributed to them some time before for that purpose by . . . the insatiable Junto *cum multis aliis*, who made the subscription, and gave out the Queen was very ill, if not dead, in order to have their treason with greater freedom.[20]

The Kit-Cats also rallied direct parliamentary opposition to the Tories' peace terms, and their spirits were raised briefly when they succeeded in securing the defection of the High Church Tory Lord Nottingham. Nottingham agreed to oppose the peace in the House of Lords in exchange for the Junto's agreement to vote through a new Occasional Conformity Bill, barring Dissenters from public office. Wharton was persuaded to accept this horse-trading on the basis that nothing was more important than preventing a bad peace with France. Even the less politically active Kit-Cats were mobilized to persuade the Whig rank and file to accept this surprising, apparently hypocritical tactic: Vanbrugh advised one doubting young MP 'the matter was neither a point of honour nor Conscience, but purely political and discretional'.[21]

Kit-Cat Robert Walpole also introduced a motion in December 1711 against making any peace that would leave the Spanish throne in Bourbon hands. Walpole was backed by City men like Furnese who viewed money loaned to fund the war as investment in Britain's future trade with the Spanish Empire and did not intend to give up their investment without a fight. By focusing on trade, and by selling the Dissenters up the river, the Whigs increasingly appeared to oppose the peace for reasons of private profit. Charges of peculation were published against Marlborough before the Christmas parliamentary recess and, on 31 December 1711, the long-expected blow fell: Oxford dismissed Marlborough from all his posts, including supreme command of the Allied armies. Anne created twelve new Tory peers, the so-called 'Tory Dozen', in order to construct the narrow Tory majority in the Lords needed to vote through the peace terms. The Whigs' last power base was undermined by this action, which they viewed as unconstitutional and absolutist.

Addison's *Spectator* essay of 29 January, in this context, quivered with patriotism, saying if he could choose to live anywhere in the world, it would be in Britain: 'a Prejudice that arises from Love of my Country, and therefore such a one as I will always indulge'.[22] Being a Whig, he said, arose naturally from being proud of the 1689 constitutional balance, which Addison praised in answer to the creation of the 'Tory Dozen' and in defiance of the Tory preachers who were sure to denounce the Whigs as crypto-republicans on the following day's anniversary of Charles I's execution.[23]

In March 1712, a Tory faction with an even more anti-Court agenda than the October Club founded the 'March Club'. It started with thirty-five members, and soon rose to around fifty. This in turn prompted the Junto Whigs to inaugurate the 'Hanover Club' (or 'Hanover Society') later that year. This Club is best characterized as 'an adjunct to',[24] or satellite of, the Kit-Cat Club, with overlapping but not identical memberships and goals. Halifax and Walpole, for example, did not join the Hanover Club, and, though the Hanover Club toasted Whig ladies,[25] it never concerned itself with the Kit-Cat Club's broader cultural agenda. Instead, the thirty-plus Hanover Club members, who met weekly near Charing Cross and occasionally in Hampstead, focused on taking practical steps to secure the Hanoverian succession. They pledged, for example, to implement a tactic called 'close marking' whereby each parliamentary member was allotted a specific Tory to tackle during debates.[26] The contemporary historian Oldmixon remembered that the Hanover Club was 'very instrumental in keeping up the Whig Spirit in London and Westminster and consequently throughout the whole Kingdom'.[27] Whigs in other large cities formed clubs along similar lines.

Ambrose Philips, a protégé of Addison, was Secretary of the Hanover Club, and linked it directly to another new circle that, in 1712, began to supplement the Kit-Cat's role as a meeting place for London's writers: this was the circle of Button's Coffee House, located in Covent Garden, opposite Will's. There, in an inner room with a coffee pot kept constantly on the open fire, Addison began to hold court in Drydenesque style among his young literary apostles, including Addison's pudgy, doggedly loyal cousin and personal assistant, Eustace Budgell, and Thomas Tickell, a Fellow of Queen's College, Oxford. Addison's forms of patronage were more modest than the Kit-Cat patrons': he invited Budgell and Philips to share his lodgings, and published the work of several 'Buttonians', including Tickell, in *The Spectator*.

Playing oracle to an adoring coterie of lesser talents did Addison's character no favours. He set himself up as a big fish in a small pond, and even Macaulay admitted that Addison grew somewhat 'full of himself' (a phrase Addison coined[28]) as a result. Steele, Kneller and Garth occasionally joined the discussions at Button's, but Steele was suspicious of these new-found friends, especially Tickell, who was more moderate Tory than committed Whig and more Oxford don than town wit. Though Button's should have provided greater intellectual stimulation than the Kit-Cat Club, since it excluded those whose only qualifications for critical literary discussion were aristocratic title or electoral influence, Addison's domination had a deadening effect. None of the young Buttonians produced any literary work highly rated by posterity.

Addison also raised his social standing considerably in the spring of 1712 by purchasing Bilton Hall, near Rugby in Warwickshire, at a cost of some £10,000 (over £1 million today). Some of the capital to buy Bilton would have come from his brother Gulston's Madras estate, which was gradually being liquidated, some from Addison's savings after decades of bachelordom and frugality, but part was probably also a gift or loan from Wharton or Halifax. There is no other explanation for this impressive purchase during Addison's time of unemployment and so soon after the self-pitying complaints about his 'incredible losses'. The house was a status symbol, but also a retreat for a deeply Christian man who observed that 'in Courts and Cities we are entertained with the Works of Men, in the Country with those of God'.[29]

The Steeles were living at this time in a rented, low stone cottage on Haverstock Hill, north of London. This cottage was located near to where a pub stands today named The Sir Richard Steele. From the cottage's front gate, sheltered from the busy road up to Hampstead by a fine row of poplars, Steele had a clear view over central London's skyline, including St Paul's new dome. It was here that his son Eugene, named after Marlborough's great military ally, was born.

Addison's and Steele's rural retreats symbolized their distance from the centre of power and what they Whiggishly viewed as the Queen's now corrupt Court. May 1712 saw the British army on the Continent under strict instructions only to engage the French defensively – the infamous 'restraining orders'. On 28 May, Halifax led the Whig attack in the Lords against these orders, while fellow Kit-Cat William Pulteney led the same attack in the Commons, calling the ministry 'weak and treacherous'.[30] Not all of their followers could stomach it, however, an observer noting that when the peace terms were debated in the Lords 'Several even of the Kit-Kat Whig Lords are so satisfied with the goodness of the terms . . . as to join with the Court on this occasion.'[31]

The restraining orders' impact was soon evident: after the British troops were withdrawn from the equation, the Austro-Dutch army was soundly defeated at Denain in July 1712. This defeat was much lamented by the Kit-Cats, but was also evidence that Britain had become, in the course of the preceding decade, a first-rank military power whose presence or absence on the battlefield was decisive.

While Pulteney defended Marlborough against corruption charges in the Commons, the literary Kit-Cats supported him through their publications. Tonson, as predicted, finally published his long-awaited edition of *Caesar's Commentaries* (1712) dedicated to the Duke. *The Spectator* advertised the book by saying England gained as much glory from its printing presses and scholars as from its military victories – encapsulating a core Kit-Cat belief. Tonson's publication was, Addison wrote, 'a true Instance of the English Genius, which, though it does not come the first into any Art, generally carries it to greater heights than any other Country in the World'.[32]

On 1 July 1712, Swift observed *The Spectator* had been 'mighty impertinent' recently.[33] He saw it as his task to punish this 'impertinence' on the government's behalf. In *A Letter of Thanks from My Lord W[harto]n, to the Lord Bishop of S. Asaph, in the Name of the Kit-Cat Club* (1712), Swift satirized the Kit-Cats' religious laxity and venality. The narrator jokes that the Bishop's sermons enlist St Peter and St Paul so far to the side of the Whigs that they may soon 'be enrolled Members of our Club'. Even as his Tory friends held the upper hand in London and Dublin, Swift could not forgive Wharton or the Kit-Cat Club for having once made it clear he would never be one of them.

Swift also predicted Mr Spectator's recent 'impertinence' might mean, finally, Steele losing his Stamp Office job. Steele could ill afford to lose this last source of income. Borrowing heavily, he moved his family to a new townhouse 'handsome and neatly furnished' on the east side of Bloomsbury Square, where a visitor noted their 'table, servants, coach and everything is very genteel, and in appearance above his fortune'.[34] The new house was Steele's bid to silence his wife's constant 'dunning' for money,[35] and to fool his dying mother-in-law into thinking she could trust her money to him. Steele's wife had complained to her mother about Steele's mismanagement of their finances for years, and though he admitted to 'vast sums of money I have let slip through my hands', Steele now needed the old woman to think he had changed his ways.[36] By leasing the house in Bloomsbury Square, he succeeded in convincing her that he and Prue were living 'in the handsomest manner, supported only by my Industry'[37] and so was relieved to receive her fortune when she died soon after.

Steele's financial anxieties were equalled by Vanbrugh's. Queen Anne's 1704 promise to pay for building Blenheim had never been put into writing, and Treasury payments had been in arrears since June 1706, when the Duchess of Marlborough first started alienating the Queen's affections. The Duchess refused on principle to pay from her family's pocket what had been promised as a gift from the Royal Works, with the result that Vanbrugh had been unpaid for several years. Vanbrugh said he regarded Blenheim 'with the tenderness of a sort of Child of my Own'[38] and blamed the Duchess, whose interference in the project seems to have offended him largely because she was a woman, for the threatened abortion of his 'child' when she refused to pay the workmen from her own funds in 1710. The Duchess in turn blamed Vanbrugh for the fact that the house had already cost twice his original estimate. In May 1711, Addison was invited to inspect the Blenheim works – finally seeing the reality of the image that had appeared on his 1707 *Rosamund* stage-set. Mr Spectator reviewed the architectural design with approval. In June 1711, Oxford's vendetta against the Marlboroughs halted all payments from the Treasury and Blenheim's construction indefinitely. By this time, payment of £45,000 (or over £5.3 million today) was outstanding, including Vanbrugh's salary and expenses. Vanbrugh had prepared himself for the works' closure, however, having secured an appointment on the commission to build fifty new churches in London.

After closing down the leading Whig architectural project, Oxford sought to close down the Whig press. Failing to do so by legislation, Oxford tried undermining the Whig papers' economic viability: the Stamp Act came into effect in August 1712, levying new duties on all printed papers.[39] These new duties meant *The Spectator* had to double its price to two pence. Addison appealed to readers to pay the higher price, joking he would not want to be thought unpatriotic by halting publication and denying the Treasury taxes from England's most successful paper. With uncharacteristic venom, Addison compared those who worked behind the scenes to silence Mr Spectator to 'those Imperceptible Insects, which are discovered by the Microscope'.[40] He also suggested poorer readers wait to buy the collected *Spectator* volumes: 'My Speculations, when they are sold single, like Cherries upon the Stick, are Delights for the Rich and Wealthy; after some time they come to Market in greater Quantities and are every ordinary Man's Money.'[41]

The Stamp Act at first halved *The Spectator*'s sales, but Steele attracted additional advertising revenue from tradesmen, who rallied to support a paper that always spoke to them as if they mattered and subtly raised their social status. '[T]here are not more useful Members in a Commonwealth than Merchants,'[42] Addison declared. In August 1712, as if to thank the paper's saviours, Steele wrote an issue that was a hymn to English trade and the glories of London's Royal Exchange.[43]

On Thursday, 17 September 1712, Steele joined what sounds like the first Kit-Cat dinner of the London season, sending a note to Prue: 'The finest Women in nature should not detain Me an hour from You, but You must sometimes suffer the Rivalship of the Wisest Men. Lord Halifax and Somers leave this place after dinner.'[44] The gallant tone disguised Steele's growing disillusion with his marriage: he reflected in *The Spectator* on the shock of discovering 'the Creature we were enamoured of as subject to Dishumour, Age, Sickness, Impatience'[45] and on men needing the patience of Socrates to deal with shrewish wives: 'All who are married without . . . Relish of their Circumstance . . . live in the hourly Repetition of sharp Answers, eager Upbraidings, and distracting Reproaches. In a Word, the married State, with and without the Affection suitable to it, is the completest Image of Heaven and Hell.'[46]

Prue, pregnant with their fourth child, commended her own forbearance 'as a Christian as well as a Rational Creature in relation to you [Steele]'.[47] When Steele refused to let Prue have £300 from her mother's inheritance, her forbearance ran out and Steele's conjugal rights were placed in jeopardy, Steele at one point asking to spend the night with Prue if she would 'condescend to take me out of my Truckle-bed'.[48] Prue refused to let Steele join her until his debts were cleared.

In mid-November 1712, Addison and Steele met Jacob Junior at the Fountain tavern and, over a bottle, sold half the rights to the first four volumes of collected *Spectator*s for £575 (some £70,000 today). The other half was sold to Sam Buckley for the same amount. It is unknown how Addison and Steele split the proceeds. While this sum evidenced a substantial rise in literary incomes since the 1690s, it did not solve Steele's financial problems. Only learning to live within his means would do that, and Steele seemed to find this impossible.

Lord Godolphin, who had become, alongside Marlborough, a close ally of the Whigs in his final years as Lord Treasurer, died in September 1712, at the Marlboroughs' house, nursed on his deathbed by the Duchess. The Duchess and Dr Garth were also at the bedside of Kit-Cat Arthur Maynwaring when he died in November from a dose of 'Covent Garden gout' (venereal disease),[49] or possibly from taking mercury as a supposed cure. The loss of the Whigs' unofficial propaganda chief was a body blow to them in opposition. Addison, who effectively assumed this responsibility after Maynwaring's death, would be politer in his productions, and therefore less effective.

Lord Mohun was killed two days after Maynwaring's death, in a duel in Hyde Park. The Tory press speculated that this duel, ending not only in Mohun's death but also in that of his opponent the Duke of Hamilton, a crypto-Jacobite and Tory ambassador to the peace talks, was part of a Marlborough-linked Whig plot to obstruct the peace treaty.

Sir Henry Furnese then died on 30 November. Since the previous year, Furnese had been less active as a financier and more active in politics, gaining re-election as MP for Sandwich despite the Whigs' general defeat in 1710, then sitting as a City of London alderman. Lord Oxford had hoped to examine Furnese's accounts, like

Marlborough's, and bring him down on corruption charges, but Furnese's death excused the banker from this audit. Furnese's will provided generously for the poor in his constituencies, buying them plots of land from which they earned rents in perpetuity.

It is not obvious who, if anyone, took up these three vacated seats in the Kit-Cat Club, nor those of Tidcomb and Carbery, who died of natural causes in late 1712 and early 1713. The string of Kit-Cat deaths, during a season when London felt, in Addison's words, 'immersed in Sin and Sea-Coal',[50] darkened the Kit-Cats' already dejected moods. They believed their country was being sold cheap at the peace negotiations across the Channel, and their toasts in 1712 had none of the gaiety and libidinous optimism of earlier years. They wrote of themselves: 'Kit-cats grown Sage, Love's looser Flames neglect, / Toast not from Passion, but Profound respect.'[51]

On 23 October 1712, *The Spectator* announced the death of Sir Roger de Coverley, leaving the fictional Spectator Club in the same state of mourning as the Kit-Cat Club. It was the prelude for the closure of *The Spectator* on 6 December. Steele wrote the final, 555th issue, saying, 'It will not be demanded of me why I now leave off.'[52] Given the paper's popularity and the fact that we know of no specific actions by Oxford's government to force its closure, Addison and Steele may simply have agreed to quit while they were ahead, to try their pens at other things. When Steele ended the mystery of the paper's authorship in that final issue, he thanked 'all my creditors for wit and learning', and especially Addison, saying: 'I am indeed much more proud of his long continued Friendship than I should be of the Fame of being thought the Author of any Writings which he himself is capable of producing.'[53]

This declaration of pride in their friendship may also have been a conciliatory gesture, since the last few months of *Spectator* essays had contained pointed remarks showing tension between the paper's co-authors. Number 476, by Addison, seemed a jibe at Steele's increasingly lazy methods of composition: 'Irregularity and want of Method are only supportable in Men of great Learning or Genius, who . . . choose to throw down their Pearls in Heaps before the Reader.'[54] Ten days later, no. 484, by Steele, seemed to pick at Addison's insecurity about public speaking, saying 'modesty' was not, as Addison so often claimed, a justification for timidity: '[U]nder a Notion of Modesty, Men have indulged themselves in a spiritless Sheepishness, and been forever lost to themselves, their Families, their Friends and their Country.'[55] The checkmate in this coded exchange of criticisms came in mid-November 1712, when Addison advised readers to avoid letting their hopes run away with them, as this was the rock on which 'the Bankrupt, the Politician, the Alchemist and Projector are cast away in every Age'.[56] Steele was, at some stage in his life, each and every one of these things. Yet, for all these little digs, Addison and Steele remained on broadly friendly terms, united by common enemies and patrons.

Swift, whom Oxford had recently promoted to be Dean of St Patrick's Cathedral, Dublin, took a turn around the Mall with Addison and Ambrose Philips a few weeks later. He recorded that they seemed 'terrible dry and cold' and exclaimed:

> A curse of party! And do you know I have taken more pains to recommend the Whig wits to the favour and mercy of the [Tory] ministers than any other people. Steele I have kept in his place. Congreve I have got to be used kindly, and secured . . . and I set Addison so right at first that he might have been employed, and have partly secured him the place he has [Irish Record Keeper]; yet I am worse used by that faction than any man.[57]

Swift was mistaking for personal ingratitude the despond and mourning that had enveloped Addison and his friends, as they believed their country was on the verge of disaster.

Negotiations with the French were nearing completion by February 1713. The Whigs were convinced that after the peace a Jacobite invasion would follow. The 'whole club of Whig Lords' dined and cooked up 'some damned design' at Pontack's in the City,[58] while their supporters gathered for anxious Pope-burnings and Protestant anniversaries that month at London's Three Tuns and Rummer tavern. Powys House – Somers' former home in Lincoln's Inn – was now rented out to the French ambassador; when it burned to the ground, Whig arsonists were suspected. The philosopher George Berkeley, in London to publish his *Treatise on the Principles of Human Knowledge*, reported that 'Mr Addison and Mr Steele (and so far as I can find the rest of that party) seem entirely persuaded there is a design for bringing in The Pretender.'[59]

Once again the Whigs treated the press as their first line of defence. Steele launched a new paper, *The Guardian*, printed by the Tonsons, in March 1713. Its fictional narrator, Nester Ironside, was this time an old man who said he spoke his mind for the good of his country. Regarding party politics, Ironside declared: 'I shall be impartial, though I cannot be neuter.' Addison and several from the Button's crowd contributed, suggesting that Addison and Steele's friendship remained strong enough to sustain a certain level of continued collaboration.

On 11 April 1713, Britain, Holland, Portugal, Prussia, Savoy and France concluded the Treaty of Utrecht – referred to by the Kit-Cats as 'Matt's Peace' because of Prior's prominent role in its making.[60] The War of Spanish Succession was over as far as these countries were concerned, though Austria continued fighting to defend its claim to the Spanish throne for a further year.[61] Utrecht was not a bad peace, and in concluding it the Tories assisted Britain's emergence as a front-rank power. Louis XIV agreed to give up only a few towns in Flanders, but was also obliged to recognize Britain's Protestant succession and to expel The Pretender from France. Britain was allowed to keep Gibraltar and Minorca, making her the dominant power in the western Mediterranean, and to gain legal possession of the Hudson Bay territory, with obvious advantages for trade in North America. The commercial status quo in the Spanish Americas, and the balance of power within Europe, were restored by the Treaty, with Britain additionally gaining her first rights to trade (mostly slaves) in the Spanish Indies. All Britain conceded – apart from the Habsburg claim to the Spanish throne – were points offered as inducements to hold the Grand Alliance together during the war, not points of pressing national interest. Above all, Britain's new power was shown by her ability to sit alone with the French and redraw the world map (splitting North and South Carolina into two separate colonies with the sweep of a pen, for example), and for these terms to be so quickly accepted by the Dutch, the Prussians and other Allies.

The Junto Whigs, however, viewed the Treaty of Utrecht as a national humiliation that handed away several fruits of Marlborough's victories, along with colonial territories like Cape Breton. The Kit-Cat Club was despondent and directionless as its members prepared to disperse for the summer. George Berkeley observed:

> The very day peace was proclaimed, instead of associating with the Tories, I dined with several of the other party at Dr Garth's, where we drank the Duke of Marlborough's health, though they had not the heart to speak one word against the peace. Indeed the spirit of the Whigs seems quite broken.[62]

Above all, the Junto Whigs felt the Treaty betrayed several Continental allies, most notably by abandoning the Habsburg claim to the Spanish throne. This view was shared in Hanover by Britain's future George I.

After news of Utrecht's terms arrived in London, on the evening of 14 April 1713, a new play by Addison opened at Drury Lane – a Roman tragedy entitled *Cato*. Its reception by London audiences was to demonstrate exactly how highly strung the political mood had become.

Steele claimed to have seen the first draft of *Cato* as early as 1703, after Addison returned from Italy, but said Addison then did not have 'Courage enough' to stage it.[63] In 1712, as Whig prospects darkened, Addison's friends asked him to revise the play, thinking it 'a proper time to animate the Public with the Sentiments of Cato'.[64] The Kit-Cat patrons hoped the subject matter – heroic resistance to a tyrannical government – might encourage civil resistance to Oxford's government. *The Spectator* once referred to 'Cato amidst the Ruins of his Country preserving his Integrity',[65] and that was exactly how the Whigs imagined themselves since their fall from power. Addison consulted various Kit-Cats – Congreve, Garth, Halifax and, of course, Steele – as he hurriedly reworked the play.[66]

Pope, who had contributed *Cato*'s Prologue, attended the first night and observed Addison's nerves before the curtain rose. For all his talk about worldly success being but a shadow, Addison feared the audience reaction, undoubtedly recalling his last experience of an opening night at Drury Lane: the failure of the opera *Rosamund* six years before. Addison sat in a side-box with several friends, where they had a table 'and two or three flasks of Burgundy and Champagne, with which the author (who is a very sober man) thought it necessary to support his spirits'.[67] Addison need not have worried. Steele, acting, he said, as Addison's 'officious' aide-de-camp,[68] had packed the house with their friends, so that 'the Vulgar', as Steele put it, could not condemn the play too soon.

Addison also worried that such a political play might lay him open to charges of sedition. He had therefore sought the advance approval of Secretary of State Henry St John (newly created Viscount Bolingbroke, as he is called hereafter) on the play's text. In March 1713, there had been a brief reconciliation between Addison, Steele and Bolingbroke, culminating in Swift and Bolingbroke inviting Addison to a 'mighty mannerly' Good Friday meal,[69] which made this consultation possible. By *Cato*'s first night, however, the truce had broken down, as news of the Treaty of Utrecht's exact terms enraged the Whigs.

Respecting Addison's wishes, supporters of both political parties were permitted entry. From his side-box, Addison could see they had segregated themselves: the Tories sitting beneath Bolingbroke's box, the Whigs beneath the Kit-Cats'. In other boxes, footmen sent ahead to reserve seats for their masters were playing cards 'with a perfect Disregard to People of Quality sitting on each Side of them'.[70] Addison would have looked down through his 'perspective glass' (a small tube hired for six shillings) upon the women fluttering their fans in the pit below – the Whig ladies identified by orange-coloured hoods and dresses.

When the curtain went up on the Prologue, the Whig side of the house received it with such enthusiasm that Pope, its anonymous author, felt 'clapped into a staunch Whig sore against his will'.[71] Then the actors came on in their lavish costumes and very un-Roman perukes, and started declaiming the first scene. Soon it was obvious

Addison had a hit on his hands. The more patriotic lines elicited frenzied clapping from all sides, since the Kit-Cats and their followers could view the play's tyrant, Caesar, as James II or Lord Oxford, while the Tories could view him as Marlborough. The author broke into a fresh sweat of anxiety as the applause, coming 'more from the hand than the head',[72] turned into a mindless clapping match, each party trying to claim ownership of the play's patriotic sentiments.

After the final curtain, Bolingbroke publicly presented the actor playing Cato, Barton Booth, with fifty guineas '[f]or his honest Opposition to a perpetual Dictator; and his dying so bravely, in the Cause of Liberty'. The gesture seemed premeditated – a way for the government to demonstrate that Marlborough (now in exile on the Continent) was the only 'dictator' of Britain. Debate broke out among the actors as to whether it was disloyal for Booth, who admired Marlborough, to accept this prize. The situation was resolved when the Kit-Cat patrons hurriedly called the actor over to their side and offered the identical amount, so that, as Garth laughed to himself, Cato 'may have something to live upon after he dies'.[73]

Cato played to packed houses for an unprecedented twenty nights. It could have run for longer, but Mrs Oldfield, who played Cato's virginal daughter, was heavily pregnant and suddenly needed the services of 'a midwife behind the scenes'.[74] Buying a ticket for the play had become like casting a vote for the Whigs in a public opinion poll. Addison donated all his profits to the theatre company, uneasy at becoming known as such a party political author. Later, the play transferred to a theatre in Oxford, turning many student poets into Addison fans. A performance was even staged at Leghorn by an acting troupe among the British merchants.

Given the playwright's political connections, most obviously his Kit-Cat membership, the Whigs soon won total possession of *Cato* and set it within their propaganda artillery. Tonson purchased the play's copyright for the then unprecedented sum of £107. 10*s*. (nearly £12,000 today), and proceeded to publish eight editions within a year, all bestsellers. *Cato* was one of the contemporary works Tonson published in a format to match his critical Cambridge editions of English classics, thinking it would deserve such a place within the future canon. Hawkers sold copies in the street by crying out the play's most famous lines. *Cato* was also translated into several European languages, Voltaire praising it as the first 'reasonable' English tragedy.[75]

The only critic at the time who disliked *Cato* was John Dennis. Steele seems to have encouraged Pope, without Addison's authorization, to reply to Dennis' criticisms in a pamphlet so savage that Addison subsequently made Steele write letters to Pope and Pope's printer, expressing Addison's displeasure. This needless misunderstanding led to a cooling in relations between Addison and Pope. Pope afterwards wrote lines reinterpreting Addison's vaunted modesty and moderation as mealy-mouthedness, imitated by his sycophantic Buttonian protégés:

> Damn with faint praise, assent with civil leer,
> And without sneering, teach the rest to sneer;
> Willing to wound, and yet afraid to strike,
> Just hint a fault, and hesitate dislike;
> ...
> Like Cato, give his little Senate laws,
> And sit attentive to his own applause;
> While Wits and Templers ev'ry sentence raise,
> And wonder with a foolish face of praise.[76]

When Congreve saw these harsh lines, he sighed that Pope now dwelt 'among the incurables'.[77]

Addison and Steele's relationship with Swift suffered its final rupture about the same time as their falling out with Pope. Steele's *Guardian* in May 1713 heavily hinted that Swift was the author of recent *Examiner* essays celebrating the peace treaty (and one which accused the Kit-Cat Club of being the Junto's 'consistory'[78]). They were, in fact, by William Oldisworth, allowing Swift to ask Addison indignantly: 'Have I deserved this usage from Mr Steele, who knows very well that my Lord Treasurer [Oxford] has kept him in his employment upon my entreaty and intercession?'[79]

Steele was undeterred: 'You do not in direct terms say you are not concerned with him,' he replied to Swift. 'I believe you an accomplice of the Examiner.'[80] The argument continued in print through several issues of *The Examiner* and *The Guardian*, ending further social contact between Swift and the Kit-Cats. In sour mood, Swift departed for Dublin the following month.

Steele decided it was time to resign his Stamp Office post, in order to stand in the coming elections. Holding on to the post for so long under Oxford's administration had allowed even close acquaintances to mistake Addison for the 'more earnest' Whig of the pair.[81] Now, in June 1713, Steele sent a letter of resignation to Lord Oxford, accusing the chief minister of using his political talents against the nation's interests: '[I]t is impossible for anyone who thinks and has any public Spirit not to tremble at seeing His Country in its present Circumstances, in the hands of so daring a Genius as Yours.'[82]

A fortnight later, Steele told Prue he was dining with Addison who 'engaged me to meet some Whig Lords'[83] – presumably to select a safe parliamentary seat for Steele. This news did nothing to calm Prue, who was in 'lamentation'[84] over her husband resigning his only secure salary, and was subjecting him to regular 'curtain-lectures' (reproofs by spouses within curtained beds). Some of Steele's letters that July were addressed to 'Dear Tyrant' instead of 'Dear Prue'.

Steele stood for election in Stockbridge, Hampshire, a town of seventy-one voters who each sold their vote for about £60, in August. One of his electioneering gimmicks was said to be offering an apple stuck with guineas as a prize to the woman who gave birth to the first child exactly nine months after the vote – a cunning way of bribing electors with sexually willing spouses, the inspiration for which may have been his own wife's refusal of sex until their debts were cleared. The previous summer Steele had written about other enticements needed to tip the balance in an election: '[S]aluting Rows of old Women, drinking with Clowns, and being upon a Level with the lowest Part of Mankind in that wherein they themselves are lowest, their Diversions, will carry a Candidate.'[85]

Winning the Stockbridge election, Steele was soon boasting that 'as a Member of Parliament, I am accountable to no Man, but the greatest Man in England is accountable to me'.[86] Steele's status as an

MP, and the equality it gave him with friends like Addison and Stanhope, who were each returned to safe seats by their Kit-Cat patrons, were profoundly important to him. Steele had joined, he believed, the best club in England.

Tonson was in Paris on business at this time, and visited Prior, still serving as Britain's ambassador there. Prior was now so reviled by his old Kit-Cat friends for his part in the Treaty of Utrecht that he was understandably suspicious of Tonson's motives. An English Jacobite on the Continent reported to Oxford that '[a] famous printer, commonly called secretary to the Kit-Cat Club, is on this side, doing his friends all the services he can'.[87] Prior asked Bolingbroke rhetorically whether Tonson could possibly be turning Tory ('[C]an a leopard change his spots?'[88]), and promised to tell the publisher no secrets. If Tonson was attempting to use a business trip to cover some light espionage, he was inept; more probably the publisher just missed Prior's company, and felt freer to cross the Whig–Tory social divide while away from London's party tribalism.

The paper wars continued to rage unabated, and Steele was particularly active in fanning their flames. As part of his Stockbridge electioneering, he produced a pamphlet, *The Importance of Dunkirk Consider'd* (1713), accusing the Tory government of failing to insist on French compliance with the Utrecht article requiring destruction of Dunkirk's fortifications. The pamphlet also suggested Anne was easy prey for manipulative ministers because she was a woman unable to club with her ministers and learn 'the Subdivisions of Affection and Interest among Great Men . . . in their unguarded leisure'.[89] This prompted several replies from Oxford's ministry, including one by Swift, *The Importance of the Guardian Consider'd* (1713), which bitchily suggested Steele owed his literary reputation solely 'to the continual conversation and friendship of Mr Addison'.

After his election to Parliament, Steele closed *The Guardian* and opened another paper called *The Englishman*, because, as he declared in the latter's first edition, the time for inference and subtlety was over: 'It is a Jest to throw away our Care in providing for the Palate, when the whole Body is in danger of Death; or to talk of amending the Mien and Air of a Cripple that has lost his Legs and his Arms.'[90]

The Englishman – whose principal contributors were an Irishman (Steele) and a naturalized Huguenot (Abel Boyer) – was the voice of radical Whig patriotism. It was dedicated to raising the alarm about a civil war Steele believed inevitable after Anne's death, when the Jacobites, he believed, would immediately raise an insurrection.

Addison thought *The Englishman* a self-indulgent, vainglorious act of political suicide, telling a mutual friend:

> I am in a thousand troubles for poor Dick, and wish that his zeal for the public may not be ruinous to himself; he has sent me word that he is determined to go on, and that any advice I can give him in this particular will have no weight with him.[91]

Faced with Steele wilfully ignoring his advice for perhaps the first time in their long relationship, Addison claimed to be 'written out', and retired to his estate of Bilton until mid-December 1713.[92]

Steele told Prue he had 'resolved to go to the Club and ask for a Subscription myself, and, with as gay an air as I can, lay before them that I take it to be their Constitution to do it, as I am labouring in the common Cause'. At the bottom, a postscript: 'It frets my proud heart to do this, but it must be.'[93] This 'Subscription' was for yet another pamphlet, *The Crisis*, which would sound the alarm about the Oxford government's wavering commitment to the Hanoverian succession as Anne's health rapidly declined. Steele knew Bolingbroke was contemplating backing the restoration of The Pretender as 'James III', if only the Stuart exile would renounce Catholicism – a plausible option, as the English population seemed likely to have more loyalty to a Stuart son than to some unknown German. Steele's *Crisis* warned against trusting the French-backed Pretender even if he did convert, recalling the massacres of Protestants by Papists in Ireland, France and Savoy, and rallying his readers as if another civil war were already underway: 'Whatever may befall the Glory and Wealth of Great Britain, let us struggle to the last Drop of our Blood for its Religion and Liberty.'[94]

The Hanover and Kit-Cat Clubs soon responded to Steele's request by issuing 'a General Subscription for divulging *The Crisis* all over the Kingdom'.[95] Halifax from the Kit-Cats and James Craggs from the Hanoverians most actively circulated the call for subscribers, which served the additional purpose of advertising the pamphlet to the widest possible readership. At the same time, certain members of the two clubs privately asked the Elector of Hanover, via his Envoy, to finance the publication. There is no record of whether the future George I did so, but a mysterious single, sizeable pledge may have originated in Hanover.

Steele dined with Halifax on 24 December 1713, probably to deliver *The Crisis*' first draft for his patron's approval. Addison and several other Whigs assisted Steele with revising it, though Steele's name alone appeared on the title page. This recognized the fact that Oxford and the Tory press had been singling Steele out for attack since his election, so he had less than others to lose. Steele later recalled being bullied from his first parliamentary appearance, Tories jeering and interrupting his statements. Unlike most Kit-Cat politicians, Steele had no rank or family connections, with 'not one Man living of his Blood',[96] making him an easy target for the Tories and an easy sacrifice for the Whigs. They were kind to their sacrificial lamb, however: Steele likely spent the night before *The Crisis*' publication celebrating with either the Kit-Cat Club or the Hanover Club, since he wrote in *The Englishman* about how his friends teased him that night for falling asleep after dinner, quoting lines at him from Dr Garth's *Dispensary* about the God of Sloth. Steele said he hoped *The Crisis* would rouse the British nation from its own collective 'Lethargy' the following morning.[97]

The Crisis sold at least 40,000 copies, at a shilling each, by subscription alone – a sensational number, marking a turning point in the history of political propaganda. For the first time, thanks to the Kit-Cat and Hanover Clubs' coordinated publicity and distribution, Junto Whig arguments reached a truly mass audience, throughout the provinces, in Ireland and other European nations.

Socially, Addison and Steele were drifting further apart at this time. Addison was increasingly spending time with his Buttonian friends, especially Budgell and Tickell, after returning to London in December 1713. Steele turned to the company of tradesmen friends who had always bailed him out (sometimes literally, from debtors' prison) and who shared his unabashed Whiggery. The Tory *Examiner* mocked Steele for socializing with his foot doctor, haberdasher and tobacconist. One such *Examiner*, by Swift, was in the form of an open letter to 'Mr Jacob Kit-Cat, Bookseller', warning Tonson that Steele was forming a rival club among the working classes.[98]

It was, in fact, Swift who was involved during late 1713 in founding another club to rival the Kit-Cat Club: the literary clique that later became known as the 'Scriblerus Club'. It started not as a Tory club but as a proposed collaboration, coordinated by Pope, on a spoof volume of memoirs by one Martinus Scriblerus. Addison and Congreve were invited to contribute, and a piece by deceased Kit-Cat Anthony Henley was considered for inclusion. Following Pope's falling out with Addison over the pamphlet defending *Cato*, however, Swift swooped in to befriend Pope and the project then became exclusively Tory. The Kit-Cats dropped out quietly, and Swift gathered the remaining contributors (Pope, John Gay, Dr Arbuthnot and the Irish poet Thomas Parnell) for literary dinners on Saturday evenings. To these five was added Oxford, whose involvement required that the Club's dinners often took place, for the minister's convenience, at Dr Arbuthnot's lodgings in St James's Palace.

The Scriblerus Club only met regularly between the end of 1713 and spring 1714, though its friendships were to prove as lasting as the Kit-Cat Club's.[99] It cemented, and made less baldly mercenary, Oxford's relationship as patron to Swift as a propagandist. The minister commissioned, for example, a piece of counter-propaganda to answer Steele's *Crisis*, resulting in Swift's *The Publick Spirit of the Whigs* (1714). Wharton and Devonshire introduced a Lords motion to condemn this pamphlet, offering a £300 reward to uncover its author's identity, on the grounds that it contained a libellous attack on the Scottish peers. The printer was arrested, and Swift reportedly found a man who for a fee would pretend, if necessary, to be the pamphlet's author. Another anonymous Tory tract attacked Steele as a chronic debtor who had given his wife syphilis (an unverified allegation), and a satirical poem, *The Steeleids: or, the Tryal of Wit* (1714), attacked Steele's membership of the Kit-Cat Club, where 'Pert Dullness . . . acquires unjust Renown'.[100]

Oxford and Bolingbroke were grateful for anything distracting the public while they negotiated, through various secret channels, with The Pretender regarding his religion. In part to manufacture such a distraction, they started proceedings in March 1714 to expel Steele from the House of Commons. The charge was seditious libel, yet it was not a criminal prosecution, since the Kit-Cats had taken the precaution of having lawyers review *The Crisis* with an eye for libel before its publication and since Steele enjoyed parliamentary privilege.

Halifax remarked, possibly at a Kit-Cat dinner on Thursday, 11 March 1714, that if the Queen read *The Crisis* 'she would think quite otherwise of the book than they [her Tory ministers] do'.[101] During the next two days, formal charges against Steele were presented in the Commons. Steele was not present, on Halifax's advice, but afterwards accompanied Tonson to meet 'some Friends' at Walpole's house on Dover Street. Steele confided to his wife that Queen Anne's health was reported to be truly precarious. He signed this note as 'Your Faithful very Cheerful Husband',[102] suggesting that he was reassuring her, but also that he was genuinely buoyed by being at the centre of his Kit-Cat friends' supportive attention.

The ministry gave Steele less than a week to prepare his case. The Commons debate on whether Steele should be expelled took place on 18 March, running until midnight. He first formally confirmed his authorship of the two publications on which the charges were based – *The Crisis* and no. 46 of *The Englishman*. Believing it best to climb onto a very high horse in such situations, Steele declared: 'I writ them in behalf of the House of Hanover, and I own them with the same unreservedness with which I abjured the Pretender.'[103] Steele then made a three-hour speech in his own defence. Addison, who had worked with Steele on this speech throughout the previous week, sat beside him and prompted him 'upon Occasion' with little notes.[104]

'Though I had too much at Stake to be in Humour enough to enjoy the Scene,' Steele recalled, 'there was, with all the Cruelty of it, something particularly Comic in the Affair.' It had the air of a show trial, in which the verdict was predetermined: 'The Accuser arraigned a Man for Sedition with the same Indolence and Indifference as another Man pares his Nails.'[105] There were disturbances in the upper galleries and Speaker's Chamber, where rowdy Whig protesters 'refusing to withdraw, were by Order of the House taken into Custody'.[106]

The orators who defended Steele most powerfully were the same Kitlings who had spoken so brilliantly at Sacheverell's trial four years earlier: Walpole and Stanhope, aided by Pulteney. Walpole and Stanhope had each spent a year in captivity after the Whigs' fall from power in 1710. The Bourbon army had captured Stanhope in Spain when his forces surrendered at Brihuega in December 1710, a disastrous end to the Allies' Iberian campaigns, and a personal tragedy for Stanhope at the age of 37. He wrote to the Tory Secretary of State for the South, Lord Dartmouth, at the time: 'I cannot express to your Lordship how much this blow has broken my spirits, which I shall never recover.'[107] While Stanhope was in captivity, the new Tory government blocked all deals with the French and Spanish for his release and return. When he did return to Britain, Stanhope was defeated in the August 1713 election. His friends therefore had to find him the safe Whig seat of Wendover in a by-election. Stanhope's defence of Steele was therefore his first major speech since re-entering the Commons.

Walpole's defence of Steele was also his first in the Commons for some two years. In January 1712, Walpole had been convicted of corruption (while Secretary-at-War), expelled from the Commons and committed to the Tower of London. Wharton and other Kit-Cat friends visited Walpole in prison, though on his release in July 1712 he was disappointed that he was greeted with 'no music nor dinner prepared for him by the Hanover Club'.[108]

Steele said Walpole's speech that night may not have altered the vote but at least made many of those who voted with the government against him feel ashamed. Walpole pointed out that this use of parliamentary expulsion, in lieu of prosecution, threatened MPs' rights to criticize a government and hence threatened free speech in

Britain. Ironically, given his later career, Walpole defined patriotism as the bravery to criticize an unjust government, asking the crucial, provocative question: 'How comes writing for the [Hanoverian] succession to be a reflection upon this ministry?'[109]

Other Whigs used the debate to air complaints about the crypto-Jacobitism, as they saw it, of Oxford and Bolingbroke. Two Scottish peers spoke about taxpayers' money going to the Highland clans whose loyalties were with The Pretender. The Whigs, in other words, made the most of a debate they knew they could not win. Despite the full flexing of the Kit-Cat Club whip to secure the vote of every Kit-Cat's Commons clients and relations, the vote was lost by ninety-three votes, and Steele was brought back into the chamber to be found guilty of writing libels designed 'to alienate the Affections of her Majesty's good Subjects and to create Jealousies and Divisions among them'.[110] Tellingly, *The Examiner* was ready to go to press, announcing Steele's expulsion, hours before the verdict was proclaimed.

The following day, Steele wrote to the Speaker of the House to ask whether he could appeal the Commons' censure in a court of law, but was told this was impossible. That night he assured Prue: 'I am in very good Humour and in no concern, but fear of your being uneasy. I will go to the Club tonight, for as you say, I must press things well now or never.'[111] The club in question was the Kit-Cat.[112] Having been expelled from what he considered the best club in the world, Steele sought solace in the second best, to which he felt all the deeper loyalty – particularly to Walpole and Stanhope. Later Steele would dedicate a collected edition of *The Englishman* to Stanhope, complimenting his friend on his 'natural and prevailing Eloquence in Assemblies', his 'gentle and winning Behaviour in Conversation' but also his 'Plain-dealing, Generosity and Truth'.[113] Stanhope was, to Steele's mind, the new model Englishman.

When Steele spoke of the need to 'press things', however, he clearly sought more than words of comfort from the Kit-Cats: he was being sued by his wigmaker, and needed a fast cash injection to avoid another spell in debtors' prison. For once, Steele's wishes seem to have been answered; in late March 1714, he told his wife that a

Mr William Ashurst was giving him £3,000 (or £370,000 today), via a goldsmith, as an anonymous grant. Steele wrote joyously that 'all would do beyond my expectation'[114] but was unable to 'dive into the Secret by what hands I am to be obliged'.[115] It may have been thanks to his Kit-Cat patrons, or the money may even have come into Mr Ashurst's hands from Hanover. If the grant was a collected 'kitty' from the Kit-Cats, it was not pure charity, since Steele was now a famous Whig mascot and his imprisonment for debt would have been an embarrassment to their party.

On Easter Sunday 1714, financially resurrected, Steele wrote penitently to Prue, who had moved to stay with her friend Mrs Keck: '[Y]ou and Betty and Dick and Eugene and Molly shall be henceforth my principal cares.' Yet Steele was too much in love with his recent role as Whig martyr not to add that Prue and his four 'Brats', as he affectionately called them, must still come second to 'Keeping a good Conscience'.[116]

Since MPs then earned no salary, Steele's expulsion did not mean a loss of income. His only journalistic income at this time was from a non-political broadsheet, *The Lover*, narrated by one Marmaduke Myrtle, a gentleman who once again drew on reports from his 'little Club' in London.[117] Steele started producing *The Lover* as soon as he closed the first series of *The Englishman*, but *The Lover* closed in turn at the end of May 1714. Addison contributed a couple of issues to it, but this was to be the pair's last literary collaboration. Despite their teamwork at Steele's trial, the friendship had lost its former dynamic, based on a clear understanding of one man's superiority to the other.

The Whigs were given a new spurt of energy that spring, when it became public knowledge that James III had categorically refused Bolingbroke's entreaties to renounce Catholicism and conform to the Church of England. This made it highly improbable that a popular uprising in England would return the Stuarts to the throne, and made Jacobitism thereby unpatriotically synonymous with support for a French invasion. This in turn led to division in the Tories' ranks, exacerbated by deepening personal rivalry between Oxford and Bolingbroke. 'Those warm, honest Gentlemen of the Hanover Club', as Vanbrugh called them, started meeting on successive days, to capitalize on the Tories' sudden disarray, and the Tory *Postboy* reported that the Kit-Cat Club was similarly meeting every evening. The two Clubs organized, for example, parliamentary opposition to Bolingbroke's 'Schism Bill', which proposed to suppress Dissenters' schools – the kind of proposal that unified the Whigs and temporarily obscured the common ground between the majority of Whig and Tory MPs (as staunch Anglicans with no wish to see a Catholic monarchy).

Electress Sophia of Hanover died on 8 June 1714, leaving her son George the legal heir to the British throne. Queen Anne's health then took a sudden turn for the worse. The British political world sat poised, apprehensive about what might happen if and when she died. Steele predicted 'nothing but Divine Providence can prevent a Civil War within [a] few years',[118] but he and his friends were to some extent victims of their own propaganda, exaggerating the level of the Jacobite threat. Addison described the Whigs living in patriotic, vigilant martyrdom: 'Most of our Garrets are inhabited by Statesmen, who watch over the Liberties of their Country and make a Shift to keep themselves from starving.'[119]

Stanhope said he looked upon 'our liberties as good as gone' and volunteered to lead an armed civil defence of the Hanoverian succession if and when the time came.[120] He was in close communication with the exiled Duke of Marlborough, who was organizing to lead those British troops loyal to him back to Britain from garrisons in Ghent, Bruges, Dunkirk and Nieuwport, should the need arise. The journalist Abel Boyer recorded, as the Queen's death approached, that 'measures were early concerted by the Kit-Cat Club with a Major-General [Marlborough's right-hand man, Cadogan] who had a considerable Post in the Foot-Guards, to seize the Tower upon the first appearance of Danger, and to secure in it such Persons as were justly suspected to favour the Pretender'.[121]

Two surviving manuscripts strongly suggest the first military preparations to pre-empt a Jacobite uprising or invasion were plotted over a Kit-Cat dinner, and communicated from there to Marlborough on the Continent.

The Kit-Cat Club simultaneously kept up its battle for hearts and minds. Wharton engaged Steele to prepare several further anti-Jacobite pamphlets, and Steele consulted with Walpole about their content over a dinner the night before Walpole left for his Norfolk estates. As other Kit-Cat grandees likewise prepared to leave the capital, all knew it might prove a short summer recess.

In late July 1714, the crisis broke: Oxford, who had personally offended the Queen, was dismissed as Lord Treasurer on the 27th, and Bolingbroke was unable to form either a new ministry or an alliance with the Whigs to save his own political neck. Three days later, on Friday, 30 July, the Privy Council convened at Anne's bedside in Kensington Palace, where she lay too incapacitated to speak, following convulsions the previous day. After some discussion, the Tory Sir Simon Harcourt proposed Lord Shrewsbury as the man to head the government during the Queen's incapacity, and the Queen, only semi-conscious, was helped to physically pass Shrewsbury the Staff of Office. Though Shrewsbury had allied with the Tories to support the Utrecht peace, he was Whig enough to ensure the Acts of Regency and Settlement would be respected, and so his leadership was acceptable to Somers, Somerset and other Whigs in the Council. Somers, despite his own 'bodily and mental ills',[122] attended the Council for the first time in four years the following day.

With Shrewsbury's appointment, it suddenly seemed less likely that the plan of Marlborough and the Kit-Cats, to raise an armed defence force, would be necessary. Shrewsbury led the Council to authorize the taking of arms and horses from all British Catholics and the immediate closure of the ports. As Somers sat down to write to the Hanoverian Elector, apprising him of the situation and urging him to depart for Britain as soon as possible, Anne's life ebbed away. She died at seven o'clock the following Sunday morning.

XVII
BIG WHIGS: THE FIRST GEORGIANS

> A new Title or an unexpected Success throws us out of ourselves, and in a Manner destroys our Identity.
>
> JOSEPH ADDISON in *The Spectator* no. 162, 5 September 1711

STEELE RECEIVED THE momentous news of Queen Anne's death while taking his morning coffee at the Whig stronghold of St James's Coffee House. It was hard for the coffee house to suppress an unseemly celebration, with toasts drunk, before noon, to Great Britain's new King George. Afterwards, Steele walked down to the Thames where bright sunlight cast sharp shadows on the buildings and made the river sparkle, as if sharing his good mood. The Low Church divine, Archbishop Tenison, a recluse in Lambeth throughout the whole period of Tory rule, took a barge straight to Whitehall Stairs upon receiving the news, greeting Steele with the exclamation: 'Master Steele, this is a great and glorious day!'[1]

Carlisle heard the news the following day, at the York races. The local Lord Mayor proclaimed George was now King, after which most of the northern nobility abandoned the track, and commenced their own unseemly race back to London. Lady Mary Wortley Montagu complained at how she, Lord Carlisle's daughters and the other ladies were left alone and undefended in the great houses of the north – vulnerable, she implied, to a Franco-Jacobite invasion force should one land in Scotland or the northeast.

Until the King's arrival in Britain, which was delayed for some weeks, the regents ruling the country included five Kit-Cats: Halifax, Carlisle, Devonshire, Scarbrough and Somerset. Somerset may have been readmitted to the Kit-Cat Club at this juncture in recognition of his loyalty to the Hanoverian succession when it had most mattered, at the Queen's deathbed. Congreve once said the Hanoverian succession would bring 'no longer a glimpse but a glare' of good news for the Whigs.[2] Such Enlightenment imagery befitted his Kit-Cat friends' radiant mood during those summer months, as they basked in the glow of their fellowship and bright futures.

On 3 August 1714, Addison was appointed Secretary to the regents – the highest administrative post in Britain, which he received largely in recognition of his financial probity, given that such a post would be bombarded with offers of bribery from people hoping to be recommended to the new king. Addison's responsibilities included securing Britain's coastal and other domestic defences against a possible Franco-Jacobite invasion – much as he had done in the spring of 1708 – and dealing with the Tories in Ireland, who were seen as dangerously loyal to Ormonde and/or Bolingbroke.

Foreign ambassadors also had to be notified of the Queen's death and its consequences. Addison sent Prior, his former friend and guide in Paris, a poignant letter informing him that his days as a British ambassador were numbered. Prior was forced to resign before the month was out, and, on his fiftieth birthday, wrote the following epitaph for his own tumultuous career:

> Yet counting as far as fifty to his years,
> His virtues and vices were as other men's are;
> High hopes he conceived, and he smothered great fears,
> In a life party-coloured, half pleasure, half care.

Nor to business a drudge, nor to faction a slave,
He strove to make int'rest and freedom agree;
In public employments industrious and grave,
And alone with his friends, Lord! How merry was he![3]

Addison further organized the regents' role in the Queen's funeral and in George I's ceremonial welcome. To assist with this enormous list of duties, Addison turned for administrative support not to Steele (who was expectantly hanging around Westminster), but to young Thomas Tickell.

On 18 September, 54-year-old 'Georg Ludwig' finally arrived in England, having been escorted from Hanover by Lionel, Earl of Dorset. George was rowed from his ship, through the heavy fog, to the landing steps in front of Wren's great buildings at Greenwich. Waiting to greet him in the first row of the crowd, their beaming faces lit by torches in the soupy twilight, was an array of Kit-Cats. Of the regents, only Carlisle was unable to attend, due to gout. They watched as George disembarked, accompanied by no queen (his wife having eloped, been divorced, then locked away) but by two comically shaped women: the 'elephant' Kielmansegg (his illegitimate half-sister) and the 'maypole' Schulenburg (his mistress). Behind this trio came George's two Turkish manservants, Mehemet and Mustafa. This unmistakably alien retinue was quickly whisked away to a banquet inside Inigo Jones' Queen's House – a venue chosen by the Kit-Cat regents to emphasize cultural continuity with England's former monarchs.

George had visited England when a young man in 1680, but spoke little English. Many, watching his reception at Greenwich, must have assumed he would be little more than a pawn in the hands of the Whig lords who knelt before him. Lionel's role as escort, and Addison's as Secretary to the regents, together with Vanbrugh being the first man knighted after the new king set foot on the Greenwich lawns, were clear reminders of the Kit-Cats' auspicious diplomatic visit to Hanover in 1706. That Halifax, leader of that trip, should now be rewarded with the highest post of government was widely expected. Halifax was so confident that he muttered to Addison, as they waited on the waterfront, that if Addison could only overcome his 'silly

Sheepishness . . . that makes thee sit in the House and hear a Fellow prate for half an Hour altogether who has not a tenth Part of thy good Sense', then Halifax would gladly recommend Addison to become a Secretary of State, replacing Bolingbroke.

The Kit-Cats and other Whigs had spent the seven-week regency jostling for position and cutting deals with one another, knowing that they had little competition to fear from the Tories. George detested Oxford's and Bolingbroke's followers as makers of the Utrecht peace, judging Englishmen primarily by their views on international relations. The Marlboroughs had visited Hanover during their exile and reinforced these prejudices, schooling the future king in a partisan narrative of recent history in which there was no such thing as a Hanoverian Tory. Yet, despite these prejudices, George did at first try to form a mixed ministry, offering important posts to two prominent moderate Tories with relatively clean hands in terms of foreign affairs. Both refused, perhaps thinking they could do better if the forthcoming general election returned a large number of Tories. Missing this one offer of power-sharing, the Tories would not be offered another. Bolingbroke tried to console Swift that adversity would make Tory friends reunite, to which Swift replied that though the Tories had 'certainly more heads and hands than our adversaries . . . it must be confessed, they [the Whigs] have stronger shoulders and better hearts'.[4] By mid-August 1714, Swift had returned to his deanery at St Patrick's Cathedral in Dublin, where he spent the rest of his life exiled from London politics.

On 22 September, George attended the first meeting of his Privy Council, at which his decisions on ministerial appointments were announced. The roll-call of appointees confirmed that the Tories would have no share in the new government. Even Sir Simon Harcourt, who had ensured Shrewsbury was handed power at Anne's deathbed, was dismissed rather than rewarded. The Kit-Cats' alleged monopolies in the past (1696–7 and 1706–10) turned into the true monopoly of the Georgian Whig oligarchy, with purges from government and Court offices of all but those Tories who could be converted to Whiggery. One such case was Nottingham who was trusted despite his past Toryism because he had opposed Utrecht. He was joined in

George I's first Cabinet by Marlborough (who had returned to England on the day of Anne's death), Sunderland, Townshend and three Kit-Cats: Devonshire, Halifax and Somers. Halifax was appointed First Lord of the Treasury, but not Lord High Treasurer – the Treasury instead being put into commission, to be run by a board of several ministers and, at a distance, by the King himself. This was a bitter disappointment to the old Junto leader, effectively denying him the role of chief minister. Observing Halifax soon after the announcement, the Duchess of Marlborough said: 'He hardly spoke a word the whole dinnertime, looked full of rage, and as if he could have killed everybody at table.'[5]

The truth was that, at 53, Halifax's mind was not as sharp as it once was. An anecdote told by Pope, intended to demonstrate Pope's independence from patrons and especially from Halifax, illustrates this fact. One day, Garth, Addison and Congreve took Pope to meet Halifax, so that Pope could read aloud to Halifax from his manuscript translation of the *Iliad*. Halifax criticized several passages, telling Pope to alter them, which upset the author. When Pope complained about this in the carriage home, Garth laughed and told him to leave the lines exactly as they were, thank Halifax, and then read them out again in a few months' time. Pope followed this advice and, on the second reading, Halifax exclaimed, 'Ay now, Mr Pope, they are perfectly right!'[6]

Addison's hopes of replacing Bolingbroke as Secretary of State for the South were also disappointed; Stanhope instead got the job and was soon effectively acting as the King's leading minister. Addison returned to his former, relatively lowly 1708–9 post as Secretary to the Lord Lieutenant of Ireland, who was now Sunderland. Neither he nor Sunderland bothered to go to Ireland, preferring to administer the country by post and via Addison's cousin Budgell, appointed Under-Secretary. Addison complained to Halifax of this 'great fall in point of Honour from being Secretary to the Regents', begging for some post on the Board of Trade, or 'some other method to let the world see that I am not wholly disregarded'.[7] Addison also told Halifax, full of wounded pride, he would accept no less than £1,000 for the work he had done as Secretary to the regents, since anything less 'will look more like a clerk's wage than a mark of His Majesty's favour'.[8]

After Anne's death, Steele had excitedly told Prue he was being 'loaded with compliments from the regents and assured of something immediately'.[9] In fact, for all his suffering as a Whig scapegoat the previous year, Steele received relatively modest rewards from the new Georgian Court: the Governorship of the Drury Lane theatre worth £700 per year (around £93,000 today), as well as £500 (around £66,000 today) in cash from the King's Bounty, a small sinecure as Surveyor of the Royal Stables at Hampton Court and, in April 1715, a knighthood. That Steele, Stanhope's great admirer, and Vanbrugh, a distant kinsman to Stanhope, were the ones knighted – rather than Addison and Congreve – resulted from Stanhope's rise to power and the new lines of allegiance that subsequently began bisecting the Kit-Cat circle. These would grow into deep fissures during the next few years.

Before Anne's death, when Vanbrugh lost his £400 patent as Comptroller of the Royal Works as a result of expressing sympathy for Marlborough's 'bitter persecution',[10] he had had personal debts of £3,000 to £4,000 (between £330,000 and £440,000 today), in addition to debts from the Haymarket theatre. Vanbrugh therefore drew up speculative plans for a new palace in St James's that he hoped George I would commission upon his accession. George, however, held back on commissioning ostentatious new buildings in styles that might be criticized for being 'foreign'. Vanbrugh had to make do, instead, with receiving back the patent for the Royal Works, with the additional title of Surveyor of the Gardens and Waterworks.[11]

Congreve was also given two sinecures: Undersearcher of Customs for the Port of London, and Secretary to the colony of Jamaica. These posts (together worth approximately £98,500 a year by today's values) marked the end of the poet's money worries, allowing him to retire in relative comfort and to invest in various stocks. They can be attributed to Congreve's long allegiance to the Kit-Cat patrons, particularly Halifax, since the Duchess of Marlborough's disapproval of his affair with her daughter would otherwise have blocked his recommendation, and George had no particular agenda of his own to honour retired British authors.

Other politically ambitious Kit-Cats also got their cream. Wharton, who presented addresses from Britain's Dissenters to the new king in September 1714, was made Keeper of the Privy Seal. Carlisle joined the Privy Council as the First Commissioner of the Treasury in May 1715, though he only held the post for a few months before retiring. Thirty-year-old William Pulteney was appointed Secretary-at-War – one of the younger generation of Kit-Cats who would feature as key political protagonists through the next half century.[12]

George's coronation took place in Westminster Hall on 20 October 1714. One Kit-Cat noble (Grafton) bore the crown, another (Somerset) the orb. Though the Kit-Cat Club had spent almost a decade preparing the British public to accept a monarch chosen for his religious principles rather than his hereditary claim, the day was greeted with rioting in about thirty towns and villages, mostly swing constituencies, as a warm-up to Tory electioneering.

New titles were also among the Kit-Cats' rewards: Harry Boyle was created Baron Carleton, for example, and Halifax was raised from Baron to Earl. Lionel was the first Knight of the Garter invested by George I, and a full third of the thirty-five Knights of the Garter invested between August 1714 and 1733 were to be Kit-Cats. Among the slew of Court appointments bestowed upon Kit-Cats was the appointment to the King's Bedchamber of Richmond, Berkeley, Grafton and Scarbrough.[13] Provincial offices were likewise dispensed liberally to the Kit-Cat nobility, reflecting their local power bases. Only four of thirty-nine Kit-Cat members did not hold some government or Court office immediately following George's accession.

There were changes too within the Kit-Cat Club itself. A descendant of Tonson wrote that the publisher remained secretary of the Club 'till the Hanover family came to the Throne'.[14] If this is a precise statement, Tonson may, at 58, have decided to mirror the change of monarch with his resignation from the Club's 'throne'. This would make sense of the surprisingly prominent role in Club business of a new and youthful member, dating from the summer of 1714.

Twenty-one-year-old Thomas Pelham-Holles, created Earl of Clare by George I the day before the coronation, was said to have joined the Kit-Cat Club at Devonshire's nomination 'after the accession of George I',[15] though Clare had belonged to the Hanover Club during the final, tense year of Anne's reign (after which the Hanover Club disbanded, having attained its sole objective). The son of a Sussex magnate, Clare inherited a fortune – including a quarter of a million pounds' worth of land in central London and eleven other counties – from his uncle, John Holles, 1st Duke of Newcastle. This unexpected legacy propelled Clare into the national limelight while he was still a student at Cambridge. Clare started 'anticipating' his inheritance (a gross annual income of some £26,000 to £27,000, or over £3 million today) long before he received any actual income. The bankers and goldsmiths of London were more than happy to extend him credit, and Clare was soon heavily in debt, from overspending on a lifestyle intended to impress friends and neighbours. While under the Club's tutelage, Clare was at the same time its literary members' most promising patron – a man who believed that the Club's Ciceronian tradition of generosity to the arts should extend into the new Georgian period. Premature spending and precocious patronage were symptoms of a single, insecure hunger in Clare: for recognition and approbation. This insecurity showed itself in Clare's mannerisms, described as a man who babbled and fidgeted with a constant 'limb-fever'[16] as he tried desperately to impress everyone he met.

Vanbrugh became Clare's architect as early as October 1714, having turned back to the Kit-Cat Club to find employers as soon as George's reluctance to patronize palatial architecture became evident. Vanbrugh sold Clare a house called Chargate on land Vanbrugh had acquired in 1709–10 at Esher in Surrey. The architect had first built Chargate as a property development project at a time when he complained to his Kit-Cat friends that the Duchess of Marlborough was trying to bankrupt him by pursuing various disputes over the costs of Blenheim. Now Vanbrugh started building a more stately home on the same Surrey land, to be named 'Claremont' after its new owner. Clare also employed Vanbrugh to refit his London home in Lincoln's Inn Fields (formerly Somers' home, Powys House, which had been almost destroyed in the Whig arson attack against the French Envoy in 1713) and, on one of his northern estates, Nottingham Castle. Clare's architectural ambitions – particularly at Claremont – accounted for 'a sizeable portion' of his early debt.[17] After the Duchess of Marlborough's hawk-eyed accountancy, Vanbrugh must have been overjoyed to find such an extravagant and malleable patron.

Clare was a notorious hypochondriac who surrounded himself with physicians, making Dr Garth one of his favourite Kit-Cat friends. In 1715, Garth was knighted and appointed King's Physician in Ordinary, as well as Physician General to the Armed Forces, and though outsiders might have assumed these honours were thanks to Garth's friendship with the Marlboroughs, a thank-you letter from 'Sir Samuel Garth' makes clear that he also owed them to Clare.[18] Garth's indebtedness to Clare is further shown by his poem *Claremont*, published by Tonson in May 1715. After *The Dispensary*, this was Garth's most important poetic production. In it, he contrasted the generally mercenary nature of English literary patronage ('None ever can without Admirers live, / Who have a Pension or a Place to give') and the Whig tendency to pretension (the way a nobleman's piece of doggerel gets 'Horaced up') with his own sincere intention to acknowledge a deserving and generous patron in Clare. Garth describes Clare as:

> The Man who's honest, open, and a Friend,
> Glad to oblige, uneasy to offend:
> Forgiving others, to himself severe;
> Though earnest, easy; civil, yet sincere.

In a private letter sometime after writing *Claremont*, Garth thanked Clare for a surprise gift of 100 guineas: 'Though I can never overvalue the least friendship of yours, you are resolved to overvalue the greatest service of mine.'[19]

Steele was the third Kit-Cat to turn to Clare, hoping to find a reliable source of future support and an electoral patron whose influence could return him to the House of Commons. The coincidence of Garth's, Vanbrugh's and Steele's appeals to Clare's patronage in 1714 would certainly be explained if Clare had assumed Tonson's leading role within the Kit-Cat. Yet Steele felt no obligation to offer flattery to Clare, since the Whigs, by his reckoning, still owed him their favour in return for past sufferings. In one publication, Steele boldly declared to Clare: 'His Lordship and many others may perhaps have done more for the House of Hanover than I have; but I am the only man in his Majesty's dominions who did all he could.'[20]

Despite the anonymous £3,000 grant six months earlier, Steele was in debt again to the tune of £3,618 (over £445,000 today) by October 1714. He nonetheless leased a new house at 26 St James's Street. To help pay for it, Steele published two new works that month. The first, *An Apology for Himself and His Writings . . .*, was a self-justifying account of his martyrdom to the Whig cause, dedicated to Walpole. The second was a more commercial venture, at Tonson's suggestion: *The Ladies' Library*. This was an anthology of morally improving reading material for young women, the realization of a project started by Mr Spectator in 1711. Tonson advertised the three-volume set as a good 'New Year's Gift', and it proved a winter bestseller, including two editions in France.[21] There were two dedicatees. One was Steele's wife, to whom he said: 'I owe to you that for my sake you have overlooked the Prospect of living in Pomp and Plenty.' The second dedicatee, Juliana, Countess of Burlington, was a former toast of the 1690s. Now, mother of six daughters, this Whig matron was the ideal patroness for *The Ladies' Library*.

Juliana's son, Richard Boyle, 3rd Earl of Burlington, is one of those generally believed to be among the post-1714 generation of new Kit-Cat members – members who were unborn or infants when Tonson and Somers first drank together in Temple Bar after the Glorious Revolution. When Steele dedicated *The Ladies' Library* to Burlington's mother, the 19-year-old Earl was on his Grand Tour, from which he would return an ardent supporter and importer of Italian, neo-Palladian taste. Burlington became an erudite connoisseur and munificent patron of the arts, distinguished by his 'Love of Letters and Men of Learning',[22] so his inclusion among the Kit-Cats is logical. He was certainly an heir of the Club's thinking, in the sense of importing European models with the goal of reforming English style. The lack of documentation concerning Burlington's active participation in the Club, however, suggests he may have joined only to gratify Somers, who was his guardian, and Carlisle, Shannon and Harry Boyle, who were his kinsmen.

Henry Clinton, 7th Earl of Lincoln – Clare's cousin and brother-in-law – was also among the final cadre of Kit-Cats. Clare and Lincoln's double portrait was the last picture painted in the Kit-Cat series,[23] in which Clare pours wine into Kit-Cat-style glasses and in which a folly built by Vanbrugh at Claremont, the Belvedere Tower, stands in the background – emblems of the Club's importance to the two sitters.

Another of the final Kit-Cat generation was Theophilus Hastings, 9th Earl of Huntingdon. Huntingdon was only 18 and still enrolled as a student at Christ Church, Oxford, in 1714. He left without a degree but with a reputation as a wit – known to his kinsman Congreve, for example, who had been a close friend of the 8th Earl until 1705. Like Burlington, Huntingdon was admitted to the Club on his return from a Grand Tour. In Huntingdon's case, the Club's bet on who would be a leading light of the next aristocratic generation proved misplaced. Despite his talent at languages, Huntingdon hardly opened his mouth in the House of Lords and only made one appearance in any public capacity. Huntingdon's wife, Lady Selina, perhaps gave her husband the most accurate biography when she inscribed on his tomb that 'though he was capable of excelling in every form of public life, he chose to appear in none'.[24]

Kit-Cat efforts to train young men in the language and mentality of public administration and cultural patronage, if only by letting them associate and converse with more famous and powerful men, may have failed in Huntingdon's case, but they succeeded brilliantly with Walpole. Walpole had cut his teeth on the Kit-Cats' battles against the Tories for the past decade. He had been appointed Paymaster General to the Armed Forces following George's accession, but, although this post was lucrative, it did not bring Walpole the power he desired. Now, in clubbable middle age, Walpole was ready to assume what he viewed as his rightful place. He would do this by means of his leadership in the Commons and friendship with Townshend and

Stanhope, the two Secretaries of State (the bond between Walpole and Townshend having been sealed by Townshend's marriage to Walpole's sister, Dolly, in 1713).

Walpole moved his main London residence to Orford House, beside the Thames in Chelsea, and gave Vanbrugh a healthy budget to refurbish it. At his Norfolk seat of Houghton, Walpole continued to host two annual house parties: one in the spring for select friends and colleagues, and another in the shooting season, which later developed into an institution named 'The Congress', lasting six to eight weeks.[25] To some extent, Walpole's house parties replaced the Kit-Cat Club's political and social functions. Yet Walpole had little interest in patronage of literature beyond what could serve as direct government propaganda, and was sceptical of the Junto's gifting of government places to writers. He believed writers 'were guided by principles inadmissible to practical life' and therefore should be kept away from it.[26] Walpole nonetheless helped Steele, whom he regarded as a Whig activist rather than author, to re-enter Parliament at the spring 1715 general election. At Walpole's urging, Clare offered Steele a seat he controlled, representing Boroughbridge, eight miles north of York. Steele's stalling before accepting the offer, and the careful wording of his acceptance, show how desperately Steele longed to be free from such pacts with patrons: 'I know I shall express my Gratitude to you in the best manner by behaving myself with strict integrity,' Steele told Clare, knowing what Clare really hoped to buy was his strict obedience.[27]

Clare's agents handed out bribes to electors, and threatened tenants with eviction if they did not vote for Steele – £400 (over £47,000 today) was spent on such fixing. Steele also borrowed £1,100 in January 1715 which, combined with the £500 bounty from the King, gave him the cash to finish the job for himself. Steele bought votes by providing free wine and spirits for the Boroughbridge burgesses, writing home on 27 January that he was 'among Dancing, Singings, Hooping, Hallooing and Drinking'.[28]

Steele's undemocratic election did not affect his subsequent diligence as an MP. He updated his constituents by 'every post' on Westminster events, a level of direct accountability beyond the norms of his day.[29] Steele knew his main debt was to Clare, to whom he dedicated a collection of political writings in June 1715, proclaiming Clare 'the Refuge of Good Men'.[30] The dedication notably omits reference to Clare's personal charms.

Sometime after Steele and Clare returned to London, for the opening of George's first Parliament, Clare joined Vanbrugh, Carlisle and Garth (as well as two other non-Kit-Cats, and several ladies including the Duchess of Marlborough) for a daytrip from Whitehall by barge to Barn Elms. One imagines them viewing Tonson's collection of Kneller Kit-Cat portraits, by this time numerous enough to crowd the walls of several rooms. It was one of the last times Vanbrugh and the Duchess of Marlborough socialized together amiably. Vanbrugh had been trying to ingratiate himself with Clare and Marlborough by matchmaking Clare to Marlborough's granddaughter, Harriet, daughter of Congreve's lover Henrietta. Garth was employed to casually mention the girl's virtues to Clare, which needed some eloquence since Harriet was an exception to her generally handsome family. Vanbrugh reported to the Duchess of Marlborough that Clare had 'a sort of wish (expressed in a very gentle manner) that her bodily perfections had been up to those I described of her mind and understanding'.[31] When Clare stated the dowry he expected, the Duchess of Marlborough objected that her granddaughter was not *that* ugly and refused point blank. Perhaps suspecting Vanbrugh had done a deal to take a cut out of an overpriced dowry, the Duchess broke off negotiations, offending Vanbrugh irreparably – the final straw after their lengthy quarrels over Blenheim.

The general election, now involving an electorate of over 250,000 (some 50,000 more voters than in the 1690s), was a Whig victory but not a clean sweep. By different estimates, between 316 and 372 Whigs and between 186 and 217 Tories were elected – an almost exact reversal of the 1713 result. The surprisingly high number of Tories showed how uneasy the populace remained about being ruled by a German and the Junto. The Whigs failed to win a majority in the London boroughs despite tight management of the City voters via a special 'club' reporting to the Whig ministers.[32] Compton was elected Speaker of the House less because of his Kit-Cat membership than because he had served an apprenticeship in chairing the Committee of Privileges and Elections, and because of his Tory family and friends, making him a good cross-party candidate.

The Kit-Cats celebrated among themselves – a majority was still a majority. Vanbrugh remarked to Clare, who had just received the reconstituted title of Duke of Newcastle-upon-Tyne (and so is called 'Newcastle' hereafter), that the new Parliament would be 'a rare one', 'And I find our Friends disposed to make a good use on't: Hang, Whip, Pillory, etc. I wish they could love one another though, but they can't'.[33]

Intemperate Tory propaganda during the 1715 election led the King to decide once and for all that the Tories were not a party loyal to his Crown. George was therefore prepared to tolerate the vengeful temper of many Whigs in the spring of 1715 – the 'Hang, Whip, Pillory, etc.' mentioned by Vanbrugh. Halifax called for clemency for former Tory 'traitors', perhaps remembering how narrowly he had avoided choosing, like Somerset, collaboration with Oxford in 1710. Halifax was accordingly 'very earnest with the great mass of his friends to proceed moderately in the disposal of places, and was very desirous that men of ability and character, though Tories and in with the former ministry, might not be turned out, but continued in full favour'.[34]

Halifax was able to take this magnanimous view partly because he had never experienced the Tower like Walpole, or waited long months for redemption from Spanish custody like Stanhope. In April 1715, Stanhope moved to form a 'Committee of Secrecy' to investigate those involved in the original secret peace negotiations with France. Walpole was appointed its chairman, being a man with a coolly vindictive streak that must have struck terror into Tory hearts. Bolingbroke had already fled to France, which was regarded as a confession of guilt and led to a parliamentary resolution for his impeachment.

Another prominent target for Whig vengeance was Matt Prior. When Anne's health was reported to be weakening at the end of 1713, Prior had let Tonson carry warm messages home from France to his former Kit-Cat friends, prompting Halifax to write suggesting that they resume 'a correspondence about matters which no way concern the State', such as garden design.[35] Prior, seeing such correspondence as his only hope of returning to England after Anne's death, responded positively. The men exchanged a few letters with 'salading' seeds enclosed, but Prior stepped off safe ground too quickly by mentioning the Treaty of Utrecht. When Halifax cut this short, Prior sarcastically replied with regard to their gagged, horticultural correspondence: '[A] very light friendship may serve to produce a crop of chicory or lettuce.' Another silence then fell until October 1714, after George's accession. Halifax's brother Sir James Montagu played intermediary on this occasion, telling Prior that Halifax 'retains a tenderness towards you' and was willing to help Prior return to England without fear of being prosecuted for treason. Prior took the hint and wrote to Halifax that he hoped their friendship could be renewed and see them to their graves: 'Has it not been uneasy sometimes to you to have suspended the operation of it?' he asked. Just over a week later, Prior wrote again from Paris, reflecting: 'Friendship can no more be forced than Love, and those persons sometimes are the Objects of both . . . who may least have deserved our Favour.'[36]

As if restless until he replaced his old friend's pity with esteem, Prior could not resist trying to clear his name to Halifax, declaring 'as long as the fourth article either of Ryswick or of Utrecht [guaranteeing the Protestant succession] remain legible, I may as well be thought a Mahumetan as a Jacobite'.[37] With tactless speed, Prior also appealed to Halifax for help getting the Treasury to pay out his salary arrears. There was a pause of almost a month before Halifax replied to this, telling Prior they should 'let all those matters be passed over, and not mentioned any more'.[38] As for the salary payments, Halifax refused to intervene.

Six months after this final known communication with Prior, in May 1715, a bout of pneumonia unexpectedly ended Halifax's life. Politically, this death dashed Tory hopes that George might be won round by Halifax's talk of national reconciliation. It is unknown whether Prior, who had returned quietly to London and was trying to live inconspicuously, attended his old school friend's funeral in Westminster Abbey. Nor is it known whether the Kit-Cats gathered after the funeral, it being a Thursday evening, to toast the memory of one of their most historically important members.

Faithful in his infidelity, Halifax left his mistress, the former Kit-Cat toast Catherine Barton, a great fortune (the Rangership, lodge and household furniture of Bushy Park, the manor of Apscourt, a stock of jewels and £5,000 in cash) 'as a Token of the Sincere Love, Affection, and Esteem I have long had for her Person, and as a small Recompense for the Pleasure & Happiness I have had in her Conversation'.[39]

Halifax's death was the second major loss that season, closely following the death of his great Junto ally since the 1690s, Tom Wharton, on 12 April 1715. A satirical Tory elegy for 'Lord Whiglove' described Wharton as a bullying, factious, lewd republican and atheist:

> Religion o'er the Bottle was his Jest,
> And nothing more his Banter than a Priest;
> Yet oft he called on GOD, we must allow,
> But 'twas to Damn him, as he finds e'ernow.
> So Atheists sport with Heaven's avenging Ire,
> Till doomed forever to Infernal Fire.[40]

Addison must have been dismayed to find his two greatest patrons had departed the world within a matter of weeks. Somers, enfeebled by ill health, had also withdrawn from politics, leaving the stage clear for a new cast of Whig leaders, and the face of the Kit-Cat Club significantly altered.

King George's birthday fell on 28 May, two days after Halifax's funeral, and the newly knighted Sir Richard Steele used the opportunity to lift his friends' grieving spirits and advance his own career. He invited 'a Hundred Gentlemen, and as many Ladies, of leading Taste in Politeness, Wit and Learning' to subscribe to seats at an evening entertainment in the Great Room of York Buildings. Steele had been 'at no small expense' planning this edifying entertainment for some time.[41] The small matter of Steele's Commons trial for sedition had intervened to derail the project, but now he revived the venture, calling it the 'Censorium' (or 'Sensorium').[42] The two-and-a-half-hour entertainment mainly consisted of dramatized 'Incidents of

Antiquity',[43] meaning translations from Greek and Latin poetry, performed to newly composed English music, before an actress dressed as Liberty and the jury of the audience, ladies on one side, gentlemen on the other. The Prologue referred to 'Wit' and 'Beauty' – the old sexist divide of the Kit-Cat toasting ritual – as ranged facing one another.[44] Steele lit the audience so that they became 'a more beautiful Scene than any they have ever before been presented with'.[45] It was the first major private party at which the Georgian elite gathered to admire itself.

Steele emphasized that his audience was a cultural more than aristocratic elite ('rather Elegant than Great'[46]), with a very Kit-Cattish mission to educate the wider public:

> VIRGIL shall be the talk of every Beau
> And Ladies lisp the charms of CICERO.
> The land shall grow polite from You, who sit
> In chosen ranks, the CABINET OF WIT.[47]

The Epilogue, probably written by Addison, teased Steele for his life's catalogue of overambitious ventures and suggested his next would be a letter to convert the Pope to Protestantism. It was as if Addison rightly guessed that the Censorium would soon be added to Steele's list of commercial flops. The evening succeeded, on the other hand, as a model of Georgian spectacle and cultural consumption, inspiring the opening of numerous 'concert rooms' in spa towns across the country.

At home at St James's Street nothing much changed between Steele and Prue. A vinegar merchant, one of Steele's many creditors, left a valuable oral record of how he and twenty to thirty other 'dunners' would gather in the entrance hall of Steele's house every weekday morning, where they were always told Steele was not at home. If Steele were hiding upstairs and needed to leave, he would summon a friend, so they could march straight out through the front hall, knowing the tradesmen would be too polite or intimidated to harass Sir Richard in company.

Another story survives of a dinner party hosted by the Steeles for 'a great number of persons of the first quality'. The guests were surprised at the number of servants surrounding the table. After a few drinks, one of them enquired how Sir Richard could afford such a large staff, at which Steele confessed they were bailiffs, whom

> he had thought it convenient to embellish with liveries, that they might do him credit whilst they stayed. His friends were diverted with the expedient, and by paying the debt, discharged the attendance, having obliged Sir Richard to promise that they should never find him again graced with a retinue of the same kind.[48]

Some biographers have discounted this anecdote, not printed until 1753, as an eighteenth-century urban myth attached to various famous debtors, but if anyone had the humour to be its true source, it was Steele.[49] The threat of further court proceedings was, of course, no joking matter – Steele had five children, if one includes his illegitimate daughter, to support.

Steele was working on various Commons committees: to naturalize Palatine refugees; exempt Quakers from various religious oaths in law courts; and manage the wars against native tribes in South Carolina. Between these duties, which often kept him late at Whitehall, and his duties as a theatre manager, it is remarkable Steele was also writing a second series of *The Englishman*, printed twice a week. This series was not as strong as the first, written during Anne's last ministry on the adrenalin of Steele's political fears and idealism. The second *Englishman* was a production more of the head than heart: commissioned by Newcastle to win support for the government by publicizing the Committee of Secrecy's findings. Steele wanted to be fairly remunerated for these essays, and complained of working for the Whig party and public good 'without regard to myself and Family, almost to Old Age'.[50] Unfortunately, Newcastle was as deep in debt – relative to rank and income – as Steele. Newcastle and Townshend felt they had pre-paid for Steele's services by recommending him for the Hampton Court sinecure, the Royal Bounty and his knighthood. Steele viewed these differently, as payment for his pre-1714 services – the root of a festering misunderstanding.

With Halifax gone, Walpole and Stanhope convinced the King that those responsible for what they viewed as the dishonour of Utrecht should be prosecuted and punished. In June 1715, Prior was charged with high treason and placed into 'close custody' in the Covent Garden home of the Commons' Sergeant-at-Arms. Nobody was supposed to visit him without Spencer Compton's permission, but his gaoler was an easy-going man who let visitors slip in and out.[51] Prior later recounted contemptuously how the members of Walpole's Committee of Secrecy dismissed him from interrogation each time they became confused by the evidence before them. Prior laughed at their attempts to prove his associations with Papists, since that, he said, was a fair description of his entire Parisian acquaintance. Bored and deeply disillusioned, Prior spent a year detained in the Sergeant-at-Arms' house writing *Alma*, a poem that Pope considered a masterpiece.

In contrast to his 1701 betrayal of his Kit-Cat friends, Prior demonstrated great loyalty to his Tory colleagues. Only a man of Prior's ingenuity could have avoided incriminating the former ministers, Oxford and Bolingbroke, and so saved them from the death penalty – refusing to testify, for example, as to who was present at the secret talks with the French agents in his Duke Street parlour. Prior also escaped conviction, and was released in late June 1716.

Throughout the summer months, while the Committee of Secrecy was in session, the country was racked with rioting, mostly in Tory-dominated towns like Oxford. On the King's birthday, many churchwardens claimed to have lost the ropes to ring the celebratory bells, while the next day, the anniversary of the 1660 Stuart Restoration, the ropes were suddenly found and mobs smashed windows not displaying commemorative candles. On 10 June, The Pretender's birthday, the militia had to be called to quell a London riot that resulted in several deaths, and on the day Oxford was indicted for high treason, a crowd of supporters, shouting angrily against the King, accompanied the former minister to the Tower. England had not seen such unrest since the pro-Sacheverell protests. In response, Stanhope's government adopted the famous 'Riot Act', making rioting a capital offence.

This was the context in which Steele was pressed to write *The Englishman* in defence of the King and his ministers, as well as to ghost-write Newcastle's patriotic speeches in the Lords. In July 1715,

Steele warned he would have to stop such work if he were not better 'supported in it',[52] leading Newcastle to arrange a one-off payment of £500 (almost £60,000 today) for Steele from secret service funds. Kit-Cat patronage of propaganda remained as necessary as ever.

More urgent defensive measures were required when, in July, reports were received from France that The Pretender was planning to launch an invasion attempt. As in 1708 and 1714, national security was put on high alert. Stanhope directed the government's military preparations, his first step being to suspend *habeas corpus*. In September 1715, the Earl of Mar fulfilled every paranoid Whig fear by raising a Jacobite rebellion of 15–20,000 Scotsmen. Mar had favoured the Union in 1707, but was one of many Scots who afterwards grew disaffected when not offered any share in Georgian power. Mar's Scottish rebellion was premature, however – the English Jacobites were unprepared to join it, having been under close surveillance since Anne's death and having lost their leaders to exile or the Committee of Secrecy's investigations. A small uprising occurred in Northumberland in early October 1715, inspiring civil disobedience among Catholics in Lancashire, but there were no other major English rebellions. While the Whigs may have exaggerated the scale of the Jacobite threat, the Jacobites were equally deluded about the number and strength of their supporters.

The Scottish rebels were routed by government troops in bloody clashes at Preston and at Sheriffmuir in Scotland in mid-November 1715. On the sensitive anniversary of 17 November, violent hand-to-hand clashes ensued in London, and two Jacobites were shot dead. Though no records or rumours of Kit-Cat activism from this fraught month survive, we know the Club met later that winter and probably backed Whig counter-demonstrations, drawing on the grassroots members of Whig 'mug-house clubs' – large gatherings of Whig 'gentlemen, lawyers and tradesmen' who drank ale from mugs emblazoned with Whig symbols and portraits, while singing Whig drinking tunes.[53] Newcastle organized at least one Whig mob sent to intimidate London's Tory printers.

A number of Kit-Cats were also sent, through blizzards over hazardous roads, to rally government support around the country. James Dormer commanded a brigade to suppress the Jacobites in

Preston, and was badly wounded. Burlington, as Lord Lieutenant of the West Riding and the City of York, ordered the arrest of Jacobite suspects there. Garth was sent to his home district of Durham, telling Newcastle he would not go from Northumberland into Scotland 'till an Earthquake heaves me thither. I wonder that the Devil, who can be where he pleases, should at present take a fancy to be so much there.'[54] By 'the Devil' he meant The Pretender, who belatedly landed in Scotland in December 1715.

Stanhope moved to extend the suspension of *habeas corpus* in January 1716. Various lords, who felt this measure needlessly undermined civil liberties when The Pretender's attempt already seemed close to defeat, opposed the extension. Addison started a new paper, called *The Freeholder* (after the small landowners he wanted to dissuade from Jacobitism) in which he supported the suspension. Steele complained Addison's propaganda was not raising the alarm loudly enough: '[T]he Ministry made use of a lute, when they should have called for a trumpet.'[55]

Disheartened by the defeats already suffered in November, The Pretender fled back to France by 4 February 1716, ending an episode that became known in Whig history books as 'The Fifteen' (after the year 1715). Though the Jacobites were left bedraggled and humiliated by their attempt, the Whigs in London could not have been confident of the final outcome: parts of Scotland had effectively been out of Westminster's control for almost five months, and the Jacobite advance guard had reached impressively far south.

After it was over, the Whigs were relieved that the great test, so long anticipated, had been survived. Sunderland, who in August 1715 had successfully claimed the Cabinet place that Wharton's death had left vacant, hosted a celebratory banquet at his house on Piccadilly. Addison's reward for having produced *The Freeholder* during the invasion was to receive the appointment as a Commissioner of Trade and Plantations he had coveted since discovering he would not be Secretary of State. It brought a salary of £1,000 (some £120,000 today), and inside information about the progress of merchant companies and colonial investments.[56] The Board of Trade, post-Utrecht, was now at the heart of the eight-year-old Great Britain's infant empire, as the nation became one of the most prosperous and powerful in the world. Steele, meanwhile, hardly had money to pay for coal to heat his house.

Walpole, who had become Chancellor of the Exchequer in October 1715, used the mood following The Fifteen to accelerate the purging of Tories from minor Treasury offices. He also led the push, in February 1716, for execution of six Jacobite lords convicted of participating in the Scottish insurrection, including the popular Earl of Derwentwater. Addison and Steele argued for clemency. Steele saw something ruthless and not a little vindictive in the determination of his two patrons, Walpole and Stanhope, on this issue – a ruthlessness unmentioned in the literary dedications he wrote to them. Later, Steele explained to the Commons his thinking on northern England's Catholic minority: '[T]o put Severities upon men merely on account of Religion is a most grievous and Unwarrantable proceeding . . . Let Us not pursue Roman Catholics with the Spirit of Roman Catholics.'[57] On hearing this speech, more rabidly Whig colleagues jeered that Steele was turning Tory.

Addison did not oppose the government so openly, but privately suggested certain traitors be accidentally allowed to escape and those of lesser rank transported to the American plantations rather than hanged (one function of the Board of Trade on which he sat being to arrange criminal transportations). The government was determined on the harshest deterrent, however. Forty rebels were executed, including Derwentwater, some 600 of their followers were transported, and an equal number died in prison or were released. Catholic property was seized, and more repressive anti-Catholic laws were introduced.

On 26 April 1716, the Kit-Cat Club lost another founding father. At 65, the cause of Somers' death is broadly agreed to have been syphilis, this disease probably being the only legacy left to Mrs Blount, the 'housekeeper' with whom he had long cohabited at his house in Bell Bar. It is unknown whether Somers' sisters, who inherited the bulk of his estate, shared anything with Mrs Blount. Somers left a library of 9,000 volumes.

On the day of Somers' Hertfordshire funeral, Addison published a moving tribute in *The Freeholder*, praising his late patron's consistency ('his whole Conduct of a Piece') and loyalty ('so tender a Concern for his Friends, that whatever Station they were in, they usually applied to him for his Advice in every Perplexity').[58] The essay was close to a modern obituary in an age where deaths were usually noticed with no more than a tally of fortune and heirs. Somers was the Kit-Cat whom Horace Walpole later described as 'the model of Addison'.[59] Somers' softly spoken, restrained manners, admired and imitated by Addison, had been taught to the entire nation by Mr Spectator, thereby contributing to the formation of the new ideal of 'polite' Georgian male manners.

Sunderland called Somers 'the life, the soul and the spirit of his party',[60] and though he was not actively involved in Westminster politics after 1714, Somers' death seemed to mark a change for the worse in the spirit of the Whigs. It was as if a watching conscience had closed its eyes. Immediately after his death, in April 1716, the Whig majorities in both Houses of Parliament passed the Septennial Act, which extended the time permitted between elections to seven years, thereby weakening a fundamental guarantee of executive accountability. Townshend conveniently claimed Somers gave the Act his deathbed approval, but this is unverified.[61] Addison, as a leading minister, wrote in support of this Act in *The Freeholder*. Forty-three rebel Whigs, including Somerset, voted according to their consciences to defeat the Bill, however. The Act, which was not amended until 1911, brought stability to Britain, but sacrificed Whig principles to Whig party supremacy and self-interest. With the election planned for 1718 now postponed until 1722, opposition to the King's ministers was constitutionally obstructed and had to find other outlets.

The Septennial Act can be blamed for the Kit-Cat Club's demise after 1718. The Club had flourished under the constant pressures of electoral contest – coordinating campaigns before elections, commissioning propaganda, keeping underling MPs in line – and, during the war, its members had been united by the ideal of 'liberty' in its broadest sense. Referring to the threat they believed emanated from Catholic Europe, the Club's young leaders were dispensing with laws – first *habeas corpus* during The Fifteen, now the requirement of regular elections – as if consolidating the status quo of Whig control over Georgian Britain were all that mattered.

XVIII
PARADISE LOST

> Forsake not an old Friend, for the new is not comparable to him: A new Friend is as new Wine; when it is old thou shalt drink it with Pleasure.
>
> ECCLESIASTES 9:10, quoted by JOSEPH ADDISON in *The Spectator* no. 68, Friday, 18 May 1711

WITHOUT EXTERNAL ENEMIES to unite them after 1715, the ambitious Whigs of Walpole's generation began fighting bitterly over the spoils of power that the Junto had taken so many decades to win. Attempts were made to use the Kit-Cat Club to reunite old friends, but as Tonson's commitment to the Club began to wane, and as other key Kit-Cats turned their attentions elsewhere, the all-male paradise of late night London revelry began to fall away.

Steele suffered a minor stroke in the spring of 1716, but could not afford the luxury of a rest cure, his time consumed by new duties and projects. As reward for supporting the Septennial Act, he had just received a seat on the commission for redistributing Scottish estates taken from Jacobite rebels, the Commission of Forfeited Estates, which was a job with a £1,000 salary. The Commission ordered Steele's presence in Scotland in September, but he was preoccupied by a private commercial enterprise: the construction of a tanker, containing a machine to pump water through its hull, by which to transport live fish fresh from Ireland and northern England to London's Billingsgate Market. Steele called his invention the 'Fishpool', planning to launch it as a joint-stock company and believing it would make his fortune, finally freeing him from the constant need to seek patronage.

Steele was also managing the Theatre Royal on Drury Lane. He had persuaded Addison to let the theatre stage a previously unperformed play, *The Drummer*, which Steele hoped would be a hit on the back of *Cato*. Addison, however, did not want to publicize his authorship of the play, hiding his identity even from its printer, Jacob Junior. It had been written in response to the Collierite reformers' challenge to produce comedy without lewdness or immorality, but this no longer fitted with the new decadence of the early Georgians. Though attended by the Prince of Wales, *The Drummer* was not a success.

Among its themes, *The Drummer* celebrated marriage, criticizing those who ridiculed the institution, like Congreve and Vanbrugh:

> Too long has Marriage, in this tasteless Age,
> With ill-bred Raillery supplied the Stage;
> No little Scribbler is of Wit so bare,
> But has his fling at the poor Wedded Pair.

Addison and Steele emphasized that the model wife should dote on her husband, even if that were viewed as quaint and unfashionable behaviour. Steele may have promoted female literacy and liberty in print, yet privately he lectured Prue that ''tis the glory of a woman to be her husband's friend and companion and not his sovereign director'.[1] This was not a remark that Congreve, with his love and understanding of strong and intelligent women, would ever have made. Addison further argued that marriage was morally beneficial for both partners, taking the rough edges off male manners and conversation, while drawing the hysteria out of women's bodies. He believed every man needed to be softened and polished by the sensitivity and vivacity of women. As dying a bachelor would therefore have been like leaving a stylistic ugliness uncorrected in his prose, at 44, on 30 July 1716, Addison finally announced his engagement to the 36-year-old Charlotte, Countess of Warwick.

Addison had maintained his 'ambitious' courtship, as Dr Johnson called it,[2] for a full decade. While governing in Ireland, Addison quizzed the Countess' son, the Earl of Warwick, on his studies, what he thought of 'a paper called *The Tatler*' that had just appeared, and asked the boy to pass Addison's respects to 'My Lady'.[3] By 1713, Addison was writing references for Warwick to enter Oxford. Addison had postponed proposing marriage to the Countess because he felt, according to Tonson, that he needed to 'qualify himself to be owned for her husband'.[4] His seat on the Board of Trade finally provided the necessary financial security.

The couple married in September 1716 in St Edmund's, Lombard Street, one of Wren's new City churches. The newly-weds then travelled together to France, in rather grander style than Addison's journey of 1699, accompanying Lord Warwick on the first leg of his Grand Tour. The family may have crossed paths with Garth, in Paris that same September, following his own tour of France and Italy.

After they returned to London in late October 1716, Addison began living at Lady Warwick's Kensington home, Holland House. Addison had grown familiar with the fine Jacobean mansion and its extensive grounds over the years, but living there meant his lifestyle changed dramatically. His days were now full of formal visits from ladies in rustling silk, arranging themselves on stiff-backed Dutch drawing-room chairs. He could no longer, as Mr Spectator had boasted, go to bed and get up when he pleased, eat in his bedroom, or sit in his study without anyone 'bidding me be merry'.[5]

'A happy Marriage has in it all the Pleasures of Friendship,' Addison once stated,[6] a view worlds away from the cynical Restoration attitudes of Dorset or Carbery, and a view with dangerous implications for the male friendships of the Kit-Cat Club. Pope and Tonson, who claimed Addison's marriage was unhappy, said the Countess forced him to drop his club and coffee house friends. This recalls a *Spectator* essay in which Addison described a fictitious club of wives, whose rules for managing husbands included: 'To turn away all his old

Friends and Servants, that she may have the Dear Man to herself.'[7] Wives were imagined as working to destroy the Kit-Cat's all-male camaraderie. Certainly there is little evidence of Addison socializing after he married: he commemorated the Whig anniversary of King William's birthday with Steele at the Trumpet tavern soon after his return from France, when Steele said he had the 'double duty of the day upon him, as well to celebrate the immortal memory of King William . . . as to drink his friend Addison up to the conversation pitch',[8] but this is one of few such meetings on record. A proverbial pram blocked Holland House's hallway in January 1720, with the birth of a baby daughter to the 40-year-old Countess.

A few months before Addison's marriage, the Steeles lost their eldest, 6-year-old son, Richard, to an unknown illness. Whether this caused Steele's stroke around the same date, it certainly led to heavier drinking. There is an anecdote of Steele being carried, by his arms and legs, blind drunk from a Whig club to his coach. For Lady Steele (as she was now styled), her husband's drinking, combined with grief over her son's death and the permanent strain of their debts in the midst of St James's luxury, drove her to retreat, alone, to her native south Wales. Though Steele told friends that Prue was in Wales because she needed to administer her late mother's estates there, and though he may have believed this himself when she left, it was in fact a non-legal separation. She seldom replied to his letters, more usually sending him messages via a cousin, and she discouraged him from visiting her in Wales, referring to her 'indisposition'.[9] Steele's replies to her messages are revealing: 'You advise Me to take care of my soul, [but] I do not [know] what you can think of Yours when you have, and do, withhold from me your Body.'[10]

Following Prue's departure, Steele realized he had the additional chores of a single father to add to his list of employments. In mid-December 1716, Steele described himself joggling 3-year-old Molly and 4-year-old Eugene on his knees as he wrote his letters. On Christmas Day, a letter to Prue included a postscript by their eldest daughter Betty calculated to play on his wife's maternal guilt in the hope that it would bring her home. Far from being a bad wife and mother, Prue replied that remaining in Wales was 'for my children's good', to collect the rents that would keep the family afloat, even though being there gave her 'vapours to a vast degree'.[11]

Steele impatiently assured Prue he was putting himself forward: 'I do, as you advise, court and Converse with men able and willing to serve Me.'[12] She had grounds, however, for scepticism about her husband's newly turned leaves. Though some letters promised to right their finances and protect their 'Poor Babes' manfully,[13] others were written in weaker moments. One, in an obviously drunken scrawl, says simply: 'Dear Prue, Sober or not, I am Ever Yours, Richard Steele.'[14]

In March 1717, holding down the three jobs received thanks to his Kit-Cat patrons, Steele nonetheless complained to Prue about his ungrateful treatment by the Hanoverian Court and its ministers: 'I have served the Royal Family with an unreservedness due only to Heaven, and I am now (I thank my Brother Whigs) not possessed of twenty shillings from the favour of the Court.'[15]

Steele's irrepressible optimism meant he continued to hope he could 'turn a Kind inclination towards Me at present, into what is solid'. He expected to be granted a particular forfeited estate as additional payment for his work on the Commission. In the meantime, to justify not sending Prue some £800 she demanded, Steele wrote to Wales that it remained 'a Terrible Circumstance to have one's money due to others before it comes into one's own hands'.[16]

Seeking patronage in Georgian Britain was growing more complicated than it had been under William or Anne. A major rift had opened within the Whig party, and hence the Kit-Cat Club, a year earlier, in the spring of 1716, forcing every member to gamble and place his allegiance with one faction or another. Steele told Prue, 'It is not possible to describe to you the perplexities into which the business of this nation is plunged.'[17] The rift had originated in disagreement over George's emerging foreign policy, which some Kit-Cats thought served Hanover rather than Britain. Stanhope negotiated, with the King's full support, a new *entente* with France (now ruled by the Regent Duc d'Orléans), and in the summer of 1716 accompanied George back to Hanover, where good relations were further cemented with the French ambassadors. During his father's absence from London, the Prince of Wales hosted grand parties at Hampton Court and began to position himself as the figurehead for an opposition faction – a move motivated as much by personal filial hostility as any political principles. Addison's *Freeholder*, sensing the mood, warned the Whigs to treasure their unity: '[A] large diamond is of a thousand times greater value whilst it remains entire than when it is cut into a multitude of smaller stones, notwithstanding they may each of them be very curiously set.'[18]

Sunderland found an excuse to make his own way to Hanover, and there made a play for power, telling exaggerated tales of how Walpole and Townshend were plotting with the Prince against the King back in London, which both Stanhope and the King believed. The King responded by sending home instructions that Townshend should resign as Secretary of State for the North, at which news Walpole realized that his old friend Stanhope had listened to Sunderland's whispering campaign. A long, carefully worded letter to Stanhope expressed Walpole's shock and sadness: 'Such sudden changes to old sworn friends are seldom looked upon in the world with a favourable eye . . . I have heard old friends were to be valued like old gold. I never wished anything more sincerely than to bear that title, and to preserve it with you.'[19]

By 13 December 1716, Stanhope's betrayal of Townshend and Walpole, siding instead with Sunderland, was the talk of London. One observer reported: 'There never was such a jumble amongst the Whigs . . . Whether they'll carry their pet so far as to let in the Tories, God knows. Things look very dark.'[20] Another, seeing the repercussions shaking the patronage ladder to its lowest rung, laughed at 'the hurry and fright of the little placemen who did not know upon what ground they stood, nor what cue they were to follow'.[21]

After the King's return to Britain in January 1717, there was the brief appearance of party unity, but at the first Privy Council meeting in February it was obvious that Sunderland and Stanhope were in power, while Walpole and Townshend were out. Caught in the middle of this schism was the young Duke of Newcastle, and the situation brought out all Newcastle's neurosis and neediness. One memoirist found Newcastle's behaviour indecorous in a nobleman: '[H]e accosted, hugged, embraced, and promised everybody, with a seeming cordiality, but at the same time with an illiberal and degrading familiarity.'[22]

For such a man, division among his friends was personally unbearable. Newcastle therefore attempted to reconcile Walpole and Stanhope, and heal the Whig schism, by hosting a special meeting of the Kit-Cat Club on 30 March 1717.[23] Newcastle may have used the excuse of his impending marriage to Marlborough's granddaughter, Lady Harriet Godolphin, whose dowry had finally been negotiated, to beg the attendance of any Club members reluctant to bury the hatchet. The venue was Newcastle House, newly remodelled by Vanbrugh – the first time we know that the Club convened in a private house other than Barn Elms. A letter from a member tells us, however, that Newcastle was not merely the host but also 'in the Chair' of the Club. Previously this has been considered a one-off supplanting of Tonson's chairmanship, but in the context of Newcastle's role as the Club's fount of cultural patronage after 1714 – Tonson dedicated the complete set of his six *Miscellany Poems* to Newcastle in 1716, the fifth volume of which published Kit-Cat toasting verses for the first time – it may instead confirm that the Duke was generally assuming Tonson's Kit-Cat duties by this date.

Newcastle also seems to have attempted to reunify the Kit-Cats through a literary commission, funding Tonson's production of a deluxe edition of Ovid's *Metamorphoses* (1717) that combined new translations with sections previously translated by Dryden, Maynwaring, Congreve, Addison and others. Garth was asked to recruit the new contributors, and Pope, who was not one of those invited, wrote a satire about Garth drumming up 'Wits, Witlings, Prigs and Peers' like a literary recruiting officer, old Tonson inspecting the troops.[24] The book was dedicated to the Princess of Wales, while its sections were dedicated to other prominent Whig ladies, related to men on either side of the current schism. Richly illustrated, the book influenced neoclassical painting and design in the decades to come, providing motifs for the work of William Kent and later Georgians.

Newcastle's peace-making initiatives failed, the Whigs' one-party State remaining riven in two. Townshend's dismissal prompted Walpole's resignation and the pair's formation of an opposition known as the 'Prince's Party' as they did indeed now ally with the Prince of Wales. Stanhope, despite having little economic expertise, was promoted to fill Walpole's places as First Lord of the Treasury and Chancellor of the Exchequer. Newcastle, who fell in with the new Sunderland–Stanhope ministry when sitting on the fence was no longer an option, was appointed Lord Chamberlain, with control over the dispensing of nearly 500 Court places.

Among the office-holders who resigned alongside Walpole and joined the Prince's Party were many prominent Kit-Cats. They included Speaker Spencer Compton, who had become a personal friend to the Prince of Wales as Treasurer in his Household, as well as Grafton, Devonshire, Pulteney and Jack Smith. Altogether, Walpole and Townshend carried some fifty Whig MPs into opposition.

Addison's previous employment under Sunderland, and personal liking for Stanhope over Walpole, allied him to the Court faction. It was a surprise to many, however, when Addison was given the post he had long coveted as Secretary of State for the South, in charge of Britain's foreign relations with the better half of the world and worth almost £10,000 annually (over £1.2 million today). Stanhope, though in the Treasury, intended to maintain firm control over southern European and colonial foreign policy, and Addison, allergic to independent decisions, was just the kind of man he knew he could work with – diligent in managing a huge workload without complaint and unlikely to question his superiors. Enjoying direct access to the King, Addison was responsible for administering the American and West Indian colonies, the suppression of piracy, the Indian wars in Carolina and the settling of Nova Scotia. He would oversee the implementation of certain Utrecht articles, including the expulsion of Jews from Gibraltar, handle delicate Spanish trade negotiations (under Stanhope's guidance), and play a critical part in freeing British captives held in Morocco. Addison's job was so demanding that it left little time for non-professional friendships – a more plausible explanation for his retreat from the Kit-Cat Club and Button's Coffee House than his wife's alleged tyranny.

The most onerous aspect of being Secretary of State for Addison was being a Court spokesman in the Commons. Tonson gossiped that Addison only accepted a job so ill-suited to his temperament to satisfy his wife's snobbery,[25] and Lady Mary Wortley Montagu similarly remarked to Pope: 'Such a post as that, and such a wife as the Countess, do not seem to be in prudence eligible for a man that is asthmatic; and we may see the day when he will be heartily glad to resign them both.'[26] Steele, torn between loyalty to his two former defenders, Walpole and Stanhope, sent news of Addison's appointment to his wife without comment.

Despite 'gouty lameness', Steele worked long hours at the Commons, telling his wife, 'I pant for Leisure and tranquillity.'[27] Since he now had 'no money',[28] Steele was also forced to pant for favours from Stanhope and Sunderland's ministry. Not only did Steele hope Addison would help him towards something, but he also looked to his friend General William Cadogan, who was perhaps the third most powerful figure in the new ministry. Steele confided his hopes to Prue: 'They tell me I shall be something in the new changes.'[29] Three days later, however, Steele dined with 'Mr Secretary Addison' and was informed – how kindly we do not know – that his seat as a Commissioner for the Forfeited Estates prevented him receiving further offices or advancement.[30] This disappointment, in sharp contrast to Addison's elevation, made Steele start to look towards the mutinous Walpole–Townshend camp for assistance instead.

No record exists of Addison and Steele meeting for some time after this awkward dinner. Given Addison's immense salary, Steele may have found his friend's failure to loan a sum of money – say, the amount needed to cover his daughter Betty's Chelsea school fees – an unforgivable failure. In May 1717, Steele frostily told his wife: 'I do not ask Mr Secretary Addison anything.'[31]

Tonson, similarly, seems to have quarrelled with Addison after the latter became Secretary of State and failed to have the Tonsons' firm appointed official stationers to the War Office. After all Tonson had done for Addison, this does seem ungrateful, though the post may not have been in Addison's gift alone. After 1717, Tonson started admitting to other Kit-Cats that he had never really liked Addison. Mocking the pious author's weakness for drink, Tonson 'boasted of paying his court by inventing excuses for requesting a glass of Barbadoes water, in order to furnish the Secretary with an apology for indulging his own inclination'.[32]

The frontispiece to a 1793 book of engravings of Kneller's Kit-Cat portraits, by John Faber Junior. The Britannia-like goddess carries a spear and a caduceus denoting, respectively, command and commerce. She is paired with a god of war, suggesting the wars against France that defined the Club's patriotic mindset. At their feet lies Pegasus, symbol of the creative spirit, as well as other symbols of the arts (including a lyre, denoting poetry and music) and of abundant patronage (the horn of plenty). The sun of enlightened reason shines over them.

TEMPLE BARR The West-Side

LEFT: Two sides of London. The fashionable world of St James's *(top)*, near the Court, met the commercial forces and social mobility of the City of London at the Strand and Temple Bar, the lively neighbourhood where the Kit-Cat Club often convened.

THIS PAGE: Tories and High-Flyers: Jeremy Collier *(top)*, Robert Harley *(below left)* and Jonathan Swift *(below right)* were leading cultural and political adversaries of the Junto Whigs and the Kit-Cat Club.

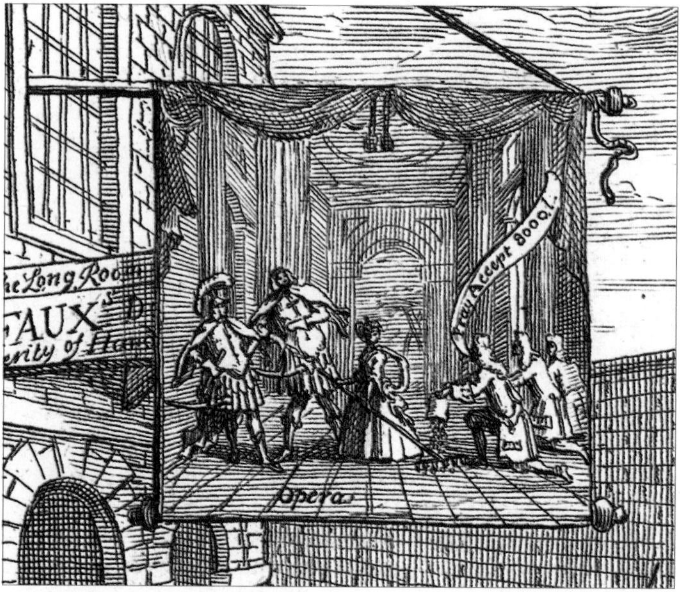

Patronage of music, especially opera, has been the most overlooked element of the Kit-Cat Club's agenda for reforming British culture. The banner in Hogarth's 'Bad Taste' *(above)* shows the interior of the Queen's Theatre, originally built by the Kit-Cats for operas. 'Rehearsal of an Opera' *(below)* shows Nicolini, one of the Italian star-singers the Club brought over to educate British audiences.

'Van's Genius without Thought or Lecture … hugely turned to Architecture': After 1698, the Kit-Cat patrons allowed Vanbrugh to become an architect, expressing their vision of Britain in stone and landscapes. Among Kit-Cat commissioned works were the innovative garden architecture of Stowe, shown above, and the equally original design of Castle Howard in Yorkshire *(below)*.

Mrs (later Lady) Steele, known to her husband Richard *(below)* as 'Prue' throughout their intimate and often tortured personal correspondence. Prue, who bore Steele four children, was left to face his creditors while he chased after patronage and improbable money-making schemes.

Spreading the Word: Bickerstaff *(below)*, *The Tatler*'s fictional narrator, at his desk with the subjects of his reforming essays against duelling, gambling and other vices lying at his feet. An original copy of *The Spectator (right)*, later described as second only to the Bible in its influence on British society.

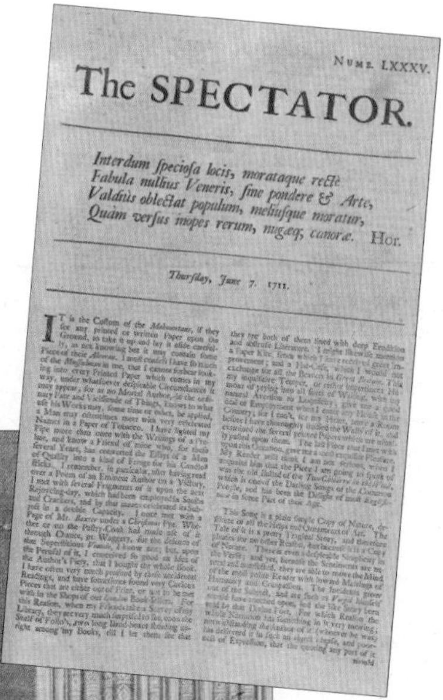

NUMB. LXXXV.

The SPECTATOR.

Interdum speciosa locis, morataque recte
Fabula nullius Veneris, sine pondere & Arte,
Valdius oblectat populum, meliusque moratur,
Quam versus inopes rerum, nugæq; canoræ. Hor.

Thursday, June 7. 1711.

Two of the younger aristocratic Kit-Cats in the only 'conversation piece' of the Club series: the Duke of Newcastle *(left)* drinking with his cousin and brother-in-law, the Earl of Lincoln, from Kit-Cat toasting glasses. The Belvedere Tower folly, built by Vanbrugh at one of Newcastle's country estates, appears in the background.

Steele decided he had to rely upon his own efforts if he could not rely on his friends. He told Prue his Fishpool prototype was now finished 'with great success, insomuch that Sir Isaac Newton is desirous the machine may stand at his House and be carried from thence to the Parliament'.[33] So soon after the ministerial schism, this was not the best time to capture politicians' attention, but the Fishpool's unveiling must have gone fairly well since Steele promised Lady Steele that, if she returned from Wales, he would hire sufficient servants to allow her to be no more than his parlour companion. 'Money is the main thing,' Steele wrote to Prue. 'Get I always could, but now I will get it and Keep it.'[34]

Steele later described himself as heartened when Prue called him 'Good Dick' in a note, in return for which he called her 'My Dear little Peevish Beautiful Wise governess'[35] and 'Poor Dear Angry Pleased Pretty Witty Silly Everything Prue'.[36] With unashamed sentimentality, Steele admitted: 'I love you with the most ardent affection and very often run over little Heats that have sometimes happened between Us with Tears in my Eyes.'[37] He enclosed a blank sheet of paper so that she could not use lack of paper as an excuse for failing to reply.

Steele, however, soon had to ask Prue to stop 'dunning' him for money again, and his autumn 1717 letters returned to complaints about her denial of his conjugal rights:

> Your Ladyship's coldness to Me as a Woman and a Wife has made me think it necessary to Suppress the expression of my Heart towards You, because it could not end in the pleasures and enjoyments I ought to expect from it, and which you obliged Me to Wean myself from till I had so much money etc.[38]

The Fishpool continued to need attention before it could turn a profit, yet Steele was compelled to leave his London enterprise to serve on the Scottish Commission. There was no time to detour via Wales for even one night with his wife. By 15 November, Steele reached Edinburgh, where he was treated well: 'You cannot imagine the civilities and honours I had done me [in Edinburgh] and never lay better, ate or drank better, or conversed with men of better sense than there.'[39]

With suspicious timing, Lady Steele returned from Wales to London after his departure. They argued over who would pay for her carriage.

By October 1717, a leading Whig was declaring that '[t]he breach between the Whigs is irreparable'.[40] Kit-Cat meetings were likely suspended, just as they had been during the temporary and comparatively minor breach between the Treasurer's Whigs and Junto Whigs back in 1708. Richard Blackmore's prophecy that the Kit-Cat Club would be destroyed not by external enemies but by internal rivalries was, more than a decade later, coming true.

An incident at a royal christening in November 1717, involving Newcastle, led to the King banishing the Prince and Princess of Wales from St James's Palace. After this, they established an alternative 'Court' at Leicester House, with Walpole and Townshend among the first to rally round. The popularity of the festivities at Leicester House forced the King to compete and make the Court proper more sociable too. He started hosting evening assemblies at St James's Palace several times a week, 'courting' public support through hospitality and cultural patronage. With two royal courts vying to be thought the more generous, stylish and enlightened, the need for a private club to promote British culture was diminished.

Theatre, music and the visual arts remained the privileged recipients of Hanoverian patronage, however, with literature lagging behind. Though George spoke fair English by 1717, he remained, like King William, unmoved by poetry not in his mother tongue. Newcastle, as Lord Chamberlain, was therefore given greater personal scope to dispense literary patronage – a role that combined perfectly with his position as the leading Kit-Cat patron.

Newcastle self-consciously saw himself as inheriting the mantle of Dorset, who had similarly worn the two hats of Lord Chamberlain and Kit-Cat patron after 1697. As Dorset had been Dryden's patron and encouraged the Kit-Cats to admire the old Tory poet, so Newcastle now funded Congreve to finally fulfil his promise to 'be kind to' Dryden's literary remains. Congreve said Newcastle had had the 'Taste and Discernment' to suggest the publication of Dryden's collected dramatic works in six volumes, and submissively commended Newcastle 'for doing a Thing which is, in truth, of a Public

Consideration'.[41] Tonson published this collection in January 1718, in which Congreve's dedication confirmed Newcastle as the arts' major patron: 'You are now in a Station by which You necessarily preside over the liberal Arts, and all the Practisers and Possessors of them.'[42] Though Dryden still lacked a monument of stone in Westminster Abbey, the Kit-Cat Club had finally given him a monument in print.

Congreve himself was nearing the time for monuments. Since the previous autumn, he had been convalescing at Ashley, the seat of fellow Kit-Cat Viscount Shannon. To memorialize his work before Congreve grew too unwell to give editorial assistance, Tonson instructed his nephew to prepare *The Works of Mr William Congreve . . . revis'd by the author*, which was published in 1719. The Whig schism made previous Whig–Tory battles seem safely in the past, allowing Tonson to also express the admiration he had never ceased to feel for Prior as a poet. Tonson produced a luxurious edition of Prior's poems in 1718, which Prior dedicated to Lionel, referring back to the debt Prior owed to Lionel's father, his first patron: 'You have a Hereditary Right to whatever may be called Mine.'[43] The profit from the enormous subscription list for this volume, including at least twenty-seven Kit-Cats and Kit-Cat relations, was sufficient to provide Prior with a pension until his death. Despite Prior's merciless savaging of Garth's poetry in *The Examiner* during the paper wars of 1710, Garth was among the first to subscribe; he had never removed the lines warmly praising Prior's poetry from later editions of *The Dispensary*.

After Prior's imprisonment by Walpole's Committee of Secrecy, however, and after losing the snakes-and-ladders board game of eighteenth-century politics, Prior never fully rekindled affection for his old Kit-Cat comrades, no matter how attracted they remained to his wit and writing. When Oxford was released from the Tower in the summer of 1717, thanks to the squabbling Whigs' inability to conclude his prosecution, Prior felt greater affinity with this fellow outcast than with the Whig oligarchs, and the two maintained a close private friendship during their final years. During a stay with Oxford in Cambridgeshire in September 1721, Prior died of cholera. He asked to be buried in Westminster Abbey next to his old schoolmate Stepney.

In contrast to the nostalgia of Tonson's relationships with Congreve and Prior, Tonson's friendship with Vanbrugh after 1714 remained as vital as in the Kit-Cat Club's beginning. With no Club meetings to tie him to London, Tonson travelled on business to France in late summer 1718, remaining there for two years. As in 1703, Vanbrugh wrote to Tonson between 1717 and 1720 about renovations at Barn Elms: '[Y]ou are so far from forgetting your old mistress, Barnes, that you are inclined to compliment her in the spring with £500 for a new petticoat. For my part, I think she deserves it, for the pleasures she has given you.'[44] Further comparing the house to a woman, Vanbrugh wrote:

> Her charms don't lie in her Beauty, but her good Conditions . . . I always found a Tete-a-Tete more pleasing with you there than I should have done at Blenheim, had the house been my own, though without my Lady Marlborough for my Wife. For one may find a great deal of Pleasure in building a Palace for another when one should find very little in living in't oneself.[45]

Nothing suggests Tonson had any mistresses other than his Barnes house. The only evidence of women in Tonson's life comes from Ned Ward:

> For kind Bocai though now he's past his Prime
> Has been an old Sheep-biter in his time;
> Not only in the Gainful skins a Dealer,
> But of the Flesh has been a Fellow-Feeler.[46]

A 'sheep-biter' was a dog that worried sheep, and in this context a man who ran after 'mutton' – that is, older women. Other than this one line, however, all of Tonson's relationships seem to have been intense friendships with men, especially Vanbrugh.

In 1713, aged 49, Vanbrugh had made (in the midst of severe money worries) a sudden, belated entrance onto the marriage market. He had been spending the winter with Carlisle at Castle Howard, and Lady Mary Wortley Montagu, also staying in York, wrote mercilessly to a London friend:

> 'Tis credibly reported that he [Vanbrugh] is endeavouring at an honourable state of matrimony and vows to lead a sinful life no more . . . Van's taste was always odd; his inclination to ruins has given him a fancy for Mrs Yarbrugh. He sighs and ogles that it would do your heart good to see him; and she is not a little pleased, in so small a proportion of men amongst such a Number of Women, a whole man should fall to her share.[47]

The object of Vanbrugh's attentions was Miss Henrietta Maria Yarbrugh, daughter of Colonel James Yarbrugh, an aide-de-camp to Marlborough and distant relation of the Dowager Duchess of Newcastle. This 'ruin' was, in fact, a 21-year-old girl – too plain to be a plausible Kit-Cat toast, but blessed with these useful connections. Lady Mary does not reveal of what Vanbrugh's previous 'sinful life' consisted, but one wonders, in light of a total lack of gossip about earlier affairs and the satire about his relationship with Peregrine Bertie, whether she was laughing at a 'confirmed bachelor' taking his first interest in the opposite sex.

He had visited Henrietta Maria again in York in the summer of 1716, full of his new appointment as Surveyor to the Royal Naval Hospital at Greenwich, and just as he was resuming work on Blenheim. By November 1716, however, Vanbrugh had fallen out with the Duchess of Marlborough and resigned from the Blenheim works for the final time, leaving the workmen under the Duchess' direction. Following the political trauma of the Whig schism of 1717–18, Vanbrugh again spent Christmas at Castle Howard, where he wrote to Newcastle that it was 'so bloody Cold, I have almost a mind to Marry to keep myself warm.'[48]

On 14 January 1719, Vanbrugh finally married Henrietta Maria, now 26 to his 54. The ceremony took place at St Lawrence's in York, Carlisle acting as best man, though crippled with gout. A short tour of Carlisle's relations followed the wedding. Vanbrugh wrote to Newcastle to tell him the news, but burying it within a lot of other architectural talk and self-mockery, suggesting that Vanbrugh guessed his friends might find his marriage cause for amusement, such that he wanted to laugh at himself first. He said Tonson would be 'frightened out of his Wits and his Religion too when he hears I've gone at last. If he is still in France, he'll certainly give himself to God, for fear he should now be ravished by a gentlewoman. I was the last man left between him and ruin.'[49]

In his cross-Channel correspondence, Vanbrugh informed Tonson of his marriage, assuring him, 'whatever evils Marriage may design me, it has not yet lessened one grain of my Affections to an old Friend'.[50] Vanbrugh joked that marriage would 'possibly do me as much good as it has mischief to many a one we know', and that the chain of matrimony 'hangs a little easy about me'. After receiving correction of a false report from Paris of Tonson's death, Vanbrugh said he had told his new wife so much about his publisher and friend 'while you were alive, after you were dead, and since you are alive again, that she knows you well enough to desire to know you better'.[51]

In August 1719, Vanbrugh was once again passed over for the top job of Surveyor of the Royal Works, writing to Tonson that it was a bitter pill 'now I come just to the time (and disgrace) of Swallowing it. I don't, however, blame anybody, nor think them wanting. But 'tis one of [the] hardest pieces of Fortune that ever fell to anybody.'[52] The reason for taking it so hard, as he confided to Tonson, was simple: 'I have no money to dispose of. I have been many years at hard labour to work through the cruel difficulties that Haymarket undertaking involved me in . . . nor are these difficulties quite at an end yet.'[53]

One grief Vanbrugh did not confide to Tonson in this letter was that his first child by Henrietta Maria, a daughter, had been stillborn. Fourteen months later, however, Vanbrugh's wife gave him a son – named Charles as much after the boy's godfather, Lord Carlisle, as after Vanbrugh's favourite brother. Tonson hinted heavily that, if Vanbrugh were not too ashamed of Tonson's 'old Testament name', he should like to stand godfather to one of Vanbrugh's future sons.[54] A couple of years after the birth of Charles, in 1722, Vanbrugh boasted to Tonson:

> I am now two Boys Strong in the Nursery but am forbid getting any more this Season for fear of killing my Wife. A Reason that in Kit-Cat days would have been stronger for it than against it: But let her live, for she's Special good, as far as I know of the Matter.[55]

Vanbrugh was genuinely surprised to find his wife so likeable, in contradiction to his deeply ingrained misogyny. Vanbrugh later told Tonson he did not repent his 'great Leap in the Dark, marriage',[56] but was 'confirmed my Old Opinion was right: That whatever there is good or bad in Marriage, it was fitter to end Our Life with than begin it'.[57] This belief that marriage was only good for a man's retirement seems to have been a common Kit-Cat view. Gentlemen did not need to marry to increase their domestic comfort, since servants took care of that, so for the more libidinous members, whatever their sexual orientations, late marriages simply prolonged their right to enjoy promiscuity without reproach. The average age of men's first marriage in this period (1700–49) was 27.5 years old, and of 118 sons of dukes born between 1680 and 1729 who reached the age of 20, forty died bachelors. At least a dozen of the fifty or so Kit-Cats never married.[58] The golden age of clubs was also, in other words, a golden age of bachelors. Not only Newcastle's meeting of March 1717 but the Kit-Cat Club as a whole can be regarded, in this light, as a kind of extended stag party. These relationships, despite the satires written about Vanbrugh and Stanhope as sodomites, were more 'homosocial' than homosexual, though the line between the two was never absolute.

To the eighteenth-century mind, family was directly associated with nature, and friendship with civilization – the first being the product of animal urges, the second the product of reason. The Kit-Cats therefore saw friendship as heroically improving upon a world based on random, biological ties (though many Kit-Cat relationships were cemented by marriages of their children). They chose as their authority Cicero, for whom same-sex friendship was a higher calling than the family, as opposed to Epicurus who, though he conceived of friendship as an escape from repressive government, included women and children in that escape. Even Steele, for all his idealization of marriage, conceived it as the rival to male friendship in coffee houses, taverns and clubs. Steele believed you had to choose, warning that 'the married Man who has not bid adieu to the Fashions and False Gallantries of the Town is perplexed with everything around him'.[59] From this viewpoint, the Kit-Cat Club was undone as much by its literary members' late marriages after 1716 as by the political schism souring public life.

Several Kit-Cats' married lives were starkly unhappier than their Club lives. Pulteney married in 1714 a woman who was beautiful but adulterous, nicknamed 'Mrs Pony' for being a good ride. They were said to argue so acerbically that they lived 'in a vinegar bottle'.[60] Edmund Dunch also married a 'lewd, handsome' woman who lived for most of their marriage with other men.[61] Walpole and his wife, likewise, agreed to live apart, and Walpole's adoring son Horace may not have been his. The most extreme case of marriage-aversion among the Kit-Cats, however, must be Scarbrough: on the eve of his late marriage to Isabella, the young widow of Lord Manchester's son, Scarbrough ordered dinner to his bedroom and a chariot to go out and meet friends for cards afterwards; then, after finishing his meal, put a gun to his mouth and blew his brains out.

Steele's marriage had long become like that of a cursed couple he described in *The Spectator*: 'In Company they are in a Purgatory, when only together, in an Hell.'[62] When Steele returned from Scotland, he seems to have quickly asserted his conjugal rights, since Prue, at 40, was soon pregnant with their fifth child. As no correspondence survives from the months they lived together at their Hampton Court home during 1718, it is impossible to know how peaceful or fractious they were. All we know is that, while Steele was restaging *Cato* at Drury Lane over Christmas, Prue suddenly fell ill, perhaps due to complications in the pregnancy. On 27 December 1718, Steele sent a note of only a couple of lines to his wife's brother, informing him that Prue had died the previous night.

Steele was devastated by the loss. He had once invented a letter to *The Spectator* from a widower who described having to excuse himself from male company to cry: 'I sat down with a Design to put you upon giving us Rules how to overcome such Griefs as these,' Steele's exemplary widower wrote, 'but I should rather advise you to teach Men to be capable of them . . . To want Sorrow when you in Decency and Truth should be afflicted, is, I should think, a greater Instance of a Man's being a Blockhead than not to know the Beauty of any Passage in Virgil.'[63]

Steele moved into bachelor's rooms in York Buildings, where he still held a lease. He instructed his 10-year-old daughter Betty that she would have to be mother to her little brother and sister now. Lady Steele's best friend, Mrs Keck, in fact, took the children in and raised them, and one might note that the way Mrs Keck had taken Prue into her cramped home above a shop during Prue's various pregnancies, and cared for Prue's infants when she was in Wales and again after her death, evidences a selfless and practical bond of trust between these two women that no Kit-Cat friendship, even between Addison and Steele, can quite match.

Steele was still in mourning for Prue when he received news of another loss. Dr Garth had fallen ill earlier in the season and, while confined to bed at his house at Harrow-on-the-Hill, judged himself to be dying. He wrote to the equally housebound Congreve in Surrey Street, to inform him he was 'going his Journey' and asking how soon it would be before Congreve followed. Congreve replied that 'he wished him a good journey but did not intend to take the same road' just yet.[64]

Among Garth's final visitors was Addison, who said he visited Garth to try to prepare him for the afterlife, but the doctor declared he had been long convinced 'that the doctrines of Christianity are incomprehensible and the religion itself an imposture'.[65] Once, when called to the deathbed of an actress named Miss Campion who was in a panic about her sins, Garth had assured her she could 'rest contented' for 'upon his honour there was neither a God nor future State'.[66] Understandably, therefore, this final, misguided interview with Garth upset Addison, who recounted it regretfully to a bishop.

Garth told another visitor he would be glad to die, 'for he was weary of having his shoes pulled off and on'.[67] Behind this brave flippancy, Garth was in excruciating pain. Once he knew himself beyond recovery, he sent for two different surgeons by two different servants. He tricked each surgeon into bleeding him from a different arm, then, when left alone, undid the bandages and tried to bleed himself to death. The attempt merely left him weakened. He did not die until 18 January 1719, four days after Vanbrugh's wedding. Garth was buried beside his late wife in a Harrow-on-the-Hill church, leaving one daughter, Martha, his only heir.

XIX
THE END OF THE CLUB

The Old Roman Friendships were a composition of several ingredients, of which the Principal was Union of Hearts (a fine Flower, which grew in several parts of that Empire), Sincerity, Frankness, Disinterestedness, Pity and tenderness, of each an equal quantity; these all mixed up together with two rich oils, which they called perpetual kind wishes and serenity of temper, and the whole was strongly perfumed with the Desire of Pleasing, which gave it a most grateful smell and was a sure restorative in all sorts of Vapours. The Cordial thus prepared was of so durable a Nature that no length of time would waste it, and what is very remarkable, says our Author, it increased in Weight and Value the longer you kept it.

The Moderns have most greatly adulterated this fine recipe; some of the Ingredients, indeed, are not to be found, but what they impose upon you for friendship is as follows: Outward Profession (a common Weed that grows everywhere) instead of the Flower of Union, the desire of being pleased, a large quantity of self-Interest, convenience, and Reservedness many handfuls, a little of pity and tenderness (but some pretend to make it up without these two last) and the common Oil of inconstancy (which, like our Linseed Oil is cold drawn every Hour) serves to mix them all together; most of these ingredients being of a perishable Nature it will not keep, and shows itself to be a counterfeit by lessening continually in Weight and Value…

JOSEPH ADDISON, *A Sketch Upon Friendship* (n.d.)[1]

IN JUNE 1717, Addison was having heart palpitations and trouble breathing as he strained to commute between London, Kensington and Hampton Court for his work as a Secretary of State. Illness confined him to Holland House later that summer, and by March 1718 Addison told the King he could not continue. He retired with a pension of £1,500 (around £196,000 today), and instead served the Sunderland–Stanhope ministry through journalism supporting their policies. Addison and Ambrose Philips, for example, produced a paper called *The Freethinker*, which discussed liberty of conscience within Protestantism, supporting Stanhope's moves to repeal the Occasional Conformity laws that the Junto Whigs had allowed to pass for tactical reasons in 1713.

Addison's other great, pro-government journalistic intervention concerned the 1719 Peerage Bill. This Bill, which proposed that membership of the House of Lords be fixed to allow the creation of only six further peers, resulted from the royal family's feud, the King attempting to ensure his son could not undo current legislation by appointing a new batch of lords the moment he came to the throne, as Anne had appointed the 'Tory Dozen' to force the Utrecht Treaty through the Lords. The government tried to argue this was a constitutional reform to strengthen the upper house's independence and prevent corruption of the honours system for party political ends. The opposition, led by Walpole and meeting at the Duke of Devonshire's house, saw it as the ministry's attempt to disempower the Lords, much as the Septennial Act had disempowered the Commons. It would turn into an important constitutional debate, which presaged many parliamentary reform debates in the centuries to come.

A printed skirmish over the Peerage Bill began immediately. Steele published *The Plebeian*, a paper attacking the Bill as tampering with Britain's constitutional balance. The paper's title pointed to Steele's conviction that his style of Whiggism was more democratic and anti-authoritarian than the present government's: '[I]f those who have a power entrusted to them by their Principals only for a few Years can seize it to themselves and their Posterity forever, what use will be made of Power so acquired[?]' he asked.[2] Steele said the peers who supported the Bill, including several Kit-Cat colleagues, were nursed on the milk of contempt for everything except their own 'imaginary dignity'.[3] Steele and Walpole criticized the Bill for aiming to establish 'the worst sort of oligarchy'.[4]

Addison, on the government's behalf, answered Steele's attacks anonymously, in a paper called *The Old Whig*. Addison regretted that *The Plebeian*'s author, whom he knew to be Steele, had resorted to an 'angry strain' rather than arguing calmly and rationally. Addison tried to present the Bill as correcting a long-standing constitutional defect and limiting the monarchy in the old Whig tradition.

Steele replied in two further issues of *The Plebeian*. Referring to *The Old Whig*'s author as 'somebody or other that is used to masquerading' – a jibe at Addison's tendency to hide his authorship – Steele cast the 'Old Whig' as old-fashioned in failing to imagine threats to English liberty from any source other than an arbitrary monarch. The line aimed at Addison's heart, however, was Steele's remark: 'I am afraid he is so old a Whig that he has quite forgot his principles.' Above all, Addison believed himself to be a man of principle, partly because Steele had admired and applauded him as such for decades. Steele also accused Addison of 'wilfully' misunderstanding *The Plebeian* because Addison was writing in the government's pay. After years of sitting on the fence during the Whig–Tory paper wars precisely to avoid such accusations, Addison must have been wounded. When Addison did not respond immediately to Steele's rebuttals, Steele smirked that 'Age is apt to be Slow' – perhaps only friendly teasing prompted by Addison's choice of the 'Old Whig' persona, but a joke suggesting Steele was unaware how sick and frail Addison was growing by this time.

When Addison's reply came, it displayed unprecedented and

uncharacteristic aggression. Steele was writing 'like a son of Grub Street', yet Addison mocked Steele's hypocrisy in calling himself a 'plebeian' when this was 'a title which he is by no means fond of retaining' – the insinuation being that Steele opposed a cap on new peerages because he himself aspired to one. Addison said he shuddered to remember, in light of Steele's radical fears about the House of Lords' exorbitant power, Steele's years of flattering peers as patrons: 'I must . . . remind this Author of the Milk with which he nurses our Nobles, not to omit [i.e. forget] his stagnated Pool.'[5] Although Addison's defenders have argued we should not read this as a personal insult to Steele's failing Fishpool project, but as referring to Steele's earlier comment that the Peerage Bill would make the House of Lords 'as corrupt and offensive as a stagnated pool',[6] any ambiguity was likely intentional. Addison concluded with a condescending recommendation to Steele, 'as a friend', to put his considerable journalistic talents to the service of some better cause.

Steele would not let Addison's condescension be the final word. He reiterated his belief that Addison was writing 'in support of vassalage' on orders from his former bosses, and that the lack of integrity was evident if one compared *The Old Whig* with Addison's earlier journalism. Steele quoted Addison's *Cato* against its author, implying Addison was a hypocrite, and concluded he was sorry to see his old friend selling out in this way.

Part of the tragedy of Addison's and Steele's public falling out was that neither was a hypocrite – the Peerage Bill simply revealed a genuine difference in the radicalism of their Whiggery. Posterity has generally sided with the more progressive Steele (even the pro-Addisonian Macaulay admitted Steele 'blundered upon the truth'[7]), but Addison's arguments were based on Lockean principles in which he sincerely believed, and on fears about the Prince of Wales' character and future actions.

Dr Johnson blamed politics for ruining this lifelong friendship and literary collaboration ('Why could not faction find other advocates?'[8]), but the friendship was over long before, broken by wounded pride, not political differences. Steele once described the consequences should the 1707 Treaty of Union be undone as follows: 'Two Warlike Nations that should separate, after being under solemn Obligation of perpetual Union, would like two private Men of Spirit that had broken Friendship, have ten thousand nameless and inexplicable Causes of Anger boiling in their Bosoms.'[9]

For Addison and Steele, the 'ten thousand nameless and inexplicable Causes' derived from failings in the carefully calibrated reciprocity necessary to keep a friendship strong despite inequalities of circumstance. Addison's elevation to Secretary of State finally tipped the balance in what had always been an unequal relationship. With the Whig schism, the Kit-Cat Club's suspension, and Addison's marriage and move to Holland House, the men had stopped meeting months before the Peerage Bill controversy.

Addison and Steele were not the only adversaries in the Peerage Bill paper war. Addison helped his former ministerial colleagues hire other journalists, while Walpole used the Prince's purse to hire writers to assist Steele, including Addison's cousin Eustace Budgell, who was angry with Addison at the time. Years later, Budgell threw himself into the Thames with pockets full of stones, leaving a note on his desk that suggested residual guilt for having betrayed his cousin in 1719: 'What Cato did [i.e. suicide] and Addison approved, Cannot be Wrong.'

The effectiveness of Addison's and Steele's competing propaganda regarding the Peerage Bill, and of Stanhope's and Walpole's competing oratory and political skills, was tested at the Commons vote. The Bill was allowed to drop, to Steele's immense satisfaction. This was a major setback for the government and a great encouragement to the Prince's party.[10] An even more dramatic Whig schism was averted only by the lucky return of an external threat: the landing of Spanish forces in Scotland to support an uprising of Jacobite Highlanders, defeated in June 1719 at Glenshiel.

That month, Addison refused to see a doctor as his condition deteriorated dramatically. He was terrified of death, admitting frankly that it was his first reason for being a Christian ('There is something so particularly gloomy and offensive to Human Nature in the Prospect of Non-Existence',[11] and if an afterlife was a delusion, 'let me enjoy it, since it makes me both the happier and better Man'[12]), but he was also morbidly fascinated by the question of how to have a heroic death. Addison was working on a tragic play about Socrates' death, and was read extracts on the deaths of ancient heroes during his last days. The mode of death, he said, was the most instructive part of any biography.

At the end, Addison summoned three people. One, to everyone's surprise, was the poet John Gay, whom he apparently begged for forgiveness over a wrong of which Gay himself was unaware – possibly blocking Gay's preferment when Addison was Secretary to the Lords Regent in 1714. Another was Milton's last surviving daughter, to whom Addison reportedly presented a purse of gold in honour of her father's genius. The third was Addison's stepson, Lord Warwick, whom Addison summoned to 'See in what peace a Christian can die.'[13] This last anecdote was quoted with much pathos by future generations, helped on by Thomas Tickell writing of Addison: 'There taught us how to live; and (oh! Too high / The price for knowledge) taught us how to die.'[14] When Virginia Woolf heard the story, her sympathies were instead 'with the foolish, and perhaps fuddled, young peer rather than with the frigid gentleman, not too far gone for a last spasm of self-complacency, upon the bed'.[15]

Addison once wrote a *Spectator* complimenting Thomas More's death as being 'of a piece with his Life. There was nothing in it new, forced or affected'[16] and, in its own way, the slight affectation or staginess of Addison's death was of a piece with his life. Self-consciousness was one of the author's intellectual assets but also his greatest handicap. Steele's unselfconscious personality was, at the height of their friendship and professional collaboration, the perfect antidote. Thus Steele wrote a very different essay on how to die in *The Tatler*, saying that '[n]one but a Tragedian can die by Rule, and wait till he discovers a Plot, or says a fine Thing upon his Exit. In real Life, this is a Chimera, and by Noble Spirits it will be done decently, without the Ostentation of it.'[17]

Addison sent no last-minute summons to Steele. Believing himself to have done no injustice to his friend, Addison saw no reason to heal their rift. This omission has negated Addison's efforts to gain posterity's admiration for his manner of dying.

Addison died on 17 June 1719, and his remains were conveyed from Holland House to Westminster Abbey in the middle of the night. He was buried, at his request, beside his first and last Kit-Cat patron, Halifax, in the north aisle of Henry VII's Chapel – next to the nation's leaders rather than in Poets' Corner, beside Dryden, Prior and Stepney. It is unknown who, if anyone, from the Kit-Cat Club was at the funeral. Tonson was still overseas, Congreve was in poor health, and Steele may not have felt welcome, though one hopes he attended in any case.

Addison's will left almost everything to his wife and baby daughter. A separate letter gave his successor as Secretary of State for the South authority over his papers. This was because there were politically sensitive items among them, but it also effectively made Thomas Tickell, Under-Secretary of State thanks to Addison's patronage, into Addison's literary executor. Though this was logical, and the donnish, devoted Tickell was the perfect administrator, the arrangement must have been difficult for Steele.

A rivalry that Tickell and Steele mastered during Addison's life soon surfaced after he died. Tickell and Addison had become friends after Addison was famous, when Addison preferred to surround himself with young acolytes rather than Kit-Cat colleagues. Like the young, last wife who often controls the materials of a great man's reputation after his death, though she may not have been the love of his life or muse of his art, Tickell earned his legacy by being physically at Addison's side at the end. Tickell had been staying at Holland House and helping Addison's wife and servants care for him in his sickness since the summer of 1717. Steele discovered Tickell was compiling a four-volume edition of Addison's collected works, for which Tickell was trawling through their collaborative publications, mostly *The Spectator* and *The Tatler*, and separating Addison's essays from Steele's. Though this was likely what Addison had instructed (touchingly, Addison seems to have ordered Tickell to omit *The Old Whig* pamphlets attacking Steele from the collection), Tickell failed to even consult Steele on the selection. The whole process was therefore felt by Steele as an insult.

Steele produced a new paper in 1720 containing his valediction to Addison. Describing their relationship as one of complementary opposites, Steele explained:

> There never was a more strict Friendship than between those Gentlemen; nor had they any Difference but what proceeded from their different Way of pursuing the same thing; the one with Patience, Foresight, and temperate Address, always waited and stemmed the Torrent; while the other often plunged himself into it, and was as often taken out by the Temper of him who stood weeping on the Bank for his Safety.[18]

Sugar-coating their lost intimacy, Steele continued:

> [T]hese two Men lived for some Years last past, shunning each other, but still preserving the most passionate Concern for their mutual Welfare. But when they met, they were as unreserved as Boys, and talked of greatest Affairs, upon which they saw where they differed, without pressing (what they knew impossible) to convert each other.[19]

In November 1721, Tickell finished editing Addison's *Collected Works*, for which Tonson and Jacob Junior compiled a list of 1,046 subscribers. Jacob Junior had the courtesy to send a copy to Steele at his lodgings in York Buildings, in which Steele found, as he expected, that Tickell had underestimated the extent of their collaboration. Tickell effectively set up a caricature of Addison as faultless scholar in contrast to Steele as boozy ex-soldier, insinuating that Steele had profited by claiming credit for Addison's work. Steele also found mistaken biographical details – Tickell did not know, for example, that it was Halifax who had persuaded Addison from taking religious orders – and that Tickell had not included *The Drummer* in the collection. Whether Addison had instructed Tickell to omit *The Drummer*, or whether Tickell was unaware of the play's true authorship, is unclear. Steele immediately bought the copyright from Tonson so he could bring it out in a new edition, with Addison named on its title page. In its dedication, addressed to Congreve, Steele answered Tickell's insinuations.[20]

Steele argued Tickell had done Addison's reputation a disservice by presenting him as faultless but also humourless. Steele reclaimed *The Spectator* and the Spectator Club framework as joint ideas, while insisting that what he had failed to attribute to Addison 'I had his direct Injunctions to hide'. This arrangement may have partially benefited Steele's reputation, he admitted, but Addison's 'oblique Stokes' against other people had also made Steele many enemies on Addison's behalf. Steele was 'a Man who had, for the greatest part of his Life, been his [Addison's] known Bosom Friend, and shielded him from all the Resentments which many of his own Works would have brought upon him'. Steele claimed he 'rejoiced in being excelled' by Addison's talent, making the double-edged boast that Addison could always send for him 'as much as he could send for any of his clerks when he was Secretary of State'. Candidly admitting Addison's 'natural Power over me', Steele said he felt 'supererogatory Affection' for his dead friend.[21] Above all, Steele credited himself with having coaxed Addison's talent into the daylight for the benefit of the British public.

Steele ultimately triumphed over Tickell to be immortalized as The Best Friend, his name and Addison's now being inseparable in literary history. As Addison, for all his love of solitude, once observed, 'neither Virgil nor Horace would have gained so great a Reputation in the World had they not been the Friends and Admirers of each other'.[22] Tickell is remembered solely for a beautiful elegy upon Addison's death, and the verse Dedication to Addison's *Collected Works*. On his tomb, Tickell correctly inscribed his life's highest achievement as having been 'the friend of Addison'.[23]

Rivalry between Tickell and Steele had been primed before Addison's death, in the autumn of 1718, when Newcastle, as Lord Chamberlain, had insisted that a prologue by Tickell to a new production of *The Beaux Stratagem* replace one by Steele. This was largely Newcastle's way of expressing his disapproval of Steele for siding with the Walpole-Townshend faction against the government. Steele interpreted it as a threat to the Drury Lane company's independence. After a series of polite remonstrations failed to move Newcastle, Steele asked Jacob Junior to act as his intermediary, saying he could no longer trust his temper to speak directly with his patron.

Steele's toleration for supplication to those above him in rank was always brittle: '[T]here is nothing to be done with those Poor Creatures called Great Men, but by an Idolatry towards them, which it is below the spirit of an Honest Free and Religious man to pay,' he once declared to Prue.[24] Now, after the Peerage Bill debates, Steele's respect for British hierarchies was at a low point.

Newcastle was frustrated by the Peerage Bill's defeat, having much to lose when the Prince of Wales, who loathed him, became king. That Steele, who owed Newcastle his seat in Parliament, should join with the Prince's Party was a humiliation he took personally. Years later, Newcastle candidly said his temper was 'such that I am often uneasy and peevish, and perhaps, what may be called wrong-headed, to my best Friends, but that always goes down with the Sun and passes off'.[25] In Steele's case, Newcastle's peevishness did not pass off so easily.

In December 1719, Newcastle again overruled Steele's management at Drury Lane by ordering the dismissal of the actor Colley Cibber, who had written a dedication critical of Newcastle. Steele refused to fire Cibber, causing Newcastle to revoke Steele's licence and suspend performances at the theatre in January until further notice. Steele was forced to resign, but took his indignation to the public in yet another journal, *The Theatre* (January–April 1720), and also a pamphlet.[26] Steele was at his nadir in early 1720, depressed by the deaths of Prue, Garth and Addison, and by his continuing inability to escape debt (a new £500 debt to Tonson appeared in Steele's accounts, probably representing the dowry for his illegitimate daughter). In *The Theatre*'s final issue, Steele complained there had been a 'Concert to undo me utterly . . . since the Beginning of this Winter' and that the paper he was closing was:

> not the Product of a Mind at Ease, but written by a Man neither out of Pain in Body or Mind; but forced to suspend the Anguish of both, with the Addition of powerful Men soliciting my Ruin, shy Looks from my Acquaintance, surly Behaviour from my Domestics, with all the Train of private and public Calamity, and that for no other Reason but pursuing what he thought just.[27]

In the tone of a son wronged by a father, the near-50-year-old Steele told his former patron, 27-year-old Newcastle, that he planned to challenge the loss of the Drury Lane licence in the law courts. Steele spoke of having been 'expelled' from the playhouse, just as he had been expelled from Parliament, as if everything in life were a matter of membership. Steele would take action for the sake of 'my Creditors and my Family, to neither of whom am I able to be just, Except I am justly dealt with by others. My Heart throbs and my Eyes flow when I talk thus to my Once Dear and Honoured Duke of Newcastle.'[28]

Despite such quarrels, the Kit-Cats did not regard their Club as formally dissolved. Many hoped it would resume when Tonson returned from the Continent. Tonson's return, however, was deferred because of his investment in a French colonial project and stock-market 'bubble' called the 'Mississippi Scheme'.[29] The publisher advised Vanbrugh to invest in the Mississippi Scheme too, which the architect said he would have done, 'But, to tell you the Truth, I have no money to dispose of.'[30] The Duchess of Marlborough was still suing Vanbrugh over Blenheim, forcing him to mortgage property to his brother. Years later, Vanbrugh assured Tonson he too would have retired, 'had I made a good voyage to the Mississippi'.[31] Tonson, it seems, received a tip-off to sell his stock just before the Mississippi Scheme crashed in May 1720.

In exchange for Tonson's financial advice, Vanbrugh recommended the South Sea Company to Tonson as 'a sort of Young Mississippi'.[32] In 1711, Oxford had founded this Company for political as much as economic reasons, to create an investment outlet for Tories long excluded from directorship of the Bank of England and to free his government from indebtedness to the Kit-Cat Furnese. The South Sea Company had assumed £8.9 million of governmental debt and raised a further £500,000 (£59.5 million today) for Oxford's ministry. Its directors' meetings were run like a Tory club, with fines for non-attendance. After the Treaty of Utrecht, the Company reaped profits from the *asiento* (the monopoly on the Atlantic slave trade), and, following the Tories' fall in 1714, the Whigs took over the Company.

The King replaced his son as the South Sea Company's Governor when the royal family feud became public in 1717. All directors related to the dissident Walpole–Townshend faction were purged.

Tonson invested £10,000 in the Company soon after this. Then, in April 1720, the King assented to a scheme by which the South Sea Company would assume much more of the national debt, and this began the bubble. Walpole publicly criticized the scheme, and Steele wrote against it in the press, pointing out that 'Credit cannot subsist without a Store'.[33] Sunderland and Stanhope nonetheless pushed the South Sea Bill through the Lords and ensured their friends had access to stock (though one letter shows James Craggs, Addison's replacement as Secretary of State, apologising to Newcastle for being unable to help him or his 'friends' obtain South Sea stock any more easily than the 'rest of the world'[34]). Vanbrugh seems to have borrowed money from his relations to invest.

The South Sea bubble's beginnings during the spring of 1720 corresponded with a period of reconciliation among the Whigs in what Steele called 'this miserable divided Nation'.[35] Walpole and Townshend recognized that the ministry was riding high on the economic boom, and that their best hope of regaining power (and a slice of the financial profits) was through conciliation. The Court meanwhile felt the Walpole–Townshend faction commanded too much influence for comfort in the Commons and wanted it on side to pass the South Sea legislation. A superficial truce was therefore engineered between the King and his son in April 1720, and one diarist recorded a snapshot of Sunderland, Stanhope, Walpole and Townshend in this state of brief and insincere friendship, walking 'all four with their arms round each other to show they are now all one'.[36]

Walpole was appointed Paymaster General and Townshend Lord President of the Privy Council.[37] On the same day, 11 June 1720, the 'Bubble Act' was passed, requiring any prospective joint-stock companies to obtain a parliamentary or Crown charter, and so preventing the foundation of any rivals to the South Sea Company.

It was lucky for the Whigs that they were even superficially unified at the time of the South Sea Company's crash in October 1720. In London, banks closed, property prices collapsed, the Strand and Exchange were deserted and a fog of disgruntled depression settled over the City. Many of the 'middling sort' had long feared, since the culture wars of the late 1690s, that urbanity might come adrift from its moral moorings, and this was how much of provincial, Christian England viewed the South Sea scandal – as the Whig oligarchs finally exposed in their true colours as crooks and conmen.

Tonson, as with the Mississippi Scheme, had the business acumen or inside information to sell just before the crash; others, like Prior, Carlisle and Vanbrugh, lost heavily, in Vanbrugh's case nearly £2,000 (over £245,000 today).[38] Kneller was another loser, to the tune of £20,000 (£2.5 million today).[39] The crash was also hard on those, like Newcastle and Steele, whose creditors were investors and now suddenly needed to call in their credit. Several subscribers in Steele's Fishpool company wanted to withdraw, and new investors were now very unlikely to step forward.

The King and his mistress lost heavily in the South Sea bubble. He returned from Hanover to face the crisis in mid-November, and the following month summoned a Parliament baying for the blood of those responsible – meaning his chief ministers. Walpole, whose hands were relatively clean, saw his chance to outmanoeuvre Sunderland and Stanhope. He and his banker devised a scheme to reorganize the South Sea Company's debt, ensuring compensation was paid out in certain cases, and key Company directors (including the King's ministers) were protected from prosecution. By the time Parliament met, Walpole had already proposed his rescue scheme to a grateful King, and brokered the necessary deal with the Bank of England.

In the House of Lords in January 1721, Wharton's son by Lucy Loftus, 23-year-old Philip, 1st Duke of Wharton,[40] launched a vicious verbal attack on his father's old friend, Stanhope, over the South Sea crisis. Philip had lost a fortune – £120,000 (or £14.8 million today) – in the crash, which explains his anger. The young man's allegations were unfair: Stanhope was not party to the criminal corruption of his fellow ministers in the South Sea project, though he did subscribe to the Company. Yet Stanhope sat looking haggard on the front benches, as Philip Wharton further accused him of having deliberately inflamed the royal family's quarrels. Wharton insinuated Stanhope was riddled with venereal disease; Stanhope was, in fact, suffering from an enormous hangover, having drowned his sorrows with Newcastle and others the night before. After this attack, Stanhope took himself home to be bled by his doctors, and did not get up again. On 5 February, Stanhope died of a brain haemorrhage. He was buried in Westminster Abbey, with a full military funeral.

Walpole's plan for economic recovery was never implemented – the wider economy was in fact healthy enough to recover on its own – but the impression that Walpole had come to the rescue in a crisis was created. Walpole's decision to 'screen' certain South Sea directors was also a masterstroke: instead of destroying men like Sunderland, who was charged with having accepted a bribe of £50,000, Walpole defended them and cast himself as the government's saviour.[41]

Steele also recommended clemency for the South Sea directors, rather as he had recommended clemency for Catholic rebels after The Fifteen. Asked how he could do so when he had argued passionately against the Bubble Act, Steele answered that he was following Walpole's lead. Steele hoped Walpole's political resurrection would revive his own fortunes, and his hopes were well placed. In April 1721, Walpole was appointed First Lord of the Treasury and Chancellor of the Exchequer – the King's now undisputed chief and, though he denied the name, Britain's first true 'Prime Minister'. The following month, Walpole reinstated Steele's Drury Lane theatre licence, and issued a warrant ordering that Steele be compensated for lost profits. Steele, thrilled to triumph over Newcastle, said he now considered himself under Walpole's permanent 'Observation and Patronage'.[42]

Walpole used his own seat of Houghton and the stately home of Eastbury in Dorset, belonging to his friend George Bubb Doddington and rebuilt by Vanbrugh, as venues for the commerce between politicians and writers, following the pattern of the Kit-Cat Club. Recalling a house party at Houghton in 1731, the Prince of Wales described a 'snug little party of about thirty odd, up to the chin in beef, venison, geese, turkeys, etc., and generally over the chin in claret, strong beer and punch . . . In public we drank loyal healths, talked of the times and cultivated popularity; in private we drew plans and cultivated the country.'[43] When Doddington fell out with Walpole, Eastbury switched to hosting the 'Patriot' anti-Walpole opposition faction – a role shared by another important Kit-Cat property.

Stowe, in Buckinghamshire, belonged to Sir Richard Temple, who in the 1690s had been an MP loyal to the Junto, a drinking companion 'six nights in seven' of Congreve and Beau Stanyan (Temple's cousin), and a founding member of the Kit-Cat Club.[44] Congreve loved Temple for his affectionate temperament ('By nature formed for love and for esteem'[45]) and intellectual candour ('Sincerest critic of my prose, or rhyme'[46]). Temple distinguished himself fighting in Spain and under Marlborough in Flanders during the War of Spanish Succession; he was described by Swift as 'the greatest Whig in the Army'.[47] Congreve, who remained his drinking companion whenever Temple was home between campaigns, described him as 'no less in arts than arms',[48] and one source suggests that Tonson was jealous of their friendship.

After Congreve's dearest childhood friend, Joe Keally, died in May 1713, Congreve retired to spend the following winter with Temple at Stowe. At that time, when the political landscape looked bleak for the Kit-Cats, Temple and Congreve discussed how to improve Temple's estates and garden landscape at Stowe. In 1714, Temple had the twin honour of being created Baron Cobham (hereafter referred to as 'Cobham') and of being dispatched to Vienna to inform Emperor Charles VI of George I's accession, where Cobham remained until 1716. Upon his return to Georgian Britain, Cobham was made a Constable of Windsor Castle and member of the Privy Council. In May 1718, Cobham was created a Viscount, and in 1719 was sent to command the expeditionary force that sacked the Spanish port of Vigo in retaliation for Spanish funding of the attempted Jacobite invasion of Scotland.

Before sailing to Spain, Cobham spent the summer at Stowe, planning its gardens. Vanbrugh, thanks to their Kit-Cat Club connection, was hired to design ornamental buildings, gleefully telling Tonson that Cobham was spending 'all he has to spare' on the property.[49] Vanbrugh designed temples, ruins, rotundas, bathhouses, orangeries and other follies, including a pyramid, secluded seats and a gothic cave, all adding picturesque variation, sometimes springing dramatically on the unsuspecting stroller amid the Charles Bridgeman-designed gardens, sometimes amusingly witty upon close inspection. Vanbrugh's Kit-Cat patrons had always encouraged him to draw on English history and classical imports, to usher in Britain's new 'golden age', and here the recipe mixed references to Augustans, English medievalism and other exotic elements. He particularly emphasized Germanic elements in tribute to Britain's new royalty, telling Carlisle that Cobham approved his designs because he had 'seen the very thing done to a great Palace in Germany'.[50] Pope's *Epistle to Burlington* (1731) praised the house and gardens at Stowe for their elegant combination of artifice and nature, neoclassicism and wilderness.[51] The gardens demonstrated control rather than rejection of nature; the manipulation of the landscape in a way symbolizing Kit-Cat ambitions to remodel the nation as a whole, right down to its very soil.

Cobham was the last of Vanbrugh's Kit-Cat architectural patrons. As if to complete the circle, one of Vanbrugh's garden features at Stowe – an amphitheatre built circa 1727 – was known to Cobham as 'The Queen's Theatre', in homage to the theatre in the Haymarket. Inspection of Vanbrugh's neoclassical temples, which still stand at Stowe today, reveals the close connection between the 'show' put on by these palatial eighteenth-century estates and the stage-sets in Vanbrugh's theatrical productions: behind the follies' creamily smooth, classical fronts, incomplete backs show they are built from cheap brick.

Since 1714, Vanbrugh had also been working on Newcastle's Claremont, designing and locating the Belvedere Tower and various temples in the grounds, while Charles Bridgeman again designed the gardens. Bridgeman's landscaping, which emphasized non-symmetrical harmony, and Vanbrugh's innovative garden buildings, were widely emulated throughout the later Georgian period. In the late 1720s, after a two-week summer visit to Stowe in 1725, Carlisle returned with Vanbrugh to build the beautiful Temple of the Four Winds in Castle Howard's grounds. As at Stowe, the design of Castle Howard's surrounding landscape celebrated English nature, including its woodlands, but treated it at the same time as a blank canvas. What Vanbrugh painted on that canvas was a visual narrative referencing the Roman Campagna, a classical landscape full of political significance to the Whigs. In its imaginative complexity, Castle Howard is now regarded as a 'quantum leap'[52] for English landscape gardening.

Vanbrugh's landscaping aesthetic can be linked to views espoused by Addison years earlier in *The Spectator* about a new, distinctively English style of garden, eschewing excessive topiary and geometry. The semi-wild garden was to Addison a place of contemplation, uniting allusions to the biblical earthly paradise and Horatian ideals of '*otium*'.[53] Years before he was able to purchase and landscape his own estate at Bilton, Addison had spoken of learning as a wealth equal to that of a peer's 'delightful Gardens, green Meadows, and fruitful Fields'.[54] Such idealization of nature and pastoral escapism, relating back to Whig pastoral poetry after Dryden's *Virgil* in 1697, resurfaced during the four years (1710–14) when the Junto Whigs roamed the political wilderness – the period in which Halifax remodelled his gardens at Bushy Park – and it was then revived again after 1720, when Walpole held power and sent every colleague who dared challenge him, even his oldest Kit-Cat confrères, to political Siberia. It was partly a practical matter of keeping occupied in unemployment, but also a question of dramatizing, through the semiotics of houses and gardens, a declaration of the individual's freedom from state control. In this sense, gardening became part of certain Kit-Cats' Whig cultural weaponry, as *The Spectator* or the opera had been in earlier years.

Cobham loyally supported Walpole for many years, though disapproving of the way he protected the South Sea directors. Only in the spring of 1733 did Cobham openly oppose Walpole, for which Walpole immediately dismissed Cobham from his army regiment, despite his heroic military record. After this, Stowe became a central venue for gatherings of the anti-Walpole, cross-party opposition, and then was opened to public tourism as early as the 1740s. Like Tonson's presses and Addison and Steele's journalism, Stowe continued the Kit-Cats' communal endeavour to educate the public in Whig styles and ideas.

Cobham's 1730s political activism did not mean he forgot his older, Kit-Cat friendships. Cobham dedicated a sixty-foot-high pyramid in the Stowe grounds to Vanbrugh, as much his friend as his architect, and still standing on an island in the middle of Stowe's Octagon Lake is Cobham's stone monument to Congreve, designed by William Kent. It shows a monkey gazing at himself in a mirror – a fitting emblem of Congreve's satire. The inscription commemorates the pleasures of Congreve's private company as much as his literary talent, complimenting: 'the piercing, polished Wit, and civilised, candid, most unaffected Manners, of WILLIAM CONGREVE.'

Congreve's 'monument' to Cobham was of words, not stone. His 'Epistle to Lord Cobham' (1729) – also known as 'Of Improving the Present Time' – is perhaps Congreve's most beautiful and subtle poem. In it, Congreve asked Cobham whether he sometimes paused from his mania for erecting Vanbrugh's temples, statues and obelisks and wandered out to

> Catch the morning breeze from fragrant meads.
> Or shun the noontide ray in wholesome shades;
> Or lowly walk along the mazy wood,
> To meditate on all that's wise and good.

In this pastoral arcadia, Congreve described Cobham in a semi-mocking tone as the man who had it all:

> Graceful in form, and winning in address,
> While well you think, what aptly you express;
> With health, with honour, with a fair estate,
> A table free, and elegantly neat.
> What can be added more to mortal bliss?
> What can he want that stands possessed of this?

Though written before Cobham opposed Walpole, and by one of the least political of the Kit-Cats, the poem alluded to the opinion that Britain was, with her current foreign policy favouring *entente* with France, staining 'with her pen the lustre of her sword'. Nonetheless, in contrast to Pope's Scriblerian pessimism about the degeneracy of modern times, and also in contrast to the bombastic Whig triumphalism of some earlier Kit-Cat poetry, Congreve concludes that little ever fundamentally changes:

For virtue now is neither more or less,
And vice is only varied in the dress:
Believe it, men have ever been the same,
And Ovid's Golden Age is but a dream.[55]

The lasting friendship between Cobham and Congreve, long after the former ceased to be an active patron to the latter, was mirrored in the friendship between Vanbrugh and Tonson, which similarly outlasted their professional usefulness to one another. The four men – Congreve, Tonson, Vanbrugh and Cobham – all Kit-Cats from the Club's earliest days, regained a striking closeness in their autumnal years. They all retired to create beautiful gardens, from which they looked back wistfully to the paradise of lost youth amid the hubbub of London.

Vanbrugh purchased some land on Greenwich Hill before his marriage, and there built a country house known locally as 'Vanbrugh Castle', which still stands today. In March 1720, he and Henrietta Maria moved there. When Vanbrugh told Tonson, several years into his marriage, that his wife gave him 'a quiet house',[56] this was the house to which he referred. Though Greenwich was hardly out of London, Vanbrugh treated it as a rural retreat and tried to convince himself it brought him greater pleasure than drunken dinner parties in his prelapsarian, Kit-Cat years. He told Carlisle in June 1721 that, compared to such a peaceful retirement, 'All other delights are but like debauches in Wine, which give three days' pain for three hours' pleasure.'[57]

If Vanbrugh hoped Greenwich would place him a short water-ferry from Tonson in Barn Elms, he was to be disappointed. That same year, 1720, Tonson bought an estate named The Hazels in Ledbury, under Herefordshire's Malvern Hills, to which he moved permanently in 1722. Tonson thought about moving the Kit-Cat portraits with him, but told Jacob Junior, 'since I find their remaining with you is so much to your satisfaction, I will never desire or think of their being removed' – especially since Tonson's eyesight was growing too weak to appreciate them, and his country neighbours would 'like a signpost as well as Van Dyke, & any sad poem with Rhyme as well as *Paradise Lost*'.[58]

As a farewell to London, Tonson 'gave a splendid entertainment at Barn Elms to the Duke and Duchess of Newcastle, Lord Lansdowne and other persons of distinction' in July 1720.[59] Steele was spending the summer in Scotland, where he still had duties as a Commissioner of the Forfeited Estates, and though he was in close contact with Jacob Junior at this date, he was probably glad to be spared an awkward encounter with Newcastle, following their Drury Lane dispute.

Tonson could afford to retire and live the life of a Herefordshire squire not only because of his Mississippi Scheme and South Sea Company profits, but also thanks to his firm receiving a forty-year patent as the official government stationers. This was Tonson's final Kit-Cat pay-off.

For a tradesman to buy an estate like The Hazels was exceptional, even in that upwardly mobile era. It was as though Tonson were living out the fictional fate of the Spectator Club's Sir Andrew Freeport, who in old age moved his money from stocks into land, became a benefactor to the rural poor, modernized his estates, concentrated on preparing his soul for death, and kept his house and garden generously open to any old Club friends who happened to drop by. With the possible exception of worrying about the state of his soul (reading in his private library was his equivalent), this was what Tonson did. Referring to Tonson's great wealth, Dr Arbuthnot had observed that 'riches will make people forget their trade as well as themselves'.[60] He never married, though Vanbrugh teased him: 'Have a Care of this retired Country Life; we shall hear of some Herefordshire Nymph in your Solitary Walks bounce out upon your heart, from Under an Apple Tree, and make you one of us.'[61]

Tonson's retirement to Herefordshire marked the true end of the Kit-Cat Club in 1720–2. Though some historians have assumed the Newcastle-hosted meeting of March 1717 was the final gathering, Steele's report on the meeting does not say so, and several satires in early 1718 imply the Club was still in existence.[62] As late as January 1719, a private letter suggests the Kit-Cat continued as an informal editorial board for the Tonsons' firm, though the sender may have been misinformed.[63] After the 1717 Whig schism, the Kit-Cat Club reverted to a focus on literary patronage under Newcastle's tutelage, but it is unlikely, given the personal heat of debates in the Commons, that members of the opposition faction, like Walpole, Pulteney and Devonshire, continued to attend. At the time of the King's reconciliation with the Prince's Party there must have been some hope of Kit-Cat reunification, but Tonson's withdrawal to Herefordshire ended such hopes.

Nonetheless, in 1725, when Vanbrugh, Cobham and Carlisle stayed together at Stowe for the summer, Vanbrugh told Tonson:

> [O]ur former Kit-Cat days were remembered with pleasure. We were one night reckoning who was left, and both Lord Carlisle & Cobham expressed a great desire of having one meeting next Winter, if you come to Town, Not as a Club, but old Friends that have been of a Club, and the best Club that ever met.[64]

The last line suggests Tonson had previously rejected Vanbrugh's entreaties to revive the Club per se, but Tonson seems to have responded positively on this occasion and suggested various dates. In October 1725, Vanbrugh wrote again from Greenwich, to say he had shown Tonson's letter to Newcastle:

> [H]e will cheerfully accept of the Club's Invitation, to dine with them one day, or one hundred, if so God pleases. I'm sorry a meeting could not be on the day and at the Place you mention; both I am sure would be highly agreeable to the Members of it. But they will not so soon be within Call: when they are, we'll try to find some other day of Happy Remembrance.[65]

It has been said the surviving Kit-Cats reunited sometime in November 1725, but it is unclear on what primary evidence (other than the above letters) this assertion may be based.[66] A letter in the spidery hand of Tonson's old age refers to a party for Newcastle, which may relate to the party Tonson threw Newcastle in 1720 but more likely points to a later event after Tonson was in Herefordshire for some time, given Tonson's statement that, 'Empowered by your Grace's Bounty', he would 'Launch out into the Oceans of Port, Claret and Champagne in which voyages I have for some years been a stranger'.[67] On another occasion, Newcastle invited Tonson to Claremont: 'Dear Jacob, you must not refuse me your good Company. Drink Water or Wine, ride or go in the Coach, Read or Laugh at Anything in the World.'[68]

Tonson and Congreve certainly met once more to take the waters in Bath in the late spring of 1728. Tonson was 72, and said he had no reason to complain of his health, especially compared to 58-year-old Congreve, who, lame and blind, required almost constant attention from his caregiver-lover Henrietta (Duchess of Marlborough since her father's death in 1722). When the publisher and author parted, they must have known they were saying their final goodbyes.

Across the expanses of the English countryside, the former Kit-Cats continued to exchange gifts of food and drink as tokens of friendship. Tonson instructed Jacob Junior to send the best batch of Barn Elms cider up to Cobham at Stowe; another year Tonson sent cider to the Vanbrughs at Greenwich, and Tonson and Newcastle exchanged gifts of cider and perry well into the 1730s. Love of food continued to unite these men: Tonson's letters show him concerned to train his Hereford servants how to butcher an ox and mutton 'the London way',[69] while a visitor to The Hazels described Tonson as an old man still excited over a breast of veal or 'a Sweetbread God damn a foot Square'.[70]

Tonson also remained in contact with Pope, the two agreeing that the 'most honest-hearted' Kit-Cat authors were Congreve, Garth and Vanbrugh.[71] When Pope and Swift together published a miscellany in 1727, their prefatory remarks repented their attacks on only two Whigs: Vanbrugh and Addison. '[W]e wish our Raillery, though ever so tender, or Resentment, though ever so just, had not been indulged.'[72] It was one of the rare occasions where, as Whigs and Kit-Cat authors, Vanbrugh and Addison were bracketed together.

In 1725, Vanbrugh took Carlisle's daughters to see the completed Blenheim Palace – probably as much to satisfy his own curiosity as theirs – and faced the humiliation of being locked out of the grounds by that 'BBBB Old B— the Duchess of Marlborough'.[73] Vanbrugh told Tonson that the old Dowager Duchess was still, out of sheer malice, trying to destroy him through legal disputes over Blenheim's costs, so as 'to throw me into an English Bastille to finish my days, as I begun them in a French one'.[74] The 1725 tour party was therefore reduced to peeking over a fence to catch a distant glimpse of Vanbrugh's remarkable creation.

Finally, in August 1725, thanks to his Kit-Cat connection to Walpole (with whom the Dowager Duchess was having her own political feud), Vanbrugh was paid from the Treasury for his work on Blenheim. This £1,700 was gained, as he put it, 'in Spite of the Hussy's teeth',[75] and meant Vanbrugh's family had something to live on when the architect died less than a year later, on 26 March 1726, from a 'quinsy in his throat'[76] – possibly severe tonsillitis. The modest size of his estate (his property consisting mainly of the Greenwich house and the cellars under the Haymarket theatre) shows Vanbrugh's life story to have been that of a writer's and artist's struggle, even amid fame and patronage, to escape endless financial anxiety.

Steele's arguments with Newcastle, and Vanbrugh's professional rivalry with a friend of Steele's, the architect William Benson, led to an estrangement between Steele and Vanbrugh at the end of their lives. Steele's reinstatement at Drury Lane in 1721 energized him into writing a new play, *The Conscious Lovers*, which proved the surprise hit of 1722–3. Literary historians view this sentimental work as Steele finally succeeding in the ambition, held since the Collier culture wars of the 1690s, to write a morally upright, Christian comedy. But Steele's last surviving son, 11-year-old Eugene, died in 1723, dragging Steele's spirits low again. He became 'paralytic', which suggests another stroke,[77] and when Vanbrugh saw him looking 'in a declining way' one day at Walpole's house, Vanbrugh immediately wrote to Newcastle, hoping to be awarded the Drury Lane patent should Steele die.[78] With their friendship so cold, it is unlikely Steele shed tears when he heard of Vanbrugh's death.

In 1724, Steele retired to one of his late wife's properties at Ty-Gwyn in Llangunnor, Wales. There Steele lived in a modest farmhouse, nursed by his two young daughters, occasionally sending out place-hunting letters to Walpole and other London friends on behalf of local friends or distant relatives, but not receiving, it seems, any of the casks of cider or other compliments that circulated so readily between Tonson, Cobham, Newcastle, Vanbrugh and Congreve. When Steele died, aged 57, on 1 September 1729, he was interred in a local church in Carmarthen. There was no outpouring of literary elegies as at Addison's death, no stone monument in Westminster Abbey, and no devoted literary follower to edit a luxurious collection of his complete works. Happily, however, Steele succeeded in his greatest ambition at the last minute: paying off his major debts and providing a decent inheritance for his children. His will even included £100 (£12,000 today) for his illegitimate daughter, now Mrs Eliza Aynston.

It is unknown whether Steele, in his paralysis and Welsh seclusion, was informed of Congreve's death seven months earlier. Congreve had continued to reside primarily in London, so he could see Henrietta. It was partly his refusal to abandon London that ensured the world fully felt his loss.

Though he had written only lyric poetry and libretti since he was 30, Congreve's reputation as a literary genius remained undimmed. This was thanks partly to his friendships with the Scriblerians, who were coming into their own in terms of literary output during the 1720s. Pope dedicated the 1720 edition of his *Iliad* to Congreve – not a pointed refusal to dedicate his work to a nobleman, as some have argued, but a sincere tribute to the Kit-Cat who, after 1709, had effectively patronized Pope with the invaluable gifts of introductions and who shared Pope's love of Greek poetry.

In September 1722, Pope complained to John Gay that Congreve needed reminding there were 'more Men and Women in the Universe' than Gay and Henrietta.[79] If Congreve suddenly became especially antisocial it must have been partly due to his health, which he was nursing in Bath, but also because he knew Henrietta had fallen pregnant with his child. When the baby, Mary, was born the following year, Congreve was 51 and Henrietta 42. Lady Mary Wortley Montagu gossiped that Henrietta was as ashamed of her 'big belly' as an unwed milkmaid.[80]

Injuries from a coach crash eventually killed Congreve. He was nursed after the crash by Henrietta – a talent, like her pride and temper, inherited from her mother Sarah – but, on 19 January 1729, Congreve died at home at Surrey Street. His corpse was taken to lie in state in the Jerusalem Chamber of Westminster Abbey, and was carried to its burial 'with great decency and solemnity'[81] by six pall-bearers, three of whom (Godolphin, Cobham and Compton) were former Kit-Cats. Henrietta, in the midst of almost deranged grief, arranged the funeral and invited these men, including her own husband, to carry her lover's casket.[82]

About a week after Congreve's funeral, Tonson urged his nephew to reissue Congreve's collected works to capitalize on the publicity surrounding his death: 'Let a man's worth be never so great, after Death it gets strangely out of the minds of his Surviving Acquaintance,' Tonson told him. This instruction reflected the old man's nose for a profit, but also a genuine concern that the version of his works edited by Congreve himself with a 'great deal of care', and copyrighted by the Tonsons, should hit the shelves before someone else produced an inferior, pirated edition.[83]

Congreve's will left almost everything to Henrietta, including his library, which Tonson, Congreve's primary bookseller since the early 1690s, advised his nephew to buy from her. The will also appointed Henrietta's husband Francis as Congreve's sole executor 'in Trust for his said Wife'.[84] Contemporaries and future generations marvelled that Congreve left his estate to a woman already so wealthy, but the explanation was their infant daughter, Mary. It was a way for Congreve to transmit his property to his only child, and Henrietta honoured this wish by buying a diamond necklace and earrings, with the initials 'W.C.' engraved on the back of each diamond,[85] worth precisely the value of what Congreve left to her (£5,300 for the necklace and £2,000 for the earrings). She then left the necklace to Mary in her own will.[86] Francis Godolphin did not interfere with this plan, which must have been discussed between the three of them before Congreve died, and Francis treated Mary as his own child, which allowed her to make a respectable marriage to the Duke of Leeds.

Edmund Curll published Congreve's will the following year, to titillate the public not only with the playwright's generosity to his titled mistress but also with details such as Congreve's legacy of £200 to his previous love, Bracey. Mrs Bracegirdle lived long enough to see the start of David Garrick's career on the stage, but never married or found any other male companion after Congreve. In the same volume, Curll (under the pseudonym Charles Wilson) also published the first Kit-Cat biography: *Memoirs of the Life, Writings and Amours of William Congreve Esq* . . . (1730). News of the death brought Pope low for some time afterwards, just when he should have been enjoying the fame and fortune brought to him by publication of *The Dunciad*: 'Every year carries away something dear with it, till we outlive all tenderness,' he mourned.[87]

Four years later, in the unseasonably snowy spring of 1733, the Archdeacon of Salop, Dr Samuel Croxall, travelled into neighbouring Herefordshire to visit Tonson at The Hazels. Croxall had a thriving ecclesiastical career – within five years he would be Chancellor of Hereford – but he had once entertained ambitions to be counted among the London literati. In 1717, Garth and Tonson recruited Croxall to translate sections of Ovid's *Metamorphoses*, through which he may have met a number of Kit-Cats who were his fellow contributors. Croxall's most famous publication, however, was a children's book: a translation of *The Fables of Aesop and Others* (1722), which taught its young readers a distinctively Whig version of the fables.

Croxall was coming to see Tonson with a proposal: he wished to write the first history of the Kit-Cat Club. When Croxall arrived, 77-year-old Tonson gave him a tour of his house including a room he called his 'museum' – a book-lined study with a roaring fire, beside which he sat and read. Tonson's eyesight had held out, but his hearing was gone, worsened on this particular occasion by a head cold. Tonson forced his guest to drink homemade sack, and they sat to talk not in any grand salon but in the kitchen, eating bread and sturgeon. Despite a healthy appetite, Tonson was 'a good deal emaciated'.[88] Pope had seen him two years earlier, and described Tonson as having become a shabby, smelly old man, wearing a thin cotton cap and a 'poor old unwadded gown', whose deafness made conversation hard going. Yet

Tonson's mind was as sharp as ever: 'so full of matter, secret history, and wit and spirit, at almost fourscore'.[89]

Croxall laid the idea before Tonson, and later reported to Jacob Junior (who would obviously be the book's publisher and may even have been the proposal's instigator):

> Though I roared like a Bull, I could hardly make him comprehend me; but when he did, he came into it at once, said nobody could tell better what to say of them than himself, for, to tell me the truth, he had been drunk with every one of them. He designs to be very exact in doing it, & will take some time for it.[90]

When Croxall asked Tonson for some 'characters' of the members to be sketched within a week, however, Tonson said that was impossible as it would take much more time for such men to be described.

Whether Tonson delivered any notes to Croxall, or whether Croxall ever began work on a manuscript, is unknown. A mostly blank, handmade notebook among Tonson's papers called 'Account of the Kitt-Catt Club' seems to have been started after Tonson's death and appears to be in Croxall's hand.[91] Perhaps something more valuable may turn up one day, amid ecclesiastical papers in Hereford or in somebody's attic, and answer the remaining Kit-Cat mysteries.

Tonson, born before any of the Kit-Cat authors, died after them all, aged 80, on 17 March 1736. His beloved nephew and heir, Jacob Junior, predeceased him by four months, probably precipitating Tonson's own death. Tonson's body was carried from Herefordshire to his great-nephew's house in the Strand, and buried on 1 April at the church of St Mary Le Strand, in the centre of the London neighbourhood where his business and Club had thrived for decades. No solemn elegies were written for the publisher, though an anonymous wit penned the epitaph:

> Death blotted out his line of life
> And he who many a scribbling elf
> Abridged, is now abridged himself.[92]

The Gentleman's Magazine carried a tiny notice, stating Tonson was 'formerly secretary to the Kit-Kat Club worth 4,000£ per annum'.[93] This was almost certainly a gross underestimate, though Tonson had already made most of his money over to his nephew and his nephew's heirs (Jacob Junior's will showed him to have been worth at least £100,000, or around £12.4 million today).[94] It has been estimated Tonson was worth at least £80,000 when he died, and the publisher's dying words were maliciously reported to have been that he regretted not making twice as much.[95]

For the next 200 years, literary historians did Tonson a similar disservice, underrating his intellect, influence and social status until he was virtually thrown back among the Grub Street publishers from whom he had consistently worked to distinguish himself. Tonson was blamed for a rash of inaccurate and scurrilous biographies that appeared in the eighteenth century, receiving the tag of 'body-snatcher'[96] that may be more fairly applied to his nemesis Curll. If anything, considering the number of great men with whom Tonson was intimate, the remarkable thing is how discreet he always remained. That Tonson never published his memoirs, or gave Croxall his history of the Kit-Cat Club, may be a loss for us, but it is also one of the reasons his authors and the Club's noble members trusted him. Tonson took to his grave the bulk of their indiscretions, committed after several bottles of wine in the hours before the dawn of a Friday morning. To posterity, instead of gossip, Tonson left an estimated 750–850 publications.

XX
LATER CLUBS AND KIT-CATS

> [W]e are of all nations the most forward to run into clubs, parties and societies.
>
> DAVID FORDYCE, *Dialogues Concerning Education* (1745)

THE KIT-CAT CLUB popularized the idea that private individuals could form their own institutions and remake their own society. The Whig idea that Englishness meant not being subject to state control of one's private life or leisure – an idea less widely accepted on the Continent – was established in practice through the proliferation of clubs that did not overtly threaten state institutions but existed alongside them. In the seventeenth century, the word 'club' carried violent, conspiratorial connotations; post-Kit-Cat, despite the Tory satirists' best efforts, it conjured something much more respectable, constructive, high-cultured and high-minded.

The Kit-Cat Club, and its fictional offspring the Spectator Club, produced a spate of contemporary and subsequent imitators and started a long-running craze for gentlemen's clubs. During the eighteenth century there were some 12,000 town-based clubs in England, another 3,000 in Scotland and some 750 in Wales. By the

1730s, the trend had spread to the American colonies. An estimated 20,000 London gentlemen were meeting in some form of club every evening by the middle of the century, and by the century's end there were also numerous female and mixed-sex 'societies'. Foreign visitors regularly remarked on the fact that what we now call 'civil society' flourished in Britain at this time when there was a degree of economic prosperity, social mobility and freedom of the press, all within the framework of a limited monarchy. This was not merely English chauvinistic pride: the French and central European governments were demonstrably more repressive of independent clubs and societies throughout the century, just as they censored their presses more rigorously. The only exception, perhaps, was the way the Austrian Emperor allowed Viennese coffee houses to flourish unchecked during the same period. French salons certainly rivalled British clubs as settings for intellectual debate, but they remained politically self-censoring because government informers infiltrated them on a scale without parallel in England.

The Kit-Cat Club's less sober face also had imitators. Its toasting rituals were revived most precisely by a club called 'The World', whose aristocratic members, including the 4th Earl of Chesterfield, met at the King's Head (formerly Queen's Head), Pall Mall, in the mid-eighteenth century. The World's members engraved their toasting glasses with diamonds, just like the Kit-Cats who had met at the same tavern before them. François de la Rochefoucauld remarked on it being a particularly English habit to end a dinner with several hours of toasting, after which the conversation became, he noted, alarmingly free.

The Union of the English Freemasons Grand Lodge was inaugurated at a tavern near St Paul's in 1717, and it was no coincidence that several younger Kit-Cats joined the Freemasons after the Kit-Cat Club's demise. The Freemasons may be viewed as the longest-lived of eighteenth-century London clubs. The earliest members were all men of property, loyal to the Hanoverian Crown, but political homogeneity was far less central than at the Kit-Cat Club. There were lodges that located themselves in opposition to one another on either side of the 1717–20 Whig schism, for example, with the Prince of

Wales himself initiated into one for the Prince's Party. Like the Kit-Cat Club, the Freemasons were committed to 'meeting upon the level' as brothers, and to mutual material support and string-pulling. And just as the Kit-Cat had a distinctive cultural agenda, so the Masonic lodges supported a cultural revival in Britain after 1717. In London, the Fountain tavern on the Strand, former Kit-Cat venue, was used for meetings of the Royal Alpha Lodge of Freemasons. But Freemasonry was not confined to a cosmopolitan London elite; by 1725 there were fifty-two lodges throughout Britain, many outside large towns. Masonic mythology and ritual were much more about a return to the rural idyll of the medieval artisan than the urbane and determinedly lax habits of the Kit-Cat Club. This may explain why Freemasonry spread almost as rapidly in France as in England.

John, Duke of Montagu, served as a Grand Master in 1721–2, and Newcastle and Walpole later joined the Freemasons, with an occasional lodge convening at Walpole's Norfolk home. There is substantial circumstantial evidence that Steele became a Freemason late in life, making his portrait by Thornhill (a Freemason) and engraved by John Faber Junior (also a Freemason) as much a 'club portrait' as his Kit-Cat portrait by Kneller. Though the pyramid monuments built at Stowe and Castle Howard were most likely allusions to the Roman mausoleum of Caius Cestius, they may also have referenced Masonic symbolism.

The Temple Bar area, where Somers and Tonson first drank together after 1688, remained the centre of London's clubland until the late eighteenth century, when clubs moved west to St James's and Pall Mall. Many St James's clubs, such as White's, focused more on gambling, a vice not derived from the Kit-Cat Club. Between 1720 and 1722, immediately after the South Sea bubble, illegal gaming houses in Covent Garden increased tenfold. Londoners complained cards were destroying the art of conversation, though each generation tended to make this complaint afresh. The Covent Garden literati's chattering in fact continued undiminished at the Bedford Coffee House throughout the 1720s, much as it had flourished at Will's before the Kit-Cat Club's foundation.

Certain clubs were founded with an emphasis on sexual and moral decadence in the 1720s. Most notable was the 'Hell-Fire Club', established by Wharton's wayward son Philip. Philip, who rejected everything his late father stood for by ending his life an avowed Jacobite and Roman Catholic, amplified the Kit-Cats' pornographic and irreligious side at the Hell-Fire Club. Its more notorious namesake started meeting in the early 1750s, mostly at West Wycombe and Medmenham Abbey, where Sir Francis Dashwood, John Wilkes and others attended pseudo-Franciscan meetings of 'The Order' or 'Brotherhood' and allegedly participated in orgiastic, satanic rituals.

Dashwood earlier founded the 'Dilettanti Society' in 1734, a club for the appreciation of ancient Greek art, comprising gentlemen home from their Grand Tours and determined to purify British taste along neoclassical lines. Like the 'Virtuosi of St Luke', a London artists' club formed after 1714, which hosted an annual members' feast, or the 'Artists' Club' at the Bull's Head tavern to which Hogarth belonged, the Dilettanti had narrow objectives compared to the multidisciplinary Kit-Cats. Indeed, after the Kit-Cat Club, there was generally a return to clubs specializing in a single profession or interest. There were also numerous Whig clubs involved in local politics of the 1720s and 1730s, like that of Sir Thomas Samwell at Upton House near Coventry, of which Philip Mercier painted a lively group portrait, but none that quite had the nationwide reach of the Kit-Cat and Hanover Clubs, or which tried to combine politics with cultural reform in the same extraordinary way.

Dr Johnson established the most self-conscious imitation of the Kit-Cat Club as cultural powerhouse. Johnson, like Tonson, came from a bookseller-stationer family and books comforted him through early, graceless years of physical debility. In 1764, Johnson and the painter Sir Joshua Reynolds founded 'The Club' at the Turk's Head tavern on Gerrard Street. Its nine founders were each concerned with different aspects of the arts in Britain, systematically exceeding the Kit-Cat Club's ambitions by including not only writers and politicians but also artists, actors, scientists and other scholars. The Club grew to about the same size as the Kit-Cat (thirty-five members by 1791), but, unlike its prototype, The Club conferred membership based on talent and charm rather than political allegiance, including both Whigs and Tories. It also contained far fewer aristocratic members – only a minority of The Club's members were even landowners. Johnson and his friends wanted to direct British arts by sheer force of intellectual influence, rather than by subsidy, patronage or commissioned propaganda. Edmund Malone, who had an antiquarian interest in the Kit-Cat Club, became a member – evidence, beyond Johnson's own scholarly interest in the individual Kit-Cat authors, that the similarities between Tonson's and Johnson's clubs were more than mere coincidence.

No political club that succeeded the Kit-Cat managed to replicate its peculiar blend of progressive and conservative elements. On the one hand, the later eighteenth century saw a resurgence of radical clubs, such as the freethinking 'Robin Hood Society' (which met after 1747 in a Temple Bar tavern, under the chairmanship of a baker named Caleb Jeacocke – a cross, it would seem, between Christopher Cat, Jacob Tonson and the 1650s republican James Harrington), or the 'Hampden Clubs' founded in the 1810s (out of which demands for universal male suffrage emerged). Political dialogue widened to the newly educated classes; societies across the country held lively debates during the 1770s on *Spectator*-like subjects, and around 800 book clubs were meeting nationwide by the 1820s. Even as *The Spectator* had been closing in 1712, its readers had written in to say that they would keep its spirit, and the new love of reading and debate it had given to them, alive: '[T]here are a number of us who have begun your Works afresh, and meet two Nights in the Week in order to give you a Rehearing . . . This we conceive to be a more useful Institution than any other Club.'[1]

At the other political and social extreme, the Regency and Victorian periods were the heyday of the St James's gentlemen's clubs, which accepted almost exclusively upper-class members and were bastions of class privilege, as expressed by the construction of grandiose, public-looking buildings for member-only use. Today their great silent rooms are the sedate descendants of the coffee house gambling clubs, whose names several still bear, rather than the more egalitarian and socially activist Kit-Cat Club.

Of the nineteenth-century clubs, the Garrick, at its foundation in

1831, perhaps most resembled the Kit-Cat Club, as it was a venue where 'actors and men of refinement and education might meet on equal terms' so that 'easy intercourse was to be promoted between artists and patrons'.[2] Tonson, Dorset and Somers would have recognized these goals, and indeed the Garrick's founders (twenty-four peers and a selection of writers, actors, musicians and publishers) replicated the Kit-Cat's balance of titled wealth and untitled talent.

Tonson's self-interest in founding the Kit-Cat as a perk for his authors and patrons, and as an informal editorial board for his firm, profoundly changed British publishers' social confidence and professional status. John Nichols, a nostalgic Kit-Cat chronicler, enjoyed the hospitality of the publishing brothers Charles and Edward Dilly, whose famous literary dinners were attended by Boswell, Johnson, Goldsmith and Joseph Priestley. In the 1810s, the drawing-room society of the publisher John Murray – attended by, among others, de Staël, Disraeli, Canning, Scott, Southey and Byron – consciously mirrored Tonson's ambition to play cultural broker. A copy of Tonson's Kit-Cat portrait graced Murray's offices in Albemarle Street.

Another notable Kit-Cat literary heir was a club of the same name founded at Yale University at the beginning of the twentieth century for 'men who have shown literary ability and interest in literary subjects'. Just as Vanbrugh's architecture remains, ironically, the most famous product of the first Kit-Cat Club's literary membership, so the most famous member of the Yale Kit-Cat Club was Robert Moses, its President in 1909 who later became the master builder of twentieth-century New York.[3]

A legitimate analogy can also be drawn between the Kit-Cat Club and the businesslike clubs for media types founded in central London since the 1980s, such as the Groucho Club, Soho House or Adam Street. The Kit-Cat Club has more in common with these ventures than with the Pall Mall institutions or the louche, early twentieth-century literary coteries of Bloomsbury and Fitzrovia. The Kit-Cats were not simply complacent, snobbish oligarchs, as they are sometimes portrayed, nor were they the anti-Establishment aesthetes, bohemians and 'angry young men' who make up London's more recent literary mythology. They were worldlier – and busier – than both.

There are remarkably few physical memorials to the Kit-Cat Club. Most of its tavern venues, like the Cat and Fiddle on Gray's Inn Lane or the Fountain on the Strand, no longer exist. Victorian antiquarians John Timbs and James Caulfield were loath to believe that such an aristocratic club could have started in Christopher Cat's pie-shop. While to us the humble origin may add charm, to these Victorians it was an embarrassment, and their efforts to gloss over the Christopher Cat connection injected various confusions into the Kit-Cat Club's geographical chronology.

There is no blue plaque or memorial to the Club at Barn Elms. When Jacob Junior died in 1735, his will specified that Kneller's Kit-Cat portraits should remain at Barn Elms, where he had 'lately at some Expence' built a special gallery for them.[4] This may have been the first instance in Britain of a gallery being purpose-built to display a single exhibition, united by subject and artist. After Tonson's death, the paintings were bequeathed to Jacob Junior's children. One of their descendants built another gallery for the paintings at Bayfordbury House in Hampshire, to which they were moved around 1812, after having been housed at a series of locations in Kent, Berkshire and Herefordshire. There was a sale in 1945, when Tonson's descendants vacated Bayfordbury, at which point those Tonson manuscripts not already dispersed or pulped went to the National Portrait Gallery archives and the Folger Shakespeare Library in Washington, DC.

The set of Kneller portraits remains the Club's single greatest monument. It was acquired by the National Arts Collection Fund at the Bayfordbury sale, and passed to the National Portrait Gallery at a time, post-Second World War, when the country was feeling particularly patriotic and the 'Whig interpretation of history' was in full swing. G. M. Trevelyan was closely involved in the purchase, assuring the National Portrait Gallery's Director they were worth every penny and writing in *The Times* to educate the public about why the Kit-Cats should be honoured as modern Britain's founding fathers – the Kneller series being their Mount Rushmore. In the catalogue accompanying the portraits' first public exhibition, the war against Louis XIV was implicitly compared with the defeat of Hitler. The catalogue's author concluded that the Kit-Cat Club 'ensured the safety of the Revolution Settlement and laid the foundations of eighteenth century England'.[5]

'Count' Johann Jacob Heidegger, who assumed the management of the Kit-Cats' Haymarket theatre, also assumed the lease at Barn Elms directly from the Tonsons and used it as his summer residence until 1750. In the nineteenth century, the radical writer and agriculturalist William Cobbett lived at the Barn Elms manor house, experimenting with various farming ideas in its gardens. Tonson's house there, despite its Vanbrugh interiors, was not preserved. In 1816, Sir Richard Phillips visited as a 'reverential pilgrim' and discovered Jacob Junior's 1730s Kit-Cat gallery in a deplorable state, having been used as a laundry, then damaged by fire and dry-rot, though '[t]he names of the members were still visible on the walls, written in chalk as they had been marked for the guidance of the man who hung up the pictures, and the marks made by the pictures were still to be seen'.[6] An article in *The Mirror* of 1832 described the same room as a separate building at the end of the old manor house's garden, with the clubroom or gallery upstairs, containing red wall hangings covered in cobwebs, holes in the floor and a swallow's nest in the ceiling.

From 1884, the whole Barn Elms property was leased to an exclusive sporting club named the Ranelagh Club. This club, instituted to supply 'an agreeable riverside resort to Gentlemen desirous of dining out of London, participating in Polo, Lawn Tennis, Pigeon Shooting, Pony Racing, etc, and for providing various outdoor entertainments during the season', was uniquely important to British social life during the 1890s and 1900s. Among the several hundred members listed in 1889, at least a handful (including the Marquess of Hartington, the Duke of Marlborough and Lord Montagu) were directly descended from the Kit-Cats, showing how little British society had altered in 200 years.

The Ranelagh Club restored the Kit-Cat gallery room for use by its members. A black and white photograph shows the entrance to 'the kit-cat room', though the image helps little in imagining the original. Thanks to the Ranelagh Club's Secretary, Mr C. J. Barrett, author of *The History of Barn Elms and the Kit-Cat Club* (1889), the sporting club also took an active interest in the site's eighteenth-century tenants, and did much to keep the Kit-Cat Club's memory alive. The winter gardens were decorated with plaster replicas of Tonson and Kneller, a picture of Tonson hung in the central stairwell, and copies of Faber's engravings adorned the clubhouse walls. The Ranelagh Club took as its insignia an ersatz coat of arms based on the emblematic frontispiece Faber added to the Kit-Cat engravings in 1735.[7] This coat of arms saying 'Kit-Cat Club, 1703' (the date Tonson leased the house at Barnes) was printed on the Ranelagh Club's menus and event programmes, and moulded on the medals, silver bowls and drinking vessels awarded at sporting competitions. It was also woven into the Club's upholstery and flags.

The Ranelagh Club closed in 1939. From June 1940 until the end of the Second World War, the Free French Army used the Barn Elms manor house as its headquarters. The property was then left unoccupied, and burned down in the 1950s. Today the bulldozed ruins are overgrown, though traces of the manor house's shape are apparent in a fenced-off wooded area beside a modest community sports club. The tree-lined drive that once connected the manor to the Thames landing survives, and within the overgrown wood one just can discern the long-dead stumps of some of the giant elms Tonson and his friends once admired.

The fortunes of the Kit-Cat's theatre on the Haymarket improved under Heidegger's management, partly thanks to his masquerade balls and Handel's operas produced there, and partly because the West End was rising around it. Another theatre, called the New Theatre, was built on the same street in 1720, and the next year the Piccadilly turnpike was moved from the end of Berkeley Street to Hyde Park Corner to mark the town's westward expansion. Vanbrugh's original building in the Haymarket burnt down in 1789; Her Majesty's Theatre now stands on the site.

The Roaring Twenties saw the Kit-Cat name's return to the Haymarket, with the opening of a nightclub called The Kit-Cat Club in 1925. Originally a private members' club, it closed following a police raid and reopened as a public restaurant and jazz cabaret in October 1927. Many early American bandleaders played with the house Kit-Cat Band, the most famous being Armand 'Al' Starita. Starita and the Kit-Cat Band (also known, after its sponsor, as Jack Hylton's Kit-Cat Band) produced some of the finest British dance records of the late 1920s. The club remained open until the Blitz.

The most famous twentieth-century 'Kit-Kat Club' is that in the 1966 stage musical *Cabaret* made into a 1972 movie starring Liza Minnelli as American singer Sally Bowles, who lives a bohemian life in 1930s Berlin and falls in love with bisexual Brian. This musical film, directed and choreographed by Bob Fosse, has become a classic, shaping most people's idea of Weimar decadence. In fact, the cabaret club in Christopher Isherwood's *Goodbye to Berlin*, and in the 1950s stage play and movie *I Am a Camera*, on which the later musical and film of *Cabaret* were based, was never called the Kit-Kat Club;[8] the 'Kit-Kat' name was instead probably borrowed for *Cabaret* from the Haymarket dance club described above.

Today in Berlin, another 'Kit-Kat Club' is run by a group of radical sexual liberationists who encourage full nakedness and performance of sexual acts on the nightclub's dance-floor. Worldwide, the 1972 movie has also spawned hundreds of strip joints and bars using the 'Kit-Cat'/'Kit-Kat' name. Sexual behaviour way beyond the Tory satirists' worst slanders against Wharton or Stanhope now occurs in Kit-Cat Clubs from Manila to Toronto.

The Kit-Cat Club was therefore a peculiar choice of name for an exclusive networking society, run by and for influential women in London, founded by Robert Maxwell's daughter Ghislaine and her friends at the end of the 1980s. Its current chair, Alice Sherwood, selects and invites speakers on a wide range of subjects, regardless of gender, to address the all-female members, and the men (often authors or journalists) are toasted from time to time – a nice inversion of the original Kit-Cat Club's election of female beauties as toasts. In other ways too, the original and current clubs have much in common: facilitating elite networking for professional gain in an atmosphere of convivial socializing, over drinks.

Of course, the main reason for the Kit-Cat name's current

familiarity worldwide is the chocolate bar. Rowntree first launched the 'biscuit' in 1935 under the uninspiring name Chocolate Crisp. In 1937, it was relaunched as the 'KitKat Chocolate Crisp', following a suggestion by a young man named Nigel Balchin who was subsidizing his efforts to become a writer through a day-job in the Rowntree factory's marketing department in York. As the original Kit-Cat Club started with the aim of helping writers pay their bills, it is a nice irony that its name was used, through this unlikely reincarnation, to do so again.

Rowntree first registered the name in 1911, when the eighteenth-century Club was still widely known in Britain and carried social cachet. When the Chocolate Crisp needed rechristening, the name may have caught Balchin's eye because it had gained, by then, fashionable associations with the Haymarket dance club, or perhaps because Balchin, being a literary man, knew something of the original club and its connections with Yorkshire via Castle Howard. Balchin became an acclaimed novelist in the 1950s.

The slogan 'Give yourself a break at teatime' was first used to market KitKats (as they quickly became known) in 1939,[9] and then as 'Have a Break, Have a KitKat' in a 1957 television advertisement. Though it would be pleasing to think there was some intention to associate the KitKat name with leisured dining, thus relating back to the original Kit-Cat Club, early posters with the slogan show a bricklayer having a KitKat with his cuppa.

The product rose steadily in popularity after the Second World War, and its brand was a key asset when the Swiss food giant Nestlé acquired Rowntree in 1988. Today, twenty-two factories around the world produce KitKats in various sizes and flavours, and in Britain, forty-seven KitKats are reportedly eaten every second. In Japan, the bars are particularly popular around school exam time, because the name sounds similar to an expression for 'good luck' in Japanese. Christopher Cat, 1690s pastry chef, would surely be proud to know his name remains attached to one of the most widely enjoyed food treats of the twenty-first century.

EPILOGUE
LEGACIES

We are always doing, says he, something for Posterity, but I would fain see Posterity do something for us.

JOSEPH ADDISON, *The Spectator* no. 583, 20 August 1714[1]

THE BREADTH OF the Kit-Cat Club's ambition is without analogy. Its members took strikingly similar approaches to criticizing and then trying to reform literature, music, architecture, gardening, interior design, portraiture, cookery, manners, parliamentary politics and philosophy. In each art form, we can now see they sought to develop hybrid, anglicized styles that combined neoclassicism with more romantic elements drawn from England's heroic past. The Club's patronage in pursuit of this goal contributed significantly to the privatization of British culture, and, in its efforts to create new readers, new audiences and new consumers, the Club established a model for elite management of British culture that essentially remains intact to this day.

The most important cultural legacies belong to Addison, Steele, Congreve, Vanbrugh and Tonson. Being 'extremely jealous of his reputation',[2] Addison was anxious how he would be presented by biographers, who he said watched for a great man's death 'like so many undertakers, on purpose to make a penny of him'.[3] His concern was not misplaced. A succession of biographers and critics has shaped posterity's opinion of the Kit-Cat Club's various literary members, and some have fared better than others.

The earliest biographies were Edmund Curll's third-person *Memoirs*, which appeared almost immediately after the deaths of Addison and Congreve.[4] Alexander Pope was another contemporary who did much to shape posterity's opinion of Addison and Steele, both through his sharp portrait of Addison in *Epistle to Dr Arbuthnot* (1734) and the anecdotes he shared in old age with an Oxford don and oral historian, Joseph Spence. Spence also recorded anecdotes told by Lady Mary Wortley Montagu and Tonson, which, after their publication in 1820, kept alive the reputation of the Kit-Cat Club throughout the nineteenth century.

The Kit-Cat poets remained high in the literary pecking order during the eighteenth century. The Club patrons who dabbled in poetry were accorded full status as authors – notably Dorset, whose handful of verses was rated above those of his Restoration pal Rochester by everyone except Swift; both Pope and Byron stated that Dorset's poetry influenced their own. Halifax's poetry, written when he was plain Charles Montagu, and Wharton's political ballads, were considered patriotic classics. When Pope satirized several minor Buttonian writers in his *Dunciad* (1728), he could not have imagined that one day virtually all the Whig poets of the early eighteenth century, including his mentors Walsh and Garth, would be forgotten.

The book generally regarded as the first true English novel, *Robinson Crusoe*, was published in 1719, approximately a year after the Kit-Cat Club ceased to meet. Defoe, the self-proclaimed outsider of Whig literature, had produced a masterpiece about isolation, intended to be read by men and women in domestic solitude, and therefore marking a dramatic shift from the Kit-Cat idea of literature as something recited aloud before a table of inebriated friends. Addison's and Steele's periodicals had helped pave the way for this development in reading habits: *The Spectator*, if read through as a single work, featuring recurring fictional characters and flowing exchanges between readers and editors on various themes, has a novelistic quality. Yet the novel's advent made Kit-Cat attempts to dictate the future of English literature appear, with hindsight, misplaced: the Club's patrons never imagined that the next big thing would be fictional prose.

After Defoe, the second intruder into the Kit-Cats' literary garden was the young poet Richard Savage, whom Steele befriended towards the end of his life.[5] Savage dramatized himself as a martyred outcast, going far beyond Steele's occasional blurts of self-pity, and Savage's emphasis on self-expression signalled the beginnings of the Romantic literary revolution. His introspective image conflicted with the Kit-Cat view of writing as primarily communication with an audience – a social gesture among friends, or to a larger audience whom one flattered by addressing as though they were one's friends. Because the Kit-Cat Club also existed before the first great age of literary biography, its authors had few preconceptions about how they were supposed to live. Samuel Johnson's *Life of Savage* (1744) changed all that, prefiguring the Romantic depiction of poets as bardic visionaries and social rebels. Johnson's *Savage* put the glamour into starving in a garret, and within a generation struggling authors no longer clamoured to join the Establishment by charming a political patron, or gaining a Court place. Nobility of genius no longer needed the nobility's endorsement.

Johnson nonetheless admired Addison's prose as the supreme model of 'English style',[6] and Johnson's essay periodicals respectfully imitated Addison's. Johnson was less convinced about the literary merits of Addison's Kit-Cat friends, however. He disapproved of Stepney's overly loose classical translations, and Stepney's reputation as a poet has never recovered since. Johnson believed Garth lacked 'poetical ardour',[7] while Prior was 'never low, nor very often sublime'.[8] Though Prior remained, in 1781, a household name, Walsh was already 'known more by his familiarity with greater men, than by anything done or written by himself'.[9] Johnson largely dismissed Congreve, who died while Johnson was a student at Oxford, for writing in what seemed to him an affected style. He said Congreve's writing contained 'more bustle than sentiment', yet at the same time complimented some lines from Congreve's *Mourning Bride* as the 'most poetical' in 'the whole mass of English poetry'.[10]

Johnson and Oliver Goldsmith weighed in on the debate, started by Tickell and Steele, over the relative merits – as writers and men – of Addison and Steele. Johnson empathized with Addison and underestimated Steele's contribution to *The Tatler* and *The Spectator*, though he recognized Steele's personal charms. Goldsmith, perhaps informed by his friendship with Johnson, described Steele as 'self-victimised by a competitive intimacy with his friend [Addison]'.[11] The Addison–Steele relationship was then reimagined through the friendship of Wordsworth and Coleridge, which uncannily reincarnated and exaggerated it in several ways. Coleridge championed Steele over Addison, arguing Steele had a 'pure humanity springing from the gentleness, the kindness of his heart'.[12] Coleridge apparently read a 1787 edition of Steele's letters to Prue and felt a sense of kinship, at least with Steele's constant battles to keep his creditors at bay. William Hazlitt similarly preferred Steele to Addison, for writing with the 'stamp of nature'.[13]

Though Romantic poets often collaborated intensely, they (particularly Wordsworth in his 1800 Preface to *Lyrical Ballads*) also glossed over this fact to form the myth of the solo, inspired artist, 'Voyaging through strange seas of Thought, alone'.[14] This established a widespread prejudice against collaborations like those published by Tonson or sponsored by the Kit-Cat Club, and against writing as witty banter improved on paper, detached from deep personal feelings. The growing cult of the artist shrank the Kit-Cats' stature, though drawing heavily upon authors whom Tonson and Addison had popularized, like Milton and Shakespeare. When Byron wished to mock the affectation of a rich businessman and politician who hosted literary evenings in order to be thought a cultured patron, he used the Club's name:

> 'Kit-Cat', the famous conversationalist,
> Who in his commonplace book had a page,
> Prepared each morn for evenings.[15]

Nineteenth-century critics nonetheless assumed the place of Addison and Steele in the English canon was secure, partly because of endless reprintings of *The Spectator* and *The Tatler*, including cheap editions for schools, home libraries and export to the colonies. Throughout the 1800s, Steele's plays – *The Funeral*, *The Tender Husband* and *The Conscious Lovers* – were staples of English repertory, alongside Addison's *Cato*. The strait-laced Victorians carefully picked out their pieces of Kit-Cat literature, and their image of the Kit-Cat Club, to fit a tamed, tea-drinking, sentimental picture.[16]

Addison's first major biographer, Lucy Aikin, returned Addison's reputation to its pedestal in 1843, after the criticisms of the Romantics. Addison could do no wrong in Aikin's eyes, and she rejected evidence that he had ever been cold or ungenerous to Steele. If Addison's writing ever showed too much levity or moral weakness for her taste, she attributed the passage in question to Steele. Aikin was responsible for characterizing Addison as her own contemporary: 'the first Victorian'.[17]

In the 1850s, William Thackeray praised Steele's candour and contagious delight in the world ('He wrote so quickly and carelessly that he was forced to make the reader his confidant, and had not time to deceive him'), imagining Addison as able to maintain his 'charming archness' only because he was so remote from ordinary life. Steele, more schooled in self-doubt and failure, was easier for Thackeray to like, albeit with the same condescension as Addison exhibited throughout their friendship:

> Poor Dick Steele stumbled and got up again, and got into jail and out again, and sinned and repented; and loved and suffered . . . If Steele is not our friend he is nothing. He is by no means the most brilliant of wits nor the deepest of thinkers: but he is our friend: we love him.[18]

The Victorians, in other words, took each man according to his own self-caricature. Preaching the underrated joys of lolling half-awake in a soft bed, 'sensible only to the present Moment', it is no wonder Steele gained a reputation as the creative partnership's lazier half.[19] In fact, in the week in 1713 when Steele wrote that particular essay, he was not only producing *The Englishman*, but also working on several parliamentary committees and corresponding with the Hanover and Kit-Cat Clubs about financing an anti-Jacobite political pamphlet. Addison similarly became the victim of his own self-caricature, such that the Victorians were able to mistake him for a humourless, morally judgemental man.

These caricatures were, at least, more positive than the Victorians' snobbish view of Tonson as 'quite as ignorant as a barber's son could be expected to be'.[20] Tonson's depiction as an avaricious, parsimonious businessman was based largely on his short quarrels with Dryden and perpetuated by Dryden's biographers. In the only previous book about the Kit-Cat Club – an illustrated work in 1849 attributed to James Caulfield – Tonson is relegated to the end as if he were the least important member, not the Club's founder and chairman. Only in recent decades has Tonson's true legacy, as a much-loved self-made man and cultural arbiter, who started not only the Kit-Cat Club but also the later eighteenth-century boom in affordable, vernacular books, begun to be appreciated. He was, in a sense, the model for every modern media mogul.

Congreve and Vanbrugh likewise suffered relative neglect by the Victorians, who, like the 1690s' Collierites, deemed their plays immoral. This had started with the Romantic critics: William Hazlitt, for example, muttered in 1819 that Vanbrugh's morality 'sits very loose upon him. It is a little upon the turn.'[21] The Orange Comedians' legacies to the nineteenth century were therefore indirect – most notably through the popularity of Oscar Wilde's comedies of manners, which, like Congreve's plays, balanced above the harsh absurdity of life on a tightrope of wit, though Wilde never explicitly acknowledged this literary lineage. Edmund Gosse's 1888 biography admitted that the brilliance and artificiality of Congreve's nimble, staccato dialogue could produce 'fatigue', but objected to those, like Thackeray, who judged 1690s plays by the standards of nineteenth-century realism.[22] Gosse rightly understood that Congreve, standing on the threshold of the eighteenth century, had had a prophetic intuition of 'all its peculiar graces'.[23] Today Congreve remains the most highly regarded and widely known of the Kit-Cat authors, vindicating the Kit-Cat patrons' generous and protective treatment of his genius throughout his lifetime.

Steele's stock rose throughout the twentieth century, with Rae Blanchard's scholarly editions of Steele's writings beginning to appear in 1932 and sealing Steele's reputation as a serious figure of English literature. By 1925, however, Virginia Woolf noted that Addison and Steele were falling out of fashion, their works borrowed less and less often from her local library. Modernism was as unsupportive as Romanticism of the Kit-Cat authors' sociability and style of writing, yet Woolf concluded: 'When we have said all that we can say against them – that many are dull, others superficial, the allegories faded, the piety conventional, the morality trite – there still remains the fact that the essays of Addison are perfect essays.'[24]

Though out of fashion, Addison, Steele, Congreve, Vanbrugh, and the Kit-Cat Club itself, remained household names among educated Britons until the 1940s, representing an Establishment against which young critics could rebel. Cyril Connolly, as if imitating his hero Coleridge's bias, rejected Addison's 'Mandarin' way of writing in *Enemies of Promise* (1938),[25] and C. S. Lewis contrasted Addison unfavourably with Pope and Swift, because Addison dealt 'only with middle things'. Lewis agreed with Connolly on Addison's smug complacency, though with more nuance:

> Almost everything which my own generation ignorantly called Victorian seems to have been expressed by Addison. It is all there in *The Spectator* – the vague religious sensibility, the insistence upon what came later to be called Good Form, the playful condescension towards women, the untroubled belief in the beneficence of commerce, the comfortable sense of security which far from excluding, perhaps renders possible the romantic relish for wildness and solitude.[26]

Lewis nonetheless admitted Addison's essential character was still superior to those of Pope and Swift, with their 'hatred and bigotry and even silliness'.[27]

Peter Otway Smithers' scholarly biography of Addison in 1955 was a necessary corrective to class-conscious rhetoric and caricature. Smithers, like Addison, was a Magdalen man and MP, and, using the first full collection of Addison's letters published in 1941, he gave equal attention to Addison's political and literary careers. Smithers concluded 'no other Englishman has influenced the social development of his country more powerfully'.[28] This was certainly a plausible conclusion in 1950s Britain, when a very Kit-Cattish ideal of what it meant to behave like an English gentleman had once again risen to the fore.

From the 1960s on, the Kit-Cats came under fresh attack. Marxist critics saw Addison and Steele as cheerleading for the bourgeoisie and coopted by the aristocracy. Later, the rise of sociological approaches (gender and race studies, most notably) in English Literature departments did the Club no favours. No collection of the poetry of any single Whig writer from the post-1688 period has been published since 1937. Brian McCrea, in *Addison and Steele Are Dead* (1990), brilliantly analysed the various causes of post-Second World War 'benign neglect'[29] of Whig literature, in contrast to growing respect for the work of the Tory Scriblerians. McCrea attributed this primarily to Kit-Cat writing's lack of ambiguity, ironic narration and other abstruse, multilayered meanings that make texts useful for the 'procedures' of academic criticism.[30]

Steele once complained that 'Modest and well-governed Imaginations' were losing out in the race for immortality to 'Satyrs, Furies and Monsters' of art,[31] and most readers today prefer Swift's dark, scatological satire to the politer Whig alternative. The Kit-Cats occasionally felt great highs and lows (as Congreve asked, 'Where is the mind which passions ne'er molest?'[32]), but were genuinely, on the whole, emotionally stable men whose dark hours came less from suffering for their art than from objective crises, such as debts and deaths. One of the Kit-Cats' key words was 'Æquanimity': a contagious state of being that could make all else go well. If a husband should find equanimity, wrote Steele, it will 'easily diffuse itself through his whole Family'.[33] If writers can find it, so might the whole nation of readers. Today, the Kit-Cat authors' essential emotional stability and unfashionable sanity partly explain their neglect.

Another prejudice has long been held against the Kit-Cats: that commissioned writing is intrinsically inferior to independent writing. The triumphal rise of the mass market, freeing authors from the tyranny of arbitrary, aristocratic patrons, became a myth of twentieth-century progress, in which the Kit-Cats were seen as the last hurrah of the old order. The alternate story, based on Congreve's advice to Cobham that 'men have ever been the same', is that authors, even geniuses, have always needed to supplement their incomes with subsidies from various sources, noble and ignoble, and that there have always been doubts about the capitalist marketplace as the most reliable judge of literary quality.

The posthumous triumph over the Kit-Cats of Swift and other writers excluded from Junto patronage is deeply ironic: it is as if posterity has formed its own club where the 'in-crowd' is suddenly 'out'. The Kit-Cats' conviction that a man's life, character and conversation were as important as his literary works, however, may mean that, if they could see how the Scriblerians' literary reputations have overtaken their own, they would not be too troubled. Steele told Pulteney with complete sincerity that '[t]he greatest Honour of Human Life is to live well with Men of Merit'[34] and on another occasion told a fan that the qualifications of a good poet were 'To be a very well-bred Man.'[35] Congreve meant something similar when, in 1727, he told Voltaire he wished to be remembered as a gentleman, not a poet. Again, the Romantics' separation and elevation of Art over Life made such well-balanced attitudes deeply unfashionable and misrepresented them as shallow social snobbery.

Very recently, there has been renewed interest in the late Stuart period and the Whig literature that dominated it. It is as if the Kit-Cats became so unfashionable that they can now be fashionable again, their obscurity giving them the sympathetic status of a minority interest. The Victorians would never have believed Addison and Steele needed rediscovering. Yet today, when *The Spectator* and *The Tatler* are mostly known in Britain as the titles of a weekly political magazine and a glossy, monthly society magazine (founded in 1828 and 1901 respectively), and when their original namesakes are no longer read for pleasure but merely quoted by historians, there is a strong case for rediscovery. Addison's and Steele's wit and wisdom merit appreciation by a new generation of readers whose values and preoccupations are probably closer to those of the early eighteenth century than at any time since the journals were first published. After 300 years, a remarkable affinity between the Kit-Cats' worldview and that of many Western, secular liberals can be discerned. Londoners and denizens of other major world cities today often identify more closely with one another, in their urbanity and cosmopolitanism, than with their rural compatriots, and, at a time when Enlightenment values are felt to be under threat from religious extremists, the witty, worldly 'moderation' of Kit-Cat writers seems more appealing, less of a smokescreen or sell-out, than once it did.

After English literature, the art form most explicitly subjected to Kit-Cat ambitions was music, a fact that has since been consistently overlooked. Vanbrugh, Congreve and their patrons deserve credit for training Londoners' taste in opera, from which Handel and the next generation of impresarios reaped the benefits. The campaign of Addison and other Kit-Cats to establish an indigenous English *opera seria* tradition may have failed, but that says more about the inadequacy of the composers they had at their disposal than the idea's intrinsic foolishness. George I founded the first Royal Academy of Music in 1719, and though this was his pet project, it also grew out of the Kit-Cat Club's pre-1714 agenda to promote English music in preparation for his reign. The Royal Academy's aristocratic support came from both sides of the Whig schism and included a few Tories, but Newcastle (the Academy's first Governor) and other former Kit-Cats were 'very prominent' in its affairs.[36] By 1722, Vanbrugh told Carlisle that, while no good new plays were being written for the English stage, 'Music has taken deep root with us.'[37] Even after the Academy as first instituted collapsed in 1728, this remained true, evidenced by Handel's popularity.

In architecture, Vanbrugh's idiosyncratic style, as shown by his masterpieces of Blenheim, Castle Howard and Stowe, at first seems to bear little relation to what immediately preceded or followed. But it becomes easier to understand when seen as a product of Kit-Cat thinking: the pursuit of an anglicized neoclassical style, importing baroque models but interpreting them loosely and romantically through visual allusions to heroic English history, such as details from medieval castles or Jacobean manors. In the 1720s, enthusiasm for neo-Palladian villas overtook and sidelined Vanbrugh's style of building, partly because Vanbrugh's houses were too grand to be replicated easily by smaller landowners. By as early as 1727, the unfavourable consensus was that Vanbrugh's houses consisted 'of great heaps of brick and thick walls, but little accommodation within'.[38] Lord Burlington had a far wider legacy, as if he found in the modest scale of his neo-Palladian Chiswick villa the architectural equivalent of the intimate Kit-Cat portrait or the brief, conversational *Spectator* essay. It was a scale more in keeping with the coming age, when epic ambitions, even in architecture, could no longer be taken quite so seriously.

Vanbrugh's most influential and imitated architecture was therefore his smaller-scale garden architecture. The oriental and gothic elements of Vanbrugh's follies were much beloved by the later eighteenth century, Sir Joshua Reynolds enthusing that they brought 'to our remembrance ancient customs and manners, such as the Castles of the Barons of ancient Chivalry'.[39] In landscape design more broadly, Vanbrugh, Carlisle, Cobham and other Kit-Cats were hugely innovative and influential, thanks to the literary (that is, narrative) and theatrical aesthetic of their creations, and the respectful incorporation of the natural English landscape into neoclassical schemas. As early patrons to men like Charles Bridgeman and William Kent, the Kit-Cats also deserve credit for the generation of gardens that followed.

In painting, Kneller's Kit-Cat series contributed to the later eighteenth-century craze for portraiture, and specifically suggested more intimate, egalitarian options than the full-length portrait in official robes. The size of Kneller's portraits is, in fact, still known by art experts as a 'Kit-Cat'. Kneller's pictures taught the new self-made men of wealth how to style themselves as cultured gentlemen by sitting for their own portraits, and Tonson taught his fellow tradesmen and professionals how to create a gallery of paintings even in a relatively modest private home.

What is astonishing is that the Kit-Cat cultural projects – the building of theatres, the funding of subscription publications, the hiring of opera singers – were only half the story, the other half being the Club's lasting impact on Britain's constitution, legislation and political culture.

The debate about the political legacy of the Kit-Cats and their fellow Whigs has swung, since the mid-1800s, between poles of idealization and cynicism. The 'Whig histories' of Macaulay and Trevelyan caricatured the period as the start of a long, linear progress towards civil and religious liberties, parliamentary freedom and British supremacy. The Whig leaders of the 1688 Glorious Revolution and their party political heirs were credited not only with this triumphal progress but also with liberal ideological motives for their actions. The clubs and coffee houses of Queen Anne's London were similarly mythologized as seedbeds of pluralist, democratic values – a view reinforced by Continental social theorists after the Second World War who sought to explain the origins of Anglo-Saxon civil society.

At the other extreme, L. B. Namier in 1929 depicted post-1688 politics as driven by competition for power between rival factions formed around bonds of kinship and vested interests, devoid of public-spirited motives. This opened the revisionist floodgates, and soon any positive consequence of Whig Junto policy was regarded as an inadvertent side effect of anti-Catholic bigotry and self-serving protectionism. The absence of a direct causal link between the 1689 constitutional settlement and later nineteenth-century constitutional reforms was easily demonstrated, and the clubs of Anne's London were reimagined, in the same revisionist spirit, as being like Vanbrugh's stage-set garden follies at Stowe: high-minded classical façades stuck onto ugly old bastions of snobbery and privilege.

J. H. Plumb, in 1969, offered the first important corrective to the revisionists, arguing that 1675–1725 saw enormous progress towards political stability in England. Plumb argued that stability emerged 'through the actions and decisions of men, as does revolution' and was neither inevitable nor accidental.[40] He attributed it to 'a sense of common identity in those who wielded economic, social and political power',[41] to which Kit-Cat Club membership clearly contributed. Plumb also attributed national stability to 'single-party government',[42] a norm which the single-party Kit-Cat Club also played its part in promoting. Just as Somers had once introduced obligatory oaths to fix Englishmen's loyalties to King William, so the Kit-Cat Club fixed its members to the Junto and to Whig 'Revolution Principles'. One or two notable failures excepted – Prior's defection to impeach his friends in 1701 and Somerset's collaboration with Oxford in 1710 – the Club proved a remarkably effective fixative, teaching its members to think in terms of political cooperation only with their 'own kind'. Plumb also attributed British stability after 1720 to a 'legislature firmly under executive control',[43] achieved partly through the Junto's use of the Kit-Cat Club as a site for 'parliamentary junketings'[44] and for exercising the Whigs' superior party and parliamentary control. It was no coincidence that the Club's lifespan correlated closely to a period of frequent electoral campaigning, being the venue for 'informal "whipping" of the party's members in both Houses' and 'marshalling the proxy votes of the Whig peers'.[45]

Once the protégés nurtured by the first generation of Kit-Cats started fighting among themselves for the spoils of power, the Club as an entity was doomed, but its 'Kitlings' nonetheless managed the country for another half century. After Walpole regained power in 1721, he exploited it more fully than any previous minister and so became what we call a 'Prime Minister'. Though it is usually argued that Walpole took Oxford as his model, Walpole's political apprenticeship was not served at Oxford's side but among the Kit-Cats, and it was from the Junto that he learned how to organize the press, politicize the culture, and wield power through patronage and partying.

Two of the youngest 'Kitlings', Newcastle and Pulteney, also later became Prime Ministers. If one counts the nominal premiership of Spencer Compton (a puppet controlled by Lord Carteret in 1742–4), there were only nine years when the British government was not in the hands of a Kit-Cat Prime Minister between 1714 and 1762, and for eight of those it was in the hands of Newcastle's younger brother, Henry Pelham.

While the rise of the first Prime Minister in this period is well recognized, it is less often remarked that the same period saw the rise of the Cabinet, as part of a general enthusiasm for collective governmental responsibility through parliamentary boards and committees. Though Cabinet meetings, as a subsection of the Privy Council, predated the Kit-Cat Club, it was during the Club's lifespan that the Cabinet became, for the first time, a 'vital organ of government'.[46] During the regency following Anne's death, when the regents' collective responsibility overlapped with the Kit-Cat Club's membership, the link between Cabinet and Club was explicit. By the time the Club dissolved, the Cabinet was meeting and taking decisions without George I's presence (though Walpole later weakened the Cabinet again, for his own ends).

Several recent historians have emphasized that Parliament in this period was not an antagonist to the Crown so much as its co-conspirator in a series of conservative changes – that the Whig aristocracy put strenuous effort into supporting, not overthrowing, the monarchy – albeit monarchs of their choosing.[47] Even Macaulay and Trevelyan admitted the Glorious Revolution was defensive and conservative, designed to preserve certain noble families' privileges. Yet this should not obscure the importance of the Junto's radically conditional style of deference to William, Anne and George – a pragmatic mixture of respect and resentment, obedience and independence, which helped define the British system of government. The early eighteenth century saw a shift from the Crown's wishes being endorsed by elections to election results forcing the royal hand and ministers audaciously twisting royal arms. The careers of the Kit-Cats were important threads connecting these two eras.

In terms of political philosophy, the Kit-Cat Club kept the soil fertile for certain ideas during the long decades between Locke and Hume. Through its mixture of members, it melded the Whig party's mainstream ideology, which was essentially conservative and aristocratic, with more meritocratic, socially progressive ideas, as promoted by the Club's non-aristocratic authors. While it did not seek to overturn social hierarchies, it helped establish the perception that social rank was no longer 'the very precondition for participating in debate'.[48] If the Kit-Cats did not always live up to their political rhet-

Red-breasted Nuthatch

Sitta canadensis

Adult male

Adult male

Nut-hatches are short-tailed and long-billed with a unique tree-climbing method; they often climb head down, feeding on insects gleaned from bark crevices.

L 4.5" WS 8.5" WT 0.35 oz (10 g)

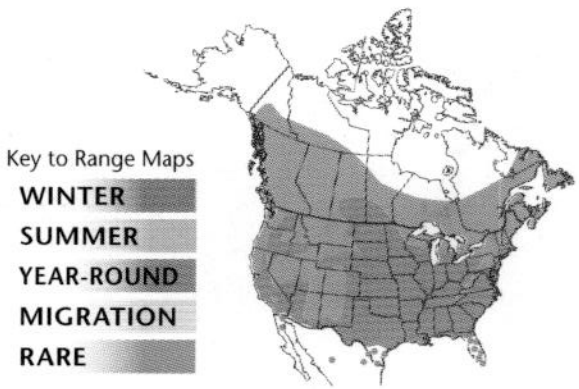

Sellers Publishing, Inc. • www.makefun.com

Monday
OCTOBER
13

Columbus Day (observed)

Thanksgiving (Canada)

October

S	M	T	W	T	F	S
			1	2	3	4
5	6	7	8	9	10	11
12	13	14	15	16	17	18
19	20	21	22	23	24	25
26	27	28	29	30	31	

oric, that rhetoric at least set the terms under which they and their political descendants were held accountable.

Late eighteenth-century French philosophers acknowledged an intellectual debt to Addison and Steele, modelling their close-knit communities on English clubs and societies. Scottish Enlightenment thinkers acknowledged a similar debt, while *The Spectator*'s assault on metaphysics 'prepared the way for the new egalitarian emphasis upon "common sense" offered by Thomas Paine'.[49] Read throughout the English-speaking world, essays like *Spectator* no. 287, which argued that liberty is best preserved by division of government among persons 'of different ranks and interests', had a crucial influence on political philosophers in the decades that followed. The definition of liberty used by American revolutionaries can be traced back to Addison's 1712 definition in the above *Spectator*, and his radical statement that: 'Liberty should reach every Individual of a People, as they all share one common Nature; if it only spreads among particular Branches, there had better be none at all, since such a Liberty only aggravates the Misfortune of those who are deprived of it.'[50]

Benjamin Franklin was hugely influenced by belonging to London's 'Honest Whigs Club', later founding his own club in America called 'The Junto'.[51] Franklin read volumes of *The Spectator* during his adolescence, and trained himself to write his first published articles, the Silence Dogood letters, by rewriting *Spectator* essays from memory.

Though Tories had been instrumental in the 1688 invitation to William, the 1701 Act of Settlement (Oxford had his portrait painted proudly holding this document), and the making of the Union in 1707, it was the Kit-Cats who achieved the greatest trick in all three cases: making these breathtakingly bold changes seem perfectly reasonable and necessary. Addison wrote of Somers: '[I]f he did not entirely project the Union of the Two Kingdoms, and the Bill of Regency ... there is none who will deny him to have been the chief Conductor in both.'[52] The Whig party in general, and the Kit-Cat Club in particular, should be given just such measured credit for both achievements. While there has been widespread historical agreement, at least until very recently, that the impact of the Union with Scotland was positive for the Scots, the verdict on the Whig and Kit-Cat legacy in Ireland is less straightforward. Wharton and Addison certainly handled Ireland in the English interest, without encouraging the union of kingdoms that the Irish oligarchy desired and without opposing the persecution of the Catholic majority. In 1720, a former Kit-Cat, Grafton, became Irish Lord Lieutenant, and in 1730–7 and 1750–5, Dorset's son Lionel also held this office.

The Kit-Cats not only made it look easy to reform a nation constitutionally, but also to reform the fundamental attitudes and aspirations of that nation. Far more important than any single play, journal, opera or building left behind by a Kit-Cat, was the Club's legacy of spreading Whig attitudes in Britain, which, by the 1730s, could no longer be considered strictly 'Whig' because they had become so commonplace. Steele's *Guardian* had once lectured that a 'Fine Gentleman' of Britain should be 'properly a Compound' – of military courage, political honour, literary talent and other virtues.[53] It was as if, instead of mixing neoclassicism and English historicism to make a palace or an opera, Steele was mixing his 'Compound' ideal English character from the qualities he admired in his friends and patrons. Tonson's printing presses were the progenitors of this new national identity, conveying metropolitan values to the rest of the country through the tri-weekly post. Addison, Steele and their fellow Kit-Cats were in this way responsible for writing a story about the nature of Englishness and the conduct of English men and women, which thousands of ordinary people began to repeat unconsciously to themselves and imitate in their daily lives.

BIBLIOGRAPHY

Secondary Sources

Acres, W. Marston, *The Bank of England from Within, 1694–1900*, vol. 1 (London, 1931)

Adair, Richard, *Courtship, Illegitimacy and Marriage in Early Modern England* (Manchester, 1996)

Adams, Robert, 'In Search of Baron Somers', in P. Zagorin (ed.), *Culture and Politics from Puritanism to the Enlightenment* (Berkeley, Calif., 1980)

Aikin, Lucy, *The Life of Joseph Addison*, 2 vols (London, 1843)

Aitken, G. A., *The Life of Richard Steele*, 2 vols (London, 1889)

Allen, David, 'Political Clubs in Restoration London', *Historical Journal* 19, 3 (1976), pp. 561–80

Allen, Robert J., 'The Kit-Cat Club and the Theatre', *Review of English Studies* 7 (1931), pp. 56–61

——*The Clubs of Augustan London* (Cambridge, Mass., 1933)

Alsop, J. D., 'New Light on Joseph Addison', *Modern Philology* 80 (August 1982), pp. 13–34

Anderson, Robert, *The Poets of Great Britain*, vol. 6 (London, 1795 edn)

Anon., *Ranelagh Club, Barn Elms: Rules, Regulations and List of Members* (London, 1889)

Anthony, Sister Rose, *The Jeremy Collier Stage Controversy, 1698–1726* (Milwaukee, Wis., 1937)

Arciszewska, Barbara, *The Hanoverian Court and the Triumph of Palladio* (London, 2002)

Ashe, Geoffrey, *The Hell-Fire Clubs* (London, 1974 and 2005 edn)

Ashton, J., *Social Life in the Reign of Queen Anne*, 2 vols (London, 1882)

Avery, Emmett L., *Congreve's Plays on the Eighteenth-Century Stage* (New York, 1951)

Bahlman, Dudley, *The Moral Revolution of 1688* (New Haven, Conn., 1957)

Bailyn, Bernard, *The Ideological Origins of the American Revolution* (London, 1992 edn)

Balen, Malcolm, *A Very English Deceit: The Secret History of the South Sea Bubble and the First Great Financial Scandal* (London, 2002)

Barlow, Graham F., 'Vanbrugh's Queens Theatre in the Haymarket', *Early Music* 17 (November 1989), pp. 515–21

Barnard, Toby, *A New Anatomy of Ireland: The Irish Protestants 1649–1770* (New Haven, Conn. and London, 2003)

——and J. Clark (eds), *Lord Burlington: Architecture, Art and Life* (London, 1995)

Barrett, C. J., *The History of Barn Elms and the Kit-Cat Club* (London, 1889)

Baxter, Stephen B., *The Development of the Treasury 1660–1702* (Cambridge, Mass., 1957)

——(ed.), *England's Rise to Greatness, 1660 –1763* (Berkeley, Calif., 1983)

Beljame, Alexandre, *Men of Letters and the English Public in the Eighteenth Century*, trans. E. O. Lorimer, ed. Bonamy Dobrée (London, 1948)

Berkeley, George Monck, *Literary Relics* (London, 1789)

Berry, Elizabeth, 'A Household Account Book of Thomas Wharton 5th Baron Wharton (1648-1715)', *Records of Buckinghamshire* 36 (Aylesbury, 1996), pp. 86–97

Bingham, Madeleine, *Masks and Façades: Sir John Vanbrugh, the Man and his Setting* (London, 1974)

Black, Jeremy, *A System of Ambition: British Foreign Policy, 1660–1793* (London, 1991)

—— *The English Press 1621–1861* (London, 2001)

——*Walpole in Power* (London, 2001)

Blanchard, Rae, 'Was Sir Richard Steele a Freemason?', *Publications of the Modern Language Association of America* 63 (1948), pp. 903–17

——Review of Peter Smithers' *Life of Joseph Addison*, *Philological Quarterly* 34 (1955), pp. 267–9

Blanning, Tim, *The Pursuit of Glory: Europe 1648–1815* (London, 2007)

Bloom, E. A. and Lillian D. Bloom, *Joseph Addison's Sociable Animal* (Providence, R.I.,1971)

——*Addison and Steele: The Critical Heritage* (London, 1980)

——and Edmund Leites, *Educating an Audience: Addison, Steele and Eighteenth Century Culture* (Los Angeles, Calif., 1984)

Bond, Donovan and W. R. McLeod (eds), *Newsletters to Newspapers: Eighteenth-Century Journalism* (Morgantown, W.Va., 1977)

Bond, Richmond P., *The Tatler: The Making of a Literary Journal* (Cambridge, Mass., 1971)

Booth, C. C., 'Sir Samuel Garth, FRS: The Dispensary Poet', *Notes and Records of the Royal Society of London* 40 (May 1986)

Borsay, P., *The English Urban Renaissance: Culture and Society in the Provincial Town, 1660–1770* (Oxford, 1989)

Brewer, John, 'Commercialization and Politics', in Neil McKendrick (ed.), *The Birth of a Consumer Society* (London, 1982), pp. 217–30

——*The Sinews of Power: War, Money and the English State, 1688–1783* (London, 1989)

——and A. Bermingham (eds), *The Consumption of Culture, 1600–1800* (London, 1995)

——*The Pleasures of the Imagination: English Culture in the Eighteenth Century* (London, 1997)

Brown, Peter, *Pyramids of Pleasure: Eating and Dining in 18th Century England*, an exhibition at Fairfax House, York, 1 July to 31 October 1990 (York, 1990)

Brown, Peter Hume (ed.), *Letters Relating to Scotland in the Reign of Queen Anne by James Ogilvy First Earl of Seafield and Others*, no. 11, Scottish History Society, 2nd Series (Edinburgh, 1915)

Brunt, P. A., 'Amicitia in the Roman Republic', in *The Fall of the Roman Republic and Related Essays* (Oxford, 1988)

Bucholz, R. O., *The Augustan Court: Queen Anne and the Decline of Court Culture* (Stanford, Calif., 1993)

Bull, John, *Vanbrugh and Farquhar* (London, 1998)

Burgess, Glenn (ed.), *The New British History: Founding a Modern State 1603–1715* (London and New York, 1999)

Burney, Charles, *A General History of Music*, 4 vols (London, 1776–89)

Carswell, J., *The South Sea Bubble* (London, 1960)

Carter, Philip, *Men and the Emergence of Polite Society 1660–1830* (Oxford, 2000)

Castro, J. Paul de, '"Over Against Catherine Street in the Strand"', *Notes and Queries*, 12th series, 7 (23 October 1920), p. 321

Caulfield, James, *Memoirs of the Celebrated Persons Composing the Kit-Cat Club; with a prefatory account of the origin of the association, illustrated with forty-eight portraits from the original paintings by Sir Godfrey Kneller* (London, 1849)

Cibber, Theophilus, *The Lives of the Poets of Great Britain and Ireland to the Time of Dean Swift*, 5 vols (London, 1753)
Ciletti, Frederick M., 'The Kit-Cat Club', MA Thesis, Penn State University, 1953
Cipolla, C., *Before the Industrial Revolution* (London, 1981)
Clapham, Sir John, *The Bank of England: A History*, 2 vols (Cambridge, 1944)
Clark, Sir George, *History of the Royal College of Physicians of London*, 3 vols (Oxford, 1964–6)
Clark, J. C. D., *English Society 1688–1832* (Cambridge, 2000 edn)
Clark, Peter, *British Clubs and Societies, 1580–1800: The Origins of an Associational World* (Oxford, 2000)
—— (ed.), *The Cambridge Urban History of Britain* (Cambridge, 2000)
Clark, William Smith, *The Early Irish Stage: The Beginnings to 1720* (Oxford, 1973 edn)
Claydon, Tony, *William and the Godly Revolution* (Cambridge, 1996)
Cobbett, William (ed.), *Parliamentary History of England*, 36 vols (London, 1806–20)
Cokayne, G. E., *The Complete Peerage* (London, 1936)
Colley, Linda, *In Defiance of Oligarchy* (London, 1982)
——*Forging the Nation 1707–1837* (London, 1992)
——*Captives* (London, 2002)
Colvin, H. M. et al. (eds), *The History of the King's Works 1660–1782*, vol. 5 (London, 1976)
Connely, William, *Sir Richard Steele* (London, 1934)
Connolly, S. J., *Religion, Law and Power: The Making of Protestant Ireland, 1660–1760* (Oxford, 1992)
Cook, Chris and John Stevens, *British Historical Facts 1688–1760* (Basingstoke, 1988)
Cook, Richard I., *Sir Samuel Garth* (Boston, Mass., 1980)
Cooke, Arthur L., 'Addison vs. Steele, 1708', *PMLA* 68 (1953), pp. 313–20
——'Addison's Aristocratic Wife', *PMLA* 72, 1 (June 1957), pp. 373–89
Cordner, Michael, 'Marriage Comedy after the 1688 Revolution: Southerne to Vanbrugh', *Modern Language Review* 85, 2 (1990), pp. 273–89
Couper, Ramsay W., 'John Dryden's First Funeral', *The Athenaeum* no. 4005 (July 1904), pp. 145–6
Coxe, William, *Memoirs of the Life and Administration of Sir Robert Walpole, Earl of Orford*, 3 vols (London, 1798)
Cruickshanks, Eveline, Stuart Handley and D. W. Hayton, *The House of Commons 1690–1715*, 3 vols (Cambridge, 2002)

Cushing, Harvey, *Dr. Garth: The Kit-Cat Poet* (Baltimore, Md., 1906)

Dammers, Richard H., *Richard Steele* (Boston, Mass., 1982)

Davies, Godfrey, 'The Seamy Side of Marlborough's War', *Huntington Library Quarterly* 15 (1951–2), pp. 21–44

Delany, Patrick, *Observations upon Lord Orrery's Remarks* (London, 1754)

Dickinson, H. T. (ed.), *The Correspondence of Sir James Clavering*, vol. 178, The Surtees Society Series (Gateshead, 1967)

——*Companion to Eighteenth Century History* (Oxford, 2002)

Dickson, David, *New Foundations: Ireland 1660–1800* (Dublin, 2000 edn)

Dickson, P. G. M., *The Financial Revolution in England: A Study in the Development of Public Credit 1688–1756* (London, 1967)

Diprose, John, *Some Account of the Parish of St. Clement Danes*, 2 vols (London, 1868)

Dobrée, Bonamy, *Restoration Comedy 1660–1720* (Oxford, 1924)

——*Essays in Biography 1680–1726* (Oxford, 1925)

—— 'William Congreve: A Conversation between Swift and Gay', in *As Their Friends Saw Them* (London, 1933)

Doran, John, '*Their Majesties' Servants*': *Annals of the English Stage from Thomas Betterton to Edmund Kean*, ed. Robert W. Lowe (London, 1888 edn)

Downes, Kerry, *Sir John Vanbrugh: A Biography* (London, 1987)

Dralle, L., 'Kingdom in Reversion: The Irish Viceroyalty of the Earl of Wharton 1708–10', *The Huntington Library Quarterly* 15 (1951–2), p. 393

Earle, Peter, *The Making of the English Middle Class: Business, Society and Family Life in London 1660–1730* (London, 1989)

Ede, Mary, *Arts and Society in England under William and Mary* (London, 1979)

Elias, Norbert, *The Civilizing Process*, trans. Edmund Jephcott, ed. Eric Dunning, Johan Goudsblom and Stephen Mennell (Oxford and Cambridge, Mass., 2000 edn)

Elioseff, Lee Andrew, *The Cultural Milieu of Addison's Literary Criticism* (Austin, Tex., 1963)

Escott, T. H. S., *Club Makers and Club Members* (London, 1914)

Eves, C. K., *Matthew Prior, Poet and Diplomatist* (New York, 1939)

Ferguson, Oliver W., *Jonathan Swift and Ireland* (Urbana, Ill., 1962)

Field, John, *The King's Nurseries: The Story of Westminster School* (London, 1987)

Finke, Laurie, 'Virtue in Fashion: The Fate of Women in Comedies of Cibber and Vanbrugh', in Robert Markley and Laurie Finke (eds), *From*

Renaissance to Restoration: Metamorphoses of the Drama (Cleveland, Ohio, 1984), pp. 155–79

Fitzgerald, Percy, *A New History of the English Stage*, 2 vols (London, 1882)

Fitzgerald, Robert, *Rowntree and the Marketing Revolution, 1862–1969* (Cambridge, 1995)

Fitzmaurice, S., 'Servant or Patron? Jacob Tonson and the Language of Deference and Respect', *Language Sciences* 24, 3 (May 2002), pp. 247–60

Foot, M., *The Pen and the Sword* (London, 1957)

Forster, John, 'Sir Richard Steele', in *Historical and Biographical Essays*, vol. 2 (London, 1858)

Foss, Michael, *The Age of Patronage: The Arts in England 1660–1750* (Ithaca, NY, 1972)

Foxon, David, *English Verse 1701–1750: A Catalogue of Separately Printed Poems with Notes on Contemporary Collected Editions*, 2 vols (Cambridge, 1975)

Geduld, Harry M., *Prince of Publishers: A Study of the Work and Career of Jacob Tonson* (Bloomington, Ind. and London, 1969)

Genest, John (ed.), *Some Account of the English Stage*, 10 vols (Bath, 1832)

George, Mary Dorothy, *London Life in the Eighteenth Century* (London, 1996, facsimile of 1st edn 1925)

Gibbs, G. C., 'English Attitudes towards Hanover and the Hanoverian Succession in the First Half of the Eighteenth Century', in A. M. Birke and K. Kluxen (eds), *England und Hannover* (Munich, 1986)

Gilbert, John T. (ed.), *Calendar of Ancient Records of Dublin*, vol. 6 (Dublin, 1896)

Gillespie, Stuart, 'The Early Years of the Dryden-Tonson Partnership: The Background to their Composite Translations and Miscellanies of the 1680s', *Restoration* 12 (1988), pp. 10–19

Gosse, Edmund, *Life of William Congreve* (London, 1888)

—— 'Preface', in *Critical Kit-Kats* (London, 1896)

Gregg, Edward, *Queen Anne* (London, 1984 edn)

Gregory, Jeremy and John Stevenson (eds), *The Longman Companion to Britain in the Eighteenth Century, 1688–1820* (London and New York, 2000)

Griffin, Dustin, *Literary Patronage in England 1650–1800* (Cambridge, 1996)

Grundy, Isobel, *Lady Mary Wortley Montagu: Comet of the Enlightenment* (Oxford, 1999)

Habbukuk, John, *Marriage, Debt and the Estates System* (Oxford, 1994)

Habermas, Jürgen, *The Structural Transformation of the Public Sphere* (Cambridge, Mass., 1989)

Halsband, Robert, *Life of Mary Wortley Montagu* (Oxford, 1956)

Hammond, Brean S., '"Guard the sure barrier": Pope and the Partitioning of Culture', in David Fairer (ed.), *Pope: New Contexts* (New York, 1990)

——*Professional Imaginative Writing in England 1670–1740: 'Hackney for Bread'* (Oxford, 1997)

Hans, N., *New Trends in Education in the 18th Century* (London, 1951)

Harley, G. D., *Squire Trelooby and The Cornish Squire: A Reconsideration, Philological Quarterly* 49 (1970), pp. 520–9

Harris, Bernard, *Sir John Vanbrugh* (London, 1967)

Harris, Brice, *Charles Sackville, Sixth Earl of Dorset: Patron and Poet of the Restoration, Illinois Studies in Language and Literature* 26, 3–4 (Urbana, Ill., 1940)

Harris, Tim, *Revolution: The Great Crisis of the British Monarchy, 1685–1720* (London, 2006)

Hayton, David, 'The Crisis in Ireland and the Disintegration of Queen Anne's Last Ministry', *Irish Historical Studies* 22 (March 1981), pp. 193–215

Hazlitt, William, *Lectures on the English Comic Writers* (London, 1819)

Hellman, George S., 'The Kit-Cat Club', *The Print-Collector's Quarterly* 7 (1917), pp. 3–23

Highfill, P. H. Jr et al. (eds), *A Biographical Dictionary of Actors, Actresses, Musicians, Dancers, Managers and Other Stage Personnel in London, 1660–1800*, 16 vols (Carbondale and Edwardsville, Ill., 1973–93)

Hill, Brian W., *Sir Robert Walpole* (London, 1989)

History of Parliament Trust, *The Proceedings of the House of Commons*, 10 vols (London, 1742)

Hodges, John C., 'William Congreve in the Government Service', *Modern Philology* 27 (1929), pp. 183–92

——*William Congreve the Man: A Biography from New Sources* (London, 1941)

——*The Library of William Congreve* (London, 1955)

Hodgson, Mrs Willoughby, 'Barn Elms, the Kit-Cat Club and Ranelagh of Today', *The Connoisseur* 31 (1911), pp. 199–224

Holland, Peter, *The Ornament of Action: Text and Performance in Restoration Comedy* (Cambridge, 1979)

Holmes, Geoffrey, *British Politics in the Age of Anne* (London, 1967)

——*The Trial of Doctor Sacheverell* (London, 1973)

——*Augustan England: Professions, State and Society 1680–1730* (London, 1982)

——*The Making of a Great Power: Late Stuart and Early Georgian Britain 1660–1722* (London, 1993)

Home, James A. (ed.), *Letters of Lady Louisa Stuart to Miss Louisa Clinton* (Edinburgh, 1903)

Hoppit, Julian, *A Land of Liberty? England 1689–1727* (Oxford, 2000)

Horn, D. B., *The British Diplomatic Service 1689–1789* (Oxford, 1961)

Horwitz, Henry, *Parliament, Policy and Politics in the Reign of William III* (Manchester, 1977)

——(ed.), *London Politics 1713–17: Minutes of a Whig Club 1714–17*, London Record Society publications vol. 17 (London, 1981), pp. 1–2 and 9

Howells, Catherine, 'The Kit-Cat Club: A Study of Patronage and Influence in Britain 1696–1720', PhD Thesis, University of California, 1982

Hsu, Francis L. K., *Clan, Caste and Club* (Princeton, NJ, 1963)

Hughes, Derek, 'Cibber and Vanbrugh: Language, Place and Social Order in *The Relapse*', *Comparative Drama* 21, 1 (1987), pp. 62–83

Hume, Robert D. (ed.), *The London Theatre World 1660–1800* (New Haven, Conn., 1980)

—— 'Marital Discord in English Comedy from Dryden to Fielding', *Modern Philology* 74 (1976–7), pp. 248–72

Hunt, Leigh, *A Book for a Corner*, vol. 2 (London, 1849)

Huseboe, Arthur R., *Sir John Vanbrugh* (Boston, Mass., 1976)

Ingamells, John (ed.), *A Dictionary of British and Irish Travellers in Italy 1701–1800* (New Haven, Conn. and London, 1997)

Institute for Historical Research (London), *Office-Holders in Modern Britain* series (London, 1972–)

Jacob, Margaret C., *Strangers Nowhere in the World: The Rise of Cosmopolitanism in Early Modern Europe* (Philadelphia, Pa., 2006)

Jeafferson, J. C. A., *A Book About Doctors* (New York, 1904)

Johnson, Dr Samuel, *Lives of the English Poets* (London, 1781), ed. George Birkbeck Hill, 3 vols (Oxford, 1905)

Jones, Clyve (ed.), *Britain in the First Age of Party, 1660–1750* (London and Ronceverte, W.Va., 1987)

—— 'To Dispose in Earnest, of a Place I Got in Jest: Eight New Letters of Sir John Vanbrugh,1722–1726', *Notes and Queries* 36, 4 (vol. 234 of continuous series) (December 1989), pp. 461–9

—— 'William, First Earl Cowper, Country Whiggery and the Leadership of Opposition in the House of Lords, 1720–3', in R. W. Davis (ed.), *Lords of Parliament: Studies 1714–1914* (Stanford, Calif., 1995)

—— 'The Vote in The House of Lords on the Duke of Ormond's

"Restraining Orders", 28 May 1712', *Parliamentary History* 26, part 2 (2007), pp.160–183

Jones, D. W., *War and Economy in the Age of William III and Marlborough* (Oxford, 1988)

Jones, Louis C., *The Clubs of the Georgian Rakes* (New York, 1942)

Kelch, Ray A., *Newcastle, a Duke without Money: Thomas Pelham-Holles 1693–1768* (London, 1974)

Kenyon, J. P., *Revolution Principles* (Cambridge, 1977)

Kerby-Miller, Charles (ed.), *Memoirs of the Extraordinary Life, Works, and Discoveries of Martinus Scriblerus* (Oxford, 1988)

Kitchener, Dr William, *The Housekeeper's Oracle* (London, 1829)

Klein, Lawrence E., 'Coffeehouse Civility, 1660–1714: An Aspect of Post-Courtly Culture in England', *Huntington Library Quarterly* 59 (1997), pp. 31–51

Knight, Charles, *Shadows of the Old Booksellers* (London, 1927)

Knight, Charles A., 'The Spectator's Generalizing Discourse', in J. A. Downie and Thomas N. Corns (eds), *Telling People What to Think* (London, 1993)

Knights, Mark, *Representation and Misrepresentation in Later Stuart Britain: Partisanship and Political Culture* (Oxford, 2005)

Krey, Gary Stuart de, *A Fractured Society: The Politics of London in the First Age of Party, 1688–1715* (Oxford, 1985)

Langford, Paul, *Public Life and the Propertied Englishman, 1689–1798* (Oxford, 1991)

——*Englishness Identified: Manners and Character 1650–1850* (Oxford, 2000)

——*The Eighteenth Century* (Oxford, 2002)

Leacroft, Richard, *The Development of the English Playhouse* (London, 1973)

Lehmann, Gilly, *The British Housewife: Cookery-Books, Cooking and Society in Eighteenth-Century Britain* (London, 2002)

Lemmings, David, *Gentlemen and Barristers: The Inns of Court and the English Bar 1680–1730* (Oxford, 1990)

Leslie, Major John Henry, *The History of Landguard Fort, in Suffolk* (London, 1898)

Levack, Brian P., *The Formation of the British State* (Oxford, 1987)

Lewis, C. S., 'Addison', in *Essays on the Eighteenth Century Presented to David Nichol Smith in Honour of his Seventieth Birthday* (Oxford, 1945)

Lillywhite, B., *London Coffee Houses* (London, 1963)

——*London Signs* (London, 1972)

Lindsay, Alexander and Howard Erskine-Hill (eds), *William Congreve: The Critical Heritage* (London and New York, 1989)
Loftis, John, 'Richard Steele's Censorium', *Huntington Library Quarterly* 14 (1950), pp. 43–66
—— (ed.), *The Politics of Drama in Augustan England* (Oxford, 1963)
Luckhurst, Mary and Jane Moody (eds), *Theatre and Celebrity in Britain, 1660–2000* (New York, 2005)
Lynch, Kathleen M., *A Congreve Gallery* (Cambridge, Mass., 1967)
——*Jacob Tonson, Kit-Cat Publisher* (Knoxville, Tenn., 1971)
Macaulay, T. B., 'Life and Writings of Addison', *Edinburgh Review* 78 (July 1843), pp. 193–260
——*The History of England*, 6 vols (London, 1858)
Mack, Maynard, *Alexander Pope: A Life* (London and New Haven, Conn., 1985)
Mackinnon, James, *Union of England and Scotland* (London, 1896)
Maguire, W. A. (ed.), *Kings in Conflict: The Revolutionary War in Ireland and its Aftermath* (Belfast, 1990)
Malone, Edmond (ed.), *Critical and Miscellaneous Prose Works of John Dryden*, 3 vols (London, 1800)
——*Historical Account of the English Stage* (London, 1790)
Manchester, William Drogo Montagu, 7th Duke of, *Court and Society from Elizabeth to Anne*, 2 vols (London, 1864)
Manning, J. A., *Lives of the Speakers of the House of Commons* (London, 1850)
McCormick, Frank, *Sir John Vanbrugh: The Playwright as Architect* (University Park, Pa., 1991)
——*Sir John Vanbrugh: A Reference Guide* (New York, 1992)
McCrea, Brian, *Addison and Steele Are Dead* (Newark, NJ, 1990)
McDowell, R. B. and D. A. Webb (eds), *Trinity College Dublin 1592–1952* (Cambridge, 1982)
McGreary, Thomas, 'A Satire on the Opening of the Haymarket Theatre', *Restoration and 18th Century Theatre Research* 15 (Winter 2000), pp. 18–32
McKay, D. and H. M. Scott (eds), *The Rise of the Great Powers, 1648–1815* (London, 1983)
McKeon, Michael, *The Secret History of Domesticity: Public, Private, and the Division of Knowledge* (Baltimore, Md., 2005)
McLeod, Kenneth A., 'Judgment and Choice: Politics and Ideology in Early Eighteenth-Century Masques', PhD Thesis, McGill University, Montreal, 2nd edn 1999

Milhous, Judith, 'New Light on Vanbrugh's Haymarket Theatre Project', *Theatre Survey* 17 (November 1976), pp. 143–61

——and Robert D. Hume (eds), *Register of English Theatrical Documents, 1660–1737*, 2 vols (Carbondale, Ill., 1991)

Miller, E. Arnold, 'Some Arguments Used by English Pamphleteers, 1697–1700, Concerning a Standing Army', *Journal of Modern History* 18 (December 1946), pp. 306–13

Millon, Henry A. (ed.), *Circa 1700: Architecture in Europe and the Americas* (New Haven, Conn., 2005)

Moody, T. W. and W. E. Vaughan (eds), *A New History of Ireland, vol. 4: Eighteenth-Century Ireland 1691–1800* (Oxford, 1986)

Müllenbrock, Heinz-Joachim, *The Culture of Contention: A Rhetorical Analysis of the Public Controversy about the Ending of the War of the Spanish Succession, 1710–1713* (Munich, 1997)

National Portrait Gallery, *The Portraits of Members of the Kit Cat Club* (catalogue) (London, 1971)

Naylor, J. F. (ed.), *The British Aristocracy and the Peerage Bill of 1719* (Oxford, 1968)

Newman, Donald J. (ed.), *The Spectator: Emerging Discourses* (Newark, NJ, 2005)

Nichols, John, *Select Collection of Poems* (London, 1782)

——*Literary Anecdotes of the Eighteenth Century* (London, 1812)

——*Illustrations of the Literary History of the Eighteenth Century*, 6 vols (London, 1817–31)

Noble, Mark, *A Biographical History of England from the Revolution to the End of George I's Reign; being a continuation of the Rev. J. Granger's work*, 3 vols (London, 1806)

Nokes, David, *Jonathan Swift: A Hypocrite Reversed* (Oxford, 1987)

Novak, Maximillian E., *William Congreve* (New York, 1971)

Nulle, Stebelton H., *Thomas Pelham-Holles, Duke of Newcastle: His Early Political Career 1693–1724* (Philadelphia, Pa., 1931)

Ogle, Nathaniel, *The Life of Addison* (London, 1826)

Olleson, Philip, 'Vanbrugh and the Opera at the Queens Theatre, Haymarket', *Theatre Notebook* 26, 3 (1972), pp. 94–101

The Oxford Dictionary of National Biography – electronic version, entries as noted

Papali, George Francis, *Jacob Tonson, Publisher: His Life and Work* (Auckland, 1968)

Pearson, Jacqueline, *The Prostituted Muse: Images of Women and Women Dramatists 1642–1737* (New York, 1988)

Pearson, John, *Stags and Serpents: A History of the Cavendish Family and the Dukes of Devonshire* (Bakewell, Derbyshire, 2002 edn)

Phillips, Sir Richard, *Addisoniana*, 2 vols (London, 1803)

Piper, David, *Catalogue of Seventeenth-Century Portraits in the National Portrait Gallery* (Cambridge, 1963)

Plumb, J. H., *Sir Robert Walpole: The Making of a Statesman* (Boston, Mass., 1961)

——*The Growth of Political Stability in England 1675–1725* (Harmondsworth, 1969)

Pointon, Marcia, *Hanging the Head: Portraiture and Social Formation in Eighteenth-Century England* (New Haven, Conn. and London, 1993)

Porter, Roy, *English Society in the Eighteenth Century* (Harmondsworth, 1990)

——*The Creation of the Modern World: The Untold Story of the British Enlightenment* (New York, 2000)

——*London: A Social History* (London, 2nd edn 2000)

Powell, Jocelyn, *Restoration Theatre Production* (London, 1984)

Prest, Wilfrid, *Albion Ascendant: English History 1660–1815* (Oxford, 1998)

Quick, Anthony, *Charterhouse: A History of the School* (London, 1990)

Rau, Fritz, 'Steeles Eintritt in den Kit-Cat-Club', *Germanisch-Romanische Monatschrift* 6 (1956), pp. 396–8

Rawson, Claude and Aaron Santesso (eds), *John Dryden (1631–1700): His Politics, His Plays and His Poets* (Newark, NJ, 2004)

Ribeiro, Aileen, *Fashion and Fiction: Dress in Art and Literature in Stuart England* (London, 2005)

Richardson, Tim, *The Arcadian Friends: Inventing the English Landscape Garden* (London, 2007)

Richetti, John (ed.), *The Cambridge History of English Literature 1660–1780* (Cambridge, 2005)

Ridway, Christopher and Robert Williams, *Sir John Vanbrugh and Landscape Architecture in Baroque England 1690–1730* (Stroud, 2000)

Riley, P. W. J., 'The Structure of Scottish Politics and the Union of 1707', in T. I. Rae (ed.), *The Union of 1707: Its Impact on Scotland* (Glasgow and London, 1974)

——*The Union of England and Scotland* (Manchester, 1978)

Rippy, Frances Mayhew, *Matthew Prior* (Boston, Mass., 1986)

Robbins, Caroline, *The Eighteenth-Century Commonwealthman: Studies in the Transmission, Development and Circumstances of English Liberal Thought from the Restoration of Charles II until the War with the Thirteen Colonies* (Cambridge, Mass., 1959)

Robbins, Christopher, '"The Most Universal Villain I Ever Knew": Jonathan Swift and the Earl of Wharton', *Eighteenth-Century Ireland* 18 (Dublin, 2003)

Roberts, J. M., *The Mythology of the Secret Societies* (London, 1972)

Roberts, William, *The Earlier History of English Book-Selling* (London, 1889)

Rogers, J. P. W., *Grub Street: Studies in a Subculture* (London, 1972)

Rogers, Pat, 'Matthew Prior, Sir Henry Furnese and the Kit Cat Club', *Notes and Queries*, new series, 18 (1971), pp. 46–8

Rose, Craig, *England in the 1690s: Revolution, Religion and War* (Oxford, 1999)

Rosenberg, Albert, *Sir Richard Blackmore: A Poet and Physician of the Augustan Age* (Lincoln, Nebr., 1953)

—— 'A New Move for the Censorship of Owen Swiney's *The Quacks*', *Notes and Queries* 203 (September 1958), pp. 393–6

Sachse, William L., *Lord Somers: A Political Portrait* (Manchester, 1975)

Sackville-West, Robert, *Knole* (London, 1998)

Sackville-West, Vita, *Knole and the Sackvilles* (London, 1922)

Sambrook, James, *James Thomson 1700–1748: A Life* (Oxford, 1991)

——*The Eighteenth Century: The Intellectual and Cultural Context of English Literature 1700–1789* (London and New York, 1993 edn)

Schnath, G., *Geschichte Hannovers im Zeitalter der neunten Kur und der englischen Sukzession 1674-1714*, vol. 4 (Hildesheim, 1938–82), pp. 151–62

The Scriblerian and the Kit-Cats (Philadelphia, Pa., 1972–)

Sena, John F., *The Best-Natured Man: Sir Samuel Garth, Physician and Poet* (New York, 1986)

Sennett, Richard, *The Fall of Public Man* (London, 1986)

Sherburn, George Wiley, *Early Career of Alexander Pope* (Oxford, 1934)

Smith, Charles Saumarez, *The Building of Castle Howard* (London, 1990)

——*The Rise of Design* (London, 2000)

Smithers, Peter, *The Life of Joseph Addison* (Oxford, 1968 edn)

Smollett, Tobias, *History of England*, 8 vols (London, 1794 edn)

Snyder, Henry L. (ed.), *The Marlborough-Godolphin Correspondence*, 3 vols (Oxford, 1975)

Solkin, David H., *Painting for Money: The Visual Arts and the Public Sphere in Eighteenth-Century England* (New Haven, Conn. and London, 1993)

Speck, W. A., *Tory and Whig: The Struggle in the Constituencies 1701–15* (London, 1970)

—— 'The Whig Schism under George I', *Huntington Library Quarterly* 40, 2 (February 1977), pp. 171–9

——*The Birth of Britain: A New Nation 1700–1710* (Oxford, 1994)

——*Literature and Society in Eighteenth-Century England* (London, 1998)

Spens, Susan, *George Stepney 1663–1707: Diplomat and Poet* (Cambridge, 1997)

Stallybrass, Peter and Allon White, *The Politics and Poetics of Transgression* (London, 1986)

Stater, Victor, *High Life, Low Morals: The Duel that Shook Stuart Society* (London, 1999)

Stewart, J. D., *Sir Godfrey Kneller* (London, 1971)

Stone, Lawrence (ed.), *An Imperial State at War: Britain from 1689 to 1815* (London, 1994)

——and Jeanne C. Fawtier Stone, *An Open Elite? England 1540–1880* (Oxford, 1984)

Survey of London, vols 29 and 30: *St James's Westminster, Part I* (London, 1960), pp. 223–50

Sutherland, James, 'The Last Years of Joseph Addison', in *Background for Queen Anne* (London, 1939)

Sutherland, L. S. and L. G. Mitchell (eds), *The History of the University of Oxford, vol. 5: The Eighteenth Century* (Oxford, 1986)

Sutton, Denys, 'The faire majestic Paradise of Stowe', *Apollo* 97 (1973), pp. 542ff.

Swedenberg, H. T., 'George Stepney, My Lord Dorset's Boy', *Huntington Library Quarterly* 10, 1 (November 1946), pp. 1–33

Sykes, Dr Norman, *Church and State in England in the XVIIIth Century* (Cambridge, 1934)

Taylor, D. Crane, *William Congreve* (London, 1931)

Thackeray, W. M., *The English Humourists of the Eighteenth Century* (London, 1858 edn)

Thomson, K., *Celebrated Friendships*, vol. 1 (London, 1861)

Thornbury, Walter (ed.), *Old and New London*, 6 vols (London, 1879)

Tiger, Lionel, *Men in Groups* (New Brunswick, NJ and London, 2005 edn)

Timbs, John, *Clubs and Club Life in London* (London, 1908 edn)

Tomalin, Claire, *Samuel Pepys: The Unequalled Self* (London, 2002)

Treadwell, J. M., 'Congreve, Tonson and Rowe's Reconcilement', *Notes and Queries* 22, 6 (vol. 220 of continuous series) (June 1975), pp. 265–9

Treglown, G. L. and M. C. F. Mortimer, 'Elegant and Elusive: Wine-glasses of the Kit-Cat Club', *Country Life* 170 (1981), pp. 46–8

Troyer, H. W., *Ned Ward of Grub Street: A Study of Sub-literary London in the Eighteenth Century* (London, 1968)

Turner, David M., *Fashioning Adultery: Gender, Sex and Civility in England 1660–1740* (Cambridge, 2002)

Turner, James Grantham, *Libertines and Radicals in Early Modern London* (Cambridge, 2002)

Urstad, Tone Sundt, *Sir Robert Walpole's Poets: The Use of Literature as Pro-Government Propaganda, 1721–1742* (Newark, NJ, 1999)

Voitle, Robert, *The Third Earl of Shaftesbury, 1671–1713* (Baton Rouge, La. and London, 1984)

Walpole, Horace, *A Catalogue of the Royal and Noble Authors of England* (Edinburgh, 1796 edn)

——*Anecdotes of Painting in England* (London, 1879 edn)

——*Correspondence*, ed. by W. S. Lewis et al., 48 vols (Oxford, 1937–83)

Ward, Charles E. (ed.), *The Letters of John Dryden* (Durham, NC, 1942)

Watkin, D. J. (ed.), *Sale Catalogues of Libraries of Eminent Persons* (London, 1972)

——*English Vision* (London, 1982)

West, William, *Tavern Anecdotes and Reminiscences of the Origin of Signs, Coffee Houses etc.* (London, 1825)

Wharton, E. R., *The Whartons of Wharton Hall* (Oxford, 1898)

Whistler, Laurence, *The Imagination of Vanbrugh and his Fellow Artists* (London, 1954)

——*Sir John Vanbrugh, Architect and Dramatist 1664–1726* (New York, 1978)

White, Eric Walter, *The Rise of English Opera* (London, 1951)

Williams, Abigail, *Poetry and the Creation of a Whig Literary Culture 1681–1714* (Oxford, 2005)

Williams, Basil, *Stanhope: A Study in Eighteenth-Century War and Diplomacy* (Oxford, 1932)

Wilson, Richard and Alan Mackley, *Creating Paradise: The Building of the English Country House, 1660–1800* (London and New York, 2000)

Winn, James A., *John Dryden and his World* (New Haven, Conn., 1987)

Winton, Calhoun, *Captain Steele: The Early Career of Richard Steele* (Baltimore, Md., 1964)

——*Sir Richard Steele MP* (Baltimore, Md., 1970)

Womersley, David (ed.), *Cultures of Whiggism* (Newark, NJ, 2005)

Wood, Herbert, 'Addison's Connexion with Ireland', *Royal Society of Antiquaries of Ireland Journal*, 5th series, 14 (1904), pp. 133–58

Woolf, Virginia, 'Addison', in *The Common Reader*, vol. 1 (London, 2003 edn)

Worsley, Giles, *Classical Architecture in Britain: The Heroic Age* (New Haven, Conn., 1995)

Wright, H. Bunker, 'Matthew Prior's Cloe and Lisetta', *Modern Philology* 36 (August 1938), pp. 9–23

Wrigley, E. A. and R. S. Schofield, *The Population History of England 1541–1871: A Reconstruction* (Cambridge, 1989 edn)

Yolton, Porter et al. (eds), *The Blackwell Companion to the Enlightenment* (Oxford, 1991)

York, Neil Longley, *Neither Kingdom nor Nation: The Irish Quest for Constitutional Rights 1698–1800* (Washington, DC, 1994)

Contemporary Printed Sources

Addison, Joseph, *The Whig Examiner*, nos 1–5 (London, 1710)

Remarks on Several Parts of Italy, etc, in the years 1701, 1702, 1703 (1718 edn)

The Works of the Right Honourable Joseph Addison, ed. Thomas Tickell, 4 vols (London, 1721)

The Poems of Addison, vol. 23 of *The Works of the English Poets*, ed. Dr Samuel Johnson (London, 1781)

Miscellaneous Works of Joseph Addison, ed. A. C. L. Guthkelch, 2 vols (London, 1914)

The Letters of Joseph Addison, ed. Walter Graham (Oxford, 1941)

The Freeholder, ed. J. Leheny (Oxford, 1979)

Cato: A Tragedy, and Selected Essay, ed. Christine Dunn Henderson and Mark E. Yellin (Indianapolis, Ind., 2004)

Addison, Joseph and Richard Steele, *The Lover, Written in Imitation of the Tatler, by Marmaduke Myrtle, Gent.*, ed. Walter Lewin (London, 1887)

Richard Steele's 'The Theatre', ed. John Loftis (Oxford, 1962)

The Spectator, ed. Donald F. Bond, 5 vols (Oxford, 1965)

The Guardian, ed. John Cahoun Stephens (Lexington, Ky., 1982)

The Tatler, ed. Donald F. Bond, 3 vols (Oxford, 1987)

Anon., *On Mr Pr[io]r's letters to Mr [Fleetwood] Sheppard (not omitting the last one unown'd)* (1690)

Anon., *A letter to A B C D E F, etc, concerning their argument about a standing army . . .* (1698)

Anon., *Satire on Modern Translators* (1698)

Anon. [Bevil Higgons?], *A New Ballad called The Brawny Bishop's Complaint, to the tune of Packington's Pound* (1698)

Anon., *The Patentee* (1700)

Anon., *A Choice Collection of Italian Ayres* (1703)

Anon., *The Golden Age Restor'd* (1703)

Anon., *The Golden Age Revers'd* (1703)

Anon., *Advertisement* (1704, containing false allegation that Tonson was expelled from the Kit-Cat or retired so as not to be the butt of their jokes any longer: British Library ref. 816 m.19/34)

Anon., *A Letter from Several Members of the Society for Reformation of Manners to the Most Revered Father in God Thomas Lord Archbishop of Canterbury* (1704)

Anon., *A Kit-Cat C—b Describ'd* (1705)

Anon., *A New Collection of Poems relating to State Affairs* (1705) (Pope's copy at British Library shelfmark C.28.e.15)

Anon., *The Tackers Vindicated; or, an Answer to the Whigs New Black List* (1705)

Anon., *The Loyal Calves Head Club* (1710)

Anon., *The Tryal of Dr Henry Sacheverell before the House of Peers for High Crimes and Misdemeanours* (1710)

Anon. [St John], *Letter to the Examiner* (1710) (in Somers' *Tracts*, vol. 13, p. 71)

Anon., 'A Song at the Kit-Cat Club', *The State Bell-Mans Collection of Verses for the Year 1711* (1710–11)

Anon., *The Kit-Cat Clubs Lamentation for the loss of the Pope, the Devil and the Pretender, that were taken into custody on Saturday last by the Secretary of State. Written by Jacob Door-holder to that Society* (1711)

Anon., *The Spectator Inspected* and *A Spy upon the Spectator* (1711)

Anon., *Mr Addison turned Tory* (1713)

Anon., *The Vanity of Free-Thinking Expos'd in a Satyr, Dedicated to Mr C[olli]ns, Proprietor, and the rest of the Thoughtless Members of the Kitt-Katt Club* (1713)

Anon., *Crisis upon Crisis* (1714)

Anon., *An Epistle to Joseph Addison Esq. Occasion'd by the Death of the Rt. Hon. Charles, Late Earl of Halifax* (1715)

Anon., *The Lord Whiglove's Elegy – to which is added a Pious Epitaph upon the Late Bishop of Addlebury* (1715)

Anon., *Ingratitude: to Mr Pope* (1733)

Anon., *On the Author of a Dialogue Concerning Women, pretended to be writ in Defence of the Sex* (date unknown)

Anon. [Curll?], *Cases of Divorce for Several Causes; III – The Case of John Dormer, Esq.* (1715)

Anon. [Curll?], *The Works and Life of... Charles [Montagu], late Earl of Halifax* (1715)
Anon. [Mary Pix?], *A Poem, Humbly Inscribed to the Lords Commissioners for the Union* (1707)
Arbuthnot, Dr John, *The History of John Bull* (1712), ed. Alan W. Bower and Robert A. Erickson (Oxford, 1976)
'On the Toasts of the Kit-Cat' (1716), in *Miscellanies* (Dublin, 1746)
Astell, Mary, *Bart'lemy Fair: or, an Enquiry after Wit* (1709)
Berkeley, George, *The Works of George Berkeley, Bishop of Cloyne*, ed. A. A. Luce and T. E. Jessop (London, 1956)
Betterton, T., *The History of the English Stage* (1741)
Blackmore, Sir Richard, *A Satyr against Wit* (1699)
Advice to the Poets (1706)
The Kit-Cats, A Poem (1708)
Blome, Richard, *The Gentleman's Recreation* (1710)
Boyer, Abel, *History of the Life and Reign of Queen Anne* (1722)
Anon. (Boyer?), *Letters of Wit, Politicks and Morality* (1701)
Browne, Tom, *Amusements Serious and Comical* (1702)
(ed.) *Commendatory Verses, on the Author of the Two Arthurs, and the Satyr against Wit* (1700)
Anon. (Browne), *A Description of Mr D[ryde]n's Funeral* (1700)
Bruce, Thomas (2nd Earl of Ailesbury), *Memoirs*, 2 vols, ed. W. E. Buckley (London, 1728ff.–1890 edn)
Budgell, Eustace, *The Bee* (1733)
Memoirs of the Life and Character of the Earl of Orrery and of the Family of the Boyles (1732)
Calendar of State Papers, Domestic Series, of the Reign of William III and Anne, vols 1697–1705, eds Hardy, Bateson, Mahaffy and Knighton (London, 1927–2005)
Calendar of Treasury Books, volumes 10.2 (1693) – 31.1 (1717), ed. William A. Shaw (London, 1904–62)
Carter, Charles, *Complete Practical Cook* (1730)
Chesterfield, 4th Earl of, *Characters of Lord Chesterfield* (London, 1778)
Letters of Philip Dormer Stanhope, Earl of Chesterfield, with the Characters, ed. J. Bradshaw, 3 vols (London, 1892)
Churchill, Sarah, *The Private Correspondence of Sarah Duchess of Marlborough* (London, 1838 edn)
Characters of Her Contemporaries, by Sarah Duchess of Marlborough, ed. Nathaniel Hooke (London, 1930)

Cibber, Colley, *An Apology for the Life of Mr Colley Cibber, Written by Himself* (1740), ed. B. R. S. Fone (Ann Arbor, Mich., 1968)

A Brief Supplement to Colley Cibber, Esq: his Lives of the late famous actors and actresses, ed. Anthony Aston (London, *c.* 1747)

Collier, Jeremy, *A Short View of the Immorality and Prophaness of the English Stage* (1698)

A Defence of the Short View (1699), ed. Scott McMillin (London, 1973) or Richard Hellinger (New York, 1987)

Mr Collier's Dissuasive from the Play-house (1703)

Collins, Anthony, *A Discourse of Free-Thinking* (1713)

Colman the Elder, George, 'To the Right Honourable The Earl of Bath', in *The Jealous Wife* (1761)

Congreve, William, *Letters Upon Several Occasions: written by and between Mr Dryden, Mr Wycherly, Mr ——, Mr Congreve and Mr Dennis* (1696)

Amendments to Mr Collier's False and Imperfect Citations (1698)

The Works of Mr William Congreve, 3 vols (London, 1710, 1719)

An Impossible Thing: A Tale (1720)

Mr Congreve's Last Will and Testament (1729)

The Complete Works of William Congreve, 4 vols, ed. Montague Summers (London, 1923 and New York, 1964)

The Mourning Bride, etc, ed. Bonamy Dobrée (Oxford, 1928)

William Congreve: Letters and Documents, ed. John C. Hodges (London, 1964)

The Comedies of William Congreve, ed. Eric S. Rump (London, 1985)

Croxall, Samuel, *Fables of Aesop and Others* (1728 edn)

Cunningham, Alexander, *The History of Great Britain from the Revolution in 1688 to the Accession of George I*, ed. William Thomson (Contemporary – date unknown, and ed. London, 1787)

Darby, Charles, *Bacchanalia: Or, A Description of a Drunken Club* (1680, reprinted 1698)

Davenant, Charles, *England's Enemies Exposed* (1701)

The True Picture of a Modern Whig set forth in a Dialogue between Mr Whiglove and Mr Double (1702)

De Fonvive, John, *The Post Man*

Defoe, Daniel, *The Double Welcome* (1705)

The History of the Union of Great Britain (1709), ed. D. W. Hayton, 2 vols (London, 2002)

Eleven Opinions about Mr H[arley] (1711)

The Honour and Prerogative of the Queen's Majesty Vindicated . . . in a Letter from a Country Whig to Mr Steele (1713)

Dennis, John, *Letters Upon Several Occasions* (1696)
The Usefulness of the Stage to the Happiness of Mankind, to Government, and to Religion . . . (1698) and *The True Born Englishman, A Satyr* (1701), in *The Critical Works of John Dennis*, ed. E. N. Hooker, 2 vols (Baltimore, Md., 1939–43)
The Diverting Post
The Dublin Gazette
Dryden, John and Jacob Tonson (eds), *Examen Poeticum, Being the Third Part of Miscellany Poems, Containing Variety of New Translations of the Ancient Poets. Together with many Original Copies by the Most Eminent Hands* (1693)
The Annual Miscellany: For the Year 1694, Being the Fourth Part of Miscellany Poems, etc. (1694)
Poetical Miscellanies, the Fifth Part, etc. (1704)
Poetical Miscellanies, the Sixth Part, etc. (1709)
English Gratitude, Or the Whig Miscellany (1713)
The First (-Sixth) Part of Miscellany Poems, Publish'd by Dryden, 6 vols (1716)
Dramatick Works (1718)
Dunton, John, *The Night-Walker* (1696)
The Dublin Scuffle (1699), ed. Andrew Carpenter (Dublin, 2000)
Royal Gratitude . . . To which is added . . . A Trip to the Loyal Mug-House at Night, to Drink a Health to King George and the Royal Family (1716)
D'Urfey, Thomas, *Wit and Mirth: or, Pills to Purge Melancholy* (1700)
Wonders in the Sun; or, the Kingdom of the Birds (1706)
The Examiner
Etherege, George, *The Poems of Sir George Etherege*, ed. James Thorpe (Princeton, NJ, 1963)
Faber, John Jr (ed.), *The Kit-Cat Club by Sr Godfrey Kneller* (1735)
The Flying Post or, The Post-Master
Farquhar, George, *Complete Works of George Farquhar*, ed. Charles Stonehill (New York, 1967)
Garth, Dr Samuel, *The Dispensary*, ed. Jo Allen Bradshaw (1725, 9th edn as reprinted: New York, 1975)
The Poetical Works of Samuel Garth (Glasgow, 1771)
Gay, John, *Present State of Wit* (1711)
[pseud. Sir James Baker?] *A Letter to a Buttonian K**** from Sir James Baker, admirer-general of the fair sex and late secretary of the toasts of the Kit-Cat Club* (1718)
The Gentleman's Magazine

Gildon, Charles and Gerard Langbaine, *The Lives and Characters of the English Dramatic Poets* (1691, 1698 edn, 1712 edn)
Gorden, Pat, *Geography Anatomiz'd or, The Geographical Grammar* (1708)
Hatton, Edward, *The New View of London* (1708)
Hearne, Thomas, *Remarks and Collections of Thomas Hearne*, ed. C. E. Doble et al., 11 vols (Oxford, 1885–1921)
Historical Manuscripts Commission (HMC)
Report II: Appendix (1871), The Bayfordbury Manuscripts
Report III: Appendix (1872), Correspondence of Matthew Prior
Report V: Appendix (1876), Manuscripts of Reginald Cholmondeley, of Condover Hall, Shropshire
Report VII: Appendix (1879), Copies of Letters of George Berkeley to Sir J. Percival
Report VIII: Appendix, part 1 (1881), Manuscripts of His Grace the Duke of Marlborough, at Blenheim, Co. Oxford
Report XII: Appendix, parts 1–3 (1888), Manuscripts of the Earl Cowper, K.G.
Report XIII: Appendix, part 2 (1893), Portland Papers
Report XIII: Appendix, part 7 (1893), Manuscripts of the Earl of Lonsdale
Report XIV: Appendix, part 9 (1895), Misc. manuscripts including correspondence of Francis Hare
Report on the Manuscripts of the Duke of Buccleuch & Queensberry, Montagu House, vol. 2, part 2 (1903)
Report on the Manuscripts of the Duke of Portland, vols 2, 4 and 5 (1899–1931)
Report on the Manuscripts of the Marquess of Downshire, 4 vols (1924–40)
Report on the Manuscripts of Mrs Stopford-Sackville etc., vol. 1 (1904)
Calendar of the Manuscripts of the Marquis of Bath, vol. 3, The Prior Papers (1904)
The Manuscripts of His Grace the Duke of Rutland, 4 vols (1888–1905)
Hughes, John, 'Barn-Elms', in *Poems*, vol. 1 (1735)
Jacob, Giles, *The Poetical Register*, 2 vols (1719–20)
Memoirs of the Life and Writings of the Right Hon Joseph Addison Esq., with his Character by Sir Richard Steele and a true Copy of his Last Will and Testament (1724)
The Mirrour: Or, Letters Satyrical, Panegyrical, Serious and Humorous on the Present Times (1733)
Kidder, Edward, *Receipts of Pastry and Cookery* (1740)
King, William, *Art of Cookery, in Imitation of Horace's Art of Poetry* (1708)
Lacy, John, *The Steeleids: or, the Tryal of Wit* (1714)

Lamb, Patrick, *Royal Cookery, or The Compleat Court-Cook* (1710)
Leslie, Charles, *The Rehearsal of Observator* no. 41 (5–12 May 1705)
A View of the Times, Their Principles and Practices, in the First Volumes of The Rehearsals, by Philalethes (1708)
Lister, Martin, *A Journey to Paris in the Year 1698* (1699)
Locke, John, *Essay Concerning Human Understanding* (1690)
Lord, George de Forest et al. (eds), *Poems on Affairs of State: Augustan Satirical Verse 1660–1714*, 7 vols (New Haven, Conn., 1963–75), especially vol. 7, ed. F. H. Ellis
Luttrell, Narcissus, *A Brief Historical Relation of State Affairs from September 1678 to April 1714*, 6 vols (Oxford, 1857 edn)
Macky, John, *A Journey through England* (1714)
Characters of the Court of Queen Anne (1733)
Memoirs of the Secret Services of John Macky, ed. A. R. (1733)
Manley, Mrs Mary Delariviere, *Secret Memoirs and Manners of Several Persons of Quality, of Both Sexes, from the New Atalantis* (1709), ed. Ros Ballaster (Harmondsworth, 1992)
Miège, Guy, *The Present State of Great Britain* (1707)
Montagu, Charles, *The Works and Life of the Right Hon. Charles, Late Earl of Halifax* (1715)
Nicolson, William, *The London Diaries of William Nicolson, Bishop of Carlisle, 1702–08*, ed. C. Jones and G. Holmes (Oxford, 1985)
The Observator
Oldmixon, John, *Arthur Maynwaring – Life and Posthumous Works* (1715)
Memoirs of the Life of the Most Noble Thomas, Late Marquess of Wharton; with his Speeches in Parliament both in England and Ireland. To which is added His Lordship's Character by Sir Richard Steel (1715)
The History of England during the Reigns of King William and Queen Mary, Queen Anne, King George I (1735)
Memoirs of the Press, historical and political from 1710–1740 (1742)
Patterson, William, *An Inquiry into the Reasonableness and Consequences of an Union with Scotland* (1706)
Petty, Sir William, 'Proposition for quitting Ireland & the Highlands of Scotland', in *Essays in Political Arithmetik* (1711)
Playford, Henry and Abel Roper (eds), *Luctus Britannici, or, the Tears of the British Muses for the Death of John Dryden, Esq.* (1700)
Playford, John, *The Complete Country Dance Tunes from Playford's Dancing Master (1651–1728)*, ed. Jeremy Barlow (London, 1985)

Pope, Alexander, *Works*, ed. J. W. Croker, W. Elwin and W. J. Courthope, 10 vols (London, 1871–89)

The Twickenham Edition of the Works of Alexander Pope, ed. John Butt et al., 11 vols (London 1939–69)

The Correspondence of Alexander Pope, ed. George Sherburn, 5 vols (Oxford, 1956)

Poetical Works, ed. Herbert Davis (Oxford, 1989)

The Postboy

Prior, Matthew, *Poems Upon Several Occasions* (1718)

Dialogues of the Dead, And other works in prose and verse (Cambridge, 1907)

The Literary Works of Matthew Prior, ed. H. Bunker Wright and Monroe K. Spears, 2 vols (Oxford, 1959–71 edn)

Puckle, James, *The Club: or a Dialogue between Father and Son* (1711)

Rose, Giles, *Proper School of Instructions for the Officers of the Mouth* (1682)

Rowe, Nicholas, *The Reconcilement between Jacob Tonson and Mr Congreve* (1707)

Savage, Richard, *Author To Be Let* (1729)

Shaftesbury, Anthony Ashley Cooper, 3rd Earl of, *Soliloquy: Or, Advice to an Author* (1710)

Characteristicks of Men, Manners, Opinions, Times (1711), ed. J. M. Robertson, 2 vols (New York, 1964) or ed. Philip Ayres, 2 vols (Oxford, 1999)

The Life, Unpublished Letters and Philosophical Regimen of Anthony, Earl of Shaftesbury, ed. Benjamin Rand (London, 1992)

Shippen, William, *Faction Display'd* (1704)

Somers, John (ed.), *A letter balancing the necessity of keeping a land force in times of peace, with the dangers that may follow it* (1697)

Several Orations of Demosthenes, To Encourage the Athenians to oppose the Exorbitant Power of Philip of Macedon (English'd from the Greek by several Hands) (1702)

'Dryden's Satire to his Muse', in *The Works of the Most Celebrated Minor Poets*, vol. 3 (London, 1751)

Miscellaneous State Papers from 1501 to 1726, vol. 2: Somers Papers (1778 edn)

Spence, Joseph, *Observations, Anecdotes, and Characters of Books and Men*, ed. S. W. Singer (London, 1820) or ed. James M. Osborn, 2 vols (Oxford, 1966)

St John, Henry (Lord Bolingbroke), *Letters and Correspondence*, ed. George Parke, 4 vols (London, 1798)

Steele, Richard, *The Case of Richard Steele, Esq . . .* (1714)
The Reader, nos 1–9 (London, 1714)
Chit-Chat, in a Letter to a Lady in the Country, nos 1–3 (1716)
Town-Talk, in a Letter to a Lady in the Country, nos 1–9 (1716)
The Plebeian . . . by a Member of the House of Commons, nos 1–4 (1719)
Tracts and Pamphlets by Richard Steele, ed. Rae Blanchard (Baltimore, Md., 1944)
The Occasional Verse of Richard Steele, ed. Rae Blanchard (Oxford, 1952)
The Englishman: A Political Journal by Richard Steele, ed. Rae Blanchard (Oxford, 1955)
Richard Steele's Periodical Journalism 1714–16, ed. Rae Blanchard (Oxford, 1959)
The Correspondence of Richard Steele, ed. Rae Blanchard (Oxford, 1968 edn)
The Plays of Richard Steele, ed. Shirley Strum Kenny (Oxford, 1971)
Stepney, George, *An Essay upon the Present Interest of England* (1701)
The Muses Choice (London, 1750 edn)
Sweeney, Owen, *The Quacks, or, Love's the Physician* (1705)
Swift, Jonathan, *The Tripe Club: A Satyr* (1706)
Meditations upon a Broomstick and Somewhat Beside (1710)
Mr. C[olli]ns's Discourse of Free-Thinking (1713)
Swift's marginalia on John Macky's *Characters of the Court of Britain* (1714)
'An Essay to Restore the Kit-Cat Members to their lost Abilities, for the sake of the LADIES who admire em', in *Letters, Poems and Tales: Amorous, Satyrical, and Gallant. Which passed between several persons of distinction. Now first published from respective originals found in the cabinet of . . . Mrs Anne Long* (1718)
On Poetry, A Rhapsody (1733)
The Prose Works of Jonathan Swift, ed. Temple Scott, 12 vols (London, 1897 edn) including, in vol. 5:
A Short Character of His Excellency Thomas Earl of Wharton, Lord Lieutenant of Ireland (1710)
A Letter of Thanks from My Lord W[harto]n, to the Lord Bishop of S. Asaph, in the Name of the Kit-Cat Club (1712)
The Conduct of the Allies and of the Last Ministry (1712)
The Importance of the Guardian Considered (1713)
The Publick Spirit of the Whigs (1714)

The Prose Writings of Jonathan Swift, ed. Herbert Davis et al., 16 vols (Oxford, 1939–75)

Journal to Stella, ed. Harold Williams, 2 vols (Oxford, 1948)

The Correspondence of Jonathan Swift, ed. Harold Williams, 5 vols (Oxford, 1965)

The Drapier's Letters to the People of Ireland . . . , ed. Herbert Davis (Oxford, 1965 edn)

The Correspondence of Jonathan Swift, D.D., ed. David Woolley, 4 vols (Frankfurt and Oxford, 1999–2003)

Tickell, Thomas, Preface to *Addison's Works*, vol. 1 (1721)

The Poetical Works of Thomas Tickell (1796)

Tonson, Jacob, *Jacob Tonson in Ten Letters by and about Him*, ed. Sarah Lewis Carol Clapp (Austin, Tex., 1948)

Tracts on the British Stage 1699–1726 (BL shelfmark 641.e.16)

Trapp, Joseph, *The Character and Principles of the Present Set of Whigs* (1711)

Tutchin, John, *The Observator*

Uffenbach, Zacharias Conrad von, *London in 1710, from the Travels of Zacharias Conrad von Uffenbach*, trans. and ed. W. H. Quarrell and Margaret Mare (London, 1934)

Vanbrugh, Sir John: *A Short Vindication of 'The Relapse' and 'The Provok'd Wife' from Immorality and Profaneness, by the Author* (1698)

The Complete Works of Sir John Vanbrugh, ed. Geoffrey Webb and Bonamy Dobrée, 4 vols including letters in vol. 4 (London, 1927–8)

The Relapse and Other Plays, ed. Brean Hammond (Oxford, 2004)

Voltaire, F. M. A. de, '18th Letter on The English', in *Oeuvres complètes de Voltaire*, ed. Louis Moland (Paris, 1877–85)

Wagstaffe, William, *Character of Richard Steele* (1713)

Walsh, William, *Dialogue Concerning Women* (1691)

Letters and Poems, Amorous and Gallant (1692 and reprinted in Dryden's 1716 *Miscellany*)

Ward, Edward (Ned), *The London Spy* (1698), ed. Paul Hyland (East Lansing, Mich., 1993)

The Secret History of the Calves-Head Club (1703)

The History of the London Clubs (1709)

The Secret History of Clubs: particularly the Kit-Cat . . . (1709)

Satyrical Reflections Upon Clubs in xxix chapters, vol. 5 (1710), chapter 28 on the Kit-Cat Club

The Second Part of the History of London Clubs (pamphlet, BL shelfmark 816.m.19 I-91)

A Compleat and Humorous Account of all the Remarkable Clubs and Societies in the cities of London and Westminster (1756)
Waters, Edward, *The Dublin Spy by Tom Tatler*
The Weekly Journal or Saturday's Post
The (Protestant) Dublin Intelligence (1709)
Wentworth, Thomas, *The Wentworth Papers 1705–1739*, ed. James J. Cartwright (London, 1883)
Wilson, Charles [pseud. for Edmund Curll], *Memoirs of the Life, Writings and Amours of William Congreve Esq . . .* (1730)
Woodward, Josiah, *Account of the Societies for Reformation of Manners in England and Ireland* (1698)
Wortley Montagu, Lady Mary, *The Letters and Works of Lady Mary Wortley Montagu*, ed. Lord Wharncliffe, 2 vols (London, 1861)

Manuscripts

Bank of England

Personal account records and subscription lists (e.g. First, 1694 subscription to the Bank itself)

The Bodleian, Oxford

MS Rawl D832 / Eng Hist b.209 f.79 / MS Dep d. 68 / MS Carte 79, f.420 and 80, 81 / MS Dep c. 293 / Don d. 112 / MS Eng Letters c.29 and c.129 / MS Rawl poet 152–3 / MSS Ballard / SC.25, 427 MS Montagu, d.I, f.99

Beinecke Rare Book and Manuscript Library, New Haven

The Manchester Papers / Gen MSS Misc – 1672 Item F–2 / Osborn MS File 'S', 14,451 – Various Steele papers / Osborn MS 17,972 / Osborn MS 17,500 / Osborn Shelves c.300 / Osborn MS 15,096 / Im.J637 / w791lgh v.3 / Gen MSS 310, Box 4, folder 137 / Anon., 'A True Character of the Prince of Wales's Poet' (1701)

British Library (BL)

The Kit-Cat Club in general: Add MS 40,060 / Add MS 6,321 f.5 / Add MS 21,094 f.140b / Add MS 72,495
Addison: Egerton MS 1971–4 / Add MS 7,058 f.89 / Birch (Thomas) Papers: Add 4,101(–4,478) / Add MS 61,491–665 / Add MS 61,636A f.58–9 / Add MS 61,653 f.89–155v / Add MSS 61,101–710 / Stowe MSS 227 and 241–2 / Harleian MS 694 / Sloane MS 34,075
Congreve: Add MS 4293 f.54–64
Steele: Add MS 5145 (A–C) / Add MS 61,686–88 / Add MS 32,685 / Microfilm 494

Tonson: Add MS 28,275–6 / Add MS 21,110 / Add MS 28,887 f.187 / Add MS 28,893 f.443 / Add MS 32,626 f.2 / Add MS 32,690 f.36 / Add MS 32,992 f.340 / Egerton MS 1,951 / Stowe MS 755 f.35, 155 and 97b / Add MS 61,620 f.26–33b

Vanbrugh: Add MS 70,948 / Add MS 19,611–3 / Add MS 19,592–601 / Add MS 38,056 / Add MS 32,687 and 33,064

Other: Add MS 22,510 / Egerton MS 929 / Add MS 7,121 / Add MS 32,679 / Add MS 61,619 f.196b–7 / Add MS 32,753 / Egerton MS 921 / Stowe MS 246 / Craggs Papers vol. 1, f.164 / Egerton MS 917 / Egerton MS 2,623 / Add MS 49,360 / Add MS 4,740 f.171 / Add MS 61,641 f.137 / Add MS 32,095 f.410 / Add MS 32,329 f.50 / Add MSS 28,644 / Add MS 61,609 ff.171–3 / Add MS 21, 551 / Add MS 28,875–947 / Add 61,461 f.63 / Add MS 35,854 / Add MS 4,221 / Add MS 22,851 / Add MS 70,501 / Stowe MS 751, f.142

Chatsworth, Derbyshire

Papers of William Cavendish, 2nd Duke of Devonshire

Columbia University Library, New York

Dorset's 'Book of Entrys Conserning the Knight Harbingers Place: 1688. And in Rotation to other Things at Court' (Montgomery Collection, Columbia MS)

Gilbert Collection, Dublin

Dublin Castle Improvements, 1710 – MS 195

Herefordshire County Record Office

Cowper Box 9, Diary 5, 47–8

Longleat Archives, Wiltshire

Longleat MS 393 / Charles Montagu, Duke of Manchester: Correspondence with Prior (HMC 58 Bath MSS III)

National Archives, Kew (NA)

SP 84/230 / SP 105/82 / SP 36/38 f.32 / LC7/2 / PROB 1/61 / PROB 10/7376/6 / PROB 1/103 / C11/2363/42 / SP 44/348 f.275 / 30/24/20/137

National Portrait Gallery

Tonson Papers

New York Public Library

Humanities and Social Sciences Library, Montague Collection, Boxes 7, 9, 10ff., Bolingbroke, Somers, Steele and Charles Montague

Berg Collection (Letters of Congreve, Tonson, etc.)

Nottingham University Library

Portland Papers

Rousham House, Oxfordshire
Papers of John and James Dormer
Trinity College Dublin
MSS of Archbishop King

LIST OF MEMBERS

The following are the fifty-five men who, in the view of this author, are the most likely members of the Kit-Cat Club, listed by date of birth and with their titles at the time of their deaths. For a detailed explanation of reasons for inclusion and exclusion, and for additional information about the more minor figures who barely feature in this book, please see the author's website, www.opheliafield.com.

1. John Vaughan, 3rd Earl of Carbery (1639–1713)
2. Thomas Hopkins (*c.* 1641–1720)
3. Col. John Tidcomb (1642–1713)
4. Charles Sackville, 6th Earl of Dorset and 1st Earl of Middlesex (1643–1706)
5. Thomas Wharton, 5th Baron and 1st Marquess of Wharton (1648–1715)
6. John Somers, Baron Somers of Evesham (1651–1716)
7. John Smith (1655–1723)
8. Jacob Tonson (1656–1736)
9. Sir Henry Furnese, 1st Baronet (1658–1712)
10. Charles Montagu, 4th Earl and 1st Duke of Manchester (1660/1–1722)
11. Charles Montagu, 1st Earl of Halifax (1661–1715)
12. Sir Samuel Garth (1661–1719)
13. William Walsh (1662–1708)
14. Charles Seymour, 6th Duke of Somerset (1662–1748)
15. George Stepney (1663–1707)
16. Matthew Prior (1664–1721)
17. Sir John Vanbrugh (1664–1726)
18. Charles Dartiquenave (1664–1737)
19. Evelyn Pierrepont, 1st Duke of Kingston (*c.*1665–1726)

20. Richard Norton (*c.* 1666–1732)
21. Anthony Henley (1667–1711)
22. Arthur Maynwaring (1668–1712)
23. Henry Boyle, Baron Carleton (1669–1725)
24. Abraham Stanyan (*c.* 1669–1732)
25. Charles Howard, 3rd Earl of Carlisle (1669–1738)
26. John Dormer (1669–1719) and/or James Dormer (1679–1741)
27. Algernon Capel, 2nd Earl of Essex (1670–1710)
28. William Congreve (1670–1729)
29. Richard Topham (1671–1730)
30. Joseph Addison (1672–1719)
31. Charles Lenox, 1st Duke of Richmond and Lenox (1672–1723)
32. Sir Richard Steele (1672–1729)
33. Gen. James Stanhope, 1st Earl of Stanhope (1673–1721)
34. William Cavendish, 2nd Duke of Devonshire (1673–1729)
35. Spencer Compton, 1st Earl of Wilmington (1673/4–1743)
36. Charles, 4th Baron Mohun (*c.* 1675–1712)
37. Charles, 4th Baron Cornwallis (1675–1722)
38. Edward Hopkins (1675–1736)
39. Richard Boyle, 2nd Viscount Shannon (1675–1740)
40. Sir Richard Temple, Viscount Cobham (1675–1749)
41. Sir Robert Walpole, 1st Earl of Orford (1676–1745)
42. Edmund Dunch (*c.* 1677–1719)
43. Francis, 2nd Earl of Godolphin (1678–1766)
44. James, 3rd Earl of Berkeley (1680–1736)
45. Charles Fitzroy, 2nd Duke of Grafton (1683–1757)
46. Henry Fiennes-Clinton, 7th Earl of Lincoln (1684–1728)
47. Richard Lumley, 2nd Earl of Scarbrough (1684–1740)
48. William Pulteney, 1st Earl of Bath (1684–1764)
49. John, 2nd Duke of Montagu (1690–1749)
50. Lionel Cranfield Sackville, 1st Duke of Dorset (1688–1765)
51. Thomas Holles-Pelham, Earl of Clare and Duke of Newcastle (1693/4–1768)
52. Richard Boyle, 3rd Earl of Burlington (1695–1753)
53. Theophilus Hastings, 9th Earl of Huntingdon (1696–1746)
54. Major-General John Shrimpton (?–1707)
55. John Vandom[e] (dates unknown)

NOTES

PROLOGUE

1 Edmond Malone (ed.), *Critical and Miscellaneous Prose Works of John Dryden* (London, 1800), vol. 1, part 1, pp. 347–82. Malone's version is based on Ballard MSS in the Bodleian.

2 Thomas Hearne, quoted in: Harvey Cushing, *Dr. Garth: The Kit-Cat Poet* (Baltimore, Md., 1906), p. 21.

3 HMC, *Reginald Cholmondeley MSS*, p. 333, p. 359, Edward Hinton at Westminster to his cousin the Rev. John Cooper, 14 May 1700.

4 Edward (Ned) Ward, *The London Spy* (1698), ed. Paul Hyland (East Lansing, Mich., 1993), no. 2(6), April 1700.

5 Anon. [Tom Browne], 'A Description of Mr D——n's Funeral' (1700), in *A New Collection of Poems relating to State Affairs* (1705). Alexander Pope's copy at British Library shelfmark C.28.e.15.

6 Ibid.

7 James Caulfield, *Memoirs of the Celebrated Persons Composing the Kit-Cat Club; with a prefatory account of the origin of the association, illustrated with forty-eight portraits from the original paintings by Sir Godfrey Kneller* (London, 1849), p. 249 – quoting from Dryden's 'Life of Lucian' (*c.* 1696).

8 Charles E. Ward (ed.), *The Letters of John Dryden* (Durham, NC, 1942), pp. 80–1.

9 Anon. [Tom Browne], 'A Description of Mr D——n's Funeral' (1700) in *A New Collection of Poems relating to State Affairs* (1705). Alexander Pope's copy at British Library shelfmark C.28.e.15.

10 Madeleine Bingham, *Masks and Façades: Sir John Vanbrugh, The Man and his Setting* (London, 1974), p. 76.

11 Jonathan Swift, *On Poetry, A Rhapsody* (1733).

12 Dryden's early biographer, Edmond Malone, considered this to be a libel spread by a woman who wrote an account of the event almost three decades afterwards, to pay her way out of debtors' prison. She based her account largely

on a satirical eyewitness 'Description of Mr D——n's Funeral' (1700), which said it was conducted with as much confusion as 'at St Bart's famed Fair'.

13 Charles Stonehill (ed.), *Complete Works of George Farquhar* (New York, 1967), vol. 1, p. 391.

14 Anon., 'The Seven Wise Men', Add MSS 40,060, f.51.

15 R. O. Bucholz, *The Augustan Court: Queen Anne and the Decline of Court Culture* (Stanford, Calif., 1993), p. 248.

16 Lawrence Stone (ed.), *An Imperial State at War: Britain from 1689 to 1815* (London, 1994), p. 5.

17 Anon. [Tom Browne], 'A Description of Mr D——n's Funeral' (1700), in *A New Collection of Poems relating to State Affairs* (1705). Alexander Pope's copy at British Library shelfmark C.28.e.15.

18 William Shippen, *Faction Display'd* (1704).

19 John Locke, *Essay Concerning Human Understanding* (1690).

I SELF-MADE MEN

1 Wycherley to Pope, 1709, quoted in William Roberts, *The Earlier History of English Book-Selling* (London, 1889), p. 156.

2 Donald F. Bond, *The Spectator* (Oxford, 1965), no. 69, Saturday, 19 May 1711, by Addison.

3 Daniel Defoe, *A Tour Thro The Whole Island of Great Britain . . . Letter V* (1724–7).

4 Alexander Pope, *The Dunciad* (1728). John Dryden also referred to Jacob having 'two left legs'.

5 Sarah Lewis Carol Clapp (ed.), *Jacob Tonson in Ten Letters by and about Him* (Austin, Tex., 1948), letter from Dr William Oliver to Jacob Tonson Jr, 12 July 1735.

6 From a triplet allegedly pencilled by Dryden beneath a Kneller painting of Tonson, in July 1698, and then later incorporated by William Shippen into his poem *Faction Display'd* (1704): HMC, *Bath MSS*, vol. 3, p. 238, The Prior Papers, letter from Richard Powys to Prior.

7 Matthew Prior to Jacob Tonson, 13 September 1695, quoted in: *The Gentleman's Magazine*, new series, 2 (July 1834), p. 464.

8 Alexander Pope, *The Dunciad* (1728).

9 Edward (Ned) Ward, *The Secret History of Clubs* (1709).

10 Both in Anon., *Satire on Modern Translators* (1698) and also Richard Blackmore, *A Satyr Against Wit* (1699).

11 Samuel Johnson, *A Dictionary of the English Language* (1873), entry for 'Grub Street'.

12 Edward (Ned) Ward, *The Secret History of Clubs* (1709).

13 S. Fitzmaurice, 'Servant or Patron? Jacob Tonson and the language of deference and respect', *Language Sciences* 24, 3 (May 2002), p. 247.

14 John Dunton, *Life and Errors of J. D. late Citizen of London* (1705).

15 Edward (Ned) Ward, *The Secret History of Clubs* (1709).

16 NPG, Tonson Papers. It was the NPG Director, Sir Henry Hake, who suggested in 1945 that this bill was illustrative of the Kit-Cat Club's dining habits, but there is no direct connection between the document and the Club other than Tonson's name.
17 HMC, *Bayfordbury MSS*, p. 71, no. 73.
18 John Dryden, 'Life of Lucian' (*c.* 1696).
19 Complaint of Sir Henry Chauncy in 1700, quoted in David Lemmings, *Gentlemen and Barristers: The Inns of Court and the English Bar 1680–1730* (Oxford, 1990), p. 11.
20 The War of the League of Augsburg (also known as the Nine Years War, or the War of the Grand Alliance) starting in 1689.
21 John Somers, 'Dryden's Satire to his Muse', *The Works of the Most Celebrated Minor Poets*, vol. 3 (London, 1751).
22 Charles Gildon and Gerard Langbaine, *The Lives and Characters of the English Dramatic Poets* (1712 edn), p. 21.
23 David Lemmings, *Gentlemen and Barristers: The Inns of Court and the English Bar 1680–1730* (Oxford, 1990), p. 8.
24 William Congreve, *The Way of the World*, Act 2, Scene 1.
25 Samuel Garth, *The Dispensary* (1725, 9th edn as reprinted, New York, 1975), Canto IV.
26 Dr Samuel Johnson, *Lives of the English Poets* (London, 1781), ed. George Birkbeck Hill (Oxford, 1905), vol. 1, p. 409.
27 John Dryden, *Dramatick Works* (1718).
28 John Dryden, 'To my Dear Friend Mr. Congreve, On His Comedy, call'd, The Double Dealer' (1694), prefixed to Tonson's edition of *The Double Dealer*.
29 William Congreve to the Duke of Newcastle, quoted in John C. Hodges (ed.), *William Congreve: Letters and Documents* (London, 1964), p. 76.
30 Thomas Southerne's account, Add MS 4,221, f.61.
31 Colley Cibber, *An Apology for the Life . . .*, (1740), ed. B. R. S. Fone (Ann Arbor, Mich., 1968), p. 72.
32 Ibid.
33 William Congreve, 'A Complaint to Pious Selinda', in *Poems Upon Several Occasions* (1710). This poem was about Bracegirdle according to the actor Anthony Aston.
34 Colley Cibber in the Introduction to *Ximena, or The Heroik Daughter* (1719).
35 Earl of Burlington to William Congreve's father, quoted in C. Y. Ferdinand and D. F. McKenzie, 'Congreve, William', *Oxford Dictionary of National Biography* (September 2004, online edn, October 2005).
36 Nicholas Rowe, *The Reconcilement between Jacob Tonson and Mr Congreve* (1707).
37 John Vanbrugh, *The Provok'd Wife* (1697), Act 5, Scene 2.
38 John Vanbrugh, *The Relapse* (1696), Act 1, Scene 1.

II FRIENDSHIPS FORMED

1 Donald F. Bond (ed.), *The Spectator* (Oxford, 1965), no. 313, Thursday, 28 February 1712, by Eustace Budgell.

2 Geoffrey Holmes, *Augustan England: Professions, State and Society 1680–1730* (London, 1982), p. 43.

3 Jacob Tonson Sr to Jacob Tonson Jr, quoted in Kathleen M. Lynch, *Jacob Tonson, Kit-Cat Publisher* (Knoxville, Tenn., 1971), p. 169. Original found at Bodleian MS Eng Letters c.129 f.116–17.

4 Westminster School, *Record of Old Westminsters.*

5 Prior's mother had some rather posher relations, whereby Prior was the kinsman of a later patron named Edward Villiers, Earl of Jersey, so he was not utterly obscure.

6 *Dialogues of the Dead*, quoted in C. K. Eves, *Matthew Prior, Poet and Diplomatist* (New York, 1939), p. 24.

7 Edward (Ned) Ward, *The Secret History of Clubs* (1709).

8 'Memoirs of the Life of Charles Montagu', in *The Works and Life of Charles, late Earl of Halifax* (1715), p. 17. See Brice Harris, *Charles Sackville, 6th Earl of Dorset: Patron and Poet of the Restoration* (Urbana, Ill., 1940), pp. 150–1. Prior's own direct reference to Montagu having been preferred for the Mouse poem over him: 'one Mouse eats while t'other's starved' is found in his poem, 'On Mr Pr—r's letters to Mr [Fleetwood] Sheppard (not omitting the last one unown'd)' (1690).

9 The only exception to the above resolve were the poems Montagu sometimes wrote as petitions for career advancement, such as a panegyric on King William – 'An Epistle to the Rght Hon Charles, Earl of Dorset and Middlesex, Lord Chamberlain of his Majesty's Household. Occasion'd by His Majesty's Victory in Ireland' (1690) – in which Montagu called Dorset 'The Muses' Darling, Confidant and Friend'.

10 BL Add MS 28,644, Unpublished poetry of Charles Montagu.

11 BL Add MS 7,121, Letters to Lord Halifax (1706ff.), f.45, the poem by Matthew Prior 'To Mr Charles Montagu on his Marriage with the Right Hon the Countess of Manchester' (1688).

12 NA SP 105/82, Correspondence of Montagu and Stepney.

13 Matthew Prior, 'On Mr Pr—r's letters to Mr [Fleetwood] Sheppard (not omitting the last one unown'd)' (1690).

14 T. B. Macaulay, *The History of England* (London, 1858), vol. 4, pp. 325–7; D. W. Jones, *War and Economy in the Age of William III and Marlborough* (Oxford, 1988), pp. 11–12.

15 Charles Davenant, *England's Enemies Exposed* (1701).

16 H. T. Swedenberg, 'George Stepney, My Lord Dorset's Boy', *Huntington Library Quarterly* 10, 1 (November 1946), p. 5. See also Susan Spens, *George Stepney 1663–1707: Diplomat and Poet* (Cambridge, 1997), p. 45.

17 C. K. Eves, *Matthew Prior, Poet and Diplomatist* (New York, 1939), p. 215. See also H. Bunker Wright, 'Matthew Prior's Cloe and Lisetta', *Modern Philology* 36, 1 (August 1938), pp. 9–23.

18 George Stepney to Mrs Holmes, Dresden, 7/18 December 1693, quoted in C. K. Eves, *Matthew Prior, Poet and Diplomatist* (New York, 1939), p. 88.
19 Matthew Prior, 'An Epistle to Charles Montague . . .' (1692).
20 George Stepney to Charles Montagu, 26 December 1693, quoted in Susan Spens, *George Stepney 1663–1707: Diplomat and Poet* (Cambridge, 1997), p. 86.
21 George Stepney in Dresden to his mother, *c.* 1693, quoted in Susan Spens, *George Stepney 1663–1707: Diplomat and Poet* (Cambridge, 1997), p. 84.
22 HMC, *Bath MSS*, vol. 3, The Prior Papers, Matthew Prior to Montagu.
23 Ibid., Matthew Prior to Lord Dorset, 8/18 March 1695.
24 Ibid., Matthew Prior in The Hague to Montagu (then Chancellor of the Exchequer), 5 January /25 February 1695.
25 Anthony Quick, *Charterhouse: A History of the School* (London, 1990), p. 12.
26 Donald F. Bond (ed.), *The Tatler*, 2 vols (Oxford, 1987), no. 181, Tuesday, 6 June 1710 – vol. 2, pp. 482ff.
27 Ibid.
28 Rae Blanchard (ed.), *The Correspondence of Richard Steele* (Oxford, 1968 edn), no. 1.
29 *The Theatre* no. 11, Saturday, 6 February 1720 – Steele objecting to the description of his face as 'dusky' by John Dennis. John Loftis (ed.), *Richard Steele's 'The Theatre'* (Oxford, 1962), p. 51.
30 Donald F. Bond (ed.), *The Tatler*, 2 vols (Oxford, 1987), no. 235, Tuesday, 10 October 1710 – vol. 3, p. 215. See also Mr Harwood, quoted in Peter Smithers, *The Life of Joseph Addison* (Oxford, 2nd edn 1968), pp. 8–9.
31 Dedication in the 2nd edition of *The Drummer* (1722) 'To Mr Congreve', in Rae Blanchard (ed.), *The Correspondence of Richard Steele* (Oxford, 2nd edn 1968), pp. 505ff.
32 Rae Blanchard (ed.), *The Correspondence of Richard Steele* (Oxford, 2nd edn 1968), no. 5: Steele to Henry Gascoigne, May 1690.
33 Mary Delariviere Manley, *The New Atalantis* (1709).
34 Donald F. Bond (ed.), *The Spectator* (Oxford, 1965), vol. 1, no. 54, Wednesday, 2 May 1711, by Steele.
35 'When All Thy Mercies, O My God' quoted in Bonamy Dobrée, *Essays in Biography 1680–1726* (Oxford, 1925), p. 225.
36 John Dryden and Jacob Tonson (eds), *Examen Poeticum* (1693).
37 Dedication in the 2nd edition of *The Drummer* (1722) 'To Mr Congreve', in Rae Blanchard (ed.), *The Correspondence of Richard Steele* (Oxford, 2nd edn 1968), pp. 505ff.
38 Mary Delariviere Manley, *The New Atalantis* (1709).
39 William Congreve, *Love for Love* (1695), Act 1, Scene 1.

III THE SCENT OF THE PIE-OVEN

1 Thomas Hearne, *Remarks and Collections*, ed. C. E. Doble et al. (Oxford, 1885–1921), vol. 1, p. 116, entry for 6 December 1705.

2 Edward (Ned) Ward, *The History of the London Clubs* (1709); Philip Lempriere of Bath to William Baker of Bayfordbury, 13 February 1777, NPG, Tonson Papers.

3 There are several ways in which the tavern may have acquired its name without any reference to Mr Cat, however: 'cats' and 'kittens' were also slang for the large and small pewter pots in which beer was served. The earliest tavern called the Cat and Fiddle was established in 1501, and nobody really knows when the 'Hey Diddle Diddle' rhyme was first struck up.

4 Edward (Ned) Ward, *The History of the London Clubs* (1709).

5 Some have tried to give the credit as Club founder entirely to Mr Cat, but this is highly unlikely. See T. H. S. Escott, *Club Makers and Club Members* (London, 1914), p. 90. If Cat wrote the 1711 letter mentioned above, then he was literate, but it is hard to believe he would have thought up a literary club as a scheme for increasing pie and pastry sales. Records show that a baker in London might have had annual takings of £200 (today over £18,000), with profits estimated at over of a quarter of this in a year when fruit, sugar and flour were expensive. Collaboration with Tonson did prove profitable for Cat, and he grew rich enough to eventually retire to a house in Chelsea. In the 1690s, however, the pastry-cook would have been the lowly servant of men like Somers and Dorset, and even Tonson, rather than a Club member himself.

6 Maynard Mack, *Alexander Pope: A Life* (London and New Haven, 1985), p. 122.

7 Edward (Ned) Ward, *The History of the London Clubs* (1709).

8 Some have doubted the matching claims of Ward and Blackmore that Tonson's primary motive in establishing the Kit-Cat Club was to obtain rights from authors. (E.g: 'If he had really needed fresh "copy" at the slightest possible expense, he would have been more likely to approach a hack and secure the necessary work on his own terms.' Harry M. Geduld, *Prince of Publishers: A Study of the Work and Career of Jacob Tonson* (Bloomington, Ind. and London, 1969), pp. 152–3.) Such doubters are missing the fact that Tonson was making a concerted effort to distance himself from the hacks and their paymasters.

9 George Francis Papali, *Jacob Tonson, Publisher: His Life and Work* (Auckland, 1968).

10 E.g. ibid.

11 William L. Sachse, *Lord Somers: A Political Portrait* (Manchester, 1975).

12 Edmond Malone (ed.), *Critical and Miscellaneous Prose Works of John Dryden* (London, 1800), vol. 1, part 1, p. 489.

13 Arthur Onslow, quoted in Gilbert Burnet, *History of His Own Time* (1715), p. 4 n. 5.

14 As the Tory poet Dr Arbuthnot wrote:

> Whence deathless Kit-Cat took its Name
> Few Critics can unriddle
> Some say from Pastry Cook it came,
> And some from Cat and Fiddle.

This poem is untitled and has sometimes been misattributed to Pope. Dr Arbuthnot, *Miscellanies* (Dublin, 1746) includes 'On the Toasts of the Kit-Cat Club' (*c.* 1716) at p. 317.

15 Mr Cat's name can also be written with a double t, and similarly Kit-Cat was variously spelled in the early eighteenth century as 'Kit-kat', 'Kitt-Catt', etc.

16 Four contemporaries – Joseph Addison, John Oldmixon, Thomas Hearne and Richard Blackmore – testify to this etymology of the Club's name. Edmond Malone, writing in 1800, noted: 'The Club is supposed to have derived its name from Christopher Katt, a pastry-cook, who kept the house where they dined and excelled in making mutton-pies, which always formed a part of their bill of fare. In *The Spectator* no. 9, they are said to have derived their title, not from the maker of the pie, but from the pie itself. The fact is, that on account of its excellence, it was called a Kit-Kat, as we now say a Sandwich.' Edmond Malone (ed.), *Critical and Miscellaneous Prose Works of John Dryden* (London, 1800), vol. 1, part 1, p. 525 n. 6. In William King's *Art of Cookery* (1708), there is also reference to someone 'Immortal made, as Kit-cat for his Pies.'

17 Richard Blackmore, *The Kit-Cats, A Poem* (1708).

18 Letter of 9 May 1711 signed 'Ch Chatt'. Location now unknown.

19 John Dryden, *MacFlecknoe* (1682), line 101.

20 Donald F. Bond (ed.), *The Spectator* (Oxford, 1965), vol. 3, no. 367, Thursday, 1 May 1712, by Addison.

21 William Burnaby, *The Reform'd Wife* (1700), Prologue.

22 John Dennis, *Letters Upon Several Occasions* (1696).

23 William Congreve, *The Double Dealer* (1693), Act 4, Scene 1.

24 Owen Sweeney, *The Quacks, or, Love's the Physician (29 March 1705) 'As it was Acted after being twice forbid at the Theatre Royal, Drury Lane', Translation from Moliere's L'Amour Medicin but very altered*, Act I, Stationer Freckle to Dr Medley. See also Thomas McGreary, 'A Satire on the Opening of the Haymarket Theatre', *Restoration and 18th Century Theatre Research* 15 (Winter 2000), pp. 18–32, and Albert Rosenberg, 'A New Move for the Censorship of Owen Swiney's *The Quacks*', *Notes and Queries*, vol. 203 (September 1958), pp. 393–6.

25 Edward (Ned) Ward, *The History of the London Clubs* (1709).

26 Richard Blackmore, *The Kit-Cats, A Poem* (1708).

27 George Stepney, 'Juvenal's Eighth Satire', in Dryden and Congreve's 1693 edition of Juvenal. See Robert Anderson (ed.), *The Poets of Great Britain* (London 1792–3), vol. 6, p. 525.

28 John Macky, *A Journey through England* (1714), p. 188.

29 PRO Stepney Papers, 105/82, 12 March 1694/5. Prior said Congreve's poem on Mary's death was 'only for Hanging the Rooms & painting a dismal Scene, but 'tis Mr Stepney only [who] shows the Queen'.

30 Bibliopolo the Bookseller, in William Shippen, *Faction Display'd* (1704).

31 Edward (Ned) Ward, *Satyrical Reflections Upon Clubs in xxix chapters* (1710).

32 John Brewer, *The Pleasures of the Imagination: English Culture in the Eighteenth Century* (London 1997), pp. 40–1.

33 Samuel Johnson, *Lives of the English Poets* (1781), ed. George Birkbeck Hill (Oxford, 1905 edn), vol. 2, p. 42.

34 Abigail Williams, *Poetry and the Creation of a Whig Literary Culture 1681–1714* (Oxford, 2005), p. 216: 'The patronage of contemporary writers by Whig statesmen took place under William's personal authority.' Williams argues that the greatest Kit-Cat patrons – Dorset, Somers and Halifax – acted as King William's unofficial ministers for the arts, channelling State funds towards writers in the form of jobs and sinecures at the King's behest, however there is no evidence that the King's tight control of the political sphere extended to England's literary culture and that these men were not using state resources for their own exercise of personal (or collective, Kit-Cat) patronage.

35 Donald F. Bond (ed.), *The Tatler* (Oxford, 1987), no. 79, Tuesday, 8 October 1709.

36 John Macky, *Characters of the Court of Queen Anne* (1733).

IV THE TOAST OF THE TOWN: A KIT-CAT MEETING, 1697

1 Donald F. Bond (ed.), *The Spectator* (Oxford, 1965), vol. 4, no. 508, Monday, 13 October 1712, by Steele.

2 Ibid., vol. 1, no. 119, Tuesday, 17 July 1711, by Addison.

3 Ibid., vol. 2, no. 202, Monday, 22 October 1711, by Steele.

4 Ibid., vol. 2, no. 195, Saturday, 13 October 1711, by Addison.

5 William Congreve, 'Concerning Humour in Comedy', essay written as a letter to John Dennis (of Will's Coffee House circle) on 10 July 1695.

6 Peter Conrad, *The Everyman History of English Literature* (London, 1985), p. 308.

7 Samuel Pepys quoted in William Drogo Montagu, 7th Duke of Manchester, *Court and Society from Elizabeth to Anne* (London, 1864), vol. 2, p. 61.

8 Jonathan Swift quoted in Patrick Delany, *Observations upon Lord Orrery's Remarks* (London, 1754), p. 202.

9 HMC, *Bath MSS*, The Prior Papers, Matthew Prior to Charles Montagu, 3 May (NS) 1697.

10 George Stepney to Charles Montagu, January 1697, quoted in Susan Spens, *George Stepney 1663–1707: Diplomat and Poet* (Cambridge, 1997), p. 146.

11 Henry ('Harry') Boyle, William Cavendish (the Duke of Devonshire's son, styled Marquess of Hartington in 1697), Charles Cornwallis (a Suffolk MP before his peerage of 1698), Anthony Henley, Richard Norton (a close friend of Henley's since university) and Sir Richard Temple (4th Baronet of Stowe since May 1697, but not elevated to the Lords until 1713) were the Kit-Cats with seats in the 1697–8 Commons, all essentially Junto loyalists.

12 *The Proceedings of the House of Commons*, vol. 3 (London, 1745), p. 76.

13 John Somers, 'A letter balancing the necessity of keeping a land force in times of peace, with the dangers that may follow it' (1697).

14 John Dryden et al., *The Satires of Decimus Junius Juvenalis* (1697), p. lii. Note the similarity between this movement and the recent classical popularizations by poets Ted Hughes (of Ovid) and Christopher Logue (of Homer).

15 John Dryden's Preface to William Walsh, *A Dialogue Concerning Women, being a Defence of the Fair Sex* (1691).
16 Eveline Cruickshanks, Stuart Handley and D. W. Handley, *The House of Commons 1690–1715* (Cambridge, 2002), entry on William Walsh MP (1662–1708), vol. 5, p. 785.
17 William Congreve, 'The Birth of the Muse, To the Right Honourable Charles Montague, Chancellor of the Exchequer etc' (1698).
18 Colley Cibber quoted in Madeleine Bingham, *Masks and Façades: Sir John Vanbrugh, the Man and his Setting* (London, 1974), p. 62.
19 John Coke to Thomas Coke, Cowper MSS, Hist MSS Comm, 12th Report, Appendix, Part II (London, 1888), p. 368.
20 John Dryden letter of 4 March 1699 on the playbill for *The Double Dealer* revival, quoted in John C. Hodges, *William Congreve: Letters and Documents* (London, 1964), p. 102.
21 Colley Cibber, *An Apology for the Life of Mr Colley Cibber* (1740), ed. B. R. S. Fone (Ann Arbor, Mich., 1968), p. 122.
22 Charles Gildon and Gerard Langbaine, *The Lives and Characters of the English Dramatic Poets* (1712 edn), p. 142. Despite earlier praise of Congreve's wit, Gildon concludes that 'none else can stand in Competition with [Vanbrugh]'. See also Giles Jacob, *The Poetical Register* (1719–20), vol. 2, p. 262, a biographical work on which we know Congreve was consulted about his friends, that compliments Vanbrugh's wit and 'sprightliness', original characters, and natural style.
23 John C. Hodges (ed.), *William Congreve: Letters and Documents* (London, 1964), William Congreve to Joseph Keally on 2 July 1700.
24 Ibid., Richard Steele to William Congreve, 29 December 1713 (Dedication to *Poetical Miscellanies*, 1714).
25 Edward (Ned) Ward, *The History of the London Clubs* (1709).
26 Matthew Prior, 'Jinny the Just' (n.d.) quoted in Kathleen M. Lynch, *Jacob Tonson, Kit-Cat Publisher* (Knoxville, Tenn., 1971), p. 49. Ned Ward, although he did not attend the Club's meetings, described the toasting of ladies in 1709 as a post-prandial recreation, after the board was cleared of the final course.
27 Donald F. Bond (ed.), *The Spectator* (Oxford, 1965), vol. 1, no. 9, Saturday, 10 March 1711, by Addison.
28 Donald F. Bond (ed.), *The Tatler* (Oxford, 1987), vol. 1, no. 24, Saturday, 4 June 1709, by Steele.
29 John Charlton to the Marchioness of Granby, November 1703. Charlton, a kinsman of the Earl of Rutland, was not a Kit-Cat, but knew Hartington and seems to have been close enough to the action to supply copies of the toasting poems to the curious Marchioness (the daughter of Lady Rachel Russell and married to the Marquess of Granby who later became Duke of Rutland): '[O]n the Kitcat, 'tis proper to tell your Ladyship that a great number of glasses are chose and a set number of ladies' names are writ on them, and as an addition some fine thing is to be said on every lady and writ there too . . .

Above thirty glasses will have something of the kind I send your Ladyship.' HMC, *Rutland MSS*, vol. 2, p. 177.

30 Mary Astell, *Bart'lemy Fair: or, an Enquiry after Wit* (1709), Dedication 'To the most Illustrious Society of the Kit-Cats'.

31 Donald F. Bond (ed.), *The Spectator* (Oxford, 1965), vol. 2, no. 182, Friday, 28 September 1711, by Steele.

32 Ibid., vol. 3, no. 342, Wednesday, 2 April 1712, by Steele.

33 'The First Letter from B. to Mr E[therege]' in James Thorpe (ed.), *The Poems of Sir George Etherege* (Princeton, NJ, 1963), pp. 40–5.

34 Anon., *The Patentee* (1700).

35 BL Add MS 40,060 – The Oath of the Toast, by Mr Congreve.

36 PRO Stepney Papers, 105/82 – Charles Montagu to George Stepney, 14 April 16??.

37 The story about Lady Mary Wortley Montagu being brought in by her father was reported years later by her granddaughter, Lady Louisa Stuart. See James A. Home (ed.), *Letters of Lady Louisa Stuart to Miss Louisa Clinton* (Edinburgh, 1903), vol. 1, p. 294. Note that LMWM was moved out of London at the age of 9, lending credence to Louisa's claim that this evening happened before then, in 1697 or earlier.

38 Ibid.

39 Lord Wharncliffe (ed.), *The Letters and Works of Lady Mary Wortley Montagu* (London, 1861), vol. 1, pp. 52–3.

40 James A. Home (ed.), *Letters of Lady Louisa Stuart to Miss Louisa Clinton* (Edinburgh, 1903), vol. 1, p. 294.

41 Mary Astell, *A Serious Proposal to the Ladies* (1694).

42 Edward (Ned) Ward, *The History of the London Clubs* (1709).

V CULTURE WARS

1 Richard I. Cook, *Sir Samuel Garth* (Boston, Mass., 1980), p. 112.

2 Joseph Addison, *The Freeholder*, no. 37, Friday, 27 April 1716.

3 John Dunton, Preface, *The Night-Walker* (1696).

4 *The Proceedings of the House of Commons* (London, 1745), vol. 3, p. 76.

5 Anon., 'A True Character of the Prince of Wales's Poet' (1701).

6 'A True Character of the Prince of Wales's Poet, with a Description of the new erected Folly at White-Hall' (1701), MSS at Beinecke Library, Yale.

7 Given his noble birth and his employment under Dorset until Dorset resigned as Lord Chamberlain, the fact that Bertie was not invited to join the Kit-Cat Club tells us that connections alone were not enough: if one had no major electoral influence to exert, or patronage to dispense, one needed to be considered a writer of talent.

8 Madeleine Bingham, *Masks and Façades: Sir John Vanbrugh, the Man and his Setting* (London, 1974), p. 110.

9 Kerry Downes, *Sir John Vanbrugh: A Biography* (London, 1987), p. 163.

10 Edmund Gosse, *Life of William Congreve* (London, 1888), p. 96.

11 Jeremy Collier, *A Short View of the Immorality and Prophaness of the English Stage* (1698).
12 William Congreve, *The Double Dealer* (1693), Dedication to Charles Montagu.
13 Brean Hammond (ed.), *John Vanbrugh: The Relapse and Other Plays* (Oxford, 2004 edn), p. vii.
14 Geoffrey Webb and Bonamy Dobrée (eds), *The Complete Works of Sir John Vanbrugh* (London, 1927–8), vol. 4, no. 1, to the Earl of Manchester in Paris, 25 December 1699. Henley's marriage actually took place in February 1700.
15 John Macky, *Characters of the Court of Queen Anne* (1733); the satire was the anonymous *Golden Age Revers'd* (February 1703).
16 Bodleian, MS Carte 79, f.420.
17 Lady Mary Wortley Montagu quoted in George de Forest Lord et al. (eds), *Poems on Affairs of State: Augustan Satirical Verse 1660–1714* (New Haven, Conn., 1963–75), vol. 6, p. 629 n. 65.
18 Sarah Churchill to David Mallet, September 1744, quoted in: Sarah Churchill, *The Private Correspondence of Sarah Duchess of Marlborough* (London, 1838 edn), vol. 2, pp. 144 and 147.
19 Charles Davenant, *England's Enemies Exposed* (1701), in which Charles Montagu is 'Tom Double'.
20 William Congreve, *The Double Dealer* (1693), Act 2, Scene 1.
21 John Vanbrugh, *The Relapse* (1696), Act 1, Scene 2.
22 William Shippen, *Faction Display'd* (1704).
23 Jonathan Swift, *Mr C[olli]n's Discourse on Free-Thinking Put into plain English . . .* (1713). Another religious conservative likewise answered Collins' discourse with *The Vanity of Free-Thinking Expos'd in a Satyr, Dedicated to Mr C[olli]ns, Proprietor, and the rest of the Thoughtless Members of the Kitt-Katt Club* (1713).
24 Dr John Arbuthnot, 'Notes and Memorandums of the Six Days preceding the Death of the Late Right Reverend', quoted in Richard I. Cook, *Sir Samuel Garth* (Boston, Mass., 1980), p. 38.
25 William Congreve, *Amendments of Mr Collier's False and Imperfect Citations* (1698).
26 Madeleine Bingham, *Masks and Façades: Sir John Vanbrugh, the Man and his Setting* (London, 1974), p. 319.
27 Sister Rose Anthony, *The Jeremy Collier Stage Controversy 1698–1726* (Milwaukee, Wis., 1937), p. 99.
28 William Congreve, *Amendments of Mr Collier's False and Imperfect Citations* (1698).
29 D. Crane Taylor, *William Congreve* (London, 1931), p. 127.
30 There was a split within the Church between senior clerical figures (often Whig) and the more Tory lower orders, who were paradoxically known as 'high flyers' because of their beliefs: they preached 'non-resistance' to the monarchy (thereby denying legitimacy of the 1688 Revolution).
31 John Dennis, *The Usefulness of the Stage to the Happiness of Mankind, to Government, and to Religion . . .* (1698).

32 'Letter to Mr Congreve', 30 August–1 September 1698 issue of *The Post Man*, p. 7.

33 John Dennis' poem 'Sheltering Poet's Invitation to Richard Steele' (1714) publicized to the man in the street the old open secret that Somers kept a married woman (Mrs Blount) as his mistress:

[Wine] makes even Somers to disclose his art
By racking every secret from his heart
As he flings off the statesman's sly disguise
To name the cuckold's wife with whom he lies.

34 Donald F. Bond (ed.), *The Spectator* (Oxford, 1965), vol. 1, no. 51, Saturday, 28 April 1711, by Steele.

35 Richard Steele, *Apology for Himself and his Writings* (1714).

36 John C. Hodges (ed.), *William Congreve: Letters and Documents* (London, 1964), Richard Steele to William Congreve, 29 December 1713 (Dedication to *Poetical Miscellanies*, 1714).

37 Ibid., Congreve to Joseph Keally, 2 July 1700.

38 'Doris' was published in Congreve's *Collected Works* (1710) – not clear when written. Steele's Dedication 'To William Congreve' in *Poetical Miscellanies* (1714) is in Rae Blanchard (ed.), *The Correspondence of Richard Steele* (Oxford, 1968 edn).

39 Robert J. Allen, *The Clubs of Augustan London* (Cambridge, Mass., 1933), p. 236.

40 Donald F. Bond (ed.), *The Spectator* (Oxford, 1965), vol. 2, no. 203, Tuesday, 23 October 1711, by Addison.

41 Rae Blanchard (ed.), *The Correspondence of Richard Steele* (Oxford, 1968 edn), p. 437n.

42 Ibid., p. 426.

43 BL Add MSS 5,145B, f.290, Richard Steele to Mrs Manley.

44 A contemporary phrase of some complexity; see J. P. Kenyon, *Revolution Principles* (Cambridge, 1977).

45 HMC, *Bath MSS*, vol. 3, p. 394, The Prior Papers, Matthew Prior to Abraham Stanyan, 8/19 January 1700.

46 Ibid.

47 'Prologue by Sir John Falstaff' reprinted in *Wit and Mirth: or, Pills to Purge Melancholy* (1700), vol. 2.

48 *A Kit-Cat C—b Describ'd* (1705), original MS at Harvard.

49 John Macky, *A Journey Through England* (1724), vol. 1.

50 HMC, *Bath MSS*, vol. 3, p. 394, The Prior Papers, Matthew Prior to Abraham Stanyan, 8/19 January 1700.

51 Tom Browne, *Amusements Serious and Comical* (1702), p. 50.

52 John Oldmixon lists Carbery as a Kit-Cat by 1700.

53 William Congreve, *The Double Dealer* (1703), Epilogue spoken by Mrs (Susanna) Mountford.

54 Congreve's Prologue to *A Very Good Wife*, quoted in D. Crane Taylor, *William Congreve* (London, 1931), p. 43.

55 'Prologue by Sir John Falstaff' reprinted in *Wit and Mirth: or, Pills to Purge Melancholy* (1700), vol. 2.
56 Villiers Bathurst to Dr Charlett, 28 January 1700, quoted in Michael Ciletti, 'The Kit-Cat Club', MA Thesis, Penn State University, 1953, p. 46; John Genest (ed.), *Some Account of the English Stage* (Bath, 1832), vol. 2, p. 219.
57 Anon., *The Patentee* (1700).
58 Geoffrey Webb and Bonamy Dobrée (eds), *The Complete Works of Sir John Vanbrugh*, 4 vols (London, 1927–8), vol. 4, no. 1, To the Earl of Manchester in Paris, 25 December 1699.
59 William Congreve, *The Way of the World*, Dedication to Ralph Earl of Montagu.
60 Ibid., Act 1, Scene 1.
61 Ibid., Act 4, Scene 1.
62 William Congreve, 'Concerning Humour in Comedy', essay written as a letter to John Dennis, 10 July 1695.
63 William Congreve, *The Way of the World*, Act 1, Scene 1.
64 Anon., *Animadversions on Mr Congreve's Late Answer to Mr Collier* (1698).
65 Tom Browne, *Amusements Serious and Comical* (1702), p. 51.
66 P. H. Highfill Jr et al. (eds), *A Biographical Dictionary of Actors, Actresses, Musicians, Dancers, Managers and Other Stage Personnel in London, 1660–1800*, (Carbondale and Edwardsville, Ill., 1973–93); 'On the Marriage of Mr Congreve to Mrs Bracegirdle' (1702) in *Martial Redevivus*; *Poems on Affairs of State* (1707) also said that Congreve slept with his 'Angellica', 'But at length the poor Nymph did for Justice implore, / Has married her now, tho he'd — her before.'
67 John Dennis in 1717, as quoted in Emmett L. Avery, *Congreve's Plays on the Eighteenth-Century Stage* (New York, 1951), p. 32.
68 'To Mr Congreve, Occasion'd by his Comedy, call'd The Way of the World, By Mr Steele' (1700) in Rae Blanchard (ed.), *The Occasional Verse of Richard Steele* (Oxford, 1952).
69 Abigail Williams, *Poetry and the Creation of a Whig Literary Culture 1681–1714* (Oxford, 2005), p. 33.
70 Tom Browne (ed.), *Commendatory Verses, on the Author of the Two Arthurs, and the Satyr against Wit* (1700). Browne satirized both Dryden and Blackmore in various different works. Other possible Kit-Cat contributors to this anti-Blackmore collection include Richard Norton and Anthony Henley.
71 Henry Playford and Abel Roper (eds), *Luctus Britannici, or, the Tears of the British Muses for the Death of John Dryden, Esq.* (1700).
72 For example, in his first letter to the young Alexander Pope.
73 Harry M. Geduld, *Prince of Publishers: A Study of the Work and Career of Jacob Tonson* (Bloomington, Ind., and London, 1969), p. 102.
74 Dedication in the 2nd edition of *The Drummer* (1722) 'To Mr Congreve' in Rae Blanchard (ed.), *The Correspondence of Richard Steele* (Oxford, 1968 edn), pp. 505ff.
75 Edward (Ned) Ward, *The History of the London Clubs* (1709).
76 Geoffrey Webb and Bonamy Dobrée (eds), *The Complete Works of Sir John*

Vanbrugh, 4 vols (London, 1927–8), vol. 4, no. 1, To the Earl of Manchester in Paris, 25 December 1699.

77 Ibid.

78 Michael Foss, *The Age of Patronage: The Arts in England 1660–1750* (Ithaca, NY, 1972), pp. 190–1.

79 Jonathan Swift, 'Vanbrug's House' (1703 and revised 1708–9) and 'The History of Vanbrug's House' (1706). The former describes the house as 'a Thing resembling a Goose Pie'. Circulated in MSS before being printed in Jonathan Swift, *Meditations upon a Broomstick and Somewhat Beside* (1710).

80 Emmett L. Avery, *Congreve's Plays on the Eighteenth-Century Stage* (New York, 1951), p. 31.

81 Ibid. During the seventeenth and eighteenth centuries, an estimated 20,000 British captives were seized at sea by North African corsairs and held in Barbary (Morocco, Algiers, Tripoli and Tunisia). There was a nationwide drive to raise funds for such captives' redemption in the 1670s, in which Addison's father had actively participated. Now a second fundraiser was underway, mostly through parish churches, prompted by accounts of horrors in captivity. The English public donated £16,500 (some £2 million today) between 1700 and 1705, to which this one theatrical charity event contributed around £250.

82 Brean Hammond (ed.), *John Vanbrugh: The Relapse and Other Plays* (Oxford, 2004), p. xiv.

83 Some have unkindly seen Congreve's career as a case study in how material comforts can dull a great talent, tracing an inverse correlation between his income and literary output. For example, Michael Foss, *The Age of Patronage: The Arts in England 1660–1750* (Ithaca, NY, 1972), p. 159: 'Between 1693 and 1695, being as yet unrewarded, he wrote three plays; between 1695 and 1700, and now in possession of one post, he wrote two more; between 1700 and 1714, with the comfortable income of two posts, he wrote two masques and a few occasional pieces; and from 1714 to his death, while enjoying the large salary of Secretary to Jamaica, he wrote nothing of any value at all.'

VI THE EUROPEANS

1 Though stepfather and stepson were political allies, they were not close friends and sometimes competed. When Montagu's patronage helped Sir Isaac Newton, the uncle of Montagu's long-standing mistress, become Master of the Mint, for example, Vanbrugh, who was grooming Manchester as a future patron for himself, was quick to send Manchester this news and wistfully contrast Newton's promotion to his own lack of support: '*Pour moi, je suis tout comme j'étais.*' William Drogo Montagu, 7th Duke of Manchester, *Court and Society from Elizabeth to Anne* (London, 1864), vol. 2, p. 55.

2 Dedication in the 2nd edition of *The Drummer* (1722) 'To Mr Congreve' in Rae Blanchard (ed.), *The Correspondence of Richard Steele* (Oxford, 1968 edn), pp. 505ff.

3 Donald F. Bond (ed.), *The Spectator* (Oxford, 1965), vol. 2, no. 255, Saturday, 22 December 1711, by Addison.
4 Walter Graham (ed.), *The Letters of Joseph Addison* (Oxford, 1941), no. 5, Addison to Somers, 1699.
5 Ibid., no. 4, Addison to Congreve, August 1699.
6 Martin Lister, *A Journey to Paris in the Year 1698* (1699), p. 7.
7 D. B. Horn, *The British Diplomatic Service 1689–1789* (Oxford, 1961), p. 141. HMC, *Bath MSS*, vol. 3, The Prior Papers, Vernon to Prior, 11 April 1699.
8 Geoffrey Webb and Bonamy Dobrée (eds), *The Complete Works of Sir John Vanbrugh*, 4 vols (London, 1927–8), vol. 4, no. 1, Vanbrugh to the Earl of Manchester, 25 December 1699.
9 Toast by Addison, *c.* 1703.
10 Bodleian SC.25, 427 MS Montagu, d.I, f.99, Prior to Montagu, 9 August 1698.
11 Matthew Prior, *Poems on Several Occasions* (1718), 'To Chloe, Jealous'.
12 HMC, *Bath MSS*, vol. 3, The Prior Papers, Prior to Montagu, 20 May (NS) 1699.
13 Ibid., Prior to Montagu, 21 May (NS) 1698.
14 Ibid., Prior to Montagu, 1 April (NS) 1699.
15 Charles Montagu, 'The Man of Honour' in Giles Jacob, *The Poetical Register* (1719–20).
16 Add MS 7,121, Letters to Lord Halifax (1706ff.), f.47, Matthew Prior to Charles Montagu, 30 August (NS) 1698; C. K. Eves, *Matthew Prior, Poet and Diplomatist* (New York, 1939), p. 104.
17 HMC, *Bath MSS*, vol. 3, The Prior Papers, Dorset to Prior, 6 March 1698.
18 Joseph Addison, *The Guardian*, no. 34, Monday, 20 April 1713 (issue by Steele).
19 Joseph Addison, *The Freeholder*, no. 1, Friday, 23 December 1715.
20 HMC, *Bath MSS*, vol. 3, The Prior Papers, Prior to Montagu, 21 May (NS) 1698.
21 Ibid., Prior to Montagu, 10 April (NS) 1698.
22 Prior's commonplace book, Prior MSS, today at Longleat House, quoted in C. K. Eves, *Matthew Prior, Poet and Diplomatist* (New York, 1939), p. 111.
23 BL Add MS 7,121, Letters to Lord Halifax (1706ff.), f.47, Matthew Prior to Charles Montagu, 30 August (NS) 1698; C. K. Eves, *Matthew Prior, Poet and Diplomatist* (New York, 1939), p. 104.
24 Walter Graham (ed.), *The Letters of Joseph Addison* (Oxford, 1941), no. 8, To Dr John Hough, October 1699.
25 Ibid., no. 11, to Montagu, December 1699.
26 Donald F. Bond (ed.), *The Spectator* (Oxford, 1965), vol. 4, no. 435, Saturday, 19 July 1712, by Addison.
27 John Macky, *Characters of the Court of Queen Anne* (1733).
28 Matthew Prior to Earl of Manchester, 12 February 1700, quoted in C. K. Eves, *Matthew Prior, Poet and Diplomatist* (New York, 1939), p. 158.
29 HMC, *Bath MSS*, vol. 3, The Prior Papers, Earl of Manchester to Prior, 22 May (NS) 1700.
30 C. K. Eves, *Matthew Prior, Poet and Diplomatist* (New York, 1939), p. 151.

31 Susan Spens, *George Stepney: Diplomat and Poet* (Cambridge, 1997), pp. 188–9: Stepney stayed with the Whig Earl of Macclesfield (2nd Earl, Charles Gerard) at his house, Bushy Park, near to Hampton Court, in mid-August and likely wrote the letter afterwards. A copy can be found in Leibniz's correspondence with Sophia, but the original MS appears to be lost.

32 HMC, *Cowper MSS*, vol. 2, p. 410, Charles Davenant to Thomas Coke, 10 December 1700.

33 Walter Graham (ed.), *The Letters of Joseph Addison* (Oxford, 1941), no. 18, Addison to Abraham Stanyan, May 1700.

34 John Ingamells (ed.), *A Dictionary of British and Irish Travellers in Italy 1701–1800* (New Haven, Conn. and London, 1997), entry on Dashwood.

35 Eveline Cruickshanks, Stuart Handley and D. W. Hayton, *The House of Commons 1690–1715* (Cambridge, 2002), vol. 4, p. 877.

36 Gilbert Burnet, *History of His Own Time* (1715), p. 234.

37 Charles Davenant, *England's Enemies Exposed* (1701).

38 BL Add MS 40,060, 'Votes'.

39 Charles Dickens, *Our Mutual Friend* (1864–5), part 2, chapter 3.

40 George de Forest Lord et al. (eds), *Poems on Affairs of State: Augustan Satirical Verse 1660–1714* (New Haven, Conn., 1963–75), vol. 5, p. 430.

41 Linda Colley, *In Defiance of Oligarchy* (London, 1982), p. 18.

42 Spencer Compton, for example, gained the seat of Eye in Suffolk on Cornwallis' orders, and Prior won the borough of East Grinstead in Sussex after nomination by Dorset.

43 Anon., *A Kit-Cat C—b Describ'd* (1705), original MS at Harvard; Lady Mary Wortley Montagu's Commonplace Book, formerly of Wortley MS, f.9, quoted in Robert Halsband, *Life of Mary Wortley Montagu* (Oxford, 1956), p. 8.

44 W. A. Speck, *The Birth of Britain: A New Nation 1700–1710* (Oxford, 1994), p. 24.

45 John C. Hodges (ed.), *William Congreve: Letters and Documents* (London, 1964), Congreve to Joe Keally, 26 March 1701.

46 W. A. Speck, *The Birth of Britain: A New Nation 1700–1710* (Oxford, 1994), p. 26.

47 'The fifth parliament of King William: First session – begins 6/2/1701', *The History and Proceedings of the House of Commons*, vol. 3 (1742), pp. 127–83.

48 Ibid.

49 Matthew Prior, 'Song. Set[t] by Mr Abel[l]' (1701).

50 Mark Noble, *A Biographical History of England from the Revolution to the End of George I's Reign; being a continuation of the Rev. J. Granger's work* (London, 1806), p. 245, extract from poem by Prior which was a dialogue between Sir Thomas More and the Vicar of Bray.

51 George Stepney to Lord Halifax, 13 August 1701, quoted in C. K. Eves, *Matthew Prior, Poet and Diplomatist* (New York, 1939), pp. 170–1.

52 S. Tufton, *The History of Faction, alias Hypocrisy, alias Moderation* (1705), pp. 74–5.

53 Jonathan Swift, 'Discourse of the Contests and Dissensions Between the Nobles

and the Commons in Athens and Rome', in Temple Scott (ed.), *Prose Works of Jonathan Swift* (London, 1897 edn), vol. 5, pp. 379–80.

54 John C. Hodges (ed.), *William Congreve: Letters and Documents* (London, 1964), Congreve to Joe Keally, 7 June 1701.

55 BL Add MS 22,851, f.131, Henry Whistler to Thomas Pitt, 20 December 1701.

VII THE WHIGS GO TO WAR

1 George de Forest Lord et al. (eds), *Poems on Affairs of State: Augustan Satirical Verse 1660–1714* , 7 vols (New Haven, Conn., 1963–75), vol. 7, 'A Vindication of the Whigs' (1702). Authors' copy when corrected by Somers and Halifax was then 'recommended to . . . their Trusty Secretary Jacob . . . to Babble it abroad by the Hawkers'.

2 Walter Graham (ed.), *The Letters of Joseph Addison* (Oxford, 1941), no. 25, To Edward Wortley, 9 December 1701.

3 Mary Delariviere Manley, *The New Atalantis* (1709), vol. 1, p. 188.

4 Rae Blanchard (ed.), *The Correspondence of Richard Steele* (Oxford, 1968 edn), no. 7, Steele to Col. Edmund Revett, nephew of Lord Cutts, 2 September 1701.

5 Richard Steele, *Mr Steele's Apology for himself and his writings* (1714).

6 Ibid.

7 Edward Gregg, *Queen Anne* (London, paperback edn 1984), p. 134.

8 Charles Davenant, *The True Picture of a Modern Whig set forth in a Dialogue between Mr Whiglove and Mr Double* (1702).

9 Eveline Cruickshanks, Stuart Handley and D. W. Hayton, *The House of Commons 1690–1715* (Cambridge, 2002), vol. 5, p. 434, entry on Sir Edward Seymour.

10 Ibid. In 1701, the French ambassador referred to Jack Smith as one of the leading Whigs in the Commons.

11 Walter Graham (ed.), *The Letters of Joseph Addison* (Oxford, 1941), no. 41, Addison to Mr Wood.

12 The Kit-Cats were Stanhope, Topham, Somers and Garth. Abigail Williams, 'Patronage and Whig Literary Culture in the Early Eighteenth Century', in David Womersley (ed.), *Cultures of Whiggism* (Newark, NJ, 2005), p. 162, has suggested that the oration translated by 'K. C.' was, in fact, a collaborative translation by several 'Kit-Cat' authors, but it was more likely the work of Dr Knightly Chetwode, a Greek scholar of the time and correspondent of Marlborough's.

13 G. M. Trevelyan, *England under Queen Anne* (London, 1930).

14 Anon., *A Kit-Cat C—b Describ'd* (1705), original MS at Harvard.

15 Anon., *The Golden Age Revers'd* (1703).

16 John Macky, *Memoirs of the Secret Services of John Macky . . .* (1733).

17 Joseph Spence, *Observations, Anecdotes, and Characters of Books and Men*, ed. James M. Osborn, 2 vols (Oxford, 1966 edn), no. 121.

18 Other Kit-Cats who were linked to Marlborough by virtue of military service included: Sir Richard Temple, who was made a colonel of a newly raised foot regiment in February 1702 and distinguished himself at the battles of Venlo

and Ruremond, and at the siege of Lille, becoming one of five lieutenant-generals in Flanders by 1710; and Major John Shrimpton, a client of Wharton's who had fought under William in the 1690s, then joined the same foot regiment as Stanhope and Steele in 1701. Colonel Tidcomb appears to have been the avuncular veteran amongst the Club's soldier-members, already 60 by the time the War of Spanish Succession began.

19 John Methuen to Alexander Stanhope, quoted in Eveline Cruickshanks, Stuart Handley and D. W. Hayton, *The House of Commons 1690–1715* (Cambridge, 2002), vol. 5, p. 540.

20 HMC, *Report XIV: Appendix*, part 9 (1895), pp. 511–12, Speaker Onslow.

21 Having had the honour of carrying news of the victory back to Anne, Shannon forfeited the Queen's good opinion forever by participating in a 'scandalous episode in St James's Church' in January 1703. Eveline Cruickshanks, Stuart Handley and D. W. Hayton, *The House of Commons 1690–1715* (Cambridge, 2002), vol. 3, entry on Richard Boyle, 2nd Viscount Shannon (1675–1740) of Shannon Park, Co. Cork.

22 Elizabeth Berry, 'A Household Account Book of Thomas Wharton 5th Baron Wharton (1648-1715)', *Records of Buckinghamshire*, vol. 36 (Aylesbury, 1996), pp. 86–97.

23 Donald F. Bond (ed.), *The Spectator* (Oxford, 1965), vol. 1, no. 105, Saturday, 30 June 1711, by Addison.

24 NPG, Tonson Papers: The names are Wharton, Carlisle, Manchester, Mohun, Hartington (that is, William Cavendish), Essex, Grafton, Cornwallis, Dormer, Stanyan, Compton, Shrimpton and Garth [and Vandome]. The list of names coincides for the most part with the names of the earliest Kit-Cats listed by Oldmixon.

25 Richard Blackmore, *The Kit-Cats, A Poem* (1708).

26 John Timbs, *Clubs and Club Life in London* (London, 1908), p. 51.

VIII KIT-CAT CONNOISSEURS

1 Third Earl of Shaftesbury, *Characteristicks of Men, Manners, Opinions, Times* (1711), ed. J. M. Robertson (New York, 1964), vol. 1, p. 74.

2 Daniel Defoe, *The Review* (1713).

3 Geoffrey Webb and Bonamy Dobrée (eds), *The Complete Works of Sir John Vanbrugh* (London, 1927–8), vol. 4, no. 165, Vanbrugh to Jacob Tonson, 12 August 1725.

4 Nicholas Rowe, 'The Reconcilement between Jacob Tonson and Mr Congreve' in the March [1707?] edition of *The Muses Mercury*. With Steele and Garth among the editors of the paper that carried this poem, and with Tonson having published two of Rowe's recent works, Rowe knew what he was talking about, though he himself was never a Kit-Cat member. Rowe may even have been trying to give his friends a gentle nudge towards a real reconcilement – perhaps resulting from the argument over publishing deals that led to Tonson's rumoured expulsion or resignation from the Kit-Cat Club back in 1704–5.

5 George Stepney to Tonson, 24 March 1703, in *The Gentleman's Magazine* (July–December 1837), vol. 8, pp. 362–4.
6 Anon. [William Walsh], *The Golden Age Restor'd* (1703), said that at this date the Jacobites were meeting at their own clubs in London, to rival the Kit-Cats ('The faithful club assembles at the Vine, / And French intrigues are broached o'er English wine').
7 Anon., *The Golden Age Revers'd* (1703).
8 Richard Blackmore, *The Kit-Cats, A Poem* (1708). Ned Ward also mocks Tonson for the 'stateliness of his brow' in his *Secret History of Clubs* (1709).
9 Vanbrugh to Tonson, quoted in Kathleen M. Lynch (ed.), *Jacob Tonson, Kit-Cat Publisher* (Knoxville, Tenn., 1971), p. 109.
10 John C. Hodges, *William Congreve: Letters and Documents* (London, 1964), Congreve to Tonson, 1 July 1703.
11 Geoffrey Webb and Bonamy Dobrée (eds), *The Complete Works of Sir John Vanbrugh* (London, 1927–8), vol. 4, no. 3, Vanbrugh to Tonson, near the Stadthouse in Amsterdam, 15 June 1703.
12 Ibid., Vanbrugh to Tonson, 13 July 1703.
13 Duke of Somerset to Tonson, 22 June 1703, quoted in Edmond Malone (ed.), *Critical and Miscellaneous Prose Works of John Dryden* (London, 1800), p. 532.
14 Geoffrey Webb and Bonamy Dobrée (eds), *The Complete Works of Sir John Vanbrugh*, 4 vols (London, 1927–8), vol. 4, no. 3, Vanbrugh to Tonson, 15 July 1703.
15 British Library shelfmark 816m.19, f.34; Osborn MS 15,096, burlesque advertisement re Tonson from 1704, contemporary hand copy.
16 Richard Blackmore, *The Kit-Cats, A Poem* (1708), but this poem was written 'some years ago', and can be dated to before June 1704 because it refers to Tom Browne alive. See Sir Albert Rosenberg, *Sir Richard Blackmore: A Poet and Physician of the Augustan Age* (Lincoln, Nebr., 1953), p. 94.
17 Anon., *A Kit-Cat C—b Describ'd* (1705), original at Harvard.
18 Halifax to Lionel, 7th Earl of Dorset, 11–12 October 1706, quoted in HMC, *Mrs Stopford-Sackville's MSS*, vol. 1, Sackville I (London, 1904), p. 34.
19 Nicholas Rowe, *The Reconcilement between Jacob Tonson and Mr Congreve . . .* (1707).
20 Jonathan Swift quoted in Madeleine Bingham, *Masks and Façades: Sir John Vanbrugh, the Man and his Setting* (London, 1974), p. 133.
21 Geoffrey Webb and Bonamy Dobrée (eds), *The Complete Works of Sir John Vanbrugh* (London, 1927–8), vol. 4, no. 168, Vanbrugh to Tonson, 25 October 1725.
22 Ibid., vol. 4, no. 4, Vanbrugh to Tonson, 13 July 1703.
23 Walter Graham (ed.), *The Letters of Joseph Addison* (Oxford 1941), no. 37, Addison to Duke of Somerset, June 1703.
24 Addison made other English friends in Holland that summer who proved influential in his later career: James Stanhope, whose regiment was at Marlborough's camp in Maastricht, travelled with him from Rotterdam to

Leiden; Addison also became acquainted with Ambrose Philips, a lean young poet who liked to wear red stockings.

25 Walter Graham (ed.), *The Letters of Joseph Addison* (Oxford, 1941), no. 42, Addison to John Wyche (resident in Hamburg), 1703.

26 Rae Blanchard (ed.), *The Correspondence of Richard Steele* (Oxford, 1968 edn), p. 510, Dedication to *The Drummer.*

27 Eustace Budgell, *Memoirs of the Life and Character of the Earl of Orrery and of the Family of the Boyles* (1732), p. ix.

28 Joseph Addison tellingly observed: 'I cannot think that Corneille, Racine, Moliere, Boileau, la Fountaine, Bruyere, Bossu or the Daciers would have written so well as they have done, had they not been Friends and Contemporaries.' See Donald F. Bond (ed.), *The Spectator* (Oxford, 1965), vol. 3, no. 409, Thursday, 19 June 1712, by Addison.

29 Richard Blackmore, *The Kit-Cats, A Poem* (1708).

30 Lytton Strachey, 'Addison, Joseph', *Dictionary of National Biography* (London, 1885). Tonson 'boasted of paying his court to the great man by giving him excuses for such indulgence'.

31 Donald F. Bond (ed.), *The Tatler* (Oxford, 1987), no. 252, 18 November 1710.

32 HMC, *Rutland MSS*, vol. 2, appendix V, p. 177, John Charlton to Lady Granby, Totteridge, 11 November 1703.

33 Lord Carlisle's shopping bill for January 1704, for example, included five quarts of brandy and a hogshead of a sweet wine known as 'canary'. A month later, he bought another hogshead of the wine, though it is unclear how many people in Yorkshire and London this may have supplied. Dorset stocked his cellar at Knole for a six-month period with an incredible inventory of booze: 425 gallons of red port, 85 gallons of sherry, 72 gallons of canary, 63 gallons of white port and a quart of hock (a dry white wine).

34 Tom Browne, *A Description of Mr D—n's Funeral* (1700).

35 Joseph Spence, *Observations, Anecdotes, and Characters of Books and Men*, ed. James M. Osborn (Oxford, 1966 edn), no. 484, quoting Alexander Pope in May 1730, Recipe for a jug of punch called 'Sir John Vanbrugh's Cup'.

36 John C. Hodges (ed.), *William Congreve: Letters and Documents* (London, 1964), Congreve to Joe Keally, 20 June 1704.

37 Ibid., Congreve to Joe Keally, 30 April 1706.

38 Donald F. Bond (ed.), *The Spectator* (Oxford, 1965), vol. 2, p. 578 n. 3, quoting G. M. Trevelyan.

39 Eveline Cruickshanks, Stuart Handley and D. W. Hayton, *The House of Commons 1690–1715* (Cambridge, 2002), vol. 4, entry on Anthony Henley.

40 Donald F. Bond (ed.), *The Spectator* (Oxford, 1965), vol. 4, no. 569, Monday, 19 July 1714, by Addison.

41 Ibid., vol. 2, no. 195, Saturday, 13 October 1711, by Addison.

42 Ibid., vol. 2, no. 205, Thursday, 25 October 1711, by Addison.

43 Ned Ward suggested there was some link between the Kit-Cat and another Whig dining club founded sometime before 1705 named the 'Beefsteak Club'

(not to be confused with the 'Sublime Society of the Beef Steaks' founded in 1735).

44 Jonathan Swift, *Journal to Stella,* 22 March 1711.

45 According to a nineteenth-century, possibly apocryphal, anecdote, 'Darty' was once out walking when he overtook a fishmonger's boy carrying home a fine turbot. The boy was amusing himself with striking the turbot against every post he met. To Darty, this was a crime not to be overlooked or forgiven. He followed the boy to the house where he was going and described what he had seen, insisting on the boy being severely punished. Another unsourced anecdote recounts how Darty was once engaged to dine with a fellow gourmand, expressly to eat one of two plums that were the only produce of a particular tree, remarkable for the richness and delicacy of its fruit. The men were to proceed after dinner to the garden and each gather and eat his plum straight from the tree. Before the dinner was over, however, Darty made some excuse to retire for a few minutes, whereupon he scurried into the garden and devoured both plums without, he said, the slightest guilt. Quoted in *The Gentleman's Magazine* 77 (July–December 1807), p. 738.

46 Alexander Pope, '1st Satire of the 2nd Book of Horace, Imitated' (1733).

47 Lord Lyttleton also wrote a 'dialogue in the shades' between *Darteneuf and Apicius* on the subject of fine dining. See *The Gentleman's Magazine* 77 (July–December 1807), p. 738.

48 Geoffrey Webb and Bonamy Dobrée (eds), *The Complete Works of Sir John Vanbrugh* (London, 1927–8), vol. 4, no. 3, Vanbrugh to Tonson, 15 July 1703.

49 Donald F. Bond (ed.), *The Spectator* (Oxford 1965), vol. 4, no. 477, Saturday, 6 September 1712, by Addison (though in the form of a reader's letter).

50 Henri Misson quoted in Peter Earle, *The Making of the English Middle Class: Business, Society and Family Life in London, 1660–1730* (London, 1989), p. 274.

51 Charles Saumarez Smith, *The Building of Castle Howard* (London, 1990), p. 80.

52 Donald F. Bond (ed.), *The Spectator* (Oxford, 1965), vol. 4, no. 538, Monday, 17 November 1712, by Addison.

53 A 1704 satire,'The Seven Wise Men' (January–March 1704), refers to the 'Kit-kat Bowl' and a 4.5lb silver salver with a Kit-Cat coat of arms in the centre, mentioning the Haymarket theatre, was allegedly sighted some twenty years ago. George de Forest Lord et al (eds), *Poems on Affairs of State: Augustan Satirical Verse 1660–1714*, 7 vols (New Haven, Conn., 1963–75), vol. 6, p. 622.

54 Edmond Malone (ed.), *Critical and Miscellaneous Prose Works of John Dryden* (London, 1800), p. 533, Vanbrugh to Tonson, 29 November 1719; Wycherley, *The Country Wife*, Act 1, Scene 2.

55 Donald F. Bond (ed.), *The Spectator* (Oxford, 1965), vol. 3, no. 409, Thursday, 19 June 1712, by Addison.

56 Richard Blackmore, *The Kit-Cats, A Poem* (1708).

57 T. B. Macaulay, 'Life and Writings of Addison' (review of Lucy Aikin's 1843 biography), *Edinburgh Review* 78 (July 1843), p. 214.

58 Joseph Addison, *The Freeholder*, no. 5, Friday, 6 January 1716.

59 Joseph Addison, *The Campaign* (1704).
60 Richard Steele, *The Diverting Post*, no. 2, 28 October–4 November 1704.
61 Anon., *A Kit-Cat C—b Describ'd* (1705), original at Harvard.
62 C. E. Doble et al. (eds), *Remarks and Collections of Thomas Hearne* (Oxford, 1885–1921), diary entry for 11 December 1705; Arthur L. Cooke, 'Addison's Aristocratic Wife', *Publications of the Modern Language Association of America (PMLA)* 72, 1 (June 1957), pp. 379–80.
63 By 1706, however, Addison recommended a petition to Halifax on the basis that it was a personal favour to Lady Warwick, without any obvious awkwardness.
64 Daniel Defoe, *The Double Welcome* (1705).

IX BY SEVERAL HANDS

1 Henley was said to have 'presided at the Opera', contributing songs to a play called *Pausanias the Betrayer of His Country* (1696) by Richard Norton. Norton was a close Oxford friend of Henley's, said to preside as a critic at the playhouse as Henley did at the opera. Mark Noble, *A Biographical History of England from the Revolution to the End of George I's Reign; being a continuation of the Rev. J. Granger's work* (London, 1806), vol. 1, p. 209.
2 William Drogo Montagu, 7th Duke of Manchester, *Court and Society from Elizabeth to Anne* (London, 1864), vol. 2, p. 287.
3 Samuel Johnson, *Lives of the English Poets*, ed. George Birkbeck Hill (Oxford, 1905 edn), vol. 2, entry on Matthew Prior.
4 Colley Cibber, *An Apology for the Life of Mr Colley Cibber* (1740), ed. B. R. S. Fone (Ann Arbor, Mich., 1968).
5 Geoffrey Webb and Bonamy Dobrée (eds), *The Complete Works of Sir John Vanbrugh*, (London, 1927–8), vol. 4, no. 4, Vanbrugh to Tonson, 13 July 1703.
6 Ibid., no. 3, Vanbrugh to Tonson, 15 June 1703.
7 HMC, *Rutland MSS*, vol. 2, appendix V, p. 177, John Charlton to Lady Granby, Totteridge, 11 November 1703.
8 Geoffrey Webb and Bonamy Dobrée (eds), *The Complete Works of Sir John Vanbrugh* (London, 1927–8), vol. 4, no. 5, Vanbrugh to Tonson, 30 July 1703.
9 Eveline Cruickshanks, Stuart Handley and D. W. Hayton, *The House of Commons 1690–1715* (Cambridge, 2002), vol. 4, entry on Charles Montagu, Baron Halifax.
10 John C. Hodges (ed.), *William Congreve: Letters and Documents* (London, 1964), Congreve to Joe Keally, 30 November 1703.
11 Jeremy Collier, *Mr Collier's Dissuasive from the Play-house* (1703).
12 Madeleine Bingham, *Masks and Façades: Sir John Vanbrugh, the Man and his Setting* (London, 1974), p. 86.
13 Also, in March 1702, a Kit-Cat document records that Lords Somerset and Manchester were suspending 'the inscription of Music till May Fair', implying that they had previously held regular subscription-concerts at their London homes, probably showcasing imported Italian musicians. BL Add MS 40,060.

14 John Hughes poem quoted in Eric Walter White, *The Rise of English Opera* (London, 1951), p. 139.

15 NPG, Tonson Papers, undated.

16 John C. Hodges (ed.), *William Congreve: Letters and Documents* (London, 1964), Congreve to Joe Keally, 20 May 1704.

17 Colley Cibber, *An Apology for the Life of Mr Colley Cibber* (1740), ed. B. R. S. Fone (Ann Arbor, Mich., 1968), p. 192.

18 HMC, *Portland MSS*, vol. 2, p. 185. One Kit-Cat subscription receipt survives, dated 8 May 1704: 'Agreement to allow the Duke of Newcastle, in consideration of the payment by him of one hundred guineas, free entrance to the theatre intended to be built in the Haymarket, and certain other privileges, Signet. Witnessed by William Congreve and another.'

19 John C. Hodges (ed.), *William Congreve: Letters and Documents* (London, 1964), Congreve to Joe Keally, 12 February 1704.

20 Add MSS 40,060 f.89:

The Kit Cats and the Toasters
Did never care a fig
For any other Beauty
Besides the little Whig.

And see Horace Walpole, *Correspondence*, ed. W. S. Lewis et al. (Oxford, 1937–83), vol. 34, p. 262: text of *A Ballad on Mrs Strawbridge* (unknown date) alleged to be by George Bubb Dodington (1690/1–1762).

21 A contemporary Tory journalist reported it was laid 'with great Solemnity by a Noble Babe of Grace' (Marlborough's daughter, Anne) and 'over or under the Foundation Stone is a Plate of Silver, on which is Graven Kit Cat on the one side, and Little Whig on the other.' Charles Leslie, *Rehearsal of Observator*, no. 41, 5–12 May 1705, in Judith Milhous and Robert D. Hume (eds), *A Register of English Theatrical Documents, 1660–1737* (Carbondale, Ill., 1991), document 1808. A nineteenth-century report, however, states that 'on March 19th, 1825, removing some portion of the walls of the Italian Opera House, the workmen discovered the first stone of the old building, with some coins and an inscription: "April 18th, 1704. This corner-stone of the Queen's Theatre was laid by his Grace Charles Duke of Somerset."' Percy Fitzgerald, *A New History of the English Stage* (London, 1882). The latter might seem incontrovertible evidence were it not that two aged stones of unknown provenance today stand outside a law office in Bedford Row, one of which is inscribed 'Kitt-Catt' and the other 'Little Whigg'. They look very much like two sides of the same stone, split in half.

22 Walter Graham (ed.), *The Letters of Joseph Addison* (Oxford, 1941), no. 18, Addison to Abraham Stanyan, May 1700.

23 It was the same argument made by a protégé of Collier who published a tract warning against opera's licentiousness and arguing for a revival of sacred works such as those by William Byrd and Thomas Tallis.

24 Daniel Defoe, *Review of the Affairs of France*, 3 May 1705.

25 Dr Samuel Garth, Prologue to *The Conquest of Granada*, quoted in Robert Anderson, *The Works of the British Poets* (London, 1795), p. 10.
26 Michael Foss, *The Age of Patronage: The Arts in England 1660–1750* (Ithaca, NY, 1972), p. 148.
27 John Dennis, *The Diverting Post*, 28 October 1704.
28 BL Lansdowne MS 1,024; reprinted in *The London Gazette* on Christmas Day (no. 4082).
29 Anon., *A Letter from Several Members of the Society for Reformation of Manners to the Most Revered Father in God Thomas Lord Archbishop of Canterbury*, 10 December 1704.
30 British Library shelfmark 816.m.19, f.35.
31 Mary Astell, *Bart'lemy Fair* (1709).
32 William Shippen, *Faction Display'd* (1704). See also the allegation that the Kit-Cat Club despised revealed religion as much as the earlier, regicide Calves Head Club: *The Observator*, Saturday, 1 May 1708, issue 23.
33 Colley Cibber, *An Apology for the Life of Mr Colley Cibber* (1740), ed. B. R. S. Fone (Ann Arbor, Mich., 1968).
34 Ibid., pp. 173–4.
35 John C. Hodges (ed.), *William Congreve: Letters and Documents* (London, 1964), Congreve to Joe Keally, 3 February 1705.
36 Robert Anderson, *The Works of the British Poets* (London, 1795).
37 BL Add MS 61,451.
38 'Lady H. Godolphin' (by Maynwaring, according to the 1716 *Miscellany*).
39 BL Add MS 61,464, Sarah Churchill to Francis Hare, October 1726.
40 John C. Hodges (ed.), *William Congreve: Letters and Documents* (London, 1964), Congreve to Joe Keally, 8 June 1706.
41 Shrimpton would be made the Governor of Gibraltar in 1705, after defending that town through its siege. Sir Richard Temple was fighting with Marlborough in the Netherlands, and would be promoted to Major-General in 1706 for the leadership he showed during the Allied siege of Lille.
42 John Downes, *Roscius Anglicanus* (1708).
43 Ibid.
44 BL Add MS 21,094, f.152–4; Anon. [Benjamin Bragg], 'The Opening Prologue Paraphras'd in a Familiar Stile, for the better Conception of the True Meaning, and for the Particular Use of Mr. Jer. Collier'; Thomas McGreary, 'A Satire on the Opening of the Haymarket Theatre', *Restoration and 18th Century Theatre Research* 15 (Winter 2000), pp. 18–32.
45 Charles Leslie, *Rehearsal of Observator*, no. 41, 5–12 May 1705, in Judith Milhous and Robert D. Hume (eds), *A Register of English Theatrical Documents, 1660–1737* (Carbondale, Ill., 1991), document 1808.
46 Congreve promoted Susanna Centlivre's work, as well as that of Mary Pix and Catharine Trotter (later Mrs Cockburn). In 1698, when a male actor plagiarized a play by Pix, Congreve helped ensure the stolen production's failure. Congreve assisted Trotter editorially on one play, *The Fatal Friendship* (1697), and helped both Trotter and Pix get their plays staged by Betterton's company.

In the Dedication to *The Unhappy Penitent* (1701), Trotter reminded Halifax of his nurturing generosity to Congreve and hinted that Halifax should become her patron too.

X THE COMEBACK KITS

1 Owen Sweeney, *The Quacks, or, Love's the Physician (29 March 1705), 'As it was Acted after being twice forbid at the Theatre Royal, Drury Lane'*, in Thomas McGreary, 'A Satire on the Opening of the Haymarket Theatre', *Restoration and 18th Century Theatre Research* 15 (Winter 2000), pp. 18–32.

2 Anon., *A Kit-Cat C—b Describ'd* (1705), original at Harvard.

3 Anon., *The Tackers Vindicated; or, an Answer to the Whigs New Black List* (1705).

4 BL Add MS 21,094 f.140b, 'New Ballad Writ by Jacob Tonson and Sung at the Kit-Kat Club . . .'

5 C. K. Eves, *Matthew Prior, Poet and Diplomatist* (New York, 1939), p. 184.

6 A Tory newspaper (*The Examiner*, no. 6), the anonymous author of which may have been Prior himself, referred in 1710 to his expulsion from the Kit-Cat Club. Some have supposed this is reported as recent news, but Prior could have been referring to an expulsion of several years earlier that still rankled. Prior mocked the idea that losing his Club membership made him any less a poet, and towards the end of his life acknowledged that his closer Kit-Cat friends never imagined it did. Prior does not, for example, seem to have overlapped with the membership of Steele, who is mentioned rarely in Prior's correspondence as a distant acquaintance.

7 Anon., *A Kit-Cat C—b Describ'd* (London, 1705), original at Harvard.

8 Donald F. Bond, *The Spectator* (Oxford 1965), vol. 2, no. 155, Tuesday, 28 August 1711, by Steele.

9 Richard Steele, 'To Joseph Addison', Prologue to *The Tender Husband*, 9 May 1705, in Rae Blanchard (ed.), *The Correspondence of Richard Steele* (Oxford, 1968 edn).

10 Calhoun Winton, *Captain Steele: The Early Career of Richard Steele* (Baltimore, Md., 1964), p. 76, Wellbore Ellis to his brother John Ellis, 1705.

11 William Congreve, *Love for Love* (1695), Act 3, Scene 1.

12 Richard Blackmore, *The Kit-Cat Club, A Poem* (1708).

13 Richard Steele, 'To Sir Samuel Garth', *The Lover and The Reader*, 1714, in Rae Blanchard (ed.), *The Correspondence of Richard Steele* (Oxford, 1968 edn).

14 Ibid.

15 John Timbs, *Clubs and Club Life in London* (London, 1908), p. 53.

16 Richard Steele, 'To Sir Samuel Garth', *The Lover and The Reader*, 1714, in Rae Blanchard (ed.), *The Correspondence of Richard Steele* (Oxford, 1968 edn).

17 Richard Steele, 'To John Lord Somers', vol. 1 of the collected *Spectator* (1712) in Rae Blanchard (ed.), *The Correspondence of Richard Steele* (Oxford, 1968 edn).

18 Ibid.

19 Richard Steele, 'To Charles Montagu Baron Halifax', vol. 2 of the collected

Spectator (1712) in Rae Blanchard (ed.), *The Correspondence of Richard Steele* (Oxford, 1968 edn).

20 Richard Steele quoted in Lawrence Stone and Jeanne C. Fawtier Stone, *An Open Elite? England 1540–1880* (Oxford, 1984), p. 213.

21 Donald F. Bond (ed.), *The Spectator* (Oxford, 1965), vol. 4, no. 471, Saturday, 30 August 1712, by Addison.

22 Ibid., no. 458, Friday, 15 August 1712, by Addison.

23 Joseph Spence, *Observations, Anecdotes, and Characters of Books and Men*, ed. James M. Osborn (Oxford, 1966 edn), no. 191.

24 BL Add MS 32,329, f.50.

25 Donald F. Bond (ed.), *The Tatler* (Oxford, 1987), no. 241, 24 October 1710.

26 Donald F. Bond (ed.), *The Spectator* (Oxford, 1965), vol. 2, no. 151, Thursday, 23 August 1711, by Steele.

27 Ibid.

28 John C. Hodges (ed.), *William Congreve: Letters and Documents* (London, 1964), Congreve to Joe Keally, 8 June 1706.

29 This sinecure was worth some £200 a year (Congreve earned the modern equivalent of £222,000 in nine years of holding it). Voltaire, Goldsmith and Boswell later marvelled enviously and nostalgically at the way the Kit-Cat patrons had elevated authors like Congreve to lucrative government posts. In doing so, they saw only the high-minded reasons for these appointments, and an admirable alliance between learning and power; they ignored the way in which the arrangement was patronage on the cheap, at the taxpayer's expense.

30 William Coxe, *Memoirs of the Life and Administration of Sir Robert Walpole, Earl of Orford* (London, 1798), vol. 1, p. 761.

31 John C. Hodges (ed.), *William Congreve: Letters and Documents* (London, 1964), Congreve to Joe Keally, 15 December 1705.

32 Nicholas Rowe, *The Reconcilement between Jacob Tonson and Mr Congreve . . .* (1707).

33 James Brydges MP quoted in Geoffrey Holmes, *British Politics in the Age of Anne* (London, 1967), p. 231.

34 Thomas Hopkins to Lord Wharton, 29 November 1705, in HMC, *Report XIII: Appendix*, part 7 (1893), Manuscripts of the Earl of Lonsdale, p. 118.

35 28 October 1703 letter from Stanhope to Walpole saying that he, Hartington, Halifax, Smith and Sunderland all wanted Walpole back in London, on both public and personal grounds. J. H. Plumb, *Sir Robert Walpole: The Making of a Statesman* (Boston, Mass., 1961), p. 116. Walpole replied on 12 November that he would come as soon as possible: '[I]f public considerations were not enough, you may easily believe I want no inclinations to kiss your hand.' Jeremy Black, *Walpole in Power* (London, 2001), p. 4.

36 Fran Beauman, *The Pineapple: King of Fruits* (London, 2005), pp. 88–9.

37 When Mrs Walpole criticized her for flirting with Wharton, Dolly moved to live at the Whartons' – an even greater public embarrassment. Walpole had a few hard words with Lady Wharton for having allowed the girl to move in, but since Mrs Walpole would not receive her back, Dolly was sent to stay with

the Townshends. This seems to have led Dolly into another romance, as she later married Townshend after his first wife's death.

38 Mary Astell, *Bart'lemy Fair* (1709).

39 Fourth Earl of Chesterfield, quoted in Julian Hoppit, *A Land of Liberty? England 1689–1727* (Oxford, 2000), p. 398.

40 Eveline Cruickshanks, Stuart Handley and D. W. Hayton, *The House of Commons 1690–1715* (Cambridge, 2002), vol. 5, entry on James Stanhope, p. 542.

41 Spencer Compton was one of the youngest Kit-Cats whom John Oldmixon lists as a founder member. In 1697, he had no parliamentary seat, though he would shortly afterwards be returned for Eye in Suffolk.

42 BL Add MS 70,501, 18 August 1705, Lord Somers to the Duke of Newcastle.

43 Eveline Cruickshanks, Stuart Handley and D. W. Hayton, *The House of Commons 1690–1715* (Cambridge, 2002), vol. 5, entry on John Smith, p. 502.

44 Quoted in J. A. Manning, *Lives of the Speakers of the House of Commons* (London, 1850), p. 410.

45 W. A. Speck, *The Birth of Britain: A New Nation 1700–1710* (Oxford, 1994), p. 94.

46 Abel Boyer, *History of the Life and Reign of Queen Anne* (1722), pp. 217–18.

47 Ibid.

48 Brice Harris, *Charles Sackville, 6th Earl of Dorset: Patron and Poet of the Restoration* (Urbana, Ill., 1940), p. 222.

49 Vita Sackville-West, *Knole and the Sackvilles* (London, 1922), p. 141.

50 Erasmus Lewis (Stepney's cousin) to George Stepney, 17 October 1704, quoted in C. K. Eves, *Matthew Prior, Poet and Diplomatist* (New York, 1939), p. 193 n. 32.

51 Robert Sackville-West, *Knole* (London, 1998), p. 75.

52 C. K. Eves, *Matthew Prior, Poet and Diplomatist* (New York, 1939), p. 193.

53 Donald F. Bond (ed.), *The Spectator* (Oxford, 1965), vol. 5, no. 6, Dedication 'To William Honeycomb Esq.'.

54 John C. Hodges (ed.), *William Congreve: Letters and Documents* (London, 1964), Congreve to Joe Keally, 8 June 1706.

55 Montague Collection, Box 7 – Charles Montagu from Hanover, 4 June 1706.

56 Peter Smithers, *The Life of Joseph Addison* (Oxford, 2nd edn 1968), p. 110.

57 Ibid.

58 Montague Collection, Box 7 – Charles Montagu from Hanover, 4 June 1706.

59 Ibid.

XI UNEASY UNIONS: 1707

1 John C. Hodges (ed.), *William Congreve: Letters and Documents* (London, 1964), Congreve to Joe Keally, 30 April 1706.

2 Robert Walpole was another Commissioner who missed most of the negotiations because of pressing business in Norfolk.

3 William L. Sachse, *Lord Somers: A Political Portrait* (Manchester, 1975), p. 248, Somers to Lord Marchmont, 23 July 1706.

4 P. W. J. Riley, *The Union of England and Scotland: A Study in Anglo-Scottish Politics in the 18th Century* (Manchester, 1978), p. 189.

5 Walter Graham (ed.), *The Letters of Joseph Addison* (Oxford, 1941), no. 52, Addison to Stepney, 3 September 1706.

6 Ibid., no. 53, Addison to Stepney, 8 November 1706.

7 Sir John Clerk of Penicuik quoted in Daniel Szechi, 'A Union of Necessity', *Parliamentary History* (Edinburgh, 1996), vol. 15, part 3, p. 400.

8 A rumour spread, however, that Wharton had privately berated Godolphin for not surrendering more offices to the Junto Whigs as thanks for their support over the union, suggesting Wharton's motives were more self-interested than patriotic; Wharton's willingness to consider a later 1713 proposal that the union be dissolved, when he thought it would embarrass his enemies, lends some credence to this charge of opportunism.

9 P. W. J. Riley, *The Union of England and Scotland: A Study in Anglo-Scottish Politics in the 18th Century* (Manchester, 1978), p. 301.

10 James Ogilvy, 1st Earl of Seafield, for example, asked Godolphin whether he could correspond directly with Somers and Sunderland, since he was unsure whether the men 'who treated with us' were friends to each other. Add MSS 28,055, f.338, James Ogilvy, 1st Earl of Seafield and Lord Chancellor of Scotland, to Sidney Godolphin, 11 November 1706.

11 Walter Graham (ed.), *The Letters of Joseph Addison* (Oxford, 1941), no. 58, Addison to Emanuel Scrope Howe, Envoy Extraordinary to Hanover, 3 December 1706.

12 Ibid., no. 75, Addison to Jean Le Clerc, 23 May 1707.

13 Ibid., no. 63, Addison to Stepney, 27 December 1706.

14 Ibid., no. 68, Addison to Newton, Envoy Extraordinary at Florence.

15 Thomas D'Urfey, *Wonders in the Sun; or, the Kingdom of the Birds* (1706); Charles Burney, *A General History of Music* (London, 1776–89), vol. 2, p. 657: statement that members of the Kit-Cat Club contributed lyrics to many of the songs in the opera; John Diprose, *Some Account of the Parish of St. Clement Danes* (London, 1868), vol. 1, pp. 262–3: on *Wonders in the Sun*, in which 'many of the most distinguished wits of that celebrated body [the Kit-Cat Club] having assisted their old favourite in writing the songs in it'.

16 Richard Steele, *The Muses Mercury*, 25 January 1707.

17 Brean Hammond notes that on 2 April 1706, ten days before the trip to Hanover, Addison presented a first draft of *Rosamund* to Sarah Churchill (now in the Houghton Library, Harvard), which does not mention stage scenery.

18 John C. Hodges (ed.), *William Congreve: Letters and Documents* (London, 1964), Congreve to Joe Keally, 10 September 1706.

19 Eric Walter White, *The Rise of English Opera* (London, 1951), p. 142.

20 Richard Steele, *The Muses Mercury*, 15 January 1707.

21 Edmund Smith, *Phaedra and Hippolitus* (1707); Eric Walter White, *The Rise of English Opera* (London, 1951), p. 143.

22 Linda Colley, *Britons: Forging the Nation 1707–1837* (London, 1996 edn), p. 12.

23 Richard Steele, *Mr Steele's Apology for himself and his writings* (1714), in Rae

Blanchard (ed.), *Tracts and Pamphlets by Richard Steele* (Baltimore, Md., 1944), p. 339.

24 Richard Steele, *The Funeral* (1701), Act 4, Scene 3.

25 Mr Cat's shop may have sold his pastries in similar fashion – a character in Steele's *The Funeral* tells some soldiers there is plenty of work to be found in London, shouting 'Puff – Puff Pies!'

26 Donald F. Bond (ed.), *The Spectator* (Oxford, 1965), vol. 2, no. 251, Tuesday, 18 December 1711, by Addison; Donald F. Bond (ed.), *The Tatler* (Oxford, 1987), no. 9.

27 Rae Blanchard (ed.), *The Correspondence of Richard Steele* (Oxford, 1968 edn), no. 263, Steele to Mary, 19 May 1708.

28 Nichols (editor of *The Tatler* in 1786) claimed to have heard this from a printer Richard Nutt. Donald F. Bond (ed.), *The Spectator* (Oxford, 1965), vol. 3, p. 162 n. 1.

29 Ibid., vol. 4, no. 576, Wednesday, 4 August 1714, by Addison.

30 John Dennis quoted in William Makepeace Thackeray, *English Humourists of the Eighteenth Century* (London, 1853).

31 BL Add MS 5,145A, Date missing from MSS – only '1707' remains. Blanchard's *Correspondence* dates it (no. 208) to 11 August (?) 1707.

32 Rae Blanchard (ed.), *The Correspondence of Richard Steele* (Oxford, 1968 edn), no. 212, Mary to her mother asking permission to marry Steele, 16 August 1707.

33 BL Add MS 5,145A, Steele to Mary, 1707 (Blanchard no. 215).

34 Ibid., Steele to Mary, late August 1707 (Blanchard no. 216).

35 Ibid., Steele to Mary, late August 1707 (Blanchard no. 217).

36 Ibid., Steele to Mary, 30 August 1707 (Blanchard no. 221).

37 Ibid., Steele to Mary, 1 September 1707 (Blanchard no. 223).

38 Ibid.

39 Ibid., Steele to Mrs Elizabeth Scurlock, 3 September 1707 (Blanchard no. 226).

40 Blanchard, no. 254 and no. 255, for example.

41 Add MS 5,145A, Steele to Mrs Steele, 8 p.m., 22 October 1707, from the Fountain tavern.

42 Three years later, Steele would still be arguing with the Tories about his belief in using the name of 'Great Britain'. See Jonathan Swift, *Journal to Stella*, 2 December 1710.

43 Walter Graham (ed.), *The Letters of Joseph Addison* (Oxford, 1941), no. 93, Addison to Lord Manchester, 1707. The new Parliament contained forty-five Scottish MPs and sixteen Scottish elected peers. These figures may not have reflected proportional representation (which would have given Scotland 103 MPs) but were a generous reflection of the ratio in the amounts the two populations paid in taxation (five to one).

44 Note possible but unverifiable connection between this story and Blanchard no. 263: Steele to Mrs Steele, 11 a.m., 19 May 1708.

45 John Nichols quoting Mr Thomas, grandson of Mrs Aynston, in the 1780s.

See BL Add MS 5,145B, and Rae Blanchard (ed.), *The Correspondence of Richard Steele* (Oxford, 1968 edn), p. 271 n. 2.

46 *The Postboy*, Tuesday, 4 November 1707.

XII BESET

1 BL Add MS 46,535, George Stepney to Robert Sutton, 2nd Lord Lexinton, 18 March (NS) 1707.

2 Susan Spens, *George Stepney 1663–1707: Diplomat and Poet* (Cambridge, 1997), pp. 314–15.

3 Walter Graham (ed.), *The Letters of Joseph Addison* (Oxford, 1941), no. 52, Addison to Stepney, 3 September 1706.

4 Ibid., no. 84, Addison to Christian Cole (Secretary to Lord Manchester), 16 September 1707.

5 William Drogo Montagu, 7th Duke of Manchester, *Court and Society from Elizabeth to Anne* (London, 1864), vol. 2, p. 253, Joseph Addison to Mr Cole, 7 October 1707.

6 BL Add MS 7,121, Letters to Lord Halifax (1706ff.), f.49, Matthew Prior to Halifax, 1707.

7 Robert Molesworth to Lord Shaftesbury, PRO 30/24/20/137, 18 December 1707.

8 John C. Hodges (ed.), *William Congreve: Letters and Documents* (London, 1964), Congreve to Joe Keally, 29 January 1708. Alexander Pope's reference (to Joseph Spence) to a time when the Kit-Cat 'broke up' probably refers to this suspension for political reasons, not the final demise of the Club.

9 Walter Graham (ed.), *The Letters of Joseph Addison* (Oxford, 1941), no. 102, Addison to Lord Manchester, 7 February 1708.

10 Harry Boyle replaced Harley, allowing Jack Smith to step into the office of Chancellor of the Exchequer. Walpole replaced St John as Secretary-at-War.

11 Eveline Cruickshanks, Stuart Handley and D. W. Hayton, *The House of Commons 1690–1715* (Cambridge, 2002), Entry on Jack Smith MP, p. 504.

12 Walter Graham (ed.), *The Letters of Joseph Addison* (Oxford, 1941), no. 103, Addison to Lord Manchester, February 1708.

13 Ibid., no. 106, Addison to Lord Manchester, 27 February 1708.

14 HMC, *Downshire MSS*, vol. 1, part 2, p. 858, Rev. Ralph Bridges to Sir William Trumbull.

15 Walter Graham (ed.), *The Letters of Joseph Addison* (Oxford, 1941), no. 109, Addison to Lord Manchester, 5 March 1708.

16 Abel Boyer, *History of the Life and Reign of Queen Anne* (1722).

17 John Oldmixon, *Memoirs of the Life of the Most Noble Thomas, Late Marquess of Wharton; with his Speeches in Parliament both in England and Ireland. To which is added His Lordship's Character by Sir Richard Steele* (1715).

18 Ibid.

19 John C. Hodges (ed.), *William Congreve: Letters and Documents* (London, 1964), Congreve to Joe Keally, 29 November 1708.

20 Geoffrey Webb and Bonamy Dobrée (eds), *The Complete Works of Sir John Vanbrugh* (London, 1927–8), vol. 4, no. 9, Vanbrugh to Lord Manchester, 24 February 1708.
21 John Vanbrugh to Thomas Coke quoted in Kerry Downes, *Sir John Vanbrugh: A Biography* (London, 1987), p. 327.
22 Walter Graham (ed.), *The Letters of Joseph Addison* (Oxford, 1941), no. 87, Addison to Lord Manchester, 7 October 1707.
23 After Sweeney's return, the licences were amended so the Queen's Theatre could stage both plays and operas, though the resultant company mixing actors and singers was never a peaceful one. Steele complained on 7 October 1708: 'The Taste for Plays is expired. We are all for Operas, performed by eunuchs every way impotent to please.' Rae Blanchard (ed.), *The Correspondence of Richard Steele* (Oxford, 1968 edn), p. 46, no. 26.
24 Geoffrey Webb and Bonamy Dobrée (eds), *The Complete Works of Sir John Vanbrugh* (London, 1927–8), vol. 4, no. 14, Vanbrugh to Lord Manchester, 27 July 1708; William Drogo Montagu, 7th Duke of Manchester, *Court and Society from Elizabeth to Anne* (London, 1864), vol. 2, p. 383, Vanbrugh to Manchester, 17 August 1708, postscript saying that London needs a good lead violinist more than a composer, and expecting arrival of Nicolini.
25 Joseph Spence, *Observations, Anecdotes, and Characters of Books and Men*, ed. James M. Osborn (Oxford, 1966 edn), no. 122.
26 Colley Cibber, *An Apology for the Life of Mr Colley Cibber* (1740), ed. B. R. S. Fone (Ann Arbor, Mich., 1968), p. 183.
27 Richard Steele, *The Muses Mercury*, April 1707.
28 James Thomson quoted in James Sambrook, *James Thomson (1700–1748): A Life* (Oxford, 1991), p. 28. Nancy remained Maynwaring's mistress until he died, bearing him a son, also named Arthur. Though he never married her, Nancy and the boy were provided for in Maynwaring's will.
29 Geoffrey Webb and Bonamy Dobrée (eds), *The Complete Works of Sir John Vanbrugh* (London, 1927–8), vol. 4, no. 7, Vanbrugh to Lord Manchester, 18 July 1707; Frank McCormick, *Sir John Vanbrugh: The Playwright as Architect* (University Park, Pa., 1991), p. 135.
30 Geoffrey Webb and Bonamy Dobrée (eds), *The Complete Works of Sir John Vanbrugh*, 4 vols (London, 1927–8), vol. 4, no. 14, Vanbrugh to Lord Manchester, 27 July 1708.
31 Ibid., no. 15, 17 August 1708, Vanbrugh to Lord Manchester.
32 HMC, *Portland MSS*, vol. 4, p. 493, Erasmus Lewis to Robert Harley, 17 June 1708.
33 Ibid.
34 Walter Graham (ed.), *The Letters of Joseph Addison* (Oxford, 1941), no. 129, To [?], Thursday, 15 July 1708.
35 BL Add MS 40,060, f.74, no date but two additional verses added at the end dated July 1708. Topham is usually listed among the members of the Kit-Cat Club on the evidence of this manuscript alone.
36 BL Add MS 40,060, f.69b, 'Toast of Great Britain for the year 1708'.

37 Donald F. Bond (ed.), *The Spectator* (Oxford, 1965), vol. 4, no. 448, Monday, 4 August 1712, by Steele.
38 Ibid., no. 280, Monday, 21 January 1712, by Steele.
39 In February 1708, for example, Steele wrote home to his wife from the Tonsons' shop at Gray's Inn Gate: 'If the man who has my Shoemaker's bill calls, let Him be answered that I shall call on Him as I come home. I stay Here in Order to get Tonson to discount a Bill for me and shall dine with Him for that end.' Rae Blanchard (ed.), *The Correspondence of Richard Steele* (Oxford, 1968 edn), no. 258, Steele to Mrs Steele, 3 February 1708. In this note, Steele addresses his wife Mary as 'Dear Prue' (the first time is in a letter of 3 January 1708), the pet name he continued to use through the rest of their married lives. 'Prudence' means modesty in several of Steele's writings. In an early love letter, he complimented Mary on 'Prudent Youth and becoming Piety' (ibid., no. 211, Steele to Mary, 16 August 1707; no. 241, Steele to Mrs Steele, 13 October 1707). In another, however, he referred to Mrs Keck, a friend of his wife's, as a 'great Prue' and from the context it is clear he meant she was a sexual and moral prude (ibid., no. 563, Steele to Lady Steele, 24 June 1717). BL Add MS 5,145A and 5,145B.
40 Dedication 'To the Right Honorable Charles Lord Halifax' (7 April 1711) in the collected *Tatler*, vol. 4, quoted in Donald F. Bond (ed.), *The Tatler* (Oxford, 1987), vol. 1, pp. 12–14.
41 Donald F. Bond (ed.), *The Tatler* (Oxford, 1987), vol. 3, no. 225, Saturday, 16 September 1710.
42 Dr Birch quoted in a note on the 1789 edition of *The Tatler*, and from thence by Samuel Johnson, *Lives of the English Poets* (1781), ed. George Birkbeck Hill (Oxford, 1905 edn), vol. 2, entry on Addison.
43 Donald F. Bond (ed.), *The Spectator* (Oxford, 1965), vol. 3, no. 293, Tuesday, 5 February 1712, by Addison.
44 Richard Steele, *The Christian Hero* (1701).
45 BL Add MS 5,145A, Steele to Mrs Steele, 8 October 1708 (Blanchard no. 306).
46 Ibid., Steele to Mrs Steele, 12 August 1708 (Blanchard no. 307, nos 281 and 282 are replies to Mrs Steele which suggest that she was writing angry notes to him complaining that he excluded her from their business, etc.).
47 Ibid., Steele to Mrs Steele, 20 October 1708 (Blanchard no. 313).
48 Ibid., Steele to Mrs Steele, 13 October 1708 (Blanchard no. 308).
49 Ibid., Steele to Mrs Steele, 30 November 1708 (Blanchard no. 329).
50 Michael Foot, *The Pen and the Sword* (London, 1957), p. 32.
51 BL Add MS 40,060, f.81: 'On Mr Hopkins; and Topham, made at the Du[c]h[ess] of Marl[borough's] by Mr Manne, November 1708 (to the tune of a French ditty)'.
52 Mary Astell, *Bart'lemy Fair* (1709).
53 Richard Blackmore, *The Kit-Cats, A Poem* (1708).
54 BL Add MS 5,145A, Steele to Mrs Steele, 16 November 1708 (Blanchard no. 324).
55 Ibid., Steele to Mrs Steele, 6 December 1708 (Blanchard no. 331).

56 Donald F. Bond (ed.), *The Spectator* (Oxford, 1965), vol. 2, no. 214, Monday, 5 November 1711, by Steele.
57 BL Add MS 32,685, Letters of the Duke of Newcastle, 25 May 1715.
58 Horace Walpole quoted in John F. Sena, *The Best-Natured Man: Sir Samuel Garth, Physician and Poet* (New York, 1986), p. 128.
59 BL Add MS 5,145A, Steele to Mrs Steele, 5 February 1709 (Blanchard no. 340).
60 Ibid., Steele to Mrs Steele, 19 April 1709 (Blanchard no. 345).
61 BL Add MS 7,121, Letters to Lord Halifax (1706ff.), f.69, Steele to Halifax, 26 January 1710.
62 Edward (Ned) Ward, *The Secret History of Clubs* (1709).
63 Mary Astell, *Bart'lemy Fair* (1709).
64 Donald F. Bond, *The Tatler* (Oxford, 1987), vol. 3, no. 202, Tuesday, 25 July 1710.
65 *The Examiner*, no. 6.
66 BL Add MS 5,145, Steele to Mrs Steele, 5 May 1709 (Blanchard no. 349).
67 Ibid., Steele to Charles Montagu, 6 October 1709 (Blanchard no. 31); BL Add MS 7,121, Letters to Lord Halifax (1706ff.), f.67, Steele to Halifax, 6 December (or October?) 1709.
68 Donald F. Bond (ed.), *The Spectator* (Oxford, 1965), vol. 1, no. 82, Monday, 4 June 1711, by Steele.
69 Samuel Johnson, *Lives of the English Poets* (1781), ed. George Birkbeck Hill (Oxford, 1905 edn), vol. 2, entry on Addison.
70 Donald F. Bond (ed.), *The Spectator* (Oxford, 1965), vol. 3, no. 284, Friday, 25 January 1712, by Steele.

XIII IRELAND: KIT-CAT COLONY

1 Archbishop King said the Irish Protestants were 'almost frightened out of their wits with the fear of an invasion' by The Pretender, even before the 1708 invasion attempt in Scotland. King to Southwell, March 1707, TCD MSS.
2 John Oldmixon, *Memoirs of the Life of the Most Noble Thomas, Late Marquess of Wharton; with his Speeches in Parliament both in England and Ireland. To which is added His Lordship's Character by Sir Richard Steele* (1715).
3 Donald F. Bond (ed.), *The Spectator* (Oxford, 1965), vol. 5, 'To Thomas Earl of Wharton' (1713).
4 John Oldmixon, *Memoirs of the Life of the Most Noble Thomas, Late Marquess of Wharton; with his Speeches in Parliament both in England and Ireland. To which is added His Lordship's Character by Sir Richard Steele* (1715).
5 Ibid.
6 Christopher Robbins, '"The Most Universal Villain I Ever Knew": Jonathan Swift and the Earl of Wharton', *Eighteenth-Century Ireland* 18 (Dublin, 2003).
7 Jonathan Swift to Col. Hunter, quoted in Herbert Wood, 'Addison's Connexion with Ireland', *Royal Society of Antiquaries of Ireland Journal*, 5th series, 14 (1904), pp. 133–58.

8 Peter Smithers, *The Life of Joseph Addison* (Oxford, 2nd edn 1968), p. 152.
9 Ibid., p. 143. Swift was then pursuing business on behalf of the Irish Church, lobbying Addison and Steele as government employees, while they in turn saw him as a potential pen for hire.
10 Ibid., p. 153.
11 Two-thirds figure given for 1732: Toby Barnard, *A New Anatomy of Ireland: The Irish Protestants 1649–1770* (New Haven, Conn. and London, 2003), p. 2; Tim Harris, *Revolution: The Great Crisis of the British Monarchy, 1685–1720* (London, 2006), p. 22 – Protestants of the Established Church (10 per cent of the population) were the only ones granted full rights at the Restoration of 1660. About 75 per cent of the population were Catholic and the remaining 15 per cent were Dissenters. T. W. Moody and W. E. Vaughan (eds), *A New History of Ireland*, vol. 4: *Eighteenth Century Ireland 1691–1800* (Oxford, 1986), p. xlix, state that the Irish Catholic population was more than four times as large as the Protestant.
12 *The Flying Post or, The Post-Master*, Monday, 14 March 1709.
13 Jonathan Swift, *The Prose Works of Jonathan Swift*, ed. Temple Scott (London, 1897 edn), vol. 2, p. 120.
14 Jonathan Swift, *The Sixth Drapier's Letter*, in Herbert Davis (ed.), *The Drapier's Letters to the People of Ireland . . .* (Oxford, 1965 edn), p. 123.
15 *The Theatre*, no. 5, Saturday, 16 January 1720, in John Loftis (ed.), *Richard Steele's 'The Theatre'* (Oxford, 1962).
16 Walter Graham (ed.), *The Letters of Joseph Addison* (Oxford, 1941), no. 191, Addison to Sidney Earl of Godolphin, 30 June 1709.
17 Pat Gorden, *Geography Anatomiz'd or, The Geographical Grammar* (1708).
18 Herbert Wood, 'Addison's Connexion with Ireland', *Royal Society of Antiquaries of Ireland Journal*, 5th series, 14 (1904), pp. 133–58. His lodgings consisted of two painted rooms and a drawing room hung with fabric; his menial servants slept on a 'settle-bed' in the loft above the stables. Next door lived Captain Pratt, the Castle's Constable, who became Addison's friend.
19 Claret being sold at 14 shillings (some £67 today) per dozen bottles, for example, in an alley off Dames Street. 'I wish you could contrive any way to send me over a Hogshead of Irish wine,' Addison once wrote to Dawson from London. 'Might not it be done in Boxes and connived at by the Commissioners of the Revenue?' See Herbert Wood, 'Addison's Connexion with Ireland', *Royal Society of Antiquaries of Ireland Journal*, 5th series, 14 (1904), pp. 133–58.
20 BL Add MS 7,121, Letters to Lord Halifax (1706ff.), Addison to Halifax, 7 May 1709: 'I have the Happiness every day to drink your Lordship's health in very good wine and with very honest gentlemen.'
21 John C. Hodges, *William Congreve the Man: A Biography from New Sources* (London, 1941), p. 83.
22 *The Dublin Gazette*, no. 422.
23 BL Add MS 7,121, Letters to Lord Halifax (1706ff.), Addison to Halifax, 7 May 1709.

24 John C. Hodges (ed.), *William Congreve: Letters and Documents* (London, 1964), Congreve to Joe Keally, 23 May 1709.

25 The story about Addison stammering in Parliament probably first appeared in the 1820 edition of Spence's *Observations, Anecdotes, and Characters of Books and Men* (Oxford, 1966 edn, vol. 2, p. 626), and was then repeated in Louis Gabriel Michaud, *Biographie universelle, ancienne et moderne* (Paris, 1843), vol. 1, p. 164. See also *The Irish Book Lover* 11 (August–September 1919), pp. 9–10.

26 See Donald F. Bond (ed.), *The Spectator* (Oxford, 1965), vol. 4, no. 556, Friday, 18 June 1714, by Addison; vol. 2, no. 231, Saturday, 24 November 1711, by Addison; vol. 3, no. 407, Tuesday, 17 June 1712, by Addison.

27 Ibid., vol. 4, no. 484, Monday, 15 September 1712, by Steele.

28 Ibid., vol. 1, no. 38, 13 April 1711, by Steele.

29 *The Dublin Intelligence*, no. 572, 21 May 1709.

30 Christopher Robbins, '"The Most Universal Villain I Ever Knew": Jonathan Swift and the Earl of Wharton', *Eighteenth-Century Ireland* 18 (Dublin, 2003), p. 32.

31 *The Dublin Gazette*, no. 456, 27 August 1709.

32 Edmund Burke quoted in L. Dralle, 'Kingdom in Reversion: The Irish Viceroyalty of the Earl of Wharton 1708–10', *The Huntington Library Quarterly* 15 (1951–2), p. 399.

33 John Dunton, *The Dublin Scuffle* (1699), ed. Andrew Carpenter (Dublin, 2000).

34 1707 Act of the Irish Parliament concerning transportation of Catholics.

35 Walter Graham (ed.), *The Letters of Joseph Addison* (Oxford, 1941), no. 185, Addison to Sidney Earl of Godolphin, 18 June 1709.

36 Ibid., no. 183, Addison to John Somers, 14 June 1709.

37 Jonathan Swift, *A Short Character of His Excellency Thomas Earl of Wharton, Lord Lieutenant of Ireland* (1710).

38 John Oldmixon, *Memoirs of the Life of the Most Noble Thomas, Late Marquess of Wharton; with his Speeches in Parliament both in England and Ireland. To which is added His Lordship's Character by Sir Richard Steele* (1715).

39 Jonathan Swift, *A Short Character of His Excellency Thomas Earl of Wharton, Lord Lieutenant of Ireland* (1710).

40 R. B. McDowell and D. A. Webb (eds), *Trinity College Dublin 1592–1952* (Cambridge, 1982), p. 34.

41 John Oldmixon, *Memoirs of the Life of the Most Noble Thomas, Late Marquess of Wharton; with his Speeches in Parliament both in England and Ireland. To which is added His Lordship's Character by Sir Richard Steele* (1715).

42 BL Add MS 21,094, poems said to have been collected *c.* 1710 by the Earl of Denbigh, f.184, 'The Earl of Godolphin to Dr Garth: Honest Daughters Running Away'.

43 John T. Gilbert (ed.), *Calendar of Ancient Records of Dublin* (Dublin, 1896), vol. 4.

44 John Oldmixon, *Memoirs of the Life of the Most Noble Thomas, Late Marquess of Wharton; with his Speeches in Parliament both in England and Ireland. To which is added His Lordship's Character by Sir Richard Steele* (1715).

45 John C. Hodges (ed.), *William Congreve: Letters and Documents* (London, 1964), Congreve to Joe Keally, 23 May 1709.
46 Walter Graham (ed.), *The Letters of Joseph Addison* (Oxford, 1941), no. 121, Addison to Lord Manchester, 20 April 1708.
47 Donald F. Bond (ed.), *The Spectator* (Oxford, 1965), no. 239, Tuesday, 4 December 1711, by Addison.
48 John Oldmixon, *Memoirs of the Life of the Most Noble Thomas, Late Marquess of Wharton; with his Speeches in Parliament both in England and Ireland. To which is added His Lordship's Character by Sir Richard Steele* (1715).
49 Robbins, Christopher , '"The Most Universal Villain I Ever Knew": Jonathan Swift and the Earl of Wharton', *Eighteenth-Century Ireland* 18 (Dublin, 2003), p. 32.
50 *The Dublin Intelligence*, no. 601, 30 August 1709, Address from the Knights, Citizens and Burgesses in Parliament.
51 Jonathan Swift, *Remarks on the Characters of the Court of Queen Anne from 'Memoirs of the Secret Services of John Macky Esq.'* (1733).
52 BL Add MS 7,121, Letters to Lord Halifax (1706ff.), f.73, Jonathan Swift to Halifax from Dublin, 13 November 1709.
53 Quoted in Christopher Robbins, '"The Most Universal Villain I Ever Knew": Jonathan Swift and the Earl of Wharton', *Eighteenth-Century Ireland* 18 (Dublin, 2003), p. 29.
54 Jonathan Swift, 'Memoirs, Relating to That Change Which Happened in the Queen's Ministry in the Year 1710', in *The Prose Works of Jonathan Swift*, ed. Herbert Davis and Irvin Ehrenpreis, vol. 8 (Oxford, 1953), p. 121.
55 Jonathan Swift, *A Short Character of His Excellency Thomas Earl of Wharton, Lord Lieutenant of Ireland* (1710).
56 Jonathan Swift, *Remarks on the Characters of the Court of Queen Anne from 'Memoirs of the Secret Services of John Macky Esq.'* (1733).
57 Jonathan Swift, *A Short Character of His Excellency Thomas Earl of Wharton, Lord Lieutenant of Ireland* (1710).

XIV THE MONOPOLY BROKEN: WHIG DOWNFALL

1 Matthew Prior, *Dialogues of the Dead, And other works in prose and verse* (Cambridge, 1907), p. 201.
2 Mary Astell, *Bart'lemy Fair* (1709).
3 BL Add MS 9,118, f.150. Note that this letter is misdated as 1708 by William Coxe and this error is repeated in its printed form: Sarah Churchill, *The Private Correspondence of Sarah Duchess of Marlborough* (London, 1838), vol. 1, pp. 159–60.
4 HMC, *Portland MSS*, vol. 2 (1893), p. 209, the Earl of Derwentwater to the Duke of Newcastle, at Welbeck, 10 December 1709; Add MS 70,502, f.112.
5 These *Caesar's Commentaries* were a new Latin edition by Dr Samuel Clarke, for the lavish publication of which Tonson had been collecting subscriptions

since as early as 1703. By the time the *Commentaries* were finally published in 1712, Marlborough would truly need such support.

6 Sarah Churchill, *The Private Correspondence of Sarah Duchess of Marlborough* (London, 1838), vol. 1, p. 272, Arthur Maynwaring to the Duchess of Marlborough, Saturday morning (probably 19 November 1709 – Coxe's memorandum).

7 HMC, *Downshire MSS*, vol. 1, part 2, pp. 885–6, John Bridges to Sir William Trumbull, 20 December 1709.

8 Sarah Churchill, *Characters of Her Contemporaries, by Sarah Duchess of Marlborough*, ed. Nathaniel Hooke (London, 1930), p. 260. This was very unlikely therefore to have been a Kit-Cat meeting, though see Lady Hyde's bitchy remark that Sarah would have to 'forget all the joys of the Kit-Cat' after the Whigs fell from power. This could mean, however, a number of things – Maynwaring, for example, once referred to some venison she sent to the Club from Windsor Lodge. BL Add 61,461, f.63, Letters of Arthur Maynwaring *c.* 1710, Maynwaring to Sarah Churchill, 22 June 1710.

9 The issue was never raised in any of the Queen's formal Cabinet meetings, since such an impeachment should have been solely within the House of Commons' competence. This explains the informal and secretive meetings throughout early December 1709.

10 Alexander Cunningham, *The History of Great Britain from the Revolution in 1688 to the Accession of George I* (London, 1787 edn), vol. 2, pp. 276–8. Sarah Churchill, *Characters of Her Contemporaries, by Sarah Duchess of Marlborough*, ed. Nathaniel Hooke (London, 1930), p. 260.

11 Anon., *The Tryal of Dr Henry Sacheverell before the House of Peers for High Crimes and Misdemeanours* (1710), p. 61.

12 Eveline Cruickshanks, Stuart Handley and D. W. Hayton, *The House of Commons 1690–1715* (Cambridge, 2002), vol. 5, entry on John Smith.

13 Geoffrey Holmes, *The Trial of Dr Sacheverell* (London, 1973), p. 51.

14 Abel Boyer, *History of the Life and Reign of Queen Anne* (1722), p. 429.

15 Eveline Cruickshanks, Stuart Handley and D. W. Hayton, *The House of Commons 1690–1715* (Cambridge, 2002), vol. 5, entry on John Smith.

16 Henry L. Snyder (ed.), *The Marlborough–Godolphin Correspondence* (Oxford, 1975), vol. 2, p. 1150, November 1708.

17 H. T. Dickinson (ed.), *The Correspondence of Sir James Clavering* (Gateshead, 1967), p. 76, Anne (James's sister) to James Clavering, 1 April 1710: 'I suppose you've heard how our neighbour of Hedley-fell has carried himself. The Duke of Rich[mond], I hear, plays him a good trick. He's to summon the Kitt-Katt to meet, to make inquiry after one of the society who has made an elopement with Robin the Trickster. A very good whim I think.'

18 John Macky, *Memoirs of the Secret Services of John Macky*, ed. A. R. (1733).

19 BL Add 61,461, f.63, Letters of Arthur Maynwaring *c.* 1710, Maynwaring to Sarah Churchill, Thursday afternoon, 22 June 1710.

20 Stowe MS 57, ii, 204, James Brydges to General Cadogan, 7 April 1710, quoted

in Kathleen M. Lynch, *Jacob Tonson, Kit-Cat Publisher* (Knoxville, Tenn., 1971), p. 59.

21 Peter Smithers, *The Life of Joseph Addison* (Oxford, 2nd edn 1968), p. 193.

22 Fourth Earl of Chesterfield, *Characters of Lord Chesterfield* (London, 1778), character of Lord Scarbrough, pp. 41–4.

23 G. E. Cokayne, *The Complete Peerage* (London, 1936), on Scarbrough, p. 511.

24 There are anecdotes of him surprising a poor family with the gift of an income for life, founding a hospital for cows and horses, showing great affection for a famously ugly pet dog, and putting itching powder into house-guests' beds. Though there is no evidence of patronage to English writers or musicians, which might have qualified this Duke for the Kit-Cat's cultural programme, he later conducted 'experiments' in educating slaves on his West Indies plantations. He sponsored one free black Jamaican to attend Cambridge University, helped free and repatriate Job Ben Solomon, an Islamic scholar, and encouraged a slave who worked at a house in Greenwich to read and educate himself. This last, Ignatius Sancho, became (besides a grocer and the first black man to vote in Britain) a composer and poet, painted by Hogarth and Gainsborough and admired by Dr Johnson.

25 Story of Manchester, Lincoln, Dunch, and some non-Kit-Cats going to Greenwich and trying to drink 'Confusion to Sacheverell' and getting into a fight with the drawer of the tavern when he refused to pledge it. BL Add 61,461, f.63, Letters of Arthur Maynwaring *c.* 1710, Maynwaring to Sarah Churchill at Windsor Lodge, Thursday afternoon, 22 June 1710.

26 *The Dublin Gazette*, no. 530; Steele's *Tatler* was reprinted by Cornelius Carter at Dublin's Old Post Office and sold at Tom's Coffee House near the Castle gate. In May 1710, a paper entitled *The Dublin Spy by Tom Tatler* was started in imitation of *The Tatler* and printed next door to the theatre in Smock Alley. Its author, Edward Waters, offered 'remarks upon the different Humours, Passions, Inclinations, Principles and Practices of Men' in Ireland.

27 R. B. McDowell and D. A. Webb (eds), *Trinity College Dublin 1592–1952* (Cambridge, 1982), p. 414.

28 *The Dublin Gazette*, no. 542, 26 June 1710; L. Dralle, 'Kingdom in Reversion: The Irish Viceroyalty of the Earl of Wharton 1708–10', *The Huntington Library Quarterly* 15 (1951–2), p. 421.

29 Donald F. Bond (ed.), *The Spectator* (Oxford, 1965), vol. 4, no. 469, Thursday, 28 August 1712, by Addison.

30 Addison's only profits above his salary were his Keepership and the emoluments from drawing up orders, making out warrants and issuing military commissions, all his by right. In private letters to Swift and Dawson, for example, he refused to free them from paying the two-guinea fee for accessing the Irish records of which he was Keeper, though they were both personal friends at the time.

31 Richard Steele, *The Lucubrations of Isaac Bickerstaff Esq.* (1710), vol. 1, 'Dedication to Mr Maynwaring'.

32 Alexander Pope to Spence, quoted in John Timbs, *Clubs and Club Life in London* (London, 1908), p. 51.

33 Donald F. Bond, *The Tatler* (Oxford, 1987), vol. 2, no. 130, Tuesday, 7 February 1710.

34 Anon. [St John], *Letter to the Examiner* (1710).

35 Rae Blanchard (ed.), *The Correspondence of Richard Steele* (Oxford, 1968 edn), no. 367, Steele to Mrs Steele, 7 April 1710.

36 Swift's note to Stella on 14 December 1710 confirms that Steele had been 'a little while in prison, or at least a sponging-house' sometime before 7 September 1710. Pamphlets of September–October 1710 suggest that Steele was sleeping at night in a sponging-house called the Bull's Head in Clare Market, from which he sent his letters to Prue in August. Rae Blanchard (ed.), *The Correspondence of Richard Steele* (Oxford, 1968 edn), p. 265 n. 1.

37 Donald F. Bond, *The Tatler* (Oxford, 1987), no. 202, Tuesday, 25 July 1710.

38 Peter Smithers, *The Life of Joseph Addison* (Oxford, 2nd edn 1968), p. 179.

39 The Act provided that 'the author of a book already printed, or the bookseller who had bought his copy, should have the sole liberty of printing it for the term of fourteen years from its publication, and no longer'. After these fourteen years, 'the sole right of printing or disposing of copies shall return to the authors thereof, if they are living, for another term of fourteen years'. For books on publishers' backlists, twenty-one years of copyright would be conferred, from the day a title was registered. Fines would be imposed, in theory, on printers who breached these terms.

40 Michael McKeon, *The Secret History of Domesticity: Public, Private, and the Division of Knowledge* (Baltimore, Md., 2005), p. 60.

41 Matthew Prior quoted in Edmond Malone (ed.), *Critical and Miscellaneous Prose Works of John Dryden* (London, 1800), pp. 546–7.

42 Anon., 'On My Lord Godolphin' (August 1710?). George de Forest Lord et al. (eds), *Poems on Affairs of State: Augustan Satirical Verse 1660–1714*, 7 vols (New Haven, Conn., 1963–75), vol. 7, p. 453 n. 4.

43 Ibid.

44 John C. Hodges (ed.), *William Congreve: Letters and Documents* (London, 1964), Congreve to Joe Keally, 10 August 1710.

45 John Oldmixon, *Life and Posthumous Works of Arthur Maynwaring* (1715), p. 158.

46 Anon., *The Loyal Calves-Head Club* (1710).

47 Anon. [Jonathan Swift], 'An Essay to Restore the Kit-Cat Members to their lost Abilities, for the sake of the LADIES who admire em', *Letters, Poems and Tales: Amorous, Satyrical, and Gallant. Which passed between several persons of distinction. Now first published from respective originals found in the cabinet of . . . Mrs Anne Long* (1711).

48 Herefordshire County Record Office MS, Cowper Box 9, Diary 5, 47–8.

49 BL Add MS 7,121, Letters to Lord Halifax (1706ff.), f.27, Defoe to Halifax, undated.

50 Mary Delariviere Manley, *The New Atalantis* (1709).

51 Herbert Davis et al (eds), *The Prose Works of Jonathan Swift* (Oxford, 1939–75), vol. 8, p. 34.

52 Donald F. Bond (ed.), *The Spectator* (Oxford, 1965), vol. 3, no. 355, Thursday, 17 April 1712, by Addison.

53 Ibid., vol. 2, no. 243, Saturday, 8 December 1711, by Addison.

54 In August 1711, Henley would die in gambling debt and intestate, and the first series of Maynwaring's *Medley* came to an end. Around the same time, a Tory named Barber replaced Tonson as *The Gazette*'s publisher, showing how the change of leadership was cascading through all levels of government contract.

55 *The Moderator*, 3 October 1710.

56 Jonathan Swift, *The Correspondence of Jonathan Swift*, ed. Harold Williams (Oxford, 1965), vol. 1, p. 166.

57 Spencer Compton, Francis Godolphin, Ned Hopkins, James Stanhope and Richard Boyle (though Richard Boyle was soon found another pocket borough by his Kit-Cat brother-in-law Lionel).

58 *The Whig Examiner*, no. 3, Thursday, 28 September 1710.

59 Anon., *The Golden Age Revers'd* (1703), accused Stanhope of sodomy, saying he 'to a Venus arms prefers a pathetic boy'.

60 J. H. Plumb, *Sir Robert Walpole: The Making of a Statesman* (Boston, Mass., 1961), vol. 1, p. 160, Walpole to James Stanhope, 19 September 1710.

61 Jonathan Swift, *Journal to Stella*, 8 October 1710.

62 Kathleen M. Lynch, *Jacob Tonson, Kit-Cat Publisher* (Knoxville, Tenn., 1971), p. 138.

63 Jonathan Swift, *Journal to Stella*, 26 October 1710 and also 5 January 1711.

64 In May 1712, Congreve wrote with relief to Joe Keally that his income as Commissioner of Wine Licences was no longer under threat; thereafter Congreve started investing in Bank of England stock (£2,400 by 1717).

65 Jonathan Swift, *Journal to Stella*, 19 October 1710.

66 Peter Smithers, *The Life of Joseph Addison* (Oxford, 2nd edn 1968), p. 199.

67 E.g. Jonathan Swift, *Journal to Stella*, 14 January 1711.

68 Jonathan Swift, *Journal to Stella*, 16 March 1711.

69 Rae Blanchard, *The Correspondence of Richard Steele* (Oxford, 1968 edn), no. 382, Steele to Mrs Steele, autumn 1710.

70 Wharton met the Queen upon his return to England, leading to a false rumour he had been dismissed as Lord Lieutenant. The Irish Lord Justices acted on this rumour and assumed interim power until a new Lord Lieutenant was appointed. Hearing of this, Addison wrote with irritation to Dawson: 'I think it is Ridiculous for the L[or]ds Justices to act otherwise than under that Commission [i.e Wharton's] (unless Her Majesty had been pleased to send them a new one) as it would have been for any other to have taken upon him the Government without any Commission at all.' Days later, Wharton was replaced by the 2nd Duke of Ormonde.

71 HMC, *Report VII: Appendix* (1879), Copies of Letters of George Berkeley to Sir J. Percival, p. 238.

72 In December 1710, Addison wrote to Joshua Dawson, defending Wharton from

Tory threats of prosecution before the Irish Commons and requesting all 'particulars that may be of service in case the Impeachment goes on'. Addison called on Dawson's conscience (despite having stood for election as a Tory) to help deny the charges against Wharton, saying: 'For my own part, though perhaps I was not the most obliged person that was near His Lordship, I shall think myself bound in Honour to do him what Right I can in case he should be attacked.' Herbert Wood, 'Addison's Connexion with Ireland', *Royal Society of Antiquarians of Ireland Journal*, 5th series, 14 (1904), pp. 133–58, Addison to Joshua Dawson, 14 December 1710. In January 1711, Addison said he hoped the impeachment proceedings had been dropped and thanked Dawson for warning that he too risked being charged as a signatory on some 'unjustifiable' orders. Ibid., Addison to Joshua Dawson, 12 January 1711.

73 Ibid., 1 September 1710.

74 Jonathan Swift, *Journal to Stella*, 8 October 1710.

75 Ibid., January 1711. At the same time, the Tory *Postboy* published an acrostic on Wharton's name, labelling him a republican, regicide and libertine, 'O'ergrown in Sin, cornuted, old, in Debt.'

76 *The Examiner*, no. 17, Thursday, 30 November 1710.

77 Ibid., no. 26, 1 February 1711.

78 Anon., 'A Song at the Kit-Cat Club', in *The State Bell-Man's Collection of Verses for the Year 1711* (1710–11), p. 13.

79 Herbert Wood, 'Addison's Connexion with Ireland', *Royal Society of Antiquarians of Ireland Journal*, 5th series, 14 (1904), pp. 133–58, Addison to Joshua Dawson, 12 January 1711.

80 Jonathan Swift, *Journal to Stella*, 14 December 1710.

81 Such as the Royston Club, which kept the bulk of Herefordshire's MPs in tune with Tory policy during 1701–34.

82 Daniel Defoe, *Eleven Opinions about Mr H[arley]* (1711).

83 Jonathan Swift, *Journal to Stella*, 2 January 1711.

84 Donald F. Bond (ed.), *The Spectator* (Oxford, 1965), vol. 1, no. 23, Tuesday, 27 March 1711, by Addison.

85 Arthur Maynwaring to Sarah Churchill said 'it is possible to scribble these men down' in 1711. That the Tories shared this belief in the power of the press was shown by efforts to tax it out of existence in 1712. J. A. Downie, 'The Development of the Political Press', in Clyve Jones, *Britain in the First Age of Party, 1660–1750* (London and Ronceverte, W.Va., 1987).

86 Donald F. Bond (ed.), *The Spectator* (Oxford, 1965), vol. 1, no. 23, Tuesday, 27 March 1711, by Addison.

87 Jonathan Swift, *Journal to Stella*, 9–20 June 1711.

88 Not to be confused with Beaufort's 'Board of Brothers'. In 1709, the crypto-Jacobite Duke of Beaufort and his friends established 'The Board of Brothers' or 'The Board of Loyal Brotherhood', but this was largely a drinking society, with limited political clout. Their meetings' minutes survive, recording gestures such as sending Dr Sacheverell, in pre-trial detention, cash and bottles of claret. In later years, the 'Board of Brothers' became a meeting

place for Tory MPs at the Cocoa Tree Coffee House, eventually evolving into the organizational base of the Tory party after 1750.

89 St John pretended the Club was a purely cultural project: 'We shall begin to meet in a small number, and that will be composed of some who have wit and learning to recommend them; of others who, from their own situations, or from their relations, have power and influence . . . None of the extravagance of the Kit-Cat, none of the drunkenness of the Beef-Steak [Club] is to be endured,' he continued. 'The improvement of friendship and the encouragement of letters are to be the two great ends of our society.' Henry St John, *Letters and Correspondence*, ed. George Parke (London, 1798), vol. 1, pp. 246–7, St John to the 4th Earl of Orrery, 12 June 1711.

90 Jonathan Swift, *Journal to Stella*, 7 December 1710.

XV IN THEIR OWN IMAGE

1 *The Medley*, 4 April 1712.

2 Peter Smithers, *The Life of Joseph Addison* (Oxford, 2nd edn 1968), p. 254.

3 Donald F. Bond (ed.), *The Spectator* (Oxford, 1965), vol. 1, no. 1, Thursday, 1 March 1711, by Addison.

4 Ibid.

5 Peter Smithers, *The Life of Joseph Addison* (Oxford, 2nd edn 1968), p. 232.

6 Donald F. Bond (ed.), *The Spectator* (Oxford, 1965), vol. 3, no. 367, Thursday, 1 May 1712, by Addison.

7 Ibid., vol. 1, no. 46, Monday, 23 April 1711, by Addison.

8 Richard Steele, Dedication to *The Drummer*, 'To Mr Congreve', in Rae Blanchard (ed.), *The Correspondence of Richard Steele* (Oxford, 1968 edn), pp. 505ff.

9 Donald F. Bond (ed.), *The Spectator* (Oxford, 1965), vol. 2, no. 221, Tuesday, 13 November 1711, by Addison.

10 Ibid., vol. 3, no. 304, Monday, 18 February 1712, by Steele.

11 Ibid., vol. 1, no. 2, Friday, 2 March 1711, by Steele.

12 Ibid.

13 Ibid., vol. 1, no. 2, Friday, 2 March 1711, by Steele.

14 C. S. Lewis, 'Addison', *Essays on the Eighteenth Century Presented to David Nichol Smith in Honour of his Seventieth Birthday* (Oxford, 1945), p. 3.

15 Donald F. Bond (ed.), *The Spectator* (Oxford, 1965), vol. 3, no. 422, Friday, 4 July 1712, by Steele.

16 Ibid., vol. 1, no. 9, Saturday, 10 March 1711, by Addison.

17 Ibid., vol. 1, no. 72, Wednesday, 23 May 1711, by Addison.

18 Jonathan Swift, *Journal to Stella*, 12 January 1711.

19 Steele's fulsome dedication to Halifax in the fourth volume of the collected *Tatler*, published three days later, was a defiant statement of Whig solidarity with the founder of the Bank of England and the New East India Company. Donald F. Bond (ed.), *The Spectator* (Oxford, 1965), vol. 2, 'To Charles Montagu Baron Halifax' (1712).

20 Abel Boyer, *History of the Life and Reign of Queen Anne* (1722), p. 496.
21 Donald F. Bond (ed.), *The Spectator* (Oxford, 1965), vol. 1, no. 124, Monday, 23 July 1711, by Addison.
22 Ibid.
23 Ibid., vol. 1, no. 10, Monday, 12 March 1711, by Addison.
24 Ibid., vol. 4, no. 512, Friday, 17 October 1712, by Addison.
25 Kathleen M. Lynch, *Jacob Tonson, Kit-Cat Publisher* (Knoxville, Tenn., 1971), p. 150.
26 In later years, Tonson said Addison was 'so eager to be the first name' among writers that he and Steele 'used to run down even Dryden's character as far as they could'. Joseph Spence, *Observations, Anecdotes, and Characters of Books and Men*, ed. James M. Osborn (Oxford, 1966), no. 814; Jacob Tonson also told Spence that Addison, envious of Dryden's laurels, used 'to decry Dryden, as far as he could, while Pope and Congreve defended him'. Edmond Malone (ed.), *Critical and Miscellaneous Prose Works of John Dryden* (London, 1800), p. 540.
27 Donald F. Bond (ed.), *The Spectator* (Oxford, 1965), vol. 2, no. 262, Monday, 31 December 1711, by Addison.
28 Ibid., no. 288, Wednesday, 30 January 1712, by Steele.
29 Letter of 1714 from an English merchant reader in Sumatra, Joseph Collet, saying that, after the Bible and John Locke, *The Spectator* and *The Tatler* were 'my constant Companions'. *Town-Talk*, no. 7, Friday, 27 January 1716.
30 Donald F. Bond (ed.), *The Spectator* (Oxford, 1965), vol. 1, no. 4, Monday, 5 March 1711, by Steele.
31 Ibid., vol. 1, no. 10, Monday, 12 March 1711, by Addison.
32 Addison answers a letter from a 13-year-old girl who is deciding whether she should marry a 'Mr Shapely'. Donald F. Bond (ed.), *The Spectator* (Oxford, 1965), vol. 4, no. 475, Thursday, 4 September 1712, by Addison.
33 Ibid., vol. 1, no. 10, Monday, 12 March 1711, by Addison.
34 Walter Graham (ed.), *The Letters of Joseph Addison* (Oxford, 1941), no. 11, Addison to Charles Montagu, from Blois, December 1699.
35 Donald F. Bond (ed.), *The Spectator* (Oxford, 1965), vol. 2, no. 135, Saturday, 4 August 1711, by Addison.
36 The traits that Langford identifies as key to the English character, by the general agreement of foreigners and the English themselves between 1650 and 1850: Energy, Candour, Decency, Taciturnity, Reserve, Eccentricity. Paul Langford, *Englishness Identified, Manners and Character 1650–1850* (Oxford, 2000), p. 15.
37 Donald F. Bond (ed.), *The Spectator* (Oxford, 1965), vol. 2, no. 126, Wednesday, 25 July 1711, by Addison.
38 Ibid., vol. 5, no. 600, Wednesday, 29 September 1714, by Addison.
39 Ibid., vol. 4, no. 495, Saturday, 27 September 1712, by Addison.
40 Ibid., vol. 4, no. 557, Monday, 21 June 1714, by Addison (quoting Archbishop Tillotson); Philip Carter, *Men and the Emergence of Polite Society 1660–1830* (Oxford, 2000), p. 10.
41 Donald F. Bond (ed.), *The Spectator* (Oxford, 1965), vol. 2, no. 119, Tuesday, 17 July 1711, by Addison.

42 Robert Sackville-West, *Knole* (London, 1998), p. 74; 'As good Nature is said . . . to belong more particularly to the ENGLISH than any other Nation, it may again be said that it belonged more particularly to the late Earl of DORSET than to any other ENGLISH Man.' *Dedication to the Right Honorable Lionel, Earl of Dorset and Middlesex, Poems on Several Occasions* (1718).

43 Donald F. Bond (ed.), *The Spectator* (Oxford, 1965), vol. 1, no. 119, Tuesday, 17 July 1711, by Addison.

44 C. S. Lewis, 'Addison', *Essays on the Eighteenth Century Presented to David Nichol Smith in Honour of his Seventieth Birthday* (Oxford, 1945), p. 7.

45 *The Guardian*, no. 38, Friday, 24 April 1713.

46 John C. Hodges (ed.), *William Congreve: Letters and Documents* (London, 1964), p. 188, Congreve to John Dennis, 11 August 1695.

47 *Town-Talk, in a letter to a Lady in the Country*, no. 1, Saturday, 17 December 1715.

48 Donald F. Bond (ed.), *The Spectator* (Oxford, 1965), vol. 1, no. 53, Tuesday, 1 May 1711, by Steele.

49 Ibid.

50 Ibid., vol. 5, no. 467, Tuesday, 26 August 1712, author unknown.

51 William Congreve, 'Concerning Humour in Comedy', Congreve to John Dennis, 10 July 1695.

52 William Congreve, *Amendments to Mr Collier's False and imperfect citations* (1698); Sister Rose Anthony, *The Jeremy Collier Stage Controversy 1698–1726* (Milwaukee, Wis., 1937), p. 112.

53 Donald F. Bond (ed.), *The Spectator* (Oxford, 1965), vol. 2, no. 169, Thursday, 13 September 1711, by Addison.

54 Ibid., vol. 1, no. 6, Wednesday, 7 March 1711, by Steele.

55 Ibid., vol. 3, no. 292, Monday, 4 February 1712, author unknown.

56 Ibid., vol. 1, no. 29, Tuesday, 3 April 1711, by Addison.

57 Ibid., vol. 1, no. 45, Saturday, 21 April 1711, by Addison; vol. 2, no. 208, Monday, 19 October 1711, by Steele; vol. 5, no. 502, Monday, 6 October 1712, by Steele.

58 Ibid., vol. 3, no. 360, Wednesday, 23 April 1712, by Steele,

59 Ibid., vol. 1, no. 58, Monday, 7 May 1711, by Addison.

60 Ibid., vol. 1, no. 62, Friday, 11 May 1711, by Addison.

61 Ibid., vol. 3, no. 409, Thursday, 19 June 1712, by Addison.

62 Ibid., vol. 1, no. 70, Monday, 21 May 1711, by Addison.

63 Ibid., vol. 1, no. 85, Thursday, 7 June 1711, by Addison.

64 Ibid., vol. 3, no. 369, Saturday, 3 May 1712, by Addison.

65 Ibid., vol. 2, no. 160, Monday, 3 September 1711, by Addison.

66 Ibid., vol. 5, no. 592, Friday, 10 September 1714, by Addison.

67 Ibid., vol. 3, no. 419, Tuesday, 1 July 1712, by Addison.

68 Abraham Cowley quoted in ibid., vol. 1, no. 123, Saturday, 21 July 1711, by Addison.

69 This absence may be evidence of their close daily contact, making letters unnecessary. It is probably also, however, evidence of Addison's discretion. He and

Steele probably 'culled' their correspondence, indeed almost obliterated it, just as Addison recommended a man should 'cull' his comments for public consumption. Ibid., vol. 2, no. 225, Saturday, 17 November 1711, by Addison.

70 Richard Steele, Dedication to *The Drummer* 'To Mr Congreve', in Rae Blanchard (ed.), *The Correspondence of Richard Steele* (Oxford, 1968 edn), pp. 505ff.

71 Ibid.

72 Joseph Addison, 'When All Thy Mercies, O My God' (1712).

73 Donald F. Bond (ed.), *The Spectator* (Oxford, 1965), vol. 1, no. 68, Friday, 18 May 1711, by Addison.

74 Ibid., vol. 2, no. 225, Saturday, 17 November 1711, by Addison.

75 Ibid., vol. 1, no. 68, Friday, 18 May 1711, by Addison.

76 In summer 1711, Addison confided to Edward Wortley Montagu that in the past year he had lost both a fortune and an unnamed mistress. This is the sole, tantalizing reference to Addison having a premarital sex life, though he may have been using the term 'mistress' in its chivalric sense, merely referring to some blip in his protracted, platonic courtship of the Countess of Warwick. This letter suggests Wortley Montagu was more of a 'bosom friend' to Addison than any of the Kit-Cats, even Steele. Walter Graham (ed.), *The Letters of Joseph Addison* (Oxford, 1941), no. 321, Addison to Edward Wortley, 21 July 1711.

77 Richard Steele quoted in Samuel Johnson, *Lives of the English Poets* (1781), ed. George Birkbeck Hill (Oxford, 1905 edn), vol. 2, entry on Addison.

78 Richard Steele, Preface affixed to vol. 4 of the collected *Tatler* (1710–11), as reprinted in Donald F. Bond (ed.), *The Tatler* (Oxford, 1987), vol. 1, pp. 3–5.

79 Donald F. Bond (ed.), *The Spectator* (Oxford, 1965), vol. 1, no. 10, Monday, 12 March 1711, by Addison.

80 Samuel Johnson, *Lives of the English Poets* (1781), ed. George Birkbeck Hill (Oxford, 1905 edn), vol. 2, entry on Addison.

81 Donald F. Bond (ed.), *The Spectator* (Oxford, 1965), vol. 4, no. 521, Tuesday, 28 October 1712, by Steele.

82 Richard Steele, *The Christian Hero*, quoted in *The Englishman*, ed. Rae Blanchard (Oxford, 1955), vol. 1, no. 48, Saturday, 23 January 1714, by Steele.

83 The first surviving manuscript reference to the project dates from June 1703, when Vanbrugh told Tonson that the Kit-Cats had not 'finished their pictures' though 'to excuse them (as well as myself) Sir Godfrey has been most in fault. The fool has got a country house near Hampton Court and is so busy about fitting it up (to receive nobody) that there is no getting him to work.' Geoffrey Webb and Bonamy Dobrée (eds), *The Complete Works of Sir John Vanbrugh* (London, 1927–8), vol. 4, no. 3, 15 June 1703, Vanbrugh to Tonson. Tonson owned a Kneller portrait of Dorset, the Kit-Cat founder, dated no later than 1697. It is of Kit-Cat dimensions, and may have been the first in the series, painted soon after the Club began. It may, alternatively, have been the model for the series, after Kit-Cat friends admired it at Tonson's house. Tonson may also have owned a 1698 Kneller portrait of Dryden, which is of similar, though not identical, pose. United by admiration for Dryden and

Dorset, the Kit-Cat authors would have liked to be painted in imitation of them. The precedent for Kneller's Kit-Cats as a series was probably his earlier half-length portraits of scholars and poets (Dryden, Prior, Locke, [Joseph] Carreras and Newton), or his portraits of the Royal Society's Fellows. After Dorset's possible 1697 starting point, the next Kit-Cat painted (though originally a slightly larger portrait) was the gourmand Dartiquenave, dated to 1702. The last single portraits – of Tonson, Pulteney and Scarbrough – were completed in 1717, then one final double portrait of two late members in 1721. The dating of most of the portraits in the series is approximate. Badges of office and medals of honour provide clues in some cases, the names pencilled on the backs suggest certain men were painted before gaining certain titles, and art experts have used stylistic and other internal evidence to propose estimated dates for others. A certain off-white powdering of the wigs tells us, for example, which were painted after 1715. Tonson's papers confirm the dates of others.

84 John Loftis (ed.), *Richard Steele's 'The Theatre'* (Oxford, 1962), no. 11, Saturday, 6 February 1720.

85 Donald F. Bond (ed.), *The Spectator* (Oxford, 1965), vol. 2, no. 226, Monday, 19 November 1711, by Steele.

86 Ibid., vol. 1, no. 83, Tuesday, 5 June 1711, by Addison.

87 Michael Foss, *The Age of Patronage: The Arts in England 1660–1750* (Ithaca, NY, 1972), p. 150.

88 John Brewer, *The Pleasures of the Imagination: English Culture in the Eighteenth Century* (London, 1997), p. 42.

89 NPG, Tonson Papers, Philip Lempriere to William Baker, 13 February 1777.

90 It is unlikely Kneller worked unpaid on the series. Though he was an unwavering Whig and old friend of Tonson's, grateful to the publisher for having boosted his early reputation by including a poetic tribute to his talent in the 1694 *Miscellany*, Kneller was notoriously businesslike about his art.

91 Tonson may not have had a special clubroom for the pictures at Barn Elms, though he talked of his intention to build one, perhaps inspired by Dorset's portrait-lined parlour at Knole. Edmond Malone's statement that the Kit-Cat canvases' size was determined by the height of the ceiling in Tonson's clubroom is therefore misleading. At least two of the less than half-length paintings predate the leasing of the Barn Elms property in 1703.

92 Anon., *A Kit-Cat C—b Describ'd* (1705), original MS at Harvard.

93 This painting was completed in 1709. It should not be confused with Kneller's first portrait of Congreve, painted at Tonson's request in 1695. This 1695 portrait was the one that looked most like him, according to his lover Henrietta Churchill. After Congreve's death, she requested that Jacob Junior exchange this portrait for 'an original one of Sir Godfrey Kneller just the same size of the Kit-Cat ones' since 'I know 'tis only the set of those pictures [the Kit-Cat series] that your uncle values and not [the one which] I would give the world for'. Henrietta got her swap, since Jacob Junior later hung a Kneller self-portrait among the Kit-Cats in his Barn Elms clubroom. NPG,

Tonson Papers, Registered Packets 3193–3235, typed transcript of the letter of 1729.

94 John C. Hodges (ed.), *William Congreve: Letters and Documents* (London, 1964), Congreve to Joe Keally, 29 January 1708.

95 Ibid., Congreve to Joe Keally, 9 October 1708; Congreve to Joe Keally, 14 October 1704.

96 John Macky quoted in G. E. Cokayne (ed.), *The Complete Peerage* (London, 1936), entry on Charles Mohun, Baron Mohun of Okehampton.

97 Rae Blanchard (ed.), *The Correspondence of Richard Steele* (Oxford, 1968 edn), no. 26, Steele to Joseph Keally, 7 October 1708.

98 Brian Masters, *The Dukes* (London, 2001), p. 88.

99 Jonathan Swift, *Remarks on the Characters of the Court of Queen Anne from 'Memoirs of the Secret Services of John Macky Esq.'* (1733).

100 Stowe MS 751, f.142.

101 This dates the painting to later than March 1704, making Vanbrugh past forty.

102 The other important reason why Kneller was not a Kit-Cat was that the Club never patronized the visual arts. Under William and Mary, painters, especially Huguenot painters, were well supported by the Court and by the English aristocracy, often through commissions of ceiling or other decorative paintings. The Club therefore did not need to subsidize this side of the arts – at least not beyond the commissioning of this single series of portraits. Vanbrugh was an anomaly because he joined as a playwright and changed career mid-life, but no other artists or architects were members. Indeed, not until the later eighteenth century were clubs of fine artists formed on the Kit-Cat model. The only contemporary example was the Rose and Crown Club, which met between 1704 and 1720 and exhibited artworks, accompanied by drinks and music. These so-called 'Rose Coronians' included several Whigs, like Sir James Thornhill and John Rysbrack, who received commissions from individual Kit-Cats over the years, but not Kneller.

103 Horace Walpole, *Anecdotes of Painting in England* (London, 1879 edn), p. 291 n. 1.

XVI THE CRISIS

1 Horace Walpole, *Anecdotes of Painting in England* (1761–71).

2 Edward (Ned) Ward, *The Secret History of Clubs* (1709).

3 Joseph Addison to Mr Wortley, 21 July 1711, and Joseph Addison to Joshua Dawson, 28 February 1712, quoted in Herbert Wood, 'Addison's Connexion with Ireland', *Royal Society of Antiquaries of Ireland Journal*, 5th series, 14 (1904), pp. 133–58.

4 Ibid.

5 Donald F. Bond (ed.), *The Spectator* (Oxford, 1965), vol. 1, no. 125, Tuesday, 24 July 1711, by Addison.

6 Ibid., vol. 2, no. 126, Wednesday, 25 July 1711, by Addison; vol. 1, no. 16, Monday, 19 March 1711, by Addison.
7 Temple Scott (ed.), *The Prose Works of Jonathan Swift* (London, 1897 edn), vol. 1, p. 7.
8 Donald F. Bond (ed.), *The Spectator* (Oxford, 1965), vol. 2, no. 152, Friday, 24 August 1711, by Steele.
9 Daniel Defoe, *An Essay on Plain Exposition of that Difficult Phrase, a Good Peace* (1711).
10 Jonathan Swift, *Remarks on the Characters of the Court of Queen Anne from 'Memoirs of the Secret Services of John Macky Esq.'* (1733).
11 Matthew Prior, 'The Conversation: A Tale' (1721).
12 HMC, *Bath MSS*, vol. 1, p. 217, Queen Anne to the Earl of Oxford, 11 November 1711.
13 Henry St John to Matthew Prior, 10 September 1712, quoted in Theophilus Cibber, *The Lives of the Poets of Great Britain and Ireland* (London, 1753).
14 Richard Steele, *Mr Steele's Apology for himself and his writings* (1714).
15 Jonathan Swift, Preface to *The Conduct of the Allies and of the Late Ministry* (1711).
16 Names listed by Abel Boyer; Jonathan Swift, *Journal to Stella*, 17 November 1711.
17 Anon., *The Kit-Cat Clubs Lamentation for the loss of the Pope, the Devil and the Pretender, that were taken into custody on Saturday last by the Secretary of State. Written by Jacob Door-holder to that Society* (1711).
18 John Oldmixon, *The History of England during the Reigns of King William and Queen Mary, Queen Anne, King George I* (1735), part 3, p. 478.
19 Abel Boyer, *History of the Life and Reign of Queen Anne* (1722), pp. 524–5.
20 John Oldmixon, *The History of England during the Reigns of King William and Queen Mary, Queen Anne, King George I* (1735), part 3, p. 479.
21 Vanbrugh explaining the matter in retrospect to the Duke of Newcastle, in Geoffrey Webb and Bonamy Dobrée (eds), *The Complete Works of John Vanbrugh*, 4 vols (London, 1927–8), vol. 4, no. 98, Vanbrugh to Newcastle, 25 December 1718.
22 Donald F. Bond (ed.), *The Spectator* (Oxford, 1965), vol. 3, no. 287, Tuesday, 29 January 1712, by Addison.
23 Ibid.
24 Eveline Cruickshanks, Stuart Handley and D. W. Hayton, *The House of Commons 1690–1715* (Cambridge, 2002), vol. 1, p. 765.
25 According to a 1713 broadside published by Ambrose Philips, the Hanover Club's Secretary, with the names of thirty-one 'Toasts Elected by the Hanover Club'.
26 Geoffrey Holmes, *British Politics in the Age of Anne* (London, 1967), p. 299.
27 John Oldmixon, *The History of England during the Reigns of King William and Queen Mary, Queen Anne, King George I* (1735).
28 Donald F. Bond (ed.), *The Spectator* (Oxford, 1965), vol. 4, no. 562, Friday, 2 July 1714, by Addison.

29 Ibid., vol. 4, no. 465, Saturday, 23 August 1712, by Addison.
30 Eveline Cruickshanks, Stuart Handley and D. W. Hayton, *The House of Commons 1690–1715* (Cambridge, 2002), vol. 5, p. 238, entry on William Pulteney MP.
31 Add MS 72,495, Ralph Bridges to Trumbull, 9 June 1712. Halifax was over-complacent and failed to rally their supporters in sufficient numbers. The Kit-Cats who 'crossed over' to vote with the Court included his own stepson Manchester and also Dorset, Manchester, Boyle, Grafton and Cornwallis. See Clyve Jones, 'The Vote in The House of Lords on the Duke of Ormond's "Restraining Orders", 28 May 1712', *Parliamentary History*, vol. 26, part 2 (2007), pp.160–83.
32 Donald F. Bond (ed.), *The Spectator* (Oxford, 1965), vol. 3, no. 367, Thursday, 1 May 1712, by Addison.
33 Jonathan Swift, *Journal to Stella*, 1 July 1712.
34 HMC, *Report VII: Appendix* (1879), Copies of Letters of George Berkeley to Sir J. Percival, p. 238, 23 February 1713.
35 Rae Blanchard (ed.), *The Correspondence of Richard Steele* (Oxford, 1968 edn), no. 400, Steele to Mrs Steele, 22 January 1712.
36 Ibid., no. 410, Steele to Mrs Scurlock, 27 September 1712.
37 Ibid., no. 411, Steele to Mrs Scurlock, 25 October 1712.
38 Laurence Whistler, *Sir John Vanbrugh, Architect and Dramatist 1664–1726* (New York, 1978), p. 155.
39 He had resorted to this tactic only after failing to pass various libel bills under which the Whig clubs and papers might have been charged with intent to incite a breach of the peace (criminal libel) or causing contempt for the Queen, Church or government (seditious libel).
40 Donald F. Bond (ed.), *The Spectator* (Oxford, 1965), vol. 4, no. 445, Thursday, 31 July 1712, by Addison.
41 Ibid., vol. 4, no. 488, Friday, 19 September 1712, by Addison.
42 Ibid., vol. 1, no. 69, Saturday, 19 May 1711, by Addison.
43 Ibid., vol. 4, no. 454, Monday, 11 August 1712, by Steele.
44 Rae Blanchard (ed.), *The Correspondence of Richard Steele* (Oxford, 1968 edn), no. 408, Steele to Mrs Steele, 17 September 1712.
45 Donald F. Bond (ed.), *The Spectator* (Oxford, 1965), vol. 4, no. 479, Tuesday, 9 September 1712, by Steele.
46 Ibid.
47 Rae Blanchard (ed.), *The Correspondence of Richard Steele* (Oxford, 1968 edn), no. 416, Mrs Steele to Steele, March 1713?
48 Ibid., no. 419, Steele to Mrs Steele, 22 April 1713.
49 John Dunton, *The Night-Walker* (1696).
50 Donald F. Bond (ed.), *The Spectator* (Oxford, 1965), vol. 4, no. 530, Friday, 7 November 1712, by Addison.
51 Anon., 'Occasioned by the Late List of Toasts', NPG, Tonson Papers.
52 Donald F. Bond (ed.), *The Spectator* (Oxford, 1965), vol. 4, no. 555, Saturday, 6 December 1712, by Steele.

53 Donald. F. Bond (ed.), *The Tatler* (Oxford, 1987), Preface to vol. 4; no. 271, Tuesday, 2 January 1710; Richard Steele, Dedication to Joseph Addison, *The Tender Husband* (1705).
54 Donald F. Bond (ed.), *The Spectator* (Oxford, 1965), vol. 4, no. 476, Friday, 5 September 1712, by Addison.
55 Ibid., vol. 4, no. 484, Monday, 15 September 1712, by Steele. It appears, however, that Steele did no better than Addison as a parliamentary speaker, blundering so badly over his first speech in the Commons in 1714 that people laughed at him. *The Wentworth Papers 1705–1739* (London, 1883), p. 358, Thomas Wentworth to his brother, 2 March 1714.
56 Ibid., vol. 4, no. 535, Thursday, 13 November 1712, by Addison.
57 Jonathan Swift, *Journal to Stella*, 27 December 1712.
58 Ibid., 26 January 1713.
59 HMC, *Report VII: Appendix* (1879), Copies of Letters of George Berkeley to Sir J. Percival, p. 238, 23 February 1713.
60 Arthur Maynwaring, 'An Excellent New Song, Called Mat's Peace, Or, The Downfall of Trade' (1711).
61 The Tories were as anxious as the French to contain the Habsburg Empire, on the rise ever since its victory over the Turks in 1699, when it gained Hungary and Transylvania, whereas the British Whigs were far less alarmed by the idea of Austrian hegemony. The Whigs formed a group of trustees to support a loan to Emperor Charles VI of Austria (formerly Archduke Charles) during this extra campaign, post-Utrecht. Abel Boyer, *The History of the Reign of Queen Anne Digested into Annals* (1722), vol. 6, pp. 126–7.
62 HMC, *Report VII: Appendix* (1879), Copies of Letters of George Berkeley to Sir J. Percival, p. 239, 7 May 1713.
63 Richard Steele quoted in Colley Cibber, *An Apology for the Life of Mr Colley Cibber*, ed. B. R. S. Fone (Ann Arbor, Mich., 1968), p. 249.
64 Ibid., p. 250.
65 Donald F. Bond (ed.), *The Spectator* (Oxford, 1965), vol. 2, no. 237, Saturday, 1 December 1711, by Addison.
66 He also showed it to Lady Mary Wortley Montagu and to Alexander Pope. Pope recalled Addison 'would show his verses to several friends, and would alter almost everything that any of them hinted at as wrong'. Pope added vainly that Addison 'did not leave a word unchanged that I made any scruple against in *Cato*'. Quoted in Joseph Spence, *Observations, Anecdotes, and Characters of Books and Men*, ed. James M. Osborn (Oxford, 1966 edn), no. 174.
67 HMC, *Report VII: Appendix* (1879), Copies of Letters of George Berkeley to Sir J. Percival, p. 238, 16 April 1713.
68 Richard Steele, Dedication to *The Drummer* 'To Mr Congreve', in Rae Blanchard (ed.), *The Correspondence of Richard Steele* (Oxford, 1968 edn), pp. 505ff.
69 Peter Smithers, *The Life of Joseph Addison* (Oxford, 1968 edn), p. 255.
70 Donald F. Bond (ed.), *The Spectator* (Oxford, 1965), vol. 2, no. 168, Wednesday, 12 September 1711, by Steele.

71 George Sherburn (ed.), *The Correspondence of Alexander Pope* (Oxford, 1956), vol. 1, p. 175.
72 Ibid., vol. 1, p. 175, Pope to Caryll.
73 Ibid.
74 HMC, *Report VII: Appendix* (1879), Copies of Letters of George Berkeley to Sir J. Percival, p. 239, 7 May 1713. The child she bore was not Maynwaring's, dead only six months earlier, but that of Brigadier-General Charles Churchill, Marlborough's nephew. The boy would grow up to marry Robert Walpole's daughter Mary.
75 F. M. A. de Voltaire, *Letters on the English* (1778), Letter 18.
76 Alexander Pope, *Essay on Criticism* (1711).
77 Anon., *Ingratitude to Mr Pope* (1733), pp. 8–9.
78 *The Examiner*, Friday, 24 April 1703.
79 Rae Blanchard (ed.), *The Correspondence of Richard Steele* (Oxford, 1968 edn), no. 75, Jonathan Swift to Joseph Addison, 13 May 1713.
80 Steele to Jonathan Swift, 19 May 1713, quoted in G. A. Aitken, *The Life of Richard Steele* (London, 1889), vol. 1, p. 380.
81 HMC, *Report VII: Appendix* (1879), Copies of Letters of George Berkeley to Sir J. Percival, p. 238, 27 March 1713.
82 Rae Blanchard (ed.), *The Correspondence of Richard Steele* (Oxford, 1968 edn), no. 80, Steele to Earl of Oxford, 4 June 1713.
83 Ibid., no. 425, Steele to Mrs Steele, 20 June 1713.
84 Ibid., no. 431, Steele to Mrs Steele, 22 July 1713.
85 Donald F. Bond (ed.), *The Spectator* (Oxford, 1965), vol. 3, no. 394, Monday, 2 June 1712, by Steele.
86 Rae Blanchard (ed.), *The Englishman: A Political Journal by Richard Steele* (Oxford, 1955), no. 1, 6 October 1713.
87 HMC, *Portland MSS*, vol. 5, p. 338, John Drummond to the Earl of Oxford, 18 September 1713.
88 Kathleen M. Lynch, *Jacob Tonson, Kit-Cat Publisher* (Knoxville, Tenn., 1971), p. 64.
89 Richard Steele, *The Importance of Dunkirk Consider'd: In Defence of the Guardian of August the 7th. In a Letter to the Bailiff of Stockbridge* (1713), p. 76.
90 Rae Blanchard (ed.), *The Englishman: A Political Journal by Richard Steele* (Oxford, 1955), no. 1, 6 October 1713.
91 Walter Graham (ed.), *The Letters of Joseph Addison* (Oxford, 1941), no. 343, Addison to John Hughes, 12 October 1713.
92 Ibid.
93 BL Add MS 5,145A, Steele to Mrs Steele at Bloomsbury Square, October 1713? (Blanchard no. 435).
94 Richard Steele, *The Crisis* (1714).
95 Add MS 5,145A, Steele to Mrs Steele, 26 January 1714 (Blanchard no. 438).
96 Richard Steele, *Mr Steele's Apology for himself and his writings* (1714).
97 Ibid.

98 *The Examiner*, vol. 4, no. 37, Friday, 9 October 1713 to Monday, 12 October 1713.

99 They reunited once or twice in the 1720s, and their relationships would prove an important stimulus to several major literary works: Swift's *Gulliver's Travels* (1726), Gay's *Beggar's Opera* (1728) and Pope's *Dunciad* (1728).

100 John Lacy, *The Steeleids: or, the Tryal of Wit* (1714).

101 BL Add MS 5,145A, Steele to Mrs Steele, 11 March 1714 (Blanchard no. 440).

102 Ibid., Steele to Mrs Steele, 12 March 1714 (Blanchard no. 441).

103 Quoted in Calhoun Winton, *Captain Steele: The Early Career of Richard Steele* (Baltimore, Md., 1964), p. 201.

104 William Cobbett (ed.), *Parliamentary History of England*, 36 vols (1806–20), vol. 6, p. 1267; Abel Boyer, *History of the Life and Reign of Queen Anne* (1722).

105 Richard Steele, *Mr Steele's Apology for himself and his writings* (1714).

106 Richard Steele, *The Case of Richard Steele, Esq . . .* (1714).

107 Basil Williams, *Stanhope: A Study in Eighteenth-Century War and Diplomacy* (Oxford, 1932), p. 112.

108 Eveline Cruickshanks, Stuart Handley and D. W. Hayton, *The House of Commons 1690–1715* (Cambridge, 2002), vol. 5, p. 782, entry on Robert Walpole.

109 J. H. Plumb, *Sir Robert Walpole: The Making of a Statesman* (Boston, Mass., 1961), p. 191.

110 Richard Steele, *The Case of Richard Steele, Esq . . .* (1714).

111 BL Add MS 5,145A, Steele to Mrs Steele, 19 March 1714 (Blanchard no. 445).

112 It was not the Hanover Club, since the next morning he was still with 'Wharton and the rest' and Wharton was not a Hanoverian member. Ibid., Steele to Mrs Steele, 20 March 1714 (Blanchard no. 446).

113 Rae Blanchard (ed.), *The Englishman: A Political Journal by Richard Steele* (Oxford, 1955), 'Dedication to General [James] Stanhope'.

114 Add MS 5,145A, Steele to Mrs Steele, probably all in late March 1714 (Blanchard nos. 447–50).

115 Ibid., Steele to Mrs Steele, 30 March 1714 (Blanchard no. 452).

116 Ibid., Steele to Mrs Steele, Easter Sunday, 28 March 1714 (Blanchard no. 451 – see also no. 450 reference to 'the brats').

117 Richard Steele, *The Lover, Written in Imitation of the Tatler, by Marmaduke Myrtle, Gent.* (1714), 'Dedication to Garth'; no. 1, Thursday, 25 February 1714; no. 27, Tuesday, 27 April 1714.

118 BL Add MS 5,145C, Steele to Mrs Steele, 30 March 1714 (Blanchard no. 452).

119 Donald F. Bond (ed.), *The Spectator* (Oxford, 1965), vol. 4, no. 556, Friday, 18 June 1714, by Addison.

120 Eveline Cruickshanks, Stuart Handley and D. W. Hayton, *The House of Commons 1690–1715* (Cambridge, 2002), vol. 1, entry on James Stanhope; Rae Blanchard (ed.), *The Englishman: A Political Journal by Richard Steele* (Oxford, 1955), 'Dedication to General [James] Stanhope'.

121 Abel Boyer, *History of the Life and Reign of Queen Anne* (1722).

122 Bothmar to George I, quoted in William L. Sachse, *Lord Somers: A Political Portrait* (Manchester, 1975), p. 313.

XVII BIG WHIGS: THE FIRST GEORGIANS

1 Thomas Bruce, 2nd Earl of Ailesbury, *Memoirs* (London, 1890 edn), vol. 1.

2 John C. Hodges (ed.), *William Congreve: Letters and Documents* (London, 1964), Congreve to Joe Keally, 29 October 1712.

3 Matthew Prior, 'For My Own Monument' (*c.* 1714).

4 Jonathan Swift, *The Correspondence of Jonathan Swift*, ed. Harold Williams (Oxford, 1965), vol. 2, p. 101 and p. 112.

5 Sarah Churchill, *Characters of Her Contemporaries, by Sarah Duchess of Marlborough*, ed. Nathaniel Hooke (London, 1930), p. 260, notes on Burnet's *History of his Own Time*.

6 Alexander Pope, quoted in Joseph Spence, *Observations, Anecdotes, and Characters of Books and Men*, ed. James M. Osborn (Oxford, 1966 edn), no. 204.

7 BL Add MS 7,121, Letters to Lord Halifax (1706ff.), f.11, Joseph Addison to Halifax, 17 October 1714.

8 Ibid., f.15, Joseph Addison to Halifax, 30 September 1714.

9 Calhoun Winton, *Captain Steele: The Early Career of Richard Steele* (Baltimore, Md., 1964), p. 212.

10 Frank McCormick, *Sir John Vanbrugh: The Playwright as Architect* (Philadelphia, Pa., 1991), p. 19.

11 As Comptroller, Vanbrugh worked with his Kit-Cat friend, Dartiquenave, Paymaster on the Board of Works.

12 Stanyan was also made a Lord of the Admiralty, and his younger brother became one of two Under-Secretaries in the Northern Department. Cornwallis was appointed joint-holder of the lucrative post of Postmaster General.

13 Somerset joined Halifax in feeling underappreciated. He was admitted to the Privy Council but only wearing the courtier's hat of Master of the Horse. Dunch was reappointed to his old Court place as Master of the Household, while Lincoln was appointed the Prince of Wales' Master of the Horse, then the Prince's Lord of the Bedchamber.

14 NPG, Tonson Papers, Philip Lempriere to William Baker, 13 February 1777.

15 Edmond Malone (ed.), *Critical and Miscellaneous Prose Works of John Dryden* (London, 1800), vol. 1, part 1, p. 525 n. 6.

16 Lord Hervey quoted in Brian Masters, *The Dukes* (London, 2001), p. 300.

17 Ray A. Kelch, *Newcastle, a Duke without Money: Thomas Pelham-Holles 1693–1768* (London, 1974), p. 51.

18 BL Add MS 32,685, Letters to the Duke of Newcastle.

19 Ibid.

20 *The State of the Case between the Lord Chamberlain of His Majesty's Household and the Governor of the Royal Company of Comedians* (1720), in Rae Blanchard (ed.), *Tracts and Pamphlets by Richard Steele* (Baltimore, Md., 1944), p. 591.

21 Calhoun Winton, *Sir Richard Steele MP* (Baltimore, Md., 1970), p. 17.

22 Eustace Budgell, *Memoirs of the Life and Character of the Earl of Orrery and of the Family of the Boyles* (1732), p. 258.

23 This 'conversation piece' could not have been completed before March 1721, when Lincoln was given the Order of the Garter, which he wears. NPG,

Tonson Papers, Philip Lempriere to William Baker, 13 February 1777, states that the double portrait of Newcastle and Lincoln was *not* by Kneller.

24 James Caulfield, *Memoirs of the Celebrated Persons Composing the Kit-Cat Club; with a prefatory account of the origin of the association, illustrated with forty-eight portraits from the original paintings by Sir Godfrey Kneller* (London, 1849), p. 84.

25 Ibid., p. 145.

26 William Coxe, *Memoirs of the Life and Administration of Sir Robert Walpole, Earl of Orford* (London, 1798), vol. 1, p. 761.

27 Rae Blanchard (ed.), *The Correspondence of Richard Steele* (Oxford, 1968 edn), no. 102, Steele to Pelham-Holles, 18 December 1714.

28 Ibid., no. 473, Steele to Mrs Steele, 27 January 1715.

29 Ibid., no. 106, Steele to Charles Wilkinson, 7 May 1715.

30 Ibid., p. 497, Dedication to Thomas Pelham-Holles, Earl of Clare, 2 June 1715 – originally published in *The Political Writings of Sir Richard Steele* (1715).

31 Geoffrey Webb and Bonamy Dobrée (eds), *The Works of John Vanbrugh*, 4 vols (London, 1927–8), vol. 4, no. 49, Vanbrugh to the Duchess of Marlborough, 16 January 1715.

32 Henry Horwitz (ed.), *London Politics 1713–17: Minutes of a Whig Club 1714–17* (London, 1981), vol. 17, pp. 1–2 and 9. H. T. Dickinson, 'The Precursors of Political Radicalism in Augustan Britain', in Clyve Jones (ed.), *Britain in the First Age of Party, 1660–1750* (London and Ronceverte, W.Va., 1987), p. 78.

33 BL Add MS 33,064, Newcastle Papers, f.44, Vanbrugh to the Earl of Clare, 5 February 1715.

34 Bishop Potter of Oxford quoted in Linda Colley, *In Defiance of Oligarchy* (London, 1982), p. 180.

35 HMC, *Bath MSS*, vol. 3, Halifax to Prior, 23 December 1713.

36 PRO, State Papers, France 105/29, f.232, Prior to Halifax, from Fontainebleau, 1 October 1714 and f.246, Prior to Halifax, from Paris, 12 October 1714.

37 Ibid., f.246, Prior to Halifax, from Paris, 12 October 1714.

38 *Longleat Papers*, vol. 3, 445, Halifax to Prior, 4 November 1714.

39 Robert Anderson, *The Poets of Great Britain* (London, 1792–3), vol. 6, p. 761; Eveline Cruickshanks, Stuart Handley and D. W. Hayton, *The House of Commons 1690–1715* (Cambridge, 2002), vol. 4, entry on Charles Montagu, Baron Halifax, p. 875.

40 Anon., *The Lord Whiglove's Elegy, to which is added a Pious Epitaph upon the Late Bishop of Addlebury* (1715).

41 By spring 1713, Steele was already redecorating the leased room, including painting its 21-foot walls with allegories of Truth and Eloquence. Inspecting the preparations at York Buildings, Steele is said to have asked one of the head carpenters to shout something from the stage to test the acoustics. The workman shouted that his men had been working for three months without pay, at which Steele answered, laughing: 'I am in raptures with the eloquence, but by no means admire the subject!' Sir Richard Phillips, *Addisoniana* (London, 1803), vol. 2, p. 25.

42 The punning ambiguity of the two spellings was apt and intentional – like a club, both inclusive and exclusive – both censorious (judgemental) and sensuous (receptive). See BL Add MS 61,688, f.21–2, definition of 'Sensorium'; *Town-Talk, in a letter to a Lady in the Country*, no. 4, 6 January 1716; no. 7, 27/8 January 1716; *The Spectator*, vol. 4, no. 565, 9 July 1714.
43 *Town-Talk, in a letter to a Lady in the Country*, no. 4, 6 January 1716.
44 Ibid., no. 7, 27/8 January 1716.
45 Ibid., no. 4, 6 January 1716.
46 Ibid., no. 7, 27/8 January 1716.
47 Ibid., Prologue to the Sensorium.
48 Theophilus Cibber, *The Lives of the Poets of Great Britain and Ireland* (London, 1753).
49 Winton discounts this anecdote: Calhoun Winton, *Sir Richard Steele MP* (Baltimore, Md., 1970), p. 118.
50 Rae Blanchard (ed.), *The Correspondence of Richard Steele* (Oxford, 1968 edn), no. 107, Steele to Lord Clare, 25 May 1715.
51 H. Bunker Wright, 'Matthew Prior's Cloe and Lisetta', *Modern Philology* 36, 1 (August 1938), pp. 16–18.
52 Rae Blanchard (ed.), *The Correspondence of Richard Steele* (Oxford, 1968 edn), no. 110, Steele to Lord Clare, 19 July 1715.
53 Wilfrid Prest, *Albion Ascendant: English History 1660–1815* (Oxford, 1998), p. 121; John Dunton, *Royal Gratitude . . . To which is added . . . A Trip to the Loyal Mug-House at Night, to Drink a Health to King George and the Royal Family* (1696).
54 BL Add MS 32,685, Letters to the Duke of Newcastle.
55 Steele quoted in Samuel Johnson, *Lives of the Poets* (1781), ed. George Birkbeck Hill (Oxford, 1905 edn), entry on Addison.
56 The Tonson firm became the Board of Trade's official stationer.
57 Calhoun Winton, *Sir Richard Steele MP* (Baltimore, Md., 1970), pp. 104–5.
58 Joseph Addison, *The Freeholder*, no. 39, Friday, 4 May 1716.
59 Horace Walpole, *A Catalogue of the Royal and Noble Authors of England* (Edinburgh, 1796 edn), p. 245.
60 William L. Sachse, *Lord Somers: A Political Portrait* (Manchester, 1975), p. 321.
61 A descendant of Townshend's claims that Townshend visited Somers as Somers lay dying and that Somers told him he supported the Septennial Act and disowned the 1694 Triennial Act: William Coxe, *Memoirs of the Life and Administration of Sir Robert Walpole* (London, 1800), vol. 1, p. 130.

XVIII PARADISE LOST

1 Quoted in Calhoun Winton, *Captain Steele: The Early Career of Richard Steele* (Baltimore, Md., 1964), p. 97.
2 Samuel Johnson, *Lives of the Poets* (1781), ed. George Birbeck Hill (Oxford, 1905 edn), entry on Addison.

3 Peter Smithers, *The Life of Joseph Addison* (Oxford, 1968 edn), p. 159.
4 Pope and Tonson quoted in Joseph Spence, *Observations, Anecdotes, and Characters of Books and Men*, ed. James M. Osborn (Oxford, 1966 edn), no. 184.
5 Donald F. Bond (ed.), *The Spectator* (Oxford, 1965), vol. 1, no. 106, Monday, 2 July 1711, by Addison.
6 Ibid., vol. 2, no. 261, Saturday, 29 December 1711, by Addison.
7 Ibid., vol. 4, no. 561, Wednesday, 30 June 1714, by Addison.
8 Rae Blanchard (ed.), *The Correspondence of Richard Steele* (Oxford, 1968 edn), p. 118.
9 BL Add MS 5,145C, To Lady Steele, 29 November 1716 (Blanchard no. 490); Steele to Lady Steele, 26 March 1717 (Blanchard no. 524).
10 Ibid., Steele to Lady Steele, mid-February 1717? (Blanchard no. 510).
11 Ibid., Lady Steele to Steele, 18 February 1717? (Blanchard no. 513).
12 Ibid., Steele to Lady Steele, mid-February 1717? (Blanchard no. 510).
13 Ibid., Steele to Lady Steele, 25 February 1717 (Blanchard no. 515); To Lady Steele, March 1717 (Blanchard no. 518).
14 Ibid., Steele to Lady Steele, 16 February 1717 (Blanchard no. 512).
15 Ibid., Steele to Lady Steele, March 1717 (Blanchard no. 518).
16 Ibid., Steele to Lady Steele, March 1717 (Blanchard no. 510).
17 Ibid., Steele to Lady Steele, 26 April 1717 (Blanchard no. 538).
18 Joseph Addison, *The Freeholder*, no. 29, Friday, 30 March 1716.
19 William Coxe, *Memoirs of the Life and Administration of Sir Robert Walpole, Earl of Orford* (London, 1798), vol. 2, pp. 143–6.
20 W. A. Speck, 'The Whig Schism under George I', *Huntington Library Quarterly* 40, 2 (February 1977), p. 171, Charles Cathcart to Lord Loudoun, 17 December 1716 [Loudoun MSS, LO 7949].
21 BL Add MS 35,584, f.163, Philip Yorke, 22 December 1716.
22 Philip Dormer Stanhope, *Characters by Lord Chesterfield* (London, 1778), p. 49.
23 Steele told Prue his letter had missed an earlier post because of 'my attendance on the Duke of Newcastle who was in the Chair of the Kitt-Katt'. BL Add MS 5,145C, Steele to Lady Steele in South Wales, 30 March 1717 (Blanchard no. 525). The fact that Steele did not remark on the Club ending, while he does name the chairman, suggests it was not consciously their last meeting.
24 Alexander Pope, 'Sandys' Ghost' (1717), referring to George Sandys, the Elizabethan translator of Ovid.
25 Pope and Tonson quoted in Joseph Spence, *Observations, Anecdotes, and Characters of Books and Men*, ed. James M. Osborn (Oxford, 1966 edn), no. 184.
26 Lady Mary Wortley Montagu to Pope, quoted in Arthur L. Cooke, 'Addison's Aristocratic Wife', *Publications of the Modern Language Association of America (PMLA)* 72, 1 (June 1957), p. 373.
27 BL Add MS 5,145C, Steele to Lady Steele, 30 March 1717 (Blanchard no. 525).
28 Ibid., Steele to Lady Steele, 10 April 1717 (Blanchard no. 528).

29 Ibid., Steele to Lady Steele, 13 April 1717 (Blanchard no. 530).
30 Ibid., Steele to Lady Steele, 16 April 1717.
31 Ibid., Steele to Lady Steele, 1 May 1717 (Blanchard no. 539).
32 John Nichols, *The Lover and the Reader*... (1789).
33 BL Add MS 5,145C, Steele to Lady Steele, 22 April 1717 (Blanchard no. 534).
34 Ibid., Steele to Lady Steele, 23 or 24 August 1717 (Blanchard no. 572).
35 Ibid., Steele to Lady Steele, 1 May 1717 (Blanchard no. 539).
36 Ibid., Steele to Lady Steele, 29 July 1717 (Blanchard no. 566).
37 Ibid., Steele to Lady Steele, May? 1717 (Blanchard no. 542).
38 Ibid., Steele to Lady Steele, October? 1717 (Blanchard no. 593).
39 Ibid., Steele to Lady Steele, 15 November 1717.
40 James Brydges, Duke of Chandos, quoted in Julian Hoppit, *A Land of Liberty? England 1689–1727* (Oxford, 2000), p. 401.
41 John C. Hodges (ed.), *William Congreve: Letters and Documents* (London, 1964), Epistolary dedication by Congreve to the Duke of Newcastle, 27 January 1718.
42 John Dryden, *The Dramatick Works of John Dryden, Esq. In Six Volumes* (1725).
43 Matthew Prior, *Poems on Several Occasions* (1718), Dedication.
44 Geoffrey Webb and Bonamy Dobrée (eds), *The Complete Works of Sir John Vanbrugh* (London, 1927–8), vol. 4, no. 114, Vanbrugh to Tonson, 29 November 1719.
45 Ibid.
46 Edward (Ned) Ward, *The Secret History of Clubs* (1709).
47 Lord Wharncliffe (ed.), *The Letters and Works of Lady Mary Wortley Montagu* (London, 1861), vol. 1, p. 206, *c.* October–November 1713.
48 BL Add MS 33,064, Newcastle Papers, Vanbrugh to the Duke of Newcastle, 25 December 1718.
49 Ibid., f.181, 24 January 1719.
50 Kathleen M. Lynch, *Jacob Tonson, Kit-Cat Publisher* (Knoxville, Tenn., 1971), p. 154.
51 Geoffrey Webb and Bonamy Dobrée (eds), *The Complete Works of Sir John Vanbrugh* (London, 1927–8), vol. 4, no. 114, Vanbrugh to Tonson, 29 November 1719. The mistaken report appeared in several London papers that Tonson had died from a fall from his horse in Paris (*The Thursday's Journal*, no. 11; *The Weekly Packet*, no. 380; *The Original Weekly Journal*, 17 October).
52 Geoffrey Webb and Bonamy Dobrée (eds), *The Complete Works of Sir John Vanbrugh* (London, 1927–8), vol. 4, no. 114, Vanbrugh to Tonson, 29 November 1719; BL Add MS 33,064, Newcastle Papers, Letters seeking, via Stanhope, the Board of Works place.
53 Geoffrey Webb and Bonamy Dobrée (eds), *The Complete Works of Sir John Vanbrugh* (London, 1927–8), vol. 4, no. 114, Vanbrugh to Tonson, 29 November 1719.
54 Tonson to Vanbrugh, June 1722, quoted in Kathleen M. Lynch, *Jacob Tonson, Kit-Cat Publisher* (Knoxville, Tenn., 1971), p. 165; original at Folger Shakespeare Library, Tonson MSS C.c.1 (74).

55 Geoffrey Webb and Bonamy Dobrée (eds), *The Complete Works of Sir John Vanbrugh* (London, 1927–8), vol. 4, no. 139, Vanbrugh to Tonson, 18 June 1722.
56 Ibid., no. 102, Vanbrugh to Tonson, 1 July 1719.
57 Ibid.
58 Including: Harry Boyle, Compton, Congreve, Maynwaring, Prior, Somers, Stanyan, Stepney, Tidcomb, Tonson and Walsh.
59 Donald F. Bond (ed.), *The Spectator* (Oxford, 1965), vol. 4, no. 479, Tuesday, 9 September 1712, by Steele.
60 Horace Walpole quoted in Stuart Handley, M. J. Rowe and W. H. McBryde, 'William Pulteney', *Oxford Dictionary of National Biography* (Oxford, September 2004, online edn, October 2005).
61 When Dunch died in 1719, his wife was said not to have seen him for years, yet would 'have no peace' until she had his Kit-Cat portrait from Tonson. (She is blamed for that painting's disappearance from the set.)
62 Donald F. Bond (ed.), *The Spectator* (Oxford, 1965), vol. 2, no. 149, Tuesday, 21 August 1711, by Steele.
63 Ibid., vol. 4, no. 520, Sunday, 27 October 1712, by Steele.
64 *The Weekly Journal or Saturday's Post*, Saturday, 24 January 1719, in BL Add MS 47,128, V, 95.
65 George Berkeley, *The Works of George Berkeley, Bishop of Cloyne*, ed. A. A. Luce and T. E. Jessop (London, 1956), vol. 4, pp. 56–7; Berkeley claimed to have the story direct from Addison.
66 Egmont MSS, quoted in Richard I. Cook, *Sir Samuel Garth* (Boston, Mass., 1980), p. 142 n. 97.
67 John Barber to Jonathan Swift, 22 April 1735 quoted in ibid., p. 37.

XIX THE END OF THE CLUB

1 BL Add MS 33,441, f.1, Addison fragment on friendship, found among his papers when he died.
2 *The Plebeian*, no. 1, Saturday, 14 March 1719.
3 Ibid.
4 Robert Walpole, *The Thoughts of a Member of the Lower House in relation to a Project for Restraining and Limiting the Power of the Crown in the Future Creation of Peers* (1719), quoted in Horace Walpole, *A Catalogue of the Royal and Noble Authors of England* (Edinburgh, 1796 edn), p. 265.
5 *The Old Whig*, 1719.
6 *The Plebeian*, no. 1, Saturday, 14 March 1719.
7 T. B. Macaulay, 'Life and Writings of Addison', *Edinburgh Review* 78 (July 1843), p. 256.
8 Samuel Johnson, *Lives of the English Poets* (1781), ed. George Birkbeck Hill (Oxford, 1905 edn), vol. 2, entry on Addison.
9 Richard Steele, *The Crisis* (1714).
10 The Peerage Bill was reintroduced in the session of 1719–20. After a ten-hour

Commons debate, in which former Kit-Cat MPs spoke according to their allegiances in the schism, and Walpole gave perhaps the most impressive speech of his career, it was once again defeated by ninety-two votes. The Prince of Wales threw a huge party afterwards, at which Steele was likely among the celebrants, but in his case guilt was mixed with the triumph. By this date, Addison had been dead for six months.

11 Donald F. Bond (ed.), *The Spectator* (Oxford, 1965), vol. 3, no. 381, Saturday, 17 May 1712, by Addison.

12 Ibid., vol. 4, no. 186, Wednesday, 3 October 1711, by Addison.

13 Edward Young, *Conjectures on Original Composition* (1759).

14 Thomas Tickell, 'To the Earl of Warwick, On the Death of Mr Addison' (1721).

15 Virginia Woolf, 'Addison', in *The Common Reader* (London, 2003 edn), vol. 1.

16 Donald F. Bond (ed.), *The Spectator* (Oxford, 1965), vol. 3, no. 349, Thursday, 10 April 1712, by Addison.

17 Donald F. Bond (ed.), *The Tatler* (Oxford, 1987), vol. 1, no. 11, Thursday, 5 May 1709.

18 John Loftis (ed.), *Richard Steele's 'The Theatre'* (Oxford, 1962), no. 12, 9 February 1720.

19 Ibid.

20 As the comedy had flopped when first performed, some discerned subconscious hostility for the reattributed reprint, but if so, it was a strange sort of revenge: the revelation of Addison's name meant the play sold out and was successfully revived on the stage for years afterwards.

21 Dedication in the 2nd edition of *The Drummer* (1722) To Mr Congreve, in Rae Blanchard (ed.), *The Correspondence of Richard Steele* (Oxford, 1968 edn), pp. 505ff.

22 Donald F. Bond (ed.), *The Spectator* (Oxford, 1965), vol. 2, no. 253, Thursday, 20 December 1711, by Addison.

23 Peter Smithers, *The Life of Joseph Addison* (Oxford, 1968 edn), p. 424.

24 BL Add MS 5,145C, Steele to Lady Steele, 24 September 1717 (Blanchard no. 582).

25 BL Add MS 32,700, ff.211–13, Newcastle (at Claremont) to Lord Hardwicke, 14 October 1739.

26 Richard Steele, *The State of the Case between the Lord Chamberlain of His Majesty's Household and the Governor of the Royal Company of Comedians* (1720).

27 John Loftis (ed.), *Richard Steele's 'The Theatre'* (Oxford, 1962), no. 28, Tuesday, 5 April 1720.

28 Rae Blanchard (ed.), *The Correspondence of Richard Steele* (Oxford, 1968 edn), no. 170, Steele to the Duke of Newcastle, February 1720 or 1721.

29 In August 1717, John Law, an Englishman favoured by the French Regent, formed the Company of the West, later known as the Mississippi Company. It held the rights to trade between France and the French colony of Louisiana (encompassing today's Louisiana, Mississippi, Arkansas, Missouri, Illinois, Iowa, Wisconsin, Minnesota and parts of Canada), and also to mine and farm

Louisiana. Law met many Kit-Cats in London, in 1714, including Steele (who tried to interest him in the Fishpool) and, it seems likely, Jacob Tonson. In 1717, Tonson decided to invest in Law's Mississippi Company. The recent diplomatic *entente* between France and Britain meant that investment in a French company was no longer unpatriotic. While Tonson was with Law in Paris in 1719, the Mississippi Company merged with the French East India and China Company to create a global trading conglomerate. The Mississippi Company's stocks immediately jumped, and by December 1719 were trading at twenty times their 1717 price. It proved lucky that a severe fever prolonged Tonson's Paris stay until 1720. It meant he was there to receive a tip-off from John Law that the Mississippi Company bubble was about to burst.

30 Geoffrey Webb and Bonamy Dobrée (eds), *The Complete Works of Sir John Vanbrugh*, 4 vols (London, 1927–8), vol. 4, no. 114, Vanbrugh to Tonson, 29 November 1719.

31 Kathleen M. Lynch, *Jacob Tonson, Kit-Cat Publisher* (Knoxville, Tenn., 1971), p. 164.

32 HMC, *Bayfordbury MSS*, p. 71, Vanbrugh to Tonson, 18 February 1720.

33 John Loftis (ed.), *Richard Steele's 'The Theatre'* (Oxford, 1962), no. 17, Saturday, 27 February 1720. In another issue, Steele went so far as to accuse the government of being a bunch of crooks ('Highway-Men') operating with impunity (ibid., no. 20, 8 March 1720).

34 Ray A. Kelch, *Newcastle, a Duke without Money: Thomas Pelham-Holles 1693–1768* (London, 1974), p. 54.

35 John Loftis (ed.), *Richard Steele's 'The Theatre'* (Oxford, 1962), no. 17, Saturday, 27 February 1720.

36 BL Add MS 35,854, f.99, William Cowper's Diary.

37 The former Lord President, asked to make way for Townshend, was the ageing Kit-Cat Duke of Kingston, who went back to being Lord of the Privy Seal, remaining so until his death.

38 The South Sea Company survived the crash and continued to pay out low but steady dividends, so that Vanbrugh reinvested and received an income from the Company (profits directly from the slave trade), which ultimately supported his widow.

39 Horace Walpole, *Anecdotes of Painting in England* (London, 1879 edn), p. 285.

40 Wharton's son Philip was the most dramatic example of a wayward son, far exceeding his father's much-exaggerated reputation as an atheist and libertine. Philip was a precocious child, raised to deliver orations before his father's friends. Addison took a particular interest in the boy's education during the years when Wharton was Addison's electoral patron in Malmesbury. At 16, Philip broke his father's heart by eloping with an unsuitable woman. Failing to annul the marriage, Wharton sent the boy, with a Huguenot escort, to study in Geneva. Philip's ultra-Whig father did not live to see him then escape Geneva to join the Jacobite Court in France. After George I's accession, Philip switched his allegiance back to the Whigs and in 1717 took up a seat in the Irish Lords. The King gave him his dukedom in January 1718, hoping it might

fix his political loyalties to the Court; Philip entered the English Lords upon his majority in December 1719. The following year, Philip founded the 'Hell-Fire Club' in London. This was a club of Whig gentlemen, but one where debauched women were admitted. Orgies and satanic rituals at the Hell-Fire were the alleged spawn of the sedate Kit-Cat toasting rituals. To contemporaries, the Hell-Fire Club sounded like one of Ned Ward's fictional inventions; although reports were exaggerated, they were based on some genuinely dissolute behaviour and the Club's reputation provided much-needed distraction for the scandalized reading public after the South Sea crisis. Not to be confused with the similar Hell-Fire Club later formed by Sir Francis Dashwood, offshoots and namesakes of this Club survived right into the twentieth century. Aligned with the first clique to oppose Walpole after 1721 – a 'Country Whig' (anti-corruption) grouping led by Lord Cowper – Philip prepared for the 1722 election by hosting a series of balls and lavish suppers in York in the summer of 1721, which Vanbrugh attended while staying at Castle Howard. One famous 'diabolical masquerade' held at Somerset House in London prompted a royal proclamation in April 1721 for the suppression of Hell-Fire Club meetings.

41 Walpole undermined the credibility of witnesses testifying to the Commons against Sunderland, and so obtained his former enemy's acquittal. Sunderland at first remained in office, but was so politically weakened by owing this debt to Walpole, and so personally weakened by the damage to his reputation, that he resigned after a month. He nonetheless retained an important Household Office with access to the King.

42 Calhoun Winton, *Sir Richard Steele MP* (Baltimore, Md., 1970), p. 170; Tone Sundt Urstad, *Sir Robert Walpole's Poets: The Use of Literature as Pro-Government Propaganda, 1721–1742* (Newark, NJ, 1999), p. 28.

43 Prince of Wales to Lord Hervey, quoted in Fran Beauman, *The Pineapple* (London, 2005), pp. 88–9.

44 Denys Sutton, 'The faire majestic Paradise of Stowe', *Apollo* 97 (1973), p. 542.

45 William Congreve, 'Of Pleasing' (1700).

46 HMC, *Bayfordbury MSS*, p. 70, MS of William Congreve, 'Of Improving the Present Time' (1729).

47 Denys Sutton, 'The faire majestic Paradise of Stowe', *Apollo* 97 (1973), p. 542.

48 Nicholas Rowe, *The Reconcilement between Jacob Tonson and Mr Congreve* (1707).

49 Geoffrey Webb and Bonamy Dobrée (eds), *The Complete Works of Sir John Vanbrugh* (London 1927–8), vol. 4, no. 102, Vanbrugh to Tonson, 1 July 1719.

50 Denys Sutton, 'The faire majestic Paradise of Stowe', *Apollo* 97 (1973), p. 544.

51 Many buildings Vanbrugh designed for Stowe were completed after the architect's death, and many were altered or destroyed as the gardens were continuously remodelled over the next century.

52 Tim Richardson, *The Arcadian Friends: Inventing the English Landscape Garden* (London, 2007), p. 58.

53 Horace, *Second Epode*.

54 Donald F. Bond (ed.), *The Spectator* (Oxford, 1965), vol. 1, no. 94, Monday, 18 June 1711, by Addison.
55 HMC, *Bayfordbury MSS*, p. 70, MS of William Congreve, 'Of Improving the Present Time' (1729).
56 Madeleine Bingham, *Masks and Façades: Sir John Vanbrugh, the Man and his Setting* (London, 1974), p. 321.
57 Geoffrey Webb and Bonamy Dobrée (eds), *The Complete Works of Sir John Vanbrugh* (London, 1927–8), vol. 4, no. 127, Vanbrugh to Lord Carlisle, June 1721.
58 Bodleian, MS Eng Letters c.129, f.127.
59 *The Weekly Pacquet*, 9 July 1720.
60 HMC, *Bath MSS*, vol. 3, p. 469, Robert Arbuthnot to Matthew Prior, 28 September 1719.
61 Geoffrey Webb and Bonamy Dobrée (eds), *The Complete Works of Sir John Vanbrugh* (London, 1927–8), vol. 4, no. 139, Vanbrugh to Tonson, 18 June 1722.
62 Anon., *A Letter to a Buttonian K***** from Sir James Baker, admirer-general of the fair sex and late secretary of the toasts of the Kit-Cat Club* (1718). 'Sir James' was a fictional narrator and pseudonym used by John Gay the previous year when he helped Pulteney and Walpole attack General Cadogan's financial probity. This 1718 piece is therefore also likely by Gay.
63 The sender, an Oxford poet, says he will understand if his submission is rejected by 'the Club' and neither Tonson nor his nephew are known to have belonged to any other club besides the Kit-Cat. BL MS 28,275, f. 82, Dr Abel Evans to Tonson, 18 January 1719.
64 Geoffrey Webb and Bonamy Dobrée (eds), *The Complete Works of Sir John Vanbrugh* (London, 1927–8), vol. 4, no. 165, Vanbrugh to Tonson, 12 August 1725.
65 Ibid., no. 168, Vanbrugh to Tonson, 25 October 1725.
66 Laurence Whistler, Vanbrugh's biographer, claimed that the surviving Kit-Cats did actually get together in November 1725, but the evidence is unclear; Sarah Lewis Carol Clapp (ed.), *Jacob Tonson in Ten Letters by and about Him* (Austin, Tex., 1948), Jacob Tonson to Jacob Tonson Jr, 22 April 1728, speaks of planning to go to Bath where he will meet 'my most worthy friend Mr Congreve'.
67 BL Add MS 32,992, f.340, Tonson to Newcastle.
68 BL Add MS 28,275, f.110, Newcastle to Tonson.
69 Sarah Lewis Carol Clapp (ed.), *Jacob Tonson in Ten Letters by and about Him* (Austin, Tex., 1948), Jacob Tonson to Jacob Tonson Jr, 29 April 1728.
70 Ibid., Dr William Oliver to Dr Alexander Small, 5 July 1732.
71 Joseph Spence, *Observations, Anecdotes, and Characters of Books and Men*, ed. James M. Osborn (Oxford, 1966 edn), vol. 1, no. 118.
72 Swift and Pope's joint Preface to their *Miscellanies* (1727), quoted in Bernard Harris, *Sir John Vanbrugh* (London, 1967), p. 36.
73 Geoffrey Webb and Bonamy Dobrée (eds), *The Complete Works of Sir John Vanbrugh* (London, 1927–8), vol. 4, no. 168, Vanbrugh to Tonson, 25 October 1725.

74 Ibid.
75 Ibid.
76 *The Weekly Journal* quoted in Kerry Downes, *Sir John Vanbrugh: A Biography* (London, 1987), p. 3.
77 Theophilus Cibber, *The Lives of the Poets of Great Britain and Ireland* (London, 1753).
78 BL Add MS 33,064, Newcastle Papers, 30 July 1723 (Blanchard no. 1 to no. 626 – misdated).
79 George Sherburn (ed.), *The Correspondence of Alexander Pope* (Oxford, 1956), vol. 2, p. 133, Pope to John Gay, 11 September 1722.
80 Lord Wharncliffe (ed.), *The Letters and Works of Lady Mary Wortley Montagu* (London, 1861), vol. 1, p. 472, Lady Mary to the Countess of Mar, 1723.
81 Theophilus Cibber, *The Lives of the Poets of Great Britain and Ireland* (London, 1753).
82 Henrietta paid for Congreve's monument in the Abbey, and it was probably the wax or clay model for this effigy, a bust of the author, that she asked if she could keep at home. This may be the source of the lewd story in *The Daily Post* and *The Amorous Duchess: or, Her Grace Grateful* (1733) that she had a wax model of her dead lover made to take to bed – a slur James Boswell repeated in *The London Journal* years later, describing the Duchess dining with her wax surrogate at the Godolphins' table.
83 Sarah Lewis Carol Clapp (ed.), *Jacob Tonson in Ten Letters by and about Him* (Austin, Tex., 1948), Jacob Tonson to Jacob Tonson Jr, 3 February 1729.
84 National Archives, PROB 1/103, Charles Wilson [Edmund Curll], *Memoirs of the Life, Writings and Amours of William Congreve Esq* (1730).
85 David Thomas, *William Congreve* (London, 1992), p. 12.
86 Joseph Spence, *Observations, Anecdotes, and Characters of Books and Men*, ed. James M. Osborn (Oxford, 1966 edn), no. 798.
87 John C. Hodges (ed.), *William Congreve: Letters and Documents* (London, 1964), p. 241, Alexander Pope to John Gay, 1728/9.
88 BL Add MSS 28,275, f.491, Samuel Croxall to Jacob Tonson Jr, 10 March 1733.
89 Sarah Lewis Carol Clapp (ed.), *Jacob Tonson in Ten Letters by and about Him* (Austin, Tex., 1948), pp. 4–5, Pope to Lord Oxford, 1731.
90 BL Add MS 28,275, f.491, Samuel Croxall to Tonson Junior, 10 March 1733.
91 Croxall's hand may match that on the undated and incomplete 'Account of the Kitt-Catt Club' in the Tonson Papers of the NPG, though in BL letters he writes 'Kit-Cat' and in the NPG MS the writer spells it 'Kitt-Catt'.
92 'Upon News of Jacob Tonson's Death', *The Gentleman's Magazine*, no. 6 (1736), p. 106.
93 Ibid., p. 168.
94 Edmond Malone (ed.), *Critical and Miscellaneous Prose Works of John Dryden* (London, 1800), p. 537 n. 3. When Jacob Junior died four months before his uncle, on 15 November 1735, he described himself in his will as a bookseller, bookbinder, stationer and a printer in partnership with J. Watts. See also National Archives, PROB 10/7376/6.

95 Ibid.
96 See, for example, Prof. Walter Raleigh on Tonson having seized on the 'many rotten corpses . . . before they were cold, and commemorated them in batches', as quoted in Michael Holroyd, *Works on Paper* (London, 2002), p. 18.

XX LATER CLUBS AND KIT-CATS

1 Donald F. Bond (ed.), *The Spectator* (Oxford, 1965), vol. 5, no. 553, Thursday, 4 December 1712, by Addison.
2 The Garrick Club official website.
3 Robert A. Caro, *The Power Broker* (New York, 1975), p. 44.
4 David Piper, *Catalogue of Seventeenth-Century Portraits in the National Portrait Gallery* (Cambridge, 1963), p. 399 n. 4, quoting the will of Jacob Junior, 1735: 'whereas I have lately at some Expence Erected an Edifice or Building at Barnes wherein the said collection of the Kit-Cat pictures are now placed'; NPG, Tonson Papers: the 1730s bills for the clubroom's construction and reframing of the pictures survive, as does a plan of how the pictures were hung by Jacob Junior. The majority of the aristocrats and patrons were at eye-level and the writers hung higher up, harder to see. The idealized society of equals was already, within a generation, being undercut by Jacob Junior's reflexive deference to rank.
5 *NPG Catalogue*, with introduction by Miss Mary Ransome (London, 1945), p. 4.
6 Unsourced newspaper clipping in the Tonson Papers, NPG.
7 It shows two figures (denoting concord): a Britannia-like woman on the left, standing in front of a lyre (symbol of lyric poetry and music), holding a spear (denoting pre-eminence and command) and with a caduceus (symbol of commerce) over her helmet; and on the right, a man, probably meant to be Mars the god of war, holding a dagger. At their feet lies Pegasus, symbol of the creative/poetic/intellectual spirit overcoming the impediments of the world, and hence of immortality, and other emblems of the arts, abundance and plentiful generosity. Over their heads shines the sun of enlightenment and power, (in some versions) with a moon inside its orb. Inside the shield that the two figures flank, instead of Faber's text, it says simply '[The] Kit-Cat Club, 1703'.
8 The nightclub in *Goodbye to Berlin* and *I Am a Camera* was named 'the Lady Windemere'. Peter Parker, Isherwood's biographer, has been unable to find a real nightclub in Berlin called either by this name or 'the Kit-Cat Club'.
9 Roger Fitzgerald, *Rowntree and the Marketing Revolution, 1862–1969* (Cambridge, 1995), p. 339.

EPILOGUE: LEGACIES

1 Donald F. Bond (ed.), *The Spectator* (Oxford, 1965), vol. 4, no. 583, Friday, 20 August 1714, by Addison.
2 Eustace Budgell quoted in Peter Smithers, *The Life of Joseph Addison* (Oxford, 1968 edn), p. 457.
3 Joseph Addison, *The Freeholder*, no. 35, Friday, 20 April 1716.

4 Steele and Vanbrugh received no such attention from Curll – the first having had the 'egotism' (a term Addison coined from the French in relation to memoirists) to publish his *Apology for Himself* in 1714.

5 Dr Johnson claimed Steele tried betrothing Elizabeth to the young poet Richard Savage, whom Steele had taken under his wing, though Steele lacked the cash to play patron. On one occasion, as if he missed the collaboration with Addison and was looking for a surrogate, Steele took Savage to write a pamphlet in a Hyde Park tavern, Savage transcribing Steele's dictation, while they enjoyed a meal. When the dinner and pamphlet were finished, Steele explained that the pamphlet must be sold to pay for the meal. Theophilus Cibber, *The Lives of the Poets of Great Britain and Ireland* (London, 1753). Note also that a play called *Richard Savage* by J. M. Barrie and H. B. Marriot was performed at the Criterion Theatre in spring 1891, the third act of which took place with Steele at a meeting of the Kit-Cat Club.

6 Samuel Johnson, *Lives of the English Poets* (1781), ed. George Birkbeck Hill (Oxford, 1905 edn), vol. 2, entry on Addison.

7 Ibid., entry on Garth.

8 Dr Samuel Johnson, *Lives of the English Poets* (London, 1781), ed. George Birkbeck Hill (Oxford, 1905), vol. 2, p. 208.

9 Ibid., vol. 1, p. 330.

10 Ibid., entry on Congreve.

11 Edward A. Bloom and Lillian D. Bloom (eds), *Addison and Steele: The Critical Heritage* (London, 1980), p. 33.

12 Ibid., p. 74.

13 William Hazlitt, *Lectures on the English Comic Writers* (London, 1819), p. 190, Lecture V.

14 William Wordsworth, *The Prelude* (1799–1850).

15 Lord Byron, *Don Juan* (1823), Canto XIII.

16 A group portrait of a male tea party in the 1690s, attributed to John Closterman or Kneller, was exhibited at the Exhibition of National Portraits at Kensington in 1867 with the label of 'The Kit-Cat Club'. Today experts think it much more likely to be a picture of key members of the Society for the Reformation of Manners. The nineteenth-century confusion in captioning has a nice irony, since the Kit-Cats tried to perform exactly this trick: co-ôpting and absorbing the public backlash against the licentiousness of the Restoration Court. They tried to show that self-reform and self-censorship could be done with more conviviality and panache and less sobriety than Jeremy Collier or the Society for the Reformation of Manners demanded.

17 C. S. Lewis, 'Addison', in *Essays on the Eighteenth Century Presented to David Nichol Smith in Honour of his Seventieth Birthday* (Oxford, 1945), p. 13.

18 William Makepeace Thackeray, *English Humourists of the Eighteenth Century* (London, 1853). Steele's reputation was finally rehabilitated by John Forster, who wrote an essay answering dismissive and condescending portraits of him by Aikin, Macaulay, Thackeray and others. John Forster, 'Sir Richard Steele', *Historical and Biographical Essays*, vol. 2 (London, 1858).

19 Rae Blanchard (ed.), *The Englishman: A Political Journal by Richard Steele* (Oxford, 1955), series 1, no. 33, Saturday, 19 December 1713.
20 James Caulfield, *Memoirs of the Celebrated Persons Composing the Kit-Cat Club; with a prefatory account of the origin of the association, illustrated with forty-eight portraits from the original paintings by Sir Godfrey Kneller* (London, 1849), p. 248.
21 William Hazlitt, *Lectures on the English Comic Writers* (London, 1819), p. 157.
22 Edmund Gosse, *Life of William Congreve* (London, 1888), p. 184.
23 Ibid.
24 Virginia Woolf, 'Addison', in *The Common Reader* (London, 2003 edn), vol. 1.
25 Cyril Connolly, *Enemies of Promise* (London, 1979 edn), pp. 23–4.
26 C. S. Lewis, 'Addison', in *Essays on the Eighteenth Century Presented to David Nichol Smith in Honour of his Seventieth Birthday* (Oxford, 1945), p. 13.
27 Ibid., p. 14.
28 Peter Smithers, *The Life of Joseph Addison* (Oxford, 1968 edn), pp. 468–9.
29 Brian McCrea, *Addison and Steele Are Dead* (Newark, NJ, 1990), p. 11.
30 Ibid., p. 38.
31 Donald F. Bond (ed.), *The Spectator* (Oxford, 1965), vol. 2, no. 172, Monday, 17 September 1711, by Steele.
32 William Congreve, 'Of Improving the Present Time' (1729).
33 Donald F. Bond (ed.), *The Spectator* (Oxford, 1965), vol. 2, no. 137, Tuesday, 7 August 1711, by Steele.
34 Richard Steele, 'To William Pulteney', *The Guardian*, vol. 2 (1714), in Rae Blanchard (ed.), *The Correspondence of Richard Steele* (Oxford, 1968 edn).
35 Donald F. Bond (ed.), *The Spectator* (Oxford, 1965), vol. 3, no. 314, Friday, 29 February 1712, by Steele.
36 Michael Foss, *The Age of Patronage: The Arts in England 1660–1750* (Ithaca, NY, 1972), p. 149. Among the subscribers were Newcastle, Grafton, Berkeley, Lincoln, Burlington, Pulteney and Manchester (on whom a dukedom was conferred in 1719, despite years of unimpressive diplomacy). The Academy's first Governor was Newcastle, with Manchester as his deputy. Grafton, Montagu, Burlington, Pulteney and Vanbrugh were among the first twenty directors.
37 Geoffrey Webb and Bonamy Dobrée (eds), *The Complete Works of Sir John Vanbrugh* (London, 1927–8), vol. 4, no. 134, Vanbrugh to the Earl of Carlisle, 6 April 1722.
38 Sir John Clerk quoted in Richard Wilson and Alan Mackley, *Creating Paradise: The Building of the English Country House, 1660–1800* (London and New York, 2000), p. 53.
39 Sir Joshua Reynolds, '13th Discourse at the Royal Academy' (1786), quoted in David Watkin, *English Vision* (London, 1982), p. 89.
40 J. H. Plumb, *The Growth of Political Stability in England 1675–1725* (Harmondsworth, 1969), p. xvii.
41 Ibid., p. xviii.
42 Ibid.
43 Ibid.

44 Ibid., p. 36.

45 Geoffrey Holmes, *The Making of a Great Power: Late Stuart and Early Georgian Britain 1660–1722* (London, 1993), p. 346.

46 Ibid., p. 224.

47 Wilfrid Prest, *Albion Ascendant: English History 1660–1815* (Oxford, 1998).

48 Jürgen Habermas quoted in Michael McKeon, *The Secret History of Domesticity: Public, Private, and the Division of Knowledge* (Baltimore, Md., 2005), p. 75.

49 Stephen Eric Bronner, *Reclaiming the Enlightenment* (New York, 2004), p. 65.

50 Donald F. Bond (ed.), *The Spectator* (Oxford, 1965), vol. 3, no. 287, Tuesday, 29 January 1712, by Addison; Bernard Bailyn, *The Ideological Origins of the American Revolution* (London, 1992 edn), p. 77.

51 Donovan Bond and W. Reynolds McLeod (eds), *Newsletters to Newspapers: Eighteenth-Century Journalism* (Morgantown, W.Va., 1977), p. 121.

52 Joseph Addison, *The Freeholder*, ed. J. Leheny (Oxford, 1979), no. 39, Friday, 4 May 1716, Addison's eulogy to Somers.

53 Joseph Addison and Richard Steele, *The Guardian*, ed. John Cahoun Stephens (Lexington, Ky., 1982), 20 April 1713.

INDEX